CRIMINAL JUSTICE TECHNOLOGY IN THE 21ST CENTURY

Second Edition

CRIMINAL JUSTICE TECHNOLOGY IN THE 21ST CENTURY

Edited by

LAURA J. MORIARTY

CHARLES C THOMAS • PUBLISHER, LTD.
Springfield • Illinois • U.S.A.

Published and Distributed Throughout the World by

CHARLES C THOMAS • PUBLISHER, LTD.
2600 South First Street
Springfield, Illinois 62704

ISBN-13 978-0-398-07559-0 (hard) ISBN-10 0-398-07559-X (hard)
ISBN-13 978-0-398-07560-6 (paper) ISBN-10 0-398-07560-3 (paper)

Library of Congress Catalog Card Number: 2004059825

With THOMAS BOOKS *careful attention is given to all details of manufacturing and design. It is the Publisher's desire to present books that are satisfactory as to their physical qualities and artistic possibilities and appropriate for their particular use.* THOMAS BOOKS *will be true to those laws of quality that assure a good name and good will.*

Printed in the United States of America
CR-R-3

Library of Congress Cataloging-in-Publication Data

Criminal justice technology in the 21st century / edited by Laura J.
Moriarty.-- 2nd ed.
p. cm.
Includes bibliographical references and index.
ISBN 0-398-07559-X -- ISBN 0-398-07560-3 (pbk.)
1. Criminal justice, Administration of--United States--Data
processing. 2. Criminal justice, Administration of--United States--
Computer assisted instruction. 3. Criminal justice, Administration
of--Study and teaching (Higher)--United States--Data processing.
I. Moriarty, Laura J.

HV9950.C76 2005
364.973--dc22

2004059825

CONTRIBUTORS

Ryan Baggett holds a Master of Science degree in Criminal Justice (with a concentration in Police Administration) from Eastern Kentucky University's (EKU) College of Justice and Safety and a Bachelor of Science degree in Criminal Justice from Murray State University. Baggett is currently the Deputy Director for Technology and Administrative Services within the EKU Justice and Safety Center (JSC), an organization that manages federal and state grants to conduct research/development, assessments/evaluations, and training/technical assistance on various aspects of public safety and security. In his current capacity at the Justice and Safety Center, Baggett manages the technical aspects of a project's life cycle for several JSC projects including the evaluation of an advanced firearm simulation system (PRISim™), the research and development of an advanced surveillance system for covert and overt applications, and the evaluation of a technology integration project in eastern Kentucky. Additionally, Baggett supports the National Rural Law Enforcement Technology Center (RULETC) in Hazard, Kentucky, and serves as an Adjunct Instructor for the EKU Department of Criminal Justice and Police Studies as well as the Department of Loss Prevention and Safety.

Marialina Bello is a faculty research assistant at the University of Maryland's Bureau of Governmental Research (BGR). For the past 5 years, she has been involved in various projects implementing the "what works" principles into the supervision field. While working with the Maryland Division of Parole and Probation (MDPP), she assisted in the design and implementation of training sessions to over 600 MDPP staff on their new model of supervision; Proactive Community Supervision (PCS). The training curriculums include Motivational

Interviewing (MI) for Offender Change and "Sizing Up." She also created various interactive tools such as the Break the Cycle (BTC) and PCS flowcharts and training games, Jeopardy and screen savers. She manages the production of the Maryland Offender Case Planning Software for Empowerment (MOCSE), which assists MDPP agents in supervising intensive offenders. She is involved in various projects such as creating "Tools of the Trade" for the National Institute of Corrections and maintains Websites.

Christine E. Bryce is a Senior Computer Forensic Examiner for the Virginia State Police Computer Evidence Recovery Unit. She also regularly instructs a variety of topics at the Virginia State Police Training Academy. Bryce frequently guest lectures and presents information around Virginia regarding "Parenting the Internet," "Identity Theft," "Internet Safety," and other related topics. Bryce has a Master of Liberal Arts in American Studies (2002) from University of Richmond and a Bachelor of Social Work (1997) from Virginia Commonwealth University, and she is currently working toward a Ph.D. in Public Policy from Virginia Commonwealth University. Her research areas include computer forensics, judicial review, 1st Amendment interpretations, 2nd Amendment interpretations, 5th Amendment interpretations, state and local policy making, and other areas that capture her interest. Bryce has written and published over 40 training and procedural manuals in topics including computers, technical skills, writing and grammar, medical billing and procedures, and computer forensics. Bryce has also published several musical and poetry compositions.

David L. Carter (Ph.D., Sam Houston State University) is a Professor in the school of Criminal Justice at Michigan State University. He also serves as the Director of the National Center for Community Policing and Director of the Criminal Justice Study Abroad Program. He has written numerous books and articles and served as a trainer and consultant to law enforcement agencies throughout the United States and several foreign countries.

Pamela A. Collins is the Director of the Justice and Safety Center, housed in the College of Justice and Safety at Eastern Kentucky University in Richmond, Kentucky. She has also held the position of Acting Dean of Graduate School, Department Chairman of Loss Prevention and Safety, and is a Professor of both undergraduate and graduate studies in the Loss Prevention and Safety Department. Dr. Collins holds a Bachelor of Science degree in Security and Public Safety, a Master of Science degree in Criminal Justice from Eastern Kentucky University, and a Doctorate in Higher Education with an emphasis in Educational Policy Studies from the University of Kentucky. She is a Certified Fraud Examiner (C.F.E.). Prior to coming to Eastern in 1986, she worked as an Industrial Security Specialist for General Electric, Aircraft Engine Business Group Division, and as a Fire and Safety Engineer for Industrial Risk Insurers.

Ann Marie Cordner (Ph.D., University of Maryland) is a senior research associate and project co-director in the Justice and Safety Center at Eastern Kentucky University, where she also teaches part-time in the Department of Criminal Justice and Police Studies. She has held faculty positions at Temple University and Niagara University and worked as a researcher/planner for the Kentucky Criminal Justice Council. Her research interests include the death penalty, prosecutorial decision-making, hate crime, and community policing.

Gary Cordner is Dean of the College of Justice and Safety (formerly the College of Law Enforcement) at Eastern Kentucky University, where he is also a Professor of Police Studies and Director of the Regional Community Policing Institute. He received his Ph.D. from Michigan State University and served as a police officer and police chief in Maryland. Cordner has co-authored textbooks on police administration and criminal justice planning and co-edited several anthologies on policing. He edited the American Journal of Police from 1987 to 1992, co-edited *Police Computer Review* from 1992 to 1995, and now edits *Police Quarterly.* Cordner is past president of the Academy of Criminal Justice Sciences, the country's largest association of criminal justice educators and researchers, and founder and former chair of that organization's Police Section. In recent years, he has worked with Abt Associates, the Police Executive Research Forum, and the Institute for Law and Justice on community policing and information technology projects, taught regularly for the Law Enforcement Management Institute of Texas, and served as a research consultant to the San Diego Police Department.

Jill A. Gordon is an Associate Professor in the School of Government and Public Affairs at Virginia Commonwealth University. She received her Ph.D. and Master of Science in Criminal Justice from the

University of Cincinnati, and a Bachelor of Science in Criminal Justice from Bowling Green State University. Her primary research interests focus on evaluative studies concerning correctional policy. In addition, she examines the attitudes held among those who work with correctional clients. She has been awarded several federal, state, and local grants and is published in a variety of journals including *Criminal Justice and Behavior,* the *Journal of Contemporary Criminal Justice,* the *American Journal of Criminal Justice,* the *Prison Journal,* the *Journal of Juvenile Justice and Detention Services,* and the *Journal of Quantitative Criminology.*

Robert C. Haas (M.A., Rutgers University) is the Chief of Police for the Westwood Police Department in Massachusetts. Prior to accepting his current position, he served fifteen years as a police officer in Morris Township Police Department in New Jersey, where he rose to the rank of lieutenant. While serving as a police officer in New Jersey, he also taught extensively at the Morris County Police Academy as a certified police instructor in a variety of topical areas and served on the Board of Directors for the New Jersey Battered Women's Services.

Janet Hutchinson is an Associate Professor and Coordinator of the Public Administration Program in the L. Douglas Wilder School of Government and Public Affairs, Virginia Commonwealth University. Her research and publications follow two threads: issues in child and family policy and feminist theory particularly in relation to public policy, and organization behavior and development. She also has a research interest in the sociology of knowledge use. She teaches courses in research methods and statistics, and women and family policy, and is affiliated with the Women's Studies program at VCU. Dr. Hutchinson received her undergraduate degree in sociology from the University of Maryland, her Master of Public Administration from American University, and her Ph.D. in Public Policy from the Graduate School of Public and International Affairs, University of Pittsburgh.

Janice O. Joseph is a Professor of Criminal Justice at the Richard Stockton College of New Jersey. She received her Ph.D. from York University (Canada). Her research interests include juvenile justice, criminology and deviance, minorities and crime, women and criminal justice, and corrections.

Andra J. Katz (Bannister) (Ph.D., Michigan State University) is an Associate Professor and Graduate Coordinator, Criminal Justice and Assistant Director at the School of Community Affairs at Wichita State University. Her research interests include computer crime, community policing, and international organized crime issues.

Robyn Diehl Lacks is an Assistant Professor of Criminal Justice in the School of Government and Public Affairs, College of Humanities and Sciences at Virginia Commonwealth University. She earned her Ph.D. in Developmental Psychology (2003) and her Masters degree in Criminal Justice (2000) from Virginia Commonwealth University and her Bachelors in Psychology (1998) from Randolph-Macon College. Her research areas include the impact of violence exposure on aggressive and delinquent acts, violent crime scene analysis and community-based program evaluation. She has published articles on DNA analysis and federal and state victim resources. She currently has articles under review on the impact of crowd behavior at homicide scenes and the impact of violence exposure on adolescent adjustment. She also has published several encyclopedia entries and community-based evaluation reports.

Dr. James E. Mays is an Associate Professor of Statistics in the Department of Statistical Sciences and Operations Research at Virginia Commonwealth University. His research interests include nonparametric and semiparametric regression techniques, with emphasis on smoothing considerations and the development of model-robust techniques. Dr. Mays is also involved in the development of introductory level (general education) statistics courses, including the implementation of interactive multimedia techniques in instruction and the development of supplement manuals to accompany numerous introductory statistics textbooks.

Lorraine Green Mazerolle (Ph.D., Rutgers University) is an Associate Professor at Griffith University in the Key Centre for Ethics, Law, Justice and Governance. Her research interests include crime prevention, policing and crime control, technology and policing, research methods.

Laura J. Moriarty is a Professor of Criminal Justice in the School of Government and Public Affairs and Associate Dean, Academic Affairs, College of Humanities and Sciences at Virginia Commonwealth University. Her earned degrees include the Ph.D., Sam Houston State University (1988), the Master of Criminal Justice (1985), and Bachelor of Criminal Justice (1984) from Louisiana State University. Her research areas include victims of crime, victimology, fear of crime, and violent crime. She is the author, co-author, or co-editor of six books: *Victims of Crime* (with Robert Jerin, Nelson-Hall, 1998), *American Prisons: An Annotated Bibliography* (with Elizabeth McConnell, Greenwood Press, 1998), *Current Issues in Victimology Research* (with Robert Jerin, Carolina Academic Press, 1998), *Criminal Justice Technology in the 21st Century* (with David Carter, Charles C. Thomas, 1998), *Policing and Victims* (Prentice/Hall, 2002), and *Controversies in Victimology* (Anderson Publishing Company, 2003). She also has published over 45 scholarly articles, book chapters, and non-refereed articles.

Larry J. Myers is President of Justice Communications Incorporated (JCI), a software application development firm located in The Woodlands, Texas. JCI specializes in criminal justice education and training, as well as the development of Web-based and wireless communication systems for improving community justice. He received his Ph.D. in Educational Human Resource Development from Texas A&M University in College Station. In addition, he received his Masters in Criminology from Florida State University. His research interests include community justice, high technology crime investigation, instructional technology, criminal justice education, and training and development. Recent publications include two articles on teaching about computer crime in the *Journal of Criminal Justice Education.*

Laura B. Myers is Professor of Juvenile Justice in the College of Juvenile Justice and Psychology at Prairie View A&M University, Prairie View, Texas. Her doctorate degree in criminology is from Florida State University. Her publication areas include criminal justice education, criminal courts, criminal justice ethics, cultural diversity, and criminal justice administration. Recent publications include two articles on teaching about computer crime in the *Journal of Criminal Justice Education*, an article on substance abuse treatment for minority females in the *Prison Journal,* an article in the *Prison Journal* on cultural diversity awareness for correctional personnel, and two editions of a book on teaching criminal justice professors how to teach. She is currently writing a book on criminal justice ethics that will be published in 2005.

Samuel Nunn is a Professor of Criminal Justice in the School of Public and Environmental Affairs at Indiana University-Purdue University, Indianapolis, and research director of the Center for Urban Policy and the Environment. He has been a consultant for, among other clients, the Indiana State Police and the Indiana Counter Terrorism and Security Council. His research focuses on criminal justice technologies and their impacts, with criminal justice-related publications in the *Public Administration Review, Journal of Policy Analysis and Management, Journal of Urban Technology, Policing: An International Journal of Police Strategies and Management, Police Practice and Research,* and *Evaluation Review.*

Timothy J. Potts has a Bachelor of Science degree in Visual Communications Technology from Bowling Green State University. He has worked in the audiovisual field for over a decade. He is currently the Senior Systems Engineer for Virginia Commonwealth University's Media Support Services department where he is in charge of the technological installations for the university. His work encompasses multimedia platforms, videoconferencing, and distance education.

Kathryn E. Scarborough is an Associate Professor at Eastern Kentucky University. She earned her Ph.D. in Criminal Justice from Sam Houston State University. She also has a Master of Arts in Applied Sociology with a Certificate in Women's Studies from Old Dominion and Norfolk State Universities, and a Bachelor of Science in Criminal Justice from the University of Southern Mississippi. Dr. Scarborough is the Director for Research and Evaluation for the Justice and Safety Center. Prior to her teaching at Eastern Kentucky University, she was a police officer in Portsmouth, Virginia, a United States Navy Hospital Corpsman/Emergency Medical Technician, and a chemical dependency technician. Her current teaching and research interests include criminal investigation, law enforcement technology, community policing, and police administration.

Eric Shepardson is a Research Assistant at the University of Maryland's Bureau of Governmental Research. For the past 5 years, he has been working extensively with the Maryland Division of Parole and Probation to assist them in implementing their "Proactive Community Supervision" initiative, which has represented a significant change in their organizational culture and structure. Included in this work has been the development and delivery of training curricula that included the Proactive Community Supervision I Training, which focused on Motivational Interviewing as a brief intervention, and the "Sizing Up" training that introduced a new assessment process. Along with the development of the curricula, he has been extensively involved in the development and deployment of various interactive training tools that have been designed to assist staff in their understanding and use of these various new concepts. Some of the tools are the "Break the Cycle CD-ROM," "Nuts and Bolts of PCS," "Proactive Community Supervision CD-ROM," and "Tools of the Trade."

Irina R. Soderstrom is an Associate Professor in the Department of Corrections and Juvenile Justice Studies at Eastern Kentucky University. She received her Bachelor of Arts in Sociology/Pre-Law at the University of Illinois, Urbana-Champaign in 1987. She received her Master of Science in Administration of Justice in 1990, and her Ph.D. in Educational Psychology/Statistics and Measurement in 1997 from Southern Illinois University at Carbondale. Her primary teaching interests include statistics, research methods, and research seminar courses at both the undergraduate and graduate levels. Her primary research focus is in program evaluation and she has conducted considerable evaluative research on parole programs, boot camps, correctional industries, teen courts, and school safety.

Faye S. Taxman is a Professor in the Wilder School of Government and Public Affairs at Virginia Commonwealth University. Dr. Taxman's work is in corrections, sentencing, and program evaluation. She is currently the principal investigator evaluating the implementation of the 12 sites in the treatment and criminal justice component of the Washington/Baltimore HIDTA program and two evaluations of substance abuse treatment programs. She is also the co-principal investigator (with James Byrne) for the grant entitled "Evaluation of Prison Culture," sponsored by the National Institute of Corrections. Dr. Taxman has published in the areas of corrections, treatment, and evaluation.

To My Godchild
Haleigh Madison Moriarty

PREFACE

This new edition of *Criminal Justice Technology in the 21st Century* is the result of many individuals inquiring about the book being updated. Apparently, there are many universities and colleges that now offer courses in criminal justice that focus on technology. I find this very interesting as my institution is only just thinking about such a course for our program. Nonetheless, many of the individuals who have used the original book found it to be very useful in their classes, but as with all technology resources, it quickly became outdated. Thus, the impetus for the second edition stems from a push to update it by those who regularly used the book.

Many of those who contacted me about updating the book are current contributors to the second edition. It only seems natural that those who are teaching, developing, and researching criminal justice technologies should be included in the text.

The text still has 14 chapters with 9 new chapters written specifically for this edition, one chapter has been updated, one chapter is a reprint, and 3 chapters remain as they were in the first edition. What I like about the second edition is the appropriate mixture of "knowledge" or information about specific types of technology with empirical studies (i.e., evaluations) of certain technology used in various subcomponents of the criminal justice system. Students, educators, and practitioners will find this edition useful as it provides practical knowledge about different technology that is useful on many levels.

The book is arranged in the same format as the first edition. However, there are three introductory chapters, one that *is* the introduction written by Samuel Nunn, and two others, one that introduces Law Enforcement Technology written by Kathryn Scarborough and Gary Cordner, and the other introduces Prison Technology, written by Janice Joseph. These three chapters provide an excellent overview of technology in criminal justice. Professor Nunn begins by defining technology, which is a very interesting discussion, and then he moves into explaining specific criminal justice technologies (as he labels it). Professors Scarborough and Cordner focus on law enforcement technologies while Professor Joseph focuses on prisons. They make a skilled presentation of all the technology available to date in their respective areas. The chapters do not overlap; they complement each other. Both the neophyte and the techno "geek" will find these chapters informative and instructive.

The education section of the text has been increased from three chapters in the previous edition to four chapters. Three of the four chapters are new additions while the third chapter has been updated. The section has been expanded to include training in this section with two of the new chapters addressing specific training opportunities. The Taxman, Bello, and Shepardson chapter actually describes how to train individuals using interactive technology tools. The beauty of this system is that any type of training can be conducted using the interactive technology tools. The authors provide Websites and specific instruction for anyone interested in training in this manner. The Baggett, Collins, and Cordner (AnnMarie this time, not Gary) chapter provides an evaluation of a computer-based training for DNA evidence collection. The focus is not on the DNA evidence collection training, rather it is on the application or protocol used to provide the training. In this case the authors compare traditionally delivered training with training delivered via technology. The authors point out that if both strategies are successful in training individuals, then consideration should be given to what type of delivery system works best for an agency given time constraints, budget restrictions, willingness to be trained, and so on.

In that same section, Laura and Larry Myers describe the evolution of the criminal justice discipline to produce cyber competent criminal justice practitioners and researchers. Their work lays the foundation for a new chapter entitled "Computer Forensics" that is presented later in the book. The point emphasized by the Myers is that we are obligated as scholars and professors to prepare the future practitioners to respond appropriately to cybercrime. And in doing so we must continue to conduct research in this area or we will neglect our fundamental charge as academicians and the discipline will become stagnant and be nonresponsive to societal changes.

The chapter by Hutchinson, Mays, and Moriarty is updated and presents technological aids that can be used in statistics courses. The authors are still developing a CD-ROM to facilitate the understanding of statistics in all courses but to date they have not completed the project. In the meantime, many other products have been published since the first chapter was written, and the authors do a very nice job at updating the readers.

The next section of the book entitled "Law Enforcement Technology" has three new chapters while one remains as it appeared in the first edition. As you will see, my colleagues at Eastern Kentucky University have been very involved in research focusing on technology. I have already discussed the Scarborough and Cordner chapter that provides an excellent update on law enforcement technology, and as you will see, Kay and Gary have also been busy conducting a national survey on technology and training needs of rural law enforcement. Their chapter with their co-authors, Pamela Collins and Irina Soderstrom, reports the results of the national study. Rural law enforcement is often ignored when we focus on policing, especially when we narrow the focus to training and technological needs. Thus, the goal of the chapter is to describe the technological capabilities and technology-related training needs of small and rural law enforcement agencies. You will find the results of their study very interesting.

The other chapters in this section focus on specific law enforcement technologies with an evaluation of them. The problem-solver chapter was in the first edition. Mazerolle and Haas provide an excellent explanation of a system used to support problem-oriented policing. The new chapter by Baggett and Cordner (AnnMarie) is an evaluation of a mobile firearm simulation system. Both chapters discuss two very important technologies that are very helpful to law enforcement.

The next section focuses on courtroom and corrections technology. The first chapter written by Gordon, Moriarty, and Potts is an evaluation of videoconferencing in one jurisdiction. The authors survey courtroom personnel to determine their attitudes and opinions about this technology. It is an interesting chapter, especially when one thinks about the average age of the respondents, what the literature suggests about age and technological savvy, and the conclusions made by the authors that the respondents would like to see the technology used in more court-related procedures and/or settings.

The second chapter in this section is entitled "Technoprison: Technology and Prisons." It is a reprinted chapter that describes all the possible technology that can be used in prisons. It is a great overview just like the chapters written by Sam Nunn and Kay Scarborough and Gary Cordner. Professor Joseph discusses the specific technology used in prisons, the potential for increasing that technology, and identifying new types of technology that can be used while not losing sight of the fact that some of these technologies might violate prisoners' rights. It is a fascinating chapter–especially when you consider how little knowledge the public really has about the potential to use technology in a prison setting.

The last section is entitled "Criminality and Technology." One new chapter is presented, "Computer Forensics," and two chapters from the first edition are included. This section is compiled as it is to help with the "evolution of the discipline." In responding to the Myers' admonishment that we must "prepare the future practitioners to respond appropriately to cybercrime," this section provides a foundation for beginning to do so. Robyn Lacks and Christine Bryce fully support the Myers' warning and provide their own justification for their chapter that parallels what Laura and Larry are advocating: With "the increase in computer-related crimes it is imperative that law enforcement agencies and prosecutors gain the technology, skills, and abilities to obtain electronic evidence stored in computers (Lacks & Bryce, Chapter 12)." With that goal in mind, the authors present an overview of computer forensics including definitions, aspects, and activities of it. They also explore the legal aspects governing information technology in the criminal justice system, major computer crimes, and they conclude with a case study from the Virginia State Police's Computer Crime Unit.

The two chapters written by Katz and Carter and Carter and Katz provide an excellent overview of computer crime victimization in the United States, and computer applications by international organized crime groups. The three chapters together add to the cybercrime literature, providing material for instructors and others to use when studying such behavior.

The second edition developed into what I think is an excellent reader/text that allows both the neophyte and the expert to learn something. As this book goes to print, we will continue to investigate current criminal justice technologies, because one thing is clear; technology development, no matter where the arena, waits for no one.

L. J. M.

ACKNOWLEDGMENTS

The second edition of this text would not have been possible without the extraordinary contributions of the many contributors to this volume. I am especially indebted to Kay Scarborough who contacted me long ago to provide feedback about the first edition. We talked and she informed me that she and her colleagues at Eastern Kentucky University were very involved in projects focusing on technology. I was intrigued and we talked more. Kay graciously volunteered to coordinate the EKU effort, making sure that all the chapters were turned in on time and that all the necessary information was correct. I am honored to publish their work in this volume, and I appreciate everyone at EKU being so willing to submit a chapter for the cause.

Other contributors in this volume were contacted directly by me, and none of them shied away from the request. I met Sam Nunn when he interviewed for a position at VCU, and immediately felt very comfortable with him. We discussed our mutual interest in technology, where he expanded on some of his recent work in the area. I asked him to write the introduction chapter to the book, and he agreed. He did a fantastic job, and I think it really sets the stage for the remainder of the text. I thank you, Sam, for your fine work.

Jill Gordon, Robyn Diehl, Christine Bryce, Janet Hutchinson, James Mays, and Faye Taxman are all colleagues of mine at VCU. They got the "call" from me asking for either an update of a chapter or for a new contribution to the book. Their work is excellent and I thank them all for responding–some on very short notice–and for the quality of their work.

Laura Myers always comes through for me and I thank her! I saw her at the ACJS conference and asked her to update the chapter. I did not expect to get a completely revised chapter, as I know her plate is full, but that is exactly what Laura and Larry provided. Without her knowing, by writing a completely new chapter, she provided a perfect lead in for the last section of the book.

I must thank Janice Joseph and Roz Muraskin for allowing me to reprint Janice's chapter from Roz's book. We were discussing the chapter at the ACJS meeting in Las Vegas and I immediately knew that I wanted it for this book. Both Janice and Roz immediately agreed to let me publish it in my volume. What I did not know was how to go about getting permission from Pearson/Prentice-Hall to do so. When I found out there was a financial charge for doing so, I did not know if I would be able to get the chapter. Our new Interim Dean and the Director of the Wilder School of Government and Public Affairs, Dr. Robert Holsworth, graciously agreed to pay the fee to reprint the chapter. I always knew Bob supported scholarship and this generous gesture reinforced that idea in my mind. Thank you, Bob!

I would also like to thank the Dean's Office staff, especially India Urbach who is so helpful with everything I need. She has an incredible amount of knowledge about the university and knows how to get anything accomplished. Eventually, I guess, I would figure it out, but honestly I am not sure that this is an accurate statement.

I would also like to thank Dr. Patricia Grant. Her technological skills are phenomenal! She was a tremendous help as I tried to prepare Janice's chapter to be reprinted. Pat is my computer wiz and I am proud to call her my colleague and friend.

I would also like to thank Charles C Thomas Publisher, especially my editor, Michael Thomas. Michael has always been very responsive and supportive of this project.

Lastly, I have to thank my family. They have always supported me no matter what I decided to do.

CONTENTS

Part II: Law Enforcement Technology

Part III: Courtroom and Corrections Technology

Part IV: Criminality and Technology

CRIMINAL JUSTICE TECHNOLOGY IN THE 21ST CENTURY

Chapter 1

THE TECHNOLOGY INFRASTRUCTURE OF CRIMINAL JUSTICE

SAMUEL NUNN

The term technology typically conjures up images of sophisticated machines doing various routine and complicated tasks rapidly and efficiently, sometimes with and other times without the assistance of humans. We speak of the technologies that put humans on the moon, or that place sophisticated imaging technologies millions of miles into space, of transportation technologies, of digital technologies, and in the case of this book, of criminal justice technologies. However, in some respects, this popular treatment of the word misses its essence. One definition of technology is simply applied science–the study of industrial arts, how to make tools do the bidding of humans. Going further back, the Greek root of the word, *techne*, actually means art or artifice (which, in turn, means skill, ingenuity, trickery, or craft). It is not too much of a stretch, then, to conceptualize criminal justice technologies as the actions and attempts by various agents of the system to use new and existing tools and apply techniques in tricky and ingenious ways to the conduct of crime, the crime prevention and control operations of the police, the judicial processing functions of the courts, and the warehousing, rehabilitation, and monitoring functions of corrections systems. The primary actors in criminal justice–the criminals, the people who measure and analyze crime, the police, judges, prosecutors, defense attorneys, and corrections officers–are all interested in using information technologies and other technological forms (e.g., electronic databases, surveillance systems, pharmaceuticals, explosives, weaponry) to achieve their various objectives.

This chapter examines the technology infrastructure of criminal justice, offering an overview of the kinds of technologies now underpinning criminal justice systems as well as how these technologies are used by the various actors within criminal justice–including criminals–to accomplish ends. It first categorizes criminal justice technologies into seven broad groups, and includes a brief description of each category. Following that, the various ways that criminal justice actors rely on technologies are briefly explored. The last section deals with some of the key issues generated by criminal justice technologies: diffusion and adoption of use, the desired outcomes of technology applications, and the impacts on criminal justice work.

BROAD CATEGORIES OF CRIMINAL JUSTICE TECHNOLOGIES

There are at least seven different–though highly related–types of technological systems in use among actors inside criminal justice. Criminals, criminal organizations, and the entire public safety, courts, and corrections systems utilize different technology systems and rely to different degrees on each of them to support their respective missions. It is assumed that all actors have personal computers (PC), or that most agencies have some version of computing power connected via local or wide area networks (LANs, WANs), or else they rely more simply on unconnected PCs. Table 1-1 offers an overlook of criminal justice system actors and the technologies important to each.

Table 1-1: Types of Technology Systems within Criminal Justice

Primary types of technological systems	Primary users in criminal justice	Examples of systems	Other synergistic requirements
1. Communications	Criminals, police, courts, corrections	Analog radio, digital wireless, mobile digital terminals, cell phones, cellular digital packet data (CDPD)	Wired and wireless LANs and WANs, (ideally) interoperability among agencies

Table 1-1: Continued

Primary types of technological systems	*Primary users in criminal justice*	*Examples of systems*	*Other synergistic requirements*
2. Database and recordkeeping	Criminals, police, courts, corrections	Criminal histories, warrants, NCIC, state systems, MAGLOCLEN, IAFIS, CODIS, property room and evidence inventories	Relational and inquiry capabilities, interconnected networks and files
3. Decision support	Police, courts	VICAP, Link analysis software, data mining software, MATRIX, case management software, CAPPS II	Human experts to evaluate output and suggestions from systems
4. Biometrics	Police, courts, corrections	Biometric access control systems, pattern recognition systems	Large databases with metrics inventory (e.g., prints, irises, DNA, etc.)
5. Monitoring	Police, corrections	Video cameras, passive scanning thermography, in-car videotaping, ECHELON, Carnivore	GPS systems, wiretapping equipment, local cable or wireless networks to connect sites
6. Imaging	Police, courts, corrections	Facial recognition software, aerial photography, GIS, thermograpics, passive scanning devices	Large databases with searchable images
7. Weaponry and personal defense	Criminals, police, corrections	Taser stun guns, rubber bullets, beanbag guns, sticky shocker, laser dazzler, pepper spray, laser "heating" weapons, body armor	Training, standard operating procedures, "rules of engagement"

Communications: Audio and Video Communications Among Agencies and Agents

Communications systems lie at the technological heart of criminal justice organizations, particularly state and local law enforcement agencies. The communications systems in place largely establishes a police agency's capacity to (a) accept citizen calls for police services, (b) deploy motorized patrol officers to service calls and initiate crime prevention activities, (c) keep track of their activities, and (d) respond to the needs of police officers in the field. Traditional analog two-way radio technologies have been the core communications system of the police, but in many agencies these older systems are being supplanted rapidly by newer digital wireless technologies (e.g., mobile digital terminals [MDTs], cell phones, laptops) that offer operational efficiencies. In 2003, the San Diego Police Department implemented a new digital communications system using laptops, touch screens that call up city maps, and a cellular digital packet data system that maximizes use of communications frequencies used by the SDPD (Roth, 2003). Cell phones, wireless laptop computers, cellular digital packet data (CDPD) systems, and MDTs are becoming at least as important as the two-way radio link between police cars and dispatch centers. As they become more important, the systems create new challenges to local agencies. Coordination of different communications systems in the same region–known as interoperability–is needed to facilitate cross-jurisdictional cooperation and emergency response management, and communications budgets are driven up by new expenses linked to cell phone usage and capital investments required to implement new systems.

Database and Recordkeeping: Maintenance of Analog and Digital Databases

All actors in criminal justice keep records so any technologies that improve data management are valued. Paper records have an ancient history in most safety bureaucracies, and have been tackled by various technologies, starting with the filing cabinet. Now, the digitalization of biometric data (fingerprints, DNA), photographic images (mugshots, crime scenes, crime victims), documents, citations, and the other paper effluvia of criminal justice requires more sophisticated relational database systems (DBS). The size, complexity, and interconnectivity of contemporary databases continue to grow, and drive the need for relational DBS in criminal justice. The FBI's national fingerprint system IAFIS (Integrated Automated Fingerprint Identification System) held 43 million sets of fingerprint images as of January 2003 (Tofig, 2003). In 2001, the Combined DNA Index System (CODIS) contained "22,000 DNA profiles from crime scenes across the nation, as well as 531,555 profiles taken from those individuals convicted of either violent crimes or sex offenses" (Trahan, 2001). As the scale and intricacy of databases increase, relational database systems often need to have data mining capabilities–the ability to pull together specific data from widely decentralized public and private sources, and to underscore patterns of interactions among people and places that are suspected of terrorist or criminal activities (McCue, Stone, & Gooch, 2003). The challenge to law enforcement officials is to know what inquiries to direct into the systems.

Some argue that focused and effective data mining of highly decentralized public and private databases can produce reliable intelligence about potential terrorist or criminal plots. It is a vision of prognostication–the ability to foretell planned terrorist attacks and criminal conspiracies in order to stop them before execution. This idea is driven by public investigations of the 9-11 terrorist plot, which suggested that all the pieces were out there in different files and different places (flight lesson records, FBI warnings, terrorist watch lists, immigrations records, etc.), but no one had responsibility for synthesis and interpretation of these disparate data (for example, see CNN, 2002). Now, some DBS applications are designed to provide synthesis. A number of states have joined MATRIX (Multistate Anti-Terrorism Information Exchange), a system that joins public criminal and prison records with other private DBS (Krouse, 2004). Under the guidance of the U.S. Department of Homeland Security and the FBI, other states are developing regional emergency response networks. The Transportation Safety Administration recently rolled out the new CAPPS II (Computer-Assisted Passenger Prescreening), which assigns levels of risk (of terrorist or criminal behavior) to airline passengers. It is considered a data mining program (Carlson, 2003).

Decision Support: Smart Software Capable of Assisting Human Decision Making

The number of federal, state, and local database systems in place within criminal justice is impressive, but the sheer volume of information available can be a major challenge to police, prosecutors, and others responsible for analyzing and making sense of these data. Various software technologies–referred to as smart software, expert systems, decision support systems, or artificial intelligence–are able to provide more than the simple records management and general inquiry capabilities of database systems. One example of a decision support system is the Violent Criminal Apprehension Program (VICAP) maintained by the FBI. VICAP is designed to isolate and identify common patterns in violent crimes that might be related and point to particular suspects. In other areas of criminal justice, software systems are available to augment case management and case investigation, including expert systems that in effect offer advice and suggestions about how to deal with the target area. Link analysis software gives investigators the capability to uncover connections among crime suspects via telephone calls, travel, or other means of communications. One system "scans arrest records, incident reports, emergency phone calls, weapon ownership data, and other information to ensure all significant clues in an investigation are found and used by detectives to solve cases" (Cook, 2003). Vendors market packages with catchy names such as CopLink, iGlass, CrimeNtel, PatternTracer, and Analysts Notebook (Miller, 2002). Decision support systems are also used for internal management purposes. The LAPD reportedly uses a data mining system that "provides monitoring of officers' detrimental behavior patterns, including excessive use of force, racial profiling, and false arrests, but also tracks commendations, rewards, and overall performance evaluations" (Mearian & Rosencrance, 2001). The idea is to identify problem officers in order to stave off potential future troubles such as the Ramparts scandals, when corrupt LAPD officers were found to have systematically stolen drugs, planted evidence and weapons on police shooting victims, and illegally killed or wounded several suspects (for the Ramparts story, see Cannon, 2000).

In their more advanced forms, the data mining capabilities in decision support systems and artificial intelligence programs are thought to be capable of creating "total information awareness" (TIA), a term made infamous by the Defense Advanced Research Projects Agency (DARPA) in 2002-2003. The TIA program was visualized as a comprehensive information management tool against terrorism, but its rollout was attacked by many public interest groups as a potentially serious invasion of personal privacy. To make matters worse, the TIA program was headed by John Poindexter, who, while President Reagan's national security advisor, had been convicted (then appealed, and reversed, on technical grounds) of lying to Congress during the Iran-Contra scandal (Schorr, 2002). Although federal funding was reportedly terminated, many components of the TIA program still receive funding, including the "Evidence Extraction and Link Discovery projects" that were comprised of nearly two dozen data mining initiatives and the "Novel Intelligence from Massive Data effort" (Sniffen, 2004). In short, smart software will continue to be developed with an eye toward improving the abilities of law enforcement investigators and intelligence officers to sift through many and massive databases.

Biometrics: Use of Biological Parameters to Control People and Places

Biometrics uses measurements of the human body to identify individuals. A biometrics system typically requires (a) an interface that extracts the remnants of an individual's biological information from the physical environment or that records some aspect of a present individual's physiognomy that is (b) coupled to an extensive database that catalogs the biological component of interest (e.g., fingerprint, palmprint, DNA sequence). Major biometric systems in criminal justice include fingerprints, DNA testing, and facial recognition, although several technologies are emerging that use other metrics. To be effective, biometric systems must have a database infrastructure holding images of fingerprints, facial photographs, voice recordings, and other templates to serve as measuring rods.

Biometrics technologies can be classified into two groups. One is based on *physical or physiological factors* that incorporate fingerprints, palm characteristics, facial structure measurements, or DNA sequences. Another biometric approach is *behavioral.* Behavioral biometrics measure characteristics of individuals based on aspects of human behavior that evolve and become unique to a particular individual (e.g., voice patterns). Biometric measures can be attached to those individuals based on templates of the behavior of interest. Signature verification, voice pattern recognition, and keystroke dynamics are behavioral biometrics. Another behavioral biometric involves individual movement and crowd interaction systems used in the surveillance of parking lots, train and subway stations, and large events such as football games in order to spot and isolate behavior associated with sociopathic or destructive behavior (e.g., car theft, arson, mugging, robbery, vandalism), such as the way an armed robber approaches a potential victim at an ATM or the manner in which car thieves examine vehicles for possible theft.

Monitoring: Direct or Remote Observation of People, Places, and Machines

Another category of criminal justice technology includes tools to monitor people, spaces, computers, and communications devices. Some of these technologies are straightforward, such as using video cameras to create areas of surveillance, electronic wiretaps of telephone conversations, or "trap and trace" and pen register systems that record incoming and outgoing phone calls. Other monitoring systems are based on global positioning systems (GPS) that track stolen cars or the location of police cruisers. For the courts and corrections systems, GPS can help track the movements of individuals under house arrest, on probation, or on parole. There are monitoring systems designed to eavesdrop monitor displays from a personal computer by capturing the electromagnetic waves emanating from the terminal, known as van Eck receptors (Denning, 1999). A similar monitoring system is called Digital Interception by Remote Transmission (DIRT), which is a software program that can be inserted into a target computer via an e-mail "Trojan horse" that reports key strokes and logs of online activity to a separate, secure file. It reportedly cannot be detected with virus programs, and is supposedly available only to law enforcement personnel (Spring, 1999). These kinds of programs are called keyloggers because they capture keyboard input information, which must then be translated. Criminals also use keyloggers: the so-called "Kinko's Caper" involved the use of keylogger software to steal personal credit information from computer users in 13 different Kinko's stores in New York City (Napoli, 2003). There are dozens of keylogger software packages available commercially that copy a variety of data to an encrypted log file for later reading. The monitoring capability of these programs is extensive, including information such as:

- Window content of most chat clients (ICQ, AIM, Yahoo, etc.)
- Content of Internet browser window
- Mail content
- Keystrokes
- Pasting text from clipboard
- File operations
- System registry operations
- Application installation/uninstallation
- Putting programs in Startup folder
- Visiting Websites

Besides cyber-monitoring tools, ongoing threats that terrorists might use biological and chemical weapons of mass destruction have created a demand for environmental sensor systems capable of alerting officials to the presence of biological vectors (anthrax, smallpox, etc.) and chemicals (sarin) linked to possible terrorist attacks. Systems are reported in "secret locations" in 31 U.S. cities, including "Philadelphia, New York, Washington, D.C., San Diego, Boston, Chicago, San Francisco, and St. Louis" (Associated Press, 2003a).

Imaging: Analog or Digital Pictures of People, Places, and Evidence

Modern imaging technologies run the gamut from digital cameras to aerial photography to thermography to remote satellite telemetry systems. These technologies are used in law enforcement to document and examine crime scenes or to deconstruct and reconstruct still photos from other still and video cameras; in turn, the documented images are used by the court system to prosecute criminal cases. Imaging technologies are essentially designed to decode information that is invisibly embedded within space (e.g., a crime scene or a suspected amphetamine lab) or hidden behind physical barriers that might literally be actual walls and partitions, or simply poorly resolved physical images in existing photographs or video imagery. Police use thermography in night vision applications, and more advanced technologies–so-called passive scanning devices–allow users to literally see through clothing and walls to uncover hidden contraband, weapons, or to simply gain a tactical advantage in hostage or "stand-off" situations (Nunn, 2002). Current aviation security uses passive scanning of carry-on luggage, and similar technologies will eventually be used "on the street" to locate hidden weapons or explosives. Another common imaging technology in wide use is geographical information systems (GIS) that provide maps and graphical analyses of crime locations and hot spots, police resource deployment, and other spatial distribution questions.

Weaponry and Personal Defense: Use of Lethal and Nonlethal Weapons

Weaponry, whether designed to kill or incapacitate, is a primary interest of the police and correction actors within criminal justice. Of course, this interest is shared by criminals, criminal groups, and terrorists who often introduce lethality and aggravated violence into criminal activities. The flip side of weapons technology is the technology of personal defense–body armor and other protective tools–that are also valued highly by police, corrections, and criminals.

The U.S. defense industry provides a direct conduit for diffusing the use of new weaponry from military applications to law enforcement and corrections environments. Among other such examples is the laser "dazzler," which is a laser-equipped green strobe light designed to disorient subjects in a crowd. Other types of so-called nonlethal weaponry have been developed for military use, then prepared for migration to civilian law enforcement applications, including pepper spray, "sticky shocker" (a wireless projectile that sticks to a target and emits an incapacitating electric shock), and "webshot" (a 10-foot octagonal kevlar net that can entangle a suspect at up to 30 feet away). Webshot, originally developed for the U.S. Army, is now used by at least 30 law enforcement agencies worldwide (U.S. Army Research Office, 1999). Additional Department of Defense (DOD) research is directed at nets that can stop fast-moving vehicles, different types of sticky foams to slow or incapacitate suspects, heat rays, and sound technologies that can disorient or sicken subjects. Alliant Techsystems markets a rifle system with laser-guided smart shells that allow for shooting over and around boulders, trenches, and walls, made possible through the use of thermal and low light imaging technologies to track a target. At the receiving end of the weapons spectrum, advanced materials and fabrics technologies are used to develop better forms of antiballistic and antistab body armor and other shielding devices.

SYNERGY AND CRIMINAL JUSTICE TECHNOLOGIES

The success of any single technology used in criminal justice is often a function of successful use and effectiveness of other independent technology systems. Capturing video images of apparent lawbreakers is more valuable if there is also a compendium of "faces" against which to compare the video still. Biometric measurements are useful only if there are databases of searchable metrics against which comparisons can be made. Furthermore, imaging systems should ideally be in place to support full development of biometrics, but at a minimum must feed their contents and output into relational data base systems. Communications systems maximize their effectiveness in emergency response and critical incidents only if they are interoperable with the communications systems of other jurisdictions. Wireless communications systems will not supplant older analog systems unless sophisticated LANs and WANs are in place within agencies and jurisdictions. Thus, many criminal justice technology systems are sequential and highly dependent on other systems.

TECHNOLOGY USAGE BY CRIMINAL JUSTICE ACTORS

At the broadest level, the criminal justice system is typically categorized into four parts: crime and its perpetrators (included because incidence of criminal activity essentially drives the entire system), the police, the courts, and corrections. Each is subdivided extensively into subfields (e.g., organized crime, juvenile corrections, drug courts, etc.), but from the perspective of analyzing technology usage, it helps to look at the general ways in which technologies have been used within these categories. This forces us to consider which technology classes actors in criminal justice rely on the most, and which they use most effectively.

Criminals and Terrorists

As tools, technologies are generally neutral–that is, like any other tool, they can be applied to good or bad ends. A hammer can be used to build a house or beat a man to death. A computer connected to the Internet gives households access to vast pools of information, but also allows an easy channel for fraud, embezzlement, identify theft, criminal impersonation, espionage, money movement and laundering–and all of these crimes have been abetted by computer technologies. The technological sophistication of criminal groups grows and evolves. Criminals–not all, but some–have become technologically proficient and use available technologies to support criminal lifestyles and exploit new targets for crime. At a minimum, the following types of crime are augmented by technologies: hacking, drug dealing, espionage, homicide, child pornography, stalking, credit card fraud, theft of trade secrets, violation of intellectual property rights, invasion of intranets (i.e., internal, secure data networks used by various organizations), sex crimes, prostitution, terrorism, fraud, and forgery.

Reliance on technologies to perpetrate crimes varies considerably. A history of the hip-hop music industry noted that inner-city drug dealers were among the first societal groups to adopt cell phone and pager technologies (George, 1998). Criminals and terrorists use advanced technologies in many crimes–the use of airplanes as weapons of mass destruction; simultaneous suicide bombings with multiple explosions at each site (which requires sophisticated planning and secure communications, not to mention complex bombing devices with different kinds of shrapnel sprays to affect casualty totals). Indeed, the Internet has enhanced the network communications capacity of criminals in the same way it has for the general public. Criminal gangs use electronic technologies to improve their crime operations, inventories of contraband, and in "planning capers" just as legitimate business organizations do. On its own, much of the illegal drug industry owes its existence to pharmaceutical technologies.

Law Enforcement Agencies

In response to this, the police community must use technologies to combat the increasing technological sophistication of criminals. As crimes of different types occur, technologies of various kinds are applied to solve particular crimes or enhance crime prevention. Considering the long history of policing, two areas in which police have used technology extensively are transportation and communications. The police have quickly acquired the most modern devices from both sectors, although the length of time they rely on a particular generation of technology varies based on budgetary, political, and managerial factors (SEASKATE, 1998). The use of motorized ground transport (cars, motorcycles) has typically stayed abreast of the times, but police reliance on older communications systems has sometimes been a problem. Once a police agency adopts a communications system operating at a particular frequency, it usually makes only marginal and incremental adjustments rather than system replacements. This has resulted in a common problem among police departments–the lack of interoperability (that is, quick and seamless intercommunications between agencies) among different departments in the same region. Some states have initiated specific communications systems initiatives to install interoperable systems across different jurisdictions, such as Operation SAFE-T in Indiana (Associated Press, 2003b).

The police rely on technologies of nearly all types. Much of the ability of police organizations to identify criminals, *modus operandi*, known associates, criminal histories, conviction records, outstanding warrants and so forth is a function of electronic databases available for secure inquiries. Database and decision support systems such as the FBI's National Crime Information Center (NCIC), regional information sharing systems (e.g., MAGLOCLEN–the Middle Atlantic-Great Lakes Organized Crime Law Enforcement Network), VICAP, Law Enforcement Online (LEO), and others make it possible for investigators to pull case files together and develop suspect dossiers that are necessary for case investigations and clearances. Fears that some police officers might provide subtle clues that they will engage in misconduct has led several police agencies to use data mining software that attempts to identify problem officers through systematic reviews of many different police databases (Mearian & Rosencrance, 2001). The police regularly use lethal and nonlethal weaponry–as well as personal protection technologies–in the course of daily activities. Advances in weapons technology–for instance, use of the Taser to incapacitate offenders or arrestees with 50,000-volt barbs–are claimed to reduce harm to suspects who resist or flee arrest but are also thought to be used in the torture or punishment of suspects in police custody or offenders in prison (Kershaw, 2004).

Another category of particularly high value to law enforcement involves monitoring and eavesdropping technologies. Some are generally routine–such as wiretapping and video surveillance devices–but some are combined with database systems to create powerful monitoring technologies. Two in particular are the FBI's e-mail monitoring system, Carnivore, and the electronic communications monitoring system known as Echelon. The Carnivore system is used to intercept and log specified e-mail traffic through an Internet service provider, based on the issuance of a court-authorized wiretap order. Echelon is managed by intelligence organizations from five countries (United States, United Kingdom, Canada, Australia, and New Zealand), and has the capacity to intercept phone calls, e-mail messages, Internet downloads, and satellite transmissions.

Forensics and Investigative Science

To extract latent clues and evidence from crime scenes, forensic and police technicians make extensive use of biometric, imaging, and recordkeeping technologies. These technological systems run from the mundane to the extraordinary. Fingerprinting continues to be a primary means of placing suspected offenders at the site of crimes or particular places. Massive national and state databases are used to inventory fingerprints. In June 1999, the FBI rolled out the Integrated Automated Fingerprint Identification System (IAFIS), which has shortened the time needed to search linked databases comparing fingerprints. The IAFIS reportedly contains more than 32 million digitized cards containing fingerprints from all ten fingers (Tofig, 2003).

Beyond traditional fingerprinting technologies, forensic units use an array of laboratory tools and equipment to examine bodily fluids, hair, skin, toxins, bullets, written documents, ink, drugs, and other materials linked to crimes and needed as evidence to prosecute accused suspects. Life science technologies have made DNA identification a common procedure, generating increasingly larger databases of DNA profiles of convicted felons and others. National DNA databases are contained in the Combined DNA Index System (CODIS), maintained by the FBI since 1990 (Rossmo, 2000, p. 55; Niezgoda & Brown, 1995), and many states have begun to build DNA libraries. Nearly all states require DNA samples from convicted sex offenders (Hibbert, 1999, p. 769). Lately, the field of computer forensics–the ability to monitor and deconstruct the various ways in which computers are used as tools in criminal activities–has become especially important because of the increasing use of computers by criminals.

Prosecution and the Courts

The judicial system obviously requires major database and recordkeeping technologies. These technologies also run the gamut of complexity, from simple filing systems to, increasingly, digital imaging technologies that are being utilized by some criminal courts to create sophisticated evidence control and presentation systems. More routine are the database management systems used by courts to develop criminal histories and conviction records of defendants, as well as to track offenders' journies through various components of the trial and sentencing system. Imaging technologies now used in various state courts include videoconferencing via closed-circuit TV (CCTV) systems utilized to perform arraignments and to minimize travel expenses and transfers of prisoners from jails to the court. In addition, prosecutors are prime consumers of the technological outputs produced by both the police agencies and forensic units charged with collecting criminal evidence, and likewise rely on electronic database management systems to assemble and collate evidence for criminal trials. Software systems assist prosecutors and the police in case investigation and management (e.g., General Evidence Management System, Case Investigative Life Cycle, PowerCase). Some of these are designed explicitly to improve the connectivity and information flow between the police and prosecutors (Miller, 2002).

Corrections

The corrections systems in criminal justice require monitoring, imaging, database and recordkeeping technologies, and lethal and nonlethal weaponry in order to function effectively. This, of course, is in addition to basic communications systems. At the extreme end of the prison technology spectrum, many prisons are currently designed to maximize monitoring technologies and minimize labor requirements (Hallinan, 2001). The technology of surveillance has become extremely advanced, and surveillance is what prisons are all about. In-person visual monitoring is strengthened or replaced by video technologies. Remote sensors, video surveillance, and perimeter monitoring systems are sometimes used in lieu of the traditional watch tower in prisons (Pfankuch, 2002). Regarding individual prisoners, Riker's Island prison in New York City uses a system called BOSS (Bodily Orifice Scanning System) that scans prisoners for weapons stored inside their bodies.

Prisons are interested in nonlethal weaponry to control unruly prisoners or respond to riots and disturbances, but there is also the possibility such weapons are applied to less seemly purposes. The use of Tasers by prison guards is considered a safer alternative than guns, without weakening control over prisoner behavior. Prison riot simulations have tested the use of pepper spray devices, as a less-than-lethal means of responding to prisoner disorders (Hayden, 2004). There are also documented instances in which nonlethal weapons (Tasers, pepper spray, incapacitating agents) are used unethically to mete out punishment–that is, the use of such weapons as a means of torture and submission–so the diffusion of nonlethal weapons works both sides of the ethics divide. Wright (2002, p. 82) cites United Nations Human Rights documents reporting that "prison guards in Arizona, California, New Mexico, and Texas have been accused of tormenting inmates with stun batons."

ISSUES IN THE USE OF TECHNOLOGIES BY CRIMINAL JUSTICE ACTORS

Like other societal sectors, the criminal justice community faces a variety of issues regarding its use of advanced information and other technologies. The primary issues involve (a) how technologies diffuse among actors and places, (b) the anticipated direct and indirect impacts of these technologies, and (c) the ways that technologies are likely to change the work process of criminal justice agencies.

Acquisition and Diffusion of Criminal Justice Technologies

When technologies are applied successfully to the operations of criminal justice agencies, managers will be interested in how to expand usage to other agencies with similar missions. Knowing how to increase the spatial diffusion of successful technologies is therefore an important part of technology management. In this respect, there are several forces affecting acquisition and diffusion of new, successful criminal justice technologies.

Military technologies for use in criminal justice. Military involvement in local police departments has introduced police personnel to advanced military technology (Kraska & Cubellis, 1997), especially through federal drug policy (Baum, 1996; Gray, 1998). As the domestic drug war escalated in the early 1980s, the 1982 U.S. Department of Defense Authorization Act included a section entitled the "Military Cooperation with Civilian Law Enforcement Agencies Act" (Diffie & Landau, 1998), which codified a level of cooperation between military and civilian law enforcement authorities. The U.S. General Accounting Office (1999) reported the DOD provided $125.9 million in crime technology assistance to state and local law enforcement agencies during the 1996-1998 period. Considering the large number of police agencies, this is not much money per agency. Of course, local agencies can buy technologies directly from defense vendors, without going through the federal government, and this happens. Haggerty and Ericson (2001) have argued that military technologies are now being introduced directly to domestic police agencies in a "dual use" format (military and civilian usages) rather than gradually "trickling down" from military to police usage. This is especially true for SWAT and other tactical police units (Kraska & Cubellis, 1997).

Diffusion of technologies among agencies. Technologies move across space, and several forces and trends have led to more new technologies in the hands of more criminal justice agencies. In the first place, system agents want the newest technological tools (SEASKATE, 1998). Diffie and Landau (1998, p. 117) note that "police have often been at the forefront of the use of new technologies." Once technologies are acquired, good and bad news about usage travels by word of mouth, professional conferences, vendors and their advertisements, interpersonal networks, and other channels. Whether technologies are adopted by justice agencies is driven by the communications networks of managers, their tolerance for risk-taking and liability concerns, peer emulation and imitation, available resources, and a department's propensity to innovate (Weiss, 1997). Newsletters from the NLECTC (National Law Enforcement and Corrections Technology Center) communicate stories, identify systems and software, and disseminate information about successes and failures in technology applications.

Federal programs and agencies. Federal initiatives and funding have sparked use of some technologies. Earlier, it was due to riots and protests; lately it is linked to antiterrorism and emergency preparedness. The U.S. Law Enforcement Assistance Administration (LEAA) delivered grants from 1968 to 1984 that allowed local police to purchase new technologies, many of which had been designed for and perfected by military users for both offensive and defensive purposes (SEASKATE, 1998). Parenti (1999, p. 23) argues that the urban riots and civil rights and war protests (more or less continuously from the late 1950s through the early 1970s) planted the seeds of police militarization and technological enhancement, leading to "the first systematic and large-scale technology transfers from the military to the civilian police." Crowd control tools (rubber bullets, incapacitating agents, sonic weapons) and military lessons from their use have drifted into local police operations. Currently, federal funds attached to homeland security, some originating from the USA PATRIOT Act of 2001, are investing in new emergency response systems that include sophisticated intranet development specific to particular regions of the country (the Dallas Southwestern Emergency Response Network [SERN], the Indiana Alert Network [IAN], and others in the Atlanta and Seattle (NWARN–Northwest Warning, Alert, and Response Network) regions (U.S. Department of Homeland Security, 2004).

Police tactics and strategies. Change in policing strategies will demand new technologies and systems of use. The attempted transition from reactive motorized patrol to proactive community policing required new decentralized forms of communications technologies such as wireless radios and MDTs. Analysts argue that these technologies were needed to control urban space, subdivided to police beats (Saunders, 1999; Herbert, 1997). Urban riots and civil disorder ushered in decentralized neighborhood-based policing (which differs from the motorized calls-for-services model). Community policing required different and more sophisticated decentralized information systems to support the localized problem-solving approaches that formed the crux of problem-oriented and community-oriented policing (Correia, 2000). This created more demand for systems such as local GIS-based mapping systems, aerial photography of urban neighborhoods, cell phones, MDTs and computer-assisted dispatch, automated fingerprint databases, and online offense reporting systems. As policing strategies change, the demand for more appropriate technologies grows.

Available financial resources. Technology use is easier when there are financial resources to purchase hardware and software systems. Asset seizure laws emerged from the racketeering in corrupt organizations (RICO) acts, and are important because dollars generated from liquidating these assets can be used to support technology acquisition. The forfeiture laws allowed local police agencies to acquire assets that could be sold, with the cash used to purchase new advanced technologies. After 1984, an expansion of police budgets was made possible with the asset forfeiture practices of the RICO acts. Police agencies could seize, then sell or use, ill-gotten gains from those arrested for selected crimes (e.g., drug dealing). Between 1979 and 2001, the U.S. Customs Service seized assets valued at an average of $756 million annually, and the U.S. Drug Enforcement Administration seized an annual average of about $586 million between 1992 and 2002 (unadjusted for inflation, calculated from data reported by U.S. Department of Justice, 2002, tables 4.42, 4.44). Parenti (1999, p. 52) tells of Glendale, CA, which used proceeds from selling asset seizures to "stock the department with infrared night vision goggles, cell phones, video surveillance and recording equipment, and a fingerprint-reading laser wand."

Combining some or all of these elements produces a steady supply of new technological tools in criminal justice organizations. On the face of it, this is a positive trend, offering as it does a supply of advanced technologies for the war on crime and terrorism. However, the widespread use and diffusion of technologies can also occur without systematic consideration of the direct outcomes–let alone unanticipated outcomes–that can result as new tools, largely untested in the field, are applied to various operating systems.

Outcomes from Criminal Justice Technologies

What are technologies designed to accomplish? Different outcomes will be associated with different technologies, and outcomes for the same or similar technologies might even be different among separate agencies. Some technological systems might have obvious outcomes–a property room inventory management system should reduce theft and improve control over evidence–but some technologies are adopted without clear ideas about potential outcomes. New communications systems are installed to improve information exchange, but how are such improvements actually measured? One evaluation of how a cellular digital packet data communications system affected a state police problem-oriented policing (POP) operation found that the technology was very suitable for overall patrol needs, but that it offered no special benefit for the POP officers (Nunn & Quinet, 2002). Will the implementation of case management systems improve the processing capabilities of U.S. courts? As a field of biometrics, DNA analysis was conceived and used originally as a means of verifying guilt, but is now used to exonerate incarcerated prisoners who were apparently innocent and thus wrongly convicted (*Frontline*, 1999). Some of the backlogs in police laboratory DNA testing have been attributed to "innocence testing" rather than developing prosecution evidence.

To see the direct and less obvious impacts of a technology, consider the mobile digital terminal now commonly used in most police vehicles. As MDTs diffused among and within police agencies, the typical pitch for their acquisition was that they would improve the speed and efficiency of dispatch operations. An argument could also be made that MDTs improve officer safety. All this might have occurred, but there have been few close examinations of the operating effect of MDTs. However, there have been indirect impacts that came to light almost accidentally. When MDTs were used as a means of messaging and requesting records checks, they become official logs of all communications and data requests from that patrol car. These logs could indicate an officer demonstrated excellent police work and proper protocols or they could suggest police malfeasance. MDTs were used to send text messages between patrol cars during the Rodney King affair in Los Angeles when racist and derogatory messages were exchanged among patrol vehicles. Police officers also began using MDTs to run vehicle identification information without having probable cause–or in some cases even reasonable suspicion–that there was any criminal activity at hand (Erickson & Haggerty, 1997).

The use of MDTs to support a new habit of running any and all license plates that struck a police officer's fancy had another indirect impact, more positive this time. It is possible that use of MDTs can generate a higher percentage of motor vehicle theft (MVT) clearances and recoveries. In a comparison of three Texas cities (two–Dallas and Fort Worth–that used MDTs, and one–Austin–that did not), there were higher clearance and recovery rates for vehicle theft in cities using police MDTs (Nunn, 1994). The aggregate theory and data suggested that patrol officers using MDTs could more easily obtain quick identification of stolen vehicles. Because MDT usage could increase the speed of identifying a vehicle as stolen, it would be possible to stop and arrest more suspects driving or holding those vehicles and would therefore increase recoveries and clearances of open offenses. The traditional reliance on two-way radio conversations between patrol officers and dispatchers would be too slow in these instances, and police without quicker MDT response capacity would miss possible arrests. Thus, two-way analog radio–an earlier public safety technology system–would begin to be supplanted by new digital and wireless telecommunications system, and eventually be overtaken in an ongoing game of technological evolution and succession. As new technologies show consistently successful outcomes, they demonstrate survival of the fittest and become more widely used.

Effect of Technologies on Criminal Justice Work Processes

Technology studies have taught us that humans and their tools combine, interact, and form new ways of doing things. The continuing use of new tools and techniques by criminals, the police, the courts, and the prison industry will evolve always, affecting the actions and comparative successes of each group. Changes in the operating procedures of criminal justice agencies go hand in hand with new technologies, just as these same technological systems enable the criminal class to execute more sophisticated crimes.

One way of looking at advanced technologies in criminal justice is to consider them, like other kinds of labor-saving machinery, as changes to the production process–they will alter the way that criminal justice professionals perform their jobs. For managers, technologies provide additional control over the discretion of labor. Consider the ways in which a police officer, using only human senses and intuition, comes to the conclusion that an individual is concealing contraband or weapons, and decides to stop that individual. That could happen if the suspect behaves in a suspicious fashion, witnessed by the police. At that point, options emerge. The officer could have probable cause or at least reasonable suspicion, and could legally detain the suspect to see if the suspicion was warranted. The police officer could also use experience and the circumstances of the moment to conclude that something is funny, and on that basis–with little or no probable cause, and less legitimacy–proceed with a stop and frisk. In both these instances, administrators are relying on the judgment and discretion of police officers to take action based on perceptions and observations. The officer could, in the end, simply decide that stopping the suspect is unnecessary or unlikely to result in revelations of illegal contraband or weaponry. When relying on police officers unaided by advanced technologies, managers must also rely on the fallible perceptions of individual officers to make decisions on the potential arrest of suspects. At best, control is loose.

Contrast this with the process involved in the use of passive scanning devices such as those made possible through thermographic technology that reveals images of items hidden under clothing or behind walls (Nunn, 2002). Here, some of the police discretion described earlier is eliminated: The officer turns on the device, scans suspects, responds to machine output, and individuals scanned by the machine are either "carrying" or not. Discretion becomes binary. Of course, the officer could have made a discretionary decision about which individuals to scan, but suppose the subject is a stream of citizens passing by the scanning device. The technological system that evolves reduces discretionary behavior; any one passing by is scanned, and the presence of contraband or weapons can be isolated and stopped. A higher level of control emerges. In the same way that industrial machine tools reduce errors associated with a human operator–that is, introduce more control by supervisors–the scanning device reduces the level of discretion exercised by police officers, and thereby institutes closer control of the public safety labor production process. Thus, police administrators could have several reasons to introduce advanced technologies to officers in the field, even if policies are ill- or loosely defined. More managerial control is exercised, and the issue of officer discretion is minimized in those situations where scanning technologies are used.

Another example includes the substitution of technology for labor in prisons, or the use of technical systems to augment human performance. One analysis of the difference in costs between using electronic monitoring technologies versus traditional prison guards noted that "with a one-time cost of about $175,000, the perimeter monitoring systems can last for at least 10 years, compared to the $800,000 annual cost of keeping armed officers on towers 24 hours a day" (Pfankuch, 2002). Thus, the job of supervising incarceration becomes qualitatively different, with less interaction between guards–who become monitors of electronic screens–and the prisoners. Also the use of less-than-lethal technologies could become more widespread in prisons, to the point that the inmate control becomes technologically based. One analyst has noted that "the design and conditions of the deployment of plastic bullets may facilitate extensive use, calmative drugs may introduce possibilities for systematic rape and the mechanized use of chemical irritants in prisons may radically alter existing relations....in other words, the availability of nonlethal weapons may lead to more coercive acts" (Rappert, 2002, p. 71).

The technologies we put in place today affect the systems we use tomorrow. Similar examples in the courts could be developed. How will case management systems affect the administration of justice by the judicial branch? Will it soon be possible (or desirable) to indict, arraign, and try offenders without their setting foot inside a courtroom? While seemingly far-fetched, the technological capacity easily exists to support such a radical change in the delivery of court-based services and procedures.

CONCLUSIONS AND OTHER ISSUES

Technologies are widely used by many actors within the criminal justice system, including its gravitational center, criminals. There are several categories of these technologies–communications, database systems, biometrics, monitoring and imaging devices, weaponry, and expert systems–and new developments emerge regularly within each category. Criminal justice technologies are used directly as tools in the wars on crime and terrorism, as well as adjuncts to the efficient management of public safety agencies, courts, and corrections. As technological systems become more (or less) effective, they replace (or are replaced by) other systems. The comparative success of these technology tools is communicated among actors and agencies, and across space. Diffusion occurs, and the process of technological evolution and succession continues into the future.

Finally, a few other issues linked to criminal justice technologies should be targeted for more focused attention. Many analysts have commented on the privacy impacts of criminal justice technologies (among many, see Lyon, 1994; Marx, 1988; Whitaker, 1999). Massive relational database systems connect many information sources that have not been extensively linked before (e.g., purchasing habits, criminal histories, travel records, library usage). How agents of the criminal justice system will use (or exploit) these newly connected systems is an evolving process, and the history of technological systems tells us there will be both expected and unexpected outcomes. Advanced imaging and monitoring technologies can reveal all things hidden from plain sight, and such technologies will integrally affect legal notions of reasonable suspicion, probable cause, and reasonable doubt. Traditional civil liberties will be affected, and the courts will be the ultimate arbiters of technology use and abuse.

REFERENCES

Associated Press. (2003a). "Secret sensors scour air for bioterrorism." *Boston Globe*, July 21. Accessed March 14, 2004, at http://www.commondreams.org/cgi-bin/print.cgi?file=/headlines03/0721-04.htm

Associated Press. (2003b). "Work begins on statewide communication system," June 8, at http://web.lexis-nexis.com

Baum, D. (1996). *Smoke and mirrors: The war on drugs and the politics of failure.* Boston: Back Bay Books.

Cannon, L. (2000). "One bad cop." *New York Times Magazine*, October 1, p. 32.

Carlson, C. (2003). "Data mining proponents defend technology." *eWeek.* May 6, at www.eweek.com/article2/0,1759,1060558,00.asp.

CNN. (2002). "Report cites warnings before 9/11," September 19. Accessed March 13, 2004, at http://www.cnn.com/2002/ALLPOLITICS/09/18/intelligence.hearings/09/18/intelligence.hearing/index.html

Cook, G. (2003). "Software helps police draw crime links." *Boston Globe*, July 17, p. A1.

Correia, M. E. (2000). "The conceptual ambiguity of community in community policing: Filtering the muddy waters." *Policing: An International Journal of Police Strategies and Management*, Vol. 23, No. 2, pp. 218-233

Denning, D. (1999). *Information warfare and security*. Reading, MA: Addison-Wesley.

Diffie, W. & Landau, S. (1998). *Privacy on the line: The politics of wiretapping and encryption*. Cambridge, MA: MIT Press.

Erickson, R. V. & Haggerty, K. D. (1997). *Policing the risk society*. Toronto: University of Toronto Press.

Frontline. (1999, November 11). *The case for innocence: DNA testing*. [Television broadcast]. WFYI-TV. Indianapolis, IN.

George, N. (1998). *Hip-hop America*. New York: Viking.

Gray, M. (1998). *Drug crazy: How we got into this mess and how we can get out*. New York: Routledge.

Haggerty, K. D. and Ericson, R. V. (2001). "The military technostructures of policing." In P.B. Kraska, (Ed.), *Militarizing the American criminal justice system: The changing roles of the armed forces and the police* (pp. 43-64). Boston: Northeastern University Press.

Hallinan, J. T. (2001). *Going up the river: Travels in a prison nation*. New York: Random House.

Hayden, T. (2004). Putting down a riot. U.S. News & World Report. June 14. Accessed 12/7/04 at http://web.Lexis-Nexis.com

Herbert, S. (1997). *Policing space: Territoriality and the Los Angeles police department*. Minneapolis: University of Minnesota Press.

Hibbert, M. (Fall, 1999). "DNA databanks: Law enforcement's greatest surveillance tool?" *Wake Forest Law Review* 34: 767-825.

Kershaw, S. (2004). "As shocks replace police bullets, deaths drop but questions arise." *New York Times*, March 7, p. 1.

Kraska, P., & Cubellis, L. J. (1997). "Militarizing Mayberry and beyond: Making sense of American paramilitary policing." *Justice Quarterly* 14 (4): pp. 608-629.

Krouse, W.J. (2004). The multi-state Anit-Terrorism information exchange (MATRIX) pilot project CRS report for Congress, Congressional Research Service. The Library of Congress. Order Code RL 32536. August 18.

Lyon, D. (1994). *The electronic eye: The rise of surveillance society*. Minneapolis: University of Minnesota Press.

Marx, G. (1988). *Undercover: Police surveillance in America*. Berkeley: University of California Press.

McCue, C., Stone, E. S., & Gooch, T. P. (2003). "Data mining and value-added analysis." FBI *Law Enforcement Bulletin* 72(11): 1-7.

Mearian, L., & Rosencrance, L. (2001). "Police policed with data mining engines." *ComputerWorld*, April 2, p. 6.

Miller, C. (2002). "Linking crimes, linking criminals." *Law Enforcement Technology* 29(5): p. 28.

Napoli, L. (2003). "The Kinko's caper: Burglary by modem," *New York Times*, August 7, p. G1.

Neizgoda, Jr., S. J. & Brown, B. (July, 1995). "The FBI Laboratory's COmbined DNA Index System Program." Federal Bureau of Investigation.

Nunn, S. (1994). "How capital technologies affect municipal service outcomes: The case of police mobile digital terminals and stolen vehicle recoveries," *Journal of Policy Analysis and Management*, 13, pp. 539-559.

Nunn, S. (2002). "When Superman used x-ray vision, did he have a search warrant? Emerging law enforcement technologies and the transformation of urban space," *Journal of Urban Technology* 9(3): 69-87.

Nunn, S., & Quinet, K. (2002). "Evaluating the effects of information technology on problem-oriented policing: If it doesn't fit, must we quit?" *Evaluation Review* 26(1): 81-108.

Pfankuch, T. B. (2002). "Technology threatens prison watchtowers," *Florida Times-Union*, January 15, p. A1.

Parenti, C. (1999). *Lockdown America: Police and prisons in the age of crisis*. New York: Verso.

Rappert, B. (2002). "Towards an understanding of nonlethality." In N. Lewer (Ed.), *The future of nonlethal weapons: Technologies, operations, ethics and law*. (p. 53-74). Portland, OR: Frank Cass Publishers.

Rossmo, D. K. (2000). *Geographic profiling*. Boca Raton, FL: CRC Press.

Roth, J. (2003). "Calling all cars." *Police* 27(11): p. 44.

Saunders, R. H. (1999. "The space community policing makes and the body that makes it." *The Professional Geographer* (1): pp. 135ff.

Schorr, D. (2002). "Poindexter redux." *Christian Science Monitor*, November 29. Accessed March 13, 2004, at http://www.csmonitor.com/2002/1129/p11s01-coop.html

SEASKATE, Inc. (July, 1998). *The Evolution and Development of Police Technology*. Technical report prepared for the National Committee on Criminal Justice Technology, National Institute of Justice.

Sniffen, M. J. (2004). "Controversial government data-mining research lives on." Associated Press, February 23.

Spring, T. (1999). "Getting DIRT on the bad guys." *PC World Online*. .http://www.pcworld.com/news/article/O,aid,11614,00.asp

Tofig, D. (2003). "43 million-print database puts the finger on suspects." *Atlanta Journal-Constitution*, January 6, p. 1A.

Trahan, J. (2001). "DNA technology, database help crack open cold cases," *Dallas Morning News*, October 14, p. 1Y.

U.S. Army Research Office. (1999). "WEBSHOT," Washington, D.C. Accessed March 14, 2004, at http://www.aro.army.mil/arowash/rt/sbir/99brochure/webshot.htm

U.S. Department of Homeland Security. (2004). "DHS INFO pilot programs," press release, February 2.

U.S. Department of Justice. (2002). *Sourcebook of Criminal Justice Statistics*, 2002. Accessed online on February 29, 2004, at http://www.albany.edu/sourcebook/

U.S. General Accounting Office. (1999). *Crime technology: Department of Defense Assistance to State and Local Law Enforcement Agencies*, letter report, GAO/GGD-00-14, October 12.

Weiss, A. (1997). "The communication of innovation in American policing." *Policing: An International Journal of Police Strategies and Management*, 20, (2): pp. 292-310.

Whitaker, R. (1999). *The end of privacy: How total surveillance is becoming a reality.* New York: The New Press.

Wright, S. (2002). "The role of sublethal weapons in human rights abuse." In N. Lewer (Ed.), *The future of non-lethal weapons: Technologies, operations, ethics and law* (pp. 75-86). Portland, OR: Frank Cass Publishers.

Part I

CRIMINAL JUSTICE EDUCATION/TRAINING AND TECHNOLOGY

Chapter 2

MEETING THE DEMAND FOR CYBER COMPETENT CRIMINAL JUSTICE PRACTITIONERS AND RESEARCHERS: THE EVOLUTION OF A DISCIPLINE

LAURA B. MYERS AND LARRY J. MYERS

A major evolution in the development and use of technology in the workplace, education, the community, and even among criminals has taken place during the last two decades. The use of desktop, laptop, and hand-held computers has become indispensable in the work environment. Cell phone technology, the Internet, and geotracking have changed the way we communicate, obtain knowledge, and locate our positions. Every major field has adapted technology to its domain. When we purchase groceries, computers scan for prices and charge our debit cards. If we want to send flowers or a card, we need only visit the Internet. Anything we want to buy can usually be found for sale on the Internet.

To function in this technology age, we must have the skills necessary to operate the technology and use the products for our everyday needs. Older generations have slowly adapted to technology use, while younger generations have benefited from cyber socialization. While many of us remember getting color television and cable television for the first time, our children and grandchildren have been raised with cell phones, a computer in the home, e-mail, and the Internet. In the 1980s a mouse was just an animal. Today, a mouse is for use with a computer. Today, children are learning to use a mouse the way older generations learned to use pens and pencils. Many children today can use a mouse before they can write.

It is no surprise that criminals and deviants have adapted technology to their own domain as well. Technology has created new venues for crime, new methods for crime commission, and new types of crime (Armstrong, 2000; Carter & Katz, 1996). Pedophiles look for their child victims on the Internet. Many types of fraud are perpetrated with computers. Corporations discover new ways to increase profit, both legally and illegally, with computer technology. Identity theft has become a major problem with so much exchange of information via technology. (For a listing of recent federal computer crime cases, see http://www.usdoj.gov/criminal/cybercrime/crimes.html).

With so many societal changes resulting from technology-related crime and victimization, the discipline of criminology and criminal justice must respond. Academic programs must conduct the research necessary to understand cybercrime and must teach students to respond appropriately as practitioners and as future researchers. The impact of this evolution includes computer crime research topics, university and college curriculums that include cybercrime knowledge, and the production of graduates prepared to meet the demands of cyber challenges in crime (Rosenblatt, 1995; White & Charney, 1995; Sharrar & Granado, 1997; President's Commission on Critical Infrastructure Protection,1997).

This chapter discusses the need for cyber evolution in criminal justice and criminology. The onset of cybercrime is presented and implications for appropriate criminal justice responses and curriculum changes are discussed. The response of the discipline to the demands for cyber competency is presented. The chapter concludes with anticipated demands, barriers, and opportunities to be faced by the discipline as it responds to changes in the substance of crime and the criminal justice response.

TECHNOLOGY AND THE IMPACT ON CRIMINAL JUSTICE

The Internet, e-mail, cell phones, and other communication and analytical technologies have significantly improved the communication process in criminal justice, as well as the ability to store and retrieve data. Many of the inefficiencies in criminal justice have been improved by these technologies. The response time of patrol officers has been increased with better dispatch technologies. The interconnections between agencies have been enhanced with the ability to interface. Crime scene investigations have been enhanced with technology. The tracking of offenders across jurisdictions has become easier. Databases of DNA and other information have led to better resolutions of crimes (University of North Texas Health Science Center, 2003; Myers & Myers, 1995).

The field technology used by practitioners has been enhanced with recent developments. Patrol cars are equipped with mobile data systems and officers carry cell phones. Judges and lawyers use computers and presentation software in the courtroom. Distance technologies allow people to observe court activity and to participate in courtroom activities from long distance. Prisons use technologies to monitor activity in prisons and to manage inmates more efficiently.

Researchers in criminology and criminal justice are able to analyze larger data sets with the creation of more sophisticated computer technology. In many cases, complete enumerations of data instead of samples can be analyzed, permitting a reduction in the potential for sampling error. Sophisticated software, including updated versions of Statistical Package for the Social Sciences (SPSS), creates the potential to conduct analyses that were once impossible.

Teaching criminology and criminal justice students also has changed with advances in technology. The use of overhead projectors and slide shows has been updated with the use of PowerPoint™ and the Internet. Typewriters are no longer necessary to complete written work. Word processing allows students to revise multiple drafts of their work. Students who are located too far from universities and colleges to obtain an education can now attend school via distance education. The software tools of Blackboard™ and WebCT™ permit professors to teach students all over the world using chat rooms and discussion boards (Myers, 2003).

The technology age has created a great potential for the advancement of the field of criminology and criminal justice, for both practitioners and educators. Although technology can make our lives more efficient, people may distrust new technologies and often lack the confidence to learn how to use those technologies. In 1997, the co-authors of this chapter conducted a study of criminal justice and criminology professors to determine their likelihood to use new technologies to teach their students (Myers & Myers, 1998). The intent of the study was to determine the degree of computer literacy among criminal justice and criminology professors as they prepared future practitioners and scholars for the field. These future practitioners and scholars would need to be exposed to and learn as much about technology as possible to meet the demands of the technology transformations in the field. A random sample of professors and instructors who were members of the Academy of Criminal Justice Sciences were surveyed.

In the 1997 study, three factors were analyzed. First, the attitudes regarding the use of technology in the teaching process were assessed. A majority of those surveyed indicated that both professors and students should use computers in the learning process and use them in courses that were not traditionally computer-based courses. Second, in addition to pro-computer attitudes, educators should have the knowledge, skills, and abilities to use computers in the learning process. The educators surveyed indicated they did possess the more traditional skills of word processing and data analysis skills they had learned during their own graduate school experiences, but few possessed the skills to use some of the newer, innovative technologies such as PowerPoint that were becoming available at that time. The third factor was an assessment of the academic support to use computers in the classroom. A majority of the educators surveyed indicated they did not have access to the necessary hardware and software, nor did they have access to technology enhanced facilities. In addition, while their administrators were placing demands on these educators to use technology, few provisions were made to help them learn and prepare for using computers. These educators also indicated there were no reward structures for using technology in the classroom, which made it difficult to add technology enhancement to already heavy workloads.

The implications from the 1997 study were that criminal justice faculty had a great potential to serve as leaders in the use of computer-based teaching, but only if administrators would provide the necessary support to enhance the skills and abilities of their faculty and would provide them the time and resources necessary to use those skills and abilities. Suggestions were made to modify the structure of faculty positions so that professors would get credit for using technology in the evaluation process. Financial incentives and awards could be provided to those who developed new teaching innovations with technology. Sabbaticals and release time, traditionally given for research, could be given for faculty development in teaching with technology.

At the same time, administrators were encouraged to find the resources necessary to provide the technology for faculty to use. Only then could criminology and criminal justice educators appropriately prepare the graduates of their programs for the growing demands of the field being transformed by technological change and advancement.

THE NEED BECOMES A DEMAND: THE ONSET OF CYBERCRIME

Since the 1997 study by Myers and Myers (1998), the transformation of criminal justice and criminology by technology has created a major demand on the discipline to respond to new forms of criminality that fall under the category of cybercrime. The increasing sophistication of technology has facilitated innovations in high technology crime. The rapid development in new forms of cybercrime has created a demand for business and the criminal justice system. This ever-increasing demand has been hard for business and criminal justice to respond to because the level of technology sophistication among cybercriminals far exceeds the capabilities of those in business and criminal justice to detect, investigate, and prosecute (Myers & Beatty, 2001).

A more proper response to the development of sophisticated cybercrimes involves better preparation for those most likely to ameliorate the problem, law enforcement investigators. It has not been enough for investigators to learn about computer crime on their own or through training workshops on the subject. The pace of cybercrime development has far outpaced this incremental learning curve. It is the responsibility of higher education to better prepare criminal justice graduates for the changes in crime, which means giving them the cybercrime knowledge, skills, and abilities necessary to respond to this critical area of criminal justice.

To determine whether criminal justice educators had risen to the level of leadership that had been predicted necessary for this demand in the 1997 study by Myers and Myers, these same researchers surveyed the academic leaders of the 100 largest criminal justice and criminology programs in the United States. The goal of this study (Myers & Myers, 2002, 2003) was to first determine the consensus of this leadership on the knowledge, skills, and attitudes that criminal justice graduates should possess to engage in high technology crime investigation. The second goal was to determine whether the programs represented by these academic leaders offered courses that would teach those knowledge, skills, and abilities and if they did not, were there plans to do so in the future.

Academic leaders of the 100 largest criminal justice and criminology programs in the United States were surveyed in 2000 and asked to review 21 knowledge elements from the Occupational Information Network, "a skill-based framework for describing knowledge, skills, and abilities across all industries and occupations" (U.S. Department of Labor, 1996). Using an 8-point scale, respondents were asked to indicate which level of a particular element was needed to detect, investigate, and prosecute high technology crime. Academic leaders, including deans, chairs, and directors, were chosen for this task because they were guiding the curriculum development of the largest criminal justice programs in the United States, producing a significant number of graduates who would be responding to high technology crime.

Three general subject matter areas were identified in the literature as the most critical areas needed to respond appropriately to cybercrime (Kovacich & Boni, 2000). The three areas were 1) criminal justice and criminology, 2) principles of accounting and auditing, and 3) computer operations and technology. When the academic leaders were asked which elements were essential to the developing area of high technology crime, they identified the knowledge elements of computers and electronics, public safety and security, economics and accounting, and law, government, and jurisprudence. The elements identified are consistent with those cited in the literature and reveal that the programs producing over half of the criminal justice and criminology graduates are led by leaders who are in line with changing trends in crime and crime control.

However, the problem is getting this knowledge to the students in these programs (Myers & Myers, 2002). Many of the programs represented in the study were not teaching these knowledge elements within their curriculums. Students were being exposed to the traditional areas of law, government, jurisprudence, sociology, and psychology, but not necessarily to advanced levels of knowledge in computers and electronics, economics and accounting, and telecommunications. Very few of the programs that were not offering this knowledge to their students in 2000 were planning to do so in the future. Potential explanations for not adapting to this technology demand included certain programs not placing an emphasis on this area of criminal justice and criminology, reliance on other departments to offer the knowledge in elective courses, or considering high technology crime to be more applied than theoretical. Finally, the most significant reason might be traced to the 1997 study of criminal justice educators (Myers & Myers, 1998). All of the issues cited in that study, including lack of faculty and administrative expertise, lack of resources and training, and insufficient administrative support may be limiting the potential of criminal justice and criminology programs to meet the current demand for competent cybercrime investigators.

CONCLUSION

In a brief period of time, the technology age has made many of us reliant on numerous hardware and software technologies designed to make our lives more efficient and productive. With the use of e-mail, voicemail, and cell phone, technology has changed the way we communicate. We can find almost anything we want to know about on the Internet. Brick and mortar libraries are no longer the primary portal of information for the scholar. In fact, most libraries can be accessed via the Internet. Research capabilities have progressed significantly from the days of card readers and computers the size of buildings. Today we can analyze large amounts of data at just the press of a button, often on our home computers. The teaching function has evolved as well. Many of us communicate with students via e-mail, voicemail, Websites, and Blackboard™ or WebCT™. We use PowerPoint and other technologies to enhance the learning process. We expect our students to use computers to word process and to do their research.

As educators have adapted to these technological changes so have criminals. Technology has made criminal activity more efficient and productive. New types of crime have evolved and the newness of these crimes has made it easier for cybercriminals to avoid detection as criminal justice and business have struggled to keep up.

The 1997 study of criminal justice educators (Myers & Myers, 1998) set the stage for the ability of the discipline to respond to the demands created on the criminal justice system with the advent of new technologies. Not only has technology become part of the tools used by the criminal justice practitioner, but technology has become a tool of the criminal. Criminal justice practitioners must be prepared to use technology tools and to respond more effectively to those who use technology in the commission of crime. Although the 1997 study showed the desire of most criminal justice educators to use computers in the learning process and the desire to make sure their students were prepared to use these tools, the subsequent studies of the knowledge elements required to properly detect, investigate, and prosecute high technology crime and the teaching of these elements in criminal justice higher education revealed the discipline of criminal justice is way behind the curve.

Not only must we prepare our graduates for increasing demands regarding cybercrime, we must also engage in the research to understand the criminology of cybercrime. It is part of our duty to the field to add this form of criminality to our understanding of crime and criminal justice. If we are not preparing people to respond appropriately to cybercrime and if we are not conducting research on cybercrime, then the discipline is failing to respond to the needs of society. Whereas administrative and resource issues may be the reasons for this failure, it is no excuse. We must find a way to respond more appropriately to cybercrime or in a few years, the next study of our progress is going to reveal we knew of our failure and again failed to make the necessary changes required to fulfill our obligations as scholars and professors.

REFERENCES

Armstrong, I. (2000). "Computer crime spreads." *SC Info Security* 11(4): p. 26.

Carter, D. L. & Katz, A. (1996). "Computer crime: An emerging challenge for law enforcement." *FBI Law Enforcement Bulletin* [Online]. Accessed on November 10, 2004 at http:// www.fbi.gov/publications/leb/1996/dec961.txt

Kovacich, G. L. and Boni, W. C. (2000). *High technology crime investigator's handbook: Working in the global information environment.* Boston: Butterworth-Heinemann.

Myers, L. B. (2003). *Criminal justice faculty development: Teaching professors to teach*, 2nd ed. Belmont, CA: Wadsworth.

Myers, L. B. & Myers, L. J. (1998). "Integrating computers in the classroom: A national survey of criminal justice educators." in L. J. Moriarty & D. L. Carter

(Eds.), *Criminal justice technology in the 21st century* (pp. 19-34). Springfield, IL: Charles C Thomas Publisher.

Myers, L.B. & Myers, L. J. (1995). "Criminal justice computer literacy: Implications for the twenty-first century." *Journal of Criminal Justice Education* 6(2): 281-298.

Myers, L. J. & Myers, L. B. (2003). "Identifying the required knowledge elements for the effective detection, investigation, and prosecution of high technology crime: The perspective of academe." *Journal of Criminal Justice Education* 14(2): 245-268.

Myers, L. J. & Myers, L. B. (2002). "Preparing for high technology crime: An educational assessment of criminal justice and criminology academic programs." *Journal of Criminal Justice Education* 13(2): 251-272.

Myers, L.J. & Beatty, P. T. (2001). "Computer information systems and the high technology offender: The need for an interdisciplinary approach in higher education curricula." *ACJS Today* 23 (1):1, 4-6.

President's Commission on Critical Infrastructure Protection. (1997). "Critical Foundations: Protecting America's Infrastructures." Washington, DC: United States President's Commission on Critical Infrastructure Protection.

Rosenblatt, K. (1995). *High technology crime: Investigating cases involving computers.* San Jose, CA: KSK Publications.

Sharrar, K. & Granado, J. (1997). "Confessions of a hard drive: Computer security." *Security Management* 41(3):73-78.

University of North Texas Health Science Center. (2003). "Texas creates DNA database to identify missing persons." [Online]. Accessed on May 1, 2004 at http://www.sciencedaily.com/print.php?url=/releases/2003/03/030318074425.ht m

U.S. Department of Labor. (1996). "The occupational information network." [Online]. Accessed on May 1, 2004 at http://www.doleta.gov/programs/onet

White, A. & Charney, S. (1995). "Search and seizure of computers: Key legal and practical issues." *Technical Bulletin.* Sacramento, CA: SEARCH, The National Consortium for Justice Information and Statistics.

Chapter 3

TECHNOLOGICAL AIDS FOR TEACHING STATISTICS IN THE 21ST CENTURY

JANET R. HUTCHINSON, JAMES E. MAYS, AND LAURA J. MORIARTY[1]

INTRODUCTION

Teaching statistics in Criminal Justice (as in other disciplines) in the 21st century offers new challenges and opportunities for both instructors and students. One such challenge is expanding traditional teaching to incorporate technological advancements such as microcomputer applications and multimedia instruction. In this chapter, we explore the methods used to teach statistics and identify the strengths and weaknesses associated with each. We explore the role played by technology in advancing student learning and comprehension of difficult statistical concepts and review a selected sample of products designed to aid student learning. We conclude by presenting a product the authors believe will address the limitations identified in the other computer products.

Teaching Statistics

It is not unusual for both undergraduate and graduate students to complain about taking statistics courses. These complaints often arise from their fear of math (sometimes referred to as "math anxiety," and in the case of older, so-called nontraditional students, "math atrophy")

1. The authors are equal contributions to this chapter. Please note that the Websites mentioned in this chapter may have changed since publication of this book.

caused by inadequate high school preparation in mathematics (Royse & Rompf, 1992, p. 271), or the forgotten math skills that often trouble the nontraditional students (adult learners). The challenge for the statistics instructor is to find a way to abate student anxiety without compromising the integrity of the course. The effective use of technology will help to meet this challenge.

A review of the literature on teaching statistics results in a variety of articles from many disciplines focusing on teaching methodologies, computer-assisted learning, and strategies to increase the quality of instruction. Betsy Becker (1996) examined the print and electronic literature focusing on teaching statistics using three electronic databases. Her review yielded well over 1,000 articles from ERIC, PsycINFO, and ACAD (Extended Academic Index). Becker combined the references, eliminated duplicates, and discarded irrelevant sources, resulting in 501 references to examine. She then sorted the articles into five categories: computer use, teaching materials, teaching approaches, individual differences, and discussions. She further divided the material into empirical and nonempirical references.

Becker found a total of 209 articles addressing computer usage and teaching, of which only 56 were empirical studies. Furthermore, she found that 53 sources focused on computer-assisted instruction with 35 being empirical sources. She identified 71 sources on the topic of software with only 6 being empirical. Lastly, she examined sources that focused on simulation activities/exercises and found 44 such articles of which only 4 were empirical sources. To summarize, Becker describes the vast majority of the literature as nonempirical, largely representing anecdotal information, and providing the reader with suggestions and recommendations from the experiences and intuition of the instructors in an effort to improve the quality of teaching statistics. We do not review all the works cited by Becker because most are not appropriate for our purposes. We do, however, present the literature focusing on improving the quality of instruction through the use of technology.

Some scholars have suggested that using technology will fill the gap in traditional teaching methods associated with teaching statistics (Gordon & Hunt, 1986, p. 66). For example, most statistics teachers demonstrate probability theory by tossing coins or drawing from a fish bowl filled with numbers. Gordon and Hunt recommend enhancing these examples by using technology, especially microcomputers with the appropriate software. They maintain that microcomputers allow for quick calculations with less effort and students find the investigations to be more interesting and captivating. Gordon and Hunt also argue that traditional teaching methods cannot teach intuition to students. They believe that "only by interaction and experimentation . . . (can) a student develop intuition . . . (and) many students are unable to achieve this by traditional methods suggest(ing) that the microcomputer (with its natural interactive ability) will prove useful" (Gordon & Hunt, 1986, p. 67).

Other researchers have examined computer software to determine the benefits of using such software in teaching statistics (Cohen et al., 1996; Cohen, Tsai, & Chechile, 1995; Cohen et al., 1994; Persell & Maisel, 1993; Dimitrova, Persell, & Maisel, 1993; Helmericks, 1993; Webster, 1992; Halley, 1991; Anderson, 1990; Fuller, 1988). Elaine Webster (1992) reviewed selected computer software to determine the relative strengths and weaknesses of each in terms of the software's ability to teach difficult concepts in statistics to students. Webster considered random sampling, the Central Limit Theorem, the binomial distribution, hypothesis testing, regression analysis, and analysis of variance as those topics most difficult for students to comprehend and for instructors to teach using the traditional teaching method of lecturing. The five computer software packages reviewed included *Stat+/Data+, Minitab, Easystat, Mystat*, and *The Data Analyst.* These products were further divided into two categories: software "associated with a statistics textbook" and "student-oriented, general statistical packages, not associated with a textbook" (Webster, 1992, p. 378). Webster concludes that both types of computer software meet the objective of increasing learning, with "*Stat+/Data+* and *Minitab* offering the most comprehensive coverage in meeting the pedagogical and technical needs of the instructor in teaching the six statistical topics discussed" (Webster, 1992, p. 384). However, these computer packages are designed mainly for data manipulation and calculation, and more efficient tools are needed for actually "teaching" and understanding the statistical concepts at a basic level.

For students to comprehend statistics, it is suggested that discipline-specific meaningfulness be attributed to such analysis (Bessant, 1992). It is important to relate statistical procedures to everyday situations in the area of greatest interest for the student. In doing so, the student receives a better appreciation of the practicality of the procedures and should show increased interest in learning the material. For example,

Bessant (1992) found that sociology students comprehended statistics more fully when the presentation of the material was carefully imbedded in sociological meaning. Rushing and Winfield (1999) incorporate content analysis of personal advertisements to demonstrate sampling and measurement concepts to students. Auster (2000) uses the candy M&Ms® to convey probability sampling and inferential statistics. Wybraniec and Wilmoth (1999) conduct in-class exercises to demonstrate difficult concepts such as sampling distributions and inferential statistics.

Researchers have suggested incorporating humor into teaching statistics. For example, cartoons have been found to reduce math anxiety (Potter, 1995; Schacht & Stewart, 1990). Placing students in creative, interactive learning environments that go beyond traditional learning experiences reduces math anxiety as well (Schacht & Stewart, 1992). Technological developments are creating vast new opportunities in this area of education.

Lastly, recent attention has been given to the infrastructure of the computer laboratory (Bills & Stanley, 2001). Instructors must keep in mind the design of the computer lab and whether changes might be made to facilitate instruction. Computer labs are often designed for individual student usage and not necessarily for instruction, resulting in a layout that may not be conducive to learning. Also, the maintenance of the computer lab in terms of upgrading hardware and software must be addressed. Instructors and students should not assume that such labs will be kept current or that the design layout will be conducive to teaching without any input from the statistics instructors.

Computer Aids (Tutorials) for Statistics Courses

A review of the tutorial resources available for statistics courses results in four broad categories of items. They include workbooks with data sets, student versions of statistical software packages, Internet applications, and CD-ROMs. Many textbooks now include their own Websites and CD-ROM products. An abbreviated list of workbooks and texts that combine CD-ROMs and Websites as a part of their packages follows. Those listed use SPSS software.

Pine Forge Press publishes a workbook specifically designed to accompany research methods and statistics texts. *Adventures in Social*

Research: Data Analysis Using SPSS 11.0/11.5, 5th edition, by Earl Babbie, Fred Halley, and Jeanne Zaino (2003) may be purchased with or without the SPSS CD-ROM. Pine Forge Press also publishes *The Practice of Social Research in Criminology and Criminal Justice* by Ronet Bachman and Russell K. Schutt (2001). The book and CD editions use SPSS 10.0 and are dated 2001. Prentice-Hall publishes *Statistical Analysis in Criminal Justice and Criminology: A User's Guide* by Gennaro F. Vito and Michael B. Blankenship (2002). In addition to the standard materials published by Prentice-Hall for the SPSS company, Allyn & Bacon has two volumes, the first a standard textbook *Social Statistics: An Introduction Using SPSS*, 2nd edition by Richard J. Kendrick (2005) and the second a workbook, *SPSS for Windows: Step by Step 11.0,* 4th edition, by Darren George and Paul Mallery (2002). The workbook gives the reader step-by-step instructions for computing statistics from basic frequencies to advanced multivariate data with pictures of SPSS screens that duplicate those on the student's computer. It can be used as a self-instructional companion to a statistics text by students with basic computer competencies and has its own Website from which 11 data files can be downloaded (*http://abacon.com/george/*). Each chapter includes a series of challenging problems that may supplement textbook assignments while reinforcing chapter content.

Although these resources may increase the students' aptitude regarding computer usage and to a lesser degree increase their mechanical knowledge of statistics (that is, they begin to understand the proper syntax to produce the statistics), in the aggregate, they offer only minimal tutorial value. In comparison to the other resources, workbooks with data sets are the least likely to emphasize mathematical principles and computations. There is even less emphasis on the underlying statistical assumptions. An exception is the George and Mallery workbook mentioned earlier. Questions at the end of each chapter expect the student to understand the statistical application as well as the commands for analyzing the data using SPSS. Most often, the student follows the instructions and produces the appropriate statistic without being challenged regarding which statistic the student thinks is the most appropriate and why. For these reasons, we feel the workbooks are not the best approach to learning statistics in the 21st century. Workbooks may be helpful, however, in instructing students in the use of statistical software procedures when used in conjunction with other teaching approaches.

The second category of tutorial resources is student versions of statistical software packages. Some of the most popular student versions include *SPSS Student Version for Windows, SYSTAT for Students 6.0 (full version 10.2)*, and *The Student Edition of Minitab 14.* These packages are the actual statistical software offered at a reduced price for students. These packages allow students to analyze data from their own computers, helping commuter students or students who work full-time and cannot take advantage of the university labs. Depending on the specific software package, there are varying degrees of help available through accompanying manuals and help menus. The main purpose of supplementary materials is to teach the students the specific software package, not to teach them the statistics. It should be noted, however, that most of the companies that sell software packages aimed at the student market have separate statistics texts for purchase. For those who view teaching statistics from a more applied perspective, these software packages provide the opportunity for students to learn how to produce the statistics using whichever package they choose. Once again, however, the problem with these statistical packages is the lack of instruction regarding which statistical procedure is appropriate to use given the underlying assumptions of the particular problem. There are some general introduction paragraphs explaining the different statistical procedures, but it is clear that the main purpose of the software is to teach the students that software package. For the purpose of teaching statistics, such a product would need a section on applications, exercises, or problems to be useful as a tutorial.

The third category of tutorial resources includes Internet applications. This is perhaps the fastest growing area for student-assisted learning and for access to supplemental course material. All students should now have access to the Web and its vast supply of learning tools. There are currently three main categories of how the Internet is being used as a teaching supplement for statistics: 1) to provide basic information and announcements for specific courses (syllabus, notes, assignments, links to other relevant sites, etc.), 2) to provide complete courses that replace the classroom, and 3) to provide access to supplemental teaching tools in the form of demonstrations of specific topics in a course. The latter two areas are relevant here and are discussed briefly.

A recent technological advancement is the development of statistics courses that are taught entirely over the Internet, allowing access to many potential students who traditionally have been unable to schedule time for such pursuits. Closely related to this is the development of statistics textbooks on the Web. For a sample of the many such courses and textbooks being developed, see the sites at *http://www.execpc.com/%7Ehelberg/statistics.html* or *http://www.uni-koeln.de/themen/Statistik/onlinebooks.html*. One of the larger scale projects in this area is the Electronic Statistics Textbook by StatSoft, Inc. Located at *http://www.statsoft.com/textbook/stathome.html*, this online textbook begins with an overview of the relevant elementary statistical concepts and continues with a more in-depth exploration of specific areas of statistics. It is organized by "modules," accessible by buttons representing classes of analytic techniques, and includes a glossary of statistical terms and list of references for further study. Projects such as these may change, or at least add to the approaches to teaching statistics, but they too would benefit from supplemental tutorials developed to help the individual student grasp difficult concepts.

This issue is being addressed by an increasing number of Web sources that contain graphical interactive demonstrations of chosen topics. Examples of such demos are applications written in Xlisp-Stat or Java applets[2]. Some of the statistical topics demonstrated by these Web sources are histograms, regression, the binomial and normal distributions, and the central limit theorem. These topics include many of the previously mentioned topics considered by Webster (1992) as "difficult to teach." For links to the most popular Java applets, see the Website at *http://www.stat.duke.edu/sites/java.html.* These types of graphical demonstrations are very appealing to the student, whether as an in-class or out-of-class supplement. However, they each address only one specific topic, and by no means do they, even as a collection, comprise a comprehensive statistics tutorial. A combination of such demos with an underlying course structure appears to be a worthwhile goal for developing supplemental material for teaching statistics. One such project in this area is the CyberStats Electronic Textbook for learning statistics through interaction, by CyberGnostics, Inc. Located at *http://statistics.cyberk.com*, CyberStats is an interactive textbook that aids student learning with "hundreds [over 600] of applets (simulations and calculations) and immediate feedback practice items." A second

2. An applet is a self-contained, precompiled batch of code that is downloaded as a separate file to a browser alongside an HTML document. HTML (Hypertext Markup Language) is the language used to create Web pages.

example of such an interactive online textbook is the HyperStat Online Textbook created by David M. Lane at Rice University. Found at *http://davidmlane.com/hyperstat/index.html*, this site includes links to analysis tools, instructional interactive demonstrations, textual explanations, tables, exercises, and other learning tools.

Three additional online sites with discipline-specific course material are mentioned here. The Research Methods in the Social Sciences: An Internet Resource List Website is maintained by the University of Miami Libraries (*http://www.library.miami.edu/netguides/psymeth.html*). This site has embedded Websites including 1) general information on social research methods, 2) tests and measures, 3) survey methods, 4) resources for quantitative and qualitative data, 5) information on research and writing, and 6) software. The Action Research Resources page (*http://www.scu.edu.au/schools/gcm/ar/arhome.html*) includes an online refereed journal, mailing lists for students (and faculty) to discuss theory and practice of action research, an online course offered each semester, archives that describe action research processes or discuss action research issues, and links to worldwide action research resources. MicroCase is a statistical data analysis program that is now available online. Anyone who uses a Wadsworth Introductory Sociology, Research Methods, or Statistics textbook has access to the MicroCase online exercises. "Specific chapter-related questions and corresponding data will allow students the opportunity to extend their exploration of sociological issues and principles presented in the texts. Based on the MicroCase ExporIt model, these Web-based exercises offer activities designed around key pieces of social science research. Basic univariate statistics, mapping and crosstabulations" examples are provided (*http://www.wadsworth.com/sociology_d/special_features/microcase.html*).

The last category of tutorial resources is CD-ROMs. George Cobb and Jonathan Cryer have developed *An Electronic Companion to Statistics* (published by Cogito Learning Media, Inc., 1997). This CD-ROM, with comprehensive workbook, is designed to complement any statistics textbook. It is a tutorial device that provides interactive review and self-testing of key concepts, including over 400 interactive testing questions in a variety of forms. Multimedia is used in the form of animations, user-controlled diagrams, and real-world videos (from the *Against All Odds: Inside Statistics* series [COMAP & Chedd/Angier, 1989]). The accompanying (optional) workbook contains hundreds of extra problems and very brief overviews of the topics presented, following the same order of progression as the CD-ROM. Many topics are included, ranging from basic statistical concepts to more advanced topics. This product is no longer marketed on the Cogito Learning Website, but copies for purchase (and reviews of this product) can be found through an Internet search on "Electronic Companion to Statistics."

Paul Velleman's *ActivStats* (originally released July 1997 by Data Description, Inc.) is a CD-ROM that contains a full introductory statistics course integrating "video, animation, narration, text, pictures, interactive experiments, Web access, and a full screen statistics package." The computer display takes the form of a lesson book that guides the student through the course. The student may select from the "contents" tab to visit lessons in any order, allowing this product to serve as a tutorial or a source for review of basic statistical concepts. However, the lessons do build on one another (using previously created data, for example), and the best use of this product appears to be for the student to chronologically complete each lesson, much like the progression of a traditional course. Quizzes, review activities, and homework assignments are included to test and increase the student's learning. *ActivStats* also provides access to the statistics software program Data Desk (also by Data Description, Inc.), which provides the data analysis and graphics capabilities for the product. *ActivStats* has been updated several times since its original release, and currently is available in the traditional individual/student version (2003-2004 release), a version for lab use, and versions for use with Excel, Minitab, JMP, or SPSS. The Website for Data Description, Inc., which contains information and links to both Data Desk and *ActivStats*, is located at *http://www.datadesk.com.* Another useful link for information on *ActivStats is http://www.aw-bc.com/activstats.*

Both of these CD-ROMs are excellent resources. One major problem, however, is the inability of these products to adapt to the specialized interests of students in diverse disciplines. As Bessant (1992) maintains, in order for students to grasp statistical concepts, the examples and tutorial aids must be discipline-specific. For the CD-ROMs listed here, the instructor does not have the flexibility of adding his or her own data sets to be analyzed, which would add to the discipline-specific effectiveness of the products.

It is clear from this discussion that the statistics instructor must expend considerable effort to compose a course that incorporates many of the tools described. The vast number of technological advances that have occurred over recent years have the potential to considerably enhance our ability to convey difficult concepts to students of statistics, yet the time and energy requirements for 1) learning the technology, 2) incorporating the technology into the classroom, 3) accommodating these new course designs to continuous software upgrades, and 4) assisting students who have not caught up with the technologies, cannot be discounted. What may have been considered timesaving devices have become for many diligent instructors more time-consuming than the traditional textbook/lecture approaches that prepared many of us for our current roles. Ideally, the medium used will help, not hinder, the instructor's ability to provide individualized instruction to those students who are struggling, while facilitating learning for their more advanced classmates. The CD-ROM discussed in the next section will, in our view, accomplish these objectives and others as well.

Proposed CD-ROM

CD-ROM production has greatly increased over the last decade, augmenting traditional teaching strategies in many disciplines. The CD-ROM has the "potential to enhance student learning, motivation, and metacognition" (Adams, 1996, p. 19). According to Adams, the CD-ROM has many educational benefits including "its quick random access of information which enables the learners to control the pace and direction of learning . . . (providing) more opportunities for cognitive processing," its ability to present a large body of knowledge from many perspectives, which leads to a robust understanding of content by students, and its creation of more positive student attitudes toward learning (Adams, 1996, p. 20). With the merits of CD-ROMs or hypermedia (Adams, 1996) well established, we put forth our design for a CD-ROM that we feel is most appropriate for use as an aid in the teaching of statistics for any specific discipline, such as Criminal Justice.

Our CD-ROM would be a multidisciplinary effort by faculty from a variety of departments or fields, including Statistics, Information Technology Support Services, Computer Science, departments with direct interest in the product (Criminal Justice, Political Science and

Public Administration, etc.), and Fine Arts (for aid in the visual presentation of the material). The program envisioned would be designed in a self-contained, modular format. Unlike other tutorial programs, it would incorporate several discipline-specific data sets of interest in applied settings, including public and private management and policy making, social policy issues of interest to students in criminology, health and social services, environmental and other public services, and business. In addition, it would have the capability of incorporating personal data sets, overcoming a major limitation of the products currently available.

The program would rely heavily on visualizing statistical concepts, using only minimal explanatory text on principal screens. Links to detailed textual and computational definitions would be incorporated into the program. We reason that the adult learner, in particular, prefers to visualize the operations first, attempting to "puzzle through" the material being presented before reading a detailed explanation of what is being seen. Furthermore, link-based definitions may be avoided by those who are revisiting the program.

The program would incorporate a multimedia approach. Animation, digital photographs, cartoons, graphs, music, and voice-overs would be used to clarify principles and enliven the presentation. Mnemonic devices would accompany visual presentations as learning aids. Each module would be self-paced, taking the average reader approximately 20 minutes to complete if all definitional and computational links are used. An appropriate reading level would be targeted.

CONCLUSIONS

According to Schacht (1990), students taking statistics courses feel introductory statistics textbooks must: "review basic algebraic operations, discuss summation notation, include and explain exercise answers, use computational rather than definitional formulas, use examples relevant to students' statistics/mathematics anxiety" (Schacht, 1990, p. 393). Schacht found that not one of the textbooks reviewed addressed all the issues outlined by the students.

We feel that our proposed CD-ROM would meet these criteria in addition to incorporating most of the suggestions found in the literature. This sophisticated yet inexpensive CD-ROM would focus on the adult learner who may have minimal or rusty mathematical skills, while maintaining appropriateness for the traditional student. Because most anxiety regarding statistics is associated with a fear of math, both groups of students, traditional and nontraditional, would benefit from this product. Perhaps the most innovative and creative aspect of the proposed CD-ROM would be its capability to incorporate personal data sets to increase the overall relevance of statistics to students in different disciplines. Both instructors and students who are well versed in computer technologies would find the ingenious, interactive learning environments, framed in their own disciplines, quite effective, practical, and even fun.[3]

REFERENCES

Adams, P. E. (1996). Hypermedia in the classroom using earth and space science CD-ROMs. *Journal of Computers in Mathematics and Science Teaching, 15*(1/2), 19-34.

Anderson, R. H. (1990). Computers, statistics, and the introductory course. *Teaching Sociology, 18*(2), 185-192.

Auster, C. J. (2000). Probability sampling and inferential statistics: An interactive exercise using M&Ms. *Teaching Sociology, 28*, 379-385.

Babbie, E., Halley, F., & Zaino, J. (2003). *Adventures in social research: Data analysis using SPSS 11.0/11.5*, 5th ed. Thousand Oaks, CA: Pine Forge Press.

Bachman, R. & Schutt, R. (2001). *The practice of social research in criminology and criminal justice.* Thousand Oaks, CA: Pine Forge Press.

Becker, B. J. (1996). A look at the literature (and other resources) on teaching statistics. *Journal of Educational and Behavioral Statistics, 21*(1), 71-90.

Bessant, K. C. (1992). Instructional design and the development of statistical literacy. *Teaching Sociology, 20*(2), 143-149.

Bills, D. B., & Stanley, A. Q. (2001). Social science computer labs as sites for teaching and learning: Challenges and solutions for their design and maintenance. *Teaching Sociology, 29*, 153-162.

Cobb, G. & Cryer, J. (1997). An Electronic Companion to Statistics. New York: Cogito Learning Media, Inc.

Cohen, S., Chechile, R., Smith, G, & Tsai, F. (1994). A method for evaluating the effectiveness of educational software. *Behavior Research Methods, Instruments, and Computers, 26*(4), 236-241.

Cohen, S., Smith, G., Chechile, R. A., Burns, G., & Tsai, F. (1996). Identifying impediments to learning probability and statistics from an assessment of instructional software. *Journal of Educational and Behavioral Statistics, 21*(1), 35-54.

3. Authors' Note: This is an ongoing project in the developmental, funding phase. Contact any of the authors for an update on the status of the CD-ROM project.

Cohen, S., Tsai, F., & Chechile, R. (1995). A model for assessing student interaction with educational software. *Behavior Research Methods, Instruments, and Computers, 27*(2), 251-256.

COMAP & Chedd/Angier. (1989). *Against All Odds: Inside Statistics* (videorecording). Santa Barbara, CA: Intellimation.

Dimitrova, G., Persell, G. H., & Maisel, R. (1993). Using and evaluating ISEE, a new computer program for teaching sampling and statistical inference. Teaching *Sociology, 21*(4), 341-351.

Fuller, M. F. (1988). MIRCOTAB and the teaching of statistics. *Teaching Statistics, 10*(1), 12-15.

George, D., & Mallery, P. (2002). *SPSS for Windows Step by Step: A Simple Guide and Reference 11.0 update.* Boston: Allyn & Bacon.

Gordon, T. J., & Hunt, D. N. (1986). Teaching statistics with the aid of a microcomputer. *Teaching Statistics, 8*(3), 66-72.

Halley, F. S. (1991). Teaching social statistics with simulated data. *Teaching Sociology, 19*(4), 518-525.

Helmericks, S. G. (1993). Collaborative testing in social statistics: Toward Gemeinstat. *Teaching Sociology, 21*(3), 287-297.

Kendrick, R. J. (2005). *Social statistics: An introduction using SPSS*, 2nd ed. Saddle River, NJ: Allyn & Bacon/Longman.

Persell, C. H., & Maisel, R. (1993). Developing the ISEE instructional software for sampling and statistical inference: Dilemmas and pitfalls. *The American Sociologist, 24*(3-4), 106-118.

Potter, A. M. (1995). Statistics for sociologists: Teaching techniques that work. *Teaching Sociology, 23*(3), 259-263.

Royse, D., & Rompf, E. L. (1992). Math anxiety: A comparison of social work and nonsocial work students. *Journal of Social Work Education, 28*(3), 270-277.

Rushing, B., & Winfield, I. (1999). Learning about sampling and measurement by doing content analysis of personal advertisements. *Teaching Sociology, 27*(2), 159-166.

Schacht, S. P. (1990). Statistics textbooks: Pedagogical tools or impediments to learning? *Teaching Sociology, 18*(3), 390-396.

Schacht, S. P., & Stewart, B. J. (1992). Interactive/User-Friendly gimmicks for teaching statistics. *Teaching Sociology, 20*(4), 329-332.

Schacht, S. P., & Stewart, B. J. (1990). What's funny about statistics? A technique for reducing student anxiety. *Teaching Sociology, 18*(1), 52-56.

Vito, G. F. & Blankenship, M. B. (2002). *Statistical analysis in criminal justice and criminology: A user's guide.* Saddle River, NJ: Prentice-Hall.

Webster, E. (1992). Evaluation of computer software for teaching statistics. *Journal of Computers in Mathematics and Science Teaching, 11*(3-4), 377-391.

Wybraniec, J., & Wilmoth, J. (1999). Teaching students inferential statistics: A "tail" of three distributions. *Teaching Statistics, 27*(1), 74-80.

Chapter 4

USING INTERACTIVE TECHNOLOGY TOOLS AS PART OF SKILL DEVELOPMENT FOR CRIMINAL JUSTICE STAFF

FAYE S. TAXMAN, MARIALINA BELLO, AND ERIC SHEPARDSON

INTRODUCTION

Criminal justice agencies struggle with the ability to provide some (enough or sufficient) training to advance the skill sets of staff. The traditional training concept is that staff should be trained, for multiple sequential days, in a setting that is away from the pressures of their jobs such as the classroom setting. Criminal justice agencies are generally able to achieve such a training process to prepare staff for their jobs (e.g., preservice) but have more logistical and manpower difficulties when the staff is already gainfully employed and engaged in work activities. However, even more importantly, when agencies are able to provide the training, staff often express concerns that the training is irrelevant to their daily work or they have a difficult time integrating the training into their concurrent work processes.

Technology offers the ability to provide the real-time training of staff in skill development that can also address some of the organizational issues that impede usage of any new skills in the workplace. An organizational development perspective, armed with the technology, can be used as a means to accomplish inservice training goals of providing staff with relevant, useful information that should improve productivity and processes. To do this, the technology must be available and the process in place to move the information to the field. Whereas traditional classroom training still plays an important role, the combination of classroom and on-site training can focus on the staff development and achievement of organizational goals.

In this chapter, we have three main goals. First, we provide description of the need for a new training model that focuses on organizational development. Second, we describe some technological advances using interactive tools and organizational development processes that were developed for a probation department to learn motivational interviewing (Miller & Rollnick, 2002) and case planning skills, and how the interactive tools are used. The organizational processes include an integrated training model that includes classroom training and the use of on-site training tools to improve staff skills. Much of this work has been put in place in the Maryland Division of Parole and Probation as part of an overarching strategy to improve staff skills. In the final section, we provide a review of how to develop some of the interactive tools and their use in an organizational development process as part of Maryland's proactive community supervision process. (Refer to the Website *www.bgr.umd.edu/proactivesupervision* for examples of many of these interactive tools and processes that are referenced in this chapter.)

TECHNOLOGY TRANSFER AND INNOVATION MANAGEMENT: LESSONS LEARNED

Within the criminal justice and other service (e.g., substance abuse treatment, public health, etc.) systems, reforms and innovations have been promulgated for nearly three decades to increase the use of science into practice. Yet, the adoption of such reforms has been met by typical barriers common to both the justice and drug treatment fields, including social attitudes about addiction, mental health, delinquency, and treatment. These attitudes have affected the ability of agencies to integrate science-based evidence to enhance services along with the general workforce issues (e.g., staff qualifications, skills, resources, attitudes, job performance, etc.). It is not surprising that technology transfer within the justice system is so difficult because staff do not often have the appropriate knowledge. Like any chicken-and-egg scenario, staff will not be able to change the way they handle offenders until their knowledge and competencies have been increased.

Historically reforms are introduced into the work environment through training and staff development workshops. Research in the effectiveness of such training efforts has found the traditional classroom training to be ineffective in altering job performance with nearly 10 percent of the exposed staff using the acquired information (Georgenson, 1982; Goldstein, 1997). In a study on the impact of training on staff performance in the probation field, Miller and Mount (2001) found that the traditional workshop approach resulted in improvements in staff self-report of change regarding the knowledge of motivational interviewing techniques, but the scholars also found that the use of the skills returned to baseline levels within four months. Bein and colleagues (2000), in a study of the impact of workshop training on brief time-limited psychotherapy, found that clinicians failed to achieve a reasonable level of competence of skills to deliver the therapy. Baldwin and Ford (1988) discuss that training outcomes can be measured in two categories–knowledge acquisition and knowledge generalization–and that little information is available about the impact of different training or technology transfer processes on desired outcomes (e.g., learning, retention, or application). Even more so, little is known about knowledge application and how it affects workplace processes. That is, there is a need to understand the degree to which different training approaches are designed to increase staff knowledge and skill sets.

The use of a single-shot workshop approach has been open to many questions since it may "even serve as a kind of inoculation against further learning, inflating clinical self-efficacy without altering practice behavior enough to improve client outcomes" (Miller & Mount, 2001, p. 17). Program evaluations of many criminal and juvenile justice programs have documented similar issues where the fidelity of program components is low (Gottfredson, 1987; Sealock, Gottfredson, & Gallagher, 1997; Taxman & Bouffard, 2003; Taxman, 2002), often attributable to the failure of staff to use the technology or technique. Many have called for the need to expand the staff qualifications as a means to address this issue while others recognize that organizations must make a commitment to advancing the skill sets of their staff.

Given the unsatisfactory outcomes from traditional training initiatives, a growing interest now exists in new strategies to affect the transfer of information into practice. Brown and Flynn (2002), in their discussion of the history and role of the federal government on technology transfer, identify four different stages of the process: development, preparation, implementation, and stabilization. Simpson (2002) puts forth a similar process for program change that ranges from exposure (training), adoption (leadership decision), and implementation (exploratory use) to practice (routine use). In Simpson's conceptualization he discusses how organizational dynamics (e.g., climate for change and staff attributes), institutional and personal readiness (motivation and resources), reception/utility, and institutional supports affect the different processes of adoption. Essentially an argument is being made that the older models of training and technology transfer that focus on information dissemination often fail to address the broad range of issues that affect the adoption and practice of a new initiative or innovation. The field is evolving from dissemination to an innovation management approach that is guided by benchmarks to determine the degree to which staff changes their practices. The underlying premise of the innovation management process is similar to client behavioral change where the emphasis is placed on the staff learning, relearning, and rehearsing the skills both in training and on the job with supportive organizational reinforcements.

An example of the application of this new model is the strategies used in transporting the Multidimensional Family Therapy (MDFT) model to an intensive outpatient treatment program (the Adolescent Day Treatment Program [ADTP]) for adolescent drug abusers (Liddle et al., & Biaggi, 2002). The long-term study goals were twofold: 1) to evaluate the impact of disseminating MDFT on clinical practices and the organizational climate of the ADTP; and 2) to evaluate the effects of these organizational changes on clinical outcomes of youth. Liddle et al. (2002) used a four-stage technology transfer process, measuring key system, organizational, and client variables along each dimension: baseline/pre-exposure, exposure (training), implementation (exploratory use), and practice (routine use). The researchers found that during the first phase the staff emphasized patient control over developing a rapport with the clientele. This dimension was then used to gauge interventions that address the organizational issues of receptivity and mission as they relate to implementing the MDFT approach. Challenges to implementation were addressed along the way as a means to increase clinical skill, competence, and accountability for the protocol. Based on the journey through the first three stages, Liddle et al. (2002) offered several recommendations: 1) have a guiding framework and a well-defined theory of change; 2) work to overcome any resistance to the proposed change; 3) keep in close contact with the staff members responsible for ultimate implementation; 4) never underestimate staffing needs; 5) allow extra time at each phase of the process; 6) realize that the technology being transferred may need to change to fit the environment; and 7) (not surprising) never expect perfection. The results from this study raise questions about the staff development and training process that deserve further consideration, particularly in interagency efforts to change multiple systems.

Together, the current research reinforces the need to move past the single-event training model to an organizational development perspective that focuses on improving the staff skills. The perception is that single-event trainings do not achieve the desired level of knowledge generalization and suggests that there is a need to integrate staff knowledge acquisition with organizational development processes. Technology can play a critical role in this process by providing on-site tools to assist the staff in applying their newly obtained skills into practice. It can also provide a forum for managers to assist staff in applying the new skills in the workplace. The following section illustrates such a model and how it has been put into place within a probation and parole setting. It draws from a case study of the Maryland Division of Parole and Probation. Before we discuss the case scenario, we will outline two pieces: the development of the interactive training tools and the organization development process that is used to focus on knowledge generalization in a probation setting.

CASE STUDY OF CHANGING THE DELIVERY OF PROBATION SERVICES

The Maryland Division of Parole and Probation, under the leadership of Judith Sachwald, has engineered a new process for the delivery of community supervision services. The goals of the Proactive Community Supervision (PCS) model are to: protect public safety, hold offenders accountable to the victims and community, and help offenders become responsible and productive members of the community. As part of the strategy, the agency has incorporated the "what works" principles into a protocol for improving the delivery of supervision services (Sachwald, 2002). The model addressed four common areas where delivery systems have been problematic: 1) assessment and case planning; 2) treatment and control services; 3) compliance management; and 4) deportment or rapport between offenders and staff (see a discussion of these issues in Taxman, 2002). As part of this strategy, the agency adopted motivational interviewing (MI) into a supervision framework to improve staff skills in each of the four areas as well as developed a quality assurance methodology to ensure that staff uses the MI skills (see the discussion by Taxman, 2002). Specialized skills were also identified in each of the areas such as assessment (learning to use better interviewing techniques and standardized protocols), treatment services (using a case plan that is based on practice guidelines), compliance management (based on contingency management and procedural justice concepts), and deportment (based on MI and rapport-building techniques).

The implementation of the PCS model accompanied a multiyear strategy focusing on skill development and role enhancement. The strategy used the following approach: 1) new policies and procedures were developed; 2) an intensive training program was developed that focused on all of the skills previously identified (see previous discussion); 3) an organizational development approach that included staff trainings during regular staff meetings using a variety of interactive training tools and specialized publications; and 4) identification of coaches and mentors within the agency that are considered "in-house experts."

The specialized tools that were developed are all available through the Maryland Division of Parole and Probation or the University of Maryland's Bureau of Governmental Research (*www.bgr.umd.edu*). The tools consist of:

Nuts and Bolts: A fact-based document explaining each of the protocols and the logic behind them. The purpose of this document is to provide a short but easy explanation and review of major concepts. Each concept is explained in less than two pages along with specific practice guidelines that can be applied in most supervision settings.

Interactive Training Tool on Phase 1 (Break the Cycle) (see Figure 4-3): This is a comprehensive technological tool that provides a graphical flow of the work process, copies of the policies and procedures, videos to role-model the new skills, and test questions. To gauge staff comprehension, at every point of the work process, specific details and expectations of staff are detailed.

Offender Flow for PCS (see Figure 4-2): This is a technological tool that basically summarizes the specialized PCS process and provides fact sheets for each component. The tool is designed to provide an overview of the process and the appropriate required forms that accompany each segment of the process. As part of the process there are specialized assessment techniques, case plans, practice guidelines for offender typologies, and measures of offender progress.

Motivational Interviewing Techniques in Supervision: This traditional three-day curriculum provides an overview of MI techniques as well as role-play for the staff to learn new skills. This training included a pretraining and booster sessions designed to bolster staff's comprehension of core concepts, and assist with knowledge generalization.

Assessment and Case Planning: This is a two-day curriculum to provide an overview of the specialized assessment tool and the case planning procedures. It focuses on using the assessment information to form a case plan. The case plan then establishes the goals and objectives to be accomplished during the supervision period.

Technological Supports for Knowledge Generalization and Application

The Maryland Division of Parole and Probation identified the need to advance the skill sets of supervision staff as part of the strategy to reengineer supervision (Taxman, 2002; Sachwald, 2002). In a partnership with the University of Maryland's Bureau of Governmental Research, an organizational development strategy was outlined that focused on bringing the skills into the workplace as part of an effect to achieve the public safety mission. That is, improving the quality of supervision services was premised on a workplace environment where the staff learns new skills and these new skills are promoted in daily use. A comprehensive organizational development process that was built on having on-site tools to assist the staff in applying the concepts and in redesigning the workflow to use the skills as mentioned earlier.

ORGANIZATIONAL DEVELOPMENT TO ACHIEVE STAFF KNOWLEDGE ON THE INNOVATION AND REQUIRED SKILLS

To avoid the perception that training is a one-shot event and the tension between the value of the training and the demands of the learning process, an organizational development process is recommended. As shown in Figure 4-1, the process includes an outline of the goals and objectives for each phase of the workflow. Each process focuses on the skills, the acquisition of the new skills, the generalization of the skills into practice, and the reinforcement within the work setting that the skills are part of the new requirements. That is, the commitment from the organization should be that the staff is expected to apply the knowledge gained during training in the workplace.

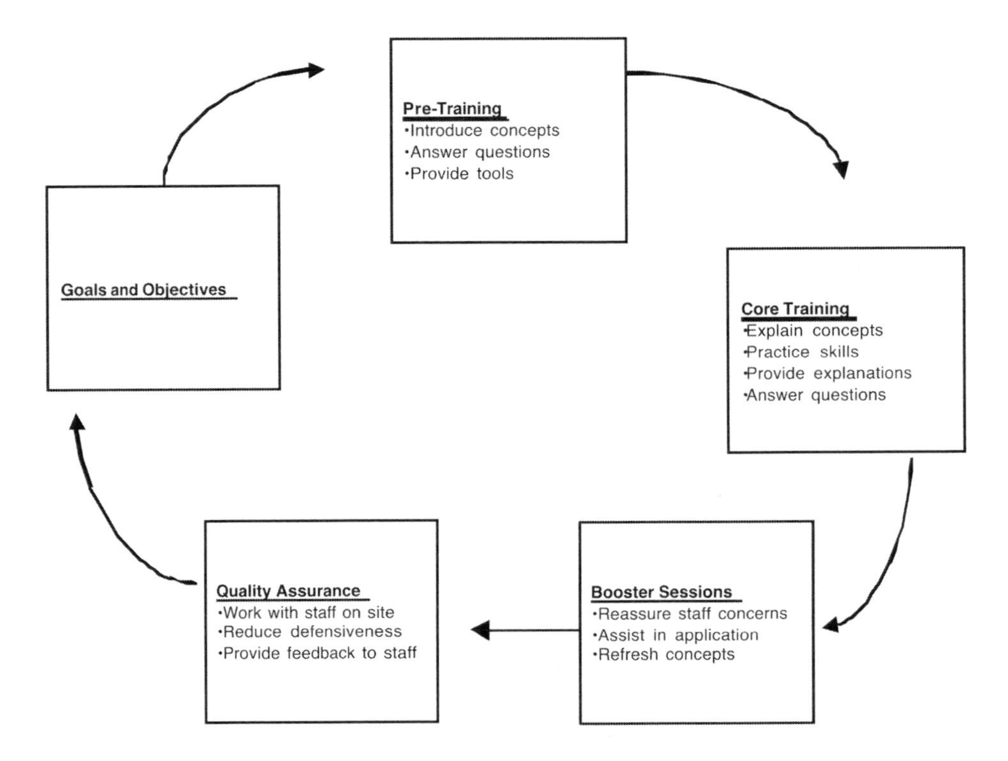

Figure 4-1: Organizational Development Process.

MANAGEMENT TASK OF OUTLINING GOALS/OBJECTIVES AND WORK PROCESSES

Before the staff is exposed to the training, it is incumbent on the management team to identify how the new skills and/or program will operate. That is, the management team of the organization must make decisions about why it is moving in this direction, and then articulate it to staff in a manner that supports the training of staff and advancement for the entire field. In other words, the purpose of the training is to assist the staff to implement the new approach but the management must provide the staff with sufficient knowledge and information to change the existing work processes. In operational terms, it involves revising the Standard Operating Procedures (SOPs) that formalize the process. For example, in the policing field, community-policing strategies had to be defined for the staff in a new process. The same is true for a community corrections program such as intensive supervision, drug treatment, drug courts, community probation, evidenced-based probation, and so on. Lengthy SOP material is usually met with trepidation because it involves the staff reading and applying the materials. Training then must be developed to incorporate the new SOPs and the staff skills necessary for the success of an initiative. The same type of problems exist in other settings where new models of service delivery are offered such as community policing for police organizations, assessment and treatment placement strategies for community correctional and drug courts, and behavioral management techniques for probation and/or correctional agencies.

Part of the management task is to identify the new skill sets that staff will need in implementing the innovation. While often the tendency is to rely on the existing skills, most innovations require staff to do *something* different. Essentially that something different requires staff to apply knowledge in a new manner that has not been previously asked of or expected, and therein lies the implementation issues commonly referred to as fidelity. If the staff does not apply their knowledge, then there is often a shortfall between the program design and implementation. This shortfall is often part of the reason that many programs do not achieve the desired goals (Sherman et al., 1997).

Pre-Training

Preparing any organization and its staff for change requires a focus on readiness to implement the innovation. Many organizations, and staff, resist new ideas because they are perceived to be of little value, time-consuming, and generally a misfit between the organizational mission and goals. To overcome this normal resistance to change, more attention should be paid to prepare staff for this new change.

This preparation generally needs to be in three areas: 1) information about the problem and the proposed change; 2) innovation design and goals; and 3) skills that the staff is expected to develop in order to implement the program. Generally these half-day sessions, which can be given by management and/or supervisors, are designed to motivate the organization for the change process. It serves to alleviate concerns that the new innovation is unnecessary or poorly designed; more importantly it provides a forum for the staff to begin to gather information about the innovation.

Pretrainings should be designed to introduce the larger concepts that will be covered in training. Pretrainings are an opportune time to use interactive tools like the flowchart or some type of game. The games can serve as a quiz to see how much advance knowledge staff has, and as stated, flowcharts are a great way to introduce policy changes to staff. An additional piece that trainers and organizations may choose to use during these pretrainings are what are called "fact sheets," or one page, stand-alone documents used to provide staff with specifics about certain aspects of the trainings. These fact sheets can address major topics and theories that staff should be versed in prior to the training session. Fact sheets can include graphics to assist aesthetically, as well as depict major themes within the piece.

Skill Development/Traditional Training

An intensive, multiday training program is generally provided to help staff learn more about innovations, SOPs, and any identified skills that are needed. Most traditional training programs are not merely classroom based, where the material is presented in a didactic style. Instead they involve case studies and role-playing that allows the staff to apply the new information and/or skills. The traditional trainings are designed to present staff with the new information that can then be applied in the workplace. To this end, well-designed curricula provide ready-to-transfer information into the workplace.

Booster Sessions/Skill Enhancement and Reinforcement

Each new innovation requires the staff to apply new or existing skills in a different manner. While the traditional training sets the stage for the innovation and the new expectations, the true test occurs in the field when the staff is busily engaged in work-related activities. Thus a challenge to the change process is to: 1) keep the momentum alive; 2) ensure that staff is using the new innovation; and 3) reinforce the innovation along with the daily work activity. Booster sessions, like the pretraining, can be designed to be in-office events focused on reinforcing the new innovation. The booster sessions should be focused on enhancing skill sets of staff as well as addressing any gaps in implementation that are likely to occur. The sessions can be designed for regular staff meetings, specialized sessions, or performance assessments of staff. That is, they are flexible to be molded into the normal workplace as part of a regular activity. In some ways, the booster sessions can become a formalized process of coaching staff in key areas. The sessions can also be perceived as events that are part of the learning process. Either way the booster sessions serve the organization by reinforcing new innovation and attending to the issues that often affect poor implementation–generalizational and application of the knowledge learned in training.

TECHNOLOGY TOOLS TO ADVANCE THE ORGANIZATIONAL DEVELOPMENT PROCESS

Training and staff development take time. Although reading materials provide background information on different topics, one of the limitations of such material is that the staff does not have the time, and more importantly the drive to read the information. Yet information can be prepared to be easy to digest, flashy, and graphical, thus allowing staff to easily translate concepts into easy steps. Interactive multimedia training tools can engage participants that increase the knowledge and application of the information.

Interactive multimedia training tools are instruments that engage participants actively while teaching them the skills encompassed in training. A flowchart that contains the work process and decision points can succinctly summarize information in a manner that narrates the steps and processes (see Figure 4-2 for an example of Maryland Division of Parole and Probation's workflow associated with the proactive community supervision initiative). Interactive training tools can range from flowcharts to videos to games. No limit exists to what can be in the tool; in fact it can be a multidimensional information sources that includes: 1) work flow; 2) criteria for different decisions; 3) policies and procedures associated with the process; 4) videos of key skills or decisions; and, 5) test questions (an example of this is in Figure 4-3 where the Break the Cycle training tool includes video role-plays as well as test questions). Interactive tools have the advantage of providing graphical representations of concepts that can assist staff in retaining information in a way that the written word cannot, especially in this fast-moving world of videos and graphic images. They capture the imagination of the staff while also being an information source.

Interactive tools encourage staff participating in training(s) to be active participants because they have to maneuver through the material. For example, an interactive flowchart allows the participant to review segments in pieces and then examine the interconnected parts. It also provides a mechanism to display pertinent information such as procedures, policies, information, research findings, or so on. When training participants have an interactive flowchart before them with layers of information and resources, they are forced to follow along with instruction uncovering the different information contained within.

Another benefit of the interactive tool is that it provides staff with a new paradigm for thinking about different information and the integration of that information into the work setting. If an organization is attempting to change their culture, introducing new ways of doing things in traditional training settings or in the booster sessions illustrates that management is willing to take chances on new ways of thinking and they are not stuck in a "business as usual" mode. Since organizational change is an ongoing process, managers must illustrate that they are committed to changing the culture of their organization. The planning and development of an interactive tool can be part of the process of change by including information that may not always be available to everyone within an organization, and in doing so it allows the organization to establish new values and expectations.

Well-designed interactive tools should have several components. The tools should begin with a graphical representation of the workflow and/or process. It allows others to visualize how the pieces fit together (see Figure 4-3). It also allows for sequencing processes, by having the information layered on top of one another. That is, often-

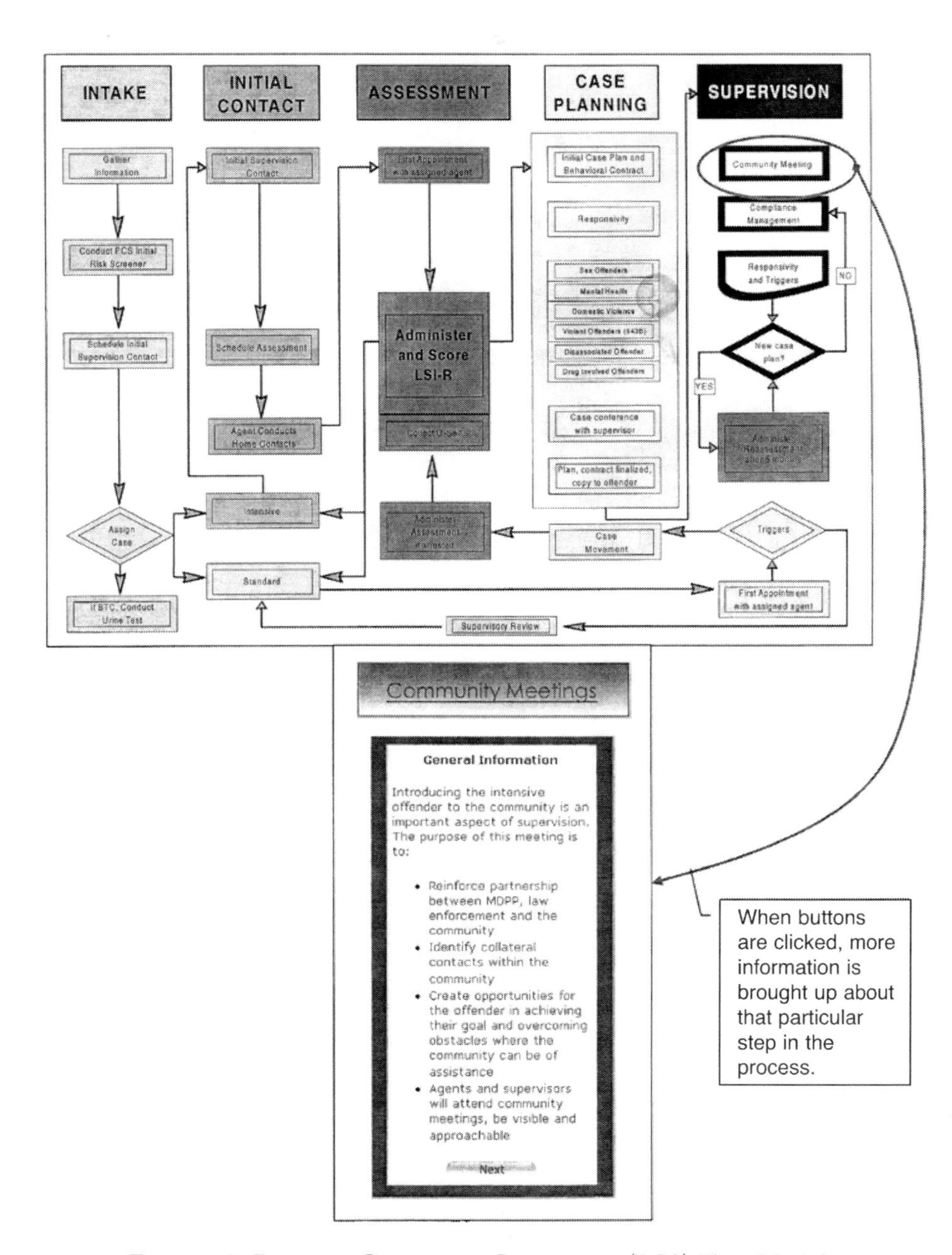

Figure 4-2: Proactive Community Supervision (PCS) Flow Model.

times the work processes are contingent on each other. If we can help staff understand the interrelationship between two given processes, then progress is being made because staff builds their own version of the process. Flowcharts are an exemplary graphical means of teaching people about new concepts. Each box of the flowchart represents a step in the process, and there is information that staff must know about each of these steps. It is now possible to turn a piece of paper into a layered computer tool that not only teaches participants what the process looks like, it can provide staff with very detailed information at each step. Each box, when tapped, will display additional information that is essential to understanding that particular process. The policies and procedures (such as the SOPs) can be provided and integrated into the tool. It also allows each phase of the flow to integrate critical pieces of information from the SOP.

Nowadays, many training curriculums are created to include role-plays or other active learning tasks for participants. Such techniques assist staff in participating in the trainings and in increasing the comprehension of the concepts. Role-plays entail providing participants with scripts, or a general outline of a situation, and asking them to act out scenarios. These are an effective way of not only allowing trainees to practice new skills, but when small groups are assigned to work together, other people can observe the new practices in action. It is advisable that the trainers designate small groups (of no more than four people) to role-play scenarios, assigning one person to play the offender, one person to play staff, and the other two people to be observers or raters. The raters can spend their time in the group critiquing the performance of the staff member and learning how such skills can be applied. A major benefit of role-playing is that participants are allowed to become familiar with the skills and make mistakes with the new techniques in a controlled environment with no level of risk as there is in the field. Interactive tools can be designed to serve the purpose of questioning staff while not raising the defensiveness by putting attendees on the spot. Interactive learning tools accomplish this goal.

Some interactive tools involve multimedias like videos. Scripting out scenarios and having personnel act out the scenes to illustrate points is a good way of presenting information. Videotapes can be used as an interactive tool for staff by having trainees score certain aspects of taped interviews and critiquing them or by having staff

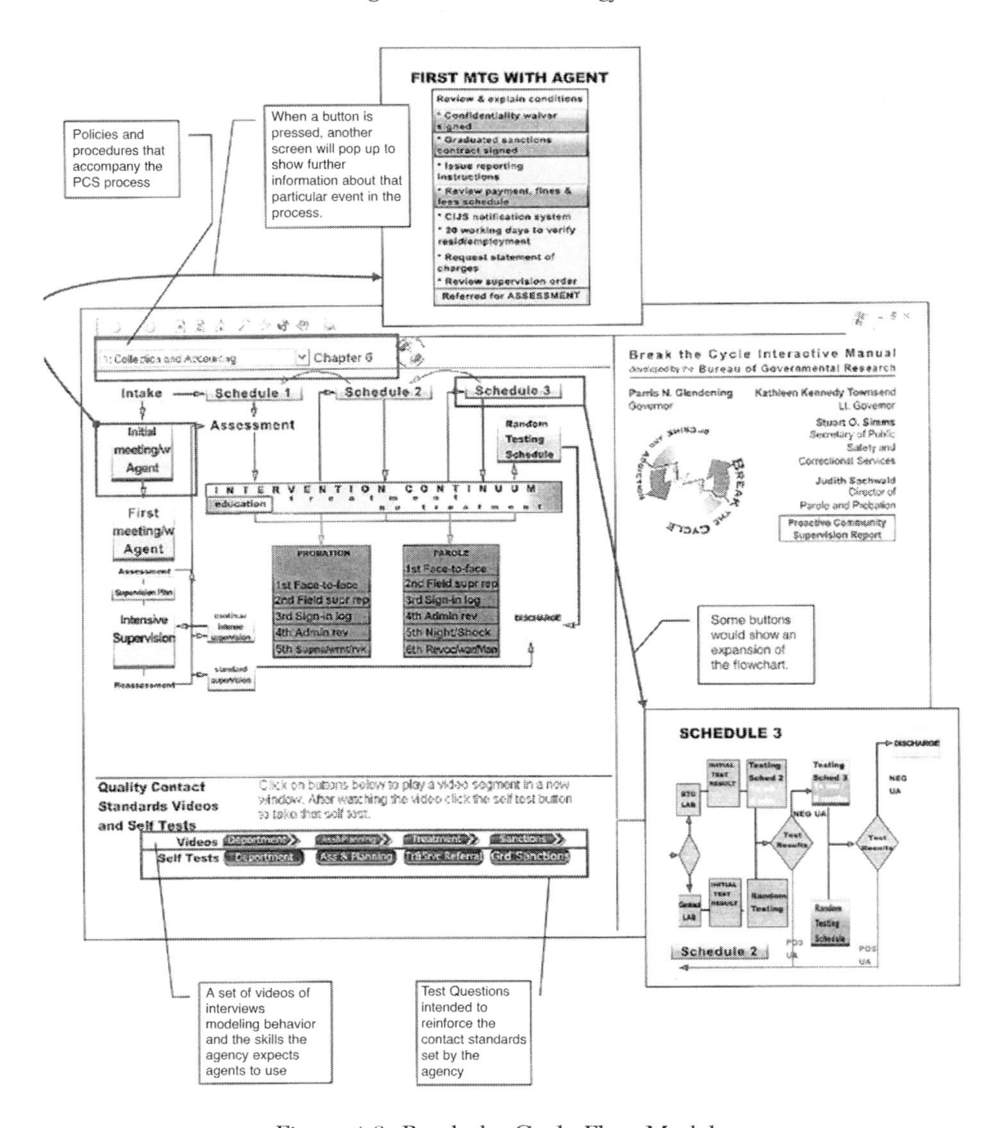

Figure 4-3: Break the Cycle Flow Model.

answer questions following segments of the video. Videos can also be created to role-model different facets of the new innovations for the purpose of establishing standards and expectations in the organization.

The term "training" can be extended to include a variety of processes that assist staff in learning new materials. Formal trainings serve to disseminate information while the booster and other processes provide opportunities to reinforce the information and allow for knowledge generalization and application. No matter which phase of training, interactive tools should be used frequently to increase the effect. Organizations committed to effective training sessions for their employees now have these alternatives to the various antiquated training tools of the past.

DEVELOPING THE INTERACTIVE TOOLS TO SUPPORT STAFF DEVELOPMENT

Preparation is crucial when creating interactive learning tools. Many decisions must be made about the tool itself, and the different components that are to be included. Figure 4-3 is a fully loaded tool that includes: 1) work processes; 2) policies and procedures; 3) background materials; 4) embedded processes and procedures; 5) video to role-model procedures; 6) test questions to test the knowledge of staff; and 7) information resources. A tool can either be loaded or have more limited options due to budgetary constraints, and of the audience. Next we are going to discuss some of the issues to consider in developing the tools. This is designed to be a general overview of the process of putting together an interactive tool but interested readers should consult with the senior author for more information about the methods for developing an interactive tool.

Purpose/Goals

Defining the goal or purpose of the project will help determine what types of tools need to be created and will help in allocating resources for it. For example, some tools are designed to be the training program itself while others are designed to supplement the training program. Some are designed to facilitate role-playing while others are not. Answering these questions will help align the tool to its intended function.

Audience

It is important to think about the needs and learning styles of the target audience and how the tool is likely to be used (e.g., individually or in a group setting like a staff meeting). Different tools can be developed for the group setting such as a flowchart or games such as Jeopardy. If the audience will be using the tool(s) individually, a word game or a smaller version of Jeopardy may work. It is also a good idea to have multiple tools available for the users to choose from. For example, a user may be more comfortable and is better at learning through reading a fact sheet rather than playing a game, or vice versa. Having multiple tools to deliver information addresses various needs and learning styles of the target audience as well as their mood and temperament. The idea is to cater the tool(s) to the target audience so as to help them learn through visual arts or through fun activities. It is essential to take into account the variety of learning styles, needs, and personalities of the audience.

When thinking about the audience, be sure that they can relate to the tool that is created. For example, in designing the tools for the Maryland Division of Parole and Probation, we realized that the audience did not like videos that were too clinical in nature. The staff could not relate to the clinicians in various videos but they could relate to the probation and/or parole agents doing the same tasks.

Another aspect to consider is the amount of time the staff/user(s) will have in using the tool. Most uses will be for short periods–less than 15 minutes for booster sessions–which means that the information must be presented in smaller segments. For example, instead of having a 30-question Jeopardy board, reduce the size to maybe 9 questions, creating a 3 x 3 matrix.

Programs to Use

Several programs can be used in creating learning tools. Helpful programs for photo editing are Macromedia Fireworks, Adobe Photoshop, or Microsoft Photo Editor. Any photo editing tool will be helpful in creating graphics and various illustrations for the tools being created. Macromedia Flash or a similar program will be most helpful in creating interactive flowcharts. Otherwise, Microsoft Visio is a great tool to create flat files or noninteractive tools (i.e., stand-alone flowcharts). Adobe InDesign, Adobe PageMaker, or Quark Express are a few software packages to choose from to create newsletters, fact sheets, or other documents for publication.

Knowledge of HTML (hypertext markup language) will come in handy when placing interactive tools online. For the more advanced users, games can be created using JavaScript and ASP. Useful tools are

Macromedia Dreamweaver or Microsoft FrontPage. Understanding of Adobe Premiere or other video editing tools will be handy when creating videos.

There are also games available online called shareware. These are ready-to-use software that is free for use by developers online. A program called FlipFop created by Luzius Schneider is an example of a shareware software program. When contacted, he only requires the software user to send him the questions being plugged into the game so that he can create a database of users and what they were being used for. Make sure to contact the owner/programmer of any program you are interested in and learn about system requirements, and their policy for use and distribution. Another example of a ready-to-use program is the screen paver created by Michael Lindell of RegSoft: "Screen Paver is an easy-to-use, make-your-own slideshow screen saver for Windows 95/98/NT4/2000/Me. The program will display an unlimited number of your own jpeg, png, or bitmap images from local and/or network directories." The company only requires a $12.95 registration fee for the full use of the program and its dissemination. There is a plethora of software ready for use on the Web and it only requires some time to do the research and contact the makers of the program.

Once the decision making has been done, then you are now ready to create the tools. Here are some detailed descriptions of interactive learning tools created by us such as the jeopardy game, flowcharts, and fact sheets/newsletters.

Jeopardy Game (see Figure 4-4)

Some of the games that can be used include quiz-like games like a "Jeopardy" type game to gauge a person's knowledge of different concepts. The benefit of using games rather than straight testing is that it allows staff to answer questions in a fun manner rather than in the atmosphere that surrounds testing situations. Games can be developed based on the needs of any organization, but if necessary they can be adapted from existing games based on agreements made between organizations. An additional benefit of developing games to test the knowledge of staff is that the questions contained in the games can be updated as newer versions are introduced.

a. Software requirements: Webpage editing tools such as Microsoft

FrontPage or Macromedia Dreamweaver, knowledge of HTML and JavaScript, graphic programs such as Macromedia Fireworks, Adobe Photoshop, or Microsoft Photo Editor.

b. Hardware requirements: Windows 98 or higher; 128mb of RAM; 900MHz of computer speed or better; Pentium or better.

Having Web-editing tools at your disposal will make the creation of a Web page much easier. Basic understanding of HTML and other programming languages are important because sometimes programs do not create Web pages that meet the layout design. If this is the case, knowledge of HTML programming language will help.

c. Layouts and Formatting. On each page, it is important to give instructions for the game clearly and have a clean and simple layout. In preparing to create a Jeopardy game, the questions and answers should first be developed and placed in clear categories. This may prove challenging at times because some topics overlap and, therefore, it is important to work on proper verbiage so as to clearly state questions and answers for each category. In general, game questions should be written prior to any development of tools. This reduces duplication and helps with arrangement of questions on the actual games.

The buttons used on this particular Jeopardy game are objects. Always prepare any graphics prior to the production of the page in order to determine Web design and layout, which will help with consistency and flow.

Flowchart

Flowcharts present graphical representations of the processes involved, and the different decision points. The flowcharts are designed to graphically display the process in such a manner that is visible.

a. Software requirements: (Animated) Macromedia Flash, Flash Player or a program that will help create dynamic/animated files; (Flat File) Microsoft Visio, PowerPoint. When placing a flowchart into the Web: Macromedia Dreamweaver or Microsoft FrontPage and knowledge of HTML is essential.

b. Hardware requirements: Windows 98 or higher; 128mb of RAM; 900MHz of computer speed or better such as a Pentium.

c. Developing the flow process. Graphics create a flowchart that displays

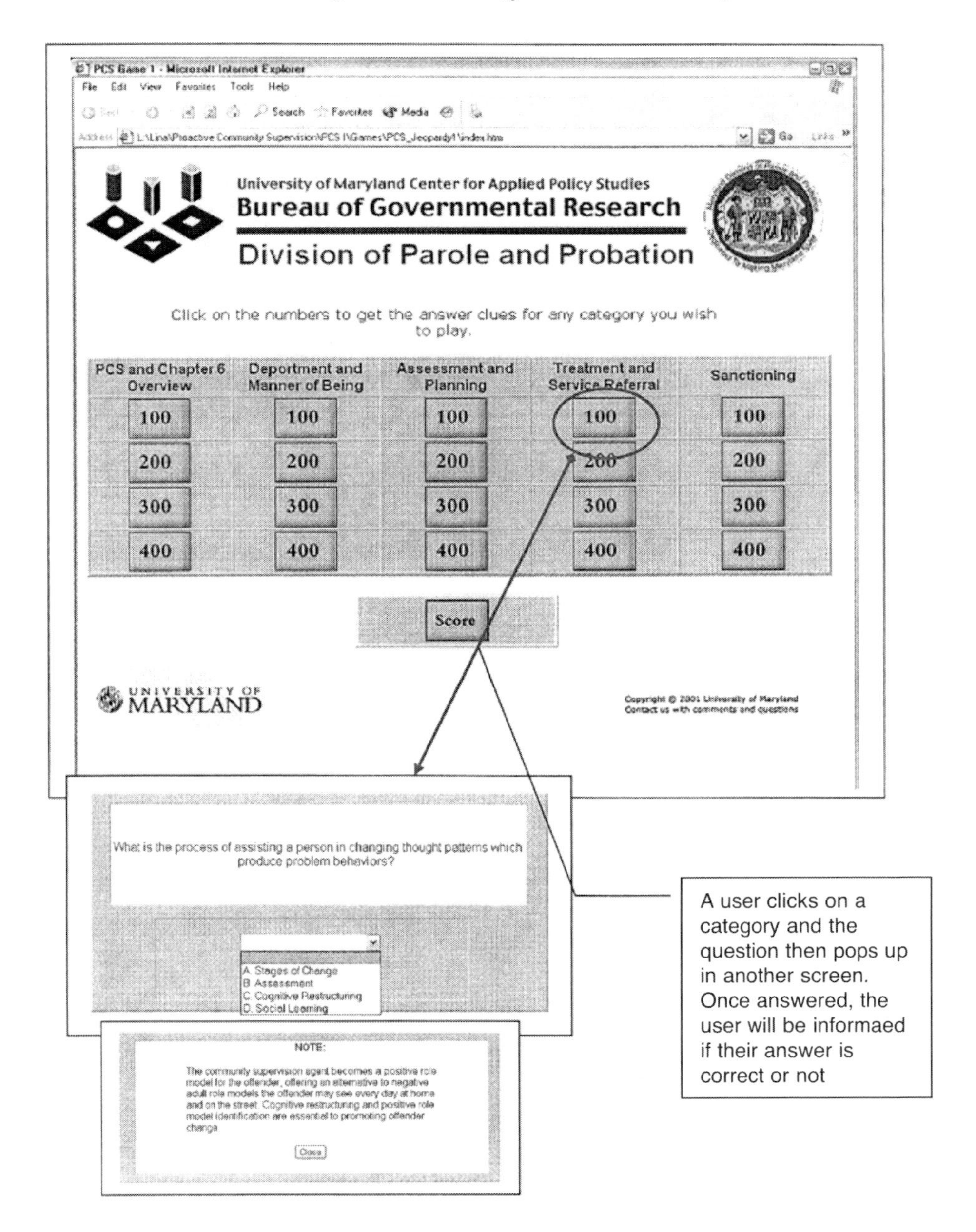

Figure 4-4: Example of a Jeopardy Game on PCS Principles.

processes and decision points. For dynamic/animated flowcharts, it will help to prepare documents that could be used as segments. Each part of the graph can be a button that opens up a new world of information.

d. Use of colors: It is advisable to stick with known meanings for colors (i.e., Red-stop, danger and warning; Green-go, proceed; Yellow–yield, promising). Colors help to display information and will often be used as visual cues for the user.

Fact Sheets/Newsletters

Information sources can be integrated into the interactive tool. The fact sheets can present a wide variety of information–research findings, operational definitions, policies, procedures, and other background information. The fact sheets are critical pieces because they provide specific details about concepts that assist in the learning process.

a. Software requirements: You will need a program or software that will allow you to create publication software, such as newsletters and other documents for publication. Some available software includes Adobe InDesign, Adobe PageMaker, and Quark Express. A photo editing program will be required for cropping photos also; it may come in handy in creating graphics for the page.

b. Hardware requirements: Windows 98 or higher; 128mb of RAM; 900MHz of computer speed or better such as a Pentium.

c. Glossary: Place the arranged article imported from a Microsoft Word file onto the page. An Object such as a picture, graphic, or enlarged quote can be placed on the page.

d. Preparation of documents/graphics: It is wise to have all documents being placed on the page to be written in Microsoft Word or a text file. Avoid having any special characters like bullets on the page for the editor, who places the article and can add these once it has been placed on the page. It will be much easier if you can prepare the graphics or photographs for the page prior to placing documents because you will be able to determine the amount of space to allocate for it, or if the article needs to be edited and made shorter/longer to accommodate the object.

If the page has a particular design, it is better to create a template to ensure uniformity throughout the document. It is better to make the design simple. Have the designs as subtle as possible and not too bold as to distract from the contents of the page. Use colors that reflect your department or the funding agency. Logos are also important to include on the page as well.

CONCLUSION

The organizational development approach, relying on technological interactive tools, underscores the efforts to improve service delivery in a probation and parole setting. The focus of the efforts is to use technology to turn the "single event training session" into an ongoing process focused on addressing staff resistance that normally occurs with most new innovations. The process relies on the interactive tools to allow the learning process to occur in the workplace, and to allow managers to use the tools to address workplace issues. That is, often the new innovations require some changes in procedures. Often these are best resolved by having staff review the protocol and then identify how the process will be modified and implemented in an office (with its own staffing issues, its own cultural issues, and its own unique attributes). To a large extent, the process then empowers midlevel managers to take more responsibility and ownership for the change process.

The technological tools provide the ability to continue the training process and to bring material to the field in an easy-to-digest manner. Instead of thick manuals that are difficult to read, the interactive tools with their flashy graphics make the information accessible. It provides a forum for anyone to see the process and to visualize it. Much of the implementation problems in the past are attributable to issues regarding the technology transfer process. The interactive tools provide a contemporary device to change that process.

Interactive tools are the future of competency development for staff and leaders. The tools take the meaning of "hands-on" to a new level by providing flexible environments to be able to assist staff in acquiring knowledge and then using it. An added benefit is that they require researchers and practitioners to partner in a manner that provides a formula for incorporating science into practical information that is designed to advance and enhance staff skills. The tools also spur a need to clarify information in a manner that is easy to understand but also thought-provoking. Copies of the tools are on *www.bgr.umd. edu.* If you desire assistance in developing the tools contact the senior author.

REFERENCES

Baldwin, T., & Ford, J. K. (1988). Transfer of training: A review and directions for future research. *Personnel Psychology*, 41(1): 63-105.

Bein, E., Anderson, T., Strupp, H. H., Henry, W. P., Schacht, T. E., Binder, J. L., & Butler, S. F. (2000). The effects of training in time-limited dynamic psychotherapy: Changes in therapeutic outcome. *Psychotherapy Research*, 10(1): 119-132.

Brown, B. S., & Flynn, P. M. (2002). The federal role in drug abuse technology transfer: A history and perspective. *Journal of Substance Abuse Treatment*, 22(4): 245-257.

Georgenson, D. (1982). The problem of transfer calls for partnership. *Training and Development Journal*, 36(10): 75-78.

Goldstein, I. (1997). *Training in organizations.* New York: Brooks/Cole.

Gottfredson, D. M. (1987). Prediction and classification in criminal justice decision making. In D. Gottfredson & M. Tonry (Eds.), *Crime and justice: A review of research* (pp. 1-20). Chicago: University of Chicago Press.

Liddle, H. A., Rowe, C. L., Quille, T. J., Dakof, G. A., Mills, D. S., Sakran, E. & Biaggi, H. (2002). Transporting a research-based adolescent drug treatment into practice. *Journal of Substance Abuse Treatment, 22*(4): 231-243.

Miller, W. R., & Mount, K. A. (2001). A small study of training in motivational interviewing: Does one workshop change clinician and client behavior? *Behavioural and Cognitive Psychotherapy*, 29(4): 457-471.

Miller, W. R, & Rollnick, S. (2002) *Motivational interviewing* (second ed.). New York: Guilford Publications Inc.

Sachwald, J. (2002). *Proactive community supervision: Bringing research into practice.* Maryland: Division of Parole and Probation.

Sealock, M., Gottfredson, D. & Gallagher, C. (1997). Drug treatment for juvenile offenders: Some good news, some bad news. *Journal of Research in Crime and Delinquency*, 34(2), 210-236.

Sherman, L. W., Gottfredson, D., MacKenzie, D. L., Eck, J., Reuter, P., & Bushway, S. (1997). *Preventing crime: What works, what doesn't, what's promising.* Washington, DC: Office of Justice Programs.

Simpson, D. D. (2002). A conceptual framework for transferring research into practice. *Journal of Substance Abuse Treatment*, 22(4): 171-182.

Taxman, F. S. (2002). Supervision: Exploring the dimensions of effectiveness, *Federal Probation*, 66(2): 14-27.

Taxman, F., & Bouffard, J. (2003). Substance abuse counselors' treatment philosophy and the content of treatment services provided to offenders in drug court programs, *Journal of Substance Abuse Treatment, 25*(2): 75-84.

Chapter 5

EVALUATION OF COMPUTER-BASED TRAINING FOR DNA EVIDENCE COLLECTION[1]

RYAN BAGGETT, PAMELA A. COLLINS, AND ANNMARIE CORDNER

The analysis of deoxyribonucleic acid (DNA), a person's genetic blueprint that is used as an investigative tool, has advanced rapidly in the last 10 years and is now a commonly accepted method for conducting criminal investigations. The 1994 Crime Act, which established the Combined DNA Index System (CODIS), a national DNA database program similar to Automated Fingerprint Identification System (AFIS), allowed crime laboratories to enhance and compare DNA information electronically. The result has been a significant increase in the number of DNA evidence submitted to crime labs. According to the Bureau of Justice Statistics (BJS), which conducted a national study of DNA laboratories, 69% of publicly operated forensic crime labs reported a DNA analyses backlog of 6,800 known and unknown subject cases and 297,000 convicted offender samples (Steadman, 2000). As demands increase on forensic laboratory staff

---

1. Points of view are those of the authors and do not necessarily represent the official position of the U.S. Department of Justice or Eastern Kentucky University. This document is not intended to create, does not create, and may not be relied on to create any rights, substantive or procedural, enforceable by any part in any matter civil or criminal.

This research was supported under award # NCJ 1999-LT-VX-K006 from the U.S. Department of Justice, Office of Justice Programs, National Institute of Justice. The products, manufacturers, and organizations discussed in this publication are presented for informational purposes only and do not constitute product approval or endorsement by the National Institute of Justice, U.S. Department of Justice, or Eastern Kentucky University.

there is an increasing demand on expanding that capability to the law enforcement officer.

The potential of DNA technology has been realized in the United Kingdom, which some believe is the most advanced country in these efforts (Cordner & Scarborough, 2004). Asplen (2003) states that the use of DNA in the United Kingdom is successful because it is not just a "forensic tool available to law enforcement...but is considered to be an integrated and routine part of the investigative process. It is not a technology to be used in special or particularly serious cases. It is a process invested in so far as to become a routine part of every investigation in which biological material may be left by the perpetrator" (p. 29).

Although there are barriers to changes in the way in which crime scene and forensic investigations are carried out, as technology advances so will the ways in which DNA evidence collection is conducted. A good comparison is the testing for alcohol intoxication, which originally was conducted by laboratory technicians, but through the advancement of sobriety testing technology and training is now primarily conducted by sworn law enforcement personnel. As DNA technology and methods for disseminating information on the proper preservation and collection of DNA evidence advances, so will the ability of law enforcement. This expansion of technology and training will allow for a forensic science capacity by law enforcement that will shift analysis from a laboratory environment to the police officer in the field (Schwabe, 1999).

The following discussion will address technology in two ways; first, the importance of training law enforcement officers on the identification and collection of DNA evidence and secondly, on the use of Computer-Based Training (CBT) as a technology tool that allows for greater access to information for end users. CBT, for purposes of this discussion, is defined as an educational method in which the computer is the primary method for instruction and learning. Modules can incorporate various media, such as text, graphics, pictures, animation, sound, and video.

Computer-Based Training (CBT) Applications

The United States Department of Defense (DOD) has been a leader in the use of distributed learning and has capitalized on an emerging network that ties together distributed instructional resources, including intelligent tutors, subject matter experts, and traditional instruction to support "learner-centric" education on a continuing basis. The DOD strategy is to "harness the power of learning and information technologies to modernize education and training" (DOD Implementation Plan for ADL, 2000). With troops stationed all over the world, the DOD has recognized the benefits of learning technologies and has utilized the technology to help support its mission into the 21st century.

Many corporations have also realized the benefits of distributed learning. Corporations are now able to deliver everything from compliance training to very specific occupational task training using CBT. For example, Daimler-Chrysler teaches maintenance engineers to troubleshoot automotive electrical systems, and companies such as Southwest Airlines have created cyber universities that provide training and development for all employees using learning technologies. Faced with retraining 50 million American workers, corporate America is using distributed learning, both internally and externally, for all aspects of training. Many major corporations save millions of dollars each year using CBT to train employees more effectively and more efficiently than with conventional methods (U.S. Distance Learning Association, 2002).

Various entities have estimated spending in the corporate e-learning market for future years. For example, the International Data Corporation (IDC) estimates that the corporate e-learning market will reach $23.7 billion in 2006, up from $6.6 billion in 2002. Cortona Consulting estimates corporate e-learning in the U.S. and Europe will reach $50 billion by 2010, up from $5 billion in 2001. Gartner Group's estimate, which is not as recent as the other two, and may account for its higher estimate, predicts the market will reach $33.6 billion by 2005, up from $2.1 billion in 2000 (eMarketer, 2004).

According to a 2002 report by the National Center for Education Statistics (NCES), the use of distributed learning at institutions of higher education is also increasing. During the 12-month 2000–2001 academic year, 56% (2,320) of all 2-year and 4-year Title IV-eligible, degree-granting institutions offered distance education courses for any level or audience, (i.e., courses designed for all types of students, including elementary and secondary, college, adult education, continuing and professional education, etc.) (NCES, 2002). Distributed learning is allowing an estimated 3 million students to take classes and obtain an education that they may not have received otherwise.

The use of computer-based learning, while commonly used by both governmental and private entities, has only recently been adopted by the law enforcement community. There are a number of reasons for the delay in the transfer of this technology. First, much of the training that has been developed was used for either military or private sector applications. Secondly, there has been and continues to be resistance by the more traditional law enforcement training academies or post commands that consider classroom time as the primary measure of an officers' knowledge on a particular subject. Because CBT has proven in many instances to often take less time to deliver than traditional platform-based instruction, many of these agencies are forced to rethink their training certification policies. Thirdly, there is also the issue of the need for the necessary infrastructure to support distributed learning to the criminal justice community (nationwide or in that particular region), and finally, the cost for development of CBTs still continues to be very costly for most law enforcement agencies. Consequently, little is known about the current state of the use of distributed learning, especially CBT, technologies in this nation's law enforcement community.

In describing CBT for law enforcement applications, this discussion will distinguish between traditional Lecture-Based Training (LBT) and CBT. Additionally, several examples of research conducted on CBT will be identified. Finally, a National Institute of Justice study on the effectiveness of a CBT module for DNA Evidence Collection will be highlighted.

Lecture vs. Computer-Based Training

There are advantages and disadvantages to both LBT and CBT training. First, the traditional approach to providing a majority of training to law enforcement is through Lecture-Based Training (LBT) taught by a qualified instructor in a classroom setting. Traditionally, law enforcement receives LBT during initial police academy training or at various inservice training sessions; the duration of both types of training varies among states. During LBT, officers are allowed face-to-face interaction with instructors and classmates. Although technology is advancing quickly, most law enforcement officers do not have access to advanced video conferencing capabilities that simulate in-person interactions with colleagues. Additionally, LBT allows for real-time training on customizable topics. Most CBT modules take months to develop and if current event information is incorporated into the module, it can become antiquated over a period of time. Despite these disadvantages, CBT also provides capabilities that are unavailable in LBT.

First, because CBT is a self-paced instructional program, students can learn at their own pace until they believe they have mastered the material. Moreover, since CBT learning is a user-centered process, studies have shown that information retention rates increase. According to Bixler (2000), this is important particularly when the training is content dense or uses a hierarchy of skill acquisition, because on average, people will remember 20% of what they see, 40% of what they see and hear, and 70% of what they see, hear, and do, therefore, the multisensory delivery of training that CBT offers has the potential to facilitate greater retention of new knowledge. Additionally, many CBT effectiveness studies have shown reduced overall training time as compared to LBT.

Second, CBT can accommodate a separation of locations during the learning process, allowing officers to take courses during slow or down times, without incurring costs for travel, hotel, and meals associated with LBT in a centralized location. Self-paced learning allows for flexibility of scheduling so that training can be taken on a 24-hour schedule, passed around among shifts.

Finally, training can be disseminated in volume throughout the world; a computer is all that is required. The decreasing prices in computer hardware, coupled with a greater dependency on information technologies, equate to a greater frequency of computer access for law enforcement agencies. CBT is a desirable method of instruction for groups other than law enforcement including the military/government, corporations, and higher education.

According to the International Association of Directors of Law Enforcement Standards (IADLEST) Survey for 2000, 18 states reported using CBT at some point during officer training programs. Thirteen states reported using CBT during entry-level training, while seventeen states used CBT during inservice or refresher training (Flink, 2000). However, based on additional phone interviews it was discovered that states used varying definitions of CBT. For example, two respondents indicated that they were referring to the use of firearm simulation systems as CBT, and one respondent indicated that they did not use CBT in any capacity. Furthermore, many of the states using CBT supplemented their platform or lecture-based instruction with the CBT module.

Several studies have been conducted on the general usefulness of CBT. For example, Hammell and Kingsley (1999) evaluated the effectiveness of CBT courses at United States Coast Guard (USCG) duty stations. The authors concluded that the CBT courses conducted at USCG duty stations were as effective as lecture-based courses conducted at shore/stateside training centers. Additionally, the cost comparison analysis showed that CBT provided to students at duty stations can save training dollars (Hammell & Kingsley, 1999).

In another study, Wegner and colleagues report on data from a two-semester university study of the effects of distance learning on student achievement as well as the impact of distance learning on student attitudes concerning their learning experiences. Students' test scores and satisfaction survey results from an Internet-based test group were compared to a control group whose instructional opportunities were from traditional, in-class models. Researchers found no significant difference between the test scores of the two groups. Additionally, while statistically significant data could not be produced in the area of student perceptions, general observations supported that, overall, and students in the experimental group had a more positive feeling about their experience than the control group (Wegner, Holloway, & Garton, 1999).

Although several research studies provide insight into the general effectiveness of CBT, little research has been conducted regarding the effectiveness of this training tool in the field of law enforcement. Although many agencies report using the technology, no information describing the effectiveness of law enforcement CBT was provided.

Based on this information, the Justice and Safety Center (JSC) at Eastern Kentucky University (EKU) was funded by the National Institute of Justice /Office of Science and Technology (NIJ/OST) to develop four CBT training modules and evaluate their effectiveness for law enforcement. The remainder of this chapter will highlight the evaluation of a DNA Evidence Collection for Law Enforcement module, provide a brief history of the CBT, outline the evaluation and findings, and discuss the implications of those findings.

DNA CBT BACKGROUND

After reading about how DNA technology was used to exonerate an innocent person, Attorney General Janet Reno requested that the National Institute of Justice establish a national commission in April of 1997 to examine the future of DNA evidence and how the Department of Justice could best encourage its effective use (Asplen, 1999). From that request, the National Commission on the Future of DNA Evidence was formed. The Commission's charter stated:

> The purpose of the *National Commission on the Future of DNA Evidence* is to provide the Attorney General with recommendations on the use of current and future DNA methods, applications, and technologies in the operation of the criminal justice system, from the crime scene to the courtroom. Over the course of its charter, the Commission will review critical policy issues regarding DNA evidence and provide recommended courses of action to improve its use as a tool of investigation and adjudication in criminal cases (National Commission on the Future of DNA Evidence Website, 2002).

The Commission focused on five areas concerning DNA evidence, one of which was the proper collection of evidence by law enforcement officials. Other areas included the use of DNA in postconviction relief cases, legal concerns and the scope of discovery in DNA cases, essential laboratory capabilities in the face of emerging technologies, and the impact of future technological developments on the use of DNA in the criminal justice system. Reports are available in most of these areas (National Commission on the Future of DNA Evidence Website, 2002).

Of particular concern to the Crime Scene Working Group of the Commission was the lack of educational and training resources to ensure proper identification, preservation, and collection of appropriate biological evidence that could yield a perpetrator's DNA profile. To remedy this problem, the Working Group developed a pamphlet for distribution to every law enforcement officer in the country. *What Every Law Enforcement Officer Should Know About DNA Evidence* (September 1999) explained the basics of DNA technology in simple terms, and outlined fundamental identification, preservation, and collection issues.

In addition to the brochure, the Working Group requested a more extensive, computer-based curriculum for training officers in DNA collection techniques. Working with the Commission, Crime Scene Working Group and a software development company, the EKU JSC managed the development of both a beginning and advanced version of "What Every Law Enforcement Officer Should Know About DNA Evidence" (Fall, 2000) in a CD-ROM/CBT format. Building on the brochure, the CBT utilizes interactive scenario training to educate officers. Specifically, the beginning level module focuses on issues that arise for the first-responding law enforcement officer, while the advanced level module delivers more in-depth information for the investigating officer and/or evidence technician.

Despite the perception that CBT modules were in great demand from law enforcement practitioners, it was not known whether the CBT was as effective in teaching the material when compared to LBT. Therefore, in November 2000, the DNA Evidence Collection CBT was evaluated using a metropolitan police department located in central Kentucky.

EVALUATION METHODOLOGY

Instrumentation

Pre- and post-instruction knowledge tests and attitudinal surveys were developed to evaluate the effectiveness of the DNA Evidence Collection-Beginning Level CBT module. The instrument's format was pen and pencil tests and surveys consisting of closed-ended questions. The tests were designed to determine the officers' knowledge before and after instruction. The surveys were designed to obtain demographic information from the officers and to determine the officers' attitudes before and after the instruction.

Sample Selection

The effectiveness of the CBT was determined through the use of a classic experimental research design. This design consists of two comparable groups: an experimental and control group. Both groups had identical curricula and were equivalent except that the experimental group was exposed to the independent variable (CBT) (Nachmias &

Nachmias, 2000). A recruit academy class of 41 was divided into two groups, 21 of which were randomly selected to participate in the LBT, with the remainder using CBT. The LBT was taught by a nationally recognized subject matter expert in the field of DNA evidence.

Evaluation Administration

The evaluation began with the dissemination of a letter of informed consent that was read aloud to the participants by the JSC staff member. The letter of informed consent described the purpose of the evaluation, authorization for study, and assured respondents of anonymity and confidentiality of the information they were providing.

Next, the LBT group was given a demographic survey, while the CBT group was given demographic and attitudinal surveys. Following the surveys, each group was given the same knowledge pretest. After both groups completed the training, they were administered the knowledge posttest. Additionally, the CBT group was given another attitudinal survey. The LBT group was not given the attitudinal survey because it was not applicable. Each group was proctored by a JSC staff member.

Data Analysis

Data were analyzed using the Statistical Package for the Social Sciences (SPSS), version 10 (2000) for the PC. Because most of the data collected were measured on rank-order scales (e.g., never, sometimes, often), most statistical analyses involved generating frequency and percentage distributions. However, inferential tests (such as paired sampled *t*-tests) were used to compare the performance between the two groups. Bivariate analyses were also conducted to determine whether a subject's performance in the computer-based course was affected by individual characteristics.

RESULTS

Descriptive Statistics

The sample consisted of 41 participants, 20 randomly selected to the computer-based training (CBT) group and 21 randomly selected to the lecture-based training (LBT) group. As displayed in Table 5-1, 78% of the participants were male (n=32). Nearly 76% of the participants were white (n=31). The average age of the subjects was 27.2 years old (s.d.=4.1). The majority had received at least some college education (80.5%, n=33), while only 4.9% held a General Equivalency Diploma (GED) (n=2).

Table 5-1: Descriptive Statistics for Background Variables

Variable	*Frequency*	*Percent*
Gender (n=41)		
Male 32	78%	
Female	9	22%
Race (n=41)		
White	31	75.6%
Non-White	10	24.4%
Education (n=41)		
Elementary	2	4.9%
High School	6	14.6%
Some College	10	24.4%
Associate's Degree	14	34.1%
Bachelor's Degree	9	22.0%
Age (n=41)		
Mean = 27.2		
Standard Deviation = 4.1		

An additional set of attitudinal questions pertaining to computer use were asked of the subjects in the CBT group. As Table 5-2 displays, 55% (n=11) reported that they had completed computer-based courses in the past and the majority owned a personal computer (75%, n=15). Only one participant reported having no computer experience; however 30% suggested that they had little to no familiarity with computers (n=6). Thirty-five percent indicated that they either had a considerable amount or a great deal of familiarity with computers (n=7). Forty percent reported that they rarely or never used computers in the course of their jobs (n=8); 35% indicated that they sometimes do (n=7); and 20% said that they usually or always use computers on the job (n = 4).

Table 5-2: Participant Computer Usage

n=20	*YES*	*NO*
Completed a computer course or training?	55% (n=11)	45% (n=9)
Do you own a personal computer?	75% (n=15)	25% (n=5)
Have you utilized CBT as a teacher or trainer?	55% (n=11)	45% (n=9)

Inferential Tests

A series of paired sample *t*-tests were conducted to examine the question of whether students improved after completing the course, beginning with an analysis of the entire sample. The average score on the pretest exam was 75.8% (SD=8.7), while the mean score on the posttest was 95% (SD=5.8). The analysis indicates that the difference between the two scores is statistically significant in the expected direction (t=-13.8, df=40). That is, the overall group improved after receiving instruction. In addition, it should also be noted that in no instance did a participant's score decrease, which suggests that all of the students benefited from their respective courses.

Further analyses separate the participants in the computer-based training from those who attended a more traditional lecture. The average pretest score for the CBT group was 74% (SD=10.1) and the average score on the posttest was 93% (SD=3.8). The *t*-test indicates that the group improved significantly on the posttest (t=-8.2, df=19). The average pretest score for the LBT group was 78% (SD=7.0), and the mean score on the posttest was 97% (SD=3.8). As expected, the difference between the pre- and posttests was significant (t=-11.849, df=20). Because the scores for both groups showed an increase, it became important to explore the question of whether the improvement was greater for one group over the other. In order to investigate this question, a variable measuring the difference between the pre- and posttest scores was created. A *t*-test was then conducted to compare the degree of improvement across the two groups. The CBT group increased their scores on the posttest by an average 19 points (SD=.10), while the scores of the LBT group increased by an average 19.4 points (SD=.08). The t-test indicates that this difference is not statistically significant (t=.15, df=39). In order to determine whether a subject's performance in the CBT group was affected by individual characteristics, analyses were conducted on the following variables: age, gender, education, prior CBT experience, whether the participant owned a personal computer, whether the participant uses a computer on the job, and the degree to which he or she is familiar with computers.[2] Bivariate analyses suggest that only the degree of computer familiarity were related to performance in the course. Participants with no or only some familiarity with computers increased their scores by 22.5 percentage points (SD=11.0), while those with considerable or a great deal of familiarity increased their scores by only 12.6 percentage points (s=4.9). The *t*-test indicates that this difference is statistically significant (t=-2.8, df=17.63).

Another important aspect of a training curriculum is the attitudes students bring to the process. The degree to which the participants felt positively about computer-based training was measured in a series of 30 attitudinal questions on a self-administered questionnaire. The survey was administered before training commenced and repeated after the course was completed. The possible responses to the questions ranged from a score of 1, which indicated the least positive response, to 5, the most positive response. The items were combined into an

---

2. Analyses of race are not reported. Given the small amount of racial diversity in the sample, the results may not hold true in the general population.

index, which was averaged across the items in order to maintain the same response scale (1-5).

Prior to going through the course, participants were generally positive about the process (mean=3.7, SD=.3). Their outlook was even more positive after having completed the course (mean=4.0, SD=.3). A *t*-test indicates that the change in attitude is statistically significant (t=-2.9, df=19). Bivariate tests revealed that posttest attitudes were not related to gender, age, education, prior experience with CBT, whether the participant owned a computer, whether the participant used a computer at work, or the degree of familiarity with computers.

Based on the results of the pre- and posttest, there were a number of interesting changes in attitudes regarding CBT. Prior to CBT instruction, 25% of the participants disagreed with the statement "I will feel concerned about not understanding the material." However, following the CBT instruction, disagreement with that statement increased to 60%, which suggests that their attitude toward understanding the material improved. Another interesting result was student concern about comparing their progress to that of their peers. For example, half of the students indicated in the pretest that it was important to know their standing in comparison with other students. However, this appeared to be of less importance in the posttest with only 25% of the students indicating this was still an issue of concern. When participants were asked if they thought they would be tested over material not presented in the CBT, half indicated that this was of concern to them. In the posttest survey, only 15% of the participants continued to express a concern. While 35% of the participants were uncertain as to whether or not the technology would enable them to learn more quickly than traditional LBT, the posttest survey attitudes reflected a 30% reduction in their level of uncertainty. Finally, a little less than half of the students indicated that they felt CBT was superior to LBT. Agreement with this statement increased to 70%, which would suggest that overall students felt that CBT was an effective tool for information dissemination.

EVALUATION CONCLUSIONS

The analyses allow several conclusions to be drawn:

1. Both lecture and computer-based training resulted in increased knowledge about DNA evidence. In fact, in no instance did a participant's score decrease, which suggests that all of the students benefited from their respective courses.
2. The amount of learning that occurs does not differ significantly across the two modes of instruction. Therefore, utilizing CBT instead of LBT to provide instruction about DNA Evidence Collection will provide the same amount of knowledge, but in less time and for less money.
3. Lack of familiarity with computers did not hamper participants in the computer-based training from learning the material. In fact, those with little or no familiarity with computers showed greater improvement than individuals who believed they had considerable knowledge of computers. Officers who have little to no formal training with computers were able to easily manipulate the program and gain knowledge from the CBT.
4. Officers were generally positive about computer-based training, both before and after course completion. In fact, attitudes were significantly more positive after the course was finished. Officers quickly understood the value of the CBT after completing the modules, and remarked that the multimedia components (sounds and movies) nicely complimented the subject matter to provide an enjoyable training experience.

The data indicate that computer-based training is an effective method of instructing officers on the use of DNA evidence. Given the lower costs associated with CBT, the results presented here suggest that this mode of instruction may be a desirable option for law enforcement agencies with limited resources.

It is, however, important to note the limitations of this evaluation. In particular, it is essential to remember that the sample size is very small and not very diverse, which means that the results may not generalize well to other groups. Further testing of the approach with larger, more diverse samples are imperative.

SUMMARY

This chapter has provided an overview of computer-based training for law enforcement applications, specifically focusing on an NIJ study on the effectiveness of a DNA Evidence Collection CBT. CBT Technology is quickly revolutionizing the way that training is conducted in many industry sectors, including law enforcement. With tightened budgets equating to fewer human resources and less opportunities for training, law enforcement must realize the potential of CBT and utilize it more often in order to maximize the amount of information provided to officers. It also focused on the importance of transferring forensic technology capacity to the law enforcement community much like what has happened with sobriety testing. As the technology advances and becomes ever more capable of field analysis, more and more agencies will have a need to use methods such as CBT to train and prepare their officers for this shift from criminal evidence collection to criminal evidence analysis. CBT will also be an invaluable tool in providing current and ongoing training to the law enforcement community and to many that would not otherwise have access to this information. As DNA evidence became a household word in the mid-1990s following the highly publicized O.J. Simpson trials, there has been an increasing demand on police departments to demonstrate their officer's knowledge in the proper collection and identification of criminal evidence such as DNA. Without the use of CBT or other distributed learning technologies the majority of law enforcement agencies in this country would continue to fall farther behind in the struggle to keep pace with advances in technology. As research continues to demonstrate that students who take a CBT course versus a platform-based course learn as well if not better, more and more law enforcement academies, post commands, and departments will embrace this technology as a necessary tool for training. Key to the breakdown of the barriers described earlier will be the acceptance by post commands and other law enforcement training authorities to accept CBT as they do platform-based training in the fulfillment of both basic and inservice police training. Issues regarding cost of development and infrastructure will continue to decline as more and more CBT training programs are developed, and law enforcement agencies have greater access and use of computers.

REFERENCES

Advanced Distributed Learning Implementation Plan. (2000, May 19). DOD Implementation Plan for ADL. Available on-line at http://www.maxwell.af.mil/au/afiadl/plans&policy/pdfs/aetcip.pdf

Asplen, C. H. (2003). *The application of DNA technology in England and Wales*, Unpublished manuscript.

Asplen, C. H. (November-December 1999). From crime scene to courtroom: Integrating DNA technology into the criminal justice system. *Judicature: Genes and Justice.* (83)3. American Judicature Society. pps. 144-147.

Bixler, B. (2000). Selecting and implementing computer-based training. Available online at http://www.personal.psu.edu/staff/b/x/bxb11/CBTGuide/Overview.htm

Cordner, G., & Scarborough, K. E. (2004, May). "Science solves crime: Myth or reality." Unpublished manuscript.

eMarketer. (2004). Available online at http://www.eMarketer.com

Flink, W. L. (ed). (2000). *A sourcebook of information by the international association of directors of law enforcement standards and training: Standards and training information in the United States.* Waynesboro: CJ Data/ Flink & Associates.

Hammell, T. J., & Kingsley, L. C. (1999). Nonresident computer-based training: Effectiveness evaluation. United States Coast Guard Research and Development Center. Available online at http://www.rdc.uscg.gov/rdcpages/pubs.html

Nachmias, C. F., & Nachmias, D. (2000). *Research methods in the social sciences.* New York: Worth Publishers.

National Center for Education Statistics (NCES). (2002). Distance learning in institutions of higher education. Available online at http://nces.ed.gov/

National Commission on the Future of DNA Evidence: Background. (2002). National Institute of Justice. Available online at http://www.ojp.usdoj.gov/nij/dna/backg.htm

Schwabe, W. (1999). *Needs and prospects for crime-fighting technology: The federal role in assisting state and local law enforcement.* Santa Monica, CA: RAND.

Steadman, G. W. (2000). *Survey of DNA Crime Laboratories, 1998.* Washington, DC: Bureau of Justice Statistics.

United States Distance Learning Association (USDLA). (2002). International Data Corporation (IDC) Corporate Spending Projections. Available online at www.usdla.org

Wegner, S., Holloway, K., & Garton, E. (1999, November). "The effects of internet-based instruction on student learning." *Journal of Asynchronous Learning Networks,* (2), 98-106.

What Every Law Enforcement Officer Should Know About DNA Evidence (Brochure). (1999, September). Department of Justice, Office of Justice Programs, National Institute of Justice. Available online at http://www.ojp.usdoj.gov/nij/pubs-sum/000614.htm

What Every Law Enforcement Officer Should Know About DNA Evidence (Beginning and Advanced Level Modules). (2000, Fall). Department of Justice, Office of Justice Programs, National Institute of Justice. Available online at www.ncjrs.org [DNA CD]

Part II

LAW ENFORCEMENT TECHNOLOGY

Chapter 6

OVERVIEW OF LAW ENFORCEMENT TECHNOLOGY

KATHRYN E. SCARBOROUGH AND GARY CORDNER

In an earlier chapter, Samuel Nunn provided an overview of technology systems in criminal justice, focusing on seven broad categories: communications, database/recordkeeping, decision support, biometrics, imaging, monitoring, and weaponry/personal defense. In this chapter, we provide an overview of technology for one specific component of criminal justice, law enforcement, with an emphasis on recent advances and key issues. We examine law enforcement technology from two different angles, police functions and police goals. Then we discuss barriers to law enforcement technology development, before concluding with a look at future technology prospects for policing.

This overview demonstrates that technology plays a very important role in policing. Only 50 years ago, police technology amounted to little more than a car, a two-way radio in that car, and a gun. Even 20 years ago, technology generally played a marginal role in policing with relatively little impact on the core functions of patrolling, handling incidents, regulating behavior, and investigating crimes (Manning, 1992). Today, it is still true that police officers rely heavily on human skills when dealing with individuals and maintaining order in neighborhoods, but more and more of the information that they use is constructed and provided technologically, and much of their day-to-day work involves new technologies, from body armor and less-lethal weapons to patrol car video cameras and in-car computers.

TECHNOLOGY AND POLICE FUNCTIONS

A logical and traditional way to classify law enforcement technology is in relation to basic police functions. We will consider six functional areas: patrol, investigations, traffic, special operations, command and control, and administration. There are other police functions, of course, but these areas represent the vast majority of employees in most police organizations.

Patrol

Patrol officers handle calls for service and otherwise patrol their assigned areas. Perhaps the biggest technological innovation in police history was the introduction of the patrol car, which allowed officers to cover larger areas, but which also changed the relationship between the beat cop and the public. When the two-way radio was combined with the patrol car, officers on patrol could be notified by headquarters that a citizen needed assistance, and they could respond quickly. Also, officers could summon help or ask for information using their radios. Ironically, research eventually demonstrated that neither preventive patrol in cars nor rapid response to reported crimes was very effective (Kelling et al., 1974; Spelman & Brown, 1981).

Today, lightweight personal radios and mobile telephones give patrol officers effective communications without dependence on the patrol car. This makes it practical for officers to patrol on foot, on bicycles, and by other means, or simply to get out of their cars more often. The biggest technology-related issue associated with modern communications equipment is interoperability, which refers to the capacity of officers to communicate directly with other officers in their own departments, with officers or agents in other law enforcement agencies, and with fire and EMS personnel in the field (National Task Force on Interoperability, 2003). Despite the fact that modern radio systems are technical marvels compared to past systems, many police officers in the field today still find themselves unable to communicate directly with other personnel during routine incidents, special operations, and emergencies.

The communication device that has had the most dramatic impact in the last decade is the mobile (cell) telephone. These phones give officers an alternative to the police radio, which is often so busy that it is difficult to transmit anything other than short, basic messages. The phones allow officers to call each other or headquarters with more extended messages. Perhaps most importantly, citizens can call officers directly if they know the officers' mobile phone numbers. Particularly in the context of community policing, it has become common for officers to distribute their cell numbers widely, and for residents to call "their officer" directly with reports of incidents, tips, and requests. Such direct contact between citizens and patrol officers arguably leads to closer relationships and better service. It also leaves police management in the dark about much of the interaction between officers and citizens, a situation that managers sometimes find distressing.

Whether patrolling or handling calls, patrol officers need access to various pieces of information. Traditionally, much of that information was not even computerized, and if it was, officers had to use the radio to ask dispatchers to run queries. Today, though, many patrol officers have computers in their cars with wireless access to a variety of local, state, and national databases. This means that officers can run "checks" on people, cars, and property directly (i.e., without going through a dispatcher), resulting in much more information being accessed and many more "hits" on wanted persons, drivers with suspended licenses, stolen cars, and the like.

As shown in a later chapter in this volume, though, there is a "technology gap" that affects many small and rural law enforcement agencies. These agencies are much less likely to have computers in patrol cars and wireless access to important police data. Some rural areas also have both poor cell phone and radio coverage. For these agencies, then, just achieving reliable two-way communication with headquarters remains a challenge; interoperability with other agencies and wireless data networks are still in the future for them.

Beyond communications and information, one of the biggest technology concerns of patrol officers is suspect control. Officers have to handle disruptive and sometimes violent people and make arrests. For many years, basic police equipment for suspect control went largely unchanged–a handgun (revolver or semiautomatic), handcuffs, and a nightstick (baton). Considerable attention has been directed toward less-lethal technology over the past 25 years, in part due to changing legal standards affecting police use of deadly force, lawsuits, and public opinion. Patrol officers today generally have several suspect control options available to them.

Probably the most important suspect control development in recent years has been pepper spray (oleoresin capsicum [OC]). Patrol officers typically carried some form of mace or "tear gas" before the advent of pepper spray, but those gases had shorter shelf lives, were more likely to be blown by the wind back into the officer's face, and most importantly, often required medical attention for those affected. Pepper spray has proven to be more effective, cheaper, less likely to be windblown, and it generally does not require medical attention. Pepper spray does not subdue every combatant in every situation, but it does seem to be very effective in many situations, allowing officers to control suspects without having to physically fight or wrestle with them or use the baton as a striking weapon (Kaminski, Edwards, & Johnson, 1998). Recent research on pepper spray indicates fewer injuries to both officers and suspects, fewer complaints of excessive force, and the only fatalities that have occurred with pepper spray were suspects who had asthma (National Institute of Justice, 2003). Although more research involving the use of pepper spray must be undertaken, its use to date has been promising.

Most recently, Tasers have become quite popular and their adoption by police is spreading (Adams, 2003; Biggs, 2003; Irwin, 2003). The taser imparts an electrical charge designed to incapacitate the suspect without causing any permanent harm. The primary use for the Taser is in those situations involving a violent or struggling suspect when pepper spray has not worked or is not feasible. It is seen as an alternative to striking the suspect with a baton, swarming the suspect with multiple officers, or possibly, shooting a suspect. Baton strikes always carry the risk of serious injury and can be perceived by the public as unnecessarily brutal. Swarming and wrestling have led to a number of suspect deaths, especially when the suspect is intoxicated (especially by drugs). Shooting a suspect armed with a knife, while often legally justified, typically arouses public sentiment and seems like it should be unnecessary in these technologically advanced times. If Tasers prove to be effective and humane alternatives in situations such as these, it can be anticipated that they will become standard equipment for patrol officers.

An aspect of suspect control that presents a continuing technological challenge relates to police pursuits. Criminal and traffic offenders sometimes flee from the police in cars, and the traditional police response has been to engage in high-speed chases. These chases are dangerous, however, often resulting in injuries or deaths to officers, suspects, or third parties. Civil lawsuits are also common. The primary technological solution to date has been stop sticks, which are hollow spikes designed to cause controlled tire blowouts. The use of these sticks is somewhat limited, though, because they have to be deployed in front of fleeing vehicles, and the suspect has to cooperate by not turning onto a different road or otherwise navigating around the sticks.

Because technological solutions to the pursuit problem have been slow to develop, the primary police management reaction has been to implement policies that control, discourage, or even prohibit high-speed chases except in narrowly defined circumstances (Alpert et al., 2000). Until a pursuit technology solution is developed that enables officers in pursuit to somehow disable or slow down the fleeing vehicle, this particular situation is likely to continue to frustrate both police managers and patrol officers. The clear trend is toward policies and practices that strongly emphasize safety, which is understandable and necessary, but that has the unfortunate consequence of allowing more offenders to escape justice.

Related to suspect control is the issue of personal protection for patrol officers. Just 30 years ago, it was very unusual for patrol officers to wear any type of body armor (often called bullet proof vests). Today, it is surprising if an officer does not wear body armor while on patrol. Vests have become much lighter, more comfortable, and more effective at protecting officers from bullets, sharp blades, and other weapons. Body armor has saved many police officers' lives over the past two decades (National Institute of Justice, 1998). Besides protecting officers from assaults, body armor has also provided life-saving protection to many officers involved in automobile crashes, especially before the advent of air bags. Body armor is still improving and issues remain, including quality control (Stearns, 2003), effectiveness in different weather conditions, and effectiveness against different types of weapons, but overall this life-saving technology has already had a big impact on policing.

Investigations

Investigating reported crimes is another important police function. Detectives have this as their primary responsibility, but patrol officers also investigate crimes, especially in smaller agencies that do not even have detectives.

The key focus of technology for criminal investigation is physical evidence. For 100 years or more, police have sought to improve their ability to collect and analyze physical evidence as a supplement and alternative to their historical reliance on eyewitnesses, informants, and confessions. At the crime scene, police now have lasers (light amplification by stimulated emission) and other forms of alternative light sources that greatly enhance their ability to find fingerprints, blood, semen, and other types of trace evidence, especially biological evidence (Fisher, 2000). Similarly, crime labs have better equipment and scientific techniques that allow scientists to draw more definitive conclusions from various types of physical evidence.

The two most striking science and technology developments affecting criminal investigation have been AFIS and DNA (Schwabe, Davis, & Jackson, 2001). AFIS (Automated Fingerprint Identification System) uses computers to scan and digitize fingerprints. This system, which operates at local, state, and national levels, has greatly improved the positive identification of arrested persons and has tremendously increased the chances of linking a latent fingerprint found at a crime scene to a suspect. The AFIS system was upgraded in 1999 to IAFIS (Integrated Automated Fingerprint Identification System), which includes not only AFIS, but also two other segments, the Interstate Identification Index (III) and the Identification Tasking and Networking (ITN). IAFIS enables agencies that have live-scan fingerprint terminals to scan prints and photographs of arrestees to numerous networks simultaneously. This is an improvement over AFIS in that the transmission and accessing of information occurs more rapidly in real time, with more quality control checks while accessing additional databases than were previously unavailable (Swanson, Chamelin, & Territo, 2003).

DNA has made it possible to conclusively demonstrate that human tissue (such as blood) found at a crime scene came from a particular suspect. With both AFIS and DNA, computers automate the process of comparing crime scene evidence to databases of known samples. Those databases contain many millions of fingerprint cards (collected from arrested persons over the years) and more and more DNA samples as the states increasingly collect DNA from persons convicted of various crimes.

Crime scene and crime lab applications are not the only arenas for technology in criminal investigation, however. Crimes are frequently captured on film by surveillance cameras, for example. Unfortunately, older analog technology often provided disappointing results, especially if the same videotape cartridge had been running for months (or if no cartridge was running at all). Today, modern digital technology can provide much better pictures, and the digital output can more easily be enhanced, transmitted to officers in the field, and stored for later use. Both technologies, however, have pros and cons. Analog technology is older, often harder to process, and full of errors. On the other hand, analog technology is the best way to record real-world events, is often faster, and can require lower amounts of power. Digital technology is newer, meaning we have less experience with it, and cannot record real-world events, but appears to be more stable and easy to process. Ideally analog and digital technologies are used in a complementary way that provides fast, stable, real-time communications in numerous environments (Kessler, 2004). Overall, the contribution of surveillance pictures and film to crime solving should increase with newer technology.

In general, modern electronic technology is far superior to older equipment. Thus, for example, the use of small transmitters to track people, cars, stolen property, drug shipments, and other items is much more practical and effective today. Technology for eavesdropping on personal and telephone conversations is quite sophisticated. Modern technology also provides some capacity to scan high volumes of telephone and e-mail communications in order to capture messages of a specific type or messages associated with specific individuals. Needless to say, of course, these powerful electronic surveillance capabilities carry with them a host of important civil liberties concerns.

Computers and databases have become standard tools of detectives. Several commercial databases are available that assist investigators in locating individuals or locating information about them. Public databases are also invaluable to investigators when it is necessary to determine who owns a piece of real estate, for example, who holds a business license, or who holds the mortgage on a property. The FBI operates the Violent Criminal Apprehension Program (ViCAP), which is a computerized database of serial offenders and unsolved crimes that are or may be part of a crime series. Recent improvements to ViCAP provide agencies with additional capabilities for matching and managing cases, as well as transmitting information including photographs and graphics (Witzig, 2003). It is also common for detectives to use Internet search engines to seek information about individuals or related crimes connected to an unusual investigation that they are conducting (sometimes called "googling" a case).

A long-term technological dream of investigators has been a device that can reveal when someone is lying. The most common type of "lie-detector" technology is the polygraph, which measures the body's physiological responses to stimuli, in this case, statements presented by a polygraph operator. Unfortunately, the ability of the polygraph to distinguish between true and false statements seems to depend greatly on the operator of the equipment, and test results are often inconclusive. The accuracy of the polygraph ranges from 62% to 98%, depending on the population studied, research design and protocols, and the actual type of polygraph machine (Swanson, Chamelin, & Territo, 2003). Consequently, the polygraph has been somewhat disappointing as an investigative aid, and in addition, test results are not generally admissible in court as evidence. Research continues into the science of lie detection, though; a technological breakthrough could certainly have a significant impact on investigative practice and crime solving.

Traffic

Traffic control and traffic enforcement are important traditional functions of the police. Three interesting technological developments have enhanced this aspect of police operations. In the realm of speed measurement, radar revolutionized the ability of police to enforce speeding laws. Newer radar technology is more accurate, more discriminating when several cars are traveling together, and more compact. Perhaps most importantly, radar equipment has been redesigned to address health concerns that arose among radar operators in the 1990s.

Drunk driving enforcement was given a tremendous boost by the development of breath-testing technology. Prior to the breathalyzer or intoxilyzer, a blood sample had to be obtained from a suspected drunk driver and then it had to be sent to a lab for analysis, if scientific evidence of intoxication was desired. This was cumbersome and difficult; as a result, most DUI prosecutions boiled down to the officer's word against the driver's. With the development and subsequent refinement of breath-testing equipment, the driver merely had to blow into a machine at the police station, which then produced a scientific analysis of his or her blood alcohol content. In recent years, preliminary breath testing (PBT) devices have also been developed that allow officers to obtain fairly accurate readings in the field. In contrast to breathalyzer results, these PBT measurements are not usually accepted in court as definitive, but they help screen out drivers who are disoriented, fatigued, or under the influence of substances other than alcoholic beverages.

Automated traffic enforcement has been the most recent development in traffic control technology. Cameras at intersections can now take pictures of cars and drivers that fail to obey traffic lights, and camera/radar combinations can record speeding violations. Technical challenges remain with respect to obtaining clear pictures of drivers through windshields in all weather and lighting conditions, but for the most part automated traffic enforcement is currently feasible and it is already used extensively in Europe. It has been slower to catch on in the United States, primarily because of privacy concerns and the uniquely American point of view that it is not quite fair to be caught by a machine. It seems obvious, though, that automated enforcement has the potential to greatly improve traffic safety by more closely regulating driver behavior.

Special Operations

Police special operations pertain to hostage situations, barricaded suspects, high-risk warrants, major crime scenes, hazardous material and weapons of mass destruction (WMD) incidents, disasters, search and rescue situations, crowd and riot control, and similar unusual circumstances. The largest police departments have special units whose full-time duties entail response to these kinds of situations. Most police departments, however, rely on specially trained personnel who work full-time in patrol and other assignments but who respond and work together as a special operations squad when needed.

The complex and challenging nature of these kinds of incidents naturally creates a need for special equipment and technology. Special operations units sometimes have specialty vehicles, including mobile command centers and armored vehicles. Individual officers often have helmets, higher-level body armor, bulletproof shields, semiautomatic rifles, and other special gear. Other military-style equipment may be available, including night-vision goggles, flash-bang grenades, laser-dazzlers, cameras that can see around corners, and microphones that can listen into closed rooms. Modern bomb squads have very specialized technology, including robots that can be used to approach and move suspected explosive devices.

The most recent technological concern in special operations is personal protective equipment (PPE) for hazardous material and chemical/biological/radiological incidents. Of course, patrol officers and other public safety first responders may need this kind of equipment as well, but where a patrol officer may have the opportunity to retreat in a WMD situation and secure the perimeter, special operations personnel will likely be expected to apprehend suspects and/or rescue victims, even in hazardous situations and contaminated areas. Technology considerations include biological and chemical field test kits, Geiger-Mueller detectors (for radioactivity detection), air purifying respirators, and self-contained breathing apparatus (Drielak & Brandon, 2000).

Command and Control

The nature of policing is such that police departments have personnel in the field at all times. Headquarters staff (managers and dispatchers), therefore, have a need to command and control those personnel–to keep track of them, deploy them to areas and assign them to specific duties, and supervise them to the extent possible (Colton, Brandeau, & Tien, 1983). To accomplish command and control, headquarter personnel need information about calls, crimes, traffic flows, officer-initiated activity, and similar events going on in the jurisdiction, as well as reliable communications with units in the field.

The basic means of command and control is the police radio system described earlier, supplemented by mobile phones and in-car computers. These are coordinated with 9-1-1 telephone systems that help the public call the police more quickly, and that give police dispatchers some information about the building or location from which a call is originating. Enhanced 9-1-1 systems go a step farther by automatically revealing the address from which a call is made, even if the caller hangs up, is lost, or cannot accurately communicate the location.

The big challenge today for 9-1-1 systems is mobile (cell) phones, with over 50 million calls coming in to emergency communications centers annually, according to the National Emergency Number Association. Because cell phones use wireless technology, it is much more difficult to pinpoint where a call coming into the police communications unit is coming from. In fact, when a 9-1-1 call is placed from a cell phone, there is no guarantee that it will be answered at the right emergency communications center, a situation that can lead to serious confusion when time is of the essence. Technological solutions are currently being implemented to improve this situation. The Federal Communications Commission (FCC) has initiated a plan that requires wireless carriers to provide emergency communications centers with geographic coordinates of callers, callback numbers, and locations of towers or satellites receiving the cell phone calls. Compliance is required by 2005, but experts estimate that carriers will not be able to fulfill the mandate by that deadline (*Technology Review*, 2004).

One interesting technological development in the command and control arena is police vehicle monitoring. Global positioning system (GPS) transmitters can now be affixed to patrol cars that allow dispatchers back at the communications center to look up at an electronic map and see a live picture of where each patrol unit is located. This makes it easier for dispatchers to select the closest unit when a serious incident occurs, and also helps dispatchers coordinate multiple units when they are responding to a call or pursuing a suspect. Interestingly, earlier versions of patrol vehicle monitoring technology (Larson & Simon, 1979) were abandoned about two decades ago because of patrol officer resistance–officers did not want to be tracked. Current technology is better, of course, but the key to its acceptance has been to sell it on the basis of officer safety. With vehicle (or even officer) tracking, officers in trouble can be located even if they cannot use their radios to call for help or specify their locations.

Another example of officer monitoring is patrol car video technology. Many police departments now have video cameras mounted in patrol cars for the purpose of videotaping pursuits and officer encounters with motorists and citizens (Maghan, O'Reilly, & Shon, 2002). Once again, this might be seen as threatening to police officer autonomy, but in the modern era it has been accepted as a practice that generally protects officers from false accusations of improper behavior. A further enhancement of this technology is a tiny camera that the officer can wear on his or her pocket or lapel, providing video coverage wherever the officer is located, rather than only in front of the patrol car. These tiny cameras transmit their video back to the same recorder in the trunk of the patrol car that also records the car-based video camera.

Not all new technologies prove to be beneficial, at least initially. This was illustrated by gunshot detection technology that was field-tested in Dallas, Texas (Mazerolle et al., 1998). Like many cities, Dallas gets numerous reports of "shots fired" from the public without definite locations, because the reporting parties did not see anyone discharge a gun and because sounds echo and bounce around city buildings. The technology involved placing several specialized receivers (listening devices) around the city so that gunshots could be quickly triangulated, approximate locations identified, and officers dispatched. The primary failing of the system was not technical, but rather that "shots fired" calls, without any associated serious crime or injured person report, were of secondary priority in Dallas. Consequently, officers were not dispatched immediately to the triangulated gunshot calls, making it more or less irrelevant that an approximate location had been identified. Not one suspect was identified or apprehended during the field test period. More recent efforts at testing this type of surveillance system are occurring in Charleston, South Carolina, where residents are not always quick to report gunfire. In a city that had 1,745 reports of gunfire, resulting in 162 people being shot in 2001-2002, investigators hope to improve their crime-solving capabilities with these technological advancements (Smith, 2003).

Administration

Beyond command and control, police organizations also need technology to make day-to-day police management more efficient and effective (Dunworth et al., 2000). This includes support services, such as records and information systems, which provide more or less continuous (around the clock) assistance to operations personnel, and administrative services, such as training and fiscal affairs, which normally provide assistance on a Monday to Friday basis (Cordner, Scarborough, & Sheehan, 2004). Technology applications in the realm of police administration mostly fall into the category of information technology (information systems, databases, and computer software).

Police departments have long maintained databases of reported crimes, arrested persons, traffic accidents and citations, seized evidence, and similar information. Traditionally, these "records" were kept on paper in file cabinets, possibly cross-referenced using index card files. Today, though, most of these records are computerized and stored electronically in Records Management Systems (RMS) that make it much easier to retrieve information and perform analyses. The RMS is a central component of any police agency's information system. It allows a police officer to determine how frequently a person's name has come up in incident reports, it allows an analyst to look for a pattern in recent burglaries, and it allows a manager to compare the productivity of various officers.

An important part of police technology today is the software that police agencies use to analyze information. An example is Geographic Information System (GIS) software that is used to analyze the locations of crimes, calls, traffic accidents, drug arrests, recovered stolen cars, and similar events (Reuland, 1997). GIS software can help analysts uncover geographic patterns, locate hot spots, produce maps that visually represent a problem, and even predict where a serial offender lives or where the next crime in a pattern might occur. Other important software can help agencies calculate optimum patrol staffing levels, draw patrol beat boundaries, and identify and track officers exhibiting problematic behaviors (so-called early-warning or early-identification systems). Most recently, a great deal of attention has been devoted to developing software that can assist police agencies with data mining of multiple databases, in order to enhance intelligence analysis and information sharing with respect to organized crime, white-collar crime, drug investigations, and domestic and international terrorism.

An aspect of police administration that is ripe for more use of technology is police training. Police agencies devote considerable time and expense to training–up to half a year for each officer's initial recruit training, up to a year of field training after that, and then a variety of refresher, recertification, update, and advanced training throughout an officer's career. If technology could reduce the amount of time required to complete training, or make the training that is provided more effective, it could have quite an impact on police organizations.

The potential for training technology is illustrated in other fields. For example, much of the training that airplane pilots and tank commanders get is in "simulators," replicas of tanks and airplanes that use computers and electronics to simulate flight and battle. Practice in simulators does not completely replace practice in real tanks and airplanes, of course, but it greatly reduces the need for such real practice and also provides the opportunity to confront trainees with a wide variety of scenarios and emergencies that would be difficult, if not impossible, to safely reproduce in real vehicles.

This type of simulation training is currently used in some police agencies and police academies to teach firearms (see the chapter later in this volume) and driving, apparently with success. Another application of simulation training in policing is the use of exercises to practice responses to disasters and WMD incidents. This use of simulation is typically more "low-tech," involving role-playing and gaming. Participants in an exercise are informed that a major incident has occurred, and instructed to respond accordingly. Then, as the response unfolds, additional complications are introduced in order to challenge the skills and adaptability of the participants. When the exercise is over, the participants go through a debriefing in order to assess what worked well, what needs improvement, and what lessons were learned. Regular practice of this type promotes learning and skill development, even though everyone who is involved is aware that the situation is simulated and not real.

A different type of application of technology to police training involves the use of computer-based training (CBT) and distance learning as alternatives to the traditional method of training (bringing 25-50 or more trainees to a room where an instructor teaches them a subject or course). With CBT, the course is "on the computer" and trainees usually proceed at their own pace. There may be no instructor at all, or one who is available only as needed. With distance learning, the instructor is located in a different place than the students (who may be together or they may each be in different places too). Distance learning normally uses the Internet and/or videoteleconferencing to deliver information and facilitate interaction, although the traditional format of the correspondence course is more low-tech, relying on postal delivery and the occasional telephone call.

The utilization of distance learning and CBT seems to be growing slowly in police training. Some resistance arises from traditionalism and fear of change, some from a shortage of existing computer-based materials and lack of funds to produce new CBT courses, and some from legitimate concerns over the degree to which CBT and distance learning can effectively transmit the core content and ethos of policing to trainees. Two things seem clear, though: (1) some police training topics can be covered more efficiently using modern technology (see the chapter on DNA evidence later in this volume), and (2) financial pressures will force police agencies to look more closely at alternative modes of training in the future, simply because police training is so time-consuming and expensive. Techniques that are either more efficient (time- and money-saving) or more effective (greater learning) will eventually be given careful consideration by many police agencies and police academies.

TECHNOLOGY AND POLICE GOALS

A different way to consider the application of technology to policing is in terms of police goals. The value of this approach is that it ties technology more directly to the ends of policing, that is, what police agencies are supposed to accomplish, instead of simply to the tasks that police traditionally perform. The discussion will focus on seven police goals: (1) reduce criminal victimization, (2) call offenders to account, (3) reduce fear and enhance personal security, (4) guarantee safety in public spaces, (5) use financial resources fairly, efficiently, and effectively, (6) use force and authority appropriately, and (7) satisfy public demands and achieve legitimacy (Moore, 2002). The discussion will be rather brief, since many police technologies and technology issues were covered in the preceding section on police functions.

Reduce Crime

Few if any of the technologies discussed earlier were specifically focused on preventing crime. This reflects the long-standing tendency of police agencies to downplay crime prevention in favor of crime reaction–responding to crimes that have already occurred and trying to apprehend those responsible. The advent of the patrol car nearly 100 years ago was rationalized on the basis of prevention, of course, but research later demonstrated that motorized patrol did not prevent crime.

Technology has real potential for preventing crime, but police agencies have generally shown little interest in emphasizing this aspect of their mandate. For example, motor vehicle theft can be reduced if manufacturers install better locks and alarms, if cars are fitted with transmitters and receivers so that they can be shut down if stolen, or if parking garages are equipped with entry/exit control devices and closed-circuit television (Clarke, 2003). Graffiti can be reduced through the use of CCTV (Closed Circuit Television) and "vandal-proof" coatings (such as textured or wash-off paints) for graffiti-prone surfaces (Weisel, 2003). If police focused more intently on the goal of crime prevention through the use of problem-oriented policing (Goldstein, 1990), situational crime prevention (Clarke, 1997), and crime science generally (Laycock, 2003), they might identify many other promising technological responses.

Call Offenders to Account

Of the seven police goals, this is probably the one toward which the most technology has been directed. Rapid response technology, night vision equipment, crime scene and crime lab enhancements, information systems and software to support crime analysis and intelligence sharing, and a host of other developments are aimed at improving the ability of the police to identify and apprehend offenders. As noted earlier, AFIS and DNA technology have had the greatest impact in recent years. For example, DNA resulted in over 1,700 matches per week in England and Wales in 2002 and a tripling of the suspect identification rate for burglary (Asplen, 2003). The utilization of DNA has been slower to develop in the United States but it is gaining momentum with additional funding for crime labs and databases.

It should be noted that calling offenders to account can also accomplish crime reduction. Incarceration of offenders results in an incapacitation effect if those offenders would have committed additional crimes. In this vein, quicker identification and apprehension of serial offenders using DNA and other technologies can prevent crimes that those offenders would otherwise commit (Lovrich et al., 2003). There is also the possibility of general deterrence when the chances of offenders being arrested and punished goes up. General deterrence effects are not very strong when only 20% of serious reported crimes are solved and even fewer result in any substantial penalties (the current state of affairs in the United States), but a significant improvement in calling offenders to account might alter the deterrence calculus.

Reduce Fear and Enhance Personal Security

The goal of making people feel safer is one that police have not emphasized with technology or with other kinds of programs. One aspect of technology that has been demonstrated to reduce fear of crime is increased street lighting (Pease, 1999). Another technology, CCTV, has had mixed results when assessed for its impact on peoples' feelings of safety (Phillips, 1999).

This area of technology for fear reduction would seem to be ripe for development. Possibilities might include panic alarms for vulnerable people (such as domestic violence victims), better surveillance technology for tracking released sex offenders, more use of reverse 9-1-1 to notify residents of specific neighborhoods about immediate threats, better technology for locating and identifying abducted children, vehicle technology that thwarts carjacking, and so on. We might hope that more police and scientific attention will be devoted to fear-reducing technology in the future.

Guarantee Safety in Public Spaces

This goal pertains not so much to safety from crime but rather safety from traffic crashes, fires, and other types of accidents. The traditional police approach to traffic safety has emphasized enforcement of traffic laws, but it is clear that road improvements, vehicle safety improvements (including air bags), and changes in public opinion in favor of the use of seatbelts and against drinking and driving have contributed much more to roadway safety.

One technological approach to traffic safety mentioned earlier was automated enforcement. Increasing the certainty of detection with speed cameras seems to have an immediate and long-term effect on driver behavior, both on roads that are known to have cameras and on other roads in the general area (Corbett & Simon, 1999). Intersection cameras might be expected to have a similar effect. Other technology applications for roadway safety include installing breath-testing devices that drivers must use before starting cars, installing "governors" (regulators) that limit the maximum speed of vehicles, and a host of traffic engineering and traffic calming techniques (Scott, 2003). Other technologies aimed at enhancing bicycle safety and pedestrian safety ought to be given consideration by the police as well.

Use Financial Resources Fairly, Efficiently, and Effectively

This goal reflects the importance for any public agency of spending tax dollars wisely. Current technology applications in line with this goal would include such things as bar-coding technology for maintaining accurate inventories of equipment, evidence, and recovered property; automated field reporting to save patrol officer report-writing time; and the use of videoconferencing for arraignment of arrested persons (saving the time and expense of transporting prisoners from jail to court).

An intriguing efficiency application is the widespread installation of CCTV and other types of sensors. Traditionally, a substantial amount of police time has been spent on patrol, essentially driving around and watching for suspicious or illegal things to happen. In the new homeland security era, police officers are also frequently assigned to guard so-called critical infrastructure, which may include bridges, transportation centers, water treatment plants, and the like. The degree to which all this human presence and effort might be replaced by technology is yet to be seen, but financial pressures guarantee that these technologies will be tested.

Use Force and Authority Appropriately

The authority and capacity to use coercive force is a defining characteristic of policing (Bittner, 1970). The public delegates that awesome authority to the police, and it follows that an important goal of police agencies is to use force and authority fairly. Technology can play an important role in helping police exercise their authority effectively as well as equitably. Powerful and sophisticated weapons, for example, can enable the police to overcome heavily armed criminals or terrorists, enter fortified facilities, and rescue hostages. More routinely, less-lethal weapons can help police subdue and arrest individuals who are violent and struggling without having to resort to more-lethal alternatives.

Information technology (IT), including databases and computer software, provides a double-edged sword with respect to police use of their authority. IT can help the police identify wanted persons as well as dangerous criminals and terrorists who may be planning violent acts. This use of IT increases police effectiveness and helps protect individual victims and society in general. In addition, with better IT police are less likely to make gross or incorrect identifications, thus reducing the chances that innocent citizens will be inconvenienced, stopped, or arrested by mistake. The inherent danger with better IT, though, is that the police will have access to more and more information about us, reducing our privacy and increasing the potential for widespread civil liberties abuses.

As discussed in the earlier section on administration, though, IT can also help police agencies monitor police officer performance, including their use of authority (stops, citations, arrests) and their use of force. This can help the agency identify individual officers and/or units that are not using force and authority appropriately. On a larger level, the same kinds of information are now being used to assess entire agencies in terms of use of force and racial profiling. Thus, modern IT has the potential to increase accountability at all levels, just as it also has the potential to improve police use of their authority and/or increase the threat that police pose to civil liberties.

Satisfy the Public and Achieve Legitimacy

In a free society, the police have to be concerned about public opinion, whether they like it or not. Although it is not possible (or expected) that police officers will please every citizen involved in every encounter, it is necessary that a police agency be generally responsive to its community, within legal parameters of course. Without public support, it is difficult for an agency to be successful in addressing crime and disorder. In the American system, it is also unlikely that a police chief or sheriff will remain in office for long if public satisfaction declines substantially or remains at a low level.

One aspect of satisfying the public is providing good service, whether that means rapid response to emergency calls or solving serious crimes. In this regard, technologies already discussed come into play, and police departments that fail to successfully adopt these modern technologies run the risk of losing ground on public satisfaction. More directly, one technology that has potential for both providing more service to the public and helping a police agency stay attuned to its "customers" is the Internet. Many police departments are now using the Internet to provide services quickly and cheaply, ranging from online crime reporting to neighborhood crime maps and chat rooms with beat officers. One agency, the Chicago Police Department, is experimenting with using online surveys to identify residents' concerns, fears, and priorities in order to guide beat-level problem solving (Rosenbaum, 2004).

BARRIERS AND OBSTACLES

The greatest obstacle to the implementation of technology in law enforcement is financial. Local law enforcement budgets are typically 80% to 90% personnel, with little remaining for equipment, supplies, facilities, and technology. Replacing worn-out patrol vehicles is often the best that departments can do each year. Many police agencies were able to secure federal funds for technology during the late 1990s from the Office of Community Oriented Policing Services, though, and more recently from the Department of Homeland Security. In addition, some police departments have periodic bonding authority that allows them to raise funds to purchase technology. Most agencies, though, especially small ones, lack sufficient local resources to take much advantage of modern technology.

Another serious obstacle is lack of knowledge. Law enforcement executives are largely self-taught, with premiums placed on operational police experience and demonstrated ability to manage and lead people. Knowledge and experience with technology is not usually high on the desired list of traits, nor is it acquired automatically as one is promoted through the police ranks. In large agencies the chief or sheriff may have expert staff to rely on to overcome a lack of personal knowledge about technology, but not in smaller agencies. This situation often puts the police executive at the mercy of city/county purchasing units or, even worse, salespersons. The end result is that, when agencies do have some funds for technology, they sometimes make unwise purchases.

Related to lack of knowledge are attitudes toward the use of technology. The majority of adults today are baby boomers who were born prior to technology being commonplace in many homes and readily available and affordable in the marketplace. This means that newer generations of police officers are more familiar with computers and technology in general. Oftentimes, new recruits will be computer savvy and willing to embrace technology, as compared to older generation decision makers who often times see technology as a hindrance rather than a help. Newer officers may become frustrated by their organization's unwillingness to embrace modern technology (Conser & Russell, 2000).

Another facet of the lack of knowledge is lack of training in the use of technology. Many law enforcement agencies have made the mistake of purchasing and distributing new technology without providing training for those who are supposed to use it. This often results in equipment being stored in a closet rather than being used, perhaps because of frustration due to an initially unsuccessful exploration with the technology. Or, as in the case of computers and software, officers and other staff often utilize only a small fraction of the technology's capabilities, never realizing what other features are available.

A different kind of obstacle to the development and deployment of law enforcement technology is the fragmented nature of the police market. Companies that decide to develop new technologies for law enforcement typically start off excited by the potential sale of their product to an industry that has over one million employees. They often get frustrated, though, when they discover that the market really consists of 18,000 different customers (law enforcement agencies) spread across the federal, state, and local levels of government, most of them small, with limited budgets and little or no coordination or standardization of equipment or purchasing procedures. Many companies have tested the waters of the law enforcement market and decided that it is too complicated for them.

The difficulty of the police market has caused two types of problems: (1) some agencies have purchased technologies from companies that then withdrew from the market (or went out of business), making maintenance and repair difficult, spare parts impossible to find, and upgrades nonexistent, and (2) most of the modern technology that is available to police departments was originally developed for some other purpose (often military) and then reengineered. Police have been creative in adapting military and off-the-shelf technologies to their own use, but the field has been fundamentally handicapped by the relatively small amount of technology research and development targeted specifically for law enforcement purposes.

One entity that has been developed to assist law enforcement with many of these obstacles is the National Law Enforcement and Corrections Technology Center system (http://www.nlectc.org/about/justnet.html). This system, composed of 10 regional and specialty centers, is federally-funded and located within the Office of Science and Technology of the National Institute of Justice. The system and its centers assist individual law enforcement agencies with technology problems, help agencies obtain surplus military equipment, evaluate and field-test new technologies, and work with the private sector to help companies meet the needs of the law enforcement and corrections fields.

FUTURE PROSPECTS

Forecasting the future of technology is easy on one level–everything will get smaller, faster, and cheaper. Major breakthroughs are more difficult to anticipate, however. For example, police have wanted portable technology to detect concealed weapons for many years, but no practical equipment acceptable to the public (i.e., not too intrusive) has yet been developed. It may be instructive that the best current "technology" to detect explosives and drugs is the dog.

Nanotechnology, wearable computers, advanced robotics, and similar high-tech developments are clearly on the military and commercial horizon along with smaller, faster, and cheaper communications, information, and video technology. It is quite likely that the police commander of the future will be in much closer contact with officers in the field than was ever possible in the past. Wearable minicameras will transmit live video and audio back to headquarters so that commanders can see and hear what their officers in the field are doing. Commanders will then actually have the opportunity to "command" by giving directions to officers over the portable radio's earphone. This scenario could revolutionize our historical understanding of police work–it will no longer be done by lone officers exercising wide discretion in low-visibility situations. It will be interesting to see how police officers and police organizations adapt to these radical new technological capabilities, and to assess whether the end result is better or worse decision making and public service.

It also seems likely that technology designed to prevent crime, automate enforcement, and enhance intelligence analysis will become more pervasive and intrusive. These technologies should result in better regulation of dangerous behavior (speeding, running red lights), constructive shaping of risky and criminal behavior, and quicker identification of violent criminals and terrorists. The people targeted by these technologies, whether speeders, car thieves, or terrorists, will certainly adapt, though. Only time will demonstrate whether technology or the determined and creative human mind of the offender will gain the upper hand in these and other contexts.

Our analysis of technology in relation to police goals pointed out several aspects of the police mission that have not received much technological attention. In the future, more research and development effort might be targeted at technologies designed to help the police reduce fear of crime (and fear of terrorism) and provide services that satisfy the public's needs and demands. Technology aimed specifically at preventing crime has also received much less attention than has been devoted to technology for catching criminals after the fact. Despite the adage that an ounce of prevention is worth a pound of cure, pennies have been invested in prevention technology compared to the dollars spent on response and investigation technology.

One final future prospect is continued federalization. The U.S. Congress has created more and more federal crimes over the past decade or two, and federal law enforcement agencies constitute a growing segment of total U.S. police employment. These large federal agencies may skew the market and affect the technologies available to state and local agencies. There are also strong efforts underway to develop national law enforcement technology standards. These standards, when coupled with federal funding provided by the Department of Homeland Security and others, are likely to lead to more centralized and standardized purchasing of law enforcement technology.

A decade from now, we may still have 18,000 police agencies in the United States, but it seems probable that more purchasing will be made from approved lists of equipment and technology. As a result, more technology will be interoperable and interchangeable, and fewer police agencies will succumb to the charms of wily equipment salespersons. Downsides to this scenario might include (1) a reduction in the number of companies serving the law enforcement field leading to collusion and reduced competition, and (2) overreliance on one product brand. Police agencies are familiar with this situation now, since Ford dominates the vehicle market to such a degree that it has little incentive to make improvements to its Crown Victoria police-package automobile. Another analogy is Microsoft–a great product, but each time a hacker finds a back door, computer systems all over the world are threatened because the software is so pervasive.

These scenarios bring to mind the adage "be careful what you wish for." As law enforcement agencies become more and more dependent on technology, they can become just that–dependent. When they are well-designed and properly implemented, modern technologies provide capacities that police agencies never had before, as well as important efficiencies. They can help the police be much more effective, greatly benefiting the public, but these technologies may also have unintended consequences for both police organizations and for society. Law enforcement executives and other public officials should pay careful attention to the pros and the cons of modern technology.

Police executives should also be careful to retain back-up and redundant low-tech systems for those days when modern technologies fail. In addition, they should continue to cultivate the human skills in their organizations that have traditionally formed the basis of police work. Even with modern technology, the effectiveness of police agencies will still largely depend on the interactions that police officers have with the public and on their skill in identifying and solving neighborhood-level and citywide problems. These front-line activities might be enhanced with technology but they will remain fundamentally human interactions.

REFERENCES

Adams, B. (2003). "City police add Taser to arsenal," Wisconsin State Journal, May 24. Avaliable online at http://www.madison.com/archives/read.php?ref=wsj%3A2003%3A05%3A24%3A268492%3ALOCAL/WISCONSIN

Alpert, G. P., Kenney, D. J., Dunham, R. G., & Smith, W. C. (2000). *Police pursuits: What we know.* Washington, DC: Police Executive Research Forum.

Asplen, C. H. (2003). *The Application of DNA Technology in England and Wales.* Unpublished manuscript.

Biggs, P. (2003). "Officers take to shock, awe of Taser guns," *The Arizona Republic,* May 13. Available online at http://www.azcentral.com/specials/special21/articles/0513tasers.html

Bittner, E. (1970). *The functions of the police in modern society.* Washington, DC: National Institute of Mental Health.

Clarke, R. V. (1997). *Situational crime prevention: Successful case studies* (2nd ed.). Guilderland, NY: Harrow and Heston.

Clarke, R. V. (2003). *Thefts of and from cars in parking facilities.* Washington, DC: Office of Community Oriented Police Services. Available online at http://www.popcenter.org/Problems/problem-theft_cars.htm

Colton, K. W., Brandeau, M. I., & Tien, J. M. (1983). *A national assessment of police command, control, and communications systems.* Washington, DC: National Institute of Justice.

Conser, J. A & Russell, G. D. (2000). *Law enforcement in the United States.* Gaithersburg, MD: Aspen Publishers.

Corbett, C. & Simon, F. (1999). "The effects of speed cameras: How drivers respond." London: Brunel University Center for Criminal Justice Research. Available online at http://www.popcenter.org/Problems/Supplemental_Material/Speeding/corbett1999.pdf

Cordner, G. W., Scarborough, K. E., & Sheehan, R. (2004). *Police administration* (5th ed.). Cincinnati, OH: Anderson Publishing.

Drielak, S. C., & Brandon, T. R. (2000). *Weapons of mass destruction: Response and investigation.* Springfield, IL: Charles C. Thomas.

Dunworth, T., Cordner, G., Greene, J., Bynum, T., Decker, S., Rich, T., Ward, S., & Webb, V. (2000). *Police Department Information Systems Technology Enhancement Project* (ISTEP). Washington, DC: Office of Community Oriented Policing Services.

Fisher, B. A. J. (2000). *Techniques of crime scene investigation.* Boca Raton, FL: CRC Press.

Goldstein, H. (1990). *Problem oriented policing.* New York: McGraw-Hill.

Irwin, A. C. (2003). "Alcoa police trained to use taser kits," *The Daily Times,* June 8. Available online at http://www.thedailytimes.com/sited/story/html/133851

Kaminski, R. J., Edwards, S. M., & Johnson, J. W. (1998). "The deterrent effects of oleoresin capsicum on assaults against police: Testing the velcro-effect hypothesis," *Police Quarterly* 1(2): 1-20.

Kelling, G. L., Pate, T., Dieckman, D., & Brown, C. E. (1974). *The Kansas City Preventive Patrol Experiment: A Summary Report.* Washington, DC: Police Foundation.

Kessler, M. (2004, May 11). Digital's domination doesn't mean analog's demise. *USA Today,* 11E.

Larson, G. C. & Simon, J. W. (1979). *Evaluation of a police automatic vehicle monitoring (AVM) system: A case study of the St. Louis experience 1976-1977.* Washington, DC: U.S. Government Printing Office.

Laycock, G. (2003). "Launching crime science," Jill Dando Institute of Crime Science, University of London. Available online at http://www.jdi.ucl.ac.uk/publications/crime_science_series/launching.php

Lovrich, N. P., Gaffney, M. J., Pratt, T. C., Johnson, C. L., Asplen, C. H., Hurst, L. H., & Schellberg, T. M. (2003). *National Forensic DNA Study Report.* Washington State University and Smith Alling Lane. Available online at http://66.155.79.168/national%20forensic%20dna%20study%20report%20%2D%20final1.pdf

Maghan, J., O'Reilly, G. W., & Shon, P. C. H. (2002). Technology, policing, and implications of in-car videos, *Police Quarterly* 5(1): 25-42.

Manning, P. K. (1992). Information technologies and the police. In M. Tonry & N. Morris, (Eds.), *Modern policing* (pp. 349-398). Chicago, IL: University of Chicago Press.

Mazerolle, L. G., Watkins, C., Rogan, D., & Frank, J. (1998). Using gunshot detection systems in police departments: The impact on police response times and officer workloads," *Police Quarterly* 1(2): 21-49.

Moore, M. with Thacher, D., Dodge, A., & Moore, T. (2002). *Recognizing value in policing: The challenge of measuring police performance.* Washington, DC: Police Executive Research Forum.

National Institute of Justice. (1998). *Selection and application guide to police body armor.* Washington, DC: Author.

National Institute of Justice. (2003). The effectiveness and safety of pepper spray. Washington, DC: Author.

National Task Force on Interoperability. (2003). *Why can't we talk? Working together to bridge the communications gap to save lives.* Washington, DC: National Institute of Justice.

Pease, K. (1999). A review of street lighting evaluations: Crime reduction effects. In K. Painter & N. Tilley (Eds.), *Surveillance of public space: CCTV, street lighting and crime prevention.* Monsey, NY: Criminal Justice Press. Available online at http://www.popcenter.org/Library/CrimePrevention/Volume%2010/pease%20street%20ligting.pdf

Phillips, C. (1999). A review of CCTV evaluations: Crime reduction effects and attitudes towards its use. in K. Painter & N. Tilley (Eds.), *Surveillance of public space: CCTV, street lighting and crime prevention.* Monsey, NY: Criminal Justice Press. Available online at http://www.popcenter.org/Library/CrimePrevention/Volume%2010/A%20Review%20of%20CCTV%20Evaluations--Attitudes%20Towards%20its%20Use.pdf

Reuland, M. M., (Ed). 1997. *Information management and crime analysis.* Washington, DC: Police Executive Research Forum.

Rosenbaum, D., Graziano, L., Thompson, E., Brown, C. & Seiden, B. (2004). Integrating Virtual and Physical Reality: Empowering the Community through Web-based Communication. Presentation to the Academy of Criminal Justice Sciences, Las Vegas, March.

Scott, M. S. (2003). *Speeding in residential areas.* Washington, DC: Office of Community Oriented Police Services. Available online at http://www.popcenter.org/Problems/problem-speeding.htm

Schwabe, W., Davis, L. M., & Jackson, B. A. (2001). *Challenges and choices for crime fighting technology: Federal and state support for state and local law enforcement.* Santa Monica, CA: Rand Corporation.

Smith, G. (2003). Surveillance system aims to curb gunfire, *The Post and Courier.* Retrieved February 12, 2003 from http://www.charleston.net/stories/012903/loc_29shotspot.shtml

Spelman, W. & Brown D. K. (1981). *Calling the police: Citizen reporting of serious crime.* Washington, DC: Police Executive Research Forum.

Stearns, J. (2003). U.S. to review policy body armor. *The Boston Globe.* Retrieved November 19, 2003, from http://www.boston.com/news/nation/articles/2003/11/19/us_to_review_police_body_armor/

Swanson, C. R., Chamelin, N. C., & Territo, L. (2003). *Criminal investigation* (8th ed.). Boston, MA: McGraw-Hill.

Technology Review. (2004, June). Wireless 911. *Technology Review,* 107(5): 78-79.

Weisel, D. L. (2003). *Graffiti.* Washington, DC: Office of Community Oriented Police Services. Available online at http://www.popcenter.org/Problems/problem-graffiti.htm

Witzig, E. (2003). "The new ViCAP: More user-friendly and used by more agencies," *FBI Law Enforcement Bulletin,* 72:6 1-7.

Chapter 7

TECHNOLOGY AND TRAINING NEEDS OF RURAL LAW ENFORCEMENT: A NATIONAL STUDY[1]

GARY CORDNER, KATHRYN E. SCARBOROUGH, PAMELA A. COLLINS, AND IRINA SODERSTROM

INTRODUCTION

Most of what is known about law enforcement comes from studies of large urban agencies. The Law Enforcement Management and Administrative Statistics (LEMAS) program, for example, which is a very useful and ongoing data collection program about American law enforcement, only includes agencies with 100 or more officers (Bureau of Justice Statistics, 2004a). Little has been done to examine small and rural law enforcement, much less the technology and training needs of those agencies. Such agencies must be understood, though, in order to guide science and technology development for small and rural law enforcement that could result in more effective and efficient policing.

1. Points of view are those of the authors and do not necessarily represent the official position of the U.S. Department of Justice or Eastern Kentucky University. This document is not intended to create, does not create, and may not be relied upon to create any rights, substantive or procedural, enforceable by any party in any matter civil or criminal.

This research was supported under award # NCJ 1999-LT-VX-K022 from the U.S. Department of Justice, Office of Justice Programs, National Institute of Justice. The products, manufacturers, and organizations discussed in this publication are presented for informational purposed only and do not constitute product approval or endorsement by the National Institute of Justice, U.S. Department of Justice, or Eastern Kentucky University.

A few works have examined crime and policing in small and rural jurisdictions (Weisheit, Falcone, & Wells, 1996, 1999; Weisheit, 2000; Schwabe, Davis, & Jackson, 2001) and report the results of studies conducted in 1992, 1996, 1999, and 2000, respectively. All of these works examined training as a significant focus, while only one focused on technology (Schwabe, Davis, & Jackson 2001).

The primary goal of this project was to describe the technological capabilities and technology-related training needs of small and rural law enforcement agencies. A focus on small police departments is necessitated by the fact that over half of the nation's local departments employ less than 10 sworn officers. Local municipal police departments are estimated to employ 565,915 full-time staff of which about 441,000 are sworn personnel. Sheriffs' offices had 293,823 full-time employees, including about 165,000 sworn personnel (Bureau of Justice Statistics, 2004b). About 90% of all local police agencies employ fewer than 50 sworn officers and serve populations of less than 25,000 (Hickman & Reaves, 2001). For purposes of this research, small refers to those agencies that serve populations of 50,000 or less.

The definition of "rural" varies widely. The federal government, the Census Bureau, the Office of Management and Budget, and the Department of Agriculture all use different definitions. Rurality can be defined based on population, population density, distance from an urban area, noninclusion in a metropolitan area, and similar criteria.

Rurality can also be defined based on economic factors. For example, we often equate rural areas with agricultural activities such as farming. Interestingly, with advances in technology, less than 10% of the rural labor force is actually farming, and less than 10% of the rural populations actually live on farms (Weisheit, Falcone, & Wells, 1999).

What the available research suggests is that small and rural law enforcement agencies are falling behind the rest of society in the use of technology. Many police departments, due to a lack of resources and training, have failed to take a proactive approach in the adoption of technology. The availability of less expensive computers, the expansion of communication capabilities, and similar advances in technology could certainly benefit the small/rural police department. Information sharing, remote site or distance training, and improved communications across large jurisdictions are examples of how technology may benefit small departments (Weisheit, Falcone, & Wells, 1999).

METHODOLOGY

Instrumentation

A mail survey was administered during the summer of 2000 as part of a National Institute of Justice award to the Justice and Safety Center (JSC) at Eastern Kentucky University (EKU). The survey was designed to assess small and rural law enforcement technology and training needs. The survey was a pen/pencil self-report and included both closed and open-ended questions. The survey was designed to determine, from a representative sample of small and rural law enforcement agencies: (1) Types and frequency of technology currently used; (2) perceived importance of technology; (3) perceived technological competency levels and technological training needs; (4) technology facilitation; and (5) organizational demographics.

Sample Selection

Using the National Public Safety Information Bureau Directory Database of police departments (both county and municipal) it was determined that 11,956 (88.5%) of agencies listed in the database serve populations of 50,000 or less. These 11,956 agencies represented the study sampling frame.

Because of the disproportionate numbers of county agencies (2,249 or 18.8%) as compared to municipal agencies (9,707 or 81.2%), stratified systematic random sampling was used to select agencies for inclusion in the sample. Thus, the sampling frame was split into separate lists of county agencies and municipal agencies.

It was determined that a random sample of 384 agencies would be required in order to obtain data that would be generalizable to the population of all small and rural police departments with reasonable sampling error (Miller & Whitehead, 1996, p. 224). This desired sample size (384) was then stratified to reflect the same proportionate breakdown of county and municipal agencies observed in the sampling frame. Seventy-two county agencies (18.8% of 384) and 312 municipal agencies (81.2% of 384) were randomly selected from their respective database lists.

Survey Administration

In October 2000, all 384 agencies selected for sample inclusion were mailed the National Assessment of Law Enforcement Technology and Training Needs survey, accompanied by a cover letter describing the purpose of the survey, authorization for the study, and assuring respondents of anonymity and confidentiality of the information they provided.

Mail surveys typically result in low response rates unless follow-up mailings occur (e.g., see Frankfort-Nachmias & Nachmias, 1996). Consequently, all surveys were given identification numbers so that nonresponders could receive follow-up mailings of the survey. In all, three separate survey administrations were undertaken in order to obtain an acceptable response rate. Surveys were sent to nonrespondents two additional times (November and December, 2000) until a 60 percent response rate was achieved.

Completed surveys were ultimately received from 43 of the county agencies that were surveyed, for a 60 percent response rate, and from 196 municipal agencies for a 63 percent response rate.

Data Analysis

Data were analyzed using the Statistical Package for the Social Sciences (SPSS), version 10 (2000) for the PC. Because most of the data collected were measured on rank-order scales (e.g., never, sometimes, often), most statistical analyses involved generating frequency and percentage distributions. These simple descriptive statistics provided the necessary information to address the goals of this project.

Additionally, narrative responses were submitted to a content analysis. This allowed similar responses to be categorized according to common themes. The frequencies and percentages of responses on these data are presented in tabular form in this chapter.

It was of additional interest to determine if differences existed between county and municipal law enforcement agencies with respect to types and frequency of technology used, perceived technological needs, attitudes toward technology, and availability of training for technology. Statistically significant differences between the two agency types were examined primarily using chi-square tests for independence (as is appropriate for ranked data); however, *t*-tests were generated when the variable being tested was measured at the interval level of measurement (allowing for a comparison between the means for the two agency types).

RESULTS

Sample Characteristics

The responding agencies were fairly evenly distributed across a total of 43 states. The average number of full-time, sworn officers (i.e., not assigned to jail, court, or lock-up units) was 18 (SD=19.92). However, the distribution was negatively skewed, meaning that the median value of 11 full-time officers, or the modal value of 7 full-time officers, may be more typical and descriptive of the responding agencies. The large amount of variability observed in responses indicated that the numbers fluctuated considerably across agencies. Furthermore, a statistically nonsignificant *t*-test ($t_{235}=-.80$, $p=.424$) indicated that county and municipal agencies did not differ in their average number of full-time, sworn officers.

Conversely, a statistically significant difference was observed between county and municipal law enforcement agencies with respect to the size of the population served ($t_{52}=4.57$, $p=.000$). While responding municipal agencies served an average of 9,702 persons (SD=11,406), county agencies served an average of 21,298 persons (SD=15,762), over twice the population of municipal law enforcement jurisdictions. The fact that municipal and county agencies differed in population served but not in agency size is not surprising. County agencies (police departments or sheriffs' offices) often include municipal residents within their "population served" because they are within the county jurisdiction, even though the municipality may have its own police department. Usually there is overlapping jurisdiction and the county agency may provide some level of secondary or specialized policing service within the municipality.

Nearly half (47%) of all survey respondents reported holding the rank of Chief, followed by Sergeant (9.4%), Captain (8.6%), and Sheriff (6.9%). Other respondents were Lieutenants, Chief Deputies, Deputies, Patrol Officers, Detectives, and others.

Types and Frequency of Technology Used

Data collected to indicate the types and frequency of technology used by responding law enforcement agencies are reported in Tables 7-1 and 7-3. The first two tables present data on specific computer-related types of technology, while Table 7-3 pertains to a variety of communications-related and in-field technologies. Table 7-4 reports the greatest technology training needs, while Table 7-5 indicates resources for the facilitation of technology. Analysis by agency type is reported later in the chapter in Table 7-6.

Table 7-1: Functions for Which Agencies Currently Use Computers (N=239)

Function	*% of Agencies Yes*
Records Management	86.6
Internet Access	73.6
Criminal Investigation	72
Dispatch (CAD)	46
Crime Analysis	41.4
In-Field Report Writing	31.1
Fleet Management	24.3
In-Field Communications	23
Resource Allocation	18.8
Crime Mapping	16.7
Other (e.g., incident or offender recordkeeping)	3.8

As can be seen in Table 7-1, majorities of the sample agencies had used computers for three different law enforcement functions. The vast majority (86.6%) of responding agencies indicated that they used computers for records management purposes. Records management systems for law enforcement are typically described as comprehensive computer programs designed to store and retrieve incident reports, enter and track crime statistical data, and provide the agency management staff with information needed to manage the agency. Additionally, 73.6% reported using computers for Internet access, and 72% indicated they used computers for criminal investigation. Nearly half (46.0%) of agencies reported using computers for dispatch, or Computer-Aided Dispatch (CAD) systems, that provide highly specialized telecommunications/geographic display technology specifically created to support Emergency Response operations. Computers for crime analysis were used by a little over 41% of respondents. Less than one-third of the sample reported using computers for crime mapping, fleet management, in-field communications, in-field report writing, and resource allocation. Other functions for which agencies used computers tended to fall in the incident or offender recordkeeping category.

The types of computerized files that are maintained by the responding agencies are presented in Table 7-2. The largest majority (85.4%) of the sample reported that incident reports are maintained in computer files. Another large majority (83.3%) reported maintaining computerized arrest files, while 71.1% said they keep calls for service in computerized files. A majority of the sample also indicated that their agency maintains computerized files for traffic citations, stolen property (both vehicle and nonvehicle), warrants, traffic accidents, criminal histories, and uniform crime reports. Only a few of the types of computerized files resulted in one-third or less of the sample responding in the affirmative, such as linked reports for crime analysis, vehicle registration, and domestic violence orders.

Table 7-2: Computerized Files Maintained by Agencies (N=239)

Type of Computerized File	*% of Agencies Yes*
Incident Reports	85.4
Arrests	83.3
Calls for Service	71.1
Traffic Citations	64.9
Stolen Property Other Than Vehicles	61.5

Table 7-2: Continued

Type of Computerized File	*% of Agencies Yes*
Traffic Accidents	61.5
Criminal Histories	57.3
Uniform Crime Reports–Incidence Based (NIBRS)	57.3
Stolen Vehicles	55.6
Warrants	54.8

When asked whether their agency had either exclusive ownership or access to an Automated Fingerprint Identification System (AFIS) terminal, the vast majority indicated that they did not. Specifically, only 8.8% of the sample reported that their agency has exclusive ownership of an AFIS, and only 4% said they operated a terminal that has access to a remote AFIS site. Of the 21 agencies reporting ownership of an AFIS, only 3 agencies indicated that the ownership was exclusive; 18 of the agencies noted that they had to share the system with another agency. When asked who they share the technology with, 16 identified a local police agency and 5 said they shared the AFIS with their state police (some agencies shared with both another local agency and the state police).

Approximately one-fourth of agencies reported that their law enforcement agency maintain an official homepage on the Internet, and had computer crime investigation capabilities. When asked what information is maintained on the homepage Website, most of the responding agencies listed general police department information, available services, and contact information. For example, the Websites described the service area of the police department, listed relevant crime data, and provide alerts regarding crimes occurring in their area.

When asked who the agency contacts for computer crime assistance if the agency does not have its own computer crime investigation capabilities, 13% of responding agencies (N=152) reported that they would contact another local police department, 37% of agencies said they would contact their state police, and 5% indicated that they would contact the FBI.

The state police, for small and rural agencies, serve as the second level of law enforcement in a state. There are 49 states that have their own police force, with the California Highway Patrol having the largest with over 6,000 full-time officers (Reaves & Hickman, 2002). In the case of some communities, the state police often represent the only law enforcement for remote areas not adequately covered by other police agencies. They also provide highway patrol coverage of many of the roadways in rural areas, and in many cases serve as the lead investigative agency.

Table 7-3 presents a wide array of technologies that respondents were specifically asked about in terms of their perceptions regarding frequency of use, importance of the technology, competency in the use of the technology, and specific technology training needs. Clearly, most of the technology currently employed by the sample agencies pertained to communication and information technology. Large majorities of the sample indicated that their agency "often" uses mobile radios (98.7%), portable radios (95.3%), base station radios (82.5%), and cellular phones (59.5%). The personal computer was the only other type of technology reported to be used "often" by a majority of the sample agencies. When "sometimes" and "often" were combined (first column of responses), mainframe computers and patrol car video cameras were also cited by a majority of agencies. All of the other technologies listed in Table 7-3 resulted in majority percentages of the sample indicating that their agency "never" used that particular type of technology (e.g., MDT, MDC, digital imaging, global positioning systems, less than lethal force weapons, night vision/electro-optic devices, and vehicle-related devices).

Table 7-3: Technology Use, Importance, Current Competence, and Training Needs

A Majority of Responding Agencies Indicated …				
	They sometimes or often used the technology	The technology was somewhat or very important	They were somewhat or fully competent with the technology	Some or much training was needed to use the technology
Communication–Mobile radios	X	X	X	
Communication–Portable radios	X	X	X	
Communication–Base station radios	X	X	X	
Personal computer (PC/ Microcomputer)	X	X	X	X
Communication–Cellular phones	X	X	X	
Mainframe computer	X	X	X	X
Video Camera (in patrol cars)	X	X	X	X
Digital Imaging–Mug Shots		X	X	X
Mini-computer		X	X	X
Car-mounted mobile digital/data terminal (MDT)		X		X
Car-mounted mobile digital/data computer (MDC)		X		X
Laptop Computer (in-field)		X	X	X
Digital Imaging–Fingerprints		X		X

Table 7-3: Continued

	A Majority of Responding Agencies Indicated ...			
	They sometimes or often used the technology	The technology was somewhat or very important	They were somewhat or fully competent with the technology	Some or much training was needed to use the technology
Video Camera (Fixed-site surveillance)		X	X	X
Video Camera (Mobile surveillance)		X	X	X
Digital Imaging–Suspect Composites		X	X	
Vehicle (Tire deflation spikes)		X	X	X
Night Vision/ Electro-Optic (Image intensifiers)		X	X	X
Night Vision/ Electro-Optic (Infrared - thermal imagers)				X
Vehicle (Stolen vehicle tracking)				X
Global Positioning Systems–Mobile surveillance				X
Night Vision/ Electro-Optic (Laser range finders)				X
Global Positioning Systems–Vehicle location				X

Table 7-3: Continued

A Majority of Responding Agencies Indicated ...				
	They sometimes or often used the technology	The technology was somewhat or very important	They were somewhat or fully competent with the technology	Some or much training was needed to use the technology
Handheld digital terminal				X
Less than lethal force–Handheld electrical device/ direct contact				X
Less than lethal force–Stun devices				X
Less than lethal force–Choke carotid hold or neck restraint				X
Less than lethal force–Flash/bang grenade				X
Less than lethal force–Three-pole trip				X
Less than lethal force–Tranquilizer darts				X
Vehicle (Electrical/ engine disruption)				X
Less than lethal force–Capture Net				X
Less than lethal force–Rubber bullets				X
Less than lethal force–Soft projectiles				X

Respondents were also asked to rate the importance to their agency of each of the technologies presented in Table 7-3 (second response column). About half of the 34 technologies were rated as somewhat or very important by a majority of respondents. Almost all of the responding agencies indicated that they perceived two communication technologies as being "very important" to their agency, namely, mobile radios (97.8%) and portable radios (97.4%). The other two types of communication technologies, base station radios (86.5%) and cellular phones (62.9%), received a rating of "very important" by a majority of the respondents as well. Three other types of technology received "very important" ratings by a majority of respondents. These included personal computers (72.4%), video cameras in patrol cars (55.2%), and a mainframe computer (53.0%). The technology receiving the next largest proportion of respondents' ratings of "very important" was digital imaging mug shots (44.1%).

It is rather interesting that a majority of respondents rated 11 types of technology as somewhat or very important, yet *not* sometimes or often actually used. This seems to identify a clear "technology gap" between needs and current availability.

Responding officers were asked to rate the knowledge or skill level of their agency for each of the specified technologies (third response column). Possible ratings were "fully competent," "somewhat competent," and "no competence." Respondents indicated that they were most competent in the areas of computers, video cameras, and communication devices such as mobile radios and cellular phones. Over 85% of the sample perceived their agency to be fully competent at all four of the communication-related technologies (i.e., base station radios, cellular phones, mobile radios, and portable radios). These are the same technologies that respondents tended to have access to in their agencies and subsequently, they perceived these devices to be important to the law enforcement efforts of their agencies.

However, the next largest proportion of the sample to indicate full competency of their agency on a specific technology was for the personal computer, and only 38% of the sample did so. Close behind the personal computer was the video camera in patrol cars (36%). For almost all of the remaining technologies, less than one-third of the respondents perceived their agency to be "fully competent" in terms of knowledge or skill in the specific technology.

Interestingly, a large majority of the respondents perceived their agency's technological knowledge or skill level to reflect "no competence" for most of the listed technologies. This paucity of knowledge or skill was associated with the following types of technology: all of the less than lethal force devices (i.e., capture net, choke carotid hold or neck restraint, flash/bang grenade, handheld electrical device/direct contact, rubber bullets, soft projectiles, stun devices, three-pole trip, and tranquilizer darts); the car-mounted digital/data terminal (MDT) and computer (MDC); digital imaging (fingerprints and suspect composites); global positioning systems (mobile surveillance and vehicle location); handheld digital terminal; mainframe computer, night vision/electro-optic devices (infrared-thermal imagers and laser range finders); vehicle engine disruption and stolen vehicle tracking devices.

The most important "knowledge gap" would seem to be in relation to in-car computers and digital imaging. These were the types of technologies that a majority of agencies rated as somewhat or very important but for which they indicated a current lack of competence.

Respondents were asked to rate the amount of training their own agency needs on each of the listed technologies (fourth response column). It should be noted that much more variability in responses was observed for these ratings than for the other ratings in the table. With respect to the perceived training needs of small law enforcement agencies, there were several technologies for which a majority of the sample indicated that there was "much training needed." These technologies included: global positioning systems (mobile surveillance and vehicle location); handheld digital terminal; digital imaging (fingerprints); vehicle engine disruption; stolen vehicle tracking device; less than lethal force (three-pole trip and capture net); and a car-mounted mobile digital/data computer (MDC).

Three of the communication technologies resulted in the largest proportion of responses for which no training was needed. Over 82% of respondents reported that their agency did not need training in the use of cellular phones, mobile radios, and portable radios. The only technology to result in a majority of the sample reporting that only "some training" is needed was the personal computer. Again, it should be noted that these are the technologies that rural law enforcement officers are most likely to have in their agency, are most likely to perceive as being important to their agency, and consider their agency to be fully competent using these communication technologies.

Respondents were also asked to list narratively, in order of greatest need, the three most important technology training needs of their agencies. These qualitative data were content analyzed and are reported in Table 7-4. The largest proportion of respondents (17.6%) identified a car-mounted mobile digital/data terminal (MDT) as the technology for which their agency needed the greatest amount of training. Another 11.3% listed some form of digital imaging as the technology for which their agency was in greatest need of training. These top two training needs match the "knowledge gap" identified in Table 7-3. Otherwise, though, what is significant about this table is the lack of consensus on what agencies consider to be their most important technology training needs.

Table 7-4: Greatest Technology-Training Needs of Agencies (N=239)

Greatest Training Need	% of Agencies
Car-mounted mobile digital/data terminal (MDT)	17.6
Digital Imaging (all types)	11.3
Personal computer (PC/Microcomputer)	9.2
Car-mounted mobile digital/data computer (MDC)	7.1
Less than lethal force (all types)	7.1
Global Positioning Systems (mobile surveillance and vehicle location)	7.1
Laptop Computer (in-field)	6.3
Video Cameras (all types)	6.3

Technology Facilitation

Respondents were asked to respond to a few narrative questions about interagency cooperation, barriers and impediments, as well as resources and facilitators, that their agency experienced in attempting to acquire technology training. Regarding interagency cooperation, a majority (64%) of the respondents indicated that their agency had interagency cooperation to provide assistance with technology. Interagency cooperation is often an informal letter of agreement or a standardized contract entered into between two agencies for necessary and authorized services or resources. In the case of law enforcement, this may be between a local police department and a federal agency such as the Federal Bureau of Investigation, for example, which could provide training in the use of technology to detect explosives.

Respondents were then asked to list the type of agency from which their agency received interagency cooperation. The most frequently listed response was other local agencies (18.0%), followed by state agencies (8.9%).

Table 7-5 details the responses to questions related to the primary barriers and impediments agencies face in acquiring necessary training on various technologies. As expected, a sizeable number of respondents (83.7%) listed funding/budget constraints, followed by limited personnel/manpower (25.9%) and a lack of available training (13.8%). The final data presented in Table 7-5 indicate the three primary resources/facilitators to an agency for meeting its technology training needs. The most frequently reported resource (31.0%) was grants (both state and federal), followed by general funding (25.5%), and state training (21.3%). Less than 10% of the agencies indicated that they also relied on community support, training provided by vendors, or other types of donations for obtaining much needed training.

Table 7-5: Facilitation of Technology (N=239)

Question	Response	% of Agencies
Three primary barriers/impediments to agency acquiring its technology training needs? (Multiple Responses Allowed)	Funding/Budget Constraints	83.7
	Limited Personnel/ Manpower	25.9
	Lack of Available Training	13.8
	Location of Training	11.7
	Time	11.7
Three primary resources/facilitators to agency acquiring its technology training needs? (Multiple Responses Allowed)	Grants (Federal and State)	31.0
	Funding	25.5

Table 7-5: Continued

Question	Response	% of Agencies
Three primary resources/facilitators to agency acquiring its technology training needs? (Multiple Responses Allowed)	State Training (Police Academy)	21.3
	Local Training (College)	13.0
	Shared Training w/ other Agencies	10.5

County versus Municipal Agencies

Finally, the last goal of this project, which pertains to municipal and county differences, was investigated by performing chi-square analyses to determine if the frequencies of responses for any given survey item were distributed in a disproportionate fashion across type of agency. The results of the statistically significant findings are reported in Table 7-6. It should be noted that a more conservative alpha rate (i.e., .01 level) was used to determine statistical significance in order to control the Type I error rate (i.e., to control the statistical probability of finding a significant difference simply by chance, a problem that arises when many of the same type of statistical tests are generated).

As revealed in Table 7-6, statistically significant differences were found between county and municipal law enforcement agencies on only six of the survey items, and most of these items pertained to the use of computerized data files.

The chi-square analyses indicated that a much higher proportion of municipal agencies (34.9%) use computers for in-field report writing than did county agencies (14.0%). Similarly, much higher proportions of municipal agencies than county agencies indicated that they maintained computerized files for alarms (52.0% vs. 18.6%, respectively), traffic accidents (66.8% vs.37.2%), and traffic citations (69.9% vs. 41.9%). Conversely, a higher proportion of county agencies than municipal agencies reported that they maintained computerized files for warrants (81.4% vs. 49.0%).

Table 7-6: Statistically Significant Chi-square Tests Between County and Municipal Agencies (N=239)

Variable	Agency	% Yes	x^2	df	p-value
Agency uses computers for in-field report writing?	Municipal County	34.9 7.20 14.0	1	.007	
Agency maintains computerized files for alarms?	Municipal County	52.0 15.87 18.6	1	.000	
Agency maintains computerized files for traffic accidents?	Municipal County	66.8 13.07 37.2	1	.000	
Agency maintains computerized files for traffic citations?	Municipal County	69.9 12.16 41.9	1	.000	
Agency maintains computerized files for warrants?	Municipal County	49.0 14.96 81.4	1	.000	
Frequency of use for Global Positioning Systems–Mobile Surveillance?*	Municipal County	6.9 15.02 17.5	2	.001	

* % sometimes or often

The final entry in Table 7-6 pertains to the agencies' frequency of use of global positioning systems–mobile surveillance. The statistically significant chi-square value indicates that fewer municipal agencies than county agencies use this technology. However, it should be noted that vast majorities of both types of agencies have not used the technology.

Summary of Results

In general, the current data suggest that rural and small law enforcement agencies nationwide do not utilize many of the types of technology at focus in this survey effort. Responding agencies tended to use, to be competently trained in, and to perceive as important to the agency, a variety of communications-related technology, as well as the personal computer.

On the other hand, they tended not to use, not to be competently trained in, and to be unclear regarding the need or importance of a variety of more sophisticated technologies, such as car-mounted mobile digital/data terminals and computers, digital imaging, and global positioning systems. This was found to be true to a lesser extent for night vision/electro-optic devices and video cameras.

Two specific gaps seem to stand out. Agencies identified a *technology gap* between what they regarded as important and what they currently had available–in-car and in-field computers, digital imaging technology, mobile and fixed video cameras, vehicle spikes, and night vision equipment were among the items falling into this technology gap. Second, agencies identified a *knowledge gap* between technologies that they deemed important but about which they did not have current competence. In-car computers and digital imaging technology were the items falling into this knowledge gap.

Not many differences were observed between county and municipal agencies on the survey items, and the ones that were observed pertained to the use of computerized files. The differences that were found seem to flow logically from the differing responsibilities of the two types of agencies. For example, municipal agencies probably focus more on traffic safety than sheriff's departments, so it is not surprising that they are more likely to maintain computerized files of accidents and citations. On the other hand, sheriffs' departments are often the repositories of all the arrest warrants issued by the courts in the county, so it is not surprising that they are more likely to have computerized warrant files. No differences were found that would suggest that the two types of agencies differ substantially in terms of their current use of technology, or their training needs.

When asked about barriers or impediments to acquiring technology training, respondents indicated that funding and budget constraints were the primary problem, followed by lack of available training. These were also the same factors that were listed to explain successful facilitation of technology training. Clearly, these issues will have to be systematically addressed in order for small and rural agencies to become adequately trained in more sophisticated law enforcement technology.

Although agencies were not specifically asked about the issue of communications interoperability, this has become one of the key communications issues among the emergency services sector following 9/11. According to the RAND Law Enforcement Technology Survey, 67% of state police agencies indicated that interoperability was a high priority compared to 45% of local agencies (Schwabe, 1999). These findings are consistent with similar studies on wireless communications and interoperability that found that agencies of all sizes and types need interoperable communications. The greatest need appeared to be between local organizations (93% indicated that they communicate at least weekly with another local agency), whereas 63% of respondents had at least a weekly need to communicate with state-level organizations (Taylor, Epper, & Toman, 1998).

With more attention being paid to the first responder community following September 11, 2001, and more particularly to small and rural communities, there will be a greater emphasis on the need to address many of the gaps in technology and training identified in this survey. It has become evident that small and rural law enforcement agencies in this country represent the majority of public law enforcement organizations and that they stand a good chance of being called on to respond to any future incidents of terrorism. These agencies represent our first line of defense against threats to a community's safety and security and thus must be better prepared to prevent, detect, respond to, and recover from incidents of terrorism or catastrophic events.

REFERENCES

Bureau of Justice Statistics. (2004a). *Law enforcement management and administrative statistics*, 2000. Available online at http://www.ojp.usdoj.gov/bjs/abstract/lemas00.htm

Bureau of Justice Statistics. (2004b). *State and local law enforcement statistics.* Available online at http://www.ojp.usdoj.gov/bjs/sandlle.htm

Frankfort-Nachmias, C., & Nachmias, D. (1996). *Research methods in the social sciences* (5th ed.). New York: St. Martin's Press.

Hickman, M. J., & Reaves, B. A. (2001). *Local police departments 1999.* Washington, DC: Bureau of Justice Statistics. Report No. NCJ 186478.

Miller, L. S., & Whitehead, J. T. (1996). *Introduction to criminal justice research and statistics.* Cincinnati, OH: Anderson Publishing.

Reaves, B. A., & Hickman, M. J. (2002). *Census of state and local law enforcement agencies, 2000.* Washington, DC: Bureau of Justice Statistics. Report No. NCJ 194066.

SPSS Version 10 for Windows. (2000). Chicago, IL: SPSS Inc.

Schwabe, W. (1999). *Needs and prospects for crime-fighting technology: The federal role in assisting state and local law enforcement.* Santa Monica, CA: Rand.

Schwabe, W., Davis, L. M., & Jackson, B. A. (2001). *Challenges and choices for crime-fighting technology: Federal support of state and local law enforcement.* Santa Monica, CA: Rand.

Taylor, M. J., Epper, R. C., & Tolman, T. K. (1998). *State and local law enforcement wireless communications and interoperability: A quantitative analysis.* National Law Enforcement and Corrections Center, Rocky Mountain Region.

Weisheit, R. A., Falcone, D. N., & Wells, L. E. (1999). *Crime and policing in rural and small-town America.* 2nd Edition. Prospect Heights, IL: Waveland Press, Inc.

Weisheit, R. A., Falcone, D. N., & Wells, L. E. (1996). *Crime and policing in rural and small-town America.* Prospect Heights, IL: Waveland Press, Inc.

Weisheity, R.A. (2000) Assessing the needs of rural, small town, and tribal law enforcement: A national survey of municipal chiefs and sheriffs in non-metropolitan counties and of tribal police. Paper presented to the National Center for State and Local Law Enforcement Training Center. Glyncoe, GA.

Chapter 8

"THE PROBLEM-SOLVER": THE DEVELOPMENT OF INFORMATION TECHNOLOGY TO SUPPORT PROBLEM-ORIENTED POLICING[1]

LORRAINE GREEN MAZEROLLE AND ROBERT C. HAAS

INTRODUCTION

The advent of community policing has increased the need for information. Police executives need information to define priority problems, design and implement solutions, and assess the strategic impact of their departments' efforts to control crime problems. Community groups demand information about crime and quality of life problems in their neighborhoods. Street-level problem-solvers need routine access to information to scan for problems, analyze these problems, and subsequently implement and assess problem-oriented policing efforts. Indeed, information technology is a critical ingredient for successful implementation of community policing in general and problem-oriented policing in particular.

Over the last decade, police departments across the nation have invested considerable resources into implementing and upgrading their police information systems. Many police departments have

1. This chapter was supported by the Inter-Police Agency Informational Sharing Grant #95-IN-15B-029 from the Massachusetts Department of Public Safety. An earlier version of this chapter was presented at the Academy of Criminal Justice Sciences conference in Louisville (March, 1997). We would like to take this opportunity to thank Ms. Margret K. Streckert and Mr. Jerrold H. Streckert of MICROSystems Integrated Public Safety Solutions, Inc. (Melrose, MA), Ms. Julie Schnobrich, and the New England Police Consortium of 52 Police Departments for their support in the development of "The Problem-Solver."

worked closely with their vendors to customize their dispatch systems and create reporting systems that allow regular access to basic police data. At the same time, many departments have made serious attempts to implement community and problem-oriented approaches to policing. However, efforts to upgrade information systems are often divorced from organizational plans to reform police agencies, creating deficiencies in departmental capabilities to access information to facilitate problem-solving activities. Our partnership activities began with the premise that implementation of problem-oriented policing should be tightly integrated with the design and implementation of information technology. Without integration, information technology may be underutilized and efforts to implement problem-oriented policing may flounder or not be sustainable.

Police departments spend considerable amounts of time, effort, and resources collecting and storing vast amounts of information. For example, most police departments these days systematically collect and store all emergency calls for service, arrests, incidents, property records, citations, traffic infringements, and field interviews. These data are typically aggregated at the end of each month and used to report demands on police resources, analyzed to identify emerging crime problems, and examined to track those problems that are on the decline. Beat officers use this type of information to communicate crime trends in their neighborhoods to community groups. The COMPSTAT process initiated in the New York City Police Department uses detailed crime trend information both as a management tool and as a method for developing more strategic responses to crime problems at the local level.

Although demand for police information is high, most police departments have struggled to develop their information systems to enable easy (and up-to-date) access to information to support problem-solving activities. Departments have extensive amounts of data, yet these data are often inaccessible to line officers, rarely accessed to support police efforts to scan and analyze the locations of hot spots of crime, and typically not well integrated with community-based information (such as census data and local social service resources) to augment problem-solving efforts.

This chapter describes a computer-based problem-solving tool ("The Problem-Solver") that was designed and developed to make police data accessible to line officers (and supervisors) with the idea of enhancing problem-oriented policing activities department wide. "The Problem-Solver" was developed through a collaboration between a private public safety computer company (MICROSystems, Inc.), a university-based researcher (Professor Lorraine Green Mazerolle), and a consortium of 52 New England Police Departments. Chief Robert Haas of the Westwood Police Department assumed the facilitation and leadership role for our consortium.

We begin our chapter by introducing the partners that were involved in developing "The Problem-Solver." We then describe the key components of "The Problem-Solver" and we conclude with a discussion about the utility of information technology in augmenting problem-oriented policing activities.

Project Partners and Partnership Background

"The Problem-Solver" is a tool that was developed to augment the problem-oriented policing efforts of a consortium of 52 police departments in New England. A private computer company (MICROSystems) and a university-based researcher (Professor Lorraine Green Mazerolle) worked extensively with the New England consortium to design "The Problem-Solver" software.

The consortium of police departments involved in the project comprise primarily suburban police departments located in the Greater Metropolitan Boston area, Western Massachusetts, New Hampshire, and Vermont. Fifty-two police departments agreed to participate in the consortium covering ten congressional districts.

Our partner departments comprise an average of about 35 full-time sworn officers, ranging from three sworn officers in the smallest department to 110 officers in the largest department in our consortium. There is an average of about seven nonsworn officers in our consortium departments. The departments serve populations ranging in size from about 5,000 people to nearly 50,000 people in larger jurisdictions (mean is nearly 20,000), covering an average area of about 20 square miles. Operating budgets for the participating departments range from $330,000 to $6.4 million (mean is $2.2 million). From our survey of participating departments, an average of about $23,000 is spent on training and officers are provided with an average of 49 hours of inservice training each year.

The New England police departments participating in our project are fairly typical of police departments in the United States: about 91 percent of local police departments in the United States employ fewer than 50 sworn officers and the average annual operating expenditure for local police departments is around $1.7 million (Reaves, 1991).

The police departments making up the consortium averaged 430 Part I crimes in 1995. The most common Part I crimes reported to police during 1994 across our consortium of departments was larceny (mean of 284), followed by aggravated assault (mean is 247), and burglary (mean is 108). The police departments recorded a total of 8 homicides and nearly 100 rapes. On average, the departments recorded about 7 robberies and 58 motor vehicle thefts during this 1-year time period.

Most of the departments in the consortium do not have what they themselves would call a community policing plan. For those that do, the nature of their plans vary considerably. One department initiated a professional development program, increasing their training budget by 900% in tuition costs alone. Another department sought to build coalitions among various municipal departments within the community. Other departments have no clear plans for implementing community policing and have traditionally been isolated from federal and state money to reform their organizations.

The common element that forms the basis to our consortium of 52 police departments is their CAD/MIS systems: over the last 12 years all departments in our consortium purchased a Computer-Aided Dispatch (CAD) and Management Information System (MIS) called *CrimeTRACK* from a private computer company called MICROSystems Integrated Public Safety Solutions, Inc. The *CrimeTRACK* system provides several attractive features among its many system modules. For example, the records management module allows users to request locations of addresses with multiple arrests for specified time periods. Additionally, a series of "queries" have been created that allow users to predict potential crime fluctuations by varying the numbers of patrol units assigned to particular beats as a means to facilitate resource allocation decisions.

In early 1995, MICROSystems, Inc., Chief Robert Haas of the Westwood Police Department, and Professor Lorraine Green Mazerolle of the University of Cincinnati began working together in an effort to develop *CrimeTRACK* in such a way to encourage, augment, and enhance the problem-solving efforts of the partnership departments. From the outset, Chief Haas assumed a facilitation role for the consortium by encouraging and mobilizing the consortium of police chiefs to work together in building a problem-oriented policing capacity within their respective agencies. Through a small state of Massachusetts Byrne Block Grant, we worked together to develop "The Problem-Solver."

We have involved the consortium police departments throughout the developmental phase of building "The Problem-Solver:" meeting monthly with representatives from each department through MICROSystem's hosted "Users' Group" meetings and by providing regular formal and informal updates on "The Problem-Solver" progress to the police chiefs in the consortium.

"The Problem-Solver:" A Problem-Oriented Policing Tool

"The Problem-Solver" was originally envisaged as an operational tool for both police managers and street-level problem-solving police officers. We wanted to create a system for accessing information already collected within the *CrimeTRACK* environment to allow easy access to the system data for problem-solving activities.[2] We also believed that "The Problem-Solver" itself could reform the way police went about their day-to-day activities by using information technology to lead officers through a Scanning, Analysis, Reponse, Assessment (SARA) approach to problem-solving (see Eck & Spelman, 1987; Goldstein, 1990). We imagined that police not versed in the SARA methodology (or problem solving in general) could change the way they responded to local crime and quality of life problems by using "The Problem-Solver." In essence, we understood "The Problem-Solver" in particular, and information technology in general, to be a medium through which we could change the way police do business. As Manning (1992) suggests, "technology is embedded in social organization; it shapes organizations and is shaped by them" (p. 349).

The main menu of "The Problem-Solver" invites users to select a stage of the problem-solving process– scanning, analysis, response, or

---

2. "The Problem-Solver" is also commercially availalbe as a Windows 95 PC-compatible software application. This PC-based application comprises four components: a database manager that includes all question, answer, and response libraries; input databases (such as call for service, arrests, field contacts, etc.); a master name file; and a geocoded master address file.

assessment–and offers users the option of approaching their problem-solving efforts either through identifying problem people or problem places. From this main menu, users are led through a series of screens that allow problem-solvers the ability to access data, identify and analyze hot "people" or hot spots of crime, input answers to specific questions about scanned problems, identify appropriate types of responses at different types of hot spots or different types of problem people, and assess the impact of the implemented responses.

The initial, "scanning" option of "The Problem-Solver" draws from police calls, arrests, incidents, citations, field interviews, traffic citations, restraining orders, warrants, and suspended licenses. Depending on whether the user wants to search for hot people or hot places, the system accesses either the master name file or the master address file. Users can search all types of incidents ("action codes") or they can select groupings of incidents such as domestics, drug, gang activity, burglaries, vice, traffic, or quality of life offenses. These groupings are all user-definable. Users can group their search in several different ways: by using existing UCR codes, existing National Incident-Based Reporting System (NIBRS) codes, or they can develop their own groupings (e.g., roller-blading incidents, all gang activity, mental health involvements, etc.). The groupings can be as specific or as general as what users choose. The flexibility within the system to group incidents in any manner they desire is an important aspect to the "The Problem-Solver." We imagine traffic enforcement officers, for example, will use the system in very different ways than general patrol officers. Similarly, we expect DARE officers to use the system and create very different problem groupings to the groupings that would be of interest to vice squad officers.

After choosing the types of incidents to search on, users can pick from a range of other search criteria: They can search between particular date ranges, they can choose specific beats or precincts to search within, they can pick the types of involvements (e.g., arrests, emergency calls, citations) from which to search from, and they can weight the involvements to search on. We created an internal weighting system to generate lists of hot people or hot places after analyzing samples of data from several participating departments. These weightings, however, can be overwritten temporarily to allow for user-defined weightings. The weightings option can also be turned on or turned off as the user chooses. Finally, users can request the system to generate any number of hot people or hot places; they can request that the scanned places or people be ordered by location or frequency of involvement, and users can request a minimum threshold of activity to be met before the system displays the list of hot people or hot places.

After the system generates lists of hot people or places, users can pick and choose the places or people they wish to "keep" in their problem file. They can then either re-scan or save their groups of people or places. The saving option allows users to give the problem groupings a "common" description (e.g., "Top 10 gang involved people" or "Top 20 traffic accident locations"). The system then generates a unique problem number.

The "analysis" option of "The Problem-Solver" allows users to systematically analyze each case listed in the "scanned" data. Users can, at the analysis stage, request which problem question group they would like to attach to their problem. For example, if a user has identified the top 20 drug hot spots in their town, they will want to request the "Drug" set of problem-solving questions; if they have identified the top 10 youths involved in quality of life problems, they will probably want to request the "Quality of Life" set of problem-solving questions. The question sets are all user-definable: system administrators can cut and paste different questions to different question sets depending on how specific they want the question groups to be (or, conversely, how general they want the question groups to be); system administrators can create their own question sets; place-specific questions can be adapted to ask questions about hot people and person-specific questions can be adapted to ask questions about hot places.

Our decision to allow for flexibility in the analysis phase of "The Problem-Solver" stems from a number of practical and theoretical concerns. On the one hand, research suggests that the problem-solving process is more likely to succeed when problems are specifically delineated one from another (see Clarke, 1992; Goldstein, 1990). For example, problem-solvers need to differentiate between different types of burglaries: commercial burglaries are found to require fundamentally different response strategies to residential burglaries. With crime prevention and problem-oriented policing research in mind, we wanted "The Problem-Solver" to reflect a degree of specificity in the analysis phase that would lead the system to generate tailormade responses. On the other hand, however, we did not want to discourage police officers who were new to the concept of problem solving by overcomplicating the problem-solving process. As such, the analysis component of "The Problem-Solver" currently provides less specificity than more experienced problem-solving officers would want, yet the flexibility of the system allows system administrators to modify the question groupings, question answers, and suggested response libraries in ways that will allow for more specificity as officers become more experienced.

In developing the question library for each problem group, we met with officers with specific expertise in solving different types of problems. Our initial process for developing the analysis questions and responses allowed individual departments and individual officers to be earmarked as the consortium experts for different types of problems, creating centers of problem-solving expertise.

The second strategy used to develop the problem-solving questions and responses was through an extensive literature search of both the academic and practitioner-based literature to glean all the different types of interventions that police have used to tackle different types of problems across the country. A list of interventions appear in our response library and each response is systematically linked to a specific analysis question.

The better and more extensive the questions and responses (and the linkages made between the questions and responses), the better the system will facilitate problem-solving efforts. We expect, however, a degree of tailoring of the supplied questions and responses to local environments. For example, if a jurisdiction using "The Problem-Solver" has a particularly serious domestic violence problem, then they may want to develop the question and response libraries in such a way to enable more precise interventions for domestic problems than the interventions that are provided in the base library. Similarly, jurisdictions can tailor the response library to accommodate idiosyncratic names of service organizations, local help groups, or local ordinances. Importantly, the linkages between the question, answer, and response libraries are user-definable: users can add, delete, and modify all questions, answers, responses, and linkages in a way that will suit their own individual departments and jurisdictions.

"The Problem-Solver" also allows users to modify and update the base question and response libraries periodically to customize the libraries to reflect new approaches to solving problems. By allowing the questions and responses to be customized and updated, all departments can benefit from the trials and tribulations of the departments that have tried different responses to specific types of problems.

The analysis phase of "The Problem-Solver" prompts users to request a question grouping from a list of more than 20 different types of problem types.[3] Based on the question group that the user requests, the system generates a series of analysis questions. For example, for the gang set of questions, the system asks the user to find out how much gang activity a person is involved in; whether the person uses violence in the gang context; or whether they are known to use graffiti to "tag" their territories (among many other gang-specific questions). The purpose of the analysis stage of "The Problem-Solver" is to encourage and suggest that officers research the causes of the problem rather than simply assuming they know the answer to the question.[4] The prompted questions cannot generally be answered without making additional inquiries about the problem person or problem place. In this regard, we aim to close the gap we have found in problem solving: that officers typically do not spend enough time on quality analysis of the problem (see Eck & Spelman, 1987). Although our system is designed to encourage officers to complete answering all analysis questions, the system does not break down if some questions are skipped or remain unanswered: The responses will only be based on the questions answered.

Based on the answers to the specific questions generated by "The Problem-Solver," the system generates a series of suggested responses. These responses are generated from a response library that is systematically linked back to the analysis questions. The response library contains weighted responses based on what we would consider urgent or the most important responses to the least or not so vital responses. The responses are specific to the problem groupings selected by the user. For example, the gang responses are specifically designed to tackle gang problems; the youth responses are specifically designed to tackle youth problems, and so forth.

Once the system has created a list of suggested responses, officers enter four pieces of information for each activity they carry out for each suggested response: They enter the date that they undertook

---

3. While 20-question groupings have already been identified, the system is built in such a way to allow system administrators to add up 999 different question groupings.

4. "The Problem-Solver" should not be viewed as a substitute for training in problem-oriented policing in particular or community policing in general. Indeed, we suggest that as a tool designed to facilitate problem-solving activities, "The Problem-Solver" should be implemented in concert with a major training program in problem-oriented policing techniques. This is especially apparent in teaching officers to conduct in-depth analysis to target problems.

action to resolve the problem; a short description of what action they took; a self-assessment as to the effectiveness of the action (on a 4-point scale); and the approximate number of minutes they spent on the action. It should be noted that the decision to include this type of action accounting system in "The Problem-Solver" was the subject of considerable debate during the developmental phase. On the one hand, we did not want to turn-off officers from "The Problem-Solver" if they saw the module as a way their supervisors could "get them." On the other hand, we believed that many police activities go unnoticed (or at least unaccounted for). For example, phone calls made to a city agency to request the boarding of an abandoned building is rarely counted in police performance measurements. Similarly, the hours that some officers spend in conversation with parents of troublesome youths or in chasing up background information on a suspected drug dealer typically go unrewarded. After carefully balancing the advantages and disadvantages of documenting the time officers spend on police problem-solving responses, we believed that for the majority of officers, the capacity to record their range of problem-solving activities and the time taken to resolve the problem would outweigh any fears that the system was a "management tool" out to undermine a problem-solver. Moreover, many of the officers we consulted with during the process of building "The Problem-Solver" saw the ability to create a paper trail of problem-solving activities as an advantage for them, particularly when they needed to go to court over an issue.

"The Problem-Solver" contains a considerable degree of flexibility in all aspects of the system. For example, our system allows departments to customize the questions and answers to their unique sets of problems in their own town or city. For example, a town bylaw (or city code) may carry with it a particular identification number. Our system allows each department to specify the town bylaw number rather than use a generic reference to a town bylaw from the response library. Users can add questions, add responses, reweight the questions and responses, relink the responses to the questions, and regroup the questions by problem type.

Finally, the "The Problem-Solver" includes an "assessment" option. This option runs some basic analysis on the numbers of calls, arrests, traffic violations, incidents or any other type of involvement data included in the system by month of the involvement. The assessment part of "The Problem-Solver" allows officers to examine the number of hours spent on a problem against the number of incidents recorded either against the problem person or problem place both before and after the intervention began. Moreover, the system allows users to examine their self-assessments regarding the effectiveness of their interventions against the time spent on solving the problem. The system also compiles an audit trail to track all entries made in "The Problem-Solver." The audit trail thus allows more than one officer to work on a defined problem at any one time and also tracks changes in the entries made to the system.

Discussion and Conclusion

"The Problem-Solver" is a tool for organizing police information and is designed to facilitate police problem-solving activities. By better organizing police data, "The Problem-Solver" seeks to augment and enhance problem-solving activities. By offering an online approach to problem solving, the software assists officers in identifying and responding to problems either in terms of those individuals who pose the greatest concern relative to specific issues or problems (hot people), or in terms of those places in the community that may require the greatest amount of police interventions (hot places). The new technology is designed so that it may be used by officers who may want to target specific problems (e.g., traffic, drugs, public drinking, assaults) or by officers who are seeking information to target general problems (or even clusters of problems).

"The Problem-Solver" draws heavily from two interrelated bodies of research: The software is designed to step officers through the SARA approach to problem-oriented policing (see Eck & Spelman, 1987) and it focuses police attention on hot places or hot people. A significant body of research demonstrates that only a small number of individuals (e.g., see Wolfgang, Figlio, & Sellin, 1972) or locations (hot spots) consume a disproportionate amount of police resources (e.g., see Pierce, Spaar, & Briggs, 1988; Sherman, Gartin, & Buerger, 1989; Sherman & Weisburd, 1995; Weisburd & Green, 1995). "The Problem-Solver" seeks to assist line officers, or those officers who specialize in any aspect of policing (e.g., traffic enforcement, narcotics, juvenile matters, domestic violence, burglaries, etc.), in focusing on those people or places that place the greatest demand on police services. Once these chronic people or places are identified, "The Problem Solver" provides officers with a tool to analyze the problem in a structured fashion, develop tailormade responses to the problem, and assess the effectiveness of their interventions. By presenting information in a format that highlights those individuals or locations that place the greatest demand on police services, "The Problem-Solver" allows street officers to look at the root causes of a problem or issue, rather than simply repeatedly responding to the symptoms.

The "Problem-Solver" not only assists line officers in dealing with identified issues or problems in a systematic way, but it also provides information for both supervisory and administrative levels of the police department to assess the impact of their investment of resources on hot people or places. We propose that "The Problem-Solver" (in concert with a problem-oriented policing training program) can promote organizational structural change by pushing operational decision making to line-level officers and developing accountability for the identification, analysis, and response undertaken by line officers to alleviate pressing crime issues and quality of life problems.

REFERENCES

Clarke, R. V. (Ed.) (1992). *Situational crime prevention: Successful case studies.* New York: Harrow and Heston.

Eck, J., & Spelman, W. (1987). *Problem solving: Problem-oriented policing in Newport news.* Washington DC: Police Executive Research Forum and National Institute of Justice.

Goldstein, H. (1990). *Problem-oriented policing.* New York: McGraw-Hill.

Manning, P. (1992). *Information technologies and the police.* In M. Tonry & N. Morris (Eds.) *Modern policing: A review of research.* (pp 349-398). Chicago, IL: University of Chicago Press.

Pierce, G. L., Spaar, L., & Briggs., L. R. (1988). *The character of police work: Strategic and tactical implications.* Boston: Center for Applied Social Research, Northeastern University.

Reaves, B. (1991). *State and local police departments, 1990.* Washington, DC: U.S. Department of Justice, Bureau of Justice Statistics.

Sherman, L., Gartin, P., & Buerger, M. (1989). Hotspots of predatory crime. *Criminology* 27(1):27-56.

Sherman, L., & Weisburd., D. (1995). General deterrent effects of police patrol in crime hot spots: A randomized controlled trial." *Justice Quarterly*, 12 (No 4): pp. 625-648.

Weisburd, D., & Green, L. (1995). Policing drug hot spots: The Jersey City drug market analysis experiment. *Justice Quarterly*, 12 (4): pp. 711-736.

Wolfgang, M., Figlio, R., & Sellin, T. (1972). *Delinquency in a birth cohort.* Chicago: University of Chicago Press.

Chapter 9

EVALUATION OF A MOBILE FIREARM SIMULATION SYSTEM[1]

RYAN BAGGETT AND ANNMARIE CORDNER

In the wake of publicized misuse of force incidents by law enforcement, the acquisition of quality use of force training has come to the forefront of the minds of many law enforcement administrators. A plausible solution to providing the required training may be the use of interactive computer simulation systems that allow trainers to recreate diverse situations in a safe, realistic environment. This chapter will briefly describe simulation training applications in other sectors (such as defense, aviation, and medical) that have provided a framework for law enforcement simulation training. Next, a historical perspective of firearms training will be provided to demonstrate the progression in training that has been made in past years. Lastly, an overview of firearm simulation training technologies for law enforcement will be provided and an evaluation of a specific mobile firearm simulation system will be highlighted.

---

1. Points of view are those of the authors and do not necessarily represent the official position of the U.S. Department of Justice or Eastern Kentucky University. This document is not intended to create, does not create, and may not be relied upon to create any rights, substantive or procedural, enforceable by any party in any matter civil or criminal.

This research was supported under award #NCJ 1999-LT-VX-K022 from the U.S. Department of Justice, Office of Justice Programs, National Institute of Justice. The products, manufacturers, and organizations discussed in this publication are presented for informational purposes only and do not constitute product approval or endorsement by the National Institute of Justice, U.S. Department of Justice, or Eastern Kentucky University.

Background

Training, as in many other occupations, provides the knowledge and skills that officers carry with them throughout their career. Gaines, Kappeler, and Vaughn (1997) state that law enforcement officers are unable to function at an acceptable level until they have successfully completed a training program that imparts an adequate amount of information.

The complexities involved in law enforcement require constant revisions to the way officers are trained. At the beginning of the 1990s, Gaines, Southerland, and Angell (1991, p. 29) reported, "The last two decades have seen a drastic increase in the quality and quantity of police training. Departments are paying more attention to curriculum, training methods, and the development of facilities." Since the early 1990s, improvements in police training have continued and advanced into more technological means of disseminating training.

In providing training, the amalgamation of technology and law enforcement has begun to bridge the training gap that currently exists in American law enforcement. Simulation training is an example of one technology that can potentially provide safe, quality training to law enforcement. Various simulation technologies have been transferred to law enforcement from sectors such as defense, aviation, and medical.

Simulation Training Technologies

Since the 1980s, the Department of Defense has actively developed and implemented computer simulation to train the military in practically every specialty to fight effectively in combat (Hormann, 1995). The emphasis on systems development has moved from a largely aviation-oriented application to land and sea weapons systems and even down to the individual soldier and Marine. In the late 1990s, simulation training began to evolve into a key element of mission planning and rehearsal (Wilson, 1998).

Even with the reduced defense spending of the 1990s, simulation continued to be a central component to the military's training and planning missions. The cost of assembling troops for training exercises in the field far exceeds the price to simulate training for personnel in similar situations using new and existing weapons and working together in joint forces and individual units (Collard, 1997).

Building on the technology introduced by the military, the aviation industry has established simulation as a primary method for training pilots. Aviation simulators range from large mechanical equipment on one end to a simplistic computer program on the other. As in other areas of simulation, the field of aviation has worked to lower the costs of systems while increasing their effectiveness. In fact, in many companies, pilots must achieve a certain level of proficiency in the simulator before they are allowed to fly a particular aircraft and must pass regular proficiency testing in the simulator to keep their licenses (Industry Canada, 2001).

Finally, the medical field has developed an emerging need to expand skills outside of the operating room. Forces such as liability, ethical dilemmas, and time restraints have placed restrictions on utilizing the operating room as the main training site for the development of surgical skills. Technological advancements in development for medical simulation include the use of force feedback, which simulates forces and pressures on an operator's hands and fingers. The feedback affects two human sensorial modalities referred to as the haptic channel. Doctors believe that the accurate simulation of these forces will enhance the realism of the overall experience and make the overall simulation system far more effective (Industry Canada, 2001).

In short, other sectors have provided a foundation on which law enforcement simulation technologies have been developed. The ability to recreate situations continuously and provide instantaneous feedback have increased simulation's desirability to many law enforcement training academies and agencies. Within these academies/agencies, the two primary training areas for which simulation is used are driving and firearms.

Driving Training Simulation Systems

Nearly every law enforcement agency in this country uses an automobile for some facet of daily activity (Hickman & Reaves, 2001). With low-cost technology becoming more available, a wide variety of virtual reality driving simulators have been developed. Due to the expense of automobile operation and maintenance, law enforcement administrators looked for another way to instruct officers on emergency vehicle operations and procedures (Olsen, 1995). Therefore, the two factors of low-cost technology and increased expense of automobile operation and maintenance provides an excellent integration of simulation technologies with law enforcement driving training. The introduction to driver simulation technology has led to the development of various simulation models to accommodate law enforcement throughout the United States.

Simulators can range from personal computer software to full vehicle cabs complete with hydraulic motion. General characteristics of law enforcement driving simulators include a three-screen display ranging from a 180- to 200-degree field of view, although 360-degree views are available. Effective simulators make officers feel as if they are inside of an emergency vehicle. A popular model simulates the Ford Crown Victoria™, a common law enforcement vehicle. The simulator is equipped with a mock dashboard of the model, complete with ignition switch, headlights, turn signals, parking brake, speedometer/odometer, fuel, oil pressure, and voltmeter. The simulator is also equipped with a two-way radio to practice radio communications as well as siren and light switches comparable to an actual law enforcement vehicle (Streit, 2000).

Inside the simulator, virtually every aspect of what the officer views can be altered. The aggressiveness or density of traffic, number of vehicles involved, and even aspects such as pedestrian involvement, can be controlled by the trainer. Furthermore, the ability to modify weather conditions is also an integral component of quality driving simulators. Conditions such as rain, snow, ice, and fog can be added at the touch of a button, thereby simulating the element of surprise that is prevalent in actual driving.

Driving simulation systems can produce quality training on procedural tactics for emergency response and can also enhance judgment, cooperation, and teamwork (Training Simulator, 2000). Generally, the more expensive the simulator, the more options such as movement, range of view, and quality of graphics and sound will be added.

As technology becomes more widely available, another type of simulation system that has grown in popularity is firearms training simulation systems. Although firearms simulation training is commonplace for many in law enforcement today, a historical look at firearms training demonstrates a vast progression of American firearms training.

Firearms Training–A Historical Perspective

Although American law enforcement officers started carrying revolvers in the mid-19th century, very few efforts in training with those weapons were made until the 1920s (Morrison & Vila, 1998). In fact, a 1919 National Rifle Association (NRA) survey of municipal departments serving a population over 25,000 found that only 12 agencies had formal firearms training (Sandler & Keysor, 1995).

Law enforcement firearms training was dominated between the world wars by the NRA who created a Police School in 1925. The school emphasized handgun proficiency and also dealt to varying degrees with other firearms, hand-to-hand fighting, and riot control. At the start of World War II, federal funding for the school ceased, bringing an end to the operation.

Due to a war on crime in the 1930s, Congress hesitantly allowed Federal Bureau of Investigation (FBI) special agents to routinely carry handguns. With that authorization came a firearms training program that became the most widely recognized post-World War II authority (FBI, 1982). J. Edgar Hoover (FBI Director) invited the nation's police to attend training in the FBI's Washington, D.C.-based Police Training School. Hence, handgun training was among the earliest of subjects included in the curriculum of what today is the FBI's National Academy (Turner, 1993).

Through these two pre- and postwar training programs/curricula, the objective of training instructors to return to their agencies to instruct fellow officers was established. By 1950, it is reported that police handgun training was common, but the effectiveness of the training was questionable (Morrison & Vila, 1998).

Historically firearms training has conveyed nonvalidated concepts and beliefs stemming from instructors' personal experiences as street officers and other anecdotal evidence (Morrison & Vila, 1998). Although some improvement has been made with the help of organizations such as the American Society of Law Enforcement Trainers (ASLET) and the International Association of Law Enforcement Firearms Instructors (IALEFI), the lack of standardization of firearms training curricula and frequency of training is still problematic. Often experts contend that the only training officers may receive is their yearly handgun qualification.

> Handgun qualification for the police, something originally conceived as a test of marksmanship proficiency for soldiers and competitive shooters, still consists of shooting at fixed numbers of clearly defined targets at well-known distances, standard firing elements and sequences, liberal time limits, and arbitrary threshold scores. The rote firing of time-honored courses and their derivatives produces well-practiced range marksmen, but it does not assess their ability to perform in gunfights. (Morrison & Vila, 1998, p. 529)

To obtain validity, handgun qualification must reflect the authenticity of armed confrontations. Morrison and Vila refer to current qualifications as "misleading and aimless activity" (1998), signifying that target practice alone does not improve an officer's judgment in a real-life situation. However, through the utilization of alternative firearms training methods, the realities of armed confrontations can be recreated and used for law enforcement firearm training.

Alternative Firearms Training Methods

The past two decades have been accompanied by advancements in alternative methods to firearms training such as interactive firearm ranges, Simunitions®, and firearm simulation systems. With the goal of exposing officers to more realistic firearms experiences, these alternative methods are utilized throughout the country.

Interactive Firearm Ranges

One of the first attempts to provide more interaction to officers in order to sharpen their judgment skills was the Federal Bureau of Investigations (FBI) Academy's Hogan Alley complex. The complex is a realistic training area that dates back to pre- World War II. The more elaborate Hogan Town complex, used for crime scene investigation and other practice problem-solving activities, was initiated in March 1987. Hogan Town, located in Quantico, Virginia, was designed to resemble a fully developed area found in almost any community throughout the United States. The complex trains FBI agents and many of the nation's police officers in tactics and arrest procedures. They use simulations that are as close to real life as possible. Thousands of local tactical police officers have been trained here in the past several years (http://www.fas.org). Based on the Hogan's

Alley and Hogan Town facilities, many law enforcement training academies as well as law enforcement agencies have constructed interactive firearm ranges. In order to increase the realism of targets while maintaining basic marksmanship principles, Simunitions® were introduced to law enforcement training.

Simunition®

Simunition® offers force-on-force training that allows officers to train with each other. Marking cartridges that come in five distinct colors leave a detergent-based, water-soluble, inert color mark that denotes hits. With a conversion kit, the round can be fired from the officer's duty weapon. Situations can be simulated with officers being able to fire on each other. Officers must wear face and body protection before engaging in Simunition® training (www.simunition.com).

Firearm Simulation Systems

As demonstrated in other sectors such as military, aviation, and medical, simulation can provide a means for practicing a particular skill, focusing on planning, assessment, and improvement. John Reintzell, Director of Training for the Baltimore Police Department, believes:

> Adults learn best by doing, not listening. Hands-on learning imprints itself, and is assimilated and recalled better. If a simulation reflects real conditions accurately, and if it "rewards" appropriate actions and "punishes" mistakes, trainees will go away better-equipped to be more effective in their jobs. And they're likely to be more receptive to learning the next time. (Reintzell, 1997, p. 41)

Interactive computer simulation can engross senses in a computer-generated environment that can provide realistic, safe, and cost-effective training. These systems are rapidly changing the training methods of many law enforcement academies and agencies.

The importance of simulation systems is emphasized in judgment or lethal/deadly force training. Although most law enforcement officers will never face an actual use of lethal force situation, it must be ensured that they have the knowledge and skills to react appropriately if they ever do. Grassi refers to use of force training as "using acquired skills in various scenarios, under varying conditions, while demonstrating discretionary decision making" (1997, p. 121).

Today's firearm simulation technology market consists of several companies who offer different varieties of interactive computerized firearm simulation systems. Although systems may vary, commonalities include interactive, digital video-based training in all aspects of the use of force and marksmanship training. These systems usually operate on the Windows platform; use a laser system or projectile rounds, with some models equipped with simulated oleoresin capsicum (OC) or pepper spray, baton, and flashlight. Most systems have a variety of weapon models so that the officer can train with his or her weapon inside the simulator. Additionally, since simulation is computer-based, many systems have branching capabilities that allow the instructor to control the outcome of the scenario based on the actions of the officer.

Historically, these systems have been stationary or required setup in a facility that required the officer to travel to that facility to receive training. Conversely, since their development in the late 1990s, mobile, trailer-housed simulation systems have increased training opportunities for many law enforcement officers by bringing the training to them. Advanced systems may also provide 360-degree training capabilities. These scenarios require trainees to encounter multiple risks, from different directions, thereby reducing tunnel vision and reinforcing use of appropriate tactics. Additionally some manufacturers have developed multiroom simulation systems for team training. Within these systems, the scenarios in each room are orchestrated with other scenarios to simulate an entry on a dwelling.

Advantages to Firearm Simulation Systems

There are several advantages to using firearm simulation systems for training. The main advantage to a simulation system is that officers are able to train in a safe, controlled environment. Officers can afford to make lethal mistakes when they are inside of a simulation system. Identifying and remedying the problem with the help of simulation could save the officer's and/or other human lives. Another advantage of these types of systems is the ability to record training for later analysis by the officer and instructor.

Second, the use of scenarios provides a variety of options. Trainers can recreate problem situations that are particularly troublesome for the officer. The scenario can also be of rarely occurring phenomena, which the officer might not otherwise observe but which could happen. Additionally, the trainer can replay the scenario as many times as necessary until the officer receives the training he or she needs. Examples of scenarios include but are not limited to common occurrences such as an intoxicated, disorderly subject to less common events such as a school shooting.

Next, mobile systems provide increased opportunities for training. Officers in rural areas who must usually travel to a central location to train on a stationary system can have training brought to them. This allows them to obtain training that they might not have had the opportunity to receive otherwise.

Disadvantages to Firearm Simulation Systems

Despite numerous advantages to firearm simulation systems, certain disadvantages do exist. Simulation technology continues to constantly improve; however, some officers still have trouble interacting with a screen. Despite branching capabilities and realistic audio, some officers are not able to comfortably interact with a projected image. Advancements in simulation may include a more lifelike image to counteract that uneasiness.

Second, a firearm simulation system is just a tool. It is the responsibility of the trainer and student to use it to maximum effectiveness. Furthermore, a poor instructor, despite the effectiveness of the system, can deliver poor training.

Finally, the cost of firearms simulation systems is prohibitive for most small and rural law enforcement agencies. It is much easier to buy ammunition and shoot at paper or even moving targets at a range. However, there are examples of agencies partnering with state training academies or other law enforcement agencies to purchase collective units that can be shared among the agencies.

With the perceived advantages and disadvantages of firearm simulation systems, prior to the year 2000, there had been no formal research conducted on the effectiveness of mobile firearm simulation systems. Therefore, only anecdotal evidence existed on the efficacy of firearm simulation systems for law enforcement applications. With no research available, the National Institute of Justice, Office of Science and Technology (NIJ/OST) funded the Eastern Kentucky University (EKU) Justice and Safety Center (JSC) to determine the effectiveness of a mobile simulation training technology, PRISim™ (Professional Range Instruction Simulator) manufactured by Advanced Interactive Systems (AIS) of Tukwila, Washington.

Professional Range Instruction Simulator (PRISim™)

The evaluation sought a simulation system that was both technologically advanced as well as mobile in order to increase training opportunities for those officers in small and rural law enforcement agencies. At the beginning of this project it was determined that the PRISim™ mobile training facility was best suited for the evaluation.

The PRISim™ mobile training facility is housed in a 36-foot triple-axle gooseneck trailer that has expandable "wings" on each side (see Figure 9-1). The overall width of the system without the wings expanded is 8'6". When the "wings" are expanded, the system's width increases to 14'3" allowing for additional training area inside the trailer. The overall height of the system is 12'5" and weighs approximately 15,000 pounds. The PRISim™ system is also equipped with electric brakes on three-axles, and an electro-hydraulic jack system. The system requires two 110 VAC, 30 amp circuits from an external power source or an optional generator is available to supplement external power. These mobile facilities are equipped with two air conditioning units totaling 41,000 BTU.

Figure 9-1. PRISim™ Mobile Training Facility.

The system is operated by two Pentium-based computers that allow for MPEG2, DVD, video, and graphics capabilities. Additionally, the system is equipped with cameras for real-time video capture, an advanced sound system, and a projector that provides the image inside the trailer. In addition to these features, the PRISim™ system is equipped with a patented ShootBackTM cannon. The instructor-aimed cannon is mounted above center-screen to fire 68 caliber nylon projectiles synchronized with the scenario. The ShootBack™ Cannon fires single, three-round bursts, or full auto "hostile fire" that provides for immediate reinforcement. The PRISim™ system also utilizes "branching technology" that allows the instructor to change the outcome of the scenarios based on the officer's behavior within the system. PRISim™ offers users a content library including different scenarios in versions tailored to patrol, schools, tactical, corrections, airport, and general law enforcement activities.

EVALUATION METHODOLOGY

The evaluation began with a site visit to observe the PRISim™ system in use by a law enforcement agency to gain a better understanding of the technology. Following the visit, an advisory council was convened consisting of subject matter experts from throughout the United States. Specifically, a psychologist, a criminal justice professor, a retired police chief, a tactical team commander, and a firearms trainer comprised the PRISim™ Evaluation Advisory Committee (PEAC). Throughout the 2-day meeting, PEAC members met with PRISim™ representatives and observed the mobile PRISim™ system. Additionally, members used a storyboarding process to identify important issues for evaluating the simulation system to assist in the project research design.

Building on the information gained from the PEAC meeting, preliminary evaluation instruments were developed for testing during a pilot test. Approximately 30 officers from five Washington law enforcement agencies participated in the 3-day test. The pilot test allowed the JSC evaluators to refine the instruments based on participant feedback and observations during the test.

There were five primary roles during the evaluation. First, the Participant, hereafter referred to as "officer," included law enforcement personnel of various ranks and agencies who received the training. Second, the Instructor provided training inside the system through direct student contact. Next, the Operator controlled the technology within the system (computers, shootback cannon, etc.). Both the Instructor and Operator positions were employees of Advanced Interactive Systems (AIS), and were cross-trained to fill both positions during the evaluation. Lastly, an Interviewer and Evaluator were directly responsible for the evaluation of the system. The Interviewer administered pretraining questionnaires and conducted posttraining interviews with the officers. The Evaluator, an experienced firearms instructor, closely monitored and evaluated the officer's performance during the training. Both the Interviewer and the Evaluator were employees of the EKU JSC and were not affiliated with AIS. Due to overlapping training schedules, the individuals who filled the roles were different in Texas than in Kentucky and Washington.

The evaluation began in June and July 2000 in the three states of Kentucky, Texas, and Washington. These three states were chosen due to their separation in geographic location enabling researchers to determine whether the simulation system had a greater impact in one region of the country as compared with another. Other differences in law enforcement training in these three states include the variance in time requirements for academy training. All three states require different durations for basic police training: Texas–14 weeks, Kentucky–16 weeks, and Washington–18 weeks. Another difference is while Kentucky and Washington both maintain centralized training academies, Texas utilizes various community colleges and regional academies throughout the state.

Data for the evaluation was obtained through three methods: 1) a pretraining questionnaire consisting of objective questions and questions about subjective experiences in a closed and an open-ended format, 2) a training assessment instrument that recorded performance measures during the actual simulation training, and 3) a post-training focused interview that took place directly after the simulation training.

Each training session, hereinafter referred to as Time 1, 2, or 3, lasted approximately one hour for the officers. First, they answered a written pretraining questionnaire regarding their backgrounds, environments, and habits. Next, officers trained inside the mobile PRISim™ system. Officers were provided a brief "warm-up" exercise (*consisting of firing their weapons at stationary and moving objects*) and were then evaluated on their performance in three scenarios. Nine scenarios were chosen by the JSC research staff with the assistance of PEAC members to maintain approximately equivalent levels of difficulty and complexity across the three training sessions. The topics of the scenarios ranged from the routine (domestic violence, intoxicated subject) to isolated incidents (officer down, school shooter). Based on the methodology prescribed by the PEAC, each session contained one no-shoot (incidents where officers were not justified in applying deadly force) and two shoot (incidents where officers were justified in using deadly force) scenarios. Within these scenarios, officers were evaluated in the four areas of Accuracy, Tactics, Judgment, and Safety, which will be discussed later in this chapter in the "Performance-Based Results" section.

On completion of the three scenarios, officers were taken to an area away from the AIS Instructor, Operator, and any other officers who had not yet undergone the training, for an oral interview to discuss their performance and their attitudes toward the system.

At the first training session, officers were asked to read and sign a letter of informed consent. The letter explained the purpose and procedures of the study, and also assured confidentiality by informing officers that all identifying characteristics would be deleted from the final data once the last training session had been completed. Information such as name and agency were included on surveys to ensure surveys were processed and organized appropriately. These items were deleted after the data had been entered for analysis.

Dependent Variables

In order to compare learning across the three time periods, a time series analysis was conducted. Time series analysis is the process of acquiring data points over a period of time to explain or prove a concept or phenomenon. In this evaluation, indices measuring the officer's behavior on each of the relevant issues across the three scenarios were created for each time period. For instance, there are three indices that measure whether the officer identified him or herself–one for the scenarios in Time 1, one for the scenarios in Time 2, and one for Time 3.

Dichotomous variables measuring positive behaviors were coded 1 if the behavior was present and 0 if the behavior was absent. The average score for each time period was calculated and multiplied by 100. These variables include identification, verbalization, drawing properly, and indexing properly. These indices have a potential range of 0 (if the officer did not demonstrate the behavior in any of the three scenarios) to 100 (if the officer performed the behavior in all three scenarios). An index measuring the officer's use of cover was created by taking the average score on this variable across the relevant scenarios. The index has a potential range of 0–100.

Dichotomous variables measuring negative behaviors were coded -1 if the behavior was present and 0 if absent. The average score for each time period was calculated and multiplied by 100. These variables include failure to decock, turning on the firing line with a loaded weapon, shooting innocent persons, and shooting without justification. These indices have a potential range of -100 (if the negative behaviors were present in all relevant scenarios) to 0 (if the behavior did not appear in any of the scenarios).

In order to measure whether accuracy improved over time, a new variable was created by dividing the number of hits by the number of rounds fired in each scenario and multiplying by 100. An index for each time period was created by averaging the values of the variables for the two scenarios in which most officers fired their weapons. The index has a potential range of 0 (no hits) to 100 (perfect accuracy).

It is important to note that not all of the learning issues were included in the analyses due to the lack of variation in some variables.

Analyses

Analyses of variance were conducted on performance measures to determine whether scores on the various indices significantly changed over time. Multiple regression analyses were also conducted in order to investigate the effect of other factors on officers' scores on the indices.

PARTICIPANT DEMOGRAPHICS

A total of 181 officers participated in the PRISim™ training at all three time periods–56 from Kentucky, 76 from Texas, and 49 from

Washington. Demographic information was obtained from the officers at Time 1 in the pretraining questionnaire. Ninety-four percent of the officers were male (n=170). Approximately 91% of the participants were Caucasian; 5% were Hispanic/Latino; 3% were Black/African American; and 1% were American Indian/Alaskan Native. The officers were, on average, 38 years old at Time 1 (SD=8.9). All of the officers had completed high school. Nearly 39% held at least a 2-year college degree.

Officers had an average 12 years of law enforcement experience (SD=7.9). Slightly more than half (54%) held the rank of officer, the remainder held higher ranks. On average, the participants had held that rank for nearly 6 years (SD=5.5). Approximately 65% were assigned to patrol, while 14% worked in the detective/investigation division, 7% were assigned to the administrative division, and 14% held other assignments. On average, the officers had been at their current assignments for slightly more than 5 years (SD=5.4). Forty-six percent worked the day shift, 21% worked the evening shift; 12% worked night shift, and the remainder (11%) worked shifts that rotated on a regular basis or some unique time frame.

The officers participated in basic training that averaged approximately 13 weeks (SD=6.1). The range of basic training was 1 to 40 weeks. Officers received an average of 26.5 hours of inservice training (SD=29.6). In the 12 months prior to Time 1, the officers received firearms training an average of three times (SD=3.5). The officers fired an average of 598 rounds in the 12 months prior to the test period (SD=1,036.7).

Slightly more than half of the participants (53.6%) were wearing body armor at Time 1. The officers worked an average of 8 hours in the 24 hours prior to the test period (SD=3.39) and slept an average of 7 hours during those 24 hours (SD=2.1).

ATTITUDINAL MEASURES

In addition to collecting measures on how the officers performed inside the simulation system, measures were also collected on the officers' attitudes about the system and the training they underwent.

After each training session, officers were asked if they felt the scenarios were realistic. Realism is an extremely important component when trying to simulate (or recreate) a specific environment. As previously stated, the scenarios at each training session were different, possibly requiring different tactics and evoking different emotions. Approximately 98% of the officers felt that the three scenarios in Times 1 and 2 were realistic, with approximately 99% of the officers finding the scenarios at Time 3 to be realistic.

Next, after Times 1 and 2, officers were asked if the instruction that they had just received would help their performance when they returned to duty or left them feeling better prepared. Almost every officer at Time 1 (99.4%) believed that the training they had received would improve their performance. Approximately 96% of the officers felt better prepared as a result of the training at Time 2.

After hearing complaints of not being able to comfortably interact with the system at Time 1, a question to determine comfort level was added to Times 2 and 3. At Time 2, approximately 90% of the officers were able to comfortably interact while approximately 8% were not. Approximately 95% of the officers reported being able to comfortably interact with the PRISim™ system at Time 3.

Moreover, officers were asked in Time 3 if they had ever been in a deadly force incident and the number (if any) incidents in which they had been involved. This information helped evaluators determine if this factor added to the performance of the officer inside the simulator. Approximately 30% of the officers had been involved in an incident that required deadly force. Of those officers, 49% reported being involved in more than one incident.

Finally, on the Time 3 pretraining survey, officers were asked to answer additional attitudinal questions about their experiences with the PRISim™ system. These questions allowed the officers to reflect on the entire experience and used a Likert scale to rate that experience.

First, officers were asked to assess the usefulness of the training at Times 1 and 2. Approximately 96% of the officers found the training at Times 1 and 2 to be useful or extremely useful. Officers were then asked to evaluate the equipment found in the PRISim™ system. *Equipment includes the Shootback™ system, weapons, and video playback.* The majority of officers (96%) believed that the PRISim™ equipment was either useful or extremely useful. Next, officers were asked to rate the value of the system's mobility. It was hypothesized that one of the most valuable components of the system was its ability to take training to the officers. Approximately 94% of the officers believed the mobility of the PRISim™ system to be either valuable or extremely valuable.

In conclusion, the attitudes of the officers involved in this evaluation were overwhelmingly favorable toward the PRISim™ system. Officers believed that the use of a mobile simulation system would better prepare them for the job. Additionally, they believed the scenarios within the system were realistic and that they were able to comfortably interact with them. Finally, they believed the equipment inside the system was useful and that the system was valuable to law enforcement.

PERFORMANCE MEASURES

As previously stated, the performance measure indices were grouped into four categories: Accuracy, Tactics, Judgment, and Safety. Table 9-1 reports the mean and standard deviation for the indices that measure the dependent variables across Times 1–3. A more detailed discussion of these results will follow.

Table 9-1: Descriptive Statistics for Dependent Variables

		Time 1	Time 2	Time 3
TACTICS: Did officer identify him or herself?	mean	38.60	30.70	37.80
	s	39.50	35.80	42.80
Did officer verbalize commands?	mean	95.00	92.00	97.10
	s	16.90	16.00	11.60
Did officer use cover appropriately?	mean	61.30	67.00	67.60
	s	20.10	23.70	28.30
JUDGMENT: Did officer draw appropriately?	mean	14.00	7.90	10.90
	s	21.70	16.70	20.00

Table 9-1: Continued

		Time 1	Time 2	Time 3
Did officer unintentionally shoot at or endanger innocent persons?				
	mean	-2.50	-0.40	-1.00
	s	8.80	3.60	6.90
Did officer shoot without justification?				
	mean	-6.80	-3.60	-1.10
	s	15.00	11.60	7.20
SAFETY: Did officer index properly?				
	mean	54.40	56.90	40.00
	s	36.50	39.50	33.60
Did officer fail to decock?				
	mean	-2.00	-1.30	-1.10
	s	8.90	6.60	9.00
Did officer turn on firing line with loaded weapon?				
	mean	-1.00	-0.40	-0.40
	s	6.80	5.00	3.80

Accuracy

Accuracy is the percentage of rounds that hit the intended target. Officers showed a dramatic improvement in Accuracy at Time 2 ($mean_{Time\ 1} = 31.9$, $mean_{Time\ 2} = 59.2$). The score attained at Time 2 is largely sustained in Time 3; however, it does not appear that additional learning occurred after Time 2 ($mean_{Time\ 3} = 58.3$).

The scores were informative; however, they did not indicate whether the finding was statistically significant. Analysis of variance is a method used to test the hypothesis that several means are equal to each other. In this case, it was used to determine whether the scores on the overall performance index were significantly different over time.

The bivariate analyses were supportive of the hypothesis that PRISim™ has value for improving accuracy. However, it is possible that other factors may account for or have a significant influence on its apparent effectiveness. For instance, the number of times the officer has received firearms training may have affected his or her score on the accuracy index. In order to help distinguish the effects of other factors, a multivariate regression analysis was also conducted. This analytical technique allows the examination of changes in the index over the time periods, while simultaneously controlling for other potentially important variables.

The analysis included individual characteristics of the officer (gender and years of law enforcement experience[2]), his or her training experiences (length of basic training, number of hours of inservice training in the 12 months prior to Time 1, number of times the officer had received firearms training during that time period, and whether the officer was a certified firearms instructor), and individual behaviors (number of rounds fired between time periods, the number of hours the officer worked in the 24 hours before the training, and the number of hours the officer slept during that period). Dummy variables representing the location of the training were also included in order to determine whether officers from different areas performed differently.

The multiple regression analysis (displayed in Appendix A) showed that after taking other factors into account, officers placed an average of 31.6% more of their shots on the target at Time 2 as compared with Time 1. The analysis also indicated that, although the gain achieved at Time 2 is retained at Time 3, further improvement did not occur.

Several other factors were important determinants of the officers' accuracy. Gender was significantly related to performance at the training. Male officers scored an average 18.6 points higher than female officers. Experience and training also appeared to be important factors. Officers' scores increased by .4 points for every year of law enforcement experience and by .5 points for each additional week of basic training. Presumably, longer basic training academies with more time for firearms training resulted in officers with better accuracy. In

2. Initial analyses also included the race, level of education, and age of the officer. None of the variables were statistically significant. Because there is no compelling theoretical argument to suggest that race or education should play a role in an officer's ability to use a firearm, the variables were dropped from further anaylyses for the sake of parsimony.

addition, a small, but significant, increase was found for each round fired by the officer in the 12 months prior to the training period (b=.003). Furthermore, officers from Texas scored an average 5.3 points lower than participants from Kentucky; officers from Washington scored nearly 8 points higher than Texas. Possible reasons for this difference may include different academy lengths or different Evaluators and Instructors within the evaluation. None of the remaining factors played a significant role in determining officers' scores on the index. The analyses suggested that, within the parameters of this model, repeated PRISim™ training has a beneficial effect on accuracy that is sustained over time.

An issue related to accuracy is the number of shots fired during each time period. It is desirable that officers fire a minimal number of shots necessary whenever use of the weapon is appropriate. Firing excessive shots can endanger others when rounds miss their intended target. Furthermore, shots that hit their intended target after the threatening behavior has ceased may be seen as excessive force. To examine this issue, the number of shots fired in the two relevant scenarios per time period was calculated. Officers fired a total of 919 shots at Time 1; 1,051 rounds at Time 2, and 1,249 rounds at Time 3. At first glance, these numbers suggest that officers became more likely to fire their weapons after repeated PRISim training. However, a closer examination of the data suggests this may not be the case.

At Time 1, officers fired an average of 3.5 shots during Scenario 1. The average number of shots fired during Scenario 3 fell to 1.6, a decrease of more than 50%. A similar pattern is found at Time 2. Officers fired an average of 3.7 shots during Scenario 2, but only an average of 2 rounds in Scenario 3. The numbers of rounds fired across these two time periods were not substantially different. Moreover, the pattern suggests that officers fired fewer rounds as the training progressed through the scenarios. Time 3, however, presented a somewhat different picture. Officers began the training in much the same way as they did in the first two scenarios. They fired an average of 3.7 rounds during the first scenario. However, they fired an average of 3.2 rounds during Scenario 3, thus accounting for the large increase in the total number of rounds fired during this time period.

It seems likely that Scenario 3 of Time 3 was qualitatively different from the other scenarios in which it was appropriate to fire the weapon. Based on posttraining interviews and anecdotal evidence,

Scenario 3 of Time 3 had a strong psychological impact on the participants. The scenario involved the officer arriving at a school where an active shooter was shooting students. The simulation included loud fire alarm horns and crying/screaming students dragging bleeding victims. The officers tended to be more emotionally aroused by this situation, according to posttraining interviews. The suspect appears, shoots another victim, and continues to move. The apparent distance between the officer and suspect is further than in other scenarios. The emotional arousal and the distance and movement of the suspect may account for the additional rounds fired. If that scenario is removed from the analysis, the picture that arises suggests that repeated PRISimTM training sessions had little effect on the number of rounds fired by officers. However, within the training period, officers became substantially less likely to fire multiple rounds.

Tactics

This group of indices is comprised of identification, verbalization, and use of cover.

Did the officer identify?

The identification index is a measure of whether the participant identified him or herself as a law enforcement officer when appropriate in each of the three scenarios presented during the test period. The data suggested that officers' performance on this skill did not vary substantially between Time 1 and Time 3 ($mean_{Time\ 1} = 38.6$, $mean_{Time\ 2} = 30.7$, $mean_{Time\ 3} = 37.8$). This conclusion was confirmed by the analysis of variance. That is, based on the bivariate analyses, PRISim™ did not appear to have a significant effect on whether officers identified themselves to the individuals they encountered in various situations. However, it is important to note that the effects of other factors may mask the true effects of the training. For example, the inconsistency of instruction from one instructor to another in this area may have masked the potential of PRISim™ to increase officer identification.

To further investigate the effect of PRISim™ on the identification index, a multiple regression analysis was conducted (see Appendix A).

The results indicated that PRISim™ did not have an impact on whether officers identified themselves at Time 2 or Time 3.

Several other variables were important predictors of this skill. Most significant, perhaps, was the role of training. Officers' scores increased significantly as the number of times they received firearms training increased. They gained 2 points for each instance of training. In addition, officers from Washington and Texas performed significantly better on this index than Kentucky officers (b=15.8 and 9.4, respectively). No other factors were found to be determinative.

Did the officer verbalize?

The verbalization index measured whether the officer verbalized appropriately during each scenario. The data suggested that officers' score on this index remained relatively stable over time ($mean_{Time\ 1}$ = 95.0, $mean_{Time\ 2}$ = 92.0, $mean_{Time\ 3}$ = 97.1). The analysis of variance indicated that significant variation did not occur (F=5.0).

The finding was clarified by the regression analysis in Appendix A, which indicated that the average score on the index did not increase at Time 2 or Time 3. The analysis also suggested that years of law enforcement experience was a significant factor in determining whether the officer verbalized appropriately. Interestingly, officers with *less* experience had higher scores on the index. A possible explanation for this could include an increased training emphasis on verbalization in recent years. Another interesting result is that officers from Texas and Washington scored somewhat higher on this index (b=5.3 and 7.5, respectively).

Did the officer use cover appropriately?

Within the PRISim™ system, two pieces of cover were set up so that officers could utilize them whenever necessary. The data suggested that some learning regarding the use of cover occurred between Time 1 and Time 2, and that the learning was sustained into Time 3 ($mean_{Time\ 1}$ = 61.3, $mean_{Time\ 2}$ = 67.0, $mean_{Time\ 3}$ = 67.6). Additionally, the analysis of variance indicated that a significant change in the average score did occur (F=3.4).

The multiple regression analysis, displayed in Appendix A, confirmed these findings. Compared to Time 1, officers did score significantly higher on the index at Time 2 (an average of 7.3 points) and at Time 3 (an average of 9.1 points).

The location of the training also played a role in determining officers' scores on this index. Officers from Texas scored significantly lower (an average 26.0 points lower) than Kentucky officers, whereas officers from Washington scored an average 6.8 points higher. Differences in locations may be related to the use of different evaluators and instructors in Texas. In addition, the centralized police academies in Kentucky and Washington as compared with the decentralized training system in Texas could have allowed for greater variation in the quality of previous firearms training. No other factors were statistically significant related to this index.

Judgment

Society expects that officers will use force, particularly deadly force, only under appropriate circumstances. Officers must choose proper actions under very difficult circumstances. Poor judgment can result in very serious consequences, including injury to officers, innocent bystanders, and suspects. The next three indices–whether the officer drew the weapon appropriately, whether innocent targets were unintentionally shot or endangered, and whether the shots fired were justified–are measures of the officer's use of judgment.

Did the officer draw appropriately?

The drawing appropriately index is a measure of whether the officer drew his or her weapon at the appropriate point in time. It should be noted that the instruments did not differentiate between drawing too soon or too late. Results suggested that officers did not improve over time with regard to this skill. In fact, compared to Time 1, officers appeared to do worse at both Time 2 and Time 3 ($mean_{Time\ 1} = 14.0$, $mean_{Time\ 2} = 7.9$, $mean_{Time\ 3} = 10.9$). The analysis of variance confirmed that the average scores were significantly different over time ($F = 3.9$). Because data were not collected to distinguish drawing too early from drawing too late, it is difficult to speculate on contributory factors to changes in this index over time.

The multiple regression analysis confirmed that officers scored an average 5.4 points lower on this index at Time 2 compared to Time 1 (see Appendix B). The average scores at Time 3 also appeared to be lower than at Time 1, but this difference was not statistically significant. The only other factor that appeared to have an influence on this index was the length of the officer's basic training. Interestingly, officers lost .4 points on the index for each additional week of training. These findings suggested that PRISim™ may not be beneficial with regard to improving officers' skills in drawing their weapons; however, additional research in this area is warranted.

Did the officer unintentionally shoot or endanger innocent persons?

This measure focuses on whether the officer unintentionally shot or endangered innocent persons at each time period. The data suggested that the officers' scores on this index increased at Time 2, but the improvement was not sustained at Time 3 ($mean_{Time\ 1} = -2.5$, $mean_{Time\ 2} = -.4$, $mean_{Time\ 3} = -1.0$). The reduction in performance between Time 2 and Time 3 was probably due to the unintended increase in the difficulty of scenarios. At Time 3, both "shoot" scenarios included more "no-shoot" human targets present near the suspects, resulting in greater opportunity for hitting innocent people. The analysis of variance confirmed that the scores differ over time (F=3.8).

These findings were further clarified by the multiple regression analysis in Appendix B, which indicated that officers improved their scores by 2.5 points on average at Time 2; that is, fewer innocent persons were endangered at Time 2. The scores at Time 3, however, were not significantly different from those at Time 1. The only other factor in the model that influences scores on this index was the number of hours worked by the officer in the 24 hours prior to the test period. Officers gained a small but statistically significant average of .2 points for each hour worked.

Did the officer shoot without justification?

The average scores on the index measuring whether officers shot their weapons without justification indicate that officers showed substantial and continued improvement at all time periods ($mean_{Time\ 1} = -6.8$, $mean_{Time\ 2} = -3.6$, $mean_{Time\ 3} = -1.11$). The conclusion is supported by the analysis of variance (F=8.9).

The ability to assess judgment is likely a primary reason that law enforcement agencies desire the use of simulators. Other performance criteria can be developed and measured by more traditional and less expensive means, but judgment in realistic situations is difficult to develop and evaluate without the assistance of a simulator.

Further support for this conclusion is found in the multiple regression analysis located in Appendix B, which suggests that, compared to Time 1, officers' scores increased by 2.8 points at Time 2 and 4.4 points at Time 3. The only other factor in the model that is statistically significant is the number of hours worked by the officer in the day prior to the training. Officers gained .2 points for every hour worked.

Safety

The final three indices are measures of behaviors related to safety. They are comprised of the indices measuring whether the officer indexed properly, whether the officer failed to decock the weapon, whether the officer turned on the firing line with a loaded weapon, and whether the officer kept his or her weapon operational.

Did the officer index properly?

Indexing refers to whether the officer keeps his or her trigger finger outside of the trigger guard until the decision to shoot has been made. Studies have shown that failing to index greatly increases the chances of a negligent discharge. Scores on the index that measured whether the officer indexed properly appeared to be stable at Time 2 and then decreased fairly dramatically at Time 3 ($mean_{Time\ 1} = 54.4$, $mean_{Time\ 2} = 56.9$, $mean_{Time\ 3} = 40.0$). The difference across the time periods was confirmed by the analysis of variance ($F=9.8$).

The multiple regression analysis in Appendix B indicated that no additional learning occurred between Time 1 and Time 2. Moreover, it confirmed that a significant decrease occurred at Time 3. Officers scored an average 14.4 points lower at Time 3 than at Time 1.

Several other factors played a significant role in determining the officers' score on this index. Male officers scored nearly 30 points lower on average than female officers. This may be explained by a relative lack of firearms experience prior to police training on the part of women, resulting in fewer bad habits to overcome. Length of law enforcement experience contributed in a small but statistically significant way to the outcome. Officers scored 1 point higher on the index for each year of experience. On the other hand, officers scored .9 points lower for each week of basic training. In addition, officers from Washington scored an average 11.8 points lower on this index.

Did the officer fail to decock?

This measure focuses on whether the officer failed to decock his or her weapon in each of the three time periods. It should be noted that due to PRISim™ equipment limitations, many officers were required to use a weapon with a "decocker" when their duty weapon did not have that feature. In addition, this performance item could not be assessed when an officer used a weapon without a "decocker" in the simulator. The data suggested that a small but noticeable improvement in this skill occurred at each time period ($mean_{Time\ 1} = -2.0$, $mean_{Time\ 2} = -1.3$, $mean_{Time\ 3} = -1.1$). However, the analysis of variance indicated that the change was not statistically significant, and therefore due to chance ($F=.5$). Further confirmation of this finding is demonstrated in the results of the multiple regression analysis (see Appendix B). No significant difference between Time 1 and the other two time periods was indicated. In fact, the only variable in the model that appeared to predict the outcome on this index was the number of hours the officer worked in the 24 hours prior to the test period. Officers who worked more hours had a slight though statistically significant improvement of .2 points for each hour worked.

Did the officer turn on the firing line with loaded weapon?

This index measured whether officers turned on the firing line with a loaded weapon. More specifically, did the officer allow the weapon to point in an unsafe direction? The data suggested that officers improved this skill between Time 1 and Time 2, and retained the improvement at Time 3 ($mean_{Time\ 1} = -.9$, $mean_{Time\ 2} = -.4$, $mean_{Time\ 3} = -.4$). However, the analysis of variance indicated that the change was not statistically significant ($F=.5$). Further support for this conclusion was found in the multiple regression analysis (see Appendix B).

Although the difference at Time 2 approached statistical significance, it was insufficient. No other variables in the model had an impact on this index.

Did the officer keep his or her weapon operational?

Officers whose weapons ceased to operate were evaluated on their ability to make the weapon operational. Possible reasons for the weapon to cease operation could include, but are not limited to: malfunctions (including officer-induced), an empty weapon, or weapon breakage.

At Time 1, there was a total of 139 malfunctions or empty weapons, with 87 instances of the weapon being returned operational, indicating a 63% success rate. At Time 2, a 61% success rate was achieved (81/133) and at Time 3, a 78% rate (100/128). These findings suggest that the officer's skill level improved between Time 2 and 3.

EVALUATION CONCLUSIONS

The analyses presented in the evaluation suggested basic conclusions with regard to the use of the PRISimTM system. Those conclusions can be found below:

1. The system does appear to be beneficial in building and/or enhancing skills that are arguably the most important for the protection of the officer and others:
   - Accuracy
   - Effective Use of Cover
   - Avoiding the Unintentional Shooting or Endangering of Innocents
   - Ensuring the Shooting is Justified

2. The greatest amount of learning appears to have occurred at Time 2, which suggests that anyone seeking to improve the training might wish to explore ways to move officers from this plateau on to greater skill development.

3. There were very few negative effects on the officers' skills as a consequence of the training. The only questionable area is whether the officer indexed properly as a result of the PRISim™ training.

4. The majority of the officers involved in the study felt that the mobility of the system made it possible to deliver training to law enforcement agencies that have limited resources and may not be able to send their officers away for training.

5. Officer's attitudes toward the PRISim™ system and training were overwhelmingly positive as identified through the pre- and post-assessments.

It should be noted that the value of any piece of training equipment is largely, if not completely, due to the operator/trainer. The PRISim™ system, when used by properly trained and motivated instructors, produces desirable outcomes. Thus, it would appear that the PRISim™ system is an effective training tool. The mobility of the system adds a dimension to this effectiveness that is judged best by needs of the end user.

STUDY LIMITATIONS

Several factors may have limited the scope of this study and should be mentioned. First, no baseline existed with which to compare officers' performance with regard to the skills examined here. Therefore, it is impossible to know how much learning occurred at Time 1. Consequently, the conclusions must be limited to whether repeated PRISim™ training is effective. We can say nothing about the extent to which a one-time exposure to the program would be beneficial.

A second limitation of this evaluation is the fact that the scenarios differed in degree of difficulty both across and within time periods. Furthermore, a means of controlling for degree of difficulty was not available for this evaluation. It should be noted that researchers were provided a very limited number of scenarios from which to choose for inclusion in the evaluation. Given the limited number of scenarios made available, it was difficult to choose nine scenarios with a similar difficulty level across the time periods. As a result, it is likely that the findings reported here underestimate, to some extent, the benefits of the program. In particular, it appears likely that at least one of the scenarios at Time 3 was significantly more difficult than those presented at Times 1 and 2. This would account for the fact that officers did not show continued improvement at Time 3.

Next, a different Evaluator (certified firearms instructor) was used in Texas than was used in Kentucky and Washington. Thus, evaluator bias cannot be controlled for. Similarly, different Advanced Interactive Systems (AIS) Instructors taught throughout the PRISim™ evaluation. Many times, these instructors emphasized different skills within their training, which may have affected the results.

Furthermore, to maintain a controlled evaluation, AIS instructors were not allowed to use the instructor-initiated branching technology of the PRISim™ system, which could have introduced instructor bias by permitting AIS instructors to determine the outcome of the scenarios. However, branching technology that responded to the officers' shots was enabled throughout the study (for more information on the branching technology, see Appendix A). Additionally, AIS was not allowed to select the scenarios used within the study for similar reasons. These were the only research constraints placed on the training.

Finally, during the course of the evaluation there were several component failures, most of which were minor and only temporarily delayed training. However, at Time 3 in Kentucky, the AIS instructor was unable to complete the training schedule due to equipment malfunctions. This required researchers to reschedule and train approximately 20 officers in February 2001. Furthermore, a limited variety of weapons required some officers to use weapons with which they were unfamiliar, making it difficult to assess an officer's true performance levels.

When the evaluation process began in January 2000, the PRISim™ system was the only firearm simulation system on the market that was deployed in a mobile trailer and that utilized a shootback mechanism. At the time of this writing (May 2004), PRISim™ remains the only simulator that is in a mobile trailer and a normal production item available for purchase by public safety. However, it should be noted that other companies have implemented a shootback mechanism on their systems since that time.

With the advances in firearm simulation systems, further research to compare PRISim™ and other firearms simulation systems is recommended. The evaluation of other simulation systems would provide a more complete evaluation of the state of simulation as a law enforcement training tool in this country.

SUMMARY

This chapter has provided an overview of simulation training and its application to law enforcement, specifically in the area of firearms training. Additionally, an evaluation of a specific system was focused on. Simulation training technologies have immense potential for the field of law enforcement. It is anticipated that law enforcement will begin to fully utilize the technology that is currently being used in other fields. Once technology is combined with the knowledge that currently exists in law enforcement, improved and more frequent training is likely to occur. Through research efforts as presented in this chapter, the hope arises that law enforcement can make an informed decision in acquiring the quality training that it needs and deserves.

Appendix A: Multivariate Regression Analyses: Accuracy and Tactics

	Tactics							
	Accuracy		Identification		Verbalization		Use of Cover	
	b	s.e.	b	s.e.	b.	s.e.	b	s.e.
Time 2	31.6	3.08*	-.7.9	4.6	-2.9	2.0	7.3	2.3*
Time 3	30.1	2.9*	-1.0	4.6	2.5	1.9	9.1	2.3*
Texas	-5.3	3.1	9.4	4.9	5.3	2.1*	-26.0	2.4*
Washington	7.8	3.5*	15.8	5.4*	7.5	2.3*	6.8	2.7*
Officer's sex	18.6	5.5*	-3.5	8.8	2.6	3.8	-1.3	4.5
Years of law enforcement experience	0.4	0.2*	0.1	0.3	-0.2	0.1	0.0	0.1
Length of basic training	0.5	0.2*	0.4	0.3	0.1	0.1	0.2	0.2
Hours of in-service training	0	0.05	0.0	0.1	0.0	0.0	0.0	0.0
Times officer received firearms training	0.2	0.5	2.1	0.7*	0.3	0.3	0.6	0.3
Number of rounds fired in 12 months prior to test period	0.003	0.001*	0.0	0.0	0.0	0.0	0.0	0.0
Whether officer is a certified firearms instructor at Time 1	-3.6	3.7	4.4	5.7	0.9	2.4	-2.2	2.8

Appendix A: Continued

	Tactics							
	Accuracy		Identification		Verbalization		Use of Cover	
	b	s.e.	b	s.e.	b.	s.e.	b	s.e.
Hours worked in 24 hours prior to test period	0	0.3	-0.2	0.4	-0.1	0.2	-0.2	0.2
Hours slept in 24 hours prior to test period	0.7	0.6	-0.6	0.9	0.3	0.4	-0.4	0.5
Constant	-4.7	8.4	27.7	13.1*	85.9	5.6*	71.0	6.6*
	$R^2 = .38$		$R^2 = .08$*		$R^2 = 0.7$		$R^2 = .43$	

Appendix B: Multivariate Regression Analyses: Judgment and Safety

	Judgment						Safety					
	Draw Appropriately		Shoot Innocents		Justification		Index Properly		Fail to Decock		Turn on Fire Line	
	b	s.e.	b	s.e.	b.	s.e.	b	s.e.	b	s.e.	b.	s.e.
Time 2	-5.4	2.3*	2.5	1*	2.8	1.4*	1.7	4.5	0.1	0.8	1.0	0.6
Time 3	-2.5	2.4	1.5	1.0	4.4	1.4*	-14.4	4.6*	0.7	0.8	0.7	0.6
Texas	0.3	2.5	-0.3	1.0	-1.5	1.5	-6.1	4.8	0.0	0.9	0.0	0.6
Washington	3.9	2.5	1.3	1.1	-2.5	1.6	-11.8	5.1*	0.1	0.9	0.6	0.6
Officer's sex	1.5	5.0	0.2	2.0	-3.8	2.9	-29.7	9.6*	-1.5	1.7	-0.5	1.2
Years of law enforcement experience	0.0	0.1	0.0	0.1	0.0	0.1	0.9	0.2*	0.0	0.0	0.0	0.0
Length of basic training	-0.4	0.2*	0.0	0.1	0.0	0.1	-0.9	0.3*	0.0	0.1	0.0	0.0
Hours of in-service training	0.0	0.0	0.0	0.0	0.0	0.0	0.0	0.1	0.0	0.0	0.0	0.0
Times officer received firearms training	-0.6	0.3	0.1	0.1	0.3	0.2	-1.1	0.7	0.1	0.1	0.0	0.1
Number of rounds fired in 12 months prior to test period	0.0	0.0	0.0	0.0	0.0	0.0	0.0	0.0	0.0	0.0	0.0	0.0

Appendix B: Multivariate Regression Analyses: Judgment and Safety

	Judgment						Safety					
	Draw Appropriately		Shoot Innocents		Justification		Index Properly		Fail to Decock		Turn on Fire Line	
	b	s.e.	b	s.e.	b.	s.e.	b	s.e.	b	s.e.	b.	s.e.
Whether officer is a certified firearms instructor at Time 1	4.9	2.7	1.4	1.2	0.5	1.7	-8.4	5.5	0.0	1.0	0.4	0.7
Hours worked in 24 hours prior to test period	0.1	0.2	0.2	0.1*	0.3	0.1	-0.1	0.4	0.2	0.1*	0.0	0.1
Hours slept in 24 hours to test period	-0.2	0.4	0.2	0.2	0.3	0.3	-0.1	0.9	0.2	0.2	0.1	0.1
Constant	15.7	7*	-7.4	3*	-4.7	4.2	93.5	13.7*	-2.5	2.5	-0.3	1.7
	$R^2 = .07$		$R^2 = .05$		$R^2 = .06$		R^2 - .15		$R^2 = .03$		$R^2 = .02$	

REFERENCES

Advanced Interactive Systems. Available online at http://www.ais-sim.com

Collard, P. (1997). The COTS revolution: As defense budgets shrink, military planners turn to smart, flexible, affordable simulators. *Military and Aerospace Electronics, 8,* (9) pp. 33-35.

Federal Bureau of Investigation (May 1982). The Bureau and the handgun. *The Investigator.* Washington, DC: FBI.

Gaines, L. K., Kappeler, V. E., & Vaughn, J. B. (1997). *Policing in America* (2nd ed.). Cincinnati, OH: Anderson Publishing Company.

Gaines, L. K., Southerland, M. D., & Angell, J. E. (1991). *Police administration.* New York: McGraw-Hill.

Grassi, R. (1997). The case for monthly firearms training. *Law and Order, 45,* (5) pps. 199-124.

Hickman, M. J., & Reaves, B. A. (2001). Local police departments 1999. Washington, D.C.: U.S. Department of Justice Bureau of Justice Statistics.

Hormann, J. S. (1995). Virtual reality: The future of law enforcement training. *FBI Law Enforcement Bulletin, 64,* (7) pps. 7-13.

Industry Canada–Life Sciences Branch. (2001, January). *Medical imaging technology–WG4 final working group report.* Available online at http://strategis.ic.gc.ca/SSG/hm00197e.html

Morrison, G. B., & Vila, B. J. (1998). Police handgun qualification: Practical measure or aimless activity? *Policing: An International Journal of Police Strategies and Management, 21*(3), 510-533.

Olsen, E. C. B. (1995). The evolution of a virtual reality driving simulator: From law enforcement training to research and assessment. *Proceedings of the Third Annual International Conference: Virtual Reality and Persons with Disabilities,* San Francisco, California. California State University, Northridge: Center on Disabilities.

Reintzell, J. F. (1997). When training saves lives. *Training and Development, 51,* 1. pps. 41-43.

Sandler, C. D., & Keysor, R. (1995, August). NRA and law enforcement: Ties that bind, *The American Rifleman, 7*(143) pps. 40-44.

Streit, C. (2000). Driving in a virtual reality world. *Law Enforcement Technology Magazine,* 27(8). 100-104.

Training Simulators Showcase. (2000). *Law Enforcement Technology Magazine,* 96-98.

Turner, W. W. (1993). *Hoover's FBI.* New York: Thunder's Mouth Press.

Wilson, J. R. (1998). Military simulation hits the wall. *Military and Aerospace Electronics, 9*(11): 15.

Part III

COURTROOM AND CORRECTIONS TECHNOLOGY

Chapter 10

VIDEOCONFERENCING: AN EXAMINATION OF COURTROOM PERSONNEL ATTITUDES

JILL A. GORDON, LAURA J. MORIARTY, AND TIMOTHY J. POTTS

Although videoconferencing has been used in the business arena for over three decades, it is only recently that the United States has applied this technology within the courtroom setting. Videoconferencing within the courtroom involves two-way interactive video (i.e., simultaneous interaction between the courtroom and the detained defendant occurs through the use of technology). Therefore, "face-to-face" court appearances can take place even though individuals are in multiple locations.

The use of videoconferencing in courtrooms has been in place, to varying degrees, throughout the United States for more than a decade. This chapter will discuss the (1) purpose of this technology, (2) the degree of implementation and support for it, (3) the legal challenges made on its use, and (4) the technology involved in videoconferencing. It will also examine the implementation of videoconferencing within one jurisdiction in one locality, gauging the support for its use within this community.

USE OF VIDEOCONFERENCING IN CRIMINAL JUSTICE SETTINGS

Originally interactive video was identified as a way to allow defendants to stay within the jail setting. In general, the use of videoconferencing stems from a need to reduce processing time, related cost, and increase public safety (Arnstein & Goodwin, 1994; Matthias & Twedt, 1997). These needs correlate with the findings of the National Sheriffs Association's survey reflecting that the major concerns among sheriff personnel are monitoring courtroom security and the transportation of detainees (National Institute of Justice, 1997).

Localities spend a great deal of time transporting accused individuals from the jail to the courthouse for related activities. To illustrate, any time a detainee enters or leaves a building the following procedures are followed: An inmate is searched prior to exiting (two deputies), detainee's transportation orders are reviewed and verified at a checkpoint, a pat search is conducted by the personnel who will conduct the transport, the detainee is received at a control point where his or her orders are again verified, and if the receiving point is the jail the detainee is subjected to a strip search in the presence of two staff members (Hemlock Business Services, 1998). Due to the complexity of this process it must be a coordinated effort and involves a significant amount of personnel and time to effectively execute a safe transfer.

The costs associated with transportation include the necessary ratio of staff to defendant, the cost of the operation and maintenance of the vehicle(s) used in transport, and the monitoring of the offenders both within the holding cell and within each courtroom of the courthouse. It must also be recognized that within the courthouse there are separate holding cells for men and women and any detainee with special needs, thus requiring additional staff persons to monitor the detainee's behavior and movement in the courtroom. Research indicates that although the initial cost of interactive video (e.g., teleconferencing) is large, the overall cost-benefit savings are substantial (Matthias & Twedt, 1997).

Videoconferencing is also seen as a way to increase public safety. The physical separation of the defendant to the public arena via the courtroom automatically reduces a chance for escape, transmission of contraband, and any physical outbursts by the defendant or other parties in the courtroom who may be provoked by the defendant.

Videoconferencing has been used more widely at arraignments, pretrial service interviews, first appearances, and bail review hearings (DiPietro, 1999). As shown by Matthias and Twedt (1997), video technology has also been implemented, on a more limited basis, for parole interviews, parole revocation hearings, emergency and review mental health hearings, domestic violence protection orders, and pretrial conferences or motions when one attorney is absent. It is also used for out-of-town witness testimony, law enforcement testimony, social security disability hearings, and signing or language interpretation. In some Florida jurisdictions the implementation of this technology is beneficial to the attorneys as well (Trost, 1997). Instead of accepting collect calls from detained clients, attorneys are now authorizing a video dial-up connection, providing incredible time-savings for the attorneys. This is due to the travel time reduction or absence of traveling to and from the jail.

DEGREE OF IMPLEMENTATION

Although it is rather challenging to identify the degree of implementation of videoconferencing throughout the United States, it is safe to say that a significant number of jurisdictions are engaging in this process. A 1995 report prepared for the National Institute of Corrections–Jails Division revealed that more than half of the states authorized the use of interactive video through case law, legislation, or court administrative rule (LIS, Inc., 1995). A more recent search to update the 1995 report was conducted for this chapter and reveals that at least 42 states have interactive video in use within at least one jurisdiction.

Limited research has been conducted on the level of support and issues regarding videoconferencing (Neimon, 2001, DiPietro, 1999; Surette & Terry, 1991). In general, the research shows support for the use of the technology. The support is greatest in jurisdictions where the judiciary embraces the concept of interactive video technology (Surette & Terry, 1991). However, there are a few areas of concern over (1) the adequacy of the right to counsel given that the defense attorney and the client are in separate locations, (2) the competency of the witnesses, and (3) the reduced deterrent effect of videoconferencing (Neimon, 2001; DiPietro, 1999; Surette & Terry, 1991). The apprehensions here are related to the question of whether videoconferencing has the same impact and protections for a detainee as provided when the defendant is physically present in court. In other words, will the client and defense attorney engage in conversations as they would if they were both physically present? Can the judge determine the mental state of the client or witnesses without their physical presence? To overcome the physical separation between the client and attorney, and to protect the client/attorney privilege some jurisdictions have installed private phone lines in order for the parties to communicate (DiPietro, 1999; Surette & Terry, 1991). In jurisdictions where videoconferencing has been discontinued, the main reason for this decision has focused on the cost of the necessary equipment rather than on any technical difficulties related to the technology or any constitutional issues (Surette & Terry, 1991).

RULES OF CRIMINAL PROCEDURE

Legal scholars have questioned whether videoconferencing can withstand legal challenges made against violations of the rules of criminal procedure. Some have argued that the "rules of criminal procedure will probably limit the use of the technology in pretrial procedures" (LexisNexis Academic, 2004a). At concern is the Sixth Amendment Confrontation Clause, in particular the "face-to-face" confrontation found in court proceedings. In general, videoconferencing has been deemed acceptable, with no violations of defendants' rights, when it is used in limited, specific court appearances, such as arraignment and other appearances made by defendants and witnesses (LexisNexis Academic, 2004b).

Other legal questions raised by videoconferencing include:

1. Does the defendant have a right to be present in a court proceeding?
2. Does videoconferencing "count" as being present?
3. Does the "presence" of the defendant via videoconferencing constitute a fair proceeding?

The issue is not whether the presence of the defendant would improve the outcome of the procedure; it is whether his or her presence in the courtroom could have contributed to the fairness of the proceedings. As stated earlier, it is generally accepted to use videoconferencing for some aspects or parts of the proceedings but not for the trial itself.

Some issues that have been identified that cannot be ascertained through videoconferencing focus on physical aspects. For instance, facial expressions and voice inflections do not translate well over video. There is also some concern that videoconferencing does not allow the defendant to readily confer with counsel. Others have raised the question about the solemnity and seriousness of the courtroom, pondering whether the absence of the defendant and substituting the videoconferencing instead has any diminishing effects on the solemnity and seriousness of the court.

Although there has been no blanket rule stating that videoconferencing counts as "appearance," it has been generally accepted as long as it is used only in proceedings thought to be less significant, such as arraignment and jury waivers. Defendants have been able to challenge videoconferencing under the issue of "plain error" when it is used in a significant proceeding. For example, in Guttendorf "the court found that a guilty plea proceeding was significant enough to warrant plain error review, but in Lindsey, the court found that neither arraignment nor a jury waiver proceeding rose to the level of plain error" (Marche, 2001).

TECHNICAL IMPLEMENTATION

There are three cost-related items to consider in the potential adoption of videoconferencing: equipment, facility, and communication.

Equipment: The hardware to conduct a two-way interactive conference requires at least two locations having cameras, monitors, videoconferencing equipment, a high-speed Internet system, audio communication, telephones, and fax machines. Optimal courtrooms will have multiple monitors, multiple cameras, and video switching equipment to be able to transmit a variety of views to the detainee at the jail.

Facility: Beyond the courtroom, the jail needs to provide a secure area to hold the detainees awaiting their appearance and a private location for the transmission of the videoconference to take place.

Communication: There are three types of connection protocols that can be used to communicate between locations: H.323 using Internet Protocol (IP), ISDN (Integrated Services Digital Network) using multiple telephone lines, or ATM (Asynchronous Transfer Mode) utilizing a Wide Area Network (WAN) or Local Area Network (LAN). Each protocol has its own strengths and weaknesses. H.323 is more subject to delays and interruptions, passing through multiple hubs via the Internet, but it is less expensive and more accessible. ISDN is less subject to delay because it uses straight connections via phone lines but, it is more expensive due to line charges (i.e., the higher the bandwidth results in more phone lines being used and long distance charges apply to this technology). ATM is a closed network that does not allow for communication with sites outside the network. Also, each location in a conference must use devices that operate on the same protocol, unless a video bridging device (Multi-point Conference Unit or MCU) is used to translate multiple protocols.

CHESTERFIELD COUNTY, VIRGINIA

Chesterfield County, Virginia, is a suburban county within the metropolitan Richmond area and has a population of 278,000 people. The county operates three different courts: General District Court, Circuit Court, and Juvenile and Domestic Court. These courts are located in two buildings within the same governmental complex. The detention of defendants occurs in one of three locations: Chesterfield County Jail, Chesterfield County Juvenile Detention facility, and Riverside Regional Jail. Both the local jail and the juvenile detention center are located approximately one mile from the governmental complex, whereas the regional jail is approximately 25 miles away. In 1998, Chesterfield transported approximately 200 defendants from the local jail for pretrial and bond hearings *each month*, approximately 85 juvenile defendants for pretrial hearings *each month*, and approximately 130 adult defendants from the Regional jail for pretrial and bond hearings *each month* (Hemlock Business Services, 1998).

The jurisdiction began inquiring about videoconferencing as an option in the early 1990s in order to reduce detainee movement. The County secured Byrne Memorial grant funds (criminal justice block grant) to begin the implementation of videoconferencing within the courtrooms in 1992. This enabled the installation of six systems, four in General District Court and two in Circuit Court. A cost-benefit analysis was conducted revealing an estimated cost savings of $153,000 annually by fully implementing videoconferencing in all courtrooms (Hemlock Business Services, 1998). Today all 15 courtrooms within Chesterfield County have videoconferencing, thus reducing transportation costs, better utilizing staff resources, and increasing public safety.

Each courtroom has five monitors set up to view the judge, the jury, the attorneys (defense and prosecution), and the courtroom observers. It was insisted on by the judiciary that the monitor be able to be hidden when not in use, so the County installed flat-panel screens at each of the stations that can easily be lowered when not in use. Each courtroom has three fixed and one portable camera. This allows for the ability to simultaneously transmit multiple images. The County uses ISDN dial-up connection to enable the videoconference to occur. Additionally, both the defendant and the defense attorney have private phone lines to ensure private conversations with clients.

The jail has one camera, monitor, fax, and phone. Each day the deputies escort the individuals who will be using videoconferencing to a secure location within the jail. The detainees sit together in a holding area until the judge calls their name. That individual then enters the room with the videoconferencing equipment accompanied by a deputy. He or she views four simultaneous pictures of the courtroom (the judge, defense counsel, Commonwealth Attorney, and overall view) and the proceeding takes place. At the end of the proceeding any release conditions are immediately faxed to the jail so that the individual is not unduly confined. Additionally, if a court-appointed attorney has been assigned, the detainee is handed his or her business card.

Each weekday, pretrial interviews are conducted beginning at 6 a.m. using the technology. The Pretrial Service Department is a remote location with the technology to conduct interviews using videoconferencing to avoid the time-intensive process of sending a pretrial officer to the jail for pretrial interviews. Beginning at 9:30 the Circuit Court followed by the General District Court conduct court proceedings via videoconferencing. This technology is primarily used for pretrial assessment, arraignments, and bond motion hearings. The court proceedings are rotated on a daily basis among the judges. In addition, the technology has been used in special circumstances when a witness is unable to attend court or in child abuse cases to keep the child out of the courtroom.

The widespread implementation of this videoconferencing has resulted in a substantial reduction in the time and cost for the Sheriff's department. Today, the Sheriff's office simply needs to assemble all individuals who need pretrial assessment in a waiting area by 6 a.m. Each individual then enters a private room to have the pretrial interviews conducted via videoconferencing. The same procedures are conducted for arraignment and bond hearings. This saves time and money as it is a departure from the more traditional procedures used when transporting detainees: performing several searches and verifying detainees' orders before transporting anyone. Additionally, the reduction of these procedures has increased public safety and security.

METHODS

A cross-sectional design was used to identify any variations in the level of support for videoconferencing based on job function. The individuals selected for inclusion in the study consist of all the Chesterfield County judges (General District, Juvenile and Domestic Relations, and Circuit Court, n=15), Commonwealth Attorneys (n=20), pretrial service officers (n=5), and sheriff personnel with direct job responsibilities to this function (e.g., court deputies, jail deputies, and jail deputies in the transportation unit, n=50). The defense attorneys chosen to participate were those who typically represented indigent defendants because their clients are less likely to make bail and thus remain in jail prior to the arraignment. The process for identifying the defense attorneys was accomplished with the assistance of the Chesterfield County Clerk who identified attorneys that are typically assigned to such cases. The total number of surveys distributed was 140.

The survey was distributed during the spring of 2004. The method of distribution was through a point of contact for the judges, pretrial service officers, sheriff personnel, and Commonwealth Attorneys. Specifically, the contact person who received the surveys simply placed them in the individual mailboxes or distributed them during roll call (sheriff personnel only). The surveys for the defense attorneys were mailed to each attorney because there is no centralized location for a similar means of distribution. The researchers had the cooperation of the pretrial service staff to mail the survey to the defense attorneys; this process eliminates the necessity of having a list of names for any of the study participants. There were no follow-up reminders or complete remailings of the survey. This process yielded 79 returned completed surveys resulting in a response rate of 56%. The response rate by position varied: 73% of the judges responded, 82% of the sheriff personnel responded, 60% of the pretrial service officers responded, 50% of the Commonwealth Attorneys responded, and 18% of defense attorneys responded. In addition, five of the returned surveys did not include an identification of the current job function.

Table 10-1 reflects the characteristics of those who responded to the survey instrument. As indicated, the majority of the respondents are white males who range in age from 26 to 67 with an average age of 45. About 40% of the participants have at least attended some college or have completed a degree. Forty-two percent of the respondents attained a graduate degree. Among the 79 respondents, 41 are sheriff personnel followed by 11 judges, 10 Commonwealth Attorneys (prosecutors), 9 defense attorneys, and 3 pretrial service officers. On average the individuals have been employed for 11 years with a range from 1 to 26 years.

Table 10-1: Demographic Characteristics of Respondents

Variable	*Number*	*Percent*
Age		
25 – 30	3	4%
31 – 40	21	26%
41 – 50	22	28%
51 – 60	16	20%
61 and older	6	8%
Missing	11	14%
Mean	45.19	
Gender		
Male	58	73%
Female	16	21%
Missing	5	6%
Race		
White	61	77%
African-American	10	13%
Missing	8	10%

Table 10-1: Continued

Variable	*Number*	*Percent*
Highest Level of Education		
High School/GED	9	12%
Some College	22	28%
Bachelor Degree	10	12%
Graduate Degree	33	42%
Missing	5	6%
Current Position		
Judge	11	14%
Sheriff personnel	41	52%
Pretrial service	3	4%
Commonwealth Attorney	10	13%
Defense Attorney	9	11%
Missing	5	6%
Years of Experience in Current Position		
1 – 5	16	19%
6 – 10	17	22%
11 – 15	17	22%
16 – 20	15	19%
21 or over	5	6%
Missing	9	12%
Mean	11.37	

The survey itself tapped a series of questions concerning attitudes toward technology in the courtroom. We asked the sample to indicate whether they strongly disagreed, disagreed, agreed, or strongly agreed that videoconferencing: is an efficient way to process offenders; increases public safety; saves the county money; reduces case processing time; enables effective assistance by counsel; restricts communication between attorney and client; reduces the "risk" to the court; reduces the ability to identify informal cues the defendant may be exhibiting; lessens the court's deterrent effect; reduces the seriousness of the court appearance; allows for adequate legal representation; and makes it difficult to assess competence. Three additional statements focused on the appropriate use of videoconferencing with the same responses: "It is appropriate to use videoconferencing for pretrial interviews"; "It is appropriate to use videoconferencing for arraignment procedures"; and "It is appropriate to use videoconferencing for felony defendants." Our goal is to determine if any of the concerns identified in the previous research are present in this jurisdiction. Specifically, how supportive are the respondents in their opinion that videoconferencing reduces time and cost, and that it increases public safety? Also, are there any concerns that exist regarding the adequacy of counsel, the competency of the defendant, and the deterrent effect of the process?

RESULTS

Table 10-2 examines attitudes regarding the appropriateness of videoconferencing in three related areas: pretrial service, arraignment, and felony cases. Although it was anticipated there would be some degree of apprehension for using this technology in felony cases because legal scholars have balked at using such technology in place of actual trials where the defendants are present, we did not find this to be the case with this sample. Overall the results show a large amount of support for videoconferencing in *all* venues. As an example, 81% indicated that this technology is appropriate for felony cases.

Table 10-2: Attitudes Toward the Use of Videoconferencing

It is appropriate to use videoconferencing for...	Strongly Disagree	Disagree	Agree	Strongly Agree	Missing
Pretrial Service	4 (5%)	4 (5%)	35 (44%)	33 (41%)	3 (4%)
Arraignment	2 (3%)	6 (7%)	31 (39%)	37 (47%)	3 (4%)
Felony Cases	7 (9%)	8 (10%)	29 (37%)	31 (39%)	4 (5%)

Table 10-3 reveals the impact videoconferencing has had on criminal justice personnel. We asked the respondents to rank order the component of the criminal justice system that has benefited the most from the use of videos within the courtrooms. [The responses ranged from 1 to 5, with 1 (low) indicating the *least* amount of impact/benefit and 5 (high) indicating the *most* impact/benefit.] Two findings of interest are noted: The respondents indicate that the sheriff's office has benefited the most from videoconferencing (71% rank it high impact) while the defense attorneys (52% rank it low impact) are seen as having had the least benefit from using the technology.

Table 10-3: Impact of Videoconferencing on Criminal Justice Personnel

	Judge	Sheriff	Pretrial	Prosecutor	Defense
1 (Low impact)	5 (6%)	13 (17%)	6 (8%)	8 (10%)	40 (52%)
2	14 (18%)	1 (1%)	13 (17%)	34 (44%)	11 (14%)
3	28 (36%)		22 (29%)	16 (21%)	9 (12%)
4	21 (27%)	8 (11%)	28 (36%)	12 (15%)	3 (4%)
5(High Impact)	9 (13%)	55 (71%)	7 (9%)	6 (9%)	13 (17%)
Missing			1 (1%)	1 (1%)	1 (1%)

Table 10-4 reports the level of support for a variety of issues related to the use of videoconferencing. An overwhelmingly favorable impact is found for three areas: public safety, case processing, and resources (i.e., saves money). At least 79% of the respondents agree or strongly agree that videos in the courtrooms increase public safety (99% agreement), reduce the court's "risk" (i.e., safety issues) (95% agreement), reduces case processing time (79% agreement), saves the county money (90% agreement), and is efficient in processing offenders (99% agreement). Additionally, moderate support is found for two additional items: 62% of the respondents believe videoconferencing enables effective assistance by counsel and 75% agree it allows adequate representation.

Table 10-4: Overall Examination of Support for Videoconferencing

The use of video in the Courtroom...	Strongly Disagree	Disagree	Strongly Agree	Agree	Missing
increases public safety.		1 (1%)	19 (24%)	59 (75%)	
reduces the "risk" to the court.	1 (1%)	3 (4%)	24 (30%)	51 (65%)	

Table 10-4: Continued

The use of video in the Courtroom...	Strongly Disagree	Disagree	Strongly Agree	Agree	Missing
is an efficient way to process offenders.	0 (0%)	1 (1%)	23 (29%)	55 (70%)	
reduces case processing time.	1 (1%)	13 (17%)	43 (54%)	20 (25%)	2 (3%)
saves county money.		4 (5%)	34 (43%)	37 (47%)	4 (5%)
enables effective assistance by counsel.	3 (4%)	25 (31%)	39 (49%)	10 (13%)	2 (3%)
restricts communication between attorney and client.	9 (11%)	34 (43%)	26 (33%)	10 (13%)	
allows adequate legal representation.	3 (4%)	13 (17%)	45 (57%)	15 (18%)	3 (4%)
reduces the ability to identify informal cues the defendant may be exhibiting.	7 (9%)	35 (44%)	23 (29%)	11 (14%)	3 (4%)
lessens the court's deterrent effect.	13 (17%)	45 (57%)	18 (22%)	2 (3%)	1 (1%)
reduces the seriousness of the court appearance.	17 (22%)	45 (57%)	11 (14%)	6 (7%)	
makes it difficult to assess competence.	11 (14%)	45 (57%)	17 (21%)	3 (4%)	3 (4%)

The respondents were not always in agreement. We found that the respondents disagreed with the following statements: Videoconferencing . . . restricts communication between attorney and client (54% disagreement), reduces the ability to identify informal cues the defendant may be exhibiting (53% disagreement), lessens the court's deterrent effect (74% disagreement), reduces the seriousness of the court appearance (79% disagreement), and makes it difficult to assess competence (71% disagreement).

LEGAL PROFESSIONALS AS A GROUP

We examined judges, prosecutors, and defense attorneys as one group. We did this because most of the challenges to videoconferencing are based on legal issues. For example, some find videoconferencing to be on the fringe of violating Sixth Amendment rights. In particular when the technology is expanded into different phases of the court proceedings, challenges to its constitutionality are raised. With this said, we wanted to see if the legal professionals as a group displayed any differences in attitudes about videoconferencing among themselves.

In general, we found relative agreement in most responses between judges and prosecutors with defense attorneys having different opinions than these groups (see Table 10-5). For example, eight of the nine defense attorneys (89%) believe videoconferencing restricts communication between attorney and client while only four out of eleven (36%) judges agree. Moreover, the judiciary (91%) and the prosecutors (80%) disagree that the video processes reduce the court's deterrent effect, whereas only 56% of the defense attorneys disagree. Lastly, only one defense attorney agreed that videoconferencing enables effective counsel compared with most of the judges and prosecutors indicating that it enables effective counsel.

Table 10-5: Examination of the Level of Agreement by Position

Variable	Judge (n=11)	Prosecutor (n=10)	Defense (n=9)
Enables effective counsel			
Agree	5 (45%)	6 (60%)	1 (11%)
Disagree	6 (55%)	3 (30%)	8 (89%)
Missing		1 (10%)	
Restricts communication between attorney and client			
Agree	4 (36%)	5 (50%)	8 (89%)
Disagree	7 (64%)	5 (50%)	1 (11%)
Reduces ability to identify informal cues			
Agree	2 (18%)	6 (60%)	8 (89%)
Disagree	8 (73%)	4 (40%)	0 (0%)
Missing	1 (9%)		1 (11%)

Table 10-5: Continued

Variable	Judge (n=11)	Prosecutor (n=10)	Defense (n=9)
Lessens the court's deterrent effect			
Agree	1 (9%)	1 (10%)	4 (44%)
Disagree	10 (91%)	8 (80%)	5 (56%)
Missing		1 (10%)	
Reduces seriousness of court appearance			
Agree	2 (18%)	1 (10%)	2 (22%)
Disagree	9 (82%)	9 (90%)	7 (78%)
Allows adequate legal representation			
Agree	8 (73%)	8 (80%)	3 (34%)
Disagree	2 (18%)	1 (10%)	6 (66%)
Missing	1 (9%)	1 (10%)	
Makes it difficult to assess competence			
Agree	1 (9%)	4 (40%)	7 (78%)
Disagree	9 (82%)	6 (60%)	1 (11%)
Missing	1 (9%)		1 (11%)

Taken together the results show strong support for the use of videoconferencing within this jurisdiction. The results are consistent with the prior literature–almost all the respondents agree that this technology has a positive impact on court costs, time savings, and public safety. These are the primary reasons for engaging in videoconferencing. The results also reflect some trepidation or hesitation among defense attorneys in a number of issues including adequacy of representation, communication restrictions, and a deterrent effect.

In addition to the quantitative questions the survey contained two open-ended questions that yielded some interesting responses. The first question asked "How does the use of video arraignment impact the defendant's due process?" Among the 57 individuals who wrote a response, 36 indicated that it has no impact, 7 point to quicker processing of the case due to the technology, while the remaining 14 responses speak to negative impacts including restriction on interaction, communication, and privacy. Some of the specific comments are presented here:

- limits conversation with counsel (Judge)
- cannot speak privately with an attorney (Sheriff personnel)
- the defendant and his or her attorney might not pursue a line of questioning due to the logistics (Sheriff personnel)
- impacts on his or her ability to communicate with his or her attorney (Prosecutor)
- it limits a confidential discussion between the defendant and his attorney during any in court legal proceedings (Prosecutor)
- On many occasions the defendant does not understand what is going on. The use of video makes it difficult to ask questions and is sometimes a barrier to effective communication. (Defense)
- It means that the defendant (in his person) is ignored and paperwork is given precedence in deciding issues such as bond (Defense)
- often defendant has a hard time hearing–very confusing (Defense)
- Some judges will allow setting bond at this time, while others will not and must wait for a bond hearing to be set. (Defense)
- It denies the client his sixth Amendment right to counsel. Defendant doesn't have the ability to discuss case with attorney during proceedings. (Defense)
- It does impede the ability for the defendant to communicate privately with his attorney. (Defense)
- The client and attorney are not able to discretely communicate; the client/ defendant cannot always see and hear events as well as he could if in courtroom. (Defense)

The second question asked: "how should the technology be expanded?" There were 43 responses to this question, which ranged from "it should not (Prosecutor)" to "as much as possible (sheriff personnel)". Here is a list of some of the responses:

- recording of judge's opening comments to bonded pretrials relating to their right to counsel (Judge)
- unsure, but not to actual trials with defendant present only by video (Judge)

- It would be helpful if all prisoners had video for civil cases–paternity, custody, etc. I worry about using it for full trials when the party is on video. (Judge)
- expert witness testimony, crime scene processing, and video presentation of scene to courtroom (Sheriff personnel)
- use of special telephone so defendant can communicate privately with their attorney. It should be used in all practical situations, even cases when inmates are incarcerated out of state. (Sheriff personnel)
- out-of-state witnesses, conferencing with other jurisdictions (Sheriff personnel)
- Perhaps pretrial arraignments could be by television. That is, pretrial officers conduct presentations from office, rather than making court appearance. (Pretrial)
- I would love to see it used for out-of-state or nonlocal witnesses. (Prosecutor)
- Hard to imagine how it could be used more without encountering due process problems (i.e., going beyond pretrial process) . . . defendant needs to be in the courtroom. Expert witness hookup should exist at various state labs so that a lab tech doesn't have to wait all day in court to testify about their blood analysis report. (Prosecutor)
- A phone line needs to be established for defense counsel to speak confidentially, so that all communication is not broadcast for the entire courtroom. (Defense)
- if at all, for child abuse and domestic violence cases (Defense).

SUMMARY AND CONCLUSIONS

The support for videoconferencing in Chesterfield County is both expected and unexpected. Because the population is older, (mean=45 years of age), we expected to find some fear or insecurity with using the new system. However, this was not the case. The majority of the respondents are very comfortable with the videoconferencing. After observing the courtrooms and speaking to the Court Administrator, we feel that the level of apprehension and fear has been significantly reduced by training provided by the Courts.

We also expected to find support for the process as long as it was limited in scope (not used for actual trials, for example). While we did find such support, the open-ended questions reveal that at least for some criminal justice actors there is a vocalized sentiment toward expanding the use of videoconferencing. Areas where expansion could benefit the county include child abuse and domestic violence cases and witness testimony, especially for out-of-state witnesses.

In conclusion, videoconferencing is an excellent way for the county to manage offenders, reducing the costs associated with pretrial interviews while ensuring public safety. And, with the criminal justice actors participating in the videoconferencing indicating they support using this technology, the county should consider expanding its usage while providing a more private means of communication between the defendant and his or her counsel.

REFERENCES

Arnstein, J., & Goodwin, J. (1994). The Technology of Video Conferencing, at 1, Fourth National Court Technology Conference, National Center for State Courts (available through the national Center for State Court's Website at www.ncsc.dni.us or from the Judicial Council). http://web.lexis-nexis.com, retrieved April 21, 2004

DiPietro, S. (1999). Fairbanks video arraignment assessment. Alaska Judicial Council: Anchorage, Alaska.

Hemlock Business Services (1998). County of Chesterfield, VA: Cost/Benefit Analysis of Video Arraignments. Unpublished document. Front Royal, VA.

LexisNexis Academic. (2004a). County officials push for expanded use of video networks. Associated Press. February 28, 2004.

Lexis Nexis Academic. (2004b). Court starts video arraignments. Associated Press. January 21, 2004. http://web.lexis-nexis.com, retrieved 4/21/04.

LIS, Inc., NIC Information Center Contractor. (1995). Use of interactive video for court proceedings: Legal status and use nationwide. Prepared for the National Institute of Corrections Jail Division. Longmont, CO: same.

Marche, C. (2001). Closed-circuit television and defendants' rights in criminal courtrooms. Illinois Bar Association (available at www.illinoisbar.org).

Matthias, J. T., & Twedt, J. C. (1997). Telejustice–Videoconferencing for the 21st Century. Fifth National Court Technology Conference (CTC5): National Center for State Courts.

National Institute of Justice. (1997). Court security and the transportation of prisoners: Summary of a research study by the National Sheriffs Association. U.S. Department of Justice, Office of Justice Programs, Washington DC.

Neimon, M. (2001). Can interactive video work in Waukesha County? An analysis and survey. Available online at www.scsonline.org/wc/educational/KIS_VidCon Guide.pdf, retrieved January 2004.

Surette, R., & Terry, W. C. (1991). The case of videotaping misdemeanor defendants. Judges Journal, pp. 20-31.

Trost, M. (1997). Video Conferencing. Available online at www.ncsconline.org/D_KIS/TechInfo/Articles/TIS_VidConTrostCTC4Art.htm, retrieved January 14, 2004.

Chapter 11

TECHNOPRISON: TECHNOLOGY AND PRISONS[1]

JANICE JOSEPH

INTRODUCTION

The great technological advances in the last 25 years are having an impact on prisons. Combined with the ever-present need to reduce prison cost and increase security, the use of technology is becoming prevalent in the penal system. Less than 15 years ago, there were perhaps very few computers, technology review committees, or technology products of any kind in prisons. Today, however, technology has emerged as a critical issue in prisons and is used in many aspects of prison life. Technological innovations have occurred in internal security with the use of advanced x-ray devices, closed-circuit monitoring, magnetic "friskers," and officer tracking/alerting systems. Drug and alcohol abuse testing packages, telemedicine, and videoconferencing all are products of advances in technology used in prison. This chapter examines several types of technological devices used in prisons and the issues surrounding their use. The chapter focuses primarily on biometrics, technology to detect illegal activities in prison, smart cards, electroshock devices, monitoring and surveillance technology, and teleconferencing technology.

---

1. Source: "Technoprisons" by Janice Joseph in Muraskin/Roberts, *Visions for Change: Crime and Justice in the Twenty-first Century*, 4th Edition, © 2004. Reprinted by permission of Pearson Education, Inc., Upper Saddle River, NJ.

BIOMETRIC SCANNING

Biometrics, which means "life measurement," is based on the principle that everyone has unique physical attributes that a computer can be programmed to recognize. It is a science of using a particular biological aspect of the human body (National Law Enforcement and Corrections Technology Center, 2000) and uses mathematical "representations of those unique physical characteristics to identify an individual (Desmarais, 2000; Wood, 2000). Biometric technologies automate the process of identifying people based on their unique physical or behavioral characteristics such as the finger, hand, eye, face, and voice.

Biometric scanning is used in the identification and verification of individuals. Identification is defined as the ability to recognize a person from among all those enrolled (all those whose biometric measurements have been collected in the database) and seeks to answer this question: Do I know who you are? It involves a one-compared-to-many match (or what is referred to as a "cold search"). Biometrics is also used for verification, which involves the authentication of a person's claimed identity from his previously enrolled pattern. Verification seeks to answer this question: Are you who you claim to be? and involves a one-to-one match (see Campbell, Alyea, and Dunn, 1996; Miller, 1996). In order to accomplish this, the system has to (1) receive biometric samples from a candidate/user; (2) extract biometric features from the sample; (3) compare the sample from the candidate with stored template(s) from known individual(s); and (4) indicate identification or verification results (Idex, 2000).

There are two phases in the system; one is the enrollment phase, and the other is the verification phase. During the enrollment phase, individuals submit a "live sample" of their biometric information (for example, the eyes, face, or fingerprints), which is scanned and stored in a database along with the subject's name and any other identification information. During the verification phase, individuals present their biometric information, and the recognition system compares the current scan with the sample stored in the database. While biometric technologies come in many forms, the procedure for storing and retrieving biometric information is uniform (Issacs, 2002a). Biometric scanning involves the scanning of the fingers, eye, hand, and face.

Finger Scanning

Finger scan technology is the oldest and most prominent biometric authentication technology used by millions of people worldwide. It measures the unique, complex swirls on a person's fingertip. The swirls are characterized and produced as a template requiring from 250-1,000 bytes. What is stored is not a full fingerprint but a small amount of data derived from the fingerprint's unique patterns (Chandrasekaran, 1997). Finger-scanning extracts certain characteristics of the image into templates known as "minutiae" that are unique to each finger. Optical, silicon, and ultrasound are mechanisms that are currently used to capture the fingerprint image with sufficient detail and resolution (Finger-Scan.com, 1999). After the fingerprints are scanned by the reader, templates are recorded and compared with the templates that are stored on the databases (ZDNet, 1999). The County of Los Angeles in California and Middlesex County in Massachusetts use finger-scanning (Esser, 2000). The Pierce County Sheriff's Department uses finger-scanning identification systems made by Tacoma, Washington-based Sagem Morpho to verify inmates upon release (Issacs, 2002). Overall, the biometric industry made $196 million in 2000, with finger imaging being the most popular tool (Pries, 2001).

Eye Scanning

Eye scanning is probably the fastest growing area of biometric research because of its promise for high scan accuracy. There are two types of eye scanning: retinal scanning and iris scanning.

Retinal scans examine the blood vessel patterns of the retina, the nerve tissue lining the inside of the eye that is sensitive to light. An infrared light source is used to illuminate the retina of the eye. The image of the enhanced blood vessel pattern of the retina is analyzed for characteristic points. A retinal scan can produce almost the same volume of data as a fingerprint image analysis. By emitting a beam of incandescent light that bounces off the person's retina and returns to the scanner, a retinal scanning system quickly maps the eye's blood vessel pattern and records it into an easily retrievable digitized database (Ritter, 1999; Tiemey, 1995).

While retinal scanning uses lasers that focus on the back of the eye, iris scanning zooms in on the front. Iris scans digitally process, record, and compare the light and dark patterns in the iris's flecks and rings, something akin to a human bar code. Iris scanning works by capturing the image of a person's iris; using a videoconferencing camera; and establishing a 512-byte code of the image's unique characteristics. Iris recognition stands out as perhaps the most "hygienic" of the biometric technologies in that no part of the user's body has to touch anything to operate the system. A retinal scan can produce almost the same volume of data as a fingerprint image analysis. Along with iris recognition technology, iris scan is perhaps the most accurate and reliable biometric technology (Woodward, 1997).

Iris recognition gives prison officials absolute assurance that the right inmate is being released and eliminates the risk of human error in matching a face with photograph identification. In addition, the iris recognition system lets the prison administration determine whether a new inmate was previously incarcerated there under a different name. The Sarasota County Detention Center in Florida uses iris scanning to prevent former prisoners from visiting former inmate friends (National Law Enforcement and Corrections Technology Center, 2000). The Lancaster County Prison and the York County Prison in Pennsylvania also use iris scanning to verify prisoners before they are released from prison at the end of their sentences and for routine events such as court appearances and medical visits (Center for Criminal Justice Technology Newsletter, 2001; Pries, 2001). There are currently 30 county prisons and 10 state prisons using iris scanning. Inmates are verified by iris recognition before they are released from prison.

Hand Scanning/Hand Geometry

With hand geometry, the biometric hand unit employs a miniaturized camera to capture a digital template of the back of the individual's hand. These photographs analyze the size, shape, width, thickness, and surface of the hand. In effect, a digital map of the outline of a person's hand is created. The biometric hand readers simultaneously analyze over 31,000 points and instantaneously record over 90 separate measurements of an individual's hand. The results are converted into a less than 10-byte code and are stored in the system's memory for future comparisons (Chandrasekaran, 1997; Zunkel, 1998).

Hand scanning/geometry has been used to identify inmates, employees, and visitors to correctional facilities. The Federal Bureau of Prisons, for example, uses hand geometry to verify and the identity of visitors and staff members in order to avoid mistakenly identifying them. Inmates use it for access to the cafeteria, recreation, lounge, and hospital. In San Antonio, Texas, hand geometry helps to prevent escape attempts. Florida Department of Corrections currently also utilizes hand scanning in 19 of its facilities (Corrections Connection, 2001).

Facial Recognition

The facial recognition technique is one of the fastest growing areas. It measures the peaks and valleys of the face, such as the tip of the nose and the depth of the eye sockets, which are known as nodal points–the human face has 80 nodal points, but only 14 to 22 are needed for recognition–concentrating on the inner region, which runs from temple to temple and just over the lip. The scan also reads the heat pattern around the eyes and cheeks and can scan the dimensions of an individual's head. It then comes up with a face print (National Law Enforcement and Corrections Technology Center, 2000). It also measures such characteristics as the distance between facial features (from pupil to pupil, for instance) or the dimensions of the features themselves (such as the width of the mouth). Facial recognition software uses a camera attached to a personal computer to capture and map key identifying features (ZDNet, 1999). In addition to photographs, the system records other identifying attributes such as scars, tattoos, and gang insignia. Identification cards are produced for department em-ployees, inmates, and offenders, and face-recognition technology is utilized for positive identification. The advantage of the facial recognition system is that it can work with people at a distance. As one approaches, the system could recognize the face and activate the system, such as turning on a computer or unlocking a door stages (Desmarais, 2000).

The Facial Recognition Vendor 2000 (FRVT, 2000) was tested at a correctional facility in Prince George's County, Maryland, to assist correctional officers in their decision to unlock an electronically controlled door providing access to the facility (Blackburn, Bone, and Philips, 2001). In 1998, the Wisconsin Department of Corrections awarded Viisage Technology, Inc., a $1.4 million contract to develop a biometric facial identification system for the state's prison system. The facial recognition system is used in more than 44 locations throughout the state (Colatosti, 1998). The Ohio Department of Rehabilitation and Corrections also uses facial recognition to identify inmates.

ILLEGAL ACTIVITIES DETECTION TECHNOLOGY

To prevent illegal activities in the prison, manufacturers have developed new detection technologies. These include technologies to detect illegal drugs, concealed weapons, and the number of heartbeats in vehicles.

Illegal Drugs

Attempts to control the influx of drugs entering prison facilities have ranged from closed-circuit television in visiting areas to an increased use of drug dogs and pat- or rub-down searches of visitors. Unfortunately, a large amount of controlled substances continue to penetrate many prisons. So today, scanners such as Ion Track Instruments' ITEMISER and VaporTracer are used to detect traces of microscopic particles associated with 40 different types of drugs. Generally, drug detection systems are categorized as trace detectors or bulk detectors. Bulk detectors are typically much larger, less mobile, and less sensitive than trace detectors. Most trace detection systems in use today are based on ion mobility spectrometry (IMS), which is a highly portable equipment and with capabilities that, until recently, were confined to the laboratory. Originally developed for medical imaging and diagnosis, trace detectors can determine whether items have been in the presence of drugs or touched by people who have been using, handling, or hiding drugs. Another use for trace detection is in the nonintrusive inspection of cargo and containers. Drug residue on the exterior or vapors seeping from the interior can be detected to signal inspectors that an enclosure needs further scrutiny. Trace detectors operate in two basic modes: vapor detection and particle detection and can use a "wipe and spray" method to detect drug residue (Wright and Butler, 2001).

These drug detection systems are used on both prisoners and visitors. In most situations, the scanner is positioned at the security checkpoint where the visitors' access into the prison is located. Before entry into visiting rooms is permitted, visitors can be screened for controlled substances. Typically, if traces of drugs are found on the visitor, either entry is refused into the visiting area or the visitor is subjected to further search procedures before being permitted entry (Ion Track, 2002). Some prisons have chosen to use trace detection technology for searching inmates' cells for drugs. Individual cells can be checked and analyzed on location with the portable, battery-operated VaporTracer or by running the ITEMISER from a portable power supply. Personal items, such as furniture and virtually any surface, can be checked for drugs. Because some drugs can easily be hidden in or on a letter or envelope, contraband screening of all incoming mail is essential. The prisons also scan multiple letters and parcels for drugs in just seconds. If a detection is made, the letter or parcel is opened and searched according to that prison's standard procedures. The machine can also search for particles that are gathered on paper used to wipe hands or clothing or through a special vacuum (Buscko, 2001).

The Department of Corrections in Pennsylvania purchased three ion scanners and 15 ITEMISERS for the prisons. In 1998, 22,074 visitors were scanned, and 734 were found to be carrying drugs (Caramanis, 1999). The Federal Bureau of Prison uses the explosive/drug detectors, from lonTrack Instruments, which can change from detecting narcotics to explosives in 10 seconds (Gaseau, 1999). California, a leader in particle-sniffing technologies, has a system that requires inmates and visitors to wipe their hands on a tissue, which is then inserted into an analyzer sensitive to trace amounts of narcotics in parts per trillion. The machine can not only indicate what narcotic the inmate has but also its quantity. California has also been using the Rapidscan 500 in its prisons to detect contraband in packages. It breaks down the molecular structure of what is inside a package and when it finds the drug, it circles it on the monitor and tells the operator it has found the preprogrammed substance (Wired News, 1997).

Concealed Weapons

Inmates can easily hide metallic objects such as tweezers, lighters, safety pins, needles, and other items in orifices on their bodies, but the

"Big BOSS" (Body Orifice Scanning System), which is a chair that scans and detects metallic objects hidden on or in the body, has been improving security in Arizona's prisons. The chair, which costs $6,500, scans an inmate's head, lower digestive tract, groin, rectum area, and feet, and sounds an alarm if any foreign objects are detected. Arizona purchased five of these chairs and with this system has caught 17 inmates hiding weapons on their bodies. The problem is that the machine cannot be used for extended periods of time so it has to be shut down to cool off before resuming operation. Physical contact, however, is still required to find nonmetallic foreign objects that inmates are hiding from officers (Directions, 2001; Lau, 2001).

Heartbeat Detectors

Perhaps one of the weakest security link in any prison has always been the sally port where trucks unload their supplies and where trash and laundry are taken out of the facility. Over the years, inmates have hidden in loads of trash, old produce, laundry–any possible container that might be exiting the facility. Oak Ridge National Laboratory has produced sound detectors or seismometers that count the number of heartbeats in service vehicles as they leave the prison, reducing the need for routine searches. Likewise Ensco, Inc. in Springfield, Virginia, and Geovox Security in Houston have developed sensors that can detect the heartbeats of those hiding inside cars or trucks at prisons. They use magnets and tiny weights to sense minute vibrations. The Advanced Vehicle Interrogation and Notification System (AVIAN)–being marketed by Geovox Security–also works by identifying the shock wave generated by the beating heart, which couples to any surface the body touches. A potential escapee can be identified in less than 2 minutes after two specialized AVIAN sensors are placed on the vehicle. Prisons can buy the system for $50,000 or lease it for $1,000 per month. The average cost of locating and capturing an escaped inmate is estimated at $750,000 (deGroot, 1997). About 6 of the 25 state prisons in Pennsylvania use the Geovox system to detect escapees before vehicles leave the prison, and one state prison in New Jersey has installed the system developed by Ensco. These devices are also now in use at other facilities, most notably at Riverbend Maximum Security Institution in Nashville, Tennessee, where four inmates escaped in a hidden compartment in a flatbed truck several years ago (Weed, 2001).

Pulsed Radar

Special Technologies Laboratories has created a new technological device, GPR-X, in which GPR stands for ground-penetrating radar, and X indicates the new generation of technology that GPR represents. It transmits energy into the ground, and by measuring the time it takes for that energy to be reflected, it can detect changes in ground material. GPR can, therefore, detect contraband buried in the recreation yard, for instance, or a tunnel being built under the prison (deGroot, 1997).

SMART CARD

A smart card is a standard-sized plastic card with an embedded computer microchip containing a central processing unit (CPU) and up to 8K bytes of electronic updatable memory. It is a photo identification card containing embedded computer chips that electronically store inmates' personal identification and medical information. Smart card technology has been emerging over the past two decades and there now are millions in circulation. The card stores all types of information about an inmate, including her movement, medical care, commissary purchases, treatment needs, and meals eaten. They can also provide access to restricted areas. Some, such as telephone calling cards and those that deduct purchases from a holder's account, are service related. Some can be used for identification purposes only; others enable remote payment, money access, and information exchange via computer, telephone, or television "set-top boxes" (Jackson, 1998b).

Australia is believed to be the first country in the world to use smart card technology as an integral part of the operation of a prison to provide greater security, efficiency, and flexibility. Fujitsu Australia's SmartCity smart card system has been incorporated throughout Western Australia's new Acacia Prison, the most advanced medium-security prison in the world. The smart cards allow prison officers to monitor the movements of individual prisoners within the jail and replace cash inside the institution. The cards are used to keep two prisoners from having any contact by restricting them from moving into the same area of the prison at the same time. The smart card also increases security considerably during prisoner transfers. Money that prisoners earn by working is credited to their smart card, and they use the card to purchase snacks, cigarettes, toiletries, and magazines or pay for telephone calls and so forth (Fujitsu Australia Limited, 2001).

Smart-card technology is still in its infancy and is used in prison primarily to dispense medication in the United States. When an inmate's smart card is inserted into a reader, the inmate's medication history is displayed on a computer screen. Any administration of medicine is entered into the record electronically, including the date and time of the dispensation–information that can be retrieved at any time by the institution's medical staff (Gaseau, 1999).

The Ohio Department of Rehabilitation and Correction (ODRC) has conducted a project funded by the National Institute of Justice to manage inmate information with "smart cards." Initially, the cards were used to track the medication activity of 2,300 inmates in a medium-security men's facility. In this system, the inmate's photo is electronically stored, indicating who the inmate is and what his inmate number is. When an inmate needs service, such as the library, he puts the card into a reader that scans the information on the microchip contained in the card. These smart cards will be integrated with the ODRC's electronic photo-imaging system so that when the card is used, it will automatically bring up a picture of the inmate on a computer screen. In the future, the smart card will be a multiuse card that will be used in prison to control many aspects of prison life. Inmate classification, medical and mental health information, education status, and parole information will be stored on the microchip (Justice Technology Information Network, 1998).

ELECTROSHOCK DEVICES

Stun Belt

The stun belt is an electronic shocking device secured to a person's waist and is available in two styles: a one-size-fits-all minimal-security belt (a slim version designed for low visibility in courts) and the high-security transport belt, complete with wrist restraints. Both come attached to a 9-volt battery. When activated, the stun belt shocks its wearer for 8 seconds, with 3 to 4 milliamps and 50,000 volts of stun power. Guards like it because they do not have to get near prisoners who wear the belt. They can set off the 8-second, 50,000-volt stun from as far away as 300 feet. It shocks the left kidney, blood channels, and nerve pathways. Stun Tech, manufacturer of the stun belt, recommends the belt as a psychological tool, an effective deterrent for potentially unruly inmates, and a humane alternative to guns or nightsticks. More than 100 county agencies have employed the belt for prisoner transport, courtroom appearances, and medical appointments (Schulz, 1999; Yeoman, 2000).

In 1995, the use of stun belts was reported to be illegal in Illinois, Hawaii, New Jersey, New York, Michigan, Massachusetts, and Rhode Island and in some municipalities. However, these shock devices have been adopted by at least 19 state prison systems including Oklahoma, Arizona, Florida, Wisconsin, and Iowa, as well as by the federal government. Seven more are considering using this device. They are currently used in both medium- and high-security prisons, on chain gangs, during prisoner transport including transport to and from medical facilities, and on prisoners deemed a "security risk" during court appearances. At Red Onion State Prison in Virginia, 10 inmates were required to wear the belts while meeting with an attorney investigating charges of human rights violations; one prisoner who refused to wear the device was barred from speaking to the lawyer. There have been few tests run to determine the safety of stun belts; those that have been conducted have led to highly suspect and vague results (Schulz, 1999; Yeoman, 2000).

Electric-Stun/Lethal Fences

Perhaps the largest contributor to keeping inmates locked up has been the introduction of electric fences, also known as lethal fences. These fences are erected around the perimeter of the facility and often carry about 10,000 volts of electricity, more than enough to take a human life. They are usually positioned between double perimeter fences and serve as unmanned lethal barriers or deterrents. The fences usually consist of galvanized posts spaced approximately 30 feet apart supporting wires powered with high voltage and are located approximately 10 feet from the outer perimeter fence and approximately 15 feet from the inner perimeter field. Any movement of the wire or variation in its current will trigger an alarm and a lethal jolt. These fences would shock would-be escapees with a lethal dose of 5,000 volts, or more than double the jolt of an electric chair. Guards in the command center can watch a graphic representation of the fenced perimeter that instantly pinpoints any change in current; the same system also sends a message to the watch commander's beeper in the event of an incident (Jackson, 1998a).

In 1992, California began installing the first electric fences around its prisons. At the time, skeptical industry observers said the system would never work and would never be widely accepted in the field. Today, all of California's 33 prisons are surrounded by electric fencing, and several other states have installed them as well (deGroot, 1997). Nevada, Colorado, Missouri, Wisconsin, Arkansas, and Alabama all use this type of fencing, and Arizona and Illinois plan to install the fence in future (deGroot, 1997).

Verichip

Applied Digital Systems of Florida has marketed the "Verichip," which is the size of a grain of rice and can be embedded beneath a person's skin. The information on this chip could include a person's medical records, banking records, how much the person owes on her mortgage, credit cards, and other personal loans. It could also be used to track a person's activities anywhere in the world. It would replace all of a person's present forms of identification such as passports, driver's licenses, social security, and credit/debit cards. The chip would also include data on family history, address, occupation, criminal record, income tax information, and so forth. The chip is powered electromagnetically through muscle movement or can be activated by an outside monitoring facility. A person will not be able to withdraw money from the bank without it, receive benefits from the government without it, or buy or sell anything without it. This is one of the dangers of the chip; once a person has it, that person can be controlled by someone else. The technology is used in some U.S. prisons where prisoners have a chip implanted in their bodies and when they become violent, the guard simply pushes a button on a remote control and paralyses the prisoner (Ultimate Scam, 2002).

MONITORING AND SURVEILLANCE TECHNOLOGY

Perimeter Security Control

A prison is only as secure as its perimeter. The basic role of a perimeter security system is fourfold: deter, detect, document, and deny/delay any intrusion of the protected area or facility. Six factors affect the probability of detection of most surveillance sensors, although to varying degrees. These are (1) the amount and pattern of emitted energy, (2) the size of the object, (3) distance to the object, (4) speed of the object, (5) direction of movement, and (6) reflection and absorption characteristics of the energy waves by the intruder and the environment (for example, open or wooded area, or shrubbery) (Jackson, 1998b). Electronic sensors monitor the tension in barbed-wire barricades, seismometers detect any suspicious shaking of chain-link fences, and microwave beams pick up motion in the deserted areas between fences. A positive signal from any of the systems sounds an alarm, swings surveillance cameras to the appropriate spot, and sets off warnings in a guard booth and the perimeter patrol car. A few of the newest prisons, including the Toledo Correctional Institution in Ohio, use "smart" perimeters that can eliminate the need for staffed watchtowers (Weed, 2001).

Control of Inmate Movement Inside Prison

The number of inmates in the United States has doubled over the past decade to nearly 2 million, so it has become difficult to monitor prisoners. Prisoners can be fitted with tamperproof transmitter wristbands that broadcast a unique serial number via radio frequency every 2 seconds. Antennas throughout the prison pick up the signals and pass the data via a local area network to a computer. This system can alert a monitor when a prisoner gets dangerously close to the perimeter fence or does not return from a furlough on time; it can even tag gang members and notify guards when rival gang members get too close to each other (prison employees also carry transmitters with panic buttons) (Roberti, 2002). Illinois recently signed a $3 million contract with the Scottsdale company Technology Systems International to outfit a state prison with a high-tech tracking system (two

Michigan prisons have also signed on). Prisons in Arizona, California, and Texas have tested a similar system developed by Motorola in which prisoners and officers wear bracelets that transmit personal radio IDs (PRI). Receivers throughout the prison pick up the signals and relay them to a computer that displays everyone's exact location in the prison. With this PRI, each prisoner can be seen on a map of the prison as a red dot, and each officer as a blue dot. A single officer monitoring the display can keep track of thousands of prisoners. The computer can alert a guard if a dangerous prisoner comes into his area or raise an alarm if someone is out of place. It can also track two prisoners who hate each other and selectively block access through certain checkpoints to make sure they never come in contact. The computer can also keep a log of everyone's movements, aiding investigations of assaults or other crimes (Weed, 2001). The Logan Correctional Center in Lincoln, Illinois, is the nation's first medium-security prison to implement Alanco Technologies Incoporation's TSI PRISM RFID officer safety and inmate management system as part of an effort to reduce operating costs and prevent inmate violence. With this system, officers wear RFID radio transmitters and inmates wear wristbands. This system allows Logan administrators to continuously monitor and track the location and movement of approximately 2,000 inmates at the 50-acre complex. Logan has become the third facility in the United States to utilize the new state-of-the-art TSI PRISM officer safety and inmate management technology, joining the California State Prison in Calipatria and the W. J. Maxey juvenile facility in Whitmore Lake, Michigan (Alanco Technologies, 2003).

VIDEO TELECONFERENCING

The uses of teleconferencing and videoconferencing have become common in prison. With it, individuals can see and talk to one another from any place around the world with picture and audio as clear as if they were having a face-to-face conversation. This tool is now readily available to all criminal justice agencies. Teleconferencing allows prisoners more virtual contact with the outside world and can be used in court hearings, prison visits, and telemedicine.

Court Hearings

Videoconferencing is used in prisons for routine court hearings, thus reducing the number of inmates transferred for their hearing. This basically enables prisoners to be arraigned without physically being present in a courtroom or allows witnesses from across the country to testify electronically, thus completing cases faster. Also, with the video technology, an inmate with an open warrant from a surrounding community is placed on the videoconferencing list. The judge can recall or resolve the warrant, appoint counsel, schedule a trial date, or resolve the case in one day. States such as Montana and Wisconsin have recently begun videoconferencing initial court appearances for inmates (Associated Press State and Local Wire, 2002; M. Miller, 2002). The use of videoconferencing in prisoner civil rights proceedings was authorized by Congress in the Prison Litigation Reform Act. The Judicial Conference also has encouraged courts to use videoconferencing in certain proceedings, and currently 100 federal court sites use the technology (Third Branch, 2001).

The cost for commercial packages for videoconferencing can run as high as $90,000 (Gaseau 1999). However, the Hampden County, Massachusetts, Correctional Center bought its own equipment and used existing fiber optics to run the technology at a cost between $7,000 and $10,000 per site. The Eastern District of Texas and the Central District of Illinois were among the first courts to receive funding for videoconferencing for prisoners court hearings (Third Branch, 2001).

The Conference Court Administration and Case Management Committee reviewed the merits of using videoconferencing in court proceedings and found that a potential for savings in personnel time and travel costs existed, which can outweigh the cost to purchase and operate videoconferencing systems in prisoner civil rights proceedings. In support of this observation, the Case Management Committee, in collaboration with the Conference Automation and Technology Committee, established the Prisoner Civil Rights Videoconferencing Project, which analyzed courts' use of videoconferencing technology for prisoner proceedings. Between 1996 and 2001, approximately 58 videoconferencing sites within the district courts were funded under this project (Third Branch, 2001).

Prison Visits/Video Visiting

Inmate visitation is required in all correctional agencies but can become difficult to manage. One facility in Colorado, however, is working on a way to automate and simplify the process. The automated visitation system, created by the Arapahoe County, Colorado, Detention Facility and AMA Technologies, allows visitors to call and schedule dates and times for visits, using an identification (ID) number (the last four digits of the photo ID that will be presented on arrival). This system is integrated with a television system at the facility. When the visitor arrives at the facility at the scheduled time, he enters by a separate entrance into a visitor reception center and sits at a 27-inch interactive screen to visit with the inmate, who will sit at one of 80 video stations throughout the facility. Inmates in the infirmary who once had to be transported to booking for a visitation can sit in their beds and have visitation directly from the infirmary. Friends and family can now save on travel and avoid standing in line by scheduling videoconferences with inmates. Because the system is considered an inmate benefit, the cost is covered by inmate welfare funds (Gaseau, 1999).

Telemedicine

Telemedicine is one of the newest and most exciting advances in medicine. The process has a doctor in the prison examine the patient with a stethoscope or perform an electrocardiogram. The results are then relayed over the Internet to a remote medical specialist who sends back a diagnosis. It could provide prisoners with adequate, cost-effective health care in the future. Taking a prisoner to a specialist outside the prison can pose a danger to the correctional officers and the community by giving the prisoner an opportunity to escape. Telemedicine allows physicians to consult with on-site medical personnel through videoconferencing and compatible medical devices such as medical microcameras. Telemedicine also helps prisons comply with a court order man-dating standardized and uniform health care for inmates. Georgia, Michigan, Ohio, Arizona, and Texas are the major states that are providing telemedicine in the field of corrections (Third Branch, 2001).

According to a report prepared by Abt Associates (1999) and funded by the National Institute of Justice (NIJ), prisons that use telemedicine systems instead of conventional care could save approximately $102 per specialist encounter. In addition, telemedicine can improve the quality of care available to prisoners by reducing the waiting time between referral and consultation with specialists and by increasing access to distant physicians who specialize in prison health care (Weed, 2001).

ISSUES REGARDING THE USE OF TECHNOLOGY

Usefulness

Many of these technological devices are very useful to the operation of the prison system. They save time and money. The smart card system, for example, can be used to process inmate data at a fast rate to dispense medication. While it could take one minute per patient to dispense medication to patients, the smart card can reduce the time for this process to a few seconds. Electric perimeter fences in California eliminated the need for 24-hour watchtower surveillance, thus saving about $32 million per year, about $1 million per prison. Heartbeat sensors used to detect inmates can be cost effective and can identify an escapee in less than 2 minutes after two specialized AVIAN sensors are placed on the vehicle. Prisons can buy the system for $50,000 or lease it for $1,000 per month. This may seem high, but the average cost of locating and capturing an escaped inmate is estimated at $750,000 (deGroot, 1997). Pennsylvania's Luzeme County has saved $120,000 in six months on court transportation, manpower, and cost on local correctional facility because of its innovative use of teleconferencing (Weiss, 2003). The benefits of telemedicine are obvious: (1) travel costs are reduced dramatically because the number of vans needed to transport inmates is substantially reduced and (2) telemedicine allows dozens of medical specialists to serve several inmates right in a prison (Weed, 2001).

Many of these technological devices used in prison can enhance the effectiveness and efficiency of institutional security. Explosive/drug detectors from Ion Track Instruments can reduce contraband, and field-monitoring devices can prevent inmates from entering restricted areas in the prison. According to Stewart (2000:8), "we are beginning to see the application of technology widely influencing virtually every aspect of institutional security. In some respects, this influence can be described as a revolution in security innovation." Telemedicine's most valuable asset may be its ability to minimize security risks associated with taking inmates outside of a corrections facility for health care (Weed, 2001).

Despite the usefulness of technological devices in prisons, there are some serious problems with their use. These include constitutional issues, reliability, cost, and their inhumane nature.

CONSTITUTIONAL ISSUES

One of the most controversial legal issues regarding technology and prisons is the right to privacy. Some of these technological devices, such as retina and iris and hand geometry biometrics, can be invasive and may capture information about a person's health and medical history. Recent scientific research suggests that finger imaging might also disclose sensitive medical information about a person. There is a relationship between an uncommon fingerprint pattern, known as a digital arch, and a medical disorder called chronic, intestinal pseudo-obstruction (CIP) that affects 50,000 people nationwide. In addition. Turner syndrome and Klinefelter syndrome and certain nonchromosomal disorders, such as leukemia, breast cancer and Rubella syndrome, may cause certain unusual fingerprint patterns (see Chen, 1988).

The availability of medical and other types of personal information on individuals whether they are inmates, employees, or visitors who are subjected to biometrics raises concern about the right to privacy. It is quite possible that personal information on individuals stored in correctional databases for the purposes of identification and verification could be disseminated to other sources because a biometric system in one correctional facility may be connected with its other databases. Once in use, therefore, a biometric system in a prison may not be confined to its original purpose. The more people who have access to a database, the less likely it is that this information will remain private.

The right to privacy becomes a bigger issue when biometrics is used in conjunction with smart cards. Smart cards, which may contain data, such as medical, financial, and health history and criminal record, can be stolen or lost. Unauthorized individuals who possess lost or stolen smart cards and have means to decrypt the biometric data could discover information that is very personal to the card owners (Esser, 2000).

Another constitutional issue relates to the Eighth Amendment concerning cruel and unusual punishment. There is a great deal of criticism of the use of electroshock devices in prisons because their use in prison is viewed as a violation of the Eighth Amendment. Stun belts, which have two metal prongs positioned just above the left kidney, leave welts that can take up to six months to heal. The belt could cause fatalities. Like the stun belt, the taser, and the stun gun, the shield is an electronic shocking device. Guards frequently use the shield when removing prisoners from their cells, but the death of a Texas corrections officer who suffered a heart attack shortly after receiving a shock from an electric shield similar in design to the stun belt raises serious questions about the belt's safety. As part of his training, Officer Landis was required to endure two 45,000-volt shocks, but on December 1, 1995, something went terribly wrong. Shortly after the second shock, Landis collapsed and died. Although the maker of the shield denied that it had killed Landis, the Coryell County justice of the peace who conducted an inquiry into Landis's death reported that Landis's autopsy showed that he died as a result of cardiac dysrhythmia due to coronary blockage following electric shock by an electronic stun shield. The electric shock threw his heart into a different rhythmic beat, causing him to die. The Texas Department of Criminal Justice, which had used the shields to subdue; prisoners since September 1995 immediately suspended their use (Cusac, 1996; Robert, 2002). In another incident in Virginia, the state used a stun gun repeatedly to shock a 50-year-old prisoner, Lawrence James Frazier, who was already in the infirmary because of his diabetes. Frazier lapsed into a coma and died five days later. Although the Virginia Department of Corrections later claimed that a "medical study" proved that the use of the stun gun did not cause Frazier's death, the study was actually only a review of policies and procedures and did not include an examination of the body or forensic reports (Amnesty International, 2000).

The electric/lethal fence has been criticized for its cruelty. At Calipatria Prison (California), the electric fence has caused the deaths of wild and endangered birds that came in contact with it. This outraged bird lovers and after the "death fence" (as it became known) had become an international environmental scandal, the state was forced to create a birdproof fence (the only one in the world) by using vertical mesh netting that envelops both sides of the electrified fence, thus making it an ecologically sensitive death fence. It also now consists of a warning wire for curious rodents, antiperching deflectors for wildfowl, and tiny passageways for burrowing owls. It has also built an attractive pond for visiting geese and ducks (Davis, 1995).

One of the greatest concerns over the user of electroshock devices is their abuse by the officers and the institution. In a prison, operators of these devices could use them (and the threats of their use) for sadistic purposes or to coerce prisoners to do whatever the operator wants. This would allow these guards to take retribution on the prison population. Amnesty International has criticized the use of high-tech weapons, especially the stun belt, in prisons as torture. It has argued that there is something frightening about them since there is no independent medical testing. Amnesty International found it outrageous that prison officials use the stun belt on inmates with HIV/AIDS in Old Parish Prison in New Orleans. At Old Parish Prison, inmates must sign a release form granting prison officials authorization to fit them with the belt for transportation to health facilities for life-saving medical treatment. What was especially disturbing to Amnesty International was that if an HIV-positive inmate refuses to sign the release, she would be denied transportation and thus denied urgent medical care (Schuiz, 1999). Amnesty International has recommended that federal, state, and local authorities (1) ban the use of remote control electroshock stun belts by law enforcement and correctional agencies and (2) prohibit the manufacture, promotion, distribution, and transfer (both within and from the U.S.) of stun belts and all other electroshock weapons, such as stun guns, stun shields, and lasers pending the outcome of a rigorous, independent, and impartial inquiry into the use and effects of the equipment. The organization also suggested that U.S. companies should cease production of the remote control stun belt and suspend all manufacture, promotion, and transfers of all other stun weapons, pending the aforementioned inquiry (William and Schuiz, 1999).

Reliability and Accuracy

One of the major issues regarding technological devices is their reliability and accuracy. Automated biometric systems, for example, are not 100 percent foolproof. Although fingerprints, the face, and the voice, for example, remain constant from day to day, small fluctuations, such as cold or moist hands, different degree of lighting for face recognition, and background noise for voice authentication can confuse the devices. Setting the sensitivity too low increases the odds of an imposter's logon being accepted (false positive). A high sensitivity setting means increased security but that an authorized user may be erroneously rejected (false negative) (Gunnerson, 1999).

Recently, a scanner that registers traces of microscopic particles associated with 40 different types of drugs at the State Correctional Institution in Woods Run, Pittsburgh, Pennsylvania, gave several false positive results, including one for a prison guard's shift commander (Bucsko, 2001). Also on January 20, 2001, six inmates escaped by circumventing a 5,000-volt malfunctioning electric fence in Alabama by using a broomstick to pry up the electric fence and slide under it. The alarms of the electric fence did not go off (News Tribute Online Edition, 2001).

The geophone-based detector for detecting heartbeats of inmates trying to escape in a vehicle is not without shortcomings as well. The main problem is that it can be used only on a vehicle that is cushioned from the ground by shock absorbers, springs, and rubber tires, for instance. If the vehicle is not cushioned from the ground, the earth itself serves as a kind of vibrational damper. That is, the vehicle and the earth virtually become one solid body. Vibrations from heartbeats are strong enough to move a truck but not strong enough to move the earth. This means that ships, which are essentially one with the water they rest in, and railroad cars, whose rigid steel wheels ride on steel tracks, will not vibrate strongly enough for geophones to detect heartbeats (Strauss, 1997).

High Cost

Although technology has reduced prison cost in many instances, start-up cost can be high. The cost for technological devices in prison is too high for some states. Although high-tech solutions may ultimately reduce staffing demands, they require funds for construction, installation, and training (Weed, 2001). The price tag attached to implementing telemedicine can be high. In Ohio, for example, the largest investment in its telemedicine program was the video hardware, which includes video codecs (coder/decoder), cameras, and monitors. The initial cost of hardware per site was approximately $87,000, and there is the possibility that the equipment will not be usable beyond 5 years (NASCIO, 2001). Likewise, in Texas, telemedicine units alone cost $50,000. The total package, including the unit, communications system, equipment on the receiving end, and software, adds up to a cost per facility of $100,000 to $300,000 (Proctor, 2000). Smart cards could be expensive; each card can cost $8.88; readers, $59; and handheld readers, $8,000. Hardware and software can cost $125,000; systems engineering, $175,000; conversion, $50,000; and support, another $50,000 (Gaseau, 1999). The installation of Arizona's lethal fence will cost $1.2 million (Tugan, 2000) and the chair in Arizona's prison that scans inmates for weapons costs $6,500 (Lau, 2001).

Apart from the specific problems discussed, there are still some general issues and questions regarding the use of technology. One is the effect that technology will have on the relationship between the inmate and correctional officers. One wonders whether the increased isolation (because of technology) between inmates and officers will increase inmates' hostilities toward officers. After years of being exposed to this coercive environment of technological devices, how would the inmates adapt to society on the outside once they are released? What are the physical and psychological effects of years of exposure of inmates to technological devices? What are the goals of all this technological gadgetry? Are these goals being achieved? Finally what types of prisoners are being created with this extensive use of technology? Will inmates be turned into robots? These are some of the unanswered questions that have not been addressed as society continues to create prisons with the prison system using the high-tech devices.

RECOMMENDATIONS

Although technological devices are beginning to revolutionalize the prison system, they are subjected to manipulation, and more needs to be done to prevent abuses. The following are some recommendations designed to improve the use of technological devices:

1. To curtail the unauthorized use of technology by prison personnel. Congress should pass legislation regulating its use. The legislation should clearly stipulate that the use of a technological device should be limited to its original purpose. Violation of the legislation should result in criminal sanctions.
2. State and federal governments should ensure that technological databases in prison are physically secured. Any physical documents pertaining to the database should be kept in a secured area protected by security personnel, alarm systems, video surveillance, and other related security devices to prevent unauthorized access to the information (see Woodward, 1997).
3. To prevent constitution challenges to the use of technology in prisons, manufacturers should work closely with legal scholars to ensure that their systems are secure and not subject to constitutional challenges.
4. To maximize the use of technology, all states should establish technology review committees in prison to evaluate various technologies before purchasing or using them. The benefit of such committees is that the prison agency becomes more knowledgeable about technological needs and requirements.
5. State and federal governments should force manufacturers of these devices to conduct comprehensive tests to determine their reliability, accuracy, and safety.

SUMMARY

Over the last decade, technological innovation has spurred the development of new devices to improve supervision in prisons. Technological advances have occurred in virtually every aspect of prison life and have led to changing roles for prison officials. Management information systems and smart cards have been introduced for a more affordable and comprehensive means of tracking inmate activities. Perimeter detectors, biometrics, and electroshock devices can prevent prison escapes. Drug and alcohol abuse testing packages, telemedicine, and videoconferencing are all advances in the use of technology in prisons.

The extensive use of technology in prison has created images of an Orwellian nightmare in which "Big Brother" watches, detects, secures, and contains inmates all across the United States through technological devices. It is expected that technology will increase its appeal to prison administrators and politicians because of its versatility. Consequently, future prisons will become more and more technologically sophisticated.

It is undeniably true that through the use of the technological gadgetry, a large number of inmates can be supervised. However, as the prisons continue to be an integral part of the technological revolution, this gadgetry presents challenges. Administrators should be cautious not to rely on technology to the point that safety is compromised. It is also important for prison officials to remember that technologies are devices that require well-trained staff to operate them. It is also perhaps too early to evaluate whether high-tech supervision will, in the long run, be the most cost-effective, efficient, and safest way to operate prisons. All new technology has negative aspects, and only time will tell how effective they really are. What is quite clear is that prisons have become part of the technological landscape and technology will continue to affect the way prisons are operated in the United States.

REFERENCES

Abt Associated. (1999). Abt Associates finds use of telemedicine can reduce health care costs in prisons. [Retrieved February 15, 2003, from http://www.abtassoc.com/html/newsroom/press-releases/pr-telemedicine.html]

Administration Office of the United States Courts. (2001). Videoconferencing in courts shows potential and possible problems. The Third Branch: Newsletter of the Federal Courts, 33(12). Available online at http://www.uscourts.gov/ttb/dec0lttb/videoconferencing.html

Alanco Technologies, Inc. (2003). Alanco completes largest TSI PRISM contract at the Logan Correctional Facility in Illinois. Available online at fhttp ://www. alanco. com/releases/051503. asp

Associated Press State and Local Wire. (2002). Prison inmates now make court appearances via TV (April 15).

Amnesty International. (2000). After prison stun gun death, Virginia refuses Amnesty International visit: Amnesty International demands VA suspend electroshock stun gun use. Washington, DC: Amnesty International. Available online at http://www.amnestyusa.org/news/2000/usa07ll2000.html1

Blackburn, D. M., Bone, J. M., & Phillips, P. J. (2001, February). Facial Recognition Vendor Test. (FRVT Evaluation Report) www.frvt.com/FRVT2000/documents. htm?tag=Nl

Buscko, M. (2001). Scanning of prison visitors under fire: Inaccurate drug detector prompts unfair penalties. *Pittsburgh Post-Gazette*: B5.

Business Wire. (2001). TELEQUIP to provide inmate calling systems for AT&T (November 1). Available online at fhttp://www.TNETIX.com/news/default.asp?a =detail&p=1&r= 1071

Business Wire. (2003). Alanco completes largest TSI PRISM contract at the Logan Correctional Facility in Illinois (May 15). Available online at http:www.business-wire.com

Campbell, J. P, Alyea, L. A., & Dunn, J. (1996). Biometric security: Government applications and operations. At 1 in CardTech/SecurTech (CTST). Government Conference Proceedings. Available online at rhttp://www.biometrics.org/ REPORTS/CTSTG9611

Caramanis, C. B. (1999). Detection and monitoring technologies help DOC become virtually drug-free. The Corrections Connection. (February). Available online at fhttp://www.corrections.com/news/technology/detection.html

Center for Criminal Justice Technology Newsletter. (2001). Biometrics at York County (Pa) prison (June 18). Available online at http://www.mitretek.org/business areas/justice/cjiti/ccjtnews/weekly/vol5-4.html

Chandrasekaran, R. (1997). Brave new whorl: ID systems using the human body are here, but privacy issues persist, *Washington Post* (March 30): HI.

Chen, H. (1988). Medical genetics handbook. St. Louis, MO: W.H. Green.

Colatosti, T. (1998). Wisconsin Department of Corrections Chooses Viisage. Viisage Technology, Inc. (November 18). Available online at http//www.viisage.com

Corrections Connection. (2001). Florida DOC increases security with identification technology. http ://www. corrections. com/technetwork/t html

Cruelty in Control? The stun belt and other electroshock weapons in law enforcement. Published by: Rights for All: Amnesty International's campaign on the United States of America, www.amnestyusa.org/rightsforall/situ

Cusac, A. (1996). Stunning technology. *Progressive, 60*(7): 18-22.

Davis, M. (1995). Hell factories in the field: A prison-industrial complex. *Nation*, 260(7): 229-234.

deGroot, G. (1997). Hot new technologies. *Corrections Today*, 59(4): 60-62.

Desmarais, N. (2000). Biometrics and network security. Information Technology Interest Group, New England Chapter (November/December), Available online at http://www.abacus.bates.edu/acrinec/sigs/itig/ tc_nov_dec2000.htm

Directions. (2001). ADC brings in the boss: 1 (8) Available online at http://www.adc.state.az.us/Directions/2001/julydirections2001]. Publications of Arizona Department of Corrections.

Esser, M. (2000). Biometric Authentication. Available online at http://www.faculty.ed.umuc.edu/-meinkej/inss690/messer/Paper

Finger-scan.com. (1999). Finger scan technology. Available online at http://www.finger-scan.com./fingerscan_technology.htm#0ptical. Silicon, Ultrasound

Fujitsu Australia. (2001). Fujitsu smart card solution for Australia's 21st century prison. Retrieved February 16, 2003, from http://www.au.fujitsu.com/FAL/CDA/Articles/0.1029.305- 1063.00.htm1

Gailiun, M. (1997). Telemedicine. *Corrections Today, 59*(4): 68-70.

Gaseau, M. (1999). Corrections technology options are expanding. *Corrections Today, 61*(6), 22-25.

Gunnerson, G. (1999). Are you ready for biometrics? Available online at http://www.zdnet.com/products/stories/reviews/0.4161.386987-2.00.html

Index (2000). M. Lockie (ed.): Biometric Technology Today Compsec Publications–dmoz.org/Computers/Security/Biometrics

Ion Track. (2002). Prisons. Available online at http://www.iontrack.com/applications/prisons/notes.html

Iosoftware. (2000). Biometrics explained. Available online at http://www.iosoftware.com/biometrics/explained•htm

Isaacs, L. (2002a). Emerging technologies use physical characteristics to verify identities of residents and employees. *American City and County, 117*(3): 22-27.

Isaacs, L. (2002b). Body language. *American City and County, 117*(3): 22-27.

Jackson, K. (1998a). Evaluating correctional technology. *Corrections Today, 60*(4,): 58-67.

Jackson, K. (1998b). The application of security measures. *Corrections Today, 60*(4): 58-67.

Justice Technology Information Network. (1998). Ohio inmates get "carded." Available online at http://www.nlectc.org/viriib/InfoDetail.asp?intInfoID=2931

Kelley, D., & Oien, K. (2000). Implementing biometric technology to enhance correctional safety and security. Available online at http://tunxis.commnet.edu/ccjci/futures/classviii/kelley_oien.html

Lau, J. (2001). Inmates hide assortment of metallic items. 08/16/2001–NLECTC News Summary. Available online at rhttp://www.mail-archive.com/justnet-news@nlectc.org/msg00068.html

Miller, B. (1996). Everything you need to know about automated biometric identification. CardTech/SecurTech (CTST) Government Conference Proceedings: 1.

Miller, M. (2002). Live video used in court case; keeps dangerous criminals in jail. *The Capital Times* (Madison, WI) (March 20): 3A.

Nascio (2001). Ohio-telemedicine-innovative use of technology. Available online at http://www.nascio.org/awards/1998awards/Innovative/ohio.cfm

National Law Enforcement and Corrections Technology Center. (2000). TechBeat Fall 2000. Available online at http://www.nlectc.org/txtfiles/tbfaU2000.html

News Tribute Online Edition. (2001). 5 of 6 Alabama escapees caught in Tennessee. Available online at http://www.newstribune.com/stories/020101/wor_0201010013.asphttp://www.new

Pries, A. (2001). Looking into the future; Iris recognition: Could replace pins and passwords. *Bergen Record* (August 6): L6.

Proctor, J. (October 2000). Medicine behind bars: Texas telemedicine experiment. *AAMC News Reporter, 9* 13. UTMB Correctional Managed Care CMC Publication.

Reid, K. (2001). Detection devices squelch escape tries in just a heartbeat: Prisons screen vehicles at gate. *Chicago Tribune* (September 10): B7.
Ritter, J. (1999). Eye scans help sheriff keep suspects in sight. *Chicago Sun-Times* (June 22):18.
Roberti, M. (2002). Big brother goes behind bars. *Fortune* (September 30): 44.
Schulz, W. (1999). Cruelty in control? The stun belt and other electroshock weapons in law enforcement. Washington, DC: Amnesty International USA. Available online at http ://www •amnestyusa.org/rightsforall/stun/press-schulz.html
Stewart, T. L. (2000). Technology and security–Opportunities and challenges. *Corrections Today, 62* (4): 8-9.
Strauss, S. (1997). Detecting stowaways. *Technology Review, 100*(1): 14-15.
Tierney, T. (1995). Eyes have it in future of law enforcement: Technology expands to identify suspects. *Chicago Tribune* (June 27): 1.
Tugan, B. (2000). $100 million prison to open September 8. *Las Vegas Sun* (Nov. 12, 2001). Available online at http://www.ndoc.state.nv.us/news/display.php?article_id=8
Ultimate Scam. (2002). Smart card 'n microchips. Available online at http://www.members.shaw.ca/theultimatescam/Smart20Card.html
Weed, W. S. (2001). Future tech: Iron bars, silicon chips: High-tech prison reform comes to America's state and federal inmates. *Discover, 22*(5). [Retrieved February 20, 2003, from http://www.discover.com/may_01/feattech.html
Weiss, D. (2003). Court teleconferencing a big money saver. *Times Leader* (May 2). Available online at http://www.timesleader.com/mld/timesleader/news/5898553.html
Wired News (1997). Prisons aim to keep, and keep ahead of, convicts. Retrieved February 23, 2003, from Available online at http://www.wired.com/news/technology/0.1282.8583.00.htm
Wood, M. (2000). Overview of biometric encryption. Information Security Reading Room. Available online at http://www.rr.sans.org/authentic/biometric3.php
Woodward, J. D. (1997). Biometric scanning, law, and policy: Identifying the concerns–Drafting the biometric blueprint. *University of Pittsburgh Law Review, 59*: 97.
Wright. S, & Butler, R. F. (2001). Can drug detection technology stop drugs from entering prisons? *Corrections Today, 63*(4): 66-69.
Yeoman, B. (2000). Shocking discipline. *Mother Jones, 25*(2): 17-18.
ZDNet. (1999). How biometrics works. Available online at http://www.zdnet.com/products/stories/reviews/0.4161.2199371.00.htm
Zunkel, R. (1998). Hand geometry based verification. In Biometrics: Personal identification in networked society. A. Jain, R. Bolle, & S. Pankanti, (Eds.), 87-102. Norwell, MA: Kluwer Academic Publishers.

Part IV

CRIMINALITY AND TECHNOLOGY

Chapter 12

COMPUTER FORENSICS

ROBYN DIEHL LACKS AND CHRISTINE BRYCE

For the past few decades, information technology (IT) has become an integral part of mainstream America. Millions of Americans spend more hours a day in front of a computer than taking part in any other daily activity (Noblett, Pollitt, & Presley, 2000). Americans spend more time sending and receiving e-mails, conducting research on the Web, and utilizing and maintaining computer databases than watching television. Just as the computer revolution has made our lives more efficient, it has made the lives of criminals more efficient as well. A large number of criminals use pagers, cell phones, computers, e-mail, and network servers to conduct their criminal enterprises: A hacker may infiltrate a computer network to obtain bank codes to embezzle money or may utilize e-mail to send death threats; a drug dealer may use pagers, cell phones, and e-mail to coordinate the manufacturing and distribution of contraband. In other cases, computers are merely used as an electronic device to store information about criminal activities: A bookie might keep a list of the money she is owed in a spreadsheet in her computer.

Computer-based crimes cost businesses throughout the United States over one billion dollars each year. In 1996, banks, insurance companies, and securities industries lost over $800 million to technologically driven crimes. In 1998 one computer-based crime alone cost a large-scale business in the United States almost $3 billion (Noblett, Pollitt, & Presley, 2000).

An FBI survey of corporations and government agencies conducted by the Computer Survey Institute (CSI) found that over 240 of those businesses surveyed had suffered some type of financial loss due to computer-based crimes (Noblett, Pollitt, & Presley, 2000). It is likely that this financial loss is only a small portion of the actual loss that occurs. The low estimate of computer-related crimes occurring in the United States is due to a lack of reporting to law enforcement by victims of computer-based crimes. In general, only 17% of businesses that suffer financial loss due to computer crimes report the crime to law enforcement each year. In the CSI survey, most businesses stated that they were not willing to report computer crimes to the authorities because they felt vulnerable when potential information about their computer network system might be exposed (Noblett, Pollitt, & Presley, 2000). For example, they may feel that reporting that someone had hacked into the company's network might make other hackers attempt to do the same or make the public believe that their personal information stored with the company is vulnerable to attack. Respondents regularly reported that they did not believe the authorities had the technology or knowledge needed to investigate, prosecute, or prevent such crimes (Noblett, Pollitt, & Presley, 2000).

On the state and local level, computer-related crimes have increased dramatically over the past 10 years. However, the computer-related crimes seen at the state and local level are typically traditional crimes involving electronic evidence. The proliferation of e-mail, Internet use, cell phones, pagers, and other computer products has made it easier and more convenient for many criminals to conduct their "business" (i.e., crime).

Based on statements such as these and the increase in computer-related crimes it is imperative that law enforcement agencies and prosecutors gain the technology, skills, and abilities to obtain electronic evidence stored in computers. This chapter addresses these issues by examining the role of information technology, specifically computer forensics, in the field of law enforcement by first presenting a high-level overview of computer forensics. Included will be various definitions, aspects, and activities as well as an exploration of the state and federal laws governing information technology in the criminal justice system. Secondly, the major computer crimes will be examined as well as the software that has been created to investigate and protect against such crimes. Finally, a case study of the Virginia State Police's Computer Crime Unit will be presented.

TYPES OF COMPUTER CRIMES

The FBI's Uniform Crime Reporting (UCR) National Incident-Based Reporting System (NIBRS) identifies over 45 criminal offenses in 22 categories including crimes perpetrated using computers (Goodman, 2001). To acquire this data NIBRS allows for the investigating agency to identify whether a computer was used during the commission of any offense. By identifying computer-related crimes in this manner, the ability to measure the extent to which computers are utilized in the commission of crimes is established as well as the ability to identify computer-related crime trends among all offense categories. According to a Department of Justice report, 42% of all crimes committed with a computer are defined as economic crimes (Barnett, 2000). The largest portion (31%) of these economic crimes in which a computer was used is larceny or theft.

Identity theft is the leading type of theft utilizing a computer. Identity theft is defined as someone appropriating another person's personal information without his or her knowledge to commit theft or fraud (U.S. Department of Justice, 2002). Identity theft most often occurs when a person divulges sensitive personal information to what they believe is a legitimate business. This personal identifying information is used to establish or assume existing credit card, bank, or utilities accounts. For example, the identity information can be used to open a credit card account and to make fraudulent charges.

Beyond identity theft, there are many other examples of computer-related fraud. Credit card schemes are a widely reported form of computer-related fraud. Credit card schemes occur when an unauthorized credit card account number is used to fraudulently obtain money or property. This most often occurs when credit card numbers are stolen from unsecured Websites. Additional computer fraud schemes include counterfeit check schemes, business/employment schemes, and online auction or retail schemes.

As previously mentioned, even though economic crime, specifically fraud, is the largest computer-related crime, computers are utilized in the commission of many other offenses. This is especially true at the state and local level. On average computers are utilized in over 50% of all other types of criminal offenses (U.S. Department of Justice, 2002). The most frequent examples are child pornography, narcotics, sexual offenses, and arson. Many researchers in the field of computer crime have stated that the number of offenses in which a computer is utilized has increased exponentially in recent years. This is not only because criminals are utilizing technology at a higher rate but also because the procedures and tools that law enforcement utilize to recover evidence from computers has been greatly enhanced. In recent years the tools and skill sets of forensic examiners to investigate computer-related crimes has allowed for more accurate computer crime data to be reported. The greatest advancement for law enforcement in investigating computer-related crimes is the increase in the complexity of the computer forensic process. The next sections explain the computer forensic processes used in criminal investigations

DEFINING COMPUTER FORENSICS

The utilization of computer technology to investigate computer-based crimes has brought forth one of the newest fields in law enforcement: computer forensics. There are several definitions of forensic computing that range from the strict policing, to the scientific, to the broad legal code definition. The *policing* definition is narrow in focus and identifies computer forensics as "the process of identifying, preserving, analyzing and presenting digital evidence in a manner that is legally acceptable" (McKemmish, 1999). The *forensic* definition is more scientific in its approach and defines the concept as the "collection of techniques and tools used to find evidence in a computer" (Caloyannides, 2001) while the *legalistic* definition is the broadest and defines computer forensics as "the preservation, identification, extraction, documentation, and interpretation of computer data" (Kruse & Heiser, 2002).

Based on the disciplines in which these definitions have been created, one can see the common aspects as well as the unique differences. Computer forensics draws on not only technical computer skills and criminal investigation skills, but also on the combination and effective utilization of both of these skill sets within the court system. Law enforcement professionals must not only understand all of the complexities and appropriate techniques associated with utilizing technology to investigate crimes and collect evidence, but they must also maintain legally acceptable procedures and have thorough knowledge of the various case law surrounding each investigation. These complexities highlight how computer forensics draws from a multitude of disciplines within the criminal justice system. As a result, it is imperative that there is a fundamental understanding of both the various definitions of computer forensics and the primary areas associated with the discipline if one hopes to accurately investigate computer crimes in a judicially appropriate manner.

COMPUTER FORENSIC ACTIVITIES

Along with the primary areas of computer forensics, there are also some uniform activities that all criminal justice professionals should recognize and should do when investigating crimes. The major activities include 1) media and electronic device analysis, 2) data communication analysis, and 3) research and development (McKemmish, 1999; Casey, 2002; Kessler, 2004).

The first activity–analysis of media and electronic devices–relates to the examination of all devices that store electronic media, which can be utilized in criminal investigations. These types of devices include computer hard disk drives, computer disks, DVDs, CDs, zip disks, thumb drives, cell phones, pagers, and personal data assistants (PDAs). The examiner must be knowledgeable of the actual structure or device holding the electronic media as well as the way in which the data are stored in the device. The efficiency of this process has greatly increased in recent years with the development of data recovery software. Software such as Encase makes the media analysis process more accessible to a larger scope of criminal justice professionals (McKemmish, 1999). It is important to note that even though software technology has enhanced the ability of law enforcement professionals to understand electronic evidence, trained examiners should still conduct the analysis.

The second activity in computer forensics is the analysis of data communication. Data communication is most directly associated with the utilization of computer forensics for Internet–based analysis. Network intrusion or misuse and data acquisition are the main

Internet-based computer forensic activities; they consist of intrusion detection, evidence preservation and activity reconstruction. Network intrusion detection activities most often involve the utilization of specialized software and hardware to monitor potentially unlawful activities utilizing the Internet. The behaviors that are most often associated with network intrusion and misuse are "unauthorized access, remote system modification, and unauthorized monitoring of data packets" (McKemmish, 1999, p. 2). To conduct these activities successfully, computer forensic examiners must be able to acquire the data from the network while working closely with software engineers and cryptographers to understand and utilize the data acquired in criminal investigations. For example, the analysis of data communication is most often utilized in tracking computer network hackers or those who transmit a computer virus.

The third activity in computer forensics–research and development–is one of the most important activities. It is in the research and development activity that computer forensic units are able to identify the newest trends in computer crimes as well as software and technology advancements for use in criminal investigations. Unfortunately, most law enforcement agencies do not have the additional resources necessary to conduct the research and development necessary to prevent electronic crimes; instead, they must utilize the devices that are currently in place.

AREAS OF COMPUTER FORENSICS AND THE COMPUTER FORENSIC EVIDENCE RECOVERY PROCESS

According to most computer forensic experts, there are four fundamental components that, if followed, increase the likelihood of the computer forensic evidence being legally acceptable. The four fundamental components of computer forensics that all criminal justice professionals should be aware of are 1) identification, 2) preservation, 3) analysis, and 4) presentation of digital evidence in a legally appropriate manner that is effective and acceptable in the courtroom. It is important to note that when examining these four components of forensic computing examiners, we are talking about not only extracting evidence from personal computers or other such computer devices but also the removal of evidence from any electronic device that stores information such as cellular phones, pagers, digital cameras, and electronic organizers (McKemmish, 1999).

The first component, the identification of technological evidence, is the process of identifying what technological evidence is present, what evidentiary material it may contain, and establishing an appropriate plan for removing the evidence from the crime scene while maintaining its authenticity (Casey, 2002). The identification component is not only the first but also the most important of the four components. This is because it allows both the lead investigator and the forensic examiner to determine what items to include in a search warrant and to form the most effective plan for the search and seizure of evidence.

The second component, the preservation of electronic evidence, is the key aspect of forensic computing concerning the judicial system. The computer forensic process commences once the computer evidence has been seized. Generally, this process begins with acquiring a **bitstream** image of the original evidence storage media, which are usually hard disk drives, but also includes diskettes, CDs, and DVDs. A bitstream image replicates all data versus a "copy" that may only contain current data accessible by the operating system. This bitstream image must be made by protecting the original evidence from change, thereby preserving the authenticity of the original electronic evidence. Thus, examiners use either hardware write-blocking devices or software **write-blocking** programs. Write-blocking prevents any data from being added, removed, or altered on the original device. Using either a hardware or software write-blocking device, additional software is used to make the bitstream image and to **hash** the image. Once the original evidence has been imaged and hashed, the original evidence is stored according to operating procedures. It is after the imaging process occurs that the actual examination begins.

It is most important during the preservation component that all processes are recorded and documented for presentation in court. To be successful in court, the forensic examiner must be able to document the process utilized in the extraction. Accurately conducted and clearly documented preservation of digital evidence allows for the effective prosecution of criminals in the courtroom. However, when the process is not accurately conducted or clearly documented the evidence instead becomes more useful for the defense to establish doubt about the case.

The third component, the analysis of electronic evidence, includes the processing and analyzing of the electronic evidence that has been bitstream imaged from the storage device in question. After the data have been extracted from the electronic medium they must be analyzed and presented in an understandable and useable manner for investigation. This component is the most commonly recognized aspect of computer forensics, allowing the forensic examiner to serve as a translator of the electronic data for the criminal investigator. When electronic data are recovered, it must be analyzed and then translated into a form that is meaningful to the investigation.

A variety of software tools allow the forensic examiner to do this. Most examiners use automated forensic software tools. The software most often used fall into two main categories: 1) primary forensic products that image, hash, and analyze, and 2) secondary/supplementary forensic products that perform limited or more narrow functions. The most frequently used products are **Encase, Forensic Toolkit (FTK)**, and **Ilook**. These all-inclusive products create bitstream images, provide hash values, have multiple search and analysis features, and create forensic reports. Each of these "big three" forensic products have a GUI-based interface that allows examiners to easily manage large volumes of data, display all data (deleted files, file slack, and unallocated), search the data, and produce report-generating options. Each of these products also has strengths and weaknesses, and it is best to have a variety of computer forensic tools available.

For special circumstances and features other forensic software products also exist. For example, **PDA Seizure** is made specifically for imaging and examining personal digital devices such as Palms, Blackberrys, and other similar devices. **E-mail Examiner** analyzes e-mails particularly well and allows the examiner to view the data in a "native" format. **NetAnalysis** processes both the Internet History files and the unallocated areas for Internet and network activity. **NavRoad** displays html and Internet image files offline. **Password Recovery Toolkit** recovers passwords on protected files and systems. **ACDSee** displays virtually all graphic files. Many other forensic tools exist as well. Overall, there has been great advancements in the tools that forensic examiners have at their disposal to investigate computer-related crimes. Ultimately, these tools allow for the examiners to offer law enforcement professionals more evidence to investigate criminal offenses.

The fourth component, the presentation of the electronic evidence is the final component of the forensic computing process. Law enforcement professionals must be able to effectively present the electronic evidence if it is to be effectual in court. The examiner or other appointed law enforcement professional must be able to explain how the evidence is extracted, maintained, analyzed, and utilized in the overall criminal investigation. The key aspect during the fourth component focuses on the training, the qualifications, and the ability of the forensic examiner and criminal investigator to present the highly technical evidence in an understandable fashion in the courtroom. The fourth component determines the effectiveness of computer forensics process and its impact on the crime (Casey, 2002).

LEGAL ISSUES ASSOCIATED WITH COMPUTER FORENSICS

The increased use of technology in criminal investigation has not only increased the utilization of computer forensics, the tools used by examiners, and the evidence offered to investigators, but has also led to an increase in the number of legal issues associated with utilizing electronic evidence in criminal investigations. These legal issues have included the creation of both state and federal statutes to prosecute computer and computer-related crimes as well as the development of laws governing electronic evidence recovery, specifically search and seizure techniques.

State and Federal Computer-Related Crime Statutes

In 1978 the Virginia General Assembly enacted one of the first computer crime statutes in response to one of the first computer crime cases prosecuted, *Lund* v. *Commonwealth of Virginia* (1977). Originally, existing offense statutes were used to criminalize "hacking" or unauthorized use of computer systems. In the 1970s several "computer crime" cases were tried without success, which led to the creation of computer crime laws.

In *Lund* v. *Virginia*, Lund was a Ph.D. candidate at Virginia Polytechnic Institute who was charged with using the university's computer system without authorization and was tried for grand larceny.

Virginia claimed that the printouts Lund created from his unauthorized use of the computer system were worth $5,000. The Supreme Court of Virginia disagreed and found that the only offense was the theft of "scrap paper."

The failure of this case brought about the movement to create the first "Computer Crime" statutes–making "theft of computer services" and "unauthorized use of computer systems" separate criminal activities (i.e., crimes). The statutes defined computer crime as "services or property which may be the subject of larceny, embezzlement, or false pretense" (Code of Virginia, 2004). The statutes were established to allow stolen computer time and/or services to be consider illegal activities. Prior to the statute, computer time and services were not deemed as "goods" thus they could not be stolen (i.e., did not meet the definition of theft or larceny).

In 1984, Virginia refined the statute by creating a clearly defined act with 14 sections and 5 identified computer crimes: 1) computer fraud, 2) computer trespass, 3) computer invasion of privacy, 4) theft of computer services, and 5) personal trespass by computers. The Virginia Computer Crimes Act of 1984 (Virginia Code, Section 18.2-152.1-16) defined computer-based offenses as a newly identified, independent crime instead of expanding an already existing crime. Following on the heels of the Virginia Computer Crime Act of 1984, the Counterfeit Access Device and Computer Fraud and Abuse Law of 1984 was established at the federal level. This federal act was created with a narrow focus to "protect classified United States" defense and foreign relations information, financial institution and consumer reporting agency files, and access to computers operated for the government" (U.S. Department of Justice, 2002).

In response to the narrow purview of the Counterfeit Access Device and Computer Fraud and Abuse Law of 1984 and the increasing number of computer-related offenses, the National Information Infrastructure Protection Act of 1996 was created. This expanded the federal jurisdiction over technology-based offenses to include not only computers used for interstate commerce activities and communications but also all federal interest computers. Later expansion of the 1996 Act included not only all federal interest computers but also five additional subsections geared toward computer-related crimes.

The first subsection [1030(a)(1)] makes accessing computer files without authorization and transmitting classified government information a crime. The second subsection [1030 (a)(2)] prohibits unauthorized obtaining or gaining access to authorized financial, government, or private sector information used in interstate commerce. The third subsection [1030 (a)(3)] directly relates to intentionally accessing U.S. Department or agency nonpublic computers without authorization, while the fourth subsection [1030 (a)(4)] addresses accessing protected computers with an intent to defraud or obtain something of value. The fifth subsection [1030 (a)(5)], the one most well known to the general public, addresses computer hacking that is intentionally, recklessly, or negligently conducted. It is important to note that only one of these criteria needs to be met to be considered a criminal act (Noblett, Politt, & Presley, 2000).

It was the National Information Infrastructure Protection Act of 1996 that limited much of the jurisdictional defenses that were formerly available under the original Act of 1994. These included computer-based crimes only being prosecutable when a computer of federal interest was accessed without authorization. It was the 1996 Act that closed many of the legal loopholes and increased the prosecutorial ammunition for the justice system when it is investigating and prosecuting computer-based crimes. The 1996 Act was one of the largest pieces of federal computer-based legislation, however, it is not the only federal statute addressing computer-based crimes. There are over 40 federal statutes that address other computer-related crimes beyond computer fraud and abuse including copyright issues, national stolen property, mail and fraud, electronic communications, privacy, and child pornography issues. However, no matter how elaborate the state and federal laws are to obtain and present electronic evidence in court the evidence must first be acquired and seized in a lawful manner in accordance with the Fourth Amendment.

Electronic Evidence Recovery: Search and Seizure Legal Requirements

The Fourth Amendment has always governed the recovery of evidence by law enforcement to be utilized in criminal prosecution; electronic evidence recovery is impacted by the amendment in the same manner. It is the Fourth Amendment that limits the government's ability to search for evidence without a warrant (U. S. Department of Justice, 2002). More specifically, the Fourth Amendment states:

> The right of the people to be secure in their persons, houses, papers, and effects, against unreasonable searches and seizures, shall not be violated, and no Warrants shall issue, but upon probable cause, supported by Oath or affirmation, and particularly describing the place to be searched, and the persons or things to be seized. (United States Constitution)

Based on the *Illinois* v. *Andreas* [463 U.S. 765, 771 (1983)] and *Illinois* v. *Rodriguez* [497 U.S. 177, 185 (1990)] cases, the Supreme Court ruled that a warrantless search does not violate the Fourth Amendment if one of two conditions are satisfied. The first condition is that the government's conduct does not violate a person's reasonable or legitimate expectation of privacy (U. S. Department of Justice, 2002). An individual's expectation of privacy is established in one of two ways: 1) "if the individual's conduct reflects an actual subjective expectation of privacy, or 2) an individual's subjective expectation of privacy is one that society is prepared to recognize as reasonable" (U. S. Department of Justice, 2002, 1).

The legal stipulations for expectation of privacy for information stored in computers and other electronic storage devices follow similar guidelines as those established by the Supreme Court in *Illinois* v. *Andreas* (1983). According to the Fourth Amendment a computer is treated like a closed container similar to a briefcase or a file cabinet. Just as the Fourth Amendment prohibits the search of either of these containers without a warrant, law enforcement professionals must also obtain a warrant to search any electronic information stored in computers or other electronic storage devices. It is important to note that law enforcement is not required to obtain a separate warrant for each file in the computer or electronic storing device because they are not treated as a separate file or closed container, but instead as one entire unit.

There are several situations in which reasonable expectations of privacy with regards to the storage of information in electronic devices is not automatically assumed, specifically in third-party possession and private search situations. Individuals may lose their Fourth Amendment rights regarding files in their computer when they turn over the information to a third party who uses the information for personal gains. For example, a stockbroker e-mails a preferred customer list of high profile clients to the competition and local law enforcement professionals search the competition's computer and find the list of customers. The list of clients obtained from the competition's computer without a warrant is not a breach of the broker's Fourth Amendment rights. This is because the broker lost his reasonable expectation of privacy when he voluntarily turned over his files to a third party, the competition, to be used for additional purposes (*United States* v. *Horowitz*, 806 F.2d 1222 (4th Cir, 1986).

Third-party possession only disregards reasonable expectation of privacy when the third party has an expectation to utilize the information obtained from the electronic device in an additional means or manner. For example, a computer that is brought to an examiner for repairs cannot be examined for information stored within the device without a warrant. Because the computer was sent to the examiner for repairs, the owner of the computer retains control over the computer and its contents. It was never the assumption of the computer's owner to give the information in the files over to the examiner for personal use. As a result, the owner's expectation of privacy is to be maintained, and a warrant is needed to search the computer (U. S. Department of Justice, 2002).

It is important to note, had the examiner conducted a private search on his own of the computer and discovered files that he felt were criminal in nature and called the police, they could have legally searched the computer without a warrant. This is because the Fourth Amendment does not apply to the rights of an owner of a computer when an individual not serving as a government agent conducts a private search and calls in law enforcement to examine what is discovered. The expectation of privacy is not assumed and thus a warrant for a search is not required for the evidence to be admissible in court.

The second condition in which a warrantless search can be conducted legally is when the reasonable expectation of privacy is violated but the search falls within the established expectation of warrant requirements (U. S. Department of Justice, 2002). For example, law enforcement professionals may search a dwelling or object without a warrant if consent for the search is given by a person of authority. This can be a business partner, spouse, parent, or owner of a residence. The scope of the consent granted by the person of authority and the evidence recovered expanding beyond the scope of the consent varies based on the facts of each case presented (*Schneckloth* v. *Bustamonte*, 412 U.S. 218, 219 [1973]). In attempting to address the parameters in which the person of authority granted the verbal consent, it is helpful for law enforcement to obtain clearly written consent in which the scope of consent includes electronic information contained in storage devices.

It is important to note, when attempting to gain consent from a person of authority for electronic information stored in computer networks, law enforcement should always address the system administrator. All computer networks have system administrators or system operators who have the ability to access all files in the network at the most fundamental level. According to the Electronic Communications Privacy Act, system administrators can grant law enforcement agents the authority to search the files of a computer network without a warrant (*Stoner* v. *California*, 376 U.S. 483 [1964]).

The advancements in computer technology and the storage of information in electronic devices have brought forth a variety of legal issues. It is clear that legally searching electronic storage devices for evidence of criminal activity is complicated at best. For law enforcement to be effective in the acquisition of information stored in electronic devices, they must be aware of all of the legal issues associated with computer- related crimes. Communication must be high among a variety of individuals, including law enforcement agents, forensic examiners, and prosecuting attorneys for such awareness to occur. Such communications establish the multidisciplinary nature of computer forensics and can more clearly be seen in an examination of the Virginia State Police's Computer Crime Unit.

VIRGINIA STATE POLICE'S COMPUTER CRIME UNIT: A CASE STUDY

The Commonwealth of Virginia has been proactive toward computer-related crimes since the seminal legislation related to computer crimes in 1978 led to the creation of the Virginia State Police's Computer Evidence Recovery Unit. In 2003 alone Virginia prosecuted over 60 cases in which technology was utilized in some aspect of the criminal act. Over 100 computers or other related equipment were seized in these criminal investigations. Based on the high number of computer-related cases that the Virginia State Police have investigated in recent years, the Computer Evidence Recovery Unit has been successful in its creation as well as its implementation and serves as a useful case study for other law enforcement agencies.

The Virginia State Police Computer Evidence Recovery Unit (CERU) began on July 1, 1996, utilizing a federal grant from the Department of Criminal Justice Services, which has since expired. CERU formed to provide assistance for local, state, and federal law enforcement agencies and assist with on-scene execution of search warrants for computer-related evidence. CERU provides computer evidence recovery services, forensic examination services, and expert testimony to Virginia law enforcement agencies through in-depth forensic examinations of computer data stored or seized during the course of a criminal investigation. CERU also provides Virginia law enforcement officer training in the areas of identifying and seizing computer-related evidence. Recently, CERU, in coordination with the Virginia Office of the Attorney General, established a child pornography images registry. CERU staff is comprised of both sworn and civilian examiners who respond to crime scenes to assist in the seizure of computer systems and related evidence and subsequently recover notable and evidentiary data from the computers. Since its inception, CERU has completed over 500 examinations for local, state, and federal criminal cases. CERU's cases typically include child pornography; embezzlement and fraudulent conversion; manufacturing, sales, and distribution of illegal drugs; sexual battery and assault; homicide; suicide; credit card offenses; rape; computer trespass; stalking; and identity theft.

CERU works closely with its companion unit, the Virginia State Police High Tech Crimes Unit (HTCU). HTCU was formed on September 1, 1998, and is comprised of eight High Technology Crime Special Agents. HTCU agents investigate crimes involving the Internet, computer fraud, computer trespass, computer invasion of privacy, theft of computer services, personal trespass by computer, and telecommunications crimes. HTCU agents bring computers seized in the aforementioned crimes to CERU for evidence recovery and forensics. Many of the HTCU agents perform on-scene forensics as well.

Both CERU and HTCU adhere to common computer forensic standards–many set forth by the Department of Justice (DOJ) and International Association of Computer Investigative Specialists (IACIS)–for the search, seizure, and forensic analysis of computer-related evidence. The Computer Evidence Recovery Unit section of the Virginia State Police manual contains written operating procedures detailing these guidelines. Each case brought to CERU, either by HTCU agents or directly from local law enforcement, must have an appropriate search warrant or consent to search form. CERU examiners carefully follow the parameters set forth by these documents. Every piece of evidence delivered with each case is "signed in" both in writing and in the Unit's database to maintain chain of custody. Each case receives a 10-digit Virginia State Police case number, which designates the year of the case, the division the case occurred in, case investigation type, and a unique identifier. Once cases are received by CERU, they are worked on a "first come, first serve" basis unless the case is marked a priority (e.g., a homicide, unattended death, etc.). When CERU examiners begin a case, they carefully make notes of the condition and details of the evidence. CERU examiners utilize the same software described earlier in this chapter.

CERU examiners have diverse backgrounds. Most have several years, if not decades, of general computer experience. Additionally, all examiners receive a variety of training, including, but not limited to, Introduction to Computer Forensics by Encase, Intermediate and Advanced Computer Forensics by Encase, Basic Data Recovery and Analysis by the National White Collar Crime Center, Automated Forensic Tools by the National White Collar Crime Center, Ilook Training, PDA Training, IACIS Training and Certification, and other courses and seminars as needed. Each examiner strives to attain the IACIS Certified Computer Forensic Examiner certification and to attend a variety of training sessions each year. CERU also participates in several trainings and conferences each year.

In addition to attending training, many CERU examiners provide training to law enforcement agents from across the United States and Canada. CERU also publishes several booklets in such areas as "Parenting the Internet" and "Identity Theft." CERU examiners frequently lecture to civic and other groups throughout Virginia on these and other related topics.

CONCLUSION

In conclusion, computer-related crimes are one of the fastest growing crimes at a local, state, and federal level, and as a result law enforcement agencies must be aware of the six major aspects of computer-related crime: 1) what it is, 2) what are the components and activities associated with it, 3) what are the types of computer-related crimes, 4) what are the available tools to process technology-based evidence, 5) what legislation is associated with obtaining technology-based evidence and successfully prosecuting the cases, and 6) a state's approach to addressing computer-related crimes. It is the intent of this chapter to offer a detailed overview of the important aspects associated with computer-related crime and computer forensics so that criminal justice professionals can have the information needed to go forth and create computer forensic programs in their communities or to enhance those that already exist.

REFERENCES

Barnett, C. (2000). *The measuring of white-collar crime using the uniform crime reporting data.* United States Department of Justice: Federal Bureau of Investigation, 3,(8). pps. 1-10.

Caloyannides, M. (2001). *Computer forensics and privacy.* Boston: Artech House.

Casey, E. (2002). *Handbook of computer crime investigation: Forensic tools and technology.* San Diego, CA: Academic Press.

Goodman, M. (2001). *Making computer crime count.* Law Enforcement Bulletin, 70(8). pps. 10-17

Kessler, G. (2004). Guide to computer forensic investigation. *Forensic Science Communications,* 6(1). pps. 212-215.

Kruse, W. and Heiser, J. (2002). *Computer forensics incident response essentials.* Boston: Addison-Wesley.

McKemmish, R. (1999). *What is forensic computing?* Australian Institute of Criminology, 118.

Noblett, M., Pollitt, M., & Presley, L. (2000). Recovering and examining computer forensic evidence. *Forensic Science Communications,* 4(2). pps. 134-149.

U.S. Department of Justice. (2002). *Searching and seizing computers and obtaining electronic evidence in criminal investigations.* Washington, D.C.: Government Printing Office.

CASES AND STATUTES

Code of Virginia (2004). www.leg1.state.va.us/cgi-bin/legp504.exe? 000+cod+18.2-152.1

Lund v. Commonwealth of Virginia (Record No. 760591, Supreme Court of Virginia, 217 Va. 688; 232 S.E.2d 745; 1977 VA).

Illinois v. Andreas, 463 U.S. 765, 771 (1983).
Illinois v. Rodriguez, 497 U.S. 177, 185 (1990).
Stoner v. California, 376 U.S. 483 (1964).
United States v. Horowitz, 806 F.2d 1222 (4th Cir, 1986).

GLOSSARY OF TERMS AND RELATED WEBSITES

Bitstream Image: An accurate digital representation of all data contained on a digital storage device (e.g., hard drive, CD-ROM, diskettes, etc.).

Write-blocking: Hardware or software means to prevent data from being written to a disk or other medium.

Hash: Using a mathematical algorithm against data to produce a numeric value that is representative of that data. Hash values for systems and files will always remain the same unless altered. (National Institute of Justice, Forensic Examination of Digital Evidence: A Guide for Law Enforcement: http://www.ojp.usdoj.gov/nij/pubs-sum/199408.htm)

Encase: www.encase.com
Forensic Toolkit (FTK): www.accessdata.com
Ilook: www.ilook-forensics.org
PDA Seizure: www.paraben-forensics.com
E-mail Examiner: www.paraben-forensics.com
NetAnalysis: www.paraben-forensics.com
NavRoad: www.faico.net/navroad
Password Recovery Toolkit (PRTK): www.accessdata.com
ACDSee: www.acdsystems.com

Chapter 13

AN ASSESSMENT OF COMPUTER CRIME VICTIMIZATION IN THE UNITED STATES

ANDRA J. KATZ AND DAVID L. CARTER

With the growth of technology and the evolution of computerization, we have not only seen new types of crime emerge, but the character of these crimes has changed rapidly as a result of developing technological capacities. Certainly there has been some empirical exploration of these offenses, most of which has been done by private security organizations largely along the lines of a risk assessment for specific industries. Although these inquiries have provided new insights, they have generally been narrowly focused and unpublished. Although there have been increasing numbers of books and publications on computer-related crime, they tend to address specific issues or cases. In essence, a comprehensive, contemporary, and empirical review of (1) the character of computer-related crime and (2) the consequences of computer-related crime appears not to exist. Given the dramatic economic impact these offenses can have, greater information is needed for policy makers, law makers, and investigators.

Several factors suggest why computer-related crime has not been comprehensively investigated:

- Given the emotional concerns of the public and criminal justice officials associated with violent crime in America today, the seemingly "distant" or impersonal nature of computer-related crime is more easily ignored (except for its victims).

- In the authors' preliminary research, it has been found that many law enforcement officials do not envision computer-related crime as a problem that effects them, thus little attention has been given to it.

- Many of the crimes–such as theft of intellectual property, unlawful transfers of money, telecommunications fraud, and data tampering–are sufficiently distinct from the types of crimes that criminal justice officials are accustomed to dealing with that they do not understand their character and impact.

- The technical nature of computer-related crime is somewhat intimidating, or at least confusing, to those with limited computer-related experience, thus the potential crime issues of these technologies are avoided.

- In the authors' experiences and preliminary research, it has been found that many view computer-related crime somewhat "unidimensionally"–that is, such as theft from a computer–not envisioning the wide array (and ever-broadening) nature of computer-related offenses. As such, the impact and breadth of the problem is diminished from their perspective.

- Technology and technological capability coupled with the innovation of computer criminals (who tend to be very bright), changes so rapidly, it is difficult to keep abreast of changes and developments.

A SYNOPSIS OF THE LITERATURE

According to Parker, the lack of attention historically paid to computer crime is no accident: "In 1970, a number of researchers concluded that the problem was merely a small part of the effort of technology on society and not worthy of specific explicit research" (1989, p. 5). However, "the increase in substantial losses associated with intentional acts involving computers proved the fallacy of this view" (Parker, 1989, p. 5).

Another setback for computer crime research came in the mid-1970s: "Researchers believed that the involvement of computers should be subordinate to the study of each specific type of crime, both manual and automated" (Parker, 1989:5). To reinforce this, researchers pointed out the fact that "the uniqueness of characteristics of computer crime across all the different types of crime was not considered sufficient to warrant explicit research" (Parker, 1989, p. 5). Consequently, research focused on "real" crimes (i.e., violence) while treating computer criminality with secondary, or even tertiary importance (Katz, 1995). Essentially, the potential impact of computer crime was not envisioned.

Just as there has been little research in this venue, law enforcement officials have given it limited attention because of its seemingly "distant and complex" nature. Preliminary research has shown that "many public law enforcement officials do not envision computer-related crime as a problem that affects them" (Carter, 1995a, p. 2). However, a wide array of anecdotes show this not to be the case. Recognition is slowly changing with the creation of computer crime units in the Secret Service, Air Force OSI, and FBI; growth of such organizations as the Florida Association of Computer Crime Investigators and the High Tech Crime Investigators Association; and computer crime specialists in local police departments as well as new units in such diverse organizations as the Royal Canadian Mounted Police, Royal Thai Police, and London Metropolitan Police. Still, as one respondent to this study observed,

> I feel the weakest link is the lack of education in [public] law enforcement relating to computer technology crimes. The law enforcement community has devoted [itself] to the high priority violent crimes lumping computer crimes into a low priority status, yet the losses to computer crime could fund a small country (Anon. Survey Response).

Despite common assumptions, computers are not used solely as a tool in white collar crime, but have also served as instrumentalities for crime against persons. Pedaphile bulletin board systems (BBS) and the "set-ups" of young people for sexual assault based on contacts and discussions through commercial online systems and the Internet are examples. Linking computers to violent crime may be one method to generate increased resources for research and planning in this arena.

Coupled with their "impersonal" nature, computer crimes are inherently technical (Katz, 1995). These crimes "are sufficiently distinct from the types of crimes that criminal justice officials are accustomed to dealing with that they do not understand their character and impact" (Carter, 1995a, p. 2). Additionally, "the technical nature of computer-related crime is intimidating to those with limited computer-related experience, thus the potential criminality related to those technologies is something which simply cannot be understood" (Carter, 1995a, p. 2).

Cyberspace in its current, largely unregulated state has created a breeding ground for a variety of criminal enterprises. Crimes and incidents of malfeasance ranging from theft, stolen services, smuggling, terrorism, pornography, sexual harassment, stalking, and the spread of hate messages by extremists, have and continue to be occurring at substantial levels (Katz, 1995).

Ingenuity on the part of criminals coupled with easy access has led to a new generation of perpetrators. The ability to commit computer-related crimes is both increasingly easy and probable. Not only does cyberspace provide a seemingly unlimited supply of information, but also an unlimited supply of victims. The frequently high stakes payoff from a computer crime, the speed at which crimes can occur (with some incursions lasting as little as three milliseconds), the ability to include a programming code instructing the software to "erase itself" after the incursion is executed, and the fact that the criminal can be in another country when executing the criminal commands, are all among the reasons to believe that computer crimes will increase at a substantial pace (Carter, 1995b).

WHO COMMITS COMPUTER CRIME: "INSIDERS" OR "OUTSIDERS"?

Although there is some debate about who poses the greatest risk as a "technocriminal," the fact remains that anyone who has the capabilities or skills may pose a threat to computer security (Katz, 1995). Determining whether a crime is the job of an employee or an outsider is often difficult to do. However, certain red flags may emerge. One example is that of companies that rely on a closed local area network

(LAN). The fact that there is only limited or, in some cases, no external network access from the company virtually eliminates the probability for outsiders to penetrate the system. Although a closed LAN is a safeguard, doing business in today's society oftentimes does not make it economically feasible for businesses to electronically cut themselves off from the outside world (Katz, 1995). Businesses that are well-connected are able to significantly surpass the commerce of those who remain electronically isolated. The pursuit of growing business options is often initiated by corporate leaders with limited thought of the security threats. A balance must be struck. One security official told the researchers, "Security is viewed as an 'add on;' 'an obstacle;' 'a necessary evil.' CEOs should view us as an investment. With effective security, profits will rise and losses will fall" (Anon. Survey Response).

While outsiders may pose a serious threat, at this point in time computer crimes tend to be "inside" jobs. According to Van Duyn (1985, p. 4), "insiders pose a far greater threat to the organization's computer security than outside 'electronic invaders' possibly could." The reason being that "insiders are familiar with their employers' data processing operations and the type of data each system and application is storing and processing" and therefore know exactly where to look for information. The emergence of networking and user-friendly protocols are beginning to change this balance.

As Van Duyn (1985) notes, vulnerability from within an organization is the most dangerous and poses the most serious threat. A number of studies support this conclusion. In fact, "one study estimated that 90% of economic computer crimes were committed by employees of the victimized companies" (U.N. Commission on Crime and Criminal Justice, 1995). A more recent study conducted in North America and Europe found that 73% of the risk to computer security was from internal sources while only 23% was attributable to external sources (U.N. Commission on Crime and Criminal Justice, 1995). Unlike outsiders attempting to break into a system, insiders are oftentimes able to more easily circumvent safeguards therefore reducing their chances of being detected. Moreover, if the employee has authorized access to the information but chooses to steal or destroy it, then detection is even more difficult.

Insiders also have a distinct advantage, for not only do they often know immediately where to look for the data, but, if in doubt, "they can reference the systems documentation which usually includes programming specifications, file and record layouts, a data element dictionary, and so on" (Van Duyn, 1985, p. 4). Most significantly, insiders have a better idea on how to locate and gain access to crucial information such as financial, marketing, manufacturing, technological, or research data.

Consistent with evidence that insiders pose the greatest threat to computer security, Parker (1989) cites several factors which alone or in conjunction with others help to create an atmosphere conducive to computer crime within organizations. The first factor identified by Parker (1989) is that perpetrators are often young. He notes that it is not youth in and of itself that translates into a generation of computer criminals. However, "younger people in data processing occupations tend to have received their education in universities and colleges where attacking computer systems has become common and is sometimes condoned as an educational activity" (Parker, 1989, p. 39).

Differential association may also help explain vulnerabilities that expose organizations to computer crime (Katz, 1995). Modifying the theory to a workplace environment, Parker (1989, p. 39) states that it "is the white-collar criminals' tendency to deviate in only small ways from the accepted practices of their associates." The vulnerability erupts from "groups of people working together and mutually encouraging and stimulating one another to engage in unauthorized acts that escalate into serious crimes" (Parker, 1989, p. 39). The potential for oneupmanship becomes magnified as the acts escalate in risk and sophistication.

METHODS

One of the difficulties in conducting exploratory research is to properly define and frame the variables to be assessed. Intuitively, one knows the issues at hand and the broad goal to be accomplished; however, operationalizing those variables can become problematic. In the current study, the research parameters were more strongly directed by current anecdotal information about computer-related abuses than previous research.

Based on a content analysis of anecdotes obtained from interviews with practitioners working on computer crime cases, information downloaded from various sources on the Internet and keyword searches of news services, the authors framed a number of variables for analysis. This was followed by further interviews with corporate security directors and investigators in order to clearly define critical information that was needed. During this process it became evident that obtaining interval and ratio information from businesses (such as explicit details on victimization, losses, active investigations, and personnel actions associated with computer abuse) would be virtually impossible. One reason was the lack of comprehensive and accessible records. More importantly, however, was the reluctance of businesses to admit their computer-based vulnerabilities.

After four iterations of the survey draft, an instrument was developed using nominal and ordinal variables that would seek much of the desired information, albeit less robust than originally planned. The survey was pretested among a small group of academicians and practitioners who reviewed it for clarity, terminology, substance, and structure. Modifications were made based on the feedback and balanced with the research project's goals.

Given the nature of the study, it was determined that the best source of information would be corporate security professionals. A purposive sampling frame was first selected from the American Society of Industrial Security (ASIS) membership. As defined by Kerlinger (1973, p. 129), purposive sampling is a nonprobability sample which is "characterized by the use of judgment and a deliberate effort to obtain representative samples by including presumably typical areas or groups in the sample." Such was the case in this study based on the sampling needs.

Since ASIS has a worldwide membership of people who hold a wide range of positions it was necessary to segregate the membership based on the member's position (i.e., corporate security directors) and businesses likely to have computers that would be the target of crime or abuse. In order to control, to the extent possible, the subjectivity of this stratification, the researchers were careful to include a broad range of business in the sampling frame. Airlines, telecommunications companies, banks, utilities, retailers, manufacturers, energy companies, the defense industry, and government agencies are examples of this range. The sampling frame was also limited to United States residents both for reduced mailing costs and because of the time and complications associated with surveying overseas members.

The actual sample of 600 people was randomly selected from the purposive sampling frame. The sample size was based on the recognition that, given the subject, the response rate would likely be low. Consequently, the researchers used a larger sample size as a means to increase the probability of representativeness of the population and ensure a sufficient number of responses to meet the assumptions needed for statistical testing.

Given that the data are at nominal and ordinal levels, the primary test for bivariate analysis was the chi-squared (X^2) test of independence to determine significant relationships between the variables. When a relationship was identified, Phi was used to determine the strength of correlation (covariance). Finally, Cramer's V was examined as a gauge of the overall strength of the association. A weakness of Cramer's V in the current study is that many of the variable scales are narrow and, as a consequence, the ability to discriminate the variance is reduced (thus Cramer's V would consistently be low). Despite this limitation, when all three statistics are viewed collectively, they provide reliable indicators from which conclusions may be drawn.

The sample members were sent a letter of introduction containing a statement of confidentiality, a survey, and a return envelope. Recipients were urged to complete the survey as soon as possible and promised a copy of the results if they sent a business card or called a toll-free number (88 people requested the survey findings.) Two weeks after the survey was mailed, a postcard reminder was sent with the closing date two weeks after that.

A total 183 surveys were returned (30.5%), however, not all could be used because they were improperly completed, not legible, or the respondent refused to complete the survey because of corporate policy. As one respondent noted, "(u)understandably, companies that have experienced some of the [computer crimes] are reluctant to disclose their experiences." There were 151 usable responses for a usable return rate of 25.2%. While the overall response rate is lower than desired, the number of usable responses is sufficiently high to provide insightful descriptive trends in addition to exceeding the assumptions and cell sizes needed for statistical testing.

VICTIMIZATION

The extent and nature of computer crime appears to be on a rapidly ascending curve. A study conducted by the American Bar Association in 1987 found that of the 300 corporations and government agencies surveyed, 72 (24%) claimed to have been the victim of a computer-related crime in the 12 months prior to the survey. (U.N. Commission on Crime and Criminal Justice, 1995). The estimated losses from these crimes ranged from $145 million to $730 million over the 1-year period. This broad range is illustrative of the problem in estimating losses. Not only is it difficult to identify and document these crimes, it is even more difficult to place a monetary value on the loss of intellectual property wherein the actual value may not be known for months or years.

Two years later, the Florida Department of Law Enforcement (FDLE) surveyed 898 public and private sector organizations that conducted business by computer. Of the 403 (44.9%) respondents, 25% reported they had been victimized by computer criminals (FDLE, 1989). The Florida study found embezzlement of funds by employees to be a major source of the crimes, however, no attempt to estimate losses was made because, according to one of the researchers interviewed, "losses would have been nothing more than a guess."

In perhaps one of the most comprehensive studies, conducted in 1991, a survey was done of 3,000 Virtual Address Extension (VAX) sites in Canada, Europe, and the United States to assess computer security threats and crimes. The results show that 72% of the respondents reported a security incident had occurred within the previous 12 months with 43% reporting the incident was criminal in nature (U.N. Commission on Crime and Criminal Justice, 1995). By far, the greatest security threats came from employees or people who had access to the computers, however, a number of external security breeches from hackers telephoning into the systems or accessing via networks was reported. The ABA and FDLE studies scarcely even mentioned this "external threat" and gave little attention to it as a growing problem. This is not surprising, however, since, as noted previously, networking in the late 1980s was predominantly used by the military, academics, and researchers. Access was comparatively limited and networking technology was more expensive. However, the 1991 United Nations study suggested that external threats via remote access was a problem that would grow in the years to come. Despite this concern, past research suggests that threats of computer crime generally come from employees, just like much of the theft in retail businesses.

The data in this study show a trend of victimization that increased significantly over previous studies, with 98.5% of the respondents reporting they had been victimized–43.3% reported being victimized more than 25 times. While these numbers seem dramatic, security professionals with whom these results were discussed stated they were surprised at the frequency of *admitted* victimization, not actual victimization. One respondent stated, "Do we know the national or even local scope of the computer crime threat? Probably not; but it has to be higher than anyone wants to admit."

This level of victimization leads one to ask who the perpetrators are. Consistent with previous research, the most common perpetrators reported in this research were employees. The primary threat comes from full-time employees, followed by part-time and outsourced employees, with computer hackers a close third; a finding which was expected since there appears to be a correlation between theft and access to computers (Herfernan, 1995). However, the important dynamic to recognize is that access is changing dramatically with networking.

THEFT

Not surprisingly, the fastest growing computer-related crime was theft. However, an interesting facet of this crime supports the forecast of Toffler–the most common "commodity" stolen was information (1990). Respondents reported that intellectual property was the most common target of thieves including such things as new product plans, new product descriptions, research, marketing plans, prospective customer lists, and similar information. One respondent observed the conflict between security and business by stating, "Outside individuals hacking into our computer is a problem and a potential threat. Its hard to stop without jeopardizing business communications and networking."

To illustrate one method of information theft, a security experiment was described to the researchers during an interview. A major corporate research laboratory uses the Internet to search for information on new product plans. In a test of the system, an information specialist "hacked" into the Internet communications of two researchers and recorded their search inquiries and the Uniform Resource Locator (URL) addresses (including both Websites and gophers) the researchers visited. The keyword search inquiries and access sites were given to an independent researcher in the same field who immediately hypothesized the type of product the company was working on and the "new dimension" of the product. When confronted with the results of this experiment, the researchers confirmed the hypotheses were correct. While this was a security experiment, the survey respondents had more concrete experiences of direct theft. One respondent, commenting on information theft, framed the problem this way, "company plans, research, products, etc. have been lost this way creating financial losses and job losses."

The research findings show there was a significant relationship between personal use of company computers and increases of intellectual property theft (X^2=15.64869, df=6, p<.01). Personal use of computers ranged from simple word processing to use of spreadsheets for personal finances to accessing the Internet. In many cases these uses were either permitted or, more typically, overlooked. Perhaps one of the problems is that when an employee has a workstation where personal activities are performed, the employee begins to view this portal as being proprietary. As a consequence, the impact of thefts, particularly that of intellectual property that does not have a tangible value, is not as readily perceived as being wrong, thereby making the theft psychologically easier.

Generally speaking, thefts were discovered by an audit trail showing access to information where the user had no legitimate need, by an informant who told the business of the theft, or the theft was surmised based on external information, such as the actions or products of a competitor. There is a wide body of research that shows the value of stolen trade secrets and intellectual property (Herfernan, 1995; Tripp, 1995; U.S. Congress, 1995). Traditionally this information was stolen by compromising employees, photocopying documents, burglary, or surveillance of company personnel and practices. Increasingly, however, theft from computers is the desired methodology because it is more comprehensive, more reliable, easier, more consumable and contains less risk for detection and capture.

Intellectual property was not the only target of thieves; there was also a significant relationship between personal use of company computers and employees stealing or attempting to steal money (X^2= 13.8424, df=6, $p<.05$). In most cases, employees who attempted to steal money were identified before an actual loss was sustained. The reason for this was that it was easier to account for monetary losses, which required some type of electronic transaction, as opposed to intellectual property theft which simply requires the copying of files. Moreover, monetary files had more security controls and were monitored more closely than information files. Finally, there are fewer monetary files than information files. As a consequence, cash accounting is easier to monitor.

Despite this, monetary thefts have nonetheless occurred. In Detroit, a "small time" computer hacker cracked a bank's computer system, opened a new account and methodically transferred small amounts of money into it from existing accounts. One survey respondent summarized the issue succinctly, "Losses are sometimes very large. We just lost $1 million."

The analysis of these variables proved insightful. When part-time employees and computer hackers were tested against the same dependent variables, no significant relationship was found. This reinforces the fact that full-time employees pose the greatest threat to theft by computer. Moreover, both the vulnerability of intellectual property and the extrinsic value it holds makes such information a tempting target.

UNAUTHORIZED ACCESS TO FILES: "SNOOPING"

The practice of "snooping" refers to a person's unauthorized opening of files in order to "see what's in there." A snooper's motive may be curiosity, the challenge of entering an unauthorized area, or evaluation of the information to determine if it has value and can be taken. Somewhat akin to a criminal trespass, it is sometimes difficult to ascertain if a law was broken, a company policy was violated, an ethical standard was breached, or the behavior was simply poor judgment. Snooping tends to vary along this continuum, depending largely on security controls, custom within the organization, and corporate policy on accessing information. One security professional told the researchers that most cases of snooping in his company were simply curiosity or "cybervoyeurism" where there was no malicious intent. Even in cases of hackers, he felt that most were interested in the challenge rather than to commit a theft.

Despite these experiences of one professional, the data indicated otherwise. There were significant relationships between snooping by full-time employees and stealing or attempting to steal intellectual property (X^2=15.48614, df=6, $p<.05$) and stealing or attempting to steal money (X^2=23.72249, df=6, $p<.001$). In the case of stealing intellectual property, it appears snooping was done to identify the nature of available information, its potential value, and the ability to steal the information. In the case of money, snooping was most likely done to better understand the file structure, determine transaction protocols, locate accounts most susceptible to theft with a lower probability of discovery, and test security for access control and authentication roadblocks (something akin to a burglar casing a target). Clearly in both cases, snooping was a significant precursor to criminality.

Significant results were also found among part-time employees' snooping and stealing or attempting to steal intellectual property (X^2=19.17477, df=6, $p<.005$) and part-time employees stealing or attempting to steal money (X^2=25.66591, df=6, $p<.001$). Importantly, the findings of both full-time and part-time employees are strongly supported and based on similar reasoning. While not as strong overall, there was a significant relationship between snooping by hackers (X^2=17.68774, df=6, $p<.01$) and stealing or attempting to steal intellectual property whereas there was no significant relationship between snooping by hackers and monetary theft. With the growth of networking, a similar analysis in the next few years or so may find different results.

Conventional wisdom seems to suggest that snoopers are more of a nuisance than a threat. However, the data suggest that snooping is an exploratory activity that leads to a theft or attempted theft in a significant number of instances. Organizational policy, employee supervision, and security measures should be reviewed to ensure that snooping activities are detected and resolved.

VIRUS INTRODUCTION

Viruses are created for a wide array of reasons and can have many different effects depending on the creator's intent. For those malcontent computer users who are looking for "ready made" viruses, there is a BBS in France, accessible via the Internet, which has a large collection of diverse viruses that can be downloaded and then introduced into the targeted computer. Certainly the capacity to infect a computer is available and is occurring on an increasing, although not epidemic, basis.

According to the data, 66.3% of the responding businesses reported viruses had been introduced into business computers over the past five years. When tested, the data show significant relationships of virus introduction by hackers attempting or stealing intellectual property (X^2=34.62849, df=9, p<.001) and by hackers attempting or stealing money (X^2=36.52177, df=9, p<.001). This is supported by anecdotal evidence that hackers would try to destroy any evidence of their presence, destroy evidence of their crime, and increase the difficulty of detecting and investigating a theft (or intrusion) by introduction of a virus. Essentially, the virus was meant to be a smokescreen for the incursion. This does not mean that hackers only used viruses to coverup a theft–indeed there is evidence that viruses are also introduced as a means to protest a company policy or simply as a game. What the strong findings suggest are that in a notable number of cases where computer thefts occur, a virus is introduced. The *caveat* to investigators is to be certain to also look for evidence of thefts whenever a virus is introduced via network or modem access.

Beyond hackers, there was also a significant relationship between a part-time employee's theft or attempted theft and a virus introduction (X^2=36.18864, df=9, p<.001). The rationale is the same for part-time employees as it is for hackers. Interestingly, there was no significant relationship between virus introduction and any behavior by full-time employees. Anecdotal evidence suggests that employees have placed viruses in computer systems for a number of reasons. According to the National Computer Security Association, an important reason for the increase in computer viruses is the massive terminations and layoffs afflicting the corporate landscape. Some employees may feel that they are being coldly dismissed after years of loyalty and a growing number see inserting a virus into the corporate computer system as a way of striking back.

Interestingly, 82.6% of the respondents reported that antivirus software had been loaded on company computers. Given the relative inexpense and ease of such software in comparison to the damage that could be caused by the virus, it would seem that virus protection would be prudent insurance for the security professional to take. Thus it was surprising that not all companies had antivirus software. While not directly comparable, it appears that the portion of respondents who do not have antivirus software is about the same as those who are not connected to the Internet nor have external modem access. One might assume that if these are the same companies, security personnel are concluding that a virus threat does not exist since the computer has no external connectivity. If this is the case, the researchers suggest that full-time employees also pose computer security risks. They obviously could–and have–introduced viruses as noted.

This leads to the reasons viruses are introduced. While not empirically measured, interviews and anecdotes shed light on these motivations. Harassment of other employees, particularly with respect to company politics serves as one reason for viruses. If a fellow employee can cause problems to others, particularly in a company where one's success is measured in a competitive atmosphere against other employees, then a virus can be a good tool to gain an advantage. Harassment could also be the intent of a person who externally introduces the virus. For example, there is evidence that activists in both the environmental and animal rights movements have infected computers of companies that the activists view as having corporate policies that are harmful to their respective causes.

Retribution is a second reason. Employees who feel they have been treated unfairly, terminated without just reason, or are not appreciated, are likely to direct some type of revenge toward the company. A computer virus seems to be one method that fulfills that need because it can cause significant damage to the company, yet there is little chance one will get caught. A third reason for infecting a computer may simply be called "gamesmanship." In these cases the virus is typically introduced by a hacker to "play with" the system but with no intent to cause permanent damage. Despite this lack of malice, the business will still suffer some financial loss because of lower productivity while the virus is present and the cost related to eradicating the problem. Moreover, there could be accidental damage caused by the virus itself or attempts to repair the problem.

Another reason for infecting a computer is to impede the commerce of a business. Whether it is a hacker working at the behest of a competitor or an employee who has "sold out," a virus intended to impede commerce will typically cause major damage such as erasing files, mixing information so that it makes no sense, or locking up hardware so that the system software has to be reloaded. Whatever the effects of the virus, there are significant losses from actual costs of the virus eradication and system repair, there are losses from commerce during operational slowdowns–and in some cases stoppages–while the problem is being resolved, and undetermined losses of market share that may occur as a result of the problem. A final reason for infecting computers is to hide evidence of thefts. If a virus erases information, disrupts audit trails, or jumbles information, losses, even if detected, may be attributed to the virus, not a theft.

Since computer viruses are readily available with new ones being written all the time and the fact they are introduced by employees and hackers alike, the problem is truly real. The need to anticipate their insertion into a computer system is a logical security precaution that policy makers should address. As computer systems are increasingly networked, the problem will only increase.

HARASSMENT

Crime and misconduct are, of course, not products of technology but the products of human behavior. The technology is simply a way to facilitate criminality. While there is no general agreement among criminologists about what causes crime, the evidence suggests that causal or precipitating factors are on a continuum that includes, as a fundamental variable, opportunity. Technology provides the opportunity to commit crimes in several ways: The opportunity to have access to a valuable commodity; the opportunity to seize that commodity with relative ease; and the opportunity to take the property with a low probability of being apprehended. With the growth of networking and new hardware configurations and software, opportunities for crime have opened into a much broader arena.

As one illustration of this phenomenon, the data show that harassment of employees significantly increased as Local Area Networks (LAN) (X^2=7.40053, df=3, p<.05) and file servers were increasingly used (X^2=8.12483, df=3, p<.05). There are a number of reasons why employees would harass others including sexual harassment, various types of jealousy of others, the "teasing" of others that gets out of control, exercising power over others, company politics, retribution for being "wronged," and competitiveness that impedes the success of another. With the ease and anonymity that can be provided over networks, harassment has been a form of misconduct which appears to have flourished.

There was a significant relationship between full-time employee computer abuse and harassment of employees (X^2=21.44211, df=9, p<.05). This statistical finding along with anecdotal evidence demonstrate a consistent theme that suggests that full-time employees who abuse their computer access privileges will do so for a number of reasons, including harassment. Perhaps one approach to minimize harassment is to have good access controls for e-mail while ensuring that the system does not permit e-mail to be delivered anonymously; instead messages should always be easily and readily identifiable. While some have argued that such controls stifle the creativity of employees who want to share innovative ideas for feedback, the process also stifles harassment. Thus, decisions have to be made on a case-by-case basis of whether harassment is a problem and a balance must be struck between competing interests and system control.

DESTRUCTION OF "VIRTUAL PROPERTY"

In this study, "virtual property" specifically refers to both computer systems operating programs and data kept in computerized files. The data indicate that when people attempt to steal intellectual property there is a significant likelihood that there will be some destruction of the computer system or file server's operating programs. This is true whether the person is a full-time employee (X^2=39.02557, df=9, p<.001), part-time employee (X^2=39.12260, df=9, p<.001), or hacker (X^2=60.49559, df=9, p<.001).

While there are very strong relationships for all three groups, the strongest was with the hackers. Perhaps this should be expected since hackers must access computers more "forcefully," thereby the probability for operating program damage would increase. Moreover, hackers do not have the same proprietary interest in virtual property that employees do nor do they have the same level of concern about identification and punishment as would an employee. Interestingly, while hackers are significantly less likely to steal information in comparison to employees, when they do attempt to steal, they are the most likely to damage operating programs.

Similar significant results were found when destruction of data files were tested against theft or attempted theft by full-time employees ($X^2=33.40446$, df=9, $p<.001$), part-time employees ($X^2=36.70534$, df=9, $p<.001$), and hackers ($X^2=42.2734$, df=9, $p<.001$). Once again, the significant relationships are all strong with the hackers being particularly noteworthy. These findings reinforce those related to destruction of operating programs and add to the significance of the results. One point that becomes imminently clear from the results is that businesses are not only the victims of intellectual property theft, but they are consistently victims of virtual property destruction.

While not explicit in the data, one may speculate why operating programs and data files were destroyed during the course of thefts or attempts. There is a probability that the damage was accidental as a result of a trespasser's probing restricted areas and attempts to take protected information. In some ways, this is similar to using an electronic sledge hammer to commit a cyberburglary–there is bound to be collateral damage as a result.

Of course, the damage could also be intentional. The thief may simply need to damage the operating program as a means to access and steal the desired information. Another reason for the destruction may be an attempt to hide evidence of the intruder's presence; essentially, covering one's tracks. A third reason is to impede both discovery and investigation of the theft. It may be inevitable that the theft will be discovered, but if an investigation can be impeded, the thief's chance of evading detection or prosecution will be increased. A final reason may be to prevent a "competitive theft." That is, if information has potentially significant payoff and competition is high, there is a likelihood that others may attempt to steal the information. As a means to prevent other thieves (i.e., competitors) from stealing the intellectual property, an intruder may destroy the operating programs.

When destruction of either operating programs or data files occurs, there is not only an intrinsic loss associated with that property, but also a loss of productivity, system repair costs, potential loss of market share, and costs associated with catching up after repairs are made and/or information is recovered. Costs grow geometrically, thus the losses can be substantial.

As a final point in this area, the data show significant relationships between the destruction of data files and the use of local area networks ($X^2=13.10538$, df=3, $p<.005$) and the use of file servers ($X^2=8.62766$, df=3, $p<.05$). There were no significant relationships between data file destruction and those companies using mainframe or minicomputers. Even when adjusting for the fact that there were fewer companies using these machines, thus lower chi-squared cell expectations, no relationships were found. Perhaps because the file servers and LANs are inherently more "network friendly" explains their relationships with property destruction.

There are some important policy implications from these findings. First, when damage to any virtual property has occurred, it should be assumed that a computer incursion has occurred until shown otherwise. The investigation should include an examination of holes in both authentication software and access control to determine if previously undetected security risks exist. Second, when an audit trail shows access to "unusual areas" of the system by a user, particularly systems operations, this may be a warning sign of a potential security breach. Somewhat surprisingly, some security officials have noted that audit trails are either inadequately used or used to ensure that an employee or intruder is not improperly using a legitimate user's access. One must recognize the painfully obvious fact that since many thieves are employees, an audit trail's notation of improper or unusual access could be an internal incursion. Third, security countermeasures should be applied to operating programs as well as data files. A number of security professionals have stated that their primary foci have been on "perimeter" and file controls, but comparatively limited security to operating programs per se. Finally, connectivity appears to have a strong relationship with property destruction. While intuitively apparent, suffice it to note that the data support this assumption and countermeasures should take "networkability" into consideration.

As a final note, there were no significant relationships found between theft or attempted theft of money (by any group of individuals) and any of the destruction variables. While cross-tabulated data indicated the probability existed, that probability is only intuitive, not statistical. Since there were notably fewer attempts to steal money and the data's scales have limited sensitivity, discrimination between the relationships could not be detected thus no conclusions can be clearly drawn on this point.

TELECOMMUNICATIONS FRAUD

Telecommunications fraud takes many forms ranging from thefts of long distance billing numbers, unauthorized access to telephone accounts, the "black market" of cellular telephone billing numbers, unauthorized access to satellite communications links, and nearly every derivative or permutation of these frauds that can be creatively developed. Regardless of how it is accomplished, telecommunications fraud is widespread.

This particular category of crime was difficult to expressly isolate as being penetrated exclusively by computer. While the researchers attempted to isolate non-computer perpetrated telecommunications fraud (such as unauthorized use of a company's long distance access) from that which was clearly computer-related, our successes were limited. One reason for this limitation was that the respondents could not always distinguish how the fraud occurred. A second reason was that most respondents had been so overwhelmed with this problem, they "forced" answers to variables that were actually not directly responsive, yet clearly indicative of a problem.

The greatest problem respondents indicated in this area was the extent of "unexplained" telecommunications fraud. Obviously fraudulent long distance and cellular billings were identified, but security investigators had difficulty locating the source of the fraud. That is, while telephone or billing numbers could be identified, the abuser typically could not be isolated; even if the number was assigned to a specific employee. In many cases, the billing times could not be correlated with employee use/abuse or the magnitude of billing costs would eliminate the employee as a suspect. Both of these factors indicate unauthorized access.

There is strong anecdotal evidence that hackers enter computer systems and take advantage of the electronic avenues open to them. This includes invasion–or in the worst case scenario, seizure–of internal telecommunications switches, use of corporate long distance and satellite channels (frequently for modem connections), or stealing long distance account numbers. In the latter case, the stolen account numbers would be either for personal use, distribution to others (usually friends) for their use, or selling the numbers on the black market. An analysis of these variables shows a significant relationship between telecommunications fraud and hacker intrusions (X^2=13.44125, df=6, p<.05), suggesting this to be a major problem.

There is a significant relationship between full-time employees who steal intellectual property via computer and increases in telecommunications fraud (X^2=18.07281, df=6, p<.005). On further examination of these variables via anecdotal evidence, it appears that employees who steal information are also likely to improperly use telecommunications access–whether land-line or cellular. It is not clear what the employees are using the long distance for (e.g., conversations, modem access, fax, or–most likely–a combination of the three.) The point to note is that the employee who is an intellectual property thief will also fraudulently use telecommunications access (they will also probably make personal copies on the company's photocopier and steal pens from the supply room).

Overall, the respondents reported that they had a major problem with telecommunications fraud. As telephone systems are increasingly managed by computer systems, particularly as interactive technology merges all telecommunications, data transmissions, networking, cable television, teleconferencing, and other facets of information transfer, the likelihood that telecommunications fraud will increase is high and its losses will grow even more.

The cellular phone industry has been particularly victimized by systems that receive billing code transmissions. Thieves, using a scanner of sorts, set up in areas where there is likely to be a heavy cellular presence and then simply snare the billing code from the air. The codes can then be downloaded from the scanner into a computer using programs available on the Internet, and entered into stolen cellular telephones that are, in turn, sold on the black market. The monetary losses are staggering. While efforts are being made to encrypt the codes as well as using other techniques such as "call profiling" and Personal Identification Numbers, technology criminals have demonstrated their creativity to meet challenges and will undoubtedly find methods to defeat these security measures. The need to constantly monitor criminal capabilities and address them via countermeasures is possibly the only way to minimize the losses. In essence, it is an ongoing process.

SECURITY COUNTERMEASURES

In light of these technological threats to proprietary information, the researchers sought to determine practices and experiences with different security countermeasures. Specifically, data encryption, operations security, surveillance of computer users, training of personnel, and use of Internet firewalls were examined. These factors were selected because preliminary research found them to be common practice in the computer security environment.

The analysis shows there was a significant relationship between file or data encryption and reduced theft of intellectual property ($X^2=9.97955$, df=3, $p<.01$). Consequently, encryption should be considered as an important security tool for confidential information. A *caveat* is provided, however. Anecdotally, it was learned that encryption must be reviewed, and perhaps changed on a regular basis–the breaking of such systems has not only occurred, it has become somewhat of a game. As an illustration, RSA-129 is a 129-digit number created in 1977 by the creators of an encryption system said to be "provably secure." At the time it was created, it was estimated to take 40 quadrillion years to factor it with methods of the time. The code's creators recognized that technology was rapidly evolving, consequently analytic capacities would also increase dramatically. In light of these changes, the encryption team projected that the code would remain secure well into the 21st century. In 1994, the code was "cracked" by a group of 600 Internet volunteers (Rosener, 1994). The point to note is that technology is challenging traditional assumptions, including the assumption of long-term security via encryption.

Another important relationship found that as operations security of companies' computer systems and file servers increased, thefts of intellectual property significantly decreased ($X^2=8.24674$, df=3, $p<.05$). Operations security included such things as monitoring users, creating audit trails of system users, and physical surveillance of users and systems. With regard to this last point, there was a significant relationship specifically found in the use of surveillance and decreased theft of intellectual property (X^2=8.90941, df=3, p<.05). As a test of reliability for these findings, an additional analysis of increased operations security was run against specific intellectual property thefts with significant results (X^2=7.51429, df=3, p<.05). An operational problem appears to emerge, however.

Anecdotal evidence suggests employee morale goes down, job satisfaction is reduced, employee productivity decreases, and individual creativity is less apparent when there is an increase in security surveillance of computer users. Balancing the need to use surveillance to reduce intellectual property thefts as opposed to the potential negative effects of this countermeasure may be a difficult one to achieve. In all likelihood, the decision will have to be made on a case-by-case basis after an evaluation of the organizational culture and the risk-benefits involved.

The protection of money, according to the respondents, poses different problems. While the value of intellectual property is difficult to assess, it can more easily be protected through encryption. However, there are unique limitations to encryption and different operations security requirements for computerized "cash accounts." Because of the inherent value of money as well as the ease of use and transfer of currencies–particularly in a "readily usable state"–virtually anywhere in the world, there was significant relationship between the need to use alternate security counter measures and the reduction of theft of money (X^2=8.89489, df=3, p<.05).

Throughout the research one constant thread which had a significant relationship between minimizing theft, thus increasing security, was increased employee training (X^2=8.00518, df=3, p<.05). Consistently, respondents reported that crimes and computer abuse (such as harassment via e-mail and use of business computer systems for personal use) were reduced after employee training.

The final countermeasure tested was the use of firewalls. While there are different methodologies, as a rule firewalls are software controls that permit system access only to users who are specifically registered with a computer. As users attempt to gain access to the system they are challenged to ensure they have an authenticated password. Typically, the user will be challenged several times–that is "layering"– for added protection. While firewalls are widely used, there were no significant relationships found between this countermeasure and protection of information. Indeed, several respondents' comments suggested that hackers had penetrated their firewalls. A number of security professionals have reported discovery of "Password Sniffer" and "Password Breaker" programs, downloaded from the Internet, which were used to breach security. What is not known was the sophistication or level of security provided by these firewalls, thus the finding of no significance could be a function of security practice rather than the countermeasure per se. That is, the finding should not be misinterpreted to say that firewalls do not work, rather there was no consensus on their success. This lack of consensus is likely based on inadequate security levels, irregular upgrade or maintenance, or an operational limitation associated with the firewall's use. The need for an organization to comprehensively review its authentication software is essential because of the comparative ease in breaking these systems as they currently exist (Bishop & Klein, 1995).

These observations are supported by Collinson who stated that ". . . firewalls are often set up incorrectly and may actually increase the risks a company faces by fostering a false sense of security" (1995, p. 217). Typically a firewall is developed to defend against known incursion methods. However, computer criminals are creative and have clearly shown their ability to penetrate many firewall systems. Moreover, when new barriers are developed, they are approached like a puzzle rather than an obstacle. The firewall is essentially a sophisticated electronic damn. Unfortunately, once an intruder finds a passage around this barrier, access to critical information becomes much easier for the hacker. Some evidence suggests that less investment is placed in internal security controls when a firewall is in place. As discussed, there are a number of vulnerabilities to this approach. Effective information system security requires a more holistic, proactive vision with an underlying assumption than any countermeasure can be compromised. Clearly, this is an area that needs closer examination, particularly given the level of reliance on this security measure.

CONCLUSIONS AND RECOMMENDATIONS

As evidenced by the research, the threat of computer crime is real. Those who maintain it is not a serious problem simply have not been awakened by the massive losses and setbacks experienced by companies worldwide. Money and intellectual property have been stolen, corporate operations have been impeded, and jobs have been lost as a result of computer crime. Similarly, information systems in government and business alike have been compromised and it has been with some luck that more damage has not been done.

There are issues of privacy, confidentiality, and ethics involved, not to mention the economic impact, which is staggering. In an interview with the British Banking Association (BBA), the authors were told that the BBA estimated the global loss to computer fraud alone to be about $8 billion a year. To add other losses as discussed previously brings the total economic effects of computer crime to a level beyond comprehension. Building on this scenario is the fact that as a result of new technologies, emerging technologies, and a growing generation of people who are not only computer literate but also network literate, the problem will grow.

Researchers must explore the problems in greater detail to learn the etiology of this growing criminal group, their methodologies, and motivations. Decision makers must react to this emerging body of knowledge by developing policies, methodologies, and regulations to detect incursions, investigate and prosecute the perpetrators, and vigilantly prevent future crimes. Our institutions have already fallen behind the criminals, at this point the question is not can we catch up, but whether we can keep the gap from widening.

The results of this study empirically support many elements of the anecdotal evidence. First, computer security incidents have significantly increased over recent years. Second, a primary target of computer thieves is the intellectual property of a business. Third, the people most likely to steal information are employees who have access to computer files. Fourth, the number of computer incursions (and attempts) by hackers outside of the business is increasing. In only a few years, the hacker threat will most likely equal if not exceed the threats posed by employees. Fifth, security professionals need to provide training to computer users about "cyberabuse," crime, the ramifications of information losses, and security precautions that must be taken (as well as the rationale for those precautions). Sixth, there must be a recognition that the threat of a virus infecting systems is real. Moreover, this threat will grow with more creative, hence destructive, viruses being created and a wider spread of the viruses as a result of the growth in networking. Seventh, the "snooping" of files is a problem that can lead to theft and damage of important information. Eighth, harassment via computer is a real problem that organizations must address, not dismiss. Ninth, destruction of virtual property is a correlate to thefts and attempted thefts. This destruction has both direct costs for reparations and indirect costs for losses of productivity. Tenth, telecommunications fraud exists on a massive scale costing millions of dollars every year. Finally, a number of established security procedures appear to work effectively; however, they can be foiled if not regularly reviewed and revised to meet changing conditions and technologies.

REFERENCES

Bishop M., & Klein, D. V. (1995). Improving system security via proactive password checking. *Computers and Security,* 14(3): 233-249.

Carter, D. L. (1995b, August.). Computer-related crime. *FBI Law Enforcement Bulletin, 3.*

Collinson, H. (1995). Recent literature. *Computers and Security,* 14:215-220.

Florida Department of Law Enforcement. (1989). *Computer crime in Florida.* An unpublished report prepared by the Florida Department of Law Enforcement, Tallahassee, Florida.

Herfernan, R. (1995, September 12). Securing Proprietary Information (SPI) Committee of the American Society of Industrial Security. Committee presentation at the ASIS Annual Meeting, New Orleans, LA.

Katz, A. J. (1995). *Computers: The changing face of criminality.* Unpublished doctoral dissertation, School of Criminal Justice, Michigan State University, East Lansing, Michigan.

Kerlinger, F. (1977). *Foundations of behavioral research.* New York: Holt, Rinehart, and Winston.

Parker, D. B. (1989). *Fighting computer crime.* New York: Charles Scribner's Sons.

Rosener, J. (1994, April). *CyberLaw.* America Online.

Toffler, A. (1990). *PowerShift.* New York: Bantam Books.

Tripp, B. (1995). *Survey of the counterintelligence needs of private industry.* Washington, DC: National Counterintelligence Center and the U.S. Department of State Overseas Security Advisory Council.

U.N. Commission on Crime and Criminal Justice. (1995). *United Nations manual on the prevention and control of computer-related crime.* New York: United Nations.

U.S. Congress. (1995). *Annual Report to Congress on Foreign Economic Collection and Industrial Espionage.* Washington, DC: Government Printing Office.

Van Duyn, J. (1985). *The human factor in computer crime.* Princeton, NJ: Petrocelli Books, Inc.

Chapter 14

COMPUTER APPLICATIONS BY INTERNATIONAL ORGANIZED CRIME GROUPS

DAVID L. CARTER AND ANDRA J. KATZ

As the global environment has changed, so has the character of international organized crime. The growth of common markets in Europe, Asia, Africa, and the Western Hemisphere; global communications networks including satellites and the Internet; the availability of easy and comparatively inexpensive travel; and evolving social and political systems–the most notable of which is the change in Eastern Europe–have all influenced an evolution in criminal enterprises. Just like any other social or economic group, organized crime continuously evolves along with the global community. It should be no surprise, therefore, to see criminal enterprises increasingly rely on computerization.

How extensive is that reliance? How are computers used by organized crime groups? Has the way that criminal enterprises "do business" changed as a result of computers? These are among the questions explored by the authors.

THE STUDY OF INTERNATIONAL ORGANIZED CRIME

This study relied on qualitative research methods including interviews with law enforcement officials, intelligence analysts, government officials, investigators, and corporate security directors all of whom work with international organized crime and have some knowledge or evidence associated with computer applications by these groups. The interviews, in most cases, followed a consistent protocol that documented the interviewees' experience and observations on current trends. The exceptions were interviews that were done under incidental situations. Even in these cases, the researchers were able to ask and record primary questions from the protocol.

Of the 47 people interviewed, most were from Europe and Asia although some interviewees were from North America and 5 were from Africa. Corporations from which security directors were interviewed are not included in this list for confidentiality reasons. Persons were selected for the interviews based on their knowledge and experience in light of the positions they hold with their organizations. Corporate security directors were included in the research because of the increasing involvement of organized crime in cargo theft, theft of intellectual property, manufacture and distribution of counterfeit commodities, and industrial espionage.

In addition, the researchers were given access to a wide range of investigative reports and documents. A content analysis was completed with these materials to the extent possible. In a few cases the authors were permitted to read and take notes from the documents, but not copy them.

An analysis matrix was designed to document the interviewees' responses to key questions. In addition, on selected variables the interviewees were asked to give their perceptions on a 5-point scale. Based on these responses and the collective observations documented in the interviews, the information was integrated for analysis in this chapter.

With respect to reporting results, because of the critical nature of information involved in this study–frequently of a classified or confidential nature–interviewees were guaranteed confidentiality in their specific responses to control questions. While the researchers were given access to some classified information, that information was used as background and to give direction for further study, but not included in this chapter.

Typically in research one reviews previous research to integrate the findings as well as to identify consistencies and inconsistencies. In the current study, there is a virtual void in the literature. Empirical research on computer crime per se is very limited–particularly recent research during the era of explosive technological growth and an exponential expansion of networking. As a result, limited literature is cited.

DEFINING ORGANIZED CRIME

Historically, organized crime has been viewed in terms of the traditional or familial crime syndicates broadly known as La Cosa Nostra or the Mafia. In the past 15 years the perspective of organized crime has been broadened, largely as a result of drug trafficking, to include the South American drug trafficking groups (e.g., Medellin and Cali Cartels; Mexican Drug Cartels), Asian crime groups (e.g., Triads, Tongs, and Yakuza) and the many emerging groups from Central and Eastern Europe. As we look toward the future it is increasingly evident that organized crime must be viewed from an even broader context–a new paradigm.

Law enforcement organizations are beginning to respond to this change. For example, Interpol defines organized crime as "any enterprise or group of persons engaged in a continuing illegal activity which has as its primary purpose the generation of profits and continuance of the enterprise regardless of national boundaries." From another perspective, the German Bundeskriminalamt (BKA) operationalizes organized crime as "the planned commission of criminal offenses, determined by the pursuit of profit and power, involving more than two persons over a prolonged or indefinite period of time, using a commercial or business license scheme, violence, and/or intimidation."

While some variance exists in these definitions, clearly the trend among international law enforcement organizations is away from the familial view and toward a more entrepreneurial perspective. The movement toward viewing organized crime as "enterprise crime" is because of its market-driven nature–any commodity where a profit can be earned is open to organized crime.

Entrepreneurial groups appear to develop through an evolutionary process. Experiences of investigators indicate that individuals–and perhaps small groups–who have common criminal interests tend to loosely amalgamate for certain criminal purposes. Just as in the case of many new business initiatives, if the crime amalgamation seems to work–that is, generate profits–then the enterprise takes on more structured characteristics. Some groups may be short-term alliances with minimal structure–essentially adhocracies–others become quite sophisticated organizations. Clearly, however, levels of structure and sophistication vary widely on a continuum with a notable degree of ebb and flow between crime groups. This fluid nature makes it difficult to develop a clear picture of these enterprises as well as to give an accurate assessment of their activities. The adoption of computer technology to criminal enterprises follows a similar developmental path.

COMPUTERS AS INSTRUMENTALITIES OF ORGANIZED CRIME

Why are computers increasingly becoming an important tool to criminal groups? The reasons are quite simple: In many venues computers permit faster, more productive work at lower cost with fewer personnel. Based on this project's interviews as well as a content analysis of other sources of information, several applications have been identified wherein criminal enterprises have used computers.

Maintaining Records of the Enterprise

Evidence by law enforcement and intelligence organizations have found crime groups keeping computerized records in a manner similar to businesses. Records that have been discovered include:

- Contraband shipment schedules
- Income and expenses of contraband or commodities
- Databases of conspirators and "customers"
- Locations, account numbers, and status of monetary transactions (typically money being laundered)
- Records of monetary transfers and payments
- Databases and "status" of bribed or vulnerable officials
- Dossiers of officials, conspirators, and others with whom the crime group has an interest.

In most cases of recordkeeping there was some type of file protection, although typically the protection was rudimentary. For example, password controls built into a word processing program or a commercial encryption program were the most common forms of protection. While these controls would keep the casual user from accessing the files, the protections could be circumvented comparatively easily by persons with the appropriate expertise. In some cases criminals attempted to erase hard drives and physically destroy floppy disks. In most of these instances computer forensics experts were able to recover much of the data. Some evidence indicates that criminals using computers for recordkeeping are becoming more technologically literate with respect to file protections and data erasure. As a result, evidence gathering could become more difficult.

An emerging issue is remote recordkeeping via networks. Rather than a criminal enterprise keeping records on a hard drive, records were kept on a remote computer in a different country that could be accessed as needed. In one case, a criminal enterprise conspirator operating out of England kept remote records on a computer in the Czech Republic. The criminal's apparent intent was that, if arrested, there would be no records of the enterprise at his home or office. While no arrests were made nor could these allegations be proven, the informant providing the information was deemed reliable. With the growth of Internet Service Providers around the world and increased ease of networking, this scenario is certainly feasible.

Using Technology to Counterfeit Currency and Documents

Computer technology has provided a revolution in the counterfeit currency and document business. Past counterfeiting activities required skilled engravers and printers as well as expensive photographic and printing equipment. Using these traditional methods, successful counterfeiting was a labor-intensive task that required expert workmanship and equipment that was bulky and somewhat uncommon, making investigations easier. In addition, because of the required skill levels and equipment, there were relatively few successful counterfeit operations.

However, with color scanners, color printers, sophisticated word processing and graphics software suites, and computer-driven color balancing photocopiers, successful counterfeiting has not only significantly broadened, but has also become much more difficult to detect. As one example, the U.S. $100 bill was the most frequently counterfeited currency in the world. With computerized counterfeiting, the global market was becoming flooded with counterfeit $100 bills (particularly in Central and Eastern Europe). As a result, the U.S. Treasury changed the bill's design and incorporated a watermark (like most of the rest of the world's currency) and other security factors. It was announced by the Treasury Department that the new $100 bill was virtually impossible to counterfeit. It was reported by interviewees that within a month of the new bill's introduction into circulation good counterfeit copies surfaced in Eastern Europe. High resolution color scanning of an original can even pick up the watermark and colors of fibers in the paper that are, in turn, reproduced by high quality printers.

The same scanning process and graphics software are used for counterfeit passports. Counterfeiters maintain scanned "masters" of various passports–Dutch and German documents appear to be particularly popular–in computer files. They are then able to readily enter appropriate names, photographs, and identity information in the files to prepare a high quality counterfeit.

Another particularly unique application of the technology has been found to make new certificates of origin and ownership papers of stolen vehicles using the actual Vehicle Identification Number (VIN) of the stolen auto. Like the passports, master files of documents–such as certificates of origin and titles–are scanned into the computer. They are then printed using the stolen vehicle's description and VIN along with the new "owner's" identification. Sophisticated auto theft rings operating from Poland to Morocco have used this method.

While this approach to counterfeiting can obviously occur anywhere, it has been most evident in Northwest Africa. However, growing use has been found in Southeast Asia.

Supporting the Distribution of Counterfeit Products

The marketing of counterfeit products–ranging from Rolex watches to Microsoft software to Levi's jeans–is well documented. The extent to which "traditional" organized crime is involved is debated; however, there is strong evidence that such groups are strongly involved in the "marketing" and distribution of these products in what is referred to by Her Majesty's Customs and Excise Service (of the United Kingdom) as the "fakes trade."

While skilled craft workers have been quite successful in designing and manufacturing counterfeit products, Customs and corporate security investigators frequently relied on product logos and subtle design and coloration characteristics to distinguish licensed products from counterfeit ones. This too is changing because of computer technology.

As in the case of counterfeit currency and documents, criminal enterprises have been using color scanners and computer-driven color printers to scan legitimate logos, product tags, and such things as "jackets" and labels of videotapes, audio tapes, and software. Using the scanned images as masters, skilled printers are able to prepare these materials to complement the knock-off products. One corporate security director told the authors that while this process was an additional wrinkle for investigators to overcome because the process made the product look more legitimate to the consumer. (In some cases, counterfeit products not only looked a great deal like the original, the quality was also good.) With authentic-appearing packaging, the enterprise could sell more of their counterfeit products at higher prices and still undercut the legitimate manufacturer's sales.

The counterfeit trade is also growing in the area of fake computer components. Particularly popular appear to be counterfeit modems and hard drives, which, apparently can be duplicated and manufactured with comparative ease. As with any counterfeit product, they are marketed under a popular brand name at a significant savings. Interestingly, these counterfeits appear to work quite well and be reliable. When consumers receive a good product at a low price there are few complaints.

By far, the vast majority of counterfeiting described in this section is occurring in southeast Asia. The exception appears to be the counterfeit movies on videocassette that are increasingly originating from Eastern Europe. Interestingly, even hard-core pornographic videotapes have been counterfeited and distributed.

Techno-Exploitation of Sexually Related Commerce

Most people have heard news accounts about various forms of individual sexually related misconduct occurring via the Internet of which organized crime has virtually no involvement. Keeping in mind that the sole purpose of a criminal enterprise is to make a profit, the focus of organized crime in cyberspace is to promote sexually related commerce.

According to investigators from Europe, North Africa, North America, and Asia, new criminal enterprises have emerged, largely consisting of intelligent, young entrepreneurs who are familiar with the capabilities and potential of computers as a tool for sexual commerce. These emerging groups do not neatly fit into traditional definitions of organized crime, yet they nonetheless are ongoing enterprises that are frequently violating the criminal law in order to gain a profit. A problem exists, however, because many of these groups' activities fall into the gray area of law. That is, some of their activities are lawful (or at least it may be debated that they are lawful). Other activities may be lawful in their country or state/province of origin but are unlawful in other areas where clientele may be served. Because of these legal ambiguities and the fact that sexual commerce is viewed as being less serious than other forms of crime, comparatively little attention is given to these groups with the exception of child pornography.

Predominantly originating from North America, Scandinavia, and Asia, among the activities of these groups are:

- International transmission of pornographic photographs
- International transmission of obscene written materials
- International transmission of child pornography
- International sales of sexual aids, particularly those related to sexual fetishes
- Advertising, negotiation, and appointments for both male and female prostitution (so-called "cyber-brothels")
- Subscription/fee e-mail services for sexual fantasies
- Live video sex shows via the Internet where customers can type instructions for the way they want live "models" to perform

Some unusual complications emerge from these enterprises. In one alleged case, Algerian and Jordanian officials were seeking to close access from a Website in Denmark that was marketing pornographic photographs of Middle Eastern women. The unique element of this case was that aspects of the photographs apparently desecrated Islam, thus the violations were deemed serious. In another unusual case it was alleged by a French firm that sexual aids being sold through a Website were actually counterfeit products violating international copyright treaties.

Officials admit it is difficult to determine which activities in this arena are unlawful. It frequently depends on the jurisdiction of the consumer, yet legal precedence has typically not advanced as quickly as the technology. One U.S. Customs investigator stated that there have been times a case was started on intuition, only to learn later that there was not a specific U.S. law violation. The investigator went on to note, however, that many people who are involved in computer-based sexual commerce are also frequently associated with some other form of criminal enterprise.

While unlawful sexual commerce does not pose the same threat as many other forms of organized crime, it does help fuel the underground economy and provide income to criminal enterprises that, in turn, may support other forms of criminality.

Unlawful Gaming

Gambling has always been a favorite–and profitable–activity for organized crime groups. Casino skimming operations in Las Vegas, panchinko rigging in Japan, and unlawful sports betting around the world have turned huge profits for criminal enterprises. It was only natural that entrepreneurial criminals would turn to computerization–particularly the Internet–in order to expand their reach, hence their profits.

At this point it appears most unlawful computerized gaming operations–notably in North America and Asia–are not networked but are accessible via modem. However, accessibility to such operations are increasingly available through the Internet. The operations generally work the same whether it is a Bulletin Board Service (BBS) or Website. Typically the user must "join a club" to be given access to the site for gambling. Part of the membership ruse is to pay "dues" that are used as bets. Most typically gamblers supply a credit card number wherein they can purchase "units" to wager–a unit is essentially an electronic poker chip. (Most typically, all wagers and transactions are converted to U.S. dollars regardless of the country of origin.)

In some cases, when a member joins and is given his or her personal identification number, they can then make a deposit–usually either by wire or money order–to a front company that serves as the "bank" for the gambling operation. All bets and communications are then conducted via the computer link. When the gambler wins he or she is typically given credits that can be used for further wagers or they can request payment, typically through the front company that serves as a bank. Credit card "credits" are typically not used for two reasons: (1) the gamblers want their winnings quickly in a readily convertible form and (2) it is feared that the issuance of too many credits to a given card number would raise questions leading to investigations.

Interestingly, one British investigator said that the financial transaction accounting procedures for these unlawful gaming operations were quite accurate and reliable. The reason: Operators make money from the "repeat business" of gamblers–if they cannot trust the enterprise, they will not bet their money.

Among the types of networked and BBS gambling operations that have been discovered are sports Books (e.g., soccer, football, horse racing, Olympics, boxing, etc.), elections, "numbers" rackets or unlawful lotteries, and video poker simulators.

Computer-Assisted Theft and Fraud

As computers are increasingly used to account for and make financial transactions, criminals are increasingly accessing them to unlawfully transfer funds, defraud, or steal information. The most common target of computer-assisted thefts by criminal enterprises is intellectual property. As information becomes an increasingly valuable commodity, organized criminals have learned how to market stolen information for high profits and substantially less risk than more traditional illicit commodity trafficking. Theft of such information as trade secrets, new product information, product pricing plans, and customer lists have proven to be highly profitable. The cost to a business competitor to pay for this stolen information is far less than original research, development, and marketing. Increasingly active in this arena are criminal enterprises in Japan, the United States, France, and Germany. While these transactions typically do not have the violence and emotional daring associated with more traditional organized crime activities, the economic toll can be far higher.

The second area of computer-assisted theft by organized crime is fraud. The Florida Division of Insurance Fraud has discovered fraud through altered computer programs that underreport insurance agency incomes. Medical and pharmaceutical overpayments through Medicare/Medicaid have also been fraudulently made in many ways through the altering of computer records and, more commonly, the use of shell companies billing the government for medical services, equipment, and pharmaceuticals. While these forms of theft net significant amounts of money, they typically are not products of broad-based organized crime, although they frequently meet the technical definition of a criminal enterprise.

Criminal enterprises have been found to be involved in frauds related to thefts of credit card numbers for which purchases are made via fax, telephone and, in some cases, over the Internet. One criminal enterprise emerging from West Africa (notably Nigeria, Liberia, Ivory Coast, and Sierra Leone) involved the purchasing of computer equipment, memory, and peripherals via telephone orders using stolen credit cards from North America and the United Kingdom where "clearance" of the credit card's validity could take weeks. The new equipment would then be sold in its original packages to individuals or commercial outlets where manufacturer's orders were small or slow to arrive. Other forms of credit card fraud using similar methods have occurred in Malaysia and South Africa. Evidence suggests that these thieves are somewhat like "outsource employees" of organized crime groups. That is, the thieves are simply paid for the "live" numbers they steal and members of the criminal enterprise "core group" perform the remaining criminal acts.

Telecommunications Fraud

Telecommunications fraud is a particularly profitable area of computer-related crime that has many approaches. Previously individual criminal entrepreneurs were committing these crimes but they are increasingly being pushed out by organized crime groups because the profits are so high and the risk is so low.

There are three types of telecommunications fraud by computer in that criminal enterprises appear to be most involved. One is the theft of telephone credit card numbers which can be gained by accessing computer records, some computerized voice mail boxes, and telephone billing files. Prime targets are large multinational corporations because discovery of the fraudulent billings takes longer. The billing numbers are either sold "on the street" or, as is increasingly the case, sold to other crime groups for their use. In one case, stolen corporate telephone billing numbers from a United States-based multinational company were being sold to various drug trafficking groups, which in turn used the stolen numbers to make arrangements for drug transactions and shipments. Payment for the stolen numbers was cheaper than paying for numerous international calls and it was more difficult for investigators to link the calls to their principle investigative targets.

The second type of telecommunications fraud, which has actually decreased, involves hacking into telecommunications "switches" (which are computers) for the purpose of routing calls and changing billing numbers. While individual hackers still break into the switches, organized efforts to do this have largely stopped as a result of more aggressive security precautions by telecommunications carriers.

The third area of telecommunications fraud is the largest and fastest growing: cellular phone theft and fraud. This too was started by individuals and small groups but is increasingly involving criminal enterprises. The process originally involved the capture of cellular telephone billing numbers being emitted from users' telephones. Using a device that detects and records the number, it could then be sold and programmed into a person's wireless phone. The number is typically usable for about one month before it is detected as being stolen. The fraudulent user would then need to purchase a new number.

Because of the large number of cellular telephones in use and the ease in which a large number of billing codes could be captured (a telephone does not have to be in use, but simply turned on in order to emit the billing code), the process became one of "assembly line theft." Essentially, a "client" pays a flat fee and receives a new billing number each month or whenever the number they are using is canceled. (It is recommended that a stolen number not be used over one month in case it is being traced by investigators.) The "service provider" typically has the computer equipment to readily reprogram the client's cell phone. Averaging about $30 a month ($60 if a "new" telephone is also obtained) with several hundred clients in a "territory" and several territories within a given geographic area, the profits can add up quickly and, again, with minimal risk.

As computer-driven telecommunications systems become more prevalent around the world, as reliance on computerized switching increases, with broader use of international telecommunications for data transmission, and as videoconferencing increases, the amounts of money that can be made through telecommunications fraud becomes staggering.

Support of Illegal Immigration Enterprises

Outside of refugees fleeing into countries such as Zambia and Thailand from neighboring countries embroiled in civil war, the European Union countries have experienced some of the largest influx of illegal immigrants (notably from Central and Eastern Europe). Seeking both peace and economic opportunity, the new immigrants have made many sacrifices–including financial ones–to achieve their goals. As in other cases when governments are slow in responding to a crisis–if they respond at all–criminal enterprises will fill the void.

In these cases, evidence has indicated that organized crime groups previously involved mostly in black market smuggling have created new processes to smuggle immigrants into Western countries with "appropriate" documentation, typically for a substantial fee. While computers play a comparatively smaller role in these enterprises, they nonetheless help expedite the scheme through the use of such processes as logistics and arrangements via e-mail, computer-forged immigration documents, and general recordkeeping related to this enterprise.

Because there has been substantially increased investigations in these human smuggling enterprises in the European Union, the criminal enterprises have explored new immigration options. For example, a Korean immigration investigative supervisor recently told the authors that his office has seen an increase in the number of immigrants from Europe, many with counterfeit passports that are of high caliber (presumably computer generated) and difficult to distinguish from legitimate documents.

While illegal immigration from Mexico and Central America into the United States remains a problem, it is actually one of a smaller scale than the European Union has experienced since the fall of the Iron Curtain. Moreover, while there are some organized groups–known as "coyotes"–smuggling the immigrants into the United States, they have not shown the same level of technological sophistication as the European enterprises.

Expanding the Reach of the Black Market

In virtually every country in the world there is a black market available to provide people with products they need or desire but simply cannot obtain through the open market processes. The black market trades in any commodity that will turn a profit, particularly if the commodity is contraband (ranging from prohibited pharmaceuticals to Cuban cigars), counterfeit (Rolex watches have remained a long-standing popular black market item), or stolen property (anything that is popular but either too expensive to purchase off the shelf or difficult to locate.) In nearly every black market, organized crime is omnipresent.

Outside of its illegal commodities and avoidance of licensing and taxes, the black market operates much like any business. It is market-driven; requires suppliers, transportation and distribution networks; it has a payroll; it must remain competitive; and is obliged to keep its customers satisfied in order to maintain repeat clientele. Because of the similarities with legitimate businesses, black market criminal enterprises have increasingly resembled legitimate business operations.

Just as in any business, the black market needs to make its inventory descriptions known to both the "sales staff" and potential clients. Photographs, product descriptions, costs, inquiry processes, and related information for a wide variety of commodities have been found in computer files; in a few cases the files are accessible through a restricted BBS. Additionally, some black market merchandise is increasingly available for order through the Internet (under the guise of a legitimate business), vastly expanding the enterprises' market, hence profits. In addition, computerization via networking or a BBS provides increased anonymity to specific individuals in the criminal group.

Black market items found to be using computerization–beyond traditional items such as clothing, watches or electronics–include such diverse commodities as high demand/popular items that have been stolen or counterfeited (e.g., electronics, designer clothing, watches, etc.); arts and antiquities; endangered species skins and by-products; armaments; body parts; and children available for adoption.

Particularly with the global expansion of the Internet, in all likelihood its application to the black market will increase. The reason: It's good business.

CONCLUSION

Given the growth and widespread accessibility of computers, it is reasonable to assume that applications of the technology by organized crime groups will increase. The conclusion that one would thus draw is that the criminal justice system must examine its policies and preparedness to deal with this criminal phenomenon. In light of this, there are several important policy implications from this research.

First, it reinforces the need for law enforcement and prosecutors to revisit their definition of organized crime. The view of criminal enterprises in the traditional familial structure remains the predominant perspective in law enforcement. Ironically, this is a particularly American police characteristic–law enforcement organizations in many other countries are more likely to accept the entrepreneurial model of organized crime (whether or not computerization is involved).

Second, with the acceptance of a new benchmark of organized crime–that is, enterprise crime–criminal justice officials must take one more step to recognize the role of technology in this genre of criminality. Computers must be as readily accepted as a criminal instrument as is a gun. These two factors alone require a substantial paradigm shift for investigators and prosecutors in organized crime cases.

Criminal justice personnel need training on the entrepreneurial model of crime, computers as a criminal instrument, investigation and evidence collection techniques, as well as an overview of the various laws and factors related to these forms of investigations. In essence, criminal justice personnel must be resocialized with respect to organized crime. This is a process that requires time, patience, and aggressive learning goals.

Given that many criminal enterprises are chameleon-like, masquerading as legitimate business, and law enforcement is comparatively slow at embracing technology as a criminal tool, the role of playing "catch up" has already been cast. Future research will provide insight on the ability of law enforcement to deal with these groups.

It took American law enforcement nearly 70 years to identify, accept, investigate, and prosecute the heart of Italian/Sicilian organized crime. While La Cosa Nostra remains, its power and influence is only a skeleton of what it once was. In many ways the Mafia has been neutralized.

Given the speed of computers, the diverse character of information and communications systems, the ease of international travel, and the growing innovation of criminals, we do not have 70 years to control these emerging entrepreneurial groups. By that time, such groups will have metastasized, becoming institutional elements in our economic and political systems.

AUTHOR INDEX

R

S

T

V

W

Y

Z

SUBJECT INDEX

The Official Guide

Linksys® Networks

Third Edition

The Official Guide

Linksys® Networks

Third Edition

Walter Glenn

McGraw-Hill Osborne

New York Chicago San Francisco Lisbon
London Madrid Mexico City Milan New Delhi
San Juan Seoul Singapore Sydney Toronto

The McGraw-Hill Companies

McGraw-Hill/Osborne
2100 Powell Street, 10th Floor
Emeryville, California 94608
U.S.A.

To arrange bulk purchase discounts for sales promotions, premiums, or fund-raisers, please contact **McGraw-Hill**/Osborne at the above address. For information on translations or book distributors outside the U.S.A., please see the International Contact Information page immediately following the index of this book.

Linksys® Networks: The Official Guide, Third Edition

567890 CUS CUS 019876

ISBN 0-07-225858-6

Executive Editor: Jane K. Brownlow
Senior Project Editor: LeeAnn Pickrell
Acquisitions Coordinator: Jessica Wilson
Technical Editor: James F. Kelly
Copy Editor: Lisa Theobald
Proofreader: Judy Wilson
Indexer: Valerie Perry
Composition: Lucie Ericksen
Illustrator: Lucie Ericksen
Series Design: Mickey Galicia
Cover Design: Pattie Lee

This book was composed with Corel VENTURA™ Publisher.

Dedication

To my mom, Lue English

About the Author

Walter Glenn has been a part of the computer industry for over 17 years and currently works in Huntsville, Alabama, as a consultant, trainer, and writer. He has helped thousands of computer users, from beginners to experts, learn more about using their computers and networks. Walter is the author or co-author of over twenty books on different versions of Windows, networking, and other computer applications. He is the author of *Windows XP Tips & Techniques,* also from McGraw-Hill/Osborne.

Contents at A Glance

Contents

Acknowledgments

As usual, there were a lot of people involved in the making of this book. At McGraw-Hill/Osborne, I'd like to thank Acquisitions Editor Jane Brownlow for this opportunity. Thanks also to Jessica Wilson for her guidance while writing this book. My thanks also goes to Technical Editor Jim Kelly, who worked diligently to make sure I got everything right. And I also owe huge thanks to Copy Editor Lisa Theobald for making sure the language in this book is appropriate and correct.

Introduction

This book is the third edition of *Linksys Networks: The Official Guide.* This edition includes updated information about new devices, new security technologies, and a major new software update from Microsoft—Windows XP Service Pack 2.

This book focuses on the hardware side of networking, rather than the usual "everything you want to know about, or do with, a network." This book helps you understand how to install, configure, maintain, and troubleshoot the hardware setup for your home network or your small business network. As I've learned over the years, people have the most trouble during the setup stage and this book should help you come through that experience relatively unscathed.

I have spent more than 17 years setting up networks of all sizes for my clients. I keep a network in my office and in my home, and I've always been a big fan of Linksys hardware. I use Linksys products throughout my own networks and those of my clients. Because Linksys is the leading vendor of network hardware for home and small business networks, it seemed natural and appropriate to present information about Linksys hardware in a book that focuses on the hardware side of networking.

Benefits of a Network

Anyone who owns more than one computer should create a network. Creating a network is easy and the resulting benefits are enormous. In fact, aside from some initial cost and a little time, there are no "downsides" to moving to a network environment.

Share an Internet Connection

Whenever the subject of connecting computers via a network is discussed, as soon as someone says, "you can share an Internet connection if you create a network," people who own multiple computers listen carefully. That's the big selling point!

If I were to list the top ten reasons homeowners and small businesses cite for creating a network, a shared Internet connection is the big one.

No matter how you connect to the Internet, without a network you have a constant battle among the computer users in your home or business for access to that Internet device. If you use a telephone modem, even if each computer has its own modem, you probably have only one telephone line dedicated to modem use. (If you've installed multiple telephone lines to accommodate multiple computers with modems, buying the hardware for a network pays for itself within a few months; after that you're saving money.)

Every time a user wants to use the modem line, he or she must check to see if a user at another computer is connected to the Internet. If so, you're probably used to hearing "get off the modem, I need to get to the Internet." Sharing a connection over a network eliminates that problem. If you have only one telephone line, period, the battle between callers and modem users is probably constant—put a second line in for modem use and share it over a network. This will stop all that yelling you hear so often, "Get off the modem, I'm expecting a call" or "Get off the modem, I want to make a call."

If you have a DSL/cable modem, it's connected to one computer. Anyone who wants to go online must use that computer (and, of course, everybody wants to go online all the time). No matter how many computers you own, everybody wants to use that computer. Sharing that device on a network means that anyone can work at any computer and reach the Internet.

Share Printers

Networking means you don't have to buy a printer for every computer. Of course, you may not have adopted that model when you bought your second (or third) computer, in which case only one computer has a printer. Users who want to print documents have to work at that computer or have to save their document on a floppy disk, carry the floppy disk to the computer with the printer, open the software that created the document (the software has to be installed on the computer with the printer), open the document in the software, and print the document. What a pain! (By the way, the technical jargon for a multiple computer setup where users have to walk floppy disks to computers in order to print or to attach a document to e-mail is called a *sneakernet*.)

Many homes and small businesses have a printer attached to each computer, but the printers are not the same. If you're working at the computer with a laser printer but want to print a particular document to an inkjet color printer, you have to wait until the computer attached to the color printer is free. When you create a network, any user working at any computer can print to any printer.

Access Files No Matter Where They Are

In most homes and businesses with multiple computers, each user has a favorite (or assigned) computer. The user (let's call her "Mom") works at that computer (let's call it "study") and saves documents on that computer's hard drive. One day Mom finds her son working on "study" (there are always more users than computers) when she wants to work on a document she's been toiling over, or she wants to start a new document based on a template she's created. She needs to tell her son to stop what he's doing and give her the computer. If her son is like most kids, he complains that he can't stop—he's doing homework or he's in the middle of an Instant Message conversation that is so important it will determine his social life and happiness for months to come. Sometimes it works the other way around—Mom is at the computer and son comes to whine that he started his homework on that computer and can't work on the computer in the kitchen (and besides, Dad is on that computer).

When you create a network, any document or template that you've created on any computer is available when you work at any other computer.

Fun and Games

If you have a network, you can play network games, where users on separate computers play against each other. Microsoft even provides a number of Internet games for free along with Windows XP. Try them; they're fun!

Is This Book for You?

This book explains and simplifies the process of installing a network. If you have multiple computers and have been thinking about creating a network, your network will be up and running quickly as a result of the information within these pages.

If you have multiple computers and haven't thought about creating a network, think again! Then read this book!

Conventions and Special Effects in This Book

To make it easier to get through the technical explanations, this book does several things:

- Makes the language as straightforward and easy to understand as possible
- Provides a glossary of networking terminology (Appendix A)
- Uses special treatment for special text:
  - **Bold type** indicates characters you type when you're supplying information to the operating system.
  - *Italic type* indicates a "geeky" technical term or jargon (and is accompanied by an explanation of the meaning).

In addition, you'll find some special effects. These effects are set apart from the regular text in the book, with special formatting and placement on the page.

- **Tips** are nuggets of information that add to your knowledge or make it easier to complete a task.
- **Notes** are informative tidbits of information that might make it easier to understand a task or to complete a task in a manner better suited to your own situation.
- **Cautions** are warnings about things that could go wrong, along with an explanation of the steps to take to avoid the problem.
- **Sidebars** are technical explanations that you don't really have to understand to perform a task, but that you might be interested in anyway.

Assumptions About You

In writing this book, I'm assuming you know how to use a computer but don't have a great deal of expertise on computer hardware, operating systems, or computer communication protocols. I'm also assuming you have multiple computers and they may not all be running the same version of Windows.

Considering current statistics on home computers and small business computers, I've concentrated on explaining how to perform tasks in Windows XP and Windows 98 Second Edition (SE). However, for some tasks, you'll find references to Windows 2000 and Windows Me, especially when performing tasks in those Windows versions differs substantially from the way you perform the tasks in Windows XP/98SE. The coverage of Windows 2000 and Windows Me isn't consistent throughout the book, but that's because of a couple of facts. First, it's unusual to find Windows 2000 running on home computers or in small businesses that don't have networks. Second, Windows Me didn't sell well and has so many problems that many Windows Me users upgraded their systems to Windows XP (and any who didn't, should). That last sentence also tells you something about the author of this book: I don't mind sharing my opinions, and you'll find them throughout this book. My opinions aren't arbitrary; they're based on many years of experience.

About Linksys

California-based Linksys is the worldwide leader in the development of both wired and wireless networking solutions for homes, small offices, and businesses. Founded in 1988, Linksys began with the vision that networking should be easy to use and affordable, helping people share documents, files, mail, and most of all—ideas.

In 2001, Linksys captured the #1 worldwide market share position in the shipments of routers and wireless solutions. You'll find Linksys' award-winning products in more than 8,400 retail stores in the U.S. and in 1,100 stores in 54 countries worldwide. Linksys' extensive selection of over 150 products are also best sellers on e-commerce Web sites and through more than 1,000 Value Added Resellers.

Part I

Getting Started

In this part, you learn about the choices you have for creating your network. The choices influence the hardware you buy and install. In the following chapters, you'll find detailed explanations about network connectivity choices, along with their pros and cons.

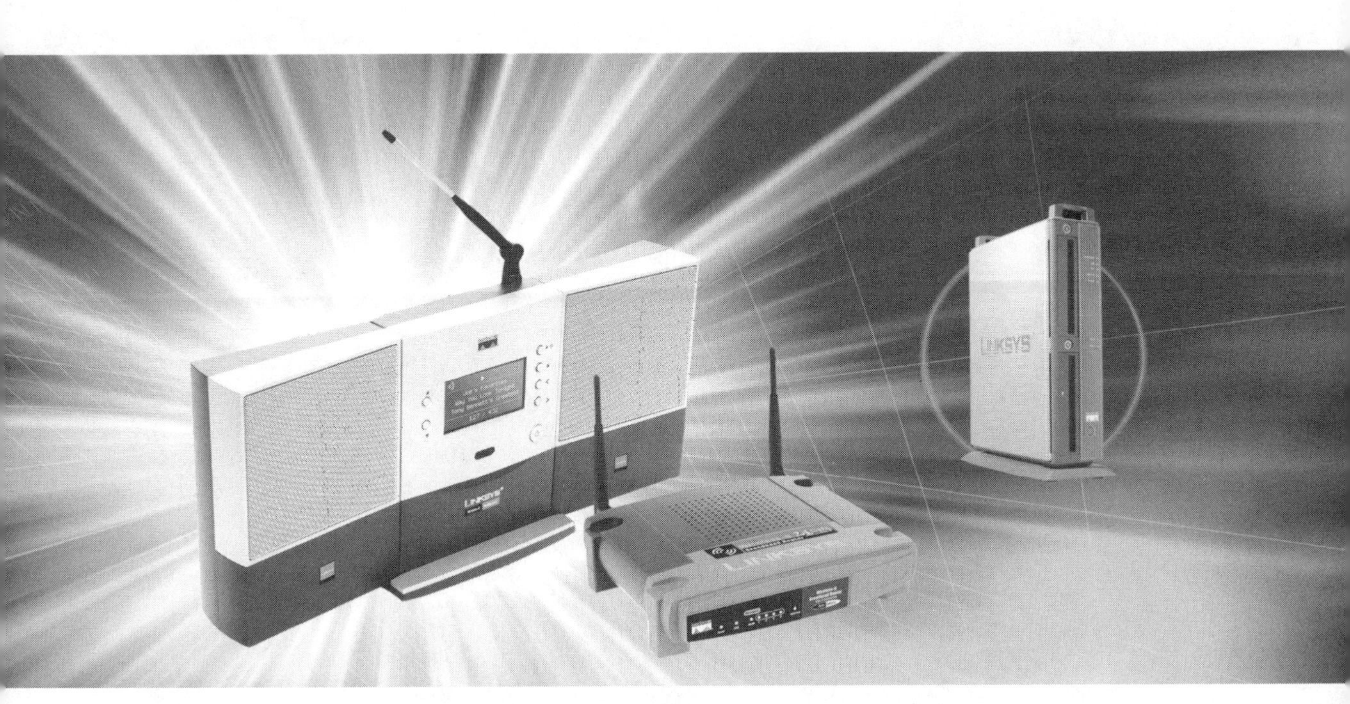

Chapter 1

Networking Choices

Before you grab a screwdriver, drill a hole for cable, or open your computer to add networking components, you need a plan. When the ultimate plan is a small network in your home or in your place of business, you need to take a step back and make some decisions before you pick up your tools. You have a lot of choices about the way you design and install your network, and you can't do anything definitive until you understand them.

In this chapter (and the following two chapters), you learn what a network is, how it works, and the pros and cons of the various network hardware options. You also learn how to install hardware networking components and how to add peripherals (printers, modems, routers, and so on) to your network.

What's a Network?

A network is nothing more than two or more computers that are connected so they can exchange data. The smallest networks are found in millions of homes, where home users have connected a few different computers so that they can share Internet access or trade files. The largest network in the world is the Internet, which is made up of servers and lots of smaller networks. At any given moment, all the computers in the world that are using the Internet are also part of the Internet network.

In between those extremes are millions of corporate and small business networks comprising anywhere from two to hundreds of thousands of connected computers. What you may not realize is that all networks, regardless of their size, share common characteristics:

- Every computer contains a hardware device that controls communication with the other computers on the network.
- Every computer has a connection method (wireless or wired) that sends data to the other computers, using the hardware communication device.

When you create a home network or a network for your business, you'll be using the same approach used by the network designers who create enormous corporate enterprises. As far as hardware and connection requirements are concerned, your network is no different than any other network in the world. While networking may seem overwhelmingly complicated, you'll be amazed at how simple and logical it is if you take it one step at a time.

You have some decisions to make regarding the type of connections you want to use between your computers and the way in which users will join the network.

This chapter provides an overview of your choices, and all the other chapters in this book will help you implement those choices.

Types of Networks

Networks are designed to be either client/server networks or peer-to-peer networks. Each type has its advantages and disadvantages, but small networks are almost always created as peer-to-peer networks. Regardless of the network type you opt for, the hardware and connection devices you have to install in each computer are the same.

Client/Server Networks

Client/server networks are built for security and controls. A server, equipped with special software tools, checks the computers and users who are logging in to the network and allows only those with valid credentials to access computers and other resources on the network. Information, including names and passwords, about each computer and user is stored in a database on one or more servers. As each computer boots and each user logs on, their logon data is checked against the information in the database (see Figure 1-1).

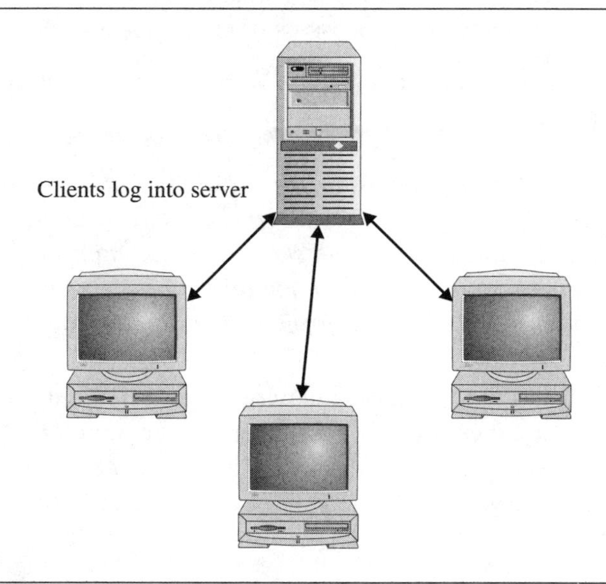

FIGURE 1-1 Client logon data is checked against server records.

The server can also limit the rights and privileges of computers and users who log on to the network. Some users may be restricted from working with files in certain folders on network computers, or they may not be able to change settings on their own computers. These controls are imposed on a computer-by-computer or user-by-user basis, but to make it easier for administrators, computers and users can be placed into *groups*. The restrictions applied to a group apply to each member of the group. Assigning rights and privileges on a group basis is easier than dealing with each computer and user one at a time.

Most client/server networks are also designed for server-based work. Servers are set up all over the network (and they must also log on and be authenticated). Most of these servers are assigned a specific task; consider the following, for instance:

- A mail server that holds the company's e-mail software and the users' mailboxes
- The accounting software server, which can be accessed only by members of the accounting department
- Print servers that control the printers attached to them, so users can share printers
- Data servers that hold the documents that users create with software applications such as word processors or spreadsheets
- Web servers that host the company's Web site or an internal intranet site for employees

NOTE *In client/server environments, the software that each user runs is often configured to save documents to a server instead of to the user's own computer. This makes it easier to share data among users and also makes it easier to back up the data. (All administrators know that users rarely obey company mandates to perform backups of their own computers.)*

In addition to being able to access network servers, client computers in a Windows client/server network can access other client computers. This permits users to exchange or share data files directly. However, access to those resources is still controlled by the servers on the network, even though the access is granted on the client computer.

Users can opt to log on to their own computers, rather than the network, if they want. They won't be able to access any network resources, but this is a way to log on if a server is down.

NOTE *This client/server discussion represents a Windows-based network, but you may come across a different operating system in corporate environments, such as UNIX, Linux, or NetWare. All of those systems authenticate users to maintain controls and security, but the methods vary. In addition, the client/server relationship is usually absolute, so individual computers on a client/server network cannot access each other in a peer-to-peer fashion, nor can users log on to their local computers—they must join the network. Those last two distinctions enhance the network security.*

The biggest advantage of a client/server network is the level of security it can achieve, but for small networks, that advantage is usually outweighed by the cost of buying a server and server software to maintain those controls and by the technical knowledge required to set up and maintain the authentication processes. Because small networks have fewer computers and users, the need to develop security controls on a user-by-user or computer-by-computer basis is less daunting.

NOTE *In a Windows client/server network, the servers that authenticate computers and users when they log on are called domain controllers. When you log on to a computer that is a member of a domain, you can log on to the local computer or to the domain. In a peer-to-peer network, computers are members of a workgroup. When you log on to a computer that is a member of a workgroup, you log on to the local computer.*

Peer-To-Peer Networks

A peer-to-peer network is exactly what the term implies—every computer is equal. No servers equipped with authentication software utilities interfere with the process of logging on to a computer or to the network. All the computers on the network can communicate directly with all the other computers on the network (see Figure 1-2).

You can apply security measures to resources, such as files and folders, on each computer on the network. In fact, if one user decides that his computer is totally private, he can refuse to share any files or folders on his computer. That doesn't stop him from being able to access resources on another computer, though, if that other computer is sharing resources.

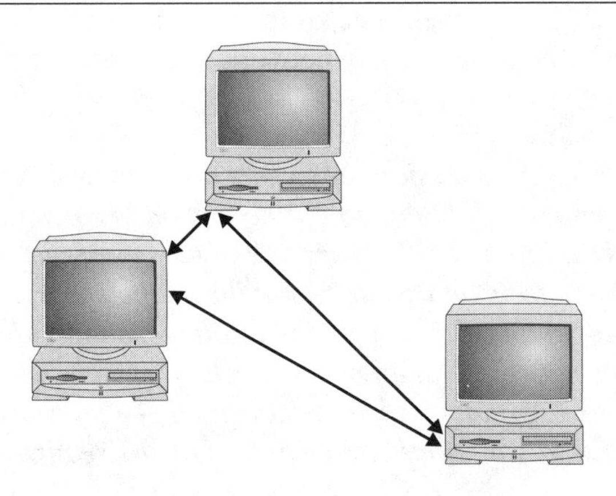

FIGURE 1-2 Computers are equivalent in a peer-to-peer network.

In addition, with peer-to-peer configuration, you don't entirely lose the concept, or efficiency, of a server. For example, you can use any computer on the network as a print server without interfering with a user's ability to work on that computer. A print server is a computer that has a printer connected to it, and that printer is configured as a shared printer, meaning others on the network with permission can use that printer. The user who works at the computer that is connected to the printer doesn't have to share any other resources, such as files or folders, because shared resources are set up on a resource-by-resource basis.

You can also maintain data files for certain software applications on one computer, which essentially treats the computer as a server. For example, many accounting software applications work in this mode (QuickBooks is an example of this file-sharing method).

The real distinction between a client/server network and a peer-to-peer network, then, is not what services computers can provide, but where the logon validation happens. On a client/server network, security is centralized on one or more servers. On a peer-to-peer network, security happens on each client computer.

In some versions of Windows (Windows 2000 and Windows XP), you can impose security on the logon process so that nobody except an existing, recognized user who knows the password can log on. In addition, each logged-on user can be restricted in his or her ability to make changes to the system's configuration.

When you log on, you join a *workgroup*, a group of computers that are connected to each other in a peer-to-peer network.

Network Administration

A certain amount of administrative work is involved in creating and maintaining a network. Luckily, if you're creating a peer-to-peer network, most of the administrative tasks don't fall into the category of "real work"; this is all more like "set it and forget it." The fact that administrative tasks must be performed is the result of some important networking concepts and rules, which I'll discuss in this section. This book is really about network hardware, and it won't cover all of the software and operating system issues involved in networking. However, it's important to present an overview of what you're going to face as you create, configure, and run your network.

Computer and Workgroup Names

Every computer that joins a network must have a name, and the name must be unique on the network. The computers communicate with each other every time a user accesses any network resource, and the computers don't have a way of determining that you meant this Bob, not the other Bob. One computer named Bob to a network, please. In addition, when you create a network, you must also name the workgroup.

You can name a computer when you install the operating system, and if you bought a computer from a manufacturer that installed the operating system for you, it may already have a name (something really creative, descriptive, and easy to remember like DEO77495FG077MR). Some people name their first computer Brown, because that's the family name; then when they buy another computer, they name it Brown, and perhaps even when a third computer arrives, it, too, is named Brown. That's neither unusual nor harmful—until you decide to create a network with all three computers.

When you install your network using one of the Windows networking wizards (available in Windows Me and Windows XP) or by setting configuration options manually (Windows 98SE and Windows 2000), you can name (or rename) the computer and the workgroup during the network setup process.

One method is to name a computer for the room in which it resides, so there's no chance of duplication and so that everyone understands where the computer is located. For example, Den, Kitchen, FrontDesk, Attic, Marysroom, and so on, are good choices.

The workgroup name can be anything you want, and each computer on your network must have the same workgroup name. The Windows networking wizards usually suggest something like *MSHome* or even *Workgroup*, but you can substitute another name for your workgroup. In fact, using the family or business name is a good option for the workgroup name.

Computer and workgroup names cannot be longer than 15 characters, and the following characters are forbidden in the name:

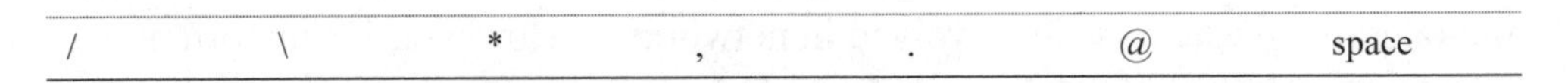

/	\	*	,	.	@	space

You can change the existing name of a computer (usually a task that's performed because of duplicate computer names) in the following way:

- In Windows XP, right-click My Computer and choose Properties from the shortcut menu. In the System Properties dialog, go to the Computer Name tab (see Figure 1-3). Click Change to enter a new name.

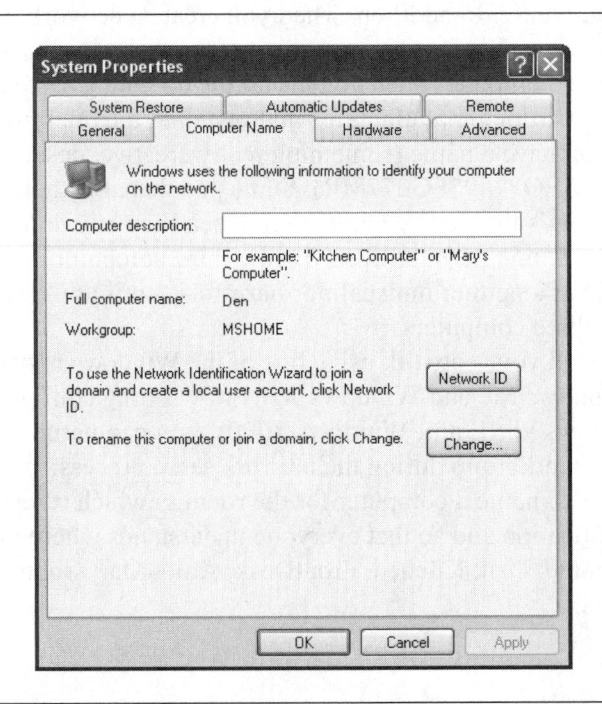

FIGURE 1-3 Changing a computer's name

- In Windows 2000, right-click My Computer and choose Properties from the shortcut menu. In the Properties dialog, go to the Network Identification tab and click Properties to change the name.
- In Windows 98SE/Me, open Control Panel, and then open the Network applet. Go to the Identification tab and type in a new name.

You'll have to restart the computer to have the change take effect.

User Settings

You can configure any computer to ask a user for a logon name and a password when the operating system starts. This approach provides several advantages to users and to your efforts to make your computers, and your network, secure.

If more than one person uses the computer, each user's configuration preferences are loaded when that user logs on—for example, desktop icons, the listings on the Start menu, the location of the My Documents folder, and other components are all exactly the way each user wants them. This is called a *user profile*, and each user's profile is stored on the computer.

For computers running Windows XP (and Windows 2000), individual logons also provide security measures that protect the computer, because you can configure the rights and privileges for each user. Users who have accounts configured for limited rights cannot perform certain functions; for instance, they may not be able to install software, and they cannot delete or modify system files (see Figure 1-4). If your network is part of your business, limited accounts make a great deal of sense. Even in a home network, a limited account may prevent damage if one of your household members tends to plunge into computer tasks without enough knowledge to stay out of trouble (usually, that means one of the parents—most kids are far more sophisticated about computers than their parents are). All network administrators can identify those users who "know enough to be dangerous"; these are the users they restrict.

For computers running Windows 98/Me, the only advantage to logons and passwords is in loading the user profile. There's no real security built into these operating systems. Any passing stranger can walk up to a Windows 98 computer, turn it on, and when the Logon dialog appears press ESC or click Cancel, and voilà—he's in the computer and can do anything he wants.

It's possible to use logon names and profiles without requiring a password (a user without a password is said to have a *null password*), and this scenario is common in many home networks. However, for a business network, where outsiders may be on the premises, it's a security risk to permit users to omit passwords.

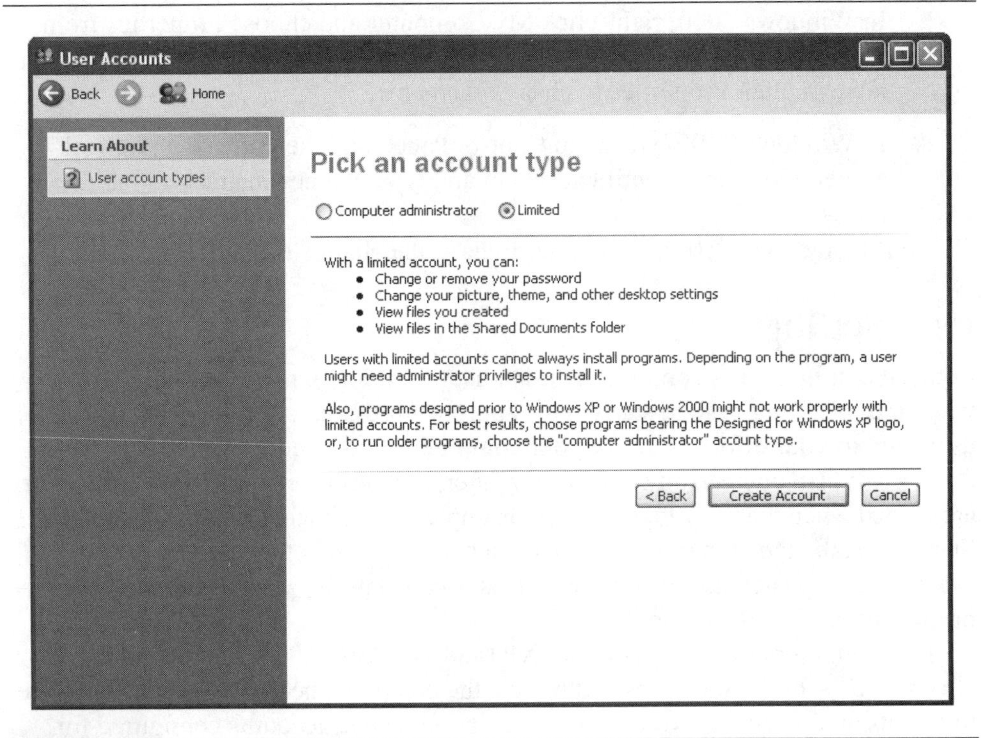

FIGURE 1-4 Creating a limited user account

Network Connection Choices

Before you can do anything about your network—before you buy the hardware—you have to choose a connection system. The decision you make affects the type of equipment you buy and the installation tasks you perform. You have several choices, and once you make your decision, you'll learn how to implement that decision by reading the appropriate chapter in this book.

But before you turn to the chapter on installation, you need to know which connection type you'll be using, because each connection type is covered in its own chapter. To help you decide, I'll present an overview of each of the following connection types:

- Ethernet cable
- Household telephone wires

- Household electrical wires
- Wireless Radio Frequency connections

The hardware devices you need to run these topologies are all available from Linksys. In the chapters that follow, I'll provide Linksys model names and numbers when appropriate.

During the discussion on connection choices, I'll be talking about the speed at which each connection type can transfer data among computers. Network speeds are rated in megabits per second (Mbps). A *megabit* is a million binary pulses, which doesn't mean anything unless you can think about it in a familiar perspective. The easiest way to do that is to think about a dial-up modem. The fastest dial-up modems available transmit data at the rate of 56,000 bits per second (or 56 kilobits

Network Connections Jargon

Even though a complete glossary of networking terms appears in Appendix A, I'll give you a brief rundown on some common terms here, so the section on connection types will be easier to understand (and you won't have to keep flipping the pages to look at Appendix A):

- *Topology* is the configuration of a network, including its layout and the type of connections used to create the network.
- *LAN*, which stands for Local Area Network, is a group of computers that are connected by a single topology in order to exchange data.
- *NIC*, which stands for Network Interface Card, is the hardware component that goes into the computer and provides the computer-side connection to the rest of the network hardware. This device gets its name from the fact that until recently, all NICs were installed, as cards, on an internal slot on the computer's systemboard (also called a motherboard). Even though the computer-side connections are now available for other ports (for instance, Universal Serial Bus [USB] ports or PC Card slots in laptops), we still call the device a NIC.
- *Concentrator* is a hardware device that is the central point for connecting computers. All the cable from all the computers on the LAN meet in the concentrator. Two types of concentrators are hubs and switches.

per second, or 56 Kbps). If you've ever used a 56 Kbps dial-up modem to download a file from the Internet, and you watched the progress bar move rather swiftly as thousands, tens of thousands, hundreds of thousands, and finally millions of bytes were delivered to your computer, think about how fast a 30 Mbps cable modem connection must be.

Ethernet Cable

Presenting the pros and cons of choosing Ethernet cable as your network topology is easy: it's almost all "pro" and very little "con." Ethernet is the cable of choice for any wired network, because it's fast, accurate, and almost always trouble-free; this is the connection type you find in corporate networks. (Instructions for cabling with Ethernet are in Chapter 4.) Absent some good reason, Ethernet is the topology to use for your network. However, I do admit that good reasons exist to opt for another topology, including the following common ones:

- You rent and the landlord doesn't want you to drill holes to bring cable through the walls (though there are clever ways to run cable without drilling).
- Your computers are located in places that are difficult to reach with a physical cable.
- The notion of running cable through your home or office strikes you as "too much work."
- The person in your household who has the final word on décor and aesthetic decisions says, "I don't want to see cable snaking out of the walls and into the room."

Ethernet can transfer data across the network at 100 Mbps, as long as the NIC and the hub or switch can support that speed. Some older NICs and hubs can send data at only 10 Mbps, but Ethernet NICs and hubs and switches can automatically sense the speed of the Ethernet devices on the network and drop or raise the speed to match the device's capabilities (this feature is called *autosensing*).

Today, Ethernet cable is purchased in the form of *100BaseT cable*, which is also called *twisted pair cable* and *category 5* (or newer implementations such as category 5e or 6) *unshielded twisted pair (UTP) cable*. The *100* in the name refers to the speed at which the cable can transmit data (100 Mbps); sometimes 100BaseT Ethernet is called *fast Ethernet*. Older Ethernet cable that can transmit data at 10 Mbps is called 10BaseT.

The term *base* is short for *baseband signaling*, which means that only Ethernet signals are carried on the wire. This differs from telephone wire, which can handle multiple types of signals. (Your telephone service uses only a portion of the wires, and you can use other portions for other technologies, including computer networks, as discussed in Chapter 6.)

The *T* stands for *twisted pair*, which describes the way the wires are twisted and paired through the cable. (Other wiring types, such as those for fiber-optic wires, which is called *100BaseF*, also exist.)

Ethernet cable looks like telephone wire (except a little thicker), and the connectors (also called *jacks*, even though the jack is the wall outlet to definition purists) look similar to the connectors on your telephone cable. However, they're not the same. The wires are twisted differently, the arrangement of wires in the connector is different (a telephone jack is an RJ-11, while an Ethernet jack is an RJ-45), and the connectors are different sizes.

Household Telephone Wires

Household telephone wires are easy to use to connect computers into a LAN, and the technology has come a long way since it was first introduced several years ago. (See Chapter 6 for instructions on creating a telephone line network.) Telephone network cable uses the wires in your telephone cable that voice communication doesn't use, so your telephone lines are still available for normal household telephone use (including a modem and a fax). The available range of frequencies within cable is called *bandwidth*, and you can use the bandwidth that your phone services don't use to create a computer network.

There are pros and cons for using your household telephone wires for networking, and they balance rather evenly. On the pro side, the only hardware you need is a NIC and length of plain telephone wire for each computer. Each computer is plugged into a regular telephone wall jack, eliminating the need to buy or install Ethernet cable. You can use your telephone wall jack for both a telephone and a network connection at the same time by installing a *splitter* (technically called a *modular duplex jack*), which is a gadget you can buy at your local supermarket. The splitter has a male jack that plugs into the wall jack and two female jacks on the outside. Plug a telephone cable from the PhoneLine network card into one jack and plug your telephone cable into the other jack.

On the con side, not every room in your house may have a telephone jack, so you must plan the location of your computers around jack availability. Also, if you use more than one telephone number at your house, all the computers on your network must be connected through the *same* number. Computers can't communicate across different telephone numbers because each number uses a different pair of wires. In addition, in many houses, the telephone wiring might not have been installed properly, which can prevent PhoneLine networking from functioning properly.

If your business uses a PBX (private branch exchange) telephone system, you can't use the jacks for your network, because the wiring is different from that of regular telephone jacks. PBX jacks are designed to deliver all the services that come with your phone system. In addition, if you use a DSL (digital subscriber line) device for your Internet connection, you'll probably have to insert a filter in your phone jacks, but that isn't very complicated (and it's covered in Chapter 6).

Another con for using telephone lines is that the maximum distance that can exist between networked computers is about 1000 feet. While you may be thinking "1000—whose house is that big," keep in mind that this actually means *1000 feet of wire between computers*. Wire often is run in a convoluted fashion through the walls in your home or business, and 1000 feet can be used before you know it. However, in most average-sized homes, this limitation really isn't very limiting.

Telephone networks operate at 10 Mbps (although much faster devices are showing up as a result of new standards that were released around the time that I wrote this). This matches the speed at which corporate networks operated until the recent introduction of fast Ethernet. In fact, plenty of networked computers still operate at 10 Mbps Ethernet, because the company's Information Technology (IT) professionals decided they didn't have a compelling reason to update the hardware. A connection speed of 10 Mbps is more than sufficient for almost any data transfer tasks. (Actually, I don't know whether to call the speed rating of telephone lines a pro or a con.)

Household Electrical Wires

You can run a network on the unused bandwidth within your household electrical lines without interfering with any of the work those lines perform to provide power to electrical appliances. In addition, the electrical appliances don't interfere with the transmission of data among the computers on your network. Best of all, since you're not using the part of the bandwidth that supplies power, the network connections don't raise your electric bill.

The NIC in each computer connects that computer to the nearest electrical outlet, and once all the NICs are installed and plugged in, you have a network. The speed of data exchange is about 14 Mbps, which is more than fast enough for anything I ever wanted to do on a network. One obvious advantage to this connection type is the fact that at least one electrical outlet exists in every room, so you can put your computers almost anywhere you want. Turn to Chapter 7 for instructions on installing your network over your household electrical wires.

Wireless Networking

Wireless networking uses RF (RadioFrequency) signals to communicate among the computers. The advances in wireless networking have been incredibly rapid in recent years, and the technology is becoming more and more popular as each new set of standards increases its power. Chapter 5 provides all the information you need to set up a wireless network.

The NIC has a transceiver (named for the fact that it both sends and receives data) and an antenna. The data communication rate varies (from about 11 Mbps to about 72 Mbps), depending on the wireless standard used by your hardware and the distance between computers. Details are in Chapter 5.

Robust security functions are built into the Linksys wireless devices, so you don't have to worry that a neighbor who also uses wireless technology could intrude on your network and gain access to your data.

The downside of wireless communication is that the signal can be interrupted by metal. So, for example, if you store your computer under a metal desk, you'll have communication problems. This is also true if the walls between computers have a lot of metal pipes inside (typical of older homes, before PVC became the standard material for drain pipes). There's also a distance maximum between computers (about 150 feet), but Linksys offers devices that extend the signal.

Mix and Match

Just to make all of these available choices more confusing (or, depending on how you look at it, more reassuring), you can also mix and match these connection types. I have been running Ethernet-cabled networks in my home and in many businesses for years. To write this book, I created separate networks for each of the connection choices and also mixed the topology, adding computers that were not running Ethernet to our original Ethernet networks. That action wasn't a "trick" to see what would happen; it was a reflection of reality. Large corporate networks that are grounded in Ethernet are adding other connection technologies to their LANs. The most prevalent example is the addition of wireless technology devices to Ethernet networks so that mobile users who visit the main office can access corporate data without having to be wired in. Small business and even home networks are increasingly using mixed topology networks as well. I routinely run into businesses that have decided to extend their Ethernet networks using wireless and other types of adapters.

Chapter 2

Purchasing and Connecting Hardware

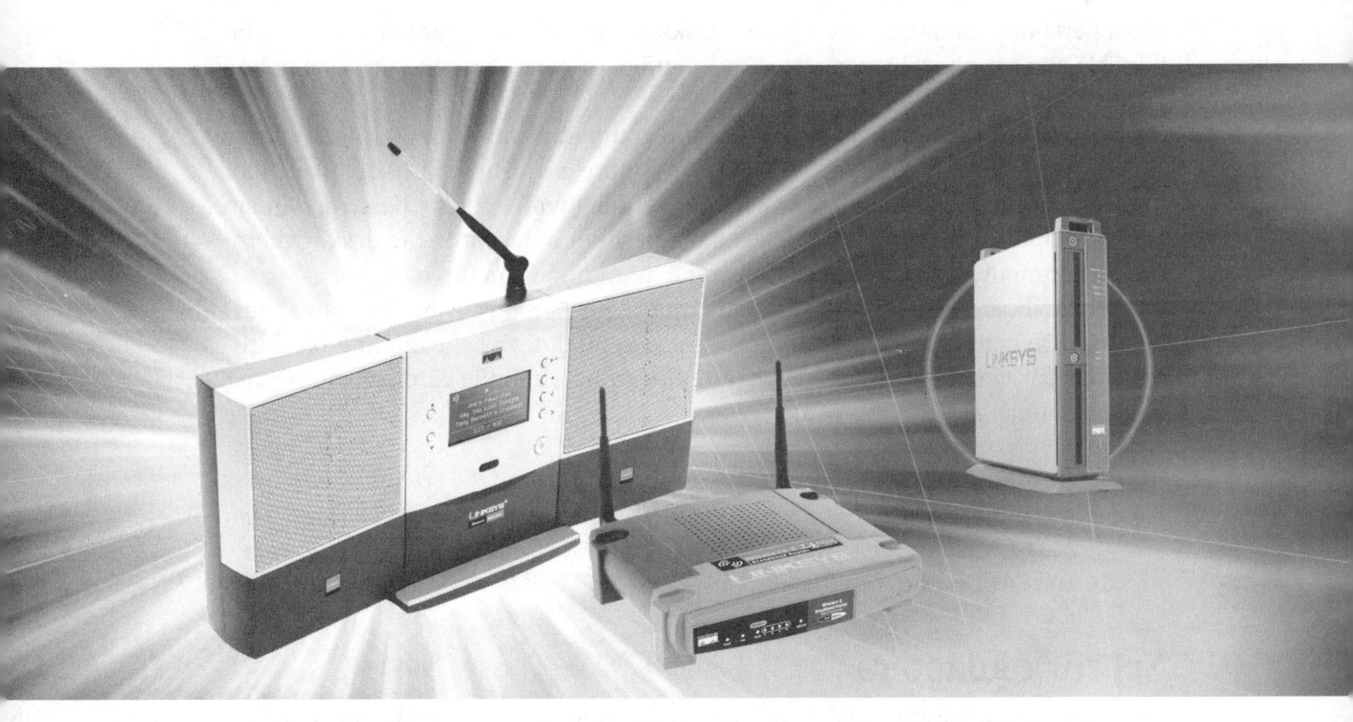

Any new computer you buy can be connected to a network, although some computers are easier to connect than others. In this chapter, you learn the basics about computer hardware and how you attach the hardware that communicates with the network.

Many years ago, adding extra hardware to a computer was tricky and required experience working with computers, but today hardware installations are much easier. Computer manufacturers, peripheral hardware vendors like Linksys, and Microsoft have all worked to accommodate a feature called Plug and Play. With this feature, you can simply plug a hardware device into your computer and Windows will recognize, install, and set up the hardware for you—automatically. In some cases, you may need to take the cover off your computer and insert a card, but even this is easy to do.

Desktop Computer Hardware

Most personal computers are of the "desktop" variety. They are not made to be portable and are typically connected to a number of other devices, such as monitors, keyboards, and mice.

Interestingly, the main part of a desktop computer (the computer itself) doesn't usually need to be on the desk, as shown in Figure 2-1. You will likely place the monitor, also called the display, on your desk, along with your keyboard and mouse. But the actual computer is often placed on the floor adjacent to the desk. Other desktop computers are designed so that the monitor sits on top of them.

The keyboard is just a keyboard, the mouse just a mouse, and the display just a display. The computer contains most of the essential devices, including disk drives, the plugs for your monitor, the keyboard, the mouse, and the card slots into which you may attach networking hardware.

NOTE *In some rare cases, the display and other parts of the computer are integrated into a single unit for space-saving and fashion purposes. The best-known example of this is the Apple iMac, but such a configuration rarely occurs in the PC world.*

Network Adapters

Computers must have a special device called a *network adapter* to connect to and communicate with a network, and that's often where products from companies like Linksys come in. These network adapters are often referred to as *NICs* (*Network*

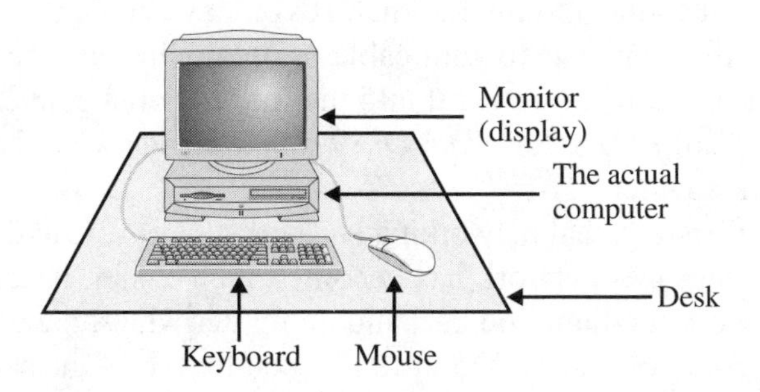

Sometimes the desktop computer's not on the desktop...

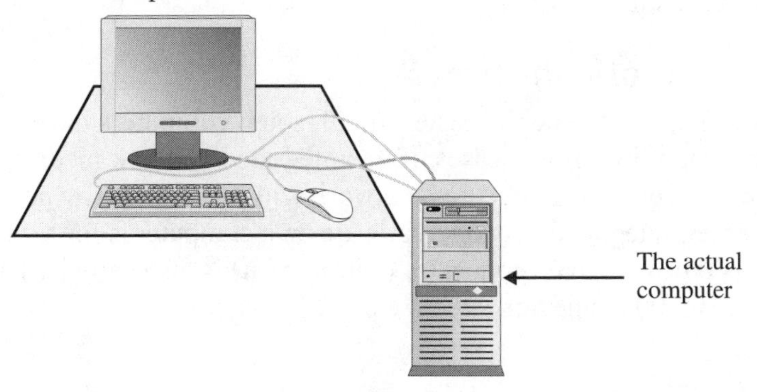

FIGURE 2-1 Desktop computers

Interface Cards). Some computers come with a network adapter built-in. Some network adapters plug into slots inside the computer, and some connect to the computer using external ports such as USB. As you will see, though, not all network adapters are cards anymore.

The job of the network adapter is to provide a physical connection—whatever the physical medium—to the network and thereby to the other computers on the network. In the most conventional case, the medium might be network wiring, but in a home it is just as likely to be your telephone wiring or a form of wireless connection. In the case of a wireless connection, the medium is the radio frequency spectrum, usually in the 2.4GHz range, but I'll discuss this in greater detail in Chapter 5. Sometimes the word *topology* is used to refer to the physical network medium.

It might be helpful for you to understand that the Internet itself is a network, so even if your system is not on a home network, you are using a type of network adapter when you connect to the Internet. If you have cable modem or DSL service, the device that connects to your cable or phone lines is a specialized type of network adapter. Even when you dial into the Internet on a conventional phone line (what techies call *POTS,* for *Plain Old Telephone Service*), the modem acts as a type of network adapter.

It's also helpful to understand that networking has both a hardware and software side. Setting up and managing a network has become much easier, because no matter what type of network medium you use, and no matter what type of network adapter you connect to your computer, Windows lets you treat it in the same way using common network software facilities.

Network adapters connect to your computer in different ways, and you work with them in different ways.

Integrated Network Adapters

The integrated system can be the easiest of all: some computers have networking hardware built right in. In such cases, if the integrated network medium is the same as your network, you can connect to a network without adding any new hardware.

In most cases, integrated network hardware on a computer is for a wired Ethernet network. This type of female connector (shown next) is also called a 10BaseT, 100BaseT, or 10/100 connector.

Yet another name for the connector, referring to the specific type of plug that fits into it, is RJ-45. The connector will probably be located on the back of the system unit near connectors for the keyboard, mouse, and other devices. Notice that the RJ-45 has an eight-wire version instead of the four wires found on the typical home telephone connector (the plug for which is called an RJ-11). The RJ-45 is also wider than the RJ-11.

You might also have an integrated network adapter for other network media, such as telephone line networking. In this case, you would probably have two RJ-11 connectors on the back of your system near all the other connectors (shown next)—one for your telephone line and one for a telephone device, such as a phone or a fax.

Line Phone

In the future, desktop system vendors may start integrating connectors for other types of network media, such as phoneline and powerline networking; as of this writing, however, these types of connectors are not yet integrated. Many desktop and portable computer vendors do integrate wireless networking into their systems, though. If you are investigating a new computer that has integrated networking, make sure it is the type of networking you want.

Network Interface Cards

Most desktop computers have *expansion slots*. On the back of your computer, you can probably see the outside of these slots, some of them with expansion cards already mounted. Expansion slots are designed to accept cards—electronic circuit boards with adapters that can be connected to various devices outside the computer. Figure 2-2 shows an example of how expansion slots look from the back of the computer. These cards add hardware functions to the computer, such as network support, that are not built into the motherboard, in the computer. When you buy your computer, it may already have expansion cards installed, such as the video card that connects to your monitor.

Before you install a networking card into your desktop computer, you should always make sure to read the instructions that come with the card. However, the following general advice should provide a helpful overview.

You must open up the system unit to access the expansion slots. First, shut down Windows, and if the system hasn't done it for you, turn off the computer. You may need to disconnect other cables from the system unit, such as the keyboard and monitor, to move the system unit so you can open it and access the insides. If you disconnect cables, take note of what you are disconnecting so that you can reconnect them correctly. Usually, these connectors are labeled and designed so that they can connect only to the proper plug, but some connectors, such as those for the keyboard

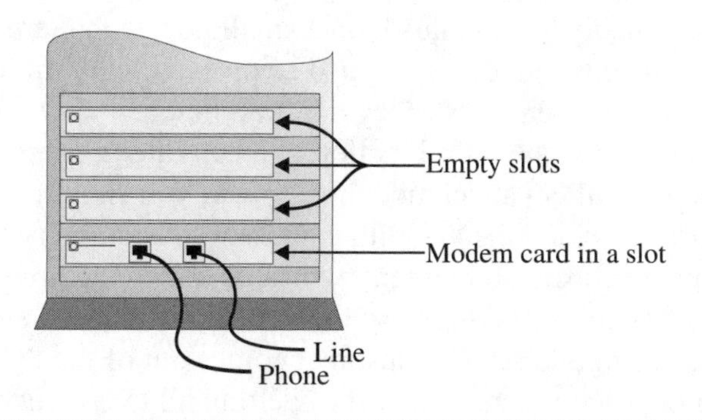

FIGURE 2-2 Expansion slots from the back of your system unit

and mouse, can be identical. Do not disconnect the power cord from the back of the computer, though. As long as the power cord is plugged in, the case is grounded and static electricity from your body will cause fewer problems.

Open the case to expose the insides. Usually, cases open in one of two ways: either a single side panel (on the left of the computer looking at it from the front) pops off or swings out to reveal the card slots, or the whole cover (both sides and top as a single piece) comes off. This may require tools, such as a Phillips screwdriver, but modern systems from quality PC companies sell "tool-less" cases that you can open using a thumbscrew or by simply pressing a button. Some cases can be tricky to open. If you cannot figure out how to open your case, or if it feels like you need to force the case in any way, stop and find the instructions for opening your case. You can usually find the instructions on the computer or case manufacturer's Web site.

After the case is open, touch any metal part of the chassis. This part is grounded, and therefore touching it will discharge any static electricity you have built up in your body. Continue to have contact with the case as much as possible; doing so will help ensure that your body is equalized to the case, thus preventing pesky static buildup on your body from going through the case.

Toward the back of the system unit case, probably in a corner, you will see the expansion slots (shown in Figure 2-3).

Yuck! What About All That Dust?

If your computer case hasn't been opened for a long time, you may see a lot of dust in there. It's a good idea to clear out this dust, but you need to be careful about how you do it. Some people use a can of compressed air to blow the dust off of the surfaces inside the PC and this practice is just fine. Many computer stores sell small, handheld vacuums with a small nozzle that are intended to let you gently suck the dust out of a system. The problem with these vacuums is that they are usually so gentle that they don't do much.

My suggestion is to use a combination of a can of compressed air and a household vacuum with an attachment hose. Now, you should never actually vacuum the surfaces inside the PC with a household vacuum (which is strong enough to damage delicate components). Instead, place the hose *near* the open case, turn on the vacuum, and then use the can of compressed air to blow the dust toward the vacuum hose. The dust that comes out of the PC is neatly sucked up into the vacuum hose instead of getting all over your desk or just settling back down inside the case.

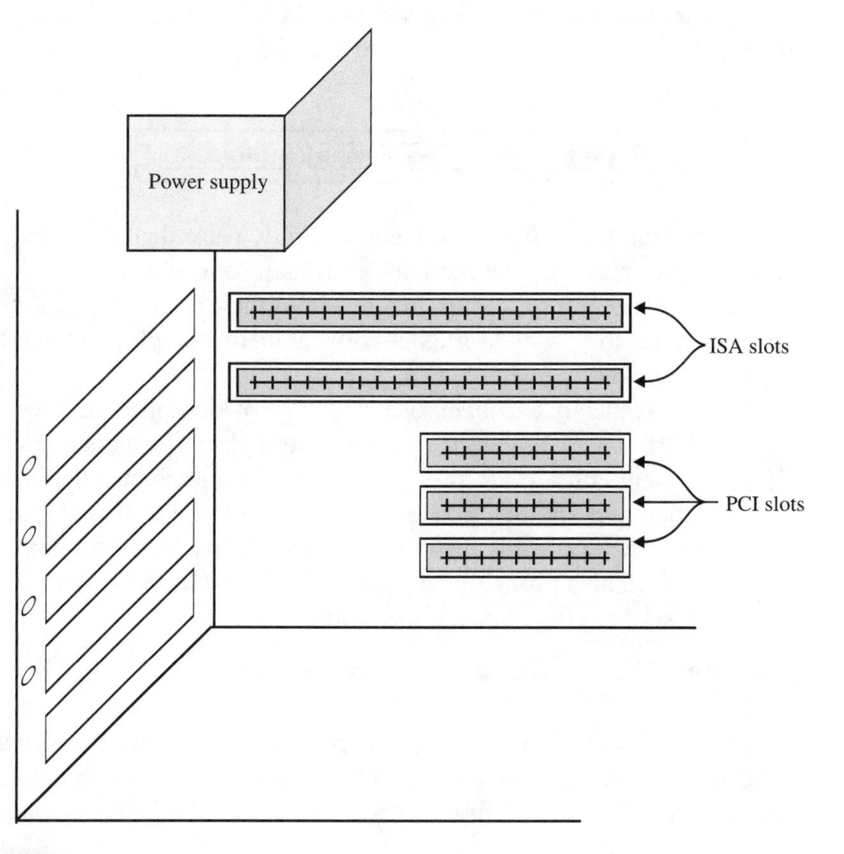

FIGURE 2-3 Expansion slots inside your computer

How to Identify the Inboard Bus (PCI/ISA) You might see two types of expansion slots on a PC motherboard: ISA (Industry Standard Architecture) and PCI (Peripheral Component Interconnect). An ISA slot (shown next) is based on an old hardware standard devised by IBM back in 1984. These slots' connections can be seen on the back of the computer case. ISA slots are included in PCs these days for compatibility with old expansion cards. No new network hardware that you are likely to buy, and nothing from Linksys, uses ISA slots.

ISA slot

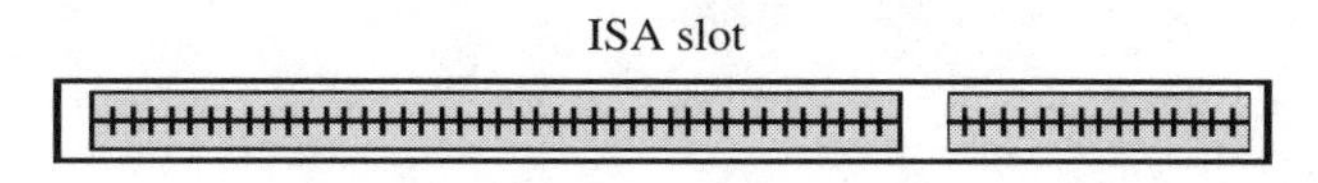

PCI slots (shown next) are shorter than ISA slots and located farther inside the case. Some modern systems are equipped with only PCI slots, and almost all modern expansion hardware that uses an internal slot uses PCI. Most network hardware you are likely to buy these days comes with PCI slots.

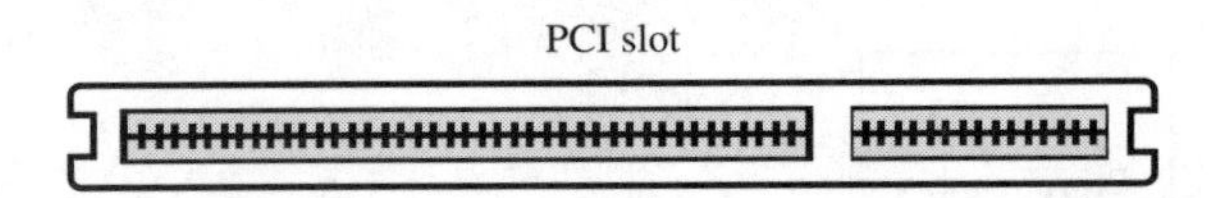

PCI Cards (see Figure 2-4) have an edge with tightly packed gold connectors that are designed to fit into a slot on the motherboard. The slot cover, the metal plate attached to the PCI Card, is exposed to the outside of the case after installation so that any outside connectors, such as the network cable, can be plugged into the card via the receptacle on the metal plate.

Finally, you will frequently encounter one other type of slot called an Accelerated Graphics Port (AGP). It's designed to accommodate high-performance graphics cards, so if your system unit has an AGP slot, there's a good chance that a card has already been installed in it and that your monitor is connected to that card. On the motherboard, this slot will probably be brown and set slightly farther from the back plate of the case. It will also probably be physically closest to the system unit and memory and the rest of the big chips on the motherboard.

Inserting the Card Here are the basics for inserting the card:

1. Locate an empty slot. You will need to remove a slot cover from an unused PCI slot. Save the screw(s) or whatever connector was used to hold the slot cover in place, as you will use it to hold the installed adapter in place.

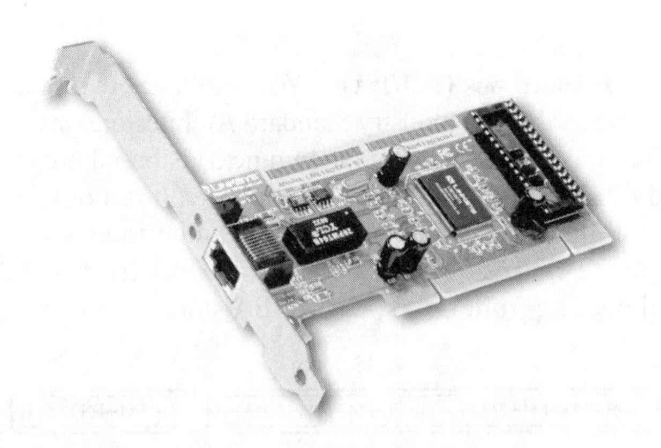

FIGURE 2-4 PCI cards, such as this Linksys network adapter, have a card edge that fits into a slot on the motherboard.

Usually, any available PCI slot will do, but sometimes certain slots are less accessible than others because of the internal cables attached to them.

2. When you handle the card, try to touch only the slot cover and card, avoiding any of the chips and the card edge; the same goes for the insides of the computer. Don't worry if you do touch anything; if you've been careful to discharge static electricity, you probably will not harm the computer. It's just a good habit to avoid touching the components.
3. Align the card vertically above the slot. Lower the card so that its edge rests in the PCI slot and so that the slot cover is sliding against the open area on the case, making sure that the card edge is set to insert directly into the slot. Press down on the top of the card to insert it into the slot.
4. Make sure the card is inserted in the slot correctly. The card edge should be inserted completely into the PCI slot; you should be able to see that it can't go down any lower because it is blocked by the lower, nonconnector edge of the card. In addition, check that the slot cover that is pressed against the back of the case and the top, which has a semicircular cut-out to expose the screw hole, is aligned to expose that hole.
5. Reinsert the screw or connector to hold the card in place.

Now that the card is in place, you can put the case back on, reattach all the cables you removed, and restart the system. Windows will recognize the new hardware through the magic of Plug and Play and begin a software installation process to load the device drivers that allow it to work with the new card. Subsequent chapters describe how this process works for various types of hardware you may be using.

Universal Serial Bus

Most people, even computer professionals, don't want to open up systems and mess with cards. That's why the computer industry came up with the Universal Serial Bus (USB), which is a standard for external devices that connect to the plugs on the PC. You use USB to connect a device to the computer. USB technology has been around since 1996, but it's become popular only within the last few years, as almost all PCs sold of late have at least one and usually between two and eight built-in USB ports.

USB devices are designed for ease of use. You just plug them in, and they usually work without further ado. After you plug in the device, Windows detects it and launches the Found New Hardware Wizard (in some versions of Windows, this wizard may have a slightly different name, such as Add New Hardware Wizard) to help you load the device drivers that allow it to communicate with the particular device.

The exact wording in the wizard differs, depending on which versions of Windows you're using, but it essentially performs the same routine: Windows tells you the name of the device it has found and says that it will now load the driver for that device. A *device driver*, as the wizard says, is a software program that allows Windows to work with the hardware product. You click Next and the wizard asks you to choose between letting Windows search for the best driver for your device or specifying the type of device you want to load. You almost certainly want to take the default option.

Next, the wizard asks you where Windows should search for the driver. The hardware product probably came with a disk—either a floppy disk or a CD-ROM—that contains the device drivers. You tell the wizard whether to use the disk that came with the device or point to a folder on your hard disk that contains the drivers you downloaded from the vendor's Web site. You may also be able to specify Microsoft Windows Update, which is a special site on the Internet where Microsoft stores updates to Windows and many current device drivers. Your best choice is usually the disks that came with the hardware product. Click Next and the wizard completes the installation of the driver. If you encounter problems, you can visit the hardware vendor's Web site and download the most recent drivers for the device, as they may be more current than those on the disk or CD that came with the product.

NOTE *Later versions of Windows include built-in drivers for many peripheral devices, so there's a chance that as you connect the device, Windows will automatically install it without requiring you to make any choices.*

USB devices have an advantage over devices that use other types of connections, such as serial ports: USB devices can usually draw power from the system over the USB line itself. This eliminates the need for a separate power supply and one of those bulky transformer boxes that ends up using at least one electrical outlet. Some USB devices, however, require more power than is supplied on the USB line, so they may include their own separate power supplies. USB hard disks and CD-ROM drives are good examples.

A variety of connectors and cables are used on USB equipment. Like most cables, USB equipment includes both male and female connectors, as shown in Figure 2-5. USB goes a step further by defining different types of connectors for the "upstream" (the A connectors) and "downstream" (the B connectors) ends of the cable.

FIGURE 2-5 USB connectors

Consider a simple example with a single USB device connected directly to the computer. The computer is upstream, and the device is downstream. The computer and device each contain female connectors, also called *receptacles*, and the cable contains male connectors, also called *plugs*. At the computer you insert the A plug into the A receptacle, and at the device you insert the B plug into the B receptacle.

Usually, when you buy a USB device, it includes a USB cable with an A plug on one end and the appropriate B connector on the other. You may also occasionally see extension cables, which, like a power extension cable, simply add some length to the connection.

NOTE *All legitimate and useful USB cables have an A connector on one end and a B connector on the other, or a male A and female A similar to the extender previously mentioned. Some vendors sell cables with the same connector on both ends. These can be dangerous; if you were to connect two computers directly via their A plugs, you could create a fire hazard because both ends are supplying power on the line. Special A-to-A cables are available from a variety of vendors, and these include a filter device through which you can connect two computers via USB; doing so directly with a simple cable is dangerous.*

Each USB connector on your computer is a separate *bus*. This means that each operates independently and that you can connect, theoretically, up to 127 devices on each connector. Realistically, you can't connect anywhere near that number, but by attaching what is called a USB *hub,* you can add extra devices to the bus.

The hub is itself a USB device, with a male connector that plugs into the female receptacle on your system or into another hub. The hub has two or more female receptacles to accept two or more USB devices or more hubs. For instance, the Linksys USBHUB4C Compact 4-Port USB Hub, shown in Figure 2-6, provides four USB ports in a small space. Because the short cable on the port hub requires you to place the device so close to the computer, you may want to buy an extender cable to run between the hub and the system so that the hub is more accessible.

Though almost all new computers come with multiple USB ports, you may come across older computers that do not include them. You may even come across new computers that don't include enough USB ports. In any event, you can buy PCI adapters from a number of vendors that add USB ports to a desktop computer, as well as PC Cards to add adapters to notebook computers.

USB 1.1 Versus USB 2.0 USBs come in two major versions: USB 1.1 (1.0 was never released to the general public) is rated at up to 12 Mbps, but you would probably get only 8 to 10 Mbps. USB 2.0, for which products began to appear in mid-2002, is rated at 480 Mbps. Yes, you saw that right—it's that much faster.

NOTE *You'll see Mbps a lot in networking, and it refers to megabits per second, or million bits per second. MBps (note the capital B) refers to megabytes per second.*

Practical terms are somewhat different from these theoretical numbers. With USB, as with most wire transfers (including networks), a certain amount of

FIGURE 2-6 USB hubs such as the Linksys USBHUB4C Compact 4-Port USB Hub allow you to use multiple devices on a single USB bus on your system.

overhead is involved in organizing the data on the wire (this is called *protocol overhead*). Plus, these ratings are for all devices on the bus, so if you are using a hub and more than one device is sharing the bus, the rated speed (12 Mbps for USB 1.1) is the *combined* limit for all devices on that bus.

Each USB connector on the system is a separate bus, so you may want to give some thought to how you plug in the various devices you have. For instance, some devices, such as joysticks and keyboards, use minimal bandwidth and can be combined on a bus easily. But a wireless network can use the whole bandwidth of the USB, so any other devices on the bus with it are likely to impede the performance of the network.

Computers with USB 2.0 ports did not appear on the market until 2002, so your older computer may not have them. You can, however, buy a PCI adapter or PC Card to add USB 2.0 ports to your system. To use a USB 2.0 connection fully, your must have a USB 2.0 port, cable, and device.

USB 2.0 ports and cables are fully compatible with USB 1.1 devices, meaning that you can plug a USB 1.1 device into a USB 2.0 port with no problem. However, you can't usually plug a USB 2.0 device into a USB 1.1 port. Either the device won't be recognized or the device won't work properly once installed.

Portable Computer Hardware

Portable computers, usually known as *laptop* or *notebook* computers, can make a lot of sense for home network use. Notebooks are also ideal candidates for wireless networks. After all, who wants to ruin that lovely portability by having to plug in a networking cable?

I'm writing this chapter on a Dell Inspiron notebook computer. At the moment, I'm sitting on the deck in my backyard watching my kids play. The notebook is connected to my wireless network, which is connected to the Internet. In the morning, I check my e-mail and read the news online while I drink my coffee. When I need to print something, I print to a printer connected to a desktop computer in my family room. I can listen to Internet radio, look up that cool insect my daughter found in the backyard, or just lie in my hammock browsing the Web—all through my wireless network, wherever my notebook and I happen to be. This is very cool stuff.

Of course, nothing this good comes for free. Notebook computers, especially quality brand-name notebook computers, are more expensive than desktop computers. But the difference in cost is nowhere near what it used to be. You can purchase a perfectly good notebook computer (it's possible that prices could go up, although that doesn't often happen) from the best companies in the business for less than $1000. On the other hand, perfectly good desktop computers, including a cheap monitor, start at around $400 to $600.

If you don't need or want a wireless network, all the other types of network hardware are available for notebook computers. In recent years, Windows has improved its ability to be disconnected from one networked environment and connected to another. For example, you might be connected to the wired Ethernet LAN at your office. At the end of the day, you can log off, disconnect the wire, and go home. When you turn on the computer back at home, Windows will find the wireless network at home, and you'll be connected to your printer and the Internet through that network. Or, you could connect the notebook to the Linksys HomeLink Phoneline or Instant PowerLine network and you'd be working on that. Like me, you might have your own wired Ethernet network (I have a lot of networks at my office and home), and you could use the same Ethernet adapter from work on your home network. Windows will find the right network resources either way.

Most new notebook computers come with an Ethernet adapter built-in. Many new notebook computers (more every day) also come with Wi-Fi hardware built in, and many more come with wired Ethernet hardware. (*Wi-Fi* stands for wireless networking. See Chapter 5 for more information.) But most users will have to buy a hardware device to connect their notebook to a network.

PC Cards

A long-established standard for expansion cards in portable computers, PCMCIA is the acronym for Personal Computer Memory Card International Association, the standards body that defines these specifications. (Perhaps, as someone suggested at the time of its invention, PCMCIA should stand for "People Cannot Memorize Computer Industry Acronyms.") The industry has moved more recently to the name PC Card for these credit card–sized adapters, especially for the more recent implementations of them.

PC Card Types

Two types of technical implementations of these cards exist, although the cards themselves appear almost identical. The initial PCMCIA specification defined a 16-bit card type that was very successful. In 1997, a 32-bit specification called CardBus was announced, and all portable computers sold in the last few years have supported this standard. In general, CardBus PC Cards are much faster than the old 16-bit PCMCIA cards and consume less power.

Most 16-bit PCMCIA cards will work in a CardBus slot, although CardBus PC Cards are "keyed" so as not to fit in a 16-bit PCMCIA slot. Some 16-bit cards are still on the market today because of this forward compatibility and the fact that many users still use older notebook computers, but look for the older 16-bit cards to disappear over time. CardBus also requires special support from the operating system or third-party device drivers. All versions of Windows since Windows 98 support CardBus. If your system supports CardBus, you should look for CardBus options.

Although all the cards are the same length and width and have the same dense, two-row, 68-pin connector, the three types of available cards offer different levels of thickness:

- Type I cards are 3.3mm thick. They are used for memory devices and you won't likely encounter them when shopping for home networking equipment.
- Type II cards are 5.0mm thick. These are the most popular types of cards and are used frequently for networking equipment as well as for modems and other devices.
- Type III cards are 10.5mm thick, which means they must be inserted in the bottom slot but consume the upper slot's space as well. They were designed for small hard drives, but they are sometimes used for other types of devices as well.

PC Card Connectors

All PC Cards are small, and it has been a challenge for vendors to find ways for users to attach relatively large cable connections to them. The initial solution that's still popular is to have a separate attachment with the necessary plugs that connects to the PC Card via a separate small plug to the card. Consider the attachment shown in Figure 2-7. Such attachments are often called *dongles* for their resemblance to devices of that name that were used for security purposes in completely different circumstances. We'll use the more descriptive and accurate name *coupler.*

In later years, the industry came up with a more convenient solution than couplers. In these cards, such as the one pictured in Figure 2-8, the cable connections are part of a plastic attachment to the card itself. These are referred to as *integrated* PC Cards. The upside to this arrangement is that you need to carry only one piece of hardware.

FIGURE 2-7 Many PC Cards come with an attachment, sometimes called a coupler or dongle, that lets you connect network cables.

Integrated PC Cards have two potential downsides. First, if you're not careful while the card is installed in the notebook computer, it's possible to break off the attachment. Actually, this is also possible with the coupler when it's plugged in, but it's less of an issue because you can detach the coupler without removing the card. So, for example, if you put your notebook in a briefcase, you may want to remove an integrated card entirely from the computer, but you'd only need to remove the coupler from the older type of card. In either case, you need to be careful not to misplace the part after you remove it.

The second potential downside to an integrated card is that the attachments are physically thicker than the cards themselves, so it's not usually possible to install

FIGURE 2-8 Other PC Cards come with the receptacles integrated into the card, which can be more convenient; however, you must be careful not to damage such a card.

two of them in the same system at once. Some older types of PCMCIA cards, notably those with the "XJACK" type connector, are physically blocked by either the coupler or integrated cards. But this is mostly history; in a home networking situation, you'll likely need to use only one card at a time, and probably just the networking card.

Working with PC Cards

The physical access to PC Cards of all types is identical. The cards slide lengthwise into a slot typically on the side of the computer. You need to press the card all the way in until it won't go any farther. At this point, the back end of the card—the point at which either the coupler or the attachment with the connectors attaches to the card—will be even with the outside edge of the computer.

To remove the card, depress the small and inconvenient button just to the side of the PC Card. In most cases, when you press and release the button, the card will pop farther out of the system, but will not yet release from the slot. When you press the button a second time, the action will push the card out of the slot and release the card from the pressure holding it in place. You can then pull it out the rest of the way with ease.

USB Connections

Like desktop computers, most modern notebook computers come with one or more USB ports. The receptacle on the notebook is an A type (mentioned earlier in the chapter).

USB-based networking hardware works fine on a notebook computer, but you will not be able to move about freely with the computer. At the least, devices will be hanging off the computer. If you keep your notebook computer in one place, a USB solution can be a good one. But if you want to be able to move the computer around and stay on the network, PC Cards are the way to go.

Notebooks often have an expensive option available called a *docking station*. It's a separate part that the notebook connects to via a large, proprietary connector on its back. The docking station, or a cheaper but similar device called a *port replicator*, has connections to printers, networks, and perhaps a full-sized mouse, keyboard, and monitor. The idea is that you can plug the notebook into the docking station and use it like a full-sized computer, or you can detach the notebook and use it by itself.

A USB hub, such as the Linksys USBHUB4C Compact 4-Port USB Hub, can be an effective "poor man's docking station." You can connect a printer, network, keyboard, and mouse to the hub and plug the hub into your notebook when you want to use the notebook in its main location. When you want to move the notebook, all you need to do is detach the USB plug. You will be logged off the network at this point, though.

Personal Digital Assistants

PDAs—especially those based on Microsoft Mobile software (used in Pocket PC devices)—are designed to work on their own and periodically synchronize with a personal computer. Some of these devices come with a Wi-Fi solution built-in. For those that don't, you can usually expand the devices using their Compact Flash Type I or II slot. Linksys makes a Wi-Fi card, the WCF12 (and WCF11) Wireless CompactFlash Card, that can be used to connect a Pocket PC PDA directly to the LAN, and thereby to the Internet.

These devices are expensive, and they would be an extravagant toy to get purely for home use. But you certainly might have one for legitimate reasons at work, and presumably you do go home at night. Why not hook up the device to your wireless network at home and surf the Web or send and receive e-mail on it? You can even use a Pocket PC device to control your Windows XP desktop computer over the network. Once again, very cool stuff.

Network Hardware

You've already learned about the different ways to connect peripherals to PCs, and perhaps you're already familiar with at least some of these concepts. The world of networking equipment has its own set of standard device types that you're likely to encounter. In this section, I'll discuss these devices in general. Throughout the rest of the book, I'll discuss specific products of these types that you might use to set up an actual network. But this section will help you to understand what they do.

Network Interface Cards

A NIC is the hardware that performs the actual network communication. As discussed earlier, it might connect to the computer in any number of ways—via PCI or USB, for example—or it might come built into the PC.

As discussed in Chapter 1, the type of network with which the NIC communicates could be wired Ethernet, Wi-Fi, your home telephone cables, or even electrical wires. In any case, you need a NIC, and you need a Windows device driver to allow Windows to control the NIC.

Cable

There was a time when many different types of cable were used in networking, but the market has shaken out a bit. In today's world of small networks, you might use two basic types of cable: Ethernet and phoneline cable.

Ethernet

Conventional wired networks usually use Ethernet cable, which is also referred to by categories that denote the physical specifications of the cable—Category 5 (cat 5), Category 5e (cat 5e), and Category 6 (cat 6). You'll learn more about the different categories in Chapter 4. For now, just know that the wire itself has four twisted pairs of copper wire with RJ-45 connectors on both ends. RJ-45s (shown next) look like RJ-11 telephone connectors, but they're larger to accommodate the fact that they hold twice as much wire.

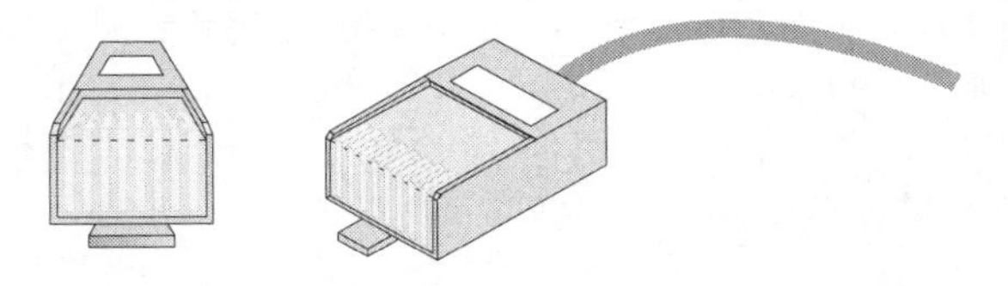

Ethernet cabling can handle network speeds up to 1000 Mbps (or 1 Gbps—gigabit per second), but almost all network equipment sold for small networks operates at 100 Mbps (or at the older standard of 10 Mbps). This speed is fast for any small network, and networking hardware that operates at this speed is much more affordable than networking hardware that operates at 1 Gbps.

When you buy a NIC or other networking equipment, it may come with a length of cable; if you need cabling that is longer than that supplied with your equipment, you may need to purchase extra cables. You can go to any computer or large business supply store and buy cable, generally labeled as network cable, Ethernet cable, and probably by category as well. You can also buy cable from Internet mail-order houses that often have a far greater selection and better prices. My network is probably more complicated than yours, but I find it useful to buy as many different colored cables as possible to make it easier to tell one from the other.

NOTE *If you buy networking equipment and it comes with wiring intended for use with the equipment, try to use the wire included with the equipment. You may not have to use the provided wire, but it is designed for that equipment, so using it decreases your chances of having a problem.*

If you are ambitious and frugal, sometimes it is handy to buy raw cable and connectors and make your own cabling. But for most people, it is worth paying a few extra bucks to get a cable that they can return if necessary. If you want instructions on making your own network wiring, see Chapter 4.

Crossover Cables In almost every case, all Ethernet cables are functionally interchangeable. But in a few situations, you need a special type of cable with a subtly different wiring scheme. It's called a *crossover cable*, and you can use it to wire two computers directly together, NIC to NIC, without any intervening hardware, to create a two-station LAN. (Such a setup is not very flexible or expandable, but it can be helpful in diagnosing some problems.) You might need a crossover cable to connect some DSL and cable modems into a regular port in a hub or to connect two hubs that don't have an uplink port (you'll learn more about all this later in the "Hubs" section).

It's not easy to tell, just by looking at a cable, whether it's a crossover or a regular cable, because the cables usually aren't specifically labeled as such. You may be able to peek into the connector and find the wiring details. Usually, it's a good idea to label a crossover cable by wrapping a paper adhesive label marked as "crossover" around some part of the cable.

Phoneline Cable

Nowadays, you can run 10 Mbps networking over your regular telephone lines. This networking is designed to work over the same phone lines in your home that already exist for your telephones, so you need only conventional telephone wire. The standard RJ-11 connectors are used, and you can still use the same phone lines for voice communications as you always have, even at the same time that the network is in use.

In general, home phoneline networking can coexist with the Asymmetric Digital Subscriber Line (ADSL) service you might have for Internet access. It can even work on an Integrated Services Digital Network (ISDN) phone line. This sort of networking does not work on phone lines connected through a private branch exchange (PBX), however. Connections to different phones are typically physically separated within a PBX, so the phoneline networking devices couldn't communicate.

Some home phoneline systems split the wires in a single cable into two different phone lines, and this can cause a problem for networking. Home phoneline systems require all four wires.

Hubs

If you want to connect more than one computer in a network, the classic option is to connect them to a hub. A hub is a box (see Figure 2-9) that brings several systems in a network together in the simplest way. Hubs are commonly used because they are simple and inexpensive. If your networking needs are uncomplicated, you will probably do well with a hub.

Most hubs have several female RJ-45 receptacles and usually an extra connector labeled "Uplink." You use cat 6 cables to connect the NICs on computers or other devices that you are placing on the network to regular ports on the hub. You can use a regular RJ-45 cable to connect an uplink port on one hub to a normal port on another.

When you plan to use a hub, it's probably better to get a hub with room to grow by buying one with a few more ports than you initially need. Although you have the option of chaining hubs together through their uplink ports, this can get messy and can adversely affect performance.

The more systems and the more traffic you put on the network, the more your performance with a hub will degrade. This is because a hub works much like the Chicago Mercantile Exchange: everyone is shouting at everyone else. All data that goes out on the network goes to every other port in the hub, and it's up to the NIC to decide whether it wants the data or not. One approach to managing the inflow of data is to use a more expensive type of hub, called a *manageable* or *intelligent hub*, which allows you to turn ports on and off and track the data going through the hub.

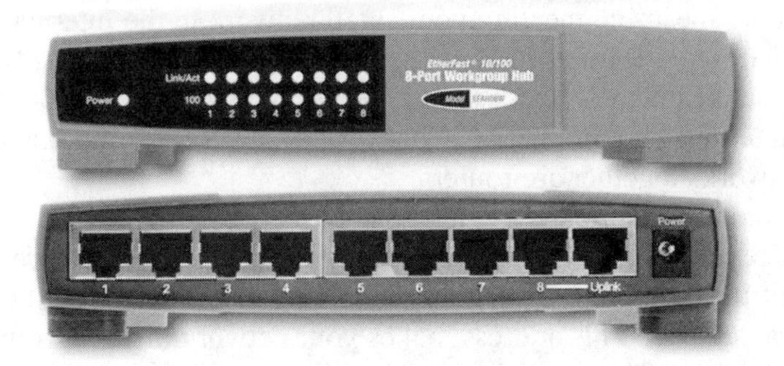

FIGURE 2-9 A hub, such as this Linksys 8-Port Workgroup Hub, has a number of ports to which computers can connect and lights to indicate whether they are connected.

Switches

A better way to connect computers together on the same network is to use a switch rather than a hub. A switch performs the same basic function as a hub—connecting networked computers together—but it does it in a faster way. All the systems connected to a hub send all their data to everyone else on the hub. This means all the systems on the network share the total potential throughput of the network, but this causes a problem. If two systems send out data at the same time, a collision occurs: a big part of the Ethernet protocol (CSMA/CD, or Carrier Sense Multiple Access with Collision Detection) deals with detecting these collisions and arranging for systems to retransmit data. But the more data is being transmitted on a network, the more likely collisions are to occur.

Switches work around this problem by creating temporary dedicated connections between systems inside the switch itself. The switch keeps track of the addresses of systems attached to it so that when a packet comes in from one system addressed to another, the switch can move the data directly to the intended port without bothering the rest of the systems. It's as if everyone is hard-wired to everyone else. The collision part of the process is eliminated.

Switches have largely replaced hubs as the connection method of choice in homes and small business networks. Switches are faster than hubs and usually no more expensive. In fact, these days it's rather difficult to purchase hubs for small networks.

Routers

A *router* connects two distinct networks. In the context of small networks, this most commonly means connecting your small network to the Internet.

A lot of hard-core techie stuff figures into this. For instance, just because your systems are "on the Internet" doesn't mean they are on the same network as everyone else on the Internet. The Internet is a "network of networks," and the devices that tie all the networks together are routers.

When your single computer is dialing into the Internet, you don't need a router because you're just a single client system on your Internet service provider's (ISP) network. But if you use a network at your home or business, you will use the system's local address. This address makes your network distinct from the rest of those on the Internet. The router knows how and when to let traffic move out to the Internet and how to send it to its destination. It also knows how to route data from the Internet to the correct systems on your network. The typical router (see Figure 2-10, for example) has one connector for the external network—probably the Internet—and one for the internal network.

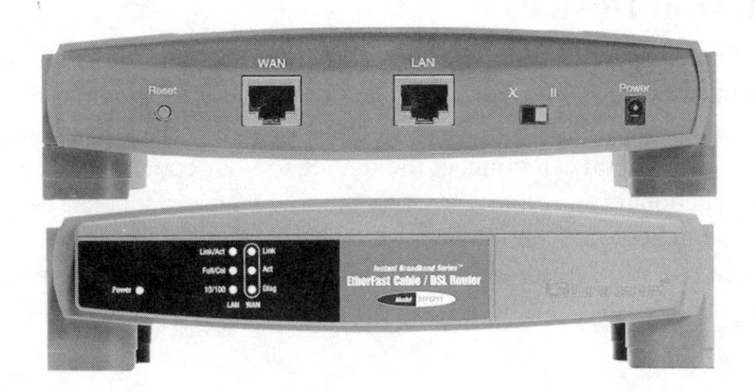

FIGURE 2-10 At its simplest, a router has connections for two networks: the LAN is your local internal network, and the WAN the external network—most likely the Internet.

Routers are often sold combined with other network functions—a switch, for example. If the combined unit has enough ports, you don't have to buy any other hardware to connect your systems to the Internet (apart from a cable modem or other Internet access hardware).

Wireless Access Points

In a wireless network, each system on the network has a wireless NIC. While it's possible to run the network just fine with the individual systems communicating via these cards, it's often a good idea to get a wireless access point—a central antenna that acts as a sort of hub for the wireless network.

You'll probably want to connect your wireless network to the Internet, so wireless access points are frequently sold with integrated routers that you can connect to a cable or DSL modem or some other Internet connection. My network is plugged into a separate hub.

Wireless access points have a few standard management capabilities. To allow client systems to choose from among multiple wireless networks, you can set a name for the network to which an access point belongs. You can also control an encryption capability available to all Wi-Fi networks called Wired Equivalent Privacy (WEP), and a newer encryption standard called Wi-Fi Protected Access (WPA). I'll discuss all this in greater detail in Chapter 5.

Combination Devices

More often than not, you'll find it easier to buy a device that offers a combination of services that fit your needs. For example, one of the more popular devices for setting up a home network combines a router, a switch, and a wireless access point into a single device. You can connect the device to your cable or DSL modem (this is the router functionality), connect any computers or devices that use network cables (through the switched ports on the back of the device), and connect any computers or devices that use WiFi (through the wireless access point). A good example of such a device is the Linksys Wireless-G Broadband Router, shown in Figure 2-11.

FIGURE 2-11 A combination device, such as the Linksys Wireless-G Broadband Router, offers an inexpensive, compact solution to creating a flexible home network.

Chapter 3

Internet Connection Hardware

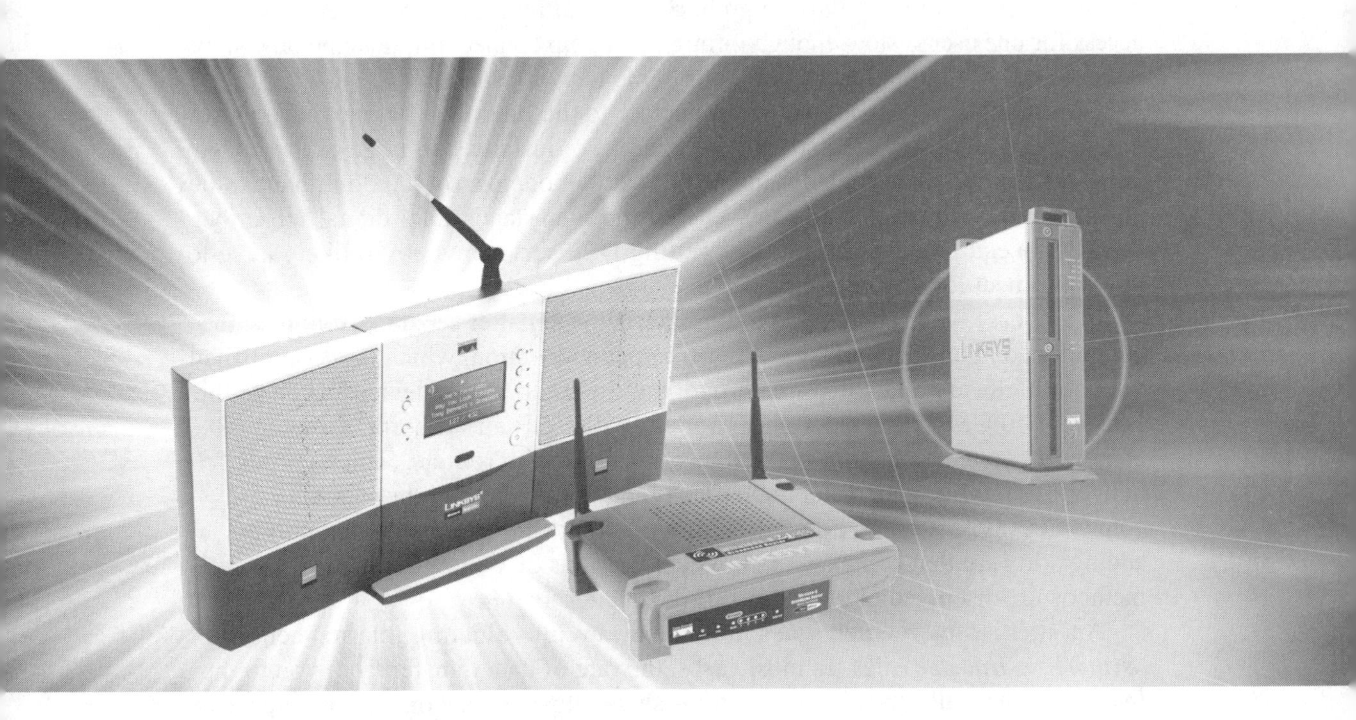

You may want a network at your home or small business for sharing files and printers and such, but most people today want a network to share access to the Internet.

You can connect your network to the Internet in many different ways. While some ways are better than others, not all of them are available to everyone. In fact, your options may be limited, depending on where you live. Such are the laws of economics and physics: high-speed Internet service may be unavailable from your phone company and/or your cable TV company, assuming cable TV is even available in your area. Not everyone can put up a satellite dish, either.

These high-speed services are usually known as *broadband*, a word that alludes to a wider pipe through which the service feeds data to you. Broadband services are becoming more and more widely available throughout the United States.

The baseline for Internet service, telephone dial-up service, will work, even to share access across a small network, but it's the kind of solution that engineers call "suboptimal," meaning that they really wish they had a better option. Once you get a taste of broadband, it's hard to go back to a plain old dial-up modem. Internet access for one user is slow enough through a dial-up connection; imagine how slow it would be with multiple users on your home network surfing the Net.

Depending on your method of connecting to the Internet, you may have more or less freedom in selecting equipment to use. For instance, all large cable modem networks support an accepted standard for cable modems, so you don't have to buy equipment from the cable company. There is no such standard for digital subscriber line (DSL) equipment, so if you are getting DSL service, you will likely have to buy equipment for it from your ISP.

In any case, your connection to the Internet is a matter separate from how the computers on your network share that Internet connection, which is accomplished via both hardware and software. Broadband Internet access devices, such as the Linksys BEFCMU10 ver. 3 Cable Modem with USB and Ethernet Connection, come with connections that make it easy to work with routers, which connect the network to the Internet. Telephone dial-up modems, on the other hand, don't connect easily to a home network, although you can make the connection by adding software that comes with all recent versions of Windows. Such software methods are discussed in greater detail in Chapter 8.

Another issue of which you should be aware in evaluating Internet access is *asymmetric transfer rates*. In most cases, the rate of data transfer from you to the Internet (often called the *upstream* rate) is slower than the rate of data coming from the Internet to you (the *downstream* rate). When the rates differ, the service is called *asymmetric*. When they are the same, it is called *symmetric*. This is not a serious concern, since in almost all cases users receive far more data than they send. But when shopping for Internet service, you should check to make sure that the upstream rate is reasonable.

Normally, a higher upstream rate is required to operate Internet servers, such as Web and mail servers, and few small network operators run such servers. In fact, operating such servers is often a violation of the terms of service for your ISP, so make sure to check your service agreement. Many teenagers join clandestine peer-to-peer (P2P) networks to share music and other files, which can easily consume all of your upstream bandwidth, potentially slowing down everyone else using the Internet on your network. One solution to this is to ban such uses on your network—good luck!

Each computer connected to the Internet needs a unique Internet address, called an IP (Internet Protocol) address. With most Internet service plans, the ISP provides your computer with a temporary address to use when it connects to the Internet. These addresses, also known as Dynamic Host Configuration Protocol (DHCP) addresses (see Chapter 8), are yours for only a period of time while you're connected. For example, you can't register a name (such as *www.linksys.com*) and have it point to your systems, because such name registrations always require what is called a *static IP address*—a permanent IP address.

Some classes of more expensive, advanced Internet service, especially from DSL providers, offer static IP addresses. It's possible that you have a legitimate need for this feature, but few home users do. The applications for which you would need static addresses, such as setting up a mail server, are beyond the scope of this book.

Telephone Modems

If nothing else is available, you can always get telephone-based Internet service. It's available in almost every country around the globe, and at any particular location in the United States you probably have several options. The hardware device you use for this is properly known as a *modem*, which is basically a telephone for the computer.

What's a Modem?

A computer modem has to use the same analog frequencies and other facilities that are used when you make a voice call. (Incidentally, sometimes you'll hear techies refer derisively to conventional telephone service as *POTS,* for *Plain Old Telephone Service*.)

The word *analog*, a shortened version of *analogous*, is often used in contrast to the word *digital*. Think of the difference between a digital clock, which displays a precise numeric time, and an analog clock, which has minute and hour hands. Since the computer is communicating *digital* information over an *analog* phone line, it has to translate the digital data it is communicating into analog sounds that it sends over the phone line. The computer also knows how to pick up the line, dial the phone, hang up, and so on. At the other end of the line, at your ISP's office (called a *Point of Presence* or *POP*), are groups of other modems receiving these calls and communicating with your computer and its modem.

When two modems talk, their main job is to turn digital data from the computer, binary 1 and 0 values, into analog data that can move over the telephone lines. This process is called *modulation*. At the other end, the modem receiving the analog signal converts it back into digital data, and this process is called *demodulation*. The shortened combination of these two terms is the basis of the word *modem*.

You can buy modems in two forms: internal and external. An internal modem is inserted as a card in your computer (probably as a PCI Card; see Chapter 2 for more detail on such hardware). Many computers, especially portable computers, come with *integrated*, or preinstalled, modems. In either case, an internal modem has two female telephone plugs exposed on the outside—one to connect to the telephone jack on the wall and probably labeled "LINE," and another to be connected to a conventional telephone for voice use when the modem is not being used for data. This other plug is probably labeled "PHONE" or shows a small drawing of a telephone.

External modems connect to the computer via a cable. In most cases, this is called a *serial* cable. On the computer side, this cable will connect to a 9-pin male plug. On the modem side, the connection will probably be a female 25-pin plug. When you buy the modem, many other types of serial cables are available, so make sure you buy a serial cable specifically meant for a modem. Some modern external modems connect to the computer using USB, as discussed in Chapter 2. Such modems use standard USB cables and probably come with one.

External modems tend to be more expensive than internal modems, but they have several advantages. You don't have to open the computer to install an external modem. You can turn it on and off separately from turning the computer on and off, which can be helpful for clearing up certain connection problems. Best of all, external modems have a series of lights that indicate the status of communications. You can see whether the modem is on, whether it has a connection to the other end, and whether data is being transmitted or received.

Modem Speeds

For many years through the 1980s and 1990s, the industry steadily increased the standard speed of modems, but now they appear to have reached a permanent plateau. The highest data rate you can expect to get downstream is about 53,000 bits per second, or 53 Kbps. The highest upstream rate that is possible with an analog modem is 33.6 Kbps.

You may see many terms referring to modems that fit the current standards, including 56K, V.90, and V.92. The term 56K is a misleading indicator that has somehow stuck with these modems, since it's not possible to get more than 53 Kbps. V.90 is a standard defined by the International Telecommunication Union (ITU). At the time that modems of this speed class were released, more than one proprietary definition for them existed, and V.90 resolved the differences between them. You may also see V.92, a compatible standard that reduces the handshake time, which is that period of time during which the modems establish a connection (when you hear the modems screeching at each other).

It's important that you understand that just because a modem is technically capable of speeds up to 53 Kbps, that doesn't mean that you will get those speeds. The quality of the telephone lines can limit the speed of connection. And even with the highest quality lines, the use of certain telephone equipment, either in your building or by your telephone company, may prevent you from getting greater than 33.6 Kbps downstream speed. (Speeds up to 53 Kbps rely on techniques that are prevented by such equipment.)

NOTE *Your modem may achieve greater throughput than the rate at which the modems are actually transmitting data because some modems compress data before transmitting it on the line.*

ISDN

Telephones are designed to use analog signals. But the phone company offers a special type of digital phone line called *ISDN,* for *Integrated Services Digital Network.*

ISDN provides three channels for communication—one D channel at 16 Kbps, and two B channels at 64 Kbps each. ISDN terminal adapters (they aren't modems because they don't modulate or demodulate) bond all these together to provide a highest theoretical throughput of 144 Kbps.

NOTE *Some ISDN services don't include all three channels, depending on what your telephone company offers. Also, note that your ISDN-based Internet service is a separate service at a separate cost from your ISDN line itself, and you will not be able to use the ISDN line for conventional voice telephony.*

If you've been shopping around for broadband Internet service using other device types such as cable modem or DSL (discussed next), you know that 144 Kbps is not a very high speed. Thus, you should choose ISDN only if it is your only option. You will have to check with all the potential providers of service to see if this is the case.

The original idea of ISDN, when it was developed in the 1980s, was for it to serve both data and enhanced voice needs, and 144 Kbps seemed like a lot. But the telephone companies and hardware manufacturers failed to agree on effective national standards until fairly recently. By that time, DSL and cable modems already provided less expensive and faster data options.

Cable Modems

A cable modem enables broadband Internet access through the same cable lines that deliver cable television. In general, considering all the cost and ease of use factors, a cable modem is usually the best option for consumers, although the specifics differ from one cable provider to another. For businesses, options can be very different, and once again you have to check the service agreement to see what is legal.

Like telephone modems, cable modems modulate and demodulate data, which actually travels on the wire in a portion of analog television bandwidth. Unlike telephone modems, this data travels at a very fast rate, allowing you, potentially, to download several megabits of data per second. Upstream data has a much narrower bandwidth and has to contend with more interference from other devices, which is one reason why cable modem connections are invariably asymmetric: your downstream bandwidth will be many times faster than your upstream bandwidth.

None of this interferes with your cable TV services on the same "wire," and since it doesn't use your phone lines, cable access doesn't interfere with your ability to make phone calls.

Older One-Way Systems

Some older cable modem systems use the cable modem only for downstream data and a telephone line for upstream data. Relatively few of these systems remain.

Such networks were built only with downstream repeaters to save money, because conventional television doesn't require upstream transmission. These systems rely on proprietary cable modem hardware, so if you are in an area served by such a system, you probably have no choice but to get your cable modem from your cable company.

Cable Modem Equipment

The actual cable modem is a device that connects on one end to the cable, just as your television or VCR does, and on the other end connects either directly to a PC or to some other network device.

The Linksys BEFCMU10 ver.3 Cable Modem with USB and Ethernet Connection is a perfect example. It is designed to support a stand-alone PC or to connect a Local Area Network (LAN) to the Internet through the cable system. You have numerous options for how to do this, which you will explore in this section.

NOTE *Most cable companies provide a cable modem when you sign up for service. So why should you purchase and use your own cable modem? The first reason is that cable companies typically rent you the cable modem for a few dollars per month. Buying your own cable modem often pays for itself in less than a year. The second reason is that Linksys cable modems are often easier to configure and more reliable than the modems that cable companies provide. And the final reason is that the Linksys cable modem stacks easily with other Linksys network gear and looks much better on your desk.*

The Linksys cable modem conforms to a well-respected standard for cable modems called DOCSIS (Data-Over-Cable Service Interface Specifications), which is administered by an organization called CableLabs *(http://www.cablemodem.com/)*. All large cable modem networks will support DOCSIS-compliant modems, such as the Linksys cable modem, so you don't have to buy or lease equipment from the cable company. All DOCSIS-compliant cable modems should work on any DOCSIS-compliant network. CableLabs tests and certifies the modems before they can be labeled as DOCSIS-certified.

Most cable modems, including the Linksys cable modem, are capable of speeds far greater than your cable modem network allows. Cable modem equipment supports standards—including Simple Network Management Protocol (SNMP), which you may recognize as a corporate network management standard as well—

to control the speeds at which cable modems operate. The cable modem network managers do this mostly to prevent a small number of users from consuming a large percentage of overall network bandwidth, although this still can occur even with the restrictions.

Setting Up the Cable Modem

Connect the power adapter (the thin wire with the transformer block attached) included in the package to the plug labeled "Power" on the cable modem. Then connect the included power cable from the transformer block to a power outlet.

NOTE *No matter how you connect your cable modem to your PC or network, you will need the TCP/IP protocol installed on the PC. If it is not installed, or if you don't know whether it is, read Chapter 8 for installation instructions.*

The BEFCMU10 ver.3 Cable Modem has five green indicator lights on its front panel that indicate the following:

- **Power** When this light is on, the cable modem is receiving power correctly. It should always be on as long as the cable modem is plugged in.
- **Cable** This light flashes on and off as the cable modem is turned on and attempts to connect to the cable modem network. When the cable modem has successfully connected to the cable network, this light will stay on. If, after 10 minutes, it keeps blinking, a problem may exist with the cable modem or more likely with the cable connection. It is also possible that your modem's MAC address is not yet registered with your cable company. Check the physical cable connection. Try resetting the cable modem by pressing the reset button on the back of the device. If the status light continues blinking, contact your cable company to determine whether a problem with the signal exists. Table 3-1 lists several flashing states and indicates the cable registration status of each.
- **Activity** This light, when lit solid, indicates a proper connection between the cable modem and the PC or router to which it is attached. When it is flashing, it indicates data moving between the cable modem and the computer(s).
- **Ethernet** This light will be solid when the modem is connected to a computer or network through the Ethernet port. This light flashes when data is being transmitted through the Ethernet port.

- **USB** This light will be solid when the modem is connected to a computer through the USB port. The light flashes when data is being transmitted through the USB port.

The Linksys cable modem has a pinhole on the back labeled "RESET." This is the reset button. If the cable modem becomes jammed somehow (cable network or electrical problems can cause such jamming, but it's rare and impossible to predict), you can use the end of a paper clip or something similarly pointed to press the internal button in the hole. This will reset the cable modem to factory defaults and cause it to restart as if you powered it up.

If you are connecting the cable modem to an Ethernet adapter in a PC, or if you are connecting the cable modem directly to the network through a router (see "Connecting the Cable Modem to the Network" later in the chapter for more on these options), you do not need to install any drivers or other special software on your PCs. You may need to configure the TCP/IP settings for each PC; Chapter 8 discusses this configuration in detail.

If you are connecting the cable modem to a PC using USB, you need to install the cable modem USB device driver. Windows helps you do this. Insert the CD-ROM that came with the cable modem into the computer's CD-ROM drive. If Windows' AutoPlay feature loads the Setup Utility, click the Exit button near the top right of the window. (If you wish, you can use the Setup Utility and read an electronic version of the cable modem manual; the box for the cable modem should also include the printed version of this manual.)

NOTE *You may also need your original Windows CD-ROM. Make sure it's available before you begin installation.*

Cable LED State	Cable Registration Status
ON	Unit is connected and registration is complete.
FLASH (0.125 sec)	Ranging process is okay.
FLASH (0.25 sec)	Downstream is locked and synchronization is okay.
FLASH (0.5 sec)	Unit is scanning for a downstream channel.
FLASH (1.0 sec)	Modem is in boot-up stage.
OFF	Error condition exists.

TABLE 3-1 BEFCMU10 ver.3 EtherFast Cable Modem Light State Definitions

Setting Up a USB Cable Modem in Windows 98 Here's how to set up a USB cable modem in Windows 98:

1. With the cable modem turned on and connected to the cable modem network (both the Power and Status lights should be on and not blinking), connect the USB cable from the computer to the cable modem. Windows will detect the new hardware and load the Add New Hardware Wizard, specifying "USB Composite Device." Click Next.

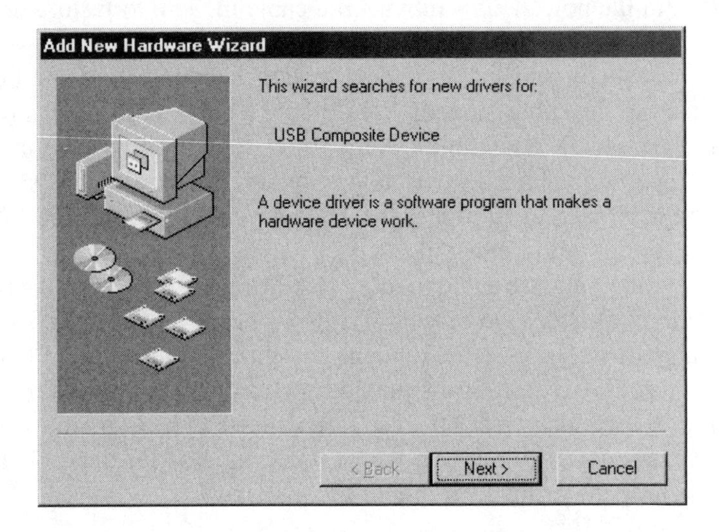

2. The next screen in the wizard asks whether it should search for the best driver or let you specify what driver to load. Almost everyone should leave the default, recommended selection to search. If you're following your own path on the setup and know what you are doing, you can choose the other option (good luck; you're on your own).

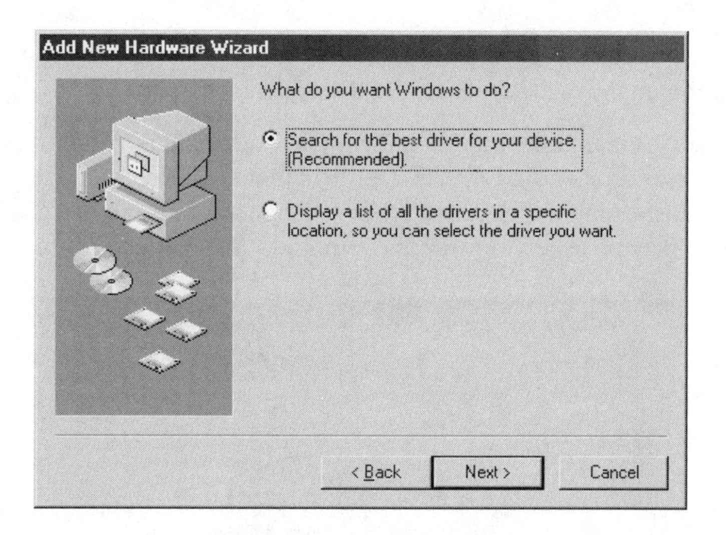

3. Next, tell Windows where to get the driver. If your cable modem came with drivers on a CD-ROM, select only the CD-ROM Drive option and Click Next. If your drivers are on a floppy disk, insert it, select Floppy Disk Drives, and then click Next. If you have downloaded the drivers from the Linksys support site, click Specify a Location and then direct Windows to the location of the downloaded files. You can also have Windows search the Windows Update site for drivers for the device, but Linksys drivers are typically not available on Windows Update.

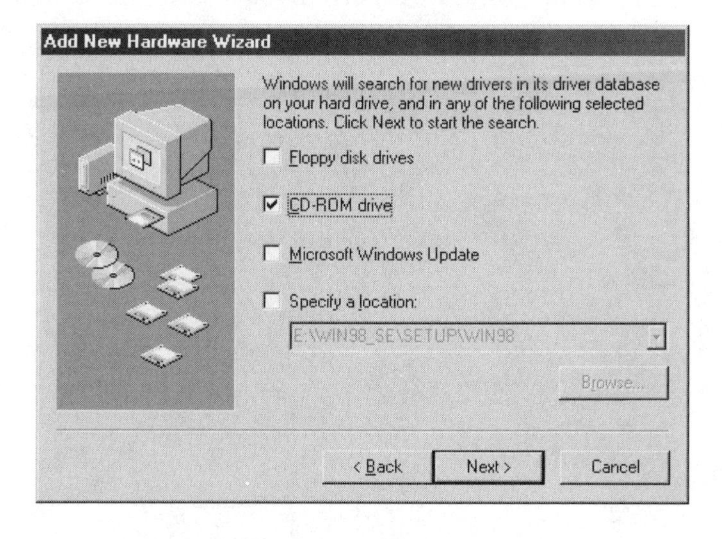

4. When Windows finds the driver at the location you specified, it displays the location on the next screen as the default choice. Click Next.

5. The next screen asks you to confirm that you want to install the specified driver for the specified device. Confirm that the correct device and driver are indicated, and click Next. After Windows copies the driver and installs it, you may be asked to insert the Windows installation disk.

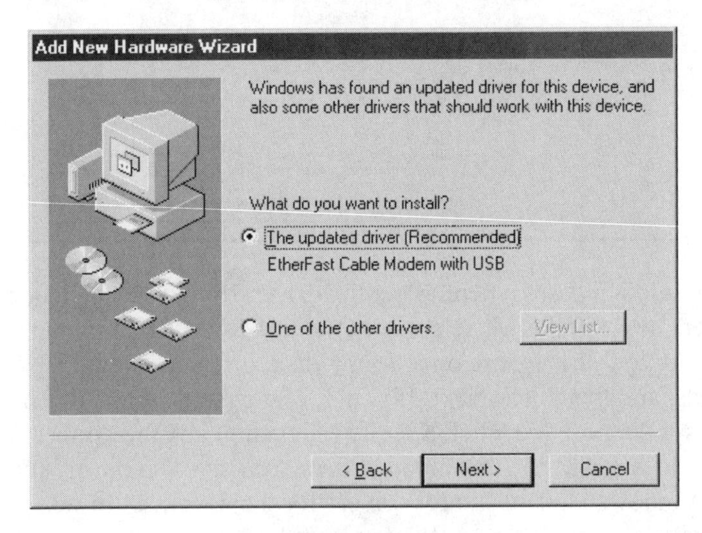

6. Finally, the wizard tells you what driver you have installed. It may then ask you to reboot the computer. Click Finish.

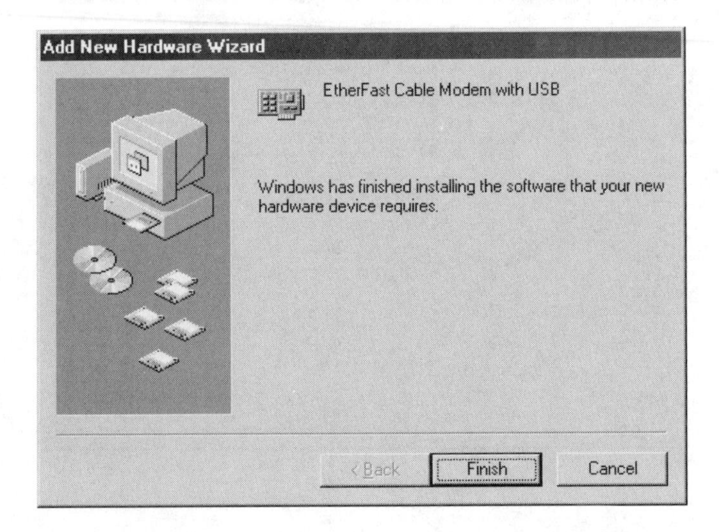

Setting Up a USB Cable Modem in Windows XP Home Edition and Windows XP Professional Here's how to set up a USB cable modem with Windows XP:

1. With the cable modem turned on and connected to the cable modem network (both the Power and Status lights should be on and not blinking), connect the USB cable from the computer to the cable modem. Windows detects the new hardware. First, a small bubble pops up in the bottom right of the screen stating "Found: USB Cable Modem." Then the Found New Hardware Wizard starts, stating that it will help you to load software for the USB cable modem. So far, so good.

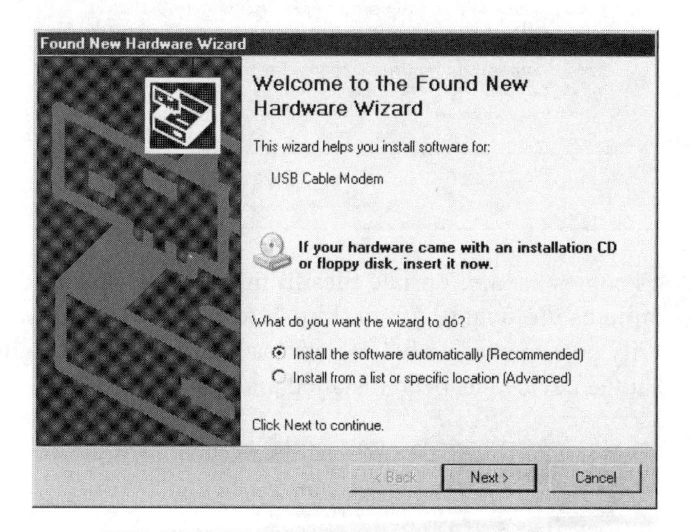

2. As the wizard says, if the driver disk for the cable modem is not yet inserted in the appropriate drive, insert it now. Leave the default selection to Install the Software Automatically (Recommended) and click Next.

3. Depending on the version of drivers that you are running, you may next see a scary dialog box telling you that the drivers for the cable modem have not passed Microsoft's compatibility tests for Windows XP. While it would be

nice for the drivers to have passed the tests, it's okay at this point to install them anyway by clicking the Continue Anyway button.

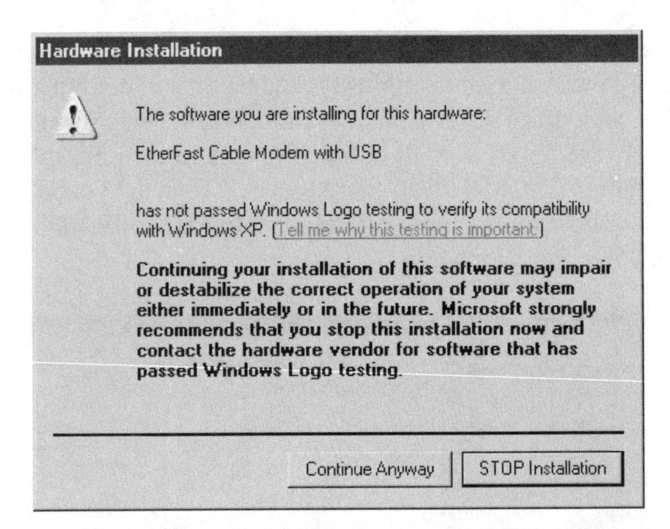

4. Windows copies the appropriate files from the driver disk to the computer and completes the wizard. Click Finish to exit it. (Windows may also temporarily pop up another balloon message in the bottom right to let you know that the device has been installed and is ready to use.)

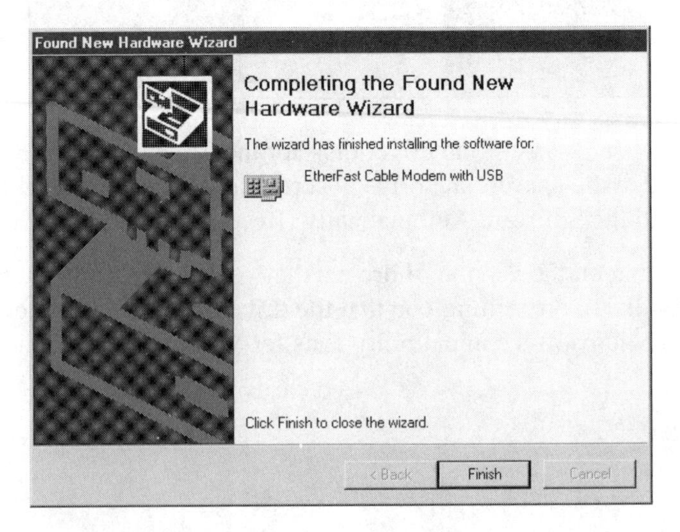

Cable Modem Service Options

Many cable modem services offer one level of service, which makes things simple. But others are beginning to offer multiple service levels to discount service to users who put a light load on the network and to get more from those who use it heavily. They usually do this not by setting a "bit quota" that limits the amount of data you can transmit for a price, but by charging more for faster service. The heavier your use, the less acceptable slower service would be. My philosophy, given such choices, is to try to get along with the slower service, with the knowledge that I can probably move up a service class if I need to. Incidentally, in almost all cases, cable modem service will prohibit you from running servers on your computers.

Business Cable Modem Plans

Read your service agreement: many cable modem service agreements state that they are intended only for personal use. I know that my cable modem service prohibits the use of Virtual Private Networks (VPNs) on its consumer service. (A cable modem service probably has no way of enforcing this rule, but if you want to follow the rules, it's an issue.) The service agreements of most cable service providers also prohibit you from hosting Web services on your computer that are accessible to the Internet. For example, you could not run a Web server on your home computer for Internet users to browse. The idea behind this is to protect the relatively limited upstream bandwidth available on the connection.

For this reason, some providers, like mine, have more expensive service plans intended for business users. The business service offered by my provider costs more than twice what the consumer service costs—pretty much just to let you run a VPN or host services. For more money (sometimes hundreds of dollars per month), some cable modem services allow you to use servers and many other fancy features such as static IP addresses.

Activating Your New Cable Modem

All network adapters have unique addresses associated with them that are of a different kind than the IP addresses discussed earlier. These addresses are called MAC (Media Access Control) addresses. All cable modems have a MAC address, too, because they are essentially network adapters on the Internet.

In the same package as your cable modem, you will find a conspicuous label with the MAC address of your cable modem as well as its serial number. Your cable modem company needs these two numbers to activate your service through that cable modem. If you don't find these numbers separate from the cable modem, they are probably printed on stickers on the cable modem itself. If you don't find them at all, bring the cable modem back to where you obtained it, because it's useless without these numbers.

If you have your cable modem before you call to set up your cable modem service from your cable provider, you can probably provide the cable company with the MAC and serial numbers at the time you set up service. If not, you will probably have to call the customer service or technical support number for your cable company to provide this information. There may be a delay of a few hours or perhaps a bit longer before your cable modem is functional on the network.

Connecting the Cable Modem to the Network

To serve a network of users, you can set up your cable modem in two basic ways. The first and most convenient way is to connect it to a router. This router can then attach to a hub or switch into which you can connect the systems in your network. The router will connect them all to the Internet through the cable modem, as shown in Figure 3-1.

Alternatively, you can use your PC as a router, as illustrated in Figure 3-2. You connect the cable modem directly to the PC, either using the USB connection or via an Ethernet adapter in the PC. Then you need a separate Ethernet adapter in the

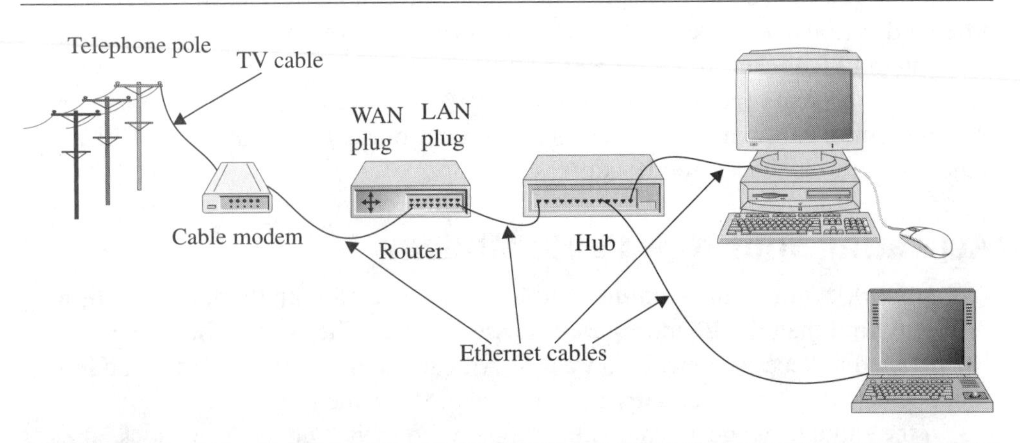

FIGURE 3-1 In a classic cable modem–based small network, the cable modem connects through a router device to a hub (the hub and router may be combined into a single box) and then to the PCs.

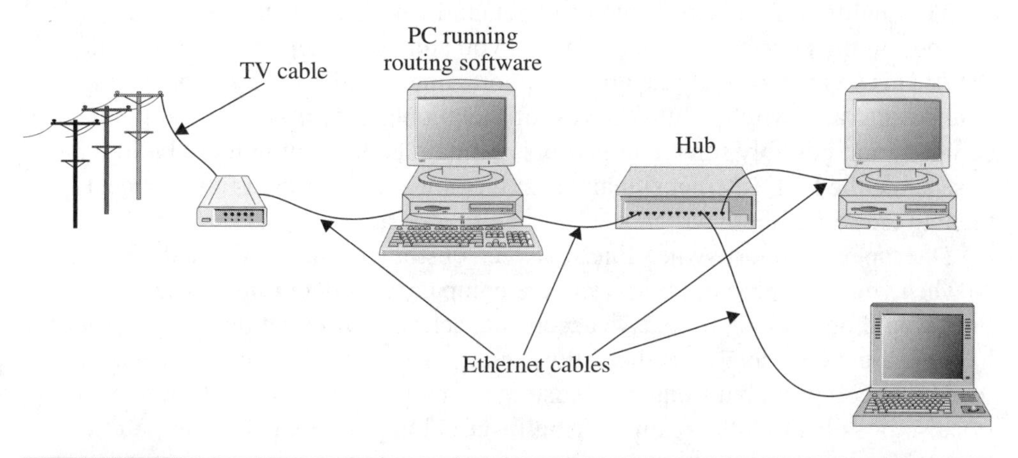

FIGURE 3-2 It's also possible to connect a cable modem directly to a PC and, optionally, run routing software on the PC to connect the rest of the network.

PC connected to the hub or switch into which all the other systems on the network are connected. At this point, the PC is on both networks: the Internet through the cable modem and the LAN through the hub.

You need routing software, such as the Internet Connection Sharing (ICS) feature that comes with Windows or third-party software, to make the connection between the two networks. It's easier to do things the first way, using a router, for a number of reasons. First, the PC doing the routing has to be turned on at all times, or the other PCs won't be able to access the Internet. If the routing PC crashes, the Internet connection to the rest of the network goes down. The routing also imposes a small performance burden on the routing PC.

Chapter 8 explores more details on how to configure such setups.

Digital Subscriber Line

DSL uses regular telephone lines for high-speed Internet access. Even though a DSL connection uses the same wires, you can continue to use your phones for normal voice and fax equipment because DSL uses different frequencies on the wires.

Several types of DSL services are available, and many offer a dizzying variety of service plans available from several ISPs. Fortunately (or unfortunately, depending on your point of view), far fewer companies are in this business today than in the past, so obtaining such a system isn't as complicated as it used to be.

The quality of DSL service you can get, and whether you can get it at all, depends on the physical distance between you and your telephone central office (CO). This CO is where all the area telephone lines from homes and businesses connect and are switched into the rest of the phone system. Your local phone company and possibly some competitors maintain equipment in these buildings to separate the DSL Internet signals from the voice transmissions and connect them to the rest of the Internet.

DSL operates poorly when lines between customers and a CO are too long, so when you attempt to order service, the company first determines whether your lines would be too long to receive acceptable service. Different phone companies have different distance limits they allow for service, so you'll have to check with your local company, but frequently customers are too far from a CO for service. It's also possible that the phone wiring installed in your area is incompatible with DSL.

Symmetric Versus Asymmetric Versus IDSL

Three basic types of DSL service are available, but one is more important than the others for most small network customers. Symmetric DSL (SDSL) and Asymmetric DSL (ADSL) are the two main types, with ADSL being far more common, affordable, and reasonable.

With SDSL, transmission speeds are the same for both upstream and downstream traffic. With ADSL they are different, which in reality means that downstream traffic moves faster than upstream traffic, as with most Internet services.

A third type of DSL, called IDSL, works over ISDN phone lines. (See the "Telephone Modems" section earlier in this chapter for an explanation of ISDN.) IDSL is relatively difficult to find and it's expensive, and it makes sense only for users who can't get other types of DSL because they are too far from a telephone CO.

IDSL is limited to 144 Kbps each way, which looks like a lot when compared to regular telephone modems, and cost (not including the cost of the ISDN line) rivals that of far faster ADSL lines. It can be supported at a much greater distance from the CO, though—up to about 50,000 feet.

How to Shop for DSL

If your local phone company sells DSL, the company has probably been sending you junk mail about it every week for years. The company may be a good choice for DSL service, but it may not be the only choice.

As a result of the Telecommunications Act of 1996, telephone companies have to allow third parties, called Competitive Local Exchange Carriers (CLECs, pronounced *see-Leks*), to rent space in the CO to run their own value-added services, including DSL. In the late 1990s, many of these companies were formed and many of them went out of business. But a few are still around, the biggest being Covad. You can buy DSL service directly from Covad (*http://www.covad.com/*) or through the many ISPs that use Covad for their DSL infrastructure. For example, my ISP is Speakeasy.net (*http://www.speakeasy.net/*), and it handles my e-mail and all the rest of the Internet part of my service, but the actual DSL service is handled by Covad and my local telephone company, Verizon.

Choosing which ISP to use can be difficult. It wouldn't be unreasonable for you to decide that your telephone company is unlikely to go out of business and just go with it. A good Web site with a lot of DSL information, including comparisons of providers, is at *http://www.dslreports.com/*.

NOTE *Remember also to check the service agreement before you sign up for DSL service. Some of the ISP's connection plans might prohibit the use of local networks to connect multiple PCs.*

DSL Equipment

Unlike with cable modems, no effective standard for DSL equipment is supported by all ISPs and phone companies. As a result, you will have to buy or lease equipment from the ISP or phone company when you get your service. These companies often have special deals for signing up new customers, involving discounted or free equipment, but you don't have the choice to go to third parties to buy equipment. This is only an issue for the device that connects to the actual phone line, not other networking equipment you may need to set up a LAN.

Like cable modems, the DSL "modem" is technically a network adapter on the Internet. One or more IP addresses will be bound to the DSL modem, and the modem will attach either to a PC or a router, such as the Linksys BEFSR41 EtherFast Cable/DSL Router.

Satellite

If you live out in the middle of nowhere, there's a decent chance you have access neither to cable modem nor DSL service. But if you have access to the sky, you may be able to get broadband Internet service via a satellite dish. This book can't provide a full guide to satellite Internet access, but this section will offer a brief overview of satellite issues for Internet access and some issues related to networks.

The main part of a satellite Internet connection is the satellite dish itself, so you will need to be able to mount a dish outdoors, either on your house or in your yard. Many companies provide satellite services, but two major providers work through smaller companies. Hughes Network Systems provides the DIRECWAY satellite service, often through partners such as Earthlink. The partner provides technical support for the product. Gilat Satellite Networks is another option for satellite broadband services.

Many satellite systems operate downstream only, so you need a simultaneous telephone connection to transfer data upstream. As you can imagine, such transmissions are rather slow. But even satellite systems that support upstream transmission to the satellite have slow upstream transmission. Actual downstream speeds can range from a few hundred Kbps to perhaps 2500 Kbps, but the high speeds come only with a lot of manual tweaking of settings. This is just one example of how satellite connectivity is generally more complicated than other broadband offerings.

Connecting the Satellite to Your Network

Another complication with satellite Internet connectivity is that current products are incompatible with hardware routers. All satellite systems need to be run in conjunction with software on a PC—specifically, the satellite transceiver, often misnamed "satellite modem," needs to be controlled by PC-based software.

Therefore, to connect the network to a satellite Internet connection, you need to run routing software, such as Windows' included ICS or a third-party product. Chapter 8 explains in detail how to set up ICS.

Part II

Installing Your Network

In this part, you get all the information you need to create your network. A chapter is devoted to each type of network configuration (Ethernet cable, wireless, telephone lines, and electric lines) so you have to read only the chapter that applies to your own network type. A separate chapter is then devoted to getting your network connected to the Internet.

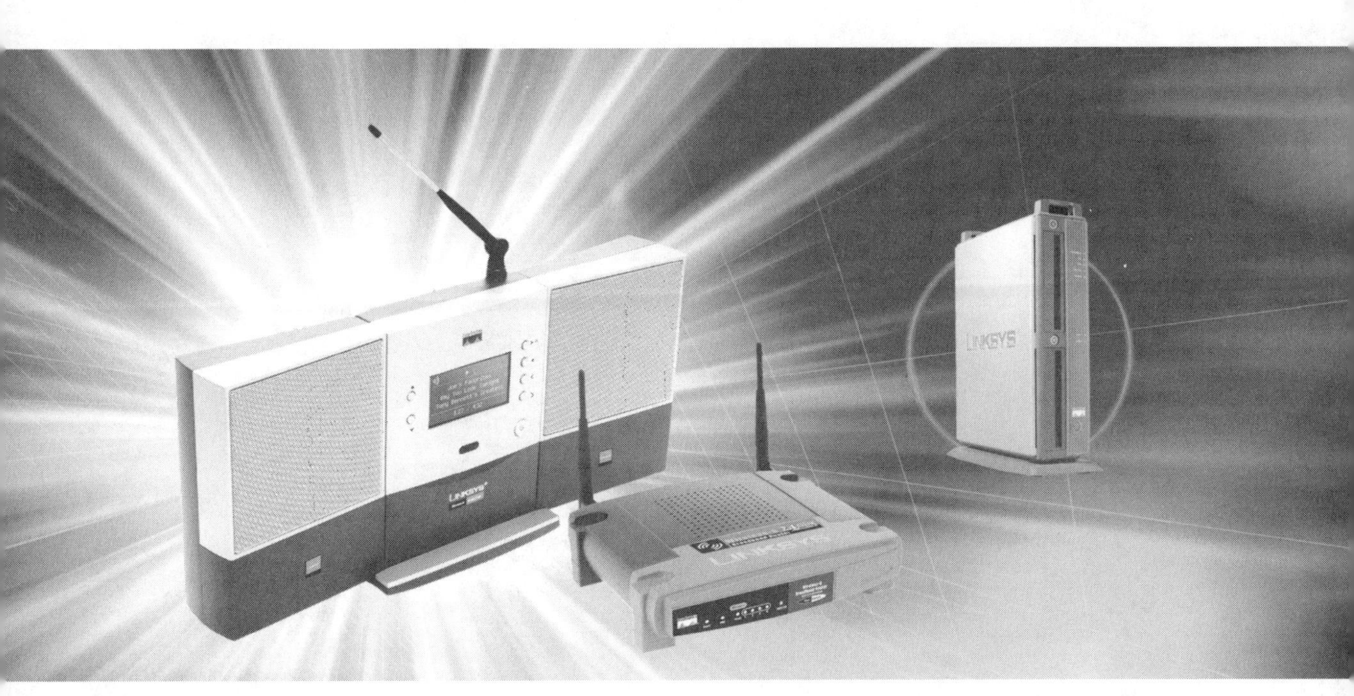

Chapter 4

Installing an Ethernet Cable Network

Now that you've made your decision about the type of network connection you want to use, it's time to install the hardware and connect the computers together. In Chapter 8, you will learn how to configure the operating system to run your network, let your computers talk to each other, and connect to the Internet.

If you decided to use Ethernet cable to connect your computers, you have some work to do, but it's easy, nontechnical work. You have to create the physical structure that runs your network. The central component of the structure is the concentrator (a hub or a switch), which accepts the Ethernet cable that arrives from each computer on the network. You must run a length of cable between the concentrator and each computer, and you also need to install a Network Interface Card (NIC) in each computer on the network to accept the computer-side connection of the cable.

The Concentrator: Central Control

The concentrator (see the sidebar "Hubs Versus Switches" in this chapter) controls the communication among the computers on the network. When one computer sends a data packet to another computer, the packet is not sent directly (because the computers aren't directly connected to each other); instead, the data packet is sent to the concentrator, which passes it along to the recipient computer.

Concentrator Speed

Concentrators come with two types of speed measurements: they operate at a specific speed, or they are *autosensing* (the concentrator communicates with each NIC at the speed that NIC can handle). If you're building a new network, all of your NICs probably operate at 100 Mbps, because that's today's standard. However, since most Linksys concentrators are autosensing, you don't have to hunt for one that operates at 100 Mbps; the device will know the speed and adjust.

I know a lot of people who created home networks by bringing home computers from work when their companies upgraded hardware. This is a great way to add computers to your home—the price is certainly right. Many of those computers have 10 Mbps NICs installed, and with autosensing concentrators, you can use those computers "as is." For the normal file exchanges that take place in a home network or a small business network, it's unlikely you'll notice the difference in speed. If you sense a difference in the 10 Mbps computer, replacing the NIC with one that supports 100 Mbps is an easy and inexpensive upgrade (see the section "Installing NICs" later in this chapter).

How Data Moves Through the Concentrator

A standard hub passes incoming data to all the computers that occupy ports in the hub, but only the computer that's meant to be the recipient pays any attention. Even though that means the hub wastes some communication bandwidth (it splits the bandwidth by sending the data to all the ports), you shouldn't notice any degradation in performance in a network that has a handful of computers.

However, on some networks (usually large business networks, but increasingly on home networks), many of the data packets are very large, especially if users are working across the network on large graphics files. As a result, the network is busy with lots of data traffic. In that case, you should consider one of the Linksys *switches* instead of a hub. A switch is a more advanced version of a hub, and it sends data only to the computer marked as the recipient. (See the sidebar "Hubs Versus Switches" if you're interested in a slightly more technical explanation.) This keeps the performance level of your network at a productive rate, even in the face of constant large data packets. In fact, you'll find it easier these days to find a switch than to find a hub, and the price difference between the two is minimal. Also, most combination products (such as the Linksys line of EtherFast Cable/DSL routers) feature built-in switches rather than built-in hubs. If you are in doubt about what you should purchase, your safest bet is to use a switch.

Hubs Versus Switches

In case you're curious, here's an explanation (admittedly oversimplified) of the differences in the methods used by hubs and switches to deliver data. When data is exchanged between networked computers, the data packet (also called a datagram) contains information beyond the data—it contains the address of the receiving computer. The receiving computer's address is its MAC (Media Access Control) address, which is unique on the network.

All the steps you take to install the operating system files for your network (running the networking wizards, installing protocols such as TCP/IP, and so on) are necessary to make sure these functions work properly. The protocol is responsible for determining the MAC address, and to accomplish this it checks a look-up table of computer names and provides all the right technical information. (Remember in Chapter 1 you learned that computer names must be unique on the network, and if you're using TCP/IP, each computer must have its own unique IP address and MAC address. MAC addresses cannot be changed; they are encoded into the NIC hardware.)

When the data packet is sent to the hub, the hub ignores the address that's contained in the packet and ships the data through all the ports, sending the data to every computer that's connected to the hub. The computers read the MAC address and only the computer that's the designated recipient accepts the packet; the others discard it.

A switch is a more intelligent device than a hub, because it can store information in its memory. Switches keep their own ARP (Address Resolution Protocol) table, which matches the MAC addresses to the port connections. When data arrives, the switch looks up the MAC address in its ARP table and isolates the circuit (the port and cable) that belongs to the receiving computer, sending the data only on that circuit. The transmission is sent at full speed, totally dedicated to the target computer. Today you can find switches that move data at the rate of a gigabyte per second, which is incredibly fast.

It's important that you realize that what I've described here is not only a simple (perhaps simplistic) overview, but it also applies only to simple switches that are commonly found on small LANs. More sophisticated switches are available that perform more sophisticated technical tasks.

Finding a Location for the Concentrator

You need to decide where to locate the concentrator, and you should choose a location that reduces the amount of cable you need to install to connect all the computers to the hub. This setup is called a *star topology*, and it requires a length of cable between each computer on the network and the hub (see Figure 4-1).

The possible permutations and combinations available for network layouts are way too numerous for me to cover with explicit detail and advice about the location of the concentrator. Where the concentrator is located and what layout you decide to use depends entirely on your location and setup. You might have two computers on the second floor and one on the first floor, so it makes sense to locate the concentrator on the second floor (so you'll have only one long cable run). If all your computers are on one floor (typical of a small business network), the logical place for the concentrator is at the mid-point. However, you can't always measure distances and put the concentrator in the location that mathematically works best in terms of distances. You have other factors to consider, which are discussed next.

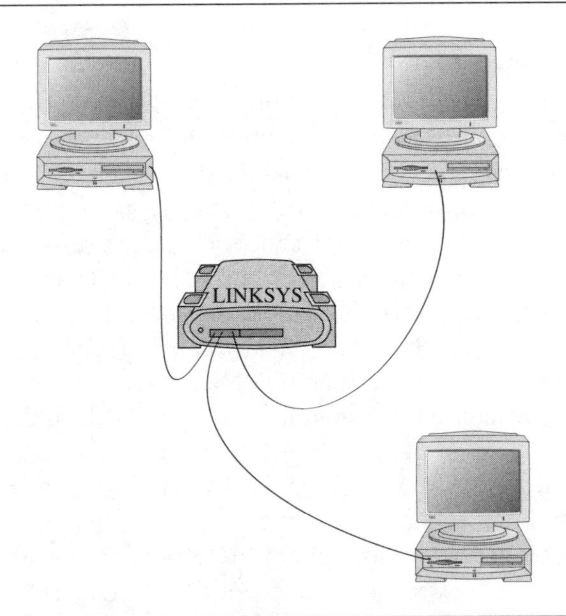

FIGURE 4-1 You need to run a cable to each computer, connecting it to the concentrator.

Access Considerations

Access to the concentrator is not an important issue. The only time you need to work at the concentrator is when you're plugging an RJ-45 connector into a port (and after you set up your network, you have to perform that task only if you add more computers to the network). There's nothing to do on a day-to-day basis—the concentrator just sits there, working dependably, without any babysitting from you. This means you can put the concentrator in some nook or niche and save desk space.

Linksys concentrators have lights that glow to indicate connections, and the lights flash to let you know data transfers are occurring. When I first installed my Ethernet network, I glanced at the lights frequently to make sure everything was working. After a few days, I took the reliability for granted and moved the concentrator off the desktop and tucked it away on a shelf.

Power and Environment

Concentrators require electrical power, so the location must have an electrical outlet. This eliminates most closets, which is a shame, because a closet is a great

Star Topology

Years ago, the term *star topology* was applied to distinguish this type of layout (using twisted-pair Ethernet cable to connect computers to a hub) from the layout of Ethernet coaxial cable (a "daisy-chain" arrangement moving from the first computer on the network to the last). In those days, we used BNC connectors (similar to the connectors that your cable company uses) to connect the Ethernet "coax," and if any connection along the daisy chain was interrupted, the whole network went down. Users had a wide variety of methods for breaking the connections—by tossing heavy objects (such as a dictionary) on the back of the desk, where it would fall behind the desk and break the connection; or by reaching for something under the desk, and accidentally yanking the coax cable; or, if the connection were within easy reach, by idly twirling the connection during telephone calls until it became unscrewed (today users play FreeCell during telephone calls).

With star topology, if you disconnect one computer, the other computers keep working because they're all still connected to the concentrator. Twisted-pair Ethernet, concentrators, and star topology have certainly made my life as a consultant much easier.

location for a concentrator. In addition, as with any electrical device, you need to protect the concentrator from excess heat and humidity. Keep the concentrator away from direct sunlight, radiators, and heaters. Don't cover it or wrap it in plastic (some people do that to avoid dust), because some air must circulate around the concentrator to prevent overheating.

And, of course, you must protect it from power surges, so plug a surge protector into the outlet and plug the concentrator into the surge protector. Also, avoid proximity to other electrical devices that might interfere with data communication—don't put the concentrator next to fluorescent lights, radios, or transmitting equipment.

Near a Gateway to the Cable Runs

The cables from all the computers on your network meet at the concentrator, so the concentrator must be near a place that can handle all the cable. If you're running cable through the walls, put the concentrator in an inconspicuous corner where you can create a hole large enough to handle multiple cables. If you're running cable along baseboards, locate the concentrator at the logical place for ending each cable run. Obviously, it's best to locate the concentrator at the edge of a room, not in the middle of a room where the cables would snake across the floor.

Incidentally, you can add concentrators to your network if your network outgrows the number of ports, or if the layout of your cable run works better if you connect one group of computers to one concentrator and another group to a different concentrator, and then connect the concentrators. See Chapter 12 to learn how to link multiple concentrators.

Near Internet Access

If your network will be connected to the Internet, you will most likely be connecting your Internet device (such as a cable or DSL modem) to your concentrator. Typically, these connections happen through a standard Ethernet cable. This means that you don't have to place the concentrator and the modem near one another, but most people like to keep all their network gear in a single place for ease of access.

Installing Cable

The way cable is strung through a building is called the *run,* and you need to create a plan for the run before you start drilling holes or uncoiling wire. The plan should match the type of access you have among the rooms that hold computers. For your Ethernet network, you must install multiple runs, one from each computer to the concentrator.

Types of Cable

Two broad categories of Ethernet cable exist: straight-through and crossover. The physical difference between them is the way the wires meet the connectors; the difference to users is the set of circumstances under which each type of cable is used.

Category 5/5e/6 cable contains eight color-coded wires that run from one end of the cable to the other. You can see the colors easily if you have a piece of cable that doesn't have a connector (you may have to strip the outer insulation of the cable to see the colors of the wires clearly). If you look at a length of cable that has a connector, point the connector away from yourself, with the little plastic tab (it's a spring clip) on the bottom, and wire #1 is on your right. Table 4-1 explains the wiring of Ethernet cable.

Wire Number	Color	Use
1	White/orange stripe	Transmit data
2	Orange	Transmit data
3	White/green stripe	Receive data
4	Blue	Not used
5	White/blue stripe	Not used
6	Green	Receive data
7	White/brown stripe	Not used
8	Brown	Not used

TABLE 4-1 Wiring Scheme for Cat 5 Cable

Two types of physical cable are available: unshielded twisted pair (UTP) and shielded twisted pair (STP). STP has a metal shield encasing the wires to reduce the possibility of interference from other electrical devices, radar, radio waves, and so on. UTP has no such shield and is less expensive, and it's almost always the cable of choice.

Crossover Cable

Crossover cable gets its name from the fact that the wires change position between connectors. (You need to consider only the wires that are actually used for Ethernet communication: 1, 2, 3, and 6.) Wires that start at one position end up at a different position, as follows:

- 1 crosses to 3
- 2 crosses to 6

Of course, if you look at the crossover from the other end (the other connector), it's the reverse:

- 3 crosses to 1
- 6 crosses to 2

Crossover cable isn't used for standard network cabling; you don't use it to connect the computers to the concentrator. It's used for special connections—

for example, you may need crossover wire to attach a DSL (digital subscriber line) device to a concentrator or to link two concentrators. The documentation for the hardware device tells you whether a crossover cable is required. It's entirely possible (and even probable) that you'll never need a crossover cable, because most concentrators have an uplink port that will cross the connection automatically.

Straight-Through Cable

Straight-through cable gets its name from the fact that the wires go through the cable without changing their positions, so that wire 1 at one connector is wire 1 at the other connector. (You need to consider only the wires that are actually used for Ethernet communication: 1, 2, 3, and 6.)

Straight-through cable is the standard used for Ethernet cable that attaches components of a network together. Taking into consideration the technical nomenclature and the technical jargon, this cable is known by several names, any of which you may hear when you're buying cable or asking for help from knowledgeable friends:

- **Twisted pair** A description of the way the wires are twisted through the length of cable. Insulated copper wires are twisted around each other to reduce crosstalk, or electromagnetic induction, between the pairs of wires.
- **Category 5/5e/6 (cat 5, cat 5e, or cat 6)** An indication of the category (level) of the cable. Other categories of twisted-pair cable exist, such as cat 2 or cat 3, for telephone lines and alarm systems. Cat 5 cabling supports Ethernet networks running at 10 Mbps or 100 Mbps. Cat 5e also supports high-speed (1 Gbps) Ethernet systems. Cat 6 is now starting to show up in most retail stores. Cat 6 is essentially the same as Cat 5e, except that Cat 6 is made to a higher standard.
- **10BaseT or 100BaseT** A technical description of twisted-pair Ethernet cable to distinguish it from 10Base2 (coaxial Ethernet cable). The *10* and *100* indicate the speed.
- **Patch cable** The term for a length of cable to which RJ-45 connectors have been added so it's ready to use. You can build your own cable by using special tools to add an RJ-45 connector to raw twisted-pair cable, but most people find that unnecessary because patch cables are inexpensive.

Making Your Own Patch Cables

If you need an extra-long cable, or you're cabling a lot of computers and want to save money (or if you just like doing it yourself), you can make your own patch cables. You're not making cable, of course—you're adding connectors to lengths of cable. It's actually quite easy—I've been making my own cables for years. You'll need the following supplies and tools:

- Bulk Ethernet cable, which sells for 10 to 20 cents per foot
- RJ-45 connectors, which cost less than 50 cents each
- A wire stripper, which costs a few dollars
- A crimper, which costs about $20 to $25

(The prices depend on the size of the order, as the more cable and connectors you buy, the lower the unit cost. I have a combo stripper/crimper that cost about $35, and it also handles RJ-11 connectors for regular phone cable in addition to the Ethernet cable.)

To make a patch cable, follow these steps:

1. Cut the cable to the length you need (plus an extra 2 or 3 feet just in case).
2. Use the stripper to remove about a half-inch of insulation and expose the wires inside. Be careful not to use too much pressure or you will also strip or damage the internal wires.
3. Push the wires into the hole on the connector (see Table 4-1 for the color order). Once you make sure the colors are lined up correctly, they slide in easily.
4. Set the crimper for RJ-45 connectors.
5. Position the crimper where the connector and the wires meet (some crimpers allow you to insert the connector), and press firmly.
6. Repeat these steps to add a connector at the other end of the cable.

Measuring the Runs

Cable doesn't run from a concentrator to a computer in a straight line—it runs along baseboards, up or down walls, and across ceilings—so you can't measure the distance "as the crow flies." The only way to measure properly is to follow the exact path the cable takes. Don't forget to measure the space between the place the cable enters the room and the RJ-45 connector on the concentrator or the NIC.

You do have one important thing to think about: the maximum length of a cable run is 328 feet (100 meters). It's unlikely that any run would be longer than that in a typical home or small business environment, but you should know that the maximum exists. If you're creating a network in a large house or office building, and the computers are spread among several floors as well as among the front and back parts of the building, you may end up with one run that is longer than the maximum distance allowed. The best solution is to use two concentrators for the network, and then link the concentrators. (Actually, the best solution is to move the computers that can't be connected within the maximum run length, but most people don't like that idea.) See Chapter 12 to learn about using multiple concentrators on an Ethernet network.

The space you use to bring the cable from the computer to the concentrator is called a *chase*. If you're lucky, you'll have a straight-line chase between the concentrator and each individual computer. The chase may be inside a wall, in a hollow space above the ceiling, through the basement or attic, along the baseboards of a room, or a combination of these paths.

After you measure, you must buy patch cable (cable with the RJ-45 connectors already attached) of the right length. Most patch cable is sold in the following lengths (in feet): 10, 15, 20, 25, 50, and 100. If you need cable longer than that, you can order patch cable in custom lengths from most computer stores (both online and brick-and-mortar) or you can make your own (see the sidebar "Making Your Own Patch Cables").

You can connect two pieces of cable with a coupler, which is a small plastic device that has two receptacles that accept RJ-45 connectors. The coupler works much like the couplers you can buy in any supermarket for telephone lines (though telephone couplers will not fit your computer cable). However, couplers don't have a terrific history of reliability. Frequently, when I've encountered problems with network communications, the cause was the coupler. Also, you should never put a coupler inside a wall or in any other location that's difficult to access, because if you have to check or replace it, you need access. The best plan is to use a coupler as a temporary measure while you wait for delivery of a custom-made patch cable that's the correct length.

Linksys sells a nifty product called Network in a Box (model number FENSK05), which comes with a hub, two NICs, and two 15-foot patch cables. This is usually sufficient for a small home network in which the computers are in the same room, adjacent rooms, or stacked rooms (one room is directly above the other room). A switched version of the Network in a Box product (model number FESWSK5) includes a 5-port switch instead of a hub. As you might expect, the price difference is small and you are better insulated against future needs by going with the switch instead of the hub.

Assembling Your Tools

Depending on the layout of the building and the placement of computers, you'll need one or more of the following tools to install your network cables:

- A fish, which is a long, thin length of metal encased in a holder (it looks like a steel tape measure on steroids). The metal is thin and flexible but very strong. The front end of the fish is a hook, which can grab cable and fish it toward you through walls. If the distance isn't very long, you can sometimes get away without buying or by borrowing a fish (do you have a friend who is an electrician?) or by using a coat hanger you've untwisted (the hook at the end grabs the cable).
- A drill, with a bit large enough to make a hole at least 7/8 inch in diameter. The connector on a patch cable is about 1/2-inch wide, but the little plastic tab may increase the size of the hole you need. You do not want to risk breaking the tab, so drill the holes large enough to avoid that risk. Some people tape down the tab, but that increases the width of the connector, so you still need a generous hole. Also, I've seen the tab break off when the tape was removed.
- Cable staples, which you can use to secure cable along baseboards, quarter-round, or doorjambs.
- A hammer for installing cable staples.
- Strong string or a length of thin chain with a small, heavy weight attached, for vertical chases (it's so much easier to drop the string or chain, attach the cable, and pull up, than to fish the cable up through the wall).
- A flashlight, for peering into the spaces between walls, or between the ceiling and floor, when you can't figure out where the cable went.

- A tennis ball and a roll of twine, if the chase is in a drop ceiling (such as in many businesses where the ceiling tiles are dropped down from the actual ceiling). Punch a hole all the way through the tennis ball (a knitting needle works well for that), thread the twine through the holes, and tie the twine. In long runs in a drop ceiling, you can throw the tennis ball from the destination toward the source of the cable. You can then tie the cable to the twine and pull the cable through the drop ceiling toward the destination.
- Cable covers, which are rubber or plastic devices that are put over cable that has to cross part of the floor after it emerges from its chase (needed when computers aren't located against the wall). Cable covers keep cable from moving, and they keep people from tripping over the cable (they're sloped at the edges to reduce the chance of tripping over them). You can even use them under a rug, which is something you shouldn't do with cable, because the rubbing of the underside of the rug against the cable can weaken or break the cable's insulation.

CAUTION *Be careful about the way you handle cable as you run it through the chase and around the room. Don't bend or install cable at a sharp angle. When you must make a turn with the cable, picture running the cable around the outer edge of a silver dollar—the turn should be no tighter than that. Also, when cable turns a corner, don't pull it taut—give it some slack.*

Cabling Within the Same Room

If all the computers on your network are in the same room (common for small business and home offices), you don't need to drill holes in walls or floors. Put the concentrator next to one computer and use a short cable to connect them. Then run longer cable from the concentrator to the other computers (see Figure 4-2).

Run the cable along the baseboard or quarter-round instead of running it across the room. If a doorway interferes with a straight chase along the wall, that's the place to put the concentrator; otherwise, use a cable cover to cross the opening, or run the cable up and around the doorway. If your computers aren't against the walls, use cable covers when you bring the cable from the wall to the computer.

Cabling Between Adjacent Rooms

If your computers are located in adjacent rooms on the same floor, you have to drill only one hole between the rooms (for the least noticeable hole, drill through the baseboard, just above the quarter-round). Put the concentrator in one of the

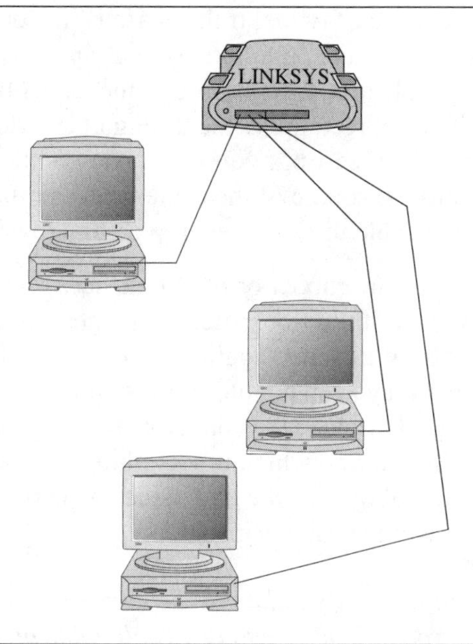

FIGURE 4-2 Creating a network is a cakewalk when all the computers are in the same room.

rooms, near a computer, and run one short length of cable between them. Run another length of cable to the computer in the other room, through the hole you drilled (see Figure 4-3).

It's easier, of course, if the computers are all located against a common wall. If they're not, run the cable along baseboards or quarter-round, not across the floor.

Cabling Between Nonadjacent Rooms on the Same Floor

If your computers are on the same floor but aren't in adjacent rooms, the most efficient cabling route is a chase along your home's beams. Most houses have beams between floors that run straight through the house, either from front to back or from side to side. You usually can expect a clear chase from one end to the other.

If your computers are on the second floor, the best chase is across the attic floor or through a crawl space above the second floor. If you run cabling across the attic, be sure to secure the cabling by running it around the periphery of the room and using cable staples or eye hooks to keep it in place. If you use your attic for storage, this will prevent you from inadvertently placing items on top of the

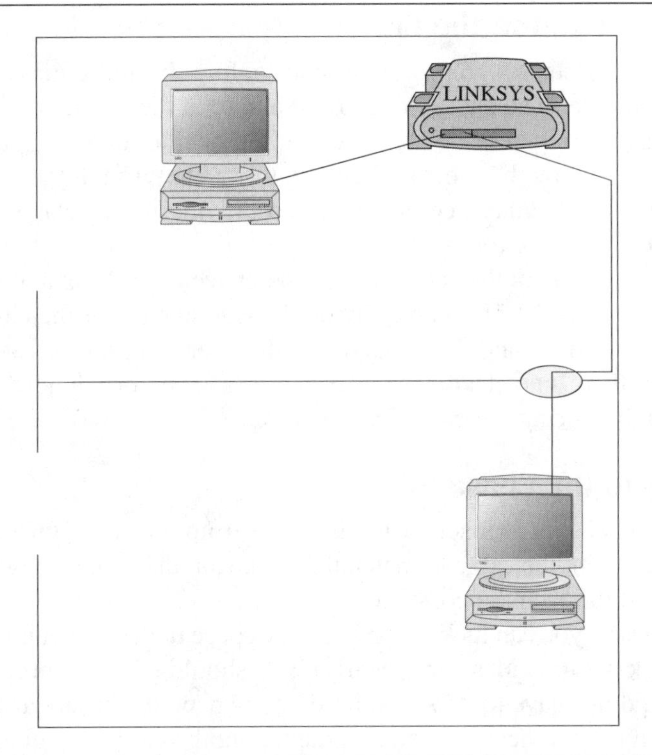

FIGURE 4-3 Cabling between adjacent rooms requires an opening between the rooms.

cabling and from tripping over it. You should also take the same precautions when you install cabling in a drop ceiling. Some manufacturers also sell cable cradles, which are simply open resting hooks that you screw into a side wall and into which you lay the cable.

If your computers are on the first floor, the best chase is across the basement ceiling or through a crawl space below the first floor. If you run cabling in a crawlspace under your house, use cable staples or screw eye-hooks into your floor joists and suspend the cable against the ceiling of the crawlspace to keep it out of the way.

The trick is to get the cable into the chase, and the logical way is to drill a hole in the ceiling or floor (depending on whether the chase is above or below the level you're working on). However, I hate drilling holes in the ceiling because it looks terrible, and even if I paint the cable to match the wall, it's visible. I have hardwood floors so I shudder at the thought of drilling into them. Instead, I use closets or walls to get to the chase.

Use a Closet to Get to the Chase

Wiring through closets is a great way to hide cabling. If you're lucky, every room that holds a computer also has a closet. Drill a hole in the ceiling or floor of each room that holds a computer (the choice of ceiling or floor depends on whether the chase is above or below the room). Then fish the cable through the chase to the closet of each room that has a computer (if a room doesn't have a closet, just bring the cable directly into the room).

Of course, a portion of the cable has to run between the closet and the computer (or concentrator, or both). If you have enough clearance under the closet door, run the cable under the door and then attach it to the quarter-round or baseboard with cable staples. If there's no clearance under the closet door, drill a hole in the bottom of the door jamb to bring the cable into the room.

Go Directly to the Chase

For any room that lacks a closet, bring the cable from the chase into the room at a corner, and then paint the cable to match the wall. Run the cable along the baseboard or quarter-round to reach the computer.

In some houses, you can tuck cabling into the space under or behind the baseboard. While this is okay (and hides cable neatly), you should take two precautions: First, make sure you don't have to press too hard or pry back the baseboard at all to get the cabling behind it; otherwise you risk damaging the cable. Second, if you have to turn a corner onto another wall, the 90-degree turn is usually too sharp for the cable. (Actually, it is difficult to get cable behind the corners of the baseboard anyway.)

Cabling Between Floors

If your computers are located on different floors, your cable length measurement must include the height of the room in addition to the horizontal length required to reach the computer. If one computer is in the basement and another is on the second floor, you need sufficient cable length to make the trip to the concentrator (which should probably be located midway, to avoid the need to purchase long cable lengths).

If the rooms are stacked one over the other, run the cable through the inside of the walls, near a corner. If closets are stacked, use them.

While it is tempting to use holes already drilled for radiators or heating pipes, you should not do so. Heat can damage cables and even cause them to melt.

If the rooms are on opposite ends of the house, you have to use both walls (closets are better) and ceilings. For the vertical chase, use any openings around pipes (not hot pipes) that are available; otherwise use the inside of the wall. For the horizontal runs, find a chase above or below the room.

Work from the top down to let gravity assist your efforts. Put a weight on the end of strong string or twine and drop it down to the lower floor. Then, tape the cable to the weight and haul it up.

You can also cable through HVAC (heating, ventilation, air condition) ducts, but many cities and towns have strict rules about this option. For example, you may be required to use shielded cable or a special cable called *plenum* cable if you're taking advantage of the duct system. Plenum cable (named after the space above a drop ceiling) is constructed so that if it burns, it does not give off poisonous fumes. However, some building codes totally forbid using HVAC for cable of any type. Never enter the duct system by drilling a hole; instead use an existing entry and exit (look for a grate over the point at which the duct meets the wall).

Adding a Professional Touch

After all the cabling is finished and the computers are connected to the concentrator, here's what happens: People in your household look at the installation and are not the least bit impressed with your efforts or with the new technology available to them. They look at all that cable coming out of walls, closets, and ceilings, and make comments in which the words *ugly*, *tacky*, or *sloppy* occur. Somebody remarks that the network at her corporate office doesn't have holes that exude cable. Professional cable installers use faceplates on the wall, and there's no reason you can't put the same finishing touch on your system.

If you run cable through walls, you can terminate the cable on the wall using an Ethernet socket (called a *keystone*) that is attached to the wall with a faceplate. You can buy keystones and faceplates at any computer store.

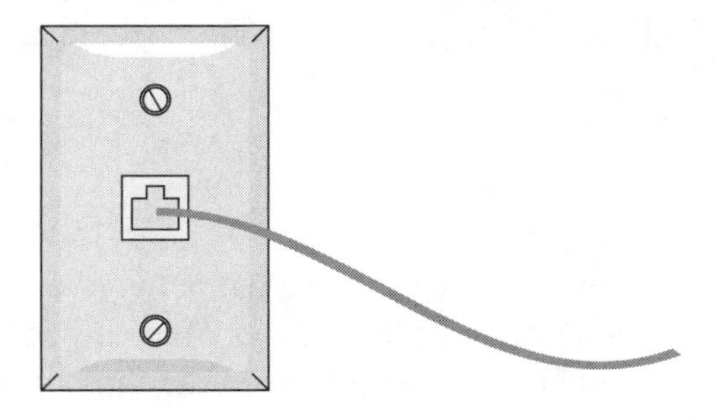

To create an Ethernet socket, pull the cable through the hole in the wall and use a stripper to remove about an inch of insulation from the cable (cut off the connector first). Then insert the wires into the socket according to a color-coded guide included with the keystone and push against the socket to seal the connection (these are similar to electrical connections that just snap into place). Attach the socket to the faceplate, and attach the faceplate to the wall (pushing the wires back into the wall).

Plan Ahead—Bring Up Other Cables

When I recabled my home recently, I had planned ahead and made my house cable-ready for anything. In addition to the network cable I placed through two stories and multiple hallways, I brought along telephone cable (8-pair), speaker cable, and electrical cable. I just tied all the cable into a bundle and hauled away. To accomplish this, I had to drill holes that were a full inch in diameter, but I was able to enter each floor through a closet and then snake each type of cable into the various rooms separately (which meant smaller holes as I entered each room).

After I set up my network outlets, the other cable just sat there, in the wall waiting for me to use it. Whenever I wanted to add a phone jack, the wire was there. When I wanted to wire the output of my stereo into every room in the house, I just had to bring up speakers—the cable was there. When I called my electrician for new outlets, the wire was there and he could hook up the circuit box and the outlet without having to fish cable through the walls (at his high hourly rate). (By the way, I do not do my own electrical wiring—that stuff is dangerous if you're not properly trained.)

Hiring a Professional

If crawling on your hands and knees in crawlspaces and attics, drilling holes in your walls, and hauling cable through tight spaces is just not your cup of tea (or if you simply want a really professional look), you can hire a professional to do it for you. Many computer companies offer networking services, such as cabling, to businesses and homes. In addition, you can also find people at alarm companies that can do the job.

Installing NICs

Every computer on the network needs an Ethernet network adapter to accept the RJ-45 connection at the end of the cable. Linksys offers a wide variety of Ethernet adapters, so you can mix and match computers on the same network. For example, you can get internal NICs for your desktop computers and a PC Card for your laptop. If a desktop computer has a USB port available, you may prefer to use it so you don't have to open the computer to install an internal NIC. You can also use a USB network adapter on your laptop (assuming a USB port is available). The following sections describe the steps you must take to install internal NICs and USB network adapters.

After you complete the tasks described here (physically installing the NICs and installing the operating system drivers), you must configure the NIC so it can find the other computers on the network. You'll find all the information you need to accomplish this in Chapter 8.

Internal NICs

To install an internal NIC, you must open the computer and insert the NIC into a slot (called a *bus*) on the systemboard. Some people find the prospect of messing around in the computer's innards rather daunting, but it's really easy, and usually the only tool you need is a Phillips screwdriver. However, pay attention to the following safety tips:

- Don't use a magnetic screwdriver. Magnets and disk drives do not get along well because magnetic forces can delete data.
- Discharge any static electricity in your body before you touch any of the components inside the computer. Leave the computer plugged in while you take the cover off and touch any exposed metal part of the computer case. Don't worry—you won't get a shock. You will just discharge the built-up static electricity in your body. Once you've done that, you can unplug the computer before installing the card, if it makes you feel more comfortable.
- Remove metal jewelry, especially gold (which conducts static electricity) and most especially rings.

Determining the Bus Type

Depending on the age of the computers in your network, you may need to purchase NICs for different bus types. (Most networks, especially home networks, comprise some older computers and some new computers.) Two types of buses accept NICs:

- A PCI (Peripheral Component Interconnect) bus is usually white, and it has a crossbar about three-quarters of the way down its length. All newer computers use PCI buses, and some older computers may have a couple of PCI buses.

- An ISA (Industry Standard Architecture) bus is usually black (an Extended ISA bus is brown), and it has a small crossbar about two-thirds of the way down its length. ISA buses are longer than PCI buses. Older computers contain ISA buses in addition to a couple of PCI buses. Although you can't really purchase new ISA NICs anymore, you might still come across them. This is particularly true if you purchase used computers or components.

NOTE *Your computer may also have a bus that's shorter than the PCI bus and is located farther away from the back of the computer than the other buses. This is an Accelerated Graphics Port (AGP) bus, and it's used for high-speed video controllers.*

For computers you've purchased within the last few years, you can automatically assume you'll need a PCI NIC. In fact, even though older computers may have PCI buses in addition to ISA buses, you have no way of knowing whether a PCI bus is empty unless you open the computer. If only an ISA bus is available, you'll have to use a NIC designed for ISA. You'll also have to make sure you've installed an autosensing 10/100 Mbps concentrator, not a pure 100 Mbps concentrator, because ISA NICs operate at 10 Mbps while your PCI NICs operate at 100 Mbps.

Inserting the NIC

Use the following steps to install your NICs:

1. Turn off the computer.
2. If your computer is easily accessible, you may be able to remove its cover without disconnecting any of the devices attached to the computer (mouse, keyboard, printer, scanner, and so on). If this is the case, skip to step 5.
3. Disconnect the cables that are attached to ports on the computer.

TIP *As you disconnect each cable, write the name of its peripheral on a small piece of paper and tape the paper to the cable. Then, on the back of the computer, use a felt tip pen to mark the ports—for instance, M for mouse and K for keyboard, Modem for the serial port, Printer for the parallel port, and so on. You'll have many occasions to thank yourself for marking everything in this manner.*

4. If your computer chassis is on the floor (common with tower computer cases), move it to a table to make it easier to work inside the computer. After moving the computer, plug it back into an electrical outlet (you'll see why in a moment).

TIP *When you move the computer to a table, vacuum the area where your computer sits, which almost certainly has a layer of dust (as computers attract dust). In addition, use a can of compressed air to clean the ports from which you just disconnected cables.*

5. Remove the cover from the case. On some computers, you can just remove the side panel (on the left as you look at the front of the computer) that covers the cards. On other computers, you must remove the entire exterior case. For most computers, you will use the Phillips screwdriver to remove the screws that hold the exterior case onto the chassis. Usually, you'll find two, four, or six screws at the back of the case. Some computers don't have screws and instead have a snap-up or pop-up device for opening and closing the case.

TIP *After opening the computer, clean out the dust inside. I recommend using a can of compressed air to blow the dust toward the hose of a standard household vacuum. Just don't use the vacuum hose to suck dust directly from inside the computer.*

6. After removing the cover, and while the computer is still plugged in, touch any exposed metal part of the case to discharge any static electricity on your body.
7. Remove the metal back plate at the end of the bus slot (at the back of the computer) by removing the small machine screw with a small Phillips screwdriver. Newer computers may require you to push out the piece of metal that is attached. Be careful not to bend the slots around it.

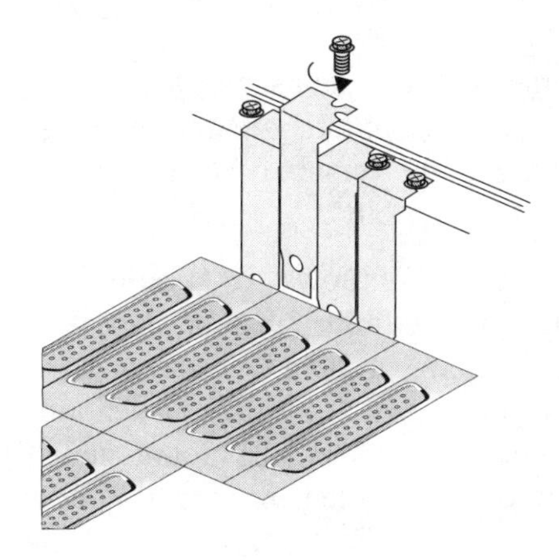

TIP

When you remove the screw, which is very, very small, place it on a piece of sticky tape. This keeps it from rolling off the table and landing in the rug, where it will probably be lost forever, or from falling on the wood or tile floor and bouncing, landing far away so you have to hunt for it for a long time and may not ever find it. Then, a week later, when you hear a funny clinking noise as you vacuum your house, you can say, "Oh, that's where that screw went." I'll bet you can guess how I learned these things.

8. Open the static-free bag that holds the NIC and remove the card. Touch the metal chassis of the computer to discharge any static electricity in your body. Always try to have contact with the chassis to prevent any component from getting damaged by static electricity.
9. Position the metal edge of the NIC in the open slot at the back of the computer (putting the RJ-45 jack in the rear opening where the metal plate used to be).
10. Position the teeth that are at the bottom of the NIC into the bus, and then push down on the NIC. The NIC is inserted properly when the back of the NIC fits neatly into the slot at the back of the computer, and the flange sits tightly on the metal rim, with the screw hole visible.
11. Replace the screw you removed when you took out the metal plate.
12. Put the cover back on the computer and replace the screws.
13. If you moved your computer or disconnected the devices attached to the computer, put your computer back in place and reconnect all of the devices.

Install the Drivers

After you reconnect all the cables to the back of the computer, plug the computer in and start it. The Windows Plug and Play feature will discover the NIC when Windows starts. Depending on the version of Windows you're running, you may have to install the drivers for your NIC.

Installing Windows XP Drivers Windows XP should automatically install the drivers for your new NIC. You may notice that the startup takes a bit longer, because it takes some time for the operating system to discover the new hardware and install the drivers. First, a message appears above the notification area of the taskbar (near the clock), telling you that Windows has found new hardware, and then another message appears to tell you the hardware has been installed.

If this doesn't occur automatically, you need to install the drivers manually. Windows XP always finds the hardware, but if it can't find the appropriate drivers, it launches the Found New Hardware Wizard so you can perform a manual installation. Put the driver CD or disk that came with your NIC into the appropriate drive (floppy or CD, depending on the type of medium that is in the package). Then follow these steps:

1. Select the option Install From a List or Specific Location (Advanced) and click Next.
2. In the next wizard window, select the option Search for the Best Driver in These Locations and clear the check box labeled Search Removable Media. In the Include This Location In The Search field, type one of the following:
   - **a:\winxp** if your Linksys drivers are on a floppy disk
   - **d:\winxp** if your Linksys drivers are on a CD (substitute the drive letter for your CD-ROM drive if it's not *d:*)
3. If the wizard displays a window telling you that the driver is not tested for Windows, click Continue Anyway (don't worry; the driver is exactly what you need for Windows XP).
4. Click Finish in the next wizard window.

Installing Windows 98 Drivers Windows 98 discovers your new hardware when it restarts, and it launches the Add New Hardware Wizard. Insert the Linksys driver disk into the appropriate drive. Then follow these steps:

1. Select the option Search For the Best Driver for Your Device (Recommended) and click Next.
2. Select the option Specify a Location and enter one of the following locations. Then click Next.
   - **a:\win98** (or **win9*x***) if your Linksys drivers are on a floppy disk
   - **d:\win98** (or **win9*x***) if your Linksys drivers are on a CD (substitute the drive letter of your CD drive if it's not d:)
3. Click Next again after Windows 98 finds the driver to begin installing the files onto your hard disk.

4. If Windows 98 needs files from the operating system CD, you'll see a message asking you to insert the CD. The file location should be d:\win98 (substitute the drive letter for your CD for *d:*).
5. When all the files are installed, click Finish.

You should see a message asking whether you want to restart your computer—take the Linksys driver disk out of the drive and click Yes.

Installing Windows 2000 Drivers Windows 2000 discovers your new NIC when it restarts, and it launches the Found New Hardware Wizard. Follow these steps to install the drivers:

1. In the Install Hardware Device Drivers window, the wizard announces it found an Ethernet Controller. Select the option Search For a Suitable Driver For My Device (Recommended) and click Next.
2. In the Locate Driver Files window, select Specify a Location and click Next.
3. Insert the Linksys driver disk and enter one of the following locations in the text box:
   - **a:\win2000** if your drivers are on a floppy disk
   - **d:\win2000** if your drivers are on a CD (substitute the correct drive letter for your CD drive if it isn't *d:*)
4. Follow the rest of the wizard's prompts and click Finish on the last wizard window.

Installing Windows Me Drivers Windows Me discovers your new NIC when it restarts, and it launches the Found New Hardware Wizard. Follow these steps to install the drivers:

1. In the Install Hardware Device Drivers window, the wizard announces it found an Ethernet Controller. Select the option Specify the Location of the Driver (Advanced) and click Next.
2. In the next wizard window, select Search For the Best Driver For Your Device (Recommended). Also select Specify a Location and enter one of the following locations in the text box:

- **a:\winME** if your drivers are on a floppy disk (may be ***win9x*** or ***win98*** if *winMe* doesn't work)
- **d:\winME** if your drivers are on a CD (substitute the correct drive letter for your CD drive if it isn't *d:*—may also be ***win9x*** or ***win98*** if *winMe* doesn't work)

3. Click Next and wait for the wizard to tell you that it has found the drivers; then click Next again.
4. If Windows Me needs files from the operating system CD, you'll see a message asking you to insert the CD. When you do, the system will find the files it needs. If you do not have the Windows Me disk, try looking in c:\windows\options\cabs, or try specifying the driver location (for example, a:\win9*x* or d:\win9*x*) if the file that Windows can't find has a .sys or .inf extension.
5. When all the files are installed, click Finish.

You should see a message asking whether you want to restart your computer—take the Linksys driver disk out of the drive and click Yes. If you don't see that message, take the Linksys driver disk out of the drive and choose Start | Shutdown. In the Shut Down Windows dialog box that opens, choose Restart and then click OK. When Windows restarts, your Linksys NIC is installed and available.

Installing a USB Network Adapter

The nifty thing about a USB network adapter is you don't have to open your computer to install it. In fact, you don't even turn off your computer to install it. All you have to do is connect the parts together properly, and Windows will automatically discover that you've installed your adapter.

Your Linksys USB network adapter has two connectors, one on each end:

- An RJ-45 connector, which accepts the Ethernet cable you use to connect the adapter to the concentrator. The RJ-45 connector resembles a telephone jack, but is slightly wider.
- A USB connector, which accepts the cable that connects the adapter to the USB port.

A USB cable for connecting the adapter to the USB port is included in the Linksys USB adapter package. Connect one end of the cable into the adapter and the other end into the USB port (the cable works in only one position, so you can't accidentally put the wrong end into the wrong device).

The Linksys USB adapter package also includes a disk with drivers for the device. As soon as you connect the adapter to the USB port, the Windows Plug and Play feature discovers the new device. At this point, you must install the drivers, using the same steps described in the previous section for installing drivers for internal NICs.

Installing NICs in Portable Computers

Almost all new portable computers (also called laptop or notebook computers) come with a built-in network adapter. On some older models, though, you may need to install a network adapter. Installing network adapters in portable computers is much like installing them in desktop systems. If your portable has a USB port (almost all of them do), you can attach a USB network adapter using the instructions in the previous section.

The other hardware choice for portables is a PC Card, which used to be called a PCMCIA card. Many of us still use the old terminology because we finally learned to say it correctly and now we can't stop reciting the sequence of letters automatically (PCMCIA stands for Personal Computer Memory Card International Association).

Ethernet is the topology used most frequently in corporate network environments, so it's common for portable computer users who take their computers to the office (in addition to using them on their home networks) to install a PC Card. In fact, the PC Card is frequently provided by the company, as is the portable computer.

NOTE *If you share your portable computer between your home and office, be sure to read Chapter 12 to learn how to adjust the settings.*

Linksys offers a variety of Ethernet PC Cards. Regardless of the model, however, the physical installation and the installation of drivers are the same.

Inserting a PC Card

Your portable computer most likely has at least one PC Card slot on the side of the chassis—most portables have two such slots. Inside the slot, way back where you can't see it, is a male connector consisting of 68 very small pins. The PC Card Ethernet network adapter has two edges: one edge has 68 small holes, and the other edge is the "business side" of the card, containing the connector you need to connect to an Ethernet network. Some PC Cards have a connector that accepts a cable (provided with the PC card), and the RJ-45 connector is at the end of the cable. (The device is called a *removable media coupler*.) Other PC Cards (called *integrated PC Cards*) have the RJ-45 connector attached directly to the card.

The Linksys documentation says to turn off the computer before you insert a PC Card into the slot, which is probably the safest approach, but actually most portables can handle installation while the computer is running (called a *hot install*).

Before you insert the card, attach the Ethernet cable that's already attached to your concentrator or router to the RJ-45 connector on the card. Then insert the PC Card into a slot with the label side up. Firmly push the card into the slot, until the little button next to the slot pops out, which means the card is properly engaged. Press that button to eject the card (this is similar to the way your floppy drive accepts and ejects disks).

NOTE *Unless the documentation for your portable has contrary instructions, it doesn't matter which slot you use.*

Installing PC Card Drivers

You must install the drivers for your PC Card Ethernet network adapter, and this task is identical to the installation of any other type of NIC. See the instructions earlier in this chapter for your version of Windows.

Now that installation of your network adapters and their drivers is complete, turn to Chapter 8 to learn how to configure the network settings so you can begin communicating with the other computers on the network.

Chapter 5

Installing a Wireless Network

If you're like most of us, you want a wireless network, especially if you have notebook computers. Wireless networks are just plain cool—and they're affordable. Wireless networks have the advantage of not requiring any wiring at all, so you can put networked computers almost anywhere.

You do need to be concerned about a few things when considering going wireless, including security and hardware considerations. This chapter explains all the issues and tells you how to set up the network.

Wireless Networking Standards and Speeds

A great deal of confusion exists over the different wireless networking standards on the market and the speeds of which they are capable. The important *Wi-Fi* standards are maintained by an industry consortium called the Wireless Ethernet Compatibility Alliance (WECA—*http://www.weca.net/*), and there is good interoperability among products from different vendors.

The first standard to market is called 802.11b and has a rated speed of 11 Mbps. A newer standard, named 802.11a, is rated at 54 Mbps. (It's odd but true that 11a was released after 11b.) Products implementing the newest standard, 802.11g, became available in mid-2003 and include many products from Linksys. They operate at 54 Mbps unless they detect 802.11b products on the network, in which case they slow down to 11 Mbps and are compatible with the 802.11b products. Linksys also makes *A+G* products, which can connect to all three types of networks. (The A+G designation means that they support both 802.11a and 802.11g.) Be sure to read the sidebar "To B or Not to B? That Is the Question" for information to help you decide between the two standards.

The network traffic for 802.11b and 802.11g products uses radio frequency in the 2.4GHz band, the same frequency used by most cordless telephones. The 802.11a products use the 5.8GHz band, which is used by a less common group of phone products.

Rated Speeds

The 11 Mbps and 54 Mbps figures used previously to describe rated speeds are not what you will actually get. Typical throughput for 802.11b products, for example, is about 4 to 5 Mbps. The 802.11g products have an actual capacity of about 20 Mbps, and 802.11a products 22 Mbps.

Exaggerations like this are not uncommon in the computer industry, where a 17-inch monitor is not really 17 inches, a 30GB hard disk has less than 30GB of

To B or Not to B? That Is the Question

Because 802.11g products are compatible with 802.11b products and have the advantage that they can run at far greater speeds, 802.11g products will eventually supplant all 802.11b products on the market. Linksys, for example, offers many 802.11b products, but many fewer products than were offered a year ago. Soon, Linksys will likely drop 802.11b products entirely in favor of 802.11g products.

As the prices of 802.11g products drop and become closer to those of 802.11b products, consumers will have less reason to buy 802.11b products. In the very long term, you should work to eliminate 802.11b products from your network. Why? Because if you have even one 802.11b device on a network that runs 802.11g devices, that one 802.11b device slows the whole network down to 802.11b speeds.

space for you to use, and 56 Kbps modems can never actually reach 56 Kbps. In all cases, the main reason for the inflated rating is that some of the missing value is taken up by overhead.

As I explain in the following section, even these lower capacities can be limited by other conditions, such as the materials in walls and distances.

SpeedBooster Products

Several of the 802.11g products now sold by Linksys include a relatively new technology named SpeedBooster, which is a specification of Broadcom's Afterburner technology. SpeedBooster products work together to increase the actual throughput you see on wireless networks by up to 35 percent. You should be aware of a couple of things when using SpeedBooster products, however, including the following:

- You will see the full effect of increased speed only when two devices that use SpeedBooster are communicating with one another. For example, if you have a computer with a SpeedBooster-equipped network adapter and a wireless router or access point with SpeedBooster, the communications between the two devices will be considerably faster.

- SpeedBooster products work just fine on networks that also include devices without the SpeedBooster technology. In fact, SpeedBooster can help increase the overall performance of a mixed wireless network running both 802.11b and 802.11g products. This means that no matter what wireless device is running, the overall performance of a network is enhanced, though not as much as it is between SpeedBooster devices.

You will see other brands of network gear that feature speed-enhancing technology. However, most of this technology will work only if every device on the network is the same brand and uses the same technology. SpeedBooster products are designed to work well with standards-compliant 802.11b and 802.11g products. SpeedBooster adapters communicating with the SpeedBooster router will perform at enhanced speeds, while other 802.11b or 802.11g products will continue to work at their designed speeds.

Positioning Computers

You need to consider two issues when deciding where to position computers on a wireless network: distance between wireless systems, and potential sources of interference with the wireless radio signals.

Distance can be tricky, although you can usually come up with ways to extend distance using signal boosters and multiple wireless access points, which I will discuss in detail in the "Improving the Wireless Signal" and "Wireless Broadband Routers and Access Points" sections.

Wi-Fi networking can function through most walls and other building structures, but the range is much better in open spaces. Linksys rates the range of its wireless adapters outdoors at up to 1500 feet (457 meters) and indoors at up to 300 feet (91 meters), but these ratings are under ideal circumstances, without interference. The indoor range is the most sensitive and really depends on structural elements in the house.

Finally, if you are using an access point or router with a wireless antenna, you should not place a computer directly beneath it or in a room directly beneath the antenna, as the signal will be weak or nonexistent there.

Interference and Conflicts Between Wireless Products

Significant amounts of metal in the walls can be a problem for wireless networking. For example, I've encountered problems with plaster walls built on a metal lath;

however, you can have problems with much less pervasive metal structures. My own house has a small wireless dead zone that I believe is caused by metal ducting from the air conditioning in the walls—and that zone is only about 30 feet from my wireless router.

Most wireless networks broadcast on the same 2.4GHz frequency as many cordless phones. These 2.4GHz devices aren't supposed to interfere with each other, but I've seen it happen occasionally. It's a good idea to keep wireless network cards some distance from cordless phones, and especially from base stations. If you're experiencing interference, you might try changing channels on the network (see the later sections "Using the Linksys WLAN Monitor Utility" and "Wireless Broadband Routers and Access Points" for how to change channels).

The 802.11a equipment, and especially the dual-band A+G products, is appealing in cases where potential conflicts exist. Specifically, if you are heavily dependent on 2.4GHz cordless phones, you should consider using 802.11a or A+G equipment so that you have more options for avoiding signal conflicts between the two devices. Better yet, consider using portable phones that operate in the 5.8GHz frequency. You'll find a lot more networking gear in the 2.4GHz range than the 5.8GHz range.

Finally, microwave ovens actually throw out signals for a short distance around them that can interfere with wireless devices, including wireless networking and cordless phones, so keep them away from microwave ovens.

Wireless NICs

Every computer on the wireless network needs a wireless network adapter. Linksys offers a wide variety of wireless adapters, so you can mix and match computers on the same network. For example, if you want to use an internal PCI NIC for your desktop computers, you can get the WMP11 Instant Wireless Network Adapter, the WMP54G Wireless-G PCI Adapter, or the WPC55AG Dual-Band Wireless A+G Notebook Adapter. If a desktop computer has a USB port available, you may prefer to use it so you don't have to open the computer to install an internal NIC. For portable computers, you can get a wireless PC Card. The following sections describe the steps you must take to install internal NICs and USB network adapters. See Chapter 8 for detailed information on installing network adapters on laptop computers.

After you complete the tasks described here (physically installing the NICs and installing the operating system drivers), you must configure the NIC so it can find the other computers on the network. You may have to do some configuration specific to the wireless network and some related to Windows networking. How you configure your computers to connect to the wireless network depends on what operating system you use, as follows:

- For computers running Windows 98, Windows Me, or Windows 2000, you will use a Linksys program called the Linksys Wireless Configuration Utility to set up your computer. See the section "Using the Linksys WLAN Monitor Utility" for more.
- For computers running Windows XP, Linksys recommends that you use the built-in wireless support in the operating system to configure wireless access rather than use the Linksys utility. See the section "Configuring Windows XP's Built-In Wireless Support" for more.

After configuring wireless access for a computer, your next step is to configure the computer to communicate with other computers on the network, and with the Internet. You'll find all the information you need about Windows networking in Chapter 8.

Internal NICs

Before you start installing the internal NIC, install the drivers first, which are provided on the CD-ROM that came with the product. The only exception to this is if you're using Windows XP. All other operating systems require that you install the drivers first. (To do this, pop in the CD-ROM—it should auto-run—and then click the Install option and follow the options.)

After installing drivers (but not in Windows XP, remember), you must physically install the NIC. To install an internal NIC, you must open the computer and put the NIC into a slot (called a *bus*) on the system board. Some people find the prospect of messing around in the computer's innards rather daunting, but it's not—it's easy, and in all likelihood the only tool you need is a Phillips screwdriver. However, pay attention to the following safety tips (which I can't emphasize enough):

- Don't use a magnetic screwdriver. Magnets and disk drives do not get along well because magnetic forces can delete data.
- Discharge any static electricity in your body before you touch any of the components inside the computer. Touch something metal in the computer to ground yourself.
- Remove metal jewelry, especially gold (which conducts static electricity) and rings.

Determining the Bus Type

Two significant types of buses (and expansion cards such as NICS to go in them) are used in computers:

- A Peripheral Component Interconnect (PCI) bus connector is usually white and has a crossbar about three-quarters of the way down its length. All newer computers use PCI buses.
- An Industry Standard Architecture (ISA) bus connector is usually black (an extended ISA bus is brown) and has a small crossbar about two-thirds of the way down its length. ISA bus connectors are longer than PCI connectors. Older computers contain ISA buses in addition to PCI. Very old computers may have only ISA buses.

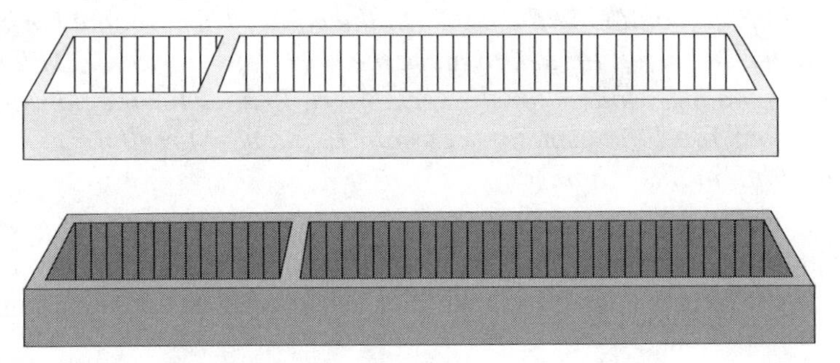

NOTE *Your computer may also have a connector that's shorter than the PCI bus and is located farther away from the back of the computer than the other connectors. This is an Accelerated Graphics Port (AGP) connector, and it's used for high-speed video controllers.*

For computers you've purchased within the last few years, you can automatically assume that you can use a PCI NIC. In fact, even though older computers may have PCI buses in addition to ISA buses, you have no way of knowing whether a PCI slot is empty without opening the computer.

If only an ISA slot is available, you may have to free up a PCI NIC somehow, because nobody makes ISA wireless network adapters. Your only alternatives are to use a USB adapter (described in the section "USB Adapters") or to use a network adapter of another type, such as an ISA card for wired Ethernet (see Chapter 4), and connect the wired network to the wireless network. At this point, though, you are adding complexity and expense to support an old computer that is probably best replaced with one that supports the PCI bus and has enough slots for you to work with.

Installing the NIC

To install a NIC:

1. Leaving your computer plugged into a power source, disconnect the cables (mouse, keyboard, printer, camera, and so on) that are attached to the ports at the back of the computer.

NOTE *Leaving the power plugged in grounds the computer, protecting it from the static electricity you carry on your body. This is a safe practice, so long as you don't go messing around with the actual power supply inside the computer.*

TIP *As you disconnect each cable, write the name of its peripheral on a small piece of paper and tape the paper to the cable. Then, on the back of the computer, use a felt tip pen to mark the ports—for instance, M for mouse, K for keyboard, Modem for the serial port, Printer for the parallel port, and so on. You'll have many occasions to thank yourself for marking everything in this manner.*

2. If your computer chassis is on the floor (common with today's tower computer cases), move it to a table to make it easier to work inside the computer.

TIP *When you move the computer to a table, vacuum the area where your computer sits, which almost certainly has a layer of dust (since computers attract dust). In addition, use a can of compressed air or a computer vacuum to clean the ports from which you just disconnected the cables.*

3. Use a Phillips screwdriver to remove the screws that hold the exterior case onto the chassis. Usually, four or six screws are used to attach the back of the case. (If your computer doesn't use screws and instead has a snap-up or pop-up device for opening and closing the case, you can skip this step, of course.)

NOTE *Once again, use compressed air to clean the inside of the computer, which I guarantee is filled with dust.*

4. Remove the metal back plate at the end of the bus slot (at the back of the computer) by removing the small machine screw with a small Phillips

screwdriver. Newer computers may require that you push out the piece of metal that is attached. Be careful not to bend the slots around it.

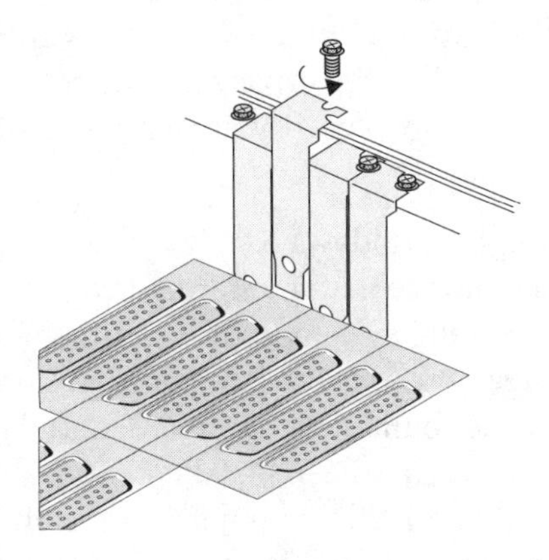

5. Open the static-free bag that holds the NIC and remove the card. Touch the metal chassis of the computer to discharge any static electricity in your body (this is why you should leave the computer plugged in); touch the metal chassis occasionally while you are working (and especially if you walk away from the computer and then come back) to prevent any component from getting damaged by static electricity.
6. Position the metal edge of the NIC in the open slot at the back of the computer (putting the screw connector for the wireless antenna in the rear opening where the metal plate used to be).
7. Position the teeth that are at the bottom of the NIC into the bus, and then push down on the NIC. The NIC is inserted properly when the back of the card fits neatly into the slot at the back of the computer and the flange sits tightly on the metal rim, with the screw hole visible.
8. Replace the screw you removed when you took out the metal plate.
9. Replace the cover on the computer and replace the screws.
10. Take the black antenna from the package the NIC came in and screw it onto the exposed connector on the card.

TIP

The best alignment for the antennas on your wireless access point or router is usually vertical—that is, pointing straight up to the sky. You can adjust them to other alignments to experiment with finding a good signal. For example, if the antennas are aligned vertically, the signal will be weak or nonexistent directly beneath the device.

Installing the Drivers

After you reconnect all the cables to the back of the computer, start the computer. The Windows Plug and Play feature will discover the wireless NIC when Windows starts. If you have already installed the drivers for the adapter, Windows will find those drivers and configure the adapter. If you've not yet installed the drivers, you will have to do so at this point.

Installing Windows XP Drivers Windows XP should automatically install the drivers for your new NIC. You may notice that the startup takes a bit longer, because it takes some time for the operating system to discover the new hardware and install the drivers. First, a message appears above the notification area of the taskbar telling you that Windows has found new hardware, and then another message appears to tell you the hardware has been installed.

If this doesn't occur automatically, you need to install the drivers manually. Windows XP always finds the hardware, but if it can't find the appropriate drivers, it launches the Found New Hardware Wizard so you can perform a manual installation. Put in the driver CD that came with your NIC, and then follow these steps:

1. Select the option Install From a List or Specific Location (Advanced) and click Next.
2. On the next wizard page, select the option Search For the Best Driver in These Locations and clear the check box labeled Search Removable Media. In the field labeled Include This Location in the Search, type **d:** if your Linksys drivers are on a CD (substitute the drive letter for your CD-ROM drive if it's not *d:*).
3. If the wizard displays a dialog box telling you that the driver is not tested for Windows, click Continue Anyway (don't worry, the driver is exactly what you need for Windows XP).
4. Click Finish in the next wizard window.
5. Windows XP may display a message above the notification area of the taskbar that a new network device is available and that you should click the notice to run the Network Setup Wizard. See Chapter 8 for more on the Network Setup Wizard.
6. After Windows finishes installing the adapter, what you see next depends on whether you have installed Windows XP Service Pack 2 on your computer (you'll learn more about the update later in the chapter in the section "Configuring Windows XP's Built-In Wireless Support").

- If Windows XP Service Pack 2 is not installed, you should see a notification in the form of a little pop-up from the system tray saying, "Wireless Connection *n*. One or more wireless networks are available. To see a list of available networks, click here." (The *n* is a real number, *1* if this is your first wireless network.) Proceed with Step 7 at this point.
- If Windows XP Service Pack 2 is installed, you will see this notification only if you have secured your wireless network. This is because Windows XP (when running Service Pack 2) does not automatically connect to unsecured networks. If this is the case, skip the rest of this procedure. You'll learn how to get connected later in the chapter, in the section "Configuring Wireless Support in Windows XP with Service Pack 2."

7. Click on the notification, and a list of available wireless networks will appear in a dialog. If you are using a multimode access point and a multimode card, such as with A+G equipment, you may see two networks available. For Linksys equipment, the default names could be linksys-a and linksys-g for the 802.11a and 802.11g networks. Select one of them and click Connect.

NOTE *If encryption is turned on for the network to which you are connecting, you will see two fields into which you must enter either a WEP or WPA key. See the "Configuring Security" section in this chapter for more details on how to proceed.*

Installing Windows 98 Drivers Follow these instructions if you did not install the drivers first.

Windows 98 discovers your new hardware when it restarts, and launches the Add New Hardware Wizard. Insert the Linksys driver disk into the appropriate drive, and then follow these steps:

1. Select the option Search For the Best Driver For Your Device (Recommended) and click Next.
2. Select the option Specify a Location. Enter **d:** (substitute the drive letter of your CD drive if it's not *d:*), and then click Next.
3. Click Next again after Windows 98 finds the driver to begin installing the files onto your hard disk.
4. If Windows 98 needs files from the operating system CD, you'll see a message asking you to insert the CD. The file location should be d:\win98 (substitute the drive letter for your CD for *d:*). If you do not have the

Windows 98 disk, then enter **c:\windows\options\cabs** or try specifying the driver location (a:\win98 or d:\win98 if the file that Windows can't find has a .sys or .inf extension).

5. When all the files are installed, click Finish.

You should see a message asking whether you want to restart your computer; click No. (If you do not get prompted, don't worry about it—just follow the instructions.) After clicking No, go to the utility folder on the Linksys CD-ROM and run setup.exe from there. You can do this by choosing Start | Run, and typing **d:\utility\setup.exe**. Once you've finished with the setup, take the Linksys driver disk out of the drive and choose Start | Shutdown. In the Shut Down Windows dialog box that opens, choose Restart and then click OK. When Windows restarts, your Linksys NIC is installed and available.

USB Adapters

You might prefer a USB adapter over an internal adapter if you don't want to open up your computer, or if your computer is under a desk and you'd rather have the antenna on top of the desk or on a shelf (on PCI adapters, the antenna sticks out of the back of your PC). Linksys offers four different USB adapters from which to choose, depending on your needs:

- The WUSB11 Instant Wireless USB Network Adapter is a full-size 802.11b product for use on networks that don't support 802.11g. It is a stand-alone unit with its own power supply. The advantage of the stand-alone model over the compact model (described next) is that you can position the unit more freely.
- The WUSB12 Wireless Compact USB Adapter is a very small 802.11b adapter (about the size of a USB memory stick). Choose this adapter when desktop space is at a premium or when you want a USB solution for your notebook computer.
- The WUSB54G Wireless-G USB Network Adapter is a stand-alone 802.11g unit with its own power supply.
- The WUSB54GP Wireless-G Portable USB Adapter is a smaller 802.11g unit that gets power from the USB port and doesn't need an external power supply.

No matter which USB wireless adapter you choose, installation is very similar. I'll cover the basics here and refer you to the user manual for the product you choose for any extra details you need.

If you buy a stand-alone unit, the package will contain the actual adapter, a power cord, and a USB cable. Connect the cable on one end to an available USB connector on the computer or USB hub and to the adapter on the other end. If you buy a compact unit, no power cord is included and the USB connector will be part of the unit—just connect it directly to your computer. Extend the antenna, and you're basically done with setup, although you may want to give some thought to the location for the adapter if it's a stand-alone unit.

NOTE *If you are running Windows 95 or Windows NT, you don't have built-in support for USB. Third-party support for USB on such operating systems is available, but Linksys does not recommend or support them.*

Installing the Drivers

When you finish the connection between the USB adapter and system, or if you turn on the system after connecting the adapter while it was off, the Windows Plug and Play feature will discover the wireless adapter. Depending on the version of Windows you're running, you may have to install the drivers for your wireless adapter.

Installing Windows XP Drivers Windows XP automatically detects the new USB wireless adapter. First, a message appears above the notification area of the taskbar telling you that Windows has found new hardware. At this point, Windows XP launches the Found New Hardware Wizard so you can perform a driver installation. Put the driver disk that came with your adapter into the CD drive. Then follow these steps:

1. Select the option Install From a List or Specific Location (Advanced) and click Next.
2. In the next wizard window, select the option Search For the Best Driver in These Locations, and clear the check box labeled Search Removable Media. In the field labeled Include This Location in the Search, type **d:\Drivers** (substitute the drive letter for your CD-ROM drive if it's not *d:*).
3. If the wizard displays a window telling you that the driver is not tested for Windows, click Continue Anyway (don't worry, the driver is exactly what you need for Windows XP).

4. Click Finish in the next wizard window.
5. Windows XP may display a message above the notification area of the taskbar that a new network device is available and that you should click the notice to run the Network Setup Wizard. See Chapter 8 for more on the Network Setup Wizard.
6. After Windows finishes installing the adapter, what you see next depends on whether you have installed a special update named Windows XP Service Pack 2 on your computer (you'll learn more about the update in the section, "Configuring Windows XP's Built-In Wireless Support").
   - If Windows XP Service Pack 2 is not installed, you should see a notification in the form of a little pop-up from the system tray saying, "Wireless Connection *n*. One or more wireless networks are available. To see a list of available networks, click here." (The *n* is a real number, *1* if this is your first wireless network.) Proceed with Step 7 at this point.
   - If Windows XP Service Pack 2 is installed, you will see this notification only if you have secured your wireless network. This is because Windows XP (when running Service Pack 2) does not automatically connect to unsecured networks. If this is the case, skip the rest of this procedure. You'll learn how to get connected later in the chapter, in the section "Configuring Wireless Support in Windows XP with Service Pack 2."
7. Click the notification, and a list of available wireless networks will appear in a dialog. If you are using a multimode access point and a multimode card, such as with A+G equipment, you may see two networks available. For Linksys equipment, the default names could be linksys-a and linksys-g for the 802.11a and 802.11g networks. Select one of them and click Connect.

NOTE *If encryption is turned on for the network to which you are connecting, you will see two fields into which you must enter either a WEP or WPA key. See the "Configuring Security" section later in this chapter for more details on how to proceed.*

Installing Windows 98 Drivers When you're using Windows 98, it is recommended that you install the drivers first, and then connect the adapter to your computer. For more information on this, see the section "Installing the Linksys WLAN Monitor Utility" later in the chapter.

If you did not install the drivers first, Windows 98 discovers your new wireless USB NIC and then launches the Add New Hardware Wizard. Insert the Linksys driver disk into the appropriate drive. Then follow these steps:

1. In the opening window, the wizard announces that it has discovered a USB Device. Click Next.
2. Select the option Search For the Best Driver For Your Device (Recommended) and click Next.
3. Select the option Specify a Location. Enter **d:\drivers** (substitute the drive letter of your CD drive if it's not *d:*). Then click Next.
4. Click Next again after Windows 98 finds the driver to begin installing the files onto your hard disk.
5. If Windows 98 needs files from the operating system CD, you'll see a message asking you to insert the CD. The file location should be d:\win98 (substitute the drive letter for your CD for *d:*).
6. If Windows 98 asks for the location of files that have names that begin with *lne* or *netlne*, enter **d:** (or whatever drive letter is appropriate) in the text box.
7. When all the files are installed, click Finish.

You should see a message asking whether you want to restart your computer; click No. Go to the utility folder on the Linksys CD-ROM and run setup.exe from there. You can do this by choosing Start | Run, and typing **d:\utility\setup.exe**. Once you've finished with the setup, take the Linksys driver disk out of the drive and choose Start | Shutdown. In the Shut Down Windows dialog box, choose Restart and then click OK. When Windows restarts, your Linksys USB wireless NIC is installed and available.

Connecting Wireless Clients to the Network

Windows XP lets you configure wireless network adapters using the operating system, but older versions of Windows require that you use a utility program supplied by Linksys with the adapter. If you are running Windows XP, skip ahead to the section "Configuring Windows XP's Built-In Wireless Support." Linksys recommends that you use Windows XP's built-in support.

Whether you are using the built-in support or the Linksys program, the function of the software is the same: you configure the adapter to find a particular wireless network and set some options for how that network operates, including security features.

Older versions of Linksys wireless adapters had a variety of configuration programs, but the company has standardized on a single program for configuration of wireless clients, the WLAN Monitor Utility. This program may not exhibit the same behavior across all Linksys adapters, but the differences are small and rather obvious; for example, if you have an adapter that supports both 802.11a and 802.11g, you will be asked to choose the standard under which the adapter will operate (it can't do both at the same time).

NOTE *These instructions are based on the 1.05 version of the WLAN Monitor for A+G products, the latest available at the time this book was written. It's likely that you will be using the same, or a slightly modified, version. Even if you are using a later version, these steps should get you through the process. Also, the initial setup screens may look a bit different depending on your specific product, but they will contain mostly the same information. If you note any discrepancies (or have any questions), check the manual for your product.*

Installing the Linksys WLAN Monitor Utility

To install the utility, place the CD-ROM that came with the adapter in your CD drive. If the Windows AutoPlay feature loads the Setup program, click the Install tab to launch the Utility install program. If not, choose Start | Run, and type **d:\utility\setup.exe** (change the drive letter to the appropriate one for your CD-ROM). Then follow these steps:

1. Click Next at the Welcome screen.
2. The next page is the copyright and warranty notices. Click Yes to agree to the terms of the warranty policy.
3. If you wish to change the destination folder indicated on the next screen, click the Browse button and do so. Click Next when you are satisfied.
4. At this point, if you are using an adapter that supports more than one type of wireless network (probably both 5GHz 802.11a and 2.4GHz 802.11g), you will be asked whether you want to use one, the other, or both (see Figure 5-1). Make the selection that's right for you and click Next.

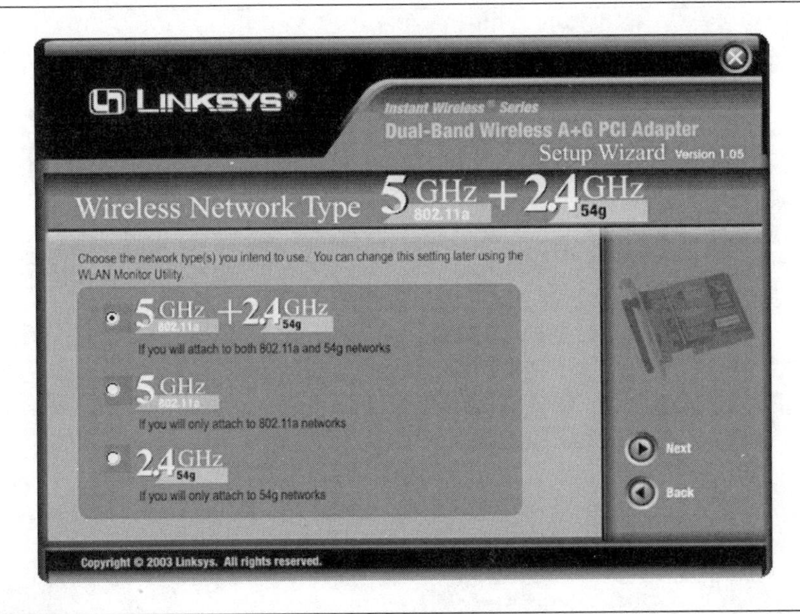

FIGURE 5-1 If you are using dual-band hardware (that supports 2.4GHz and 5.8GHz), you will need to choose which bands to support.

5. At the next screen (see Figure 5-2), choose between Infrastructure Mode and Ad-Hoc Mode. If you are using a wireless access point or router with an integrated wireless access point, choose Infrastructure Mode. If you simply have wireless cards communicating directly with each other, choose Ad-Hoc Mode. While this is an important decision for your network, don't get panicky, because you can easily change this setting later. In the lower part of the screen, enter a Service Set Identifier (SSID), which is basically the name for your wireless network. The default name is linksys—leave it as is for now, but be sure to read the "Configuring Security" section later in the chapter. Click Next.

6. In the next window, if you have configured the adapter for Ad-Hoc Mode, select a channel from 1 to 11. If you have selected Infrastructure Mode, proceed to step 7. In a sense, it doesn't matter which you choose, as long as all your systems and access points are on the same channel. I think it's a good idea to choose something other than the default channel 6 because if other networks are nearby, they are likely using the default channel. You may have the option of choosing Auto; if so, choose it, and then click Next.

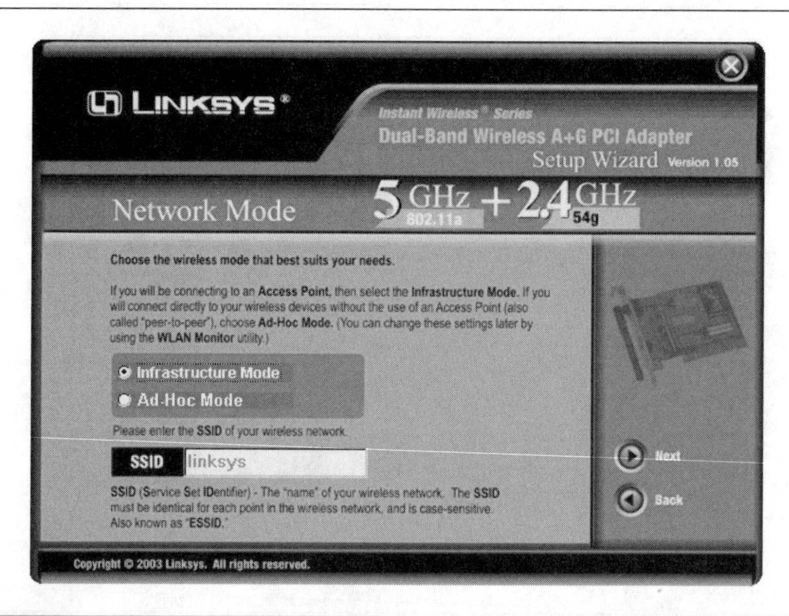

FIGURE 5-2 Infrastructure Mode enables you to use a wireless access point or wireless router, while Ad-Hoc Mode lets wireless-enabled computers communicate directly with one another.

7. Now the Install program lists your settings for confirmation before it copies the files from the install disk. Confirm they are what you want and click Next to proceed.
8. If the program asks you to reboot the computer, choose Yes.

NOTE *This procedure assumes that you have already installed the adapter and the drivers for the adapter. If you haven't done so, you can run the setup utility anyway. The process installs the drivers for you during setup. If this is the case, choose No when you are asked if you want to restart. Then shut down the computer, install the adapters, and restart the computer. Windows will find the drivers and install the adapter during startup.*

Using the Linksys WLAN Monitor Utility

After you install the WLAN Monitor Utility, a blue Linksys icon will appear in the system tray. Double-click this icon to launch the WLAN Monitor program (see Figure 5-3).

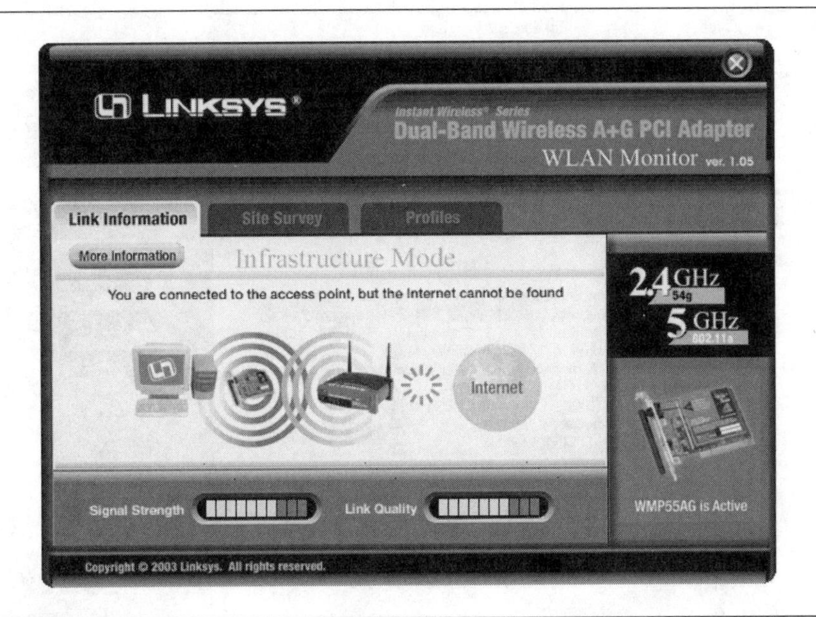

FIGURE 5-3 The Link Information tab shows the quality of the signal and network connection.

Link Information

This opening screen, which you can also reach by clicking the Link Information tab, shows you whether you are connected via Ad-Hoc or Infrastructure Mode and indicates the quality of the connection. The Signal Strength indicator measures the strength of the actual signal, and Link Quality shows the quality of the network connection, which is not exactly the same as signal strength.

If you click the More Information button, you will see two groups of settings (see Figure 5-4). On the right are your TCP/IP settings, which are the network settings used by software to connect to other computers and the Internet (see Chapter 8 for more on TCP/IP). On the left are the basic wireless network settings that describe how this wireless network card connects to and communicates with the wireless network.

What do these settings mean?

- **Status** Connected or not
- **SSID** The name of the network to which this card is connected.

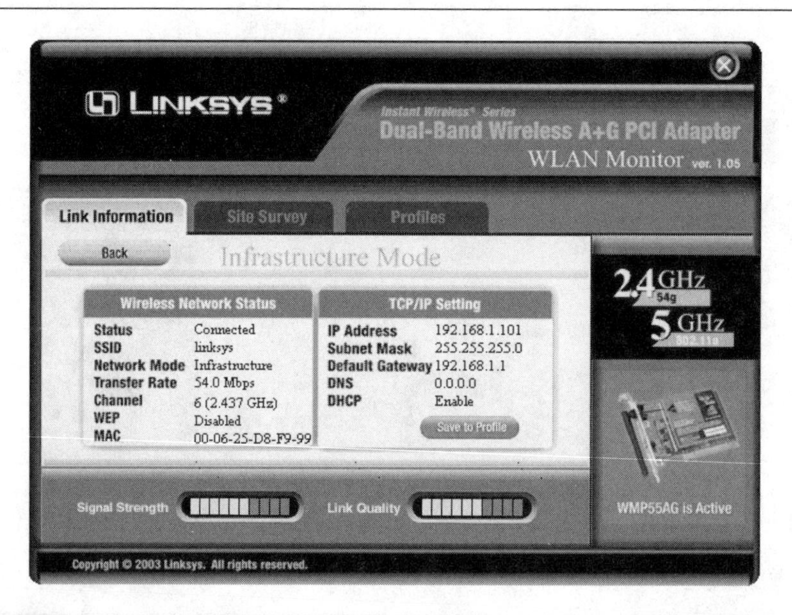

FIGURE 5-4 The Link Information tab displays details of settings for the wireless network connection.

- **Network Mode** Ad-Hoc or Infrastructure Mode.
- **Transfer Rate** The rate of data transfer on the network.
- **Channel** The number of the wireless channel being used. If you experience conflicts with other wireless devices, try changing the channel.
- **WEP** Enabled or Disabled, depending on whether WEP (Wired Equivalent Privacy), a standard for encryption of data on the network, is active.
- **MAC** Your card's Media Access Control address. Every network card has a unique address.

Site Survey

Click the Site Survey tab, shown in Figure 5-5, to reveal a list of the available wireless networks and details on each. Click the network SSID on the left to reveal the details on the right. Most of this information is the same as what appears on the Link Information tab, except that the MAC address is that of the wireless access point.

You can change the network to which you are connected on the Site Survey tab.

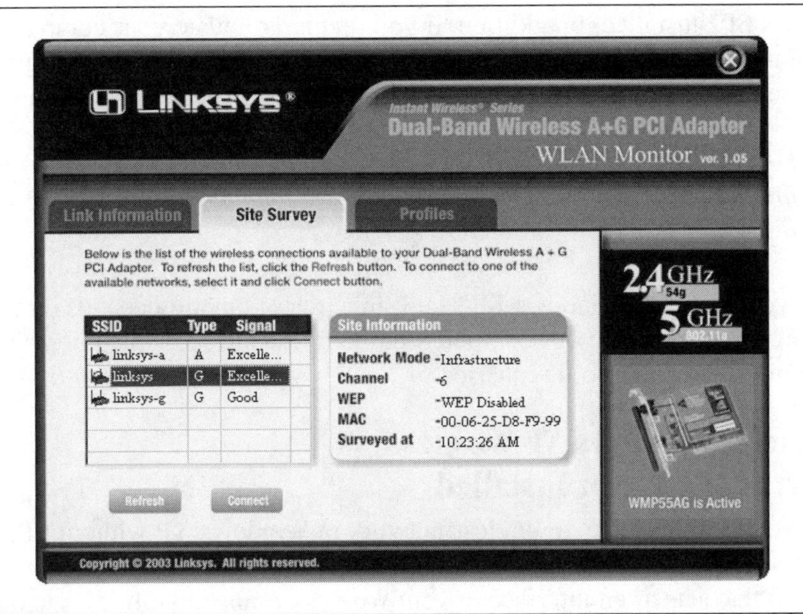

FIGURE 5-5 The Site Survey screen shows all wireless networks that the WLAN monitor finds and lets you connect to them.

Profiles

Click the Profiles tab to bring up a list of profiles, which are groups of wireless network settings. Most users will have only one profile, but if you move your computer around among multiple wireless networks, this setting can be very handy, especially since it saves you from having to remember and reenter WEP and WPA passphrases (more on WEP, WPA, and passphrases later in the chapter, especially in the "Configuring Security" section). You can even export settings to a file, save that file to a floppy, and import it on another computer on the wireless network to make it easier to set up multiple computers. The floppy can also act as a backup.

Configuring Windows XP's Built-In Wireless Support

In October 2004, Microsoft released a major (and free) update for Windows XP named Windows XP Service Pack 2 (SP2). In addition to all the updates and new security fixes released for Windows XP, SP2 also includes a host of security enhancements—including enhancements in the way Windows handles wireless connections. If you bought your computer after October 2004, the computer likely already has SP2 installed. In addition, if you regularly update your computer with the latest updates from Microsoft (or better yet, if your computer is configured to update itself automatically), your computer has probably been updated with SP2.

NOTE *For more information on SP2, software updates, and for instructions on finding out whether it's installed on your computer and how to install it if it's not, check out Chapter 9.*

How you configure Windows XP's built-in wireless support depends on whether or not SP2 is installed on your computer. In the following sections, I describe how to configure support for both scenarios.

Configuring Windows XP Wireless Support If SP2 Is Not Installed

When you are connected to a wireless network in Windows XP without SP2 installed, you will see an icon in the system tray (the icons in the bottom-right of the screen) that acts as an interface to your wireless connection. It is a picture of two computers next to each other (apparently networked computers). Right-click this icon and a menu appears.

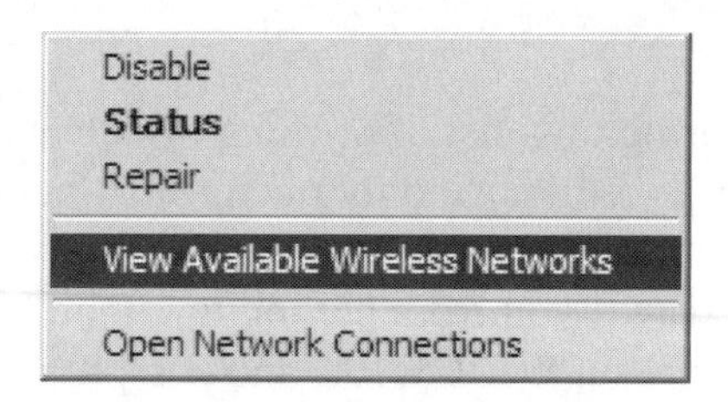

The menu lets you disable the wireless connection, which you shouldn't often need to do. The Repair option resets many settings for the network connection. For example, it renews any DHCP connection, flushes several caches, and reregisters the computer on the network. Repair can be a convenient way to clear up some problems. I describe the View Available Wireless Networks, Status, and Open Network Connections options next.

NOTE *If you have not yet connected to any network using the wireless connection, only the View Available Wireless Networks command is available. After connecting to a network, the Status and Open Network Connections options also appear.*

View Available Wireless Networks Selecting the View Available Wireless Networks option opens the Connect to Wireless Network dialog box, shown in Figure 5-6. The main feature of this dialog is a list of available networks, which are wireless networks in range of this system. The results can be surprising: if you see networks you didn't expect, they probably belong to neighbors. In any event, if you are not connected to a network, you can select the network to which you wish to connect and click the Connect button.

TIP *Use the Connect to Wireless Network dialog box when traveling to see whether any publicly available wireless networks are within range. More and more, airports, hotels, and other businesses are making wireless networks available to travelers.*

Clicking the Advanced button opens the Windows Properties dialog for the wireless network connection. Most of this dialog does not differ from the functions for nonwireless networks, so you don't need to concern yourself with them. The Wireless Networks and General tabs have some useful features, though.

The Wireless Networks tab of the Wireless Network Connection Properties dialog, shown in Figure 5-7, lets you prioritize your access to wireless networks.

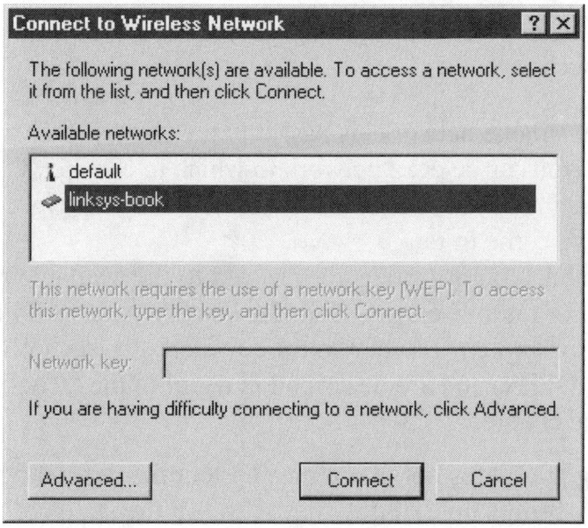

FIGURE 5-6 In Windows XP without SP2, the Connect to Wireless Network dialog box shows all wireless networks that Windows XP can locate.

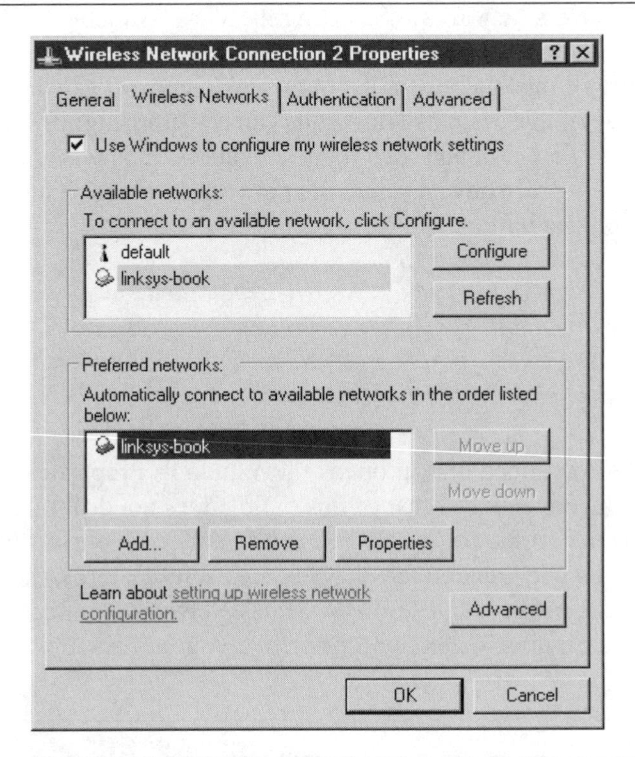

FIGURE 5-7 Windows XP (without SP2) builds in support for connections to different wireless networks.

The upper list of available networks is basically the same as the Connect to Wireless Network dialog—you can select a network to which to connect. Clicking the Refresh button repopulates the list in case some of the networks have gone out of range or new networks have come in range.

The lower list lets you prioritize your access to the available networks. You can manually add or remove entries from the list. The Add and Properties buttons bring up dialogs for implementing Wired Equivalent Privacy (WEP) or Wi-Fi Protected Access (WPA) and are described in detail in the "Configuring Security" section later in the chapter.

Status Selecting the Status option on the shortcut menu for a network connection in the system tray brings up a dialog that tells you the status of the connection (connected or disconnected), the duration (how long you have been connected to the network), the speed (on an 802.11b network, this should be 11 Mbps if all is well), and a graphical indicator of signal strength. The graphical indicator is something like the signal indicator on a cell phone. If all five bars are green, the signal is at full strength. Fewer green bars mean a weaker signal.

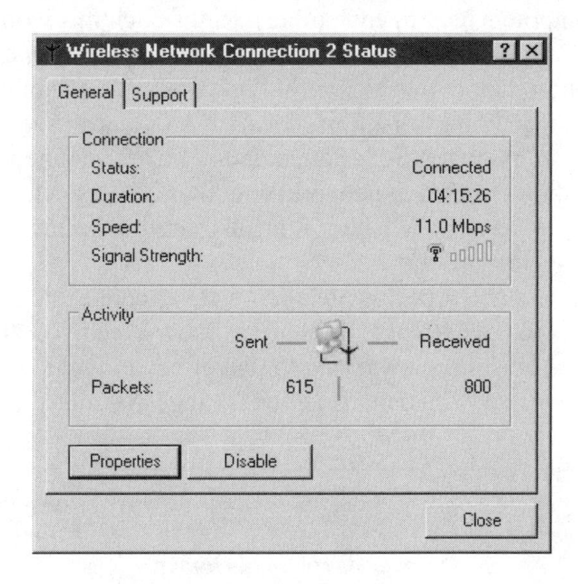

The Activity section shows how many packets or bytes of data have been sent or received through the adapter.

On the Support tab of the Status dialog, you can see some configuration information for the network connection, such as the IP address. If you click the Details button, you can see more details. The Repair button performs the same functions as the Repair menu option described previously.

Open Network Connections Selecting this option opens the Windows Network Connections window. One of the entries (perhaps the only entry) will be for your wireless connection. Double-clicking this icon opens the Status dialog described previously. If you right-click, you can perform several other options previously described. Selecting Properties opens the Windows Properties dialog for the connection, described in the previous section.

Configuring Wireless Support in Windows XP with Service Pack 2

If you are using Windows XP with SP2 installed (and you really should be, for a lot of reasons), wireless networking changes just a bit. For the most part, these changes make configuring wireless networking even easier than before.

After installing a wireless network adapter, Windows XP with SP2 shows the same icon in the system tray that you see in Windows XP without SP2 (the picture of two computers next to each other). Right-click this icon and select View Available Wireless Networks from the shortcut menu to open the Wireless Network Connection dialog box, shown in Figure 5-8. This dialog box shows the wireless networks that Windows XP has located. As you can see, Windows XP with SP2 features a completely redesigned dialog box for connecting to wireless networks, which shows you each network Windows XP has detected and also the security status of the network (whether it is unsecured or secured and what type of encryption the security uses).

Select the wireless network to which you want to connect and then click Connect to connect to the network. If the network to which you are connecting is unsecured, Windows displays a warning to that effect and asks whether you are sure you want to connect. You can also click Change Advanced Settings to bring

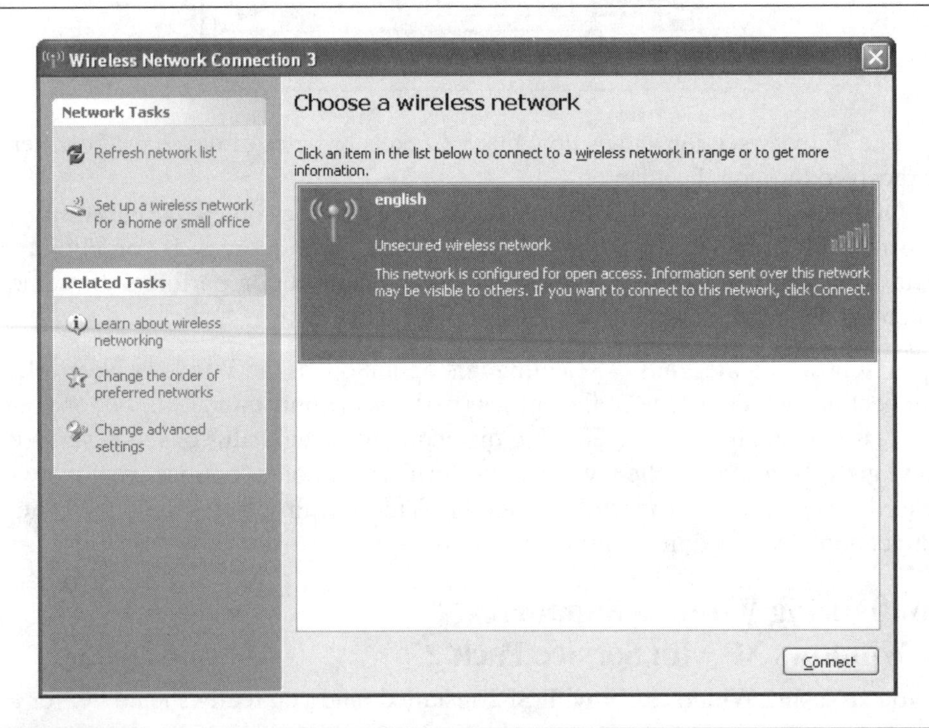

FIGURE 5-8 In Windows XP with SP2, the Wireless Network Connection dialog box shows whether networks are secured or unsecured.

up the Properties dialog box for the connection (shown next). For the most part, this dialog box works just like it does in Windows XP without SP2, with two exceptions:

- There is no Authentication tab. Rather than control authentication for a connection, Windows XP with SP2 lets you go a step further and control authentication for each network to which you connect with that connection.
- There is no list of available networks on the Wireless Networks tab. Instead, you can click the View Available Wireless Networks button to open the new Wireless Network Connection dialog box (Figure 5-8).

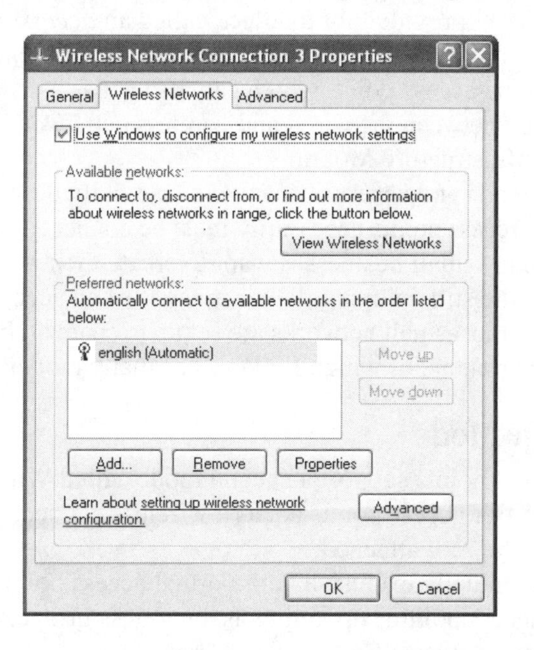

Other than these two changes (the new Wireless Network Connection dialog box and letting you control authentication on a per-network basis), working with the wireless connection is pretty much the same in Windows XP with or without SP2. After making the connection to a network, you can right-click the connection icon in the system tray to disable or repair the connection or to view open network connections. SP2 also adds shortcuts to the menu for configuring the Windows Firewall.

Wireless Broadband Routers and Access Points

As mentioned earlier, wireless networks can operate in two modes, Ad-Hoc Mode or Infrastructure Mode. In Ad-Hoc Mode, all you have is client systems with wireless network cards. Each system must communicate point-to-point with each other system. This is cheap and relatively easy to set up, but it's also slow, inefficient, and insecure. In Infrastructure Mode, all wireless client computers connect to a central wireless access point or wireless router.

Access Points

The designers of Wi-Fi provided for a device called an *access point*, a box that acts as a central antenna and is connected to a wired network. Client systems need only communicate with the access point, which can also act as a central security device and connection point between the wired and wireless networks. When so operating, the network is in Infrastructure Mode.

Infrastructure Mode and access points were originally designed with business networks in mind. Access points necessarily must be connected to a wired network; most homes and many small businesses want to create their network purely out of wireless devices while still enjoying the advantages of an access point. For this reason, and because most small networks are set up to share an Internet connection, wireless broadband routers, of which Linksys has many models, are popular.

Wireless Bridge Mode

Some Linksys access points support a special mode called Wireless Bridge Mode. In this mode, up to five access points act as a wireless connector between wired networks to which they are attached.

This feature is mutually exclusive with normal access point mode. In other words, when the access point is operating as a wireless bridge, it will not accept requests from wireless client PCs.

A special screen in the browser-based configuration program (see the section "Using the Router or Access Point Configuration Program" for more on this program) lets you turn on this feature. At the AP Mode screen of the configuration program, click the Wireless Bridge radio button. In the four fields, enter the MAC addresses of up to four other access points that support this feature. The MAC address can be read on this screen or the status screen.

Wireless Routers

A *wireless broadband router* is an access point and router combined into one box. Many such routers also include some, usually four, wired 10/100 Ethernet ports.

You can connect the router to your DSL or cable modem connection, and all your wireless clients will be able to communicate with each other and with the Internet.

NOTE *Most of the router features in Linksys wireless routers are the same as those in other Linksys routers for wired, PhoneLine, and other types of networks. See Chapter 8 for a general discussion of installing and configuring such a router.*

Dual-Band Devices

Some routers and access points will support more than one wireless networking standard. These dual-band devices can control, typically, both 802.11a and 802.11g networks and can transmit and receive in both the 2.4GHz and 5GHz bands. Certainly such features cost more, but they can be advantageous if you have users with both types of equipment or want to be able to transition from one to the other.

Connecting the Wires

An access point will have only two wires to attach: the power connector and a LAN plug. Connect an RJ-45 cable from the LAN plug to a normal plug in a hub. There; you're done.

A broadband router will also have a connector labeled either "WAN" or "Internet." Connect an RJ-45 cable from this plug to your broadband adapter, usually a DSL terminal device (sometimes inaccurately called a *modem*) or cable modem (always inaccurately called a *modem*).

If your router has Ethernet ports, you may also connect them to Ethernet devices such as wired PCs, and those devices will also share the Internet connection.

Performing the Initial Software Setup

Some access points or routers come with a setup CD that you can use to set up the router or access point on a wired network. Alternatively, if you know the default configuration settings for your access point or router, you may be able to access it with a Web browser and set it up that way.

Using the Access Point/Router Setup Wizard

This wizard will scan the wired network for access points, allow you to select the one to configure, and proceed through basic settings. You may still want to configure more advanced settings, and you can do this through the Web browser–based interface. See the next section for instructions.

To use the wizard:

1. Insert the setup CD-ROM in the CD drive. If the Windows AutoPlay feature doesn't start the setup program, you can run it manually as d:\setup.exe, where *d* is the letter of your CD-ROM drive.
2. At the Welcome screen, click the Setup button.
3. The next screen tells you that the router or access point has to be on the wired network for you to configure it this way. Click the Next button to proceed.
4. The next screen shows you the routers and access points the program found (see Figure 5-9). If only one is found, its details will be displayed in the Status box. If more than one are found, a list of their SSIDs will appear in the selection box on the left. Click the name to see its details. If the access point or router is dual-band, you will see settings for both bands. You can click No at this point to exit, but if the router or access point is new, you will certainly want to change settings, so click Yes.
5. Next, you must log in to the device. To prevent just anyone from changing settings on it, an administrative password is necessary, which, on all

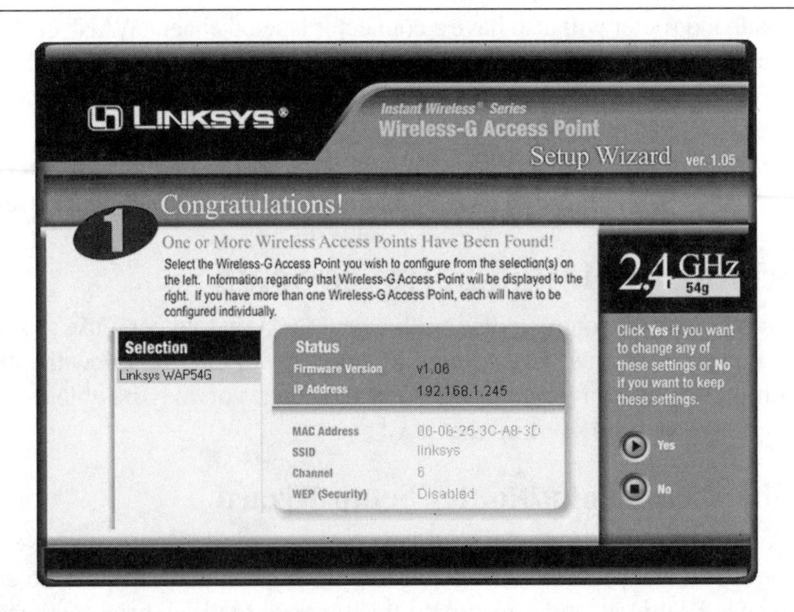

FIGURE 5-9 The Setup Wizard searches the wired network and finds access points or routers.

Linksys devices, defaults to *admin*. You'll note here the IP address of the device, which, on many Linksys devices, including routers, defaults to 192.168.1.1. Recent models of access points have defaulted to 192.168.1.245. Type **admin** into the password field and click the OK button.

6. In the IP Settings screen, you can assign a different IP address to the access point/router, if appropriate for your network. You can also change the subnet mask and assign a name to the device. Use a name you will recognize, especially if you use more than one access point or router. Click Next.

7. In the Basic Settings screen, you can assign an SSID and channel to the device. The default name will be *linksys*, *linksys-a*, or *linksys-g*, depending on the device or type of network. Regardless, you should change the name to something more difficult for outsiders to guess. You, on the other hand, should remember it. I wrote my SSIDs and other configuration information on a piece of paper on the wall near my desk. Whether this is a good idea for you depends on how private your office is, but you should save the information somewhere so you can find it if you need it. All devices on the same network need to have the same SSID. The channel also has to be the same for all devices on the network. I make a point of changing my channel from the default of 6 because I assume that the device will then be less likely to conflict with other nearby devices, which are likely also to be set to the default of 6. Click Next.

8. In the Security screen, you can either leave encryption disabled, as it is by default, or enter a passphrase for the device. See the "Configuring Security" section later in this chapter for more on how to approach security on wireless networks. Usually, though, you should turn on security sooner rather than later. Click Next once you're done.

9. If you have a dual-band router/access point, at this point the wizard asks you to configure the SSID and channel of the other network, just as in step 7. If it is an 802.11g network, you will be asked whether you want it to support 802.11g devices only, 802.11b devices only, or both. Make appropriate choices and click Next.

10. If you have a dual-band router/access point, at this point the wizard asks you to configure the security of that network just as in step 8. Click Next once you're done.

11. The next screen shows your network settings so you can confirm them (see Figure 5-10). If you want to make corrections, click No, and you can go through the process again without saving changes now. If you want to save these changes, click Yes.
12. Congratulations; you're done. Click Exit.

Setting Up or Configuring the Access Point or Router with a Web Browser

As with most networked devices these days, most of your administrative interaction with the router or access point will happen in a Web browser. The device itself contains a Web server for the purpose of administration.

To browse the device, your client needs to be on the network. See the section "Wireless NICs" earlier in this chapter for more instructions.

Guessing the Router or Access Point Settings At times you may want to connect to the device without running the CD-based setup program, which assumes a wired

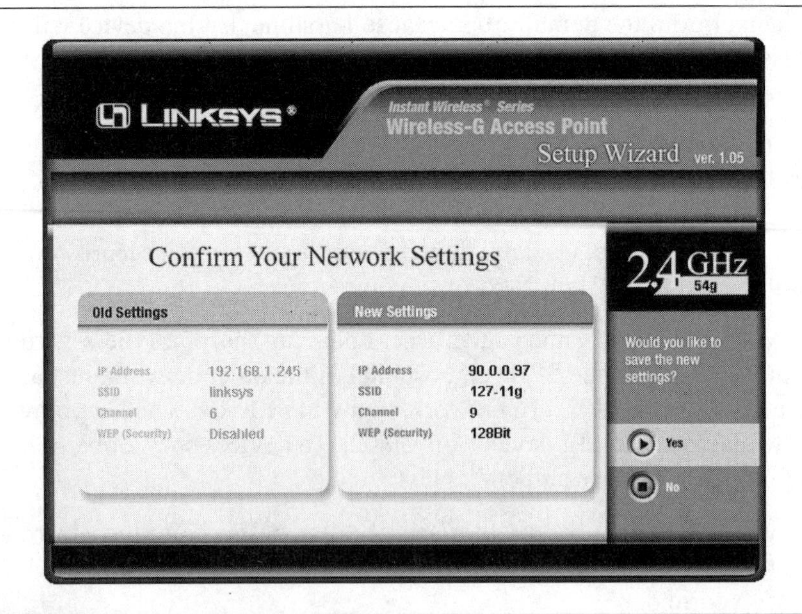

FIGURE 5-10 Confirm that the settings changes are what you want and click Yes to save them or No to start over.

network. If you know the default settings, you can get in with a browser. Here are some tips for determining your settings:

- On most Linksys devices, including routers, the IP address of the device defaults to 192.168.1.1. Recent models of access points default to 192.168.1.245 or 192.168.1.246. Some older models default to 192.168.1.250 or 192.168.1.251.
- The administrative password defaults to *admin*.
- The default SSID is *linksys*, *linksys-a*, or *linksys-g*, depending on the device or type of network.

Using the Router or Access Point Configuration Program Open a Web browser and enter **http://192.168.1.1/** (or whatever the appropriate address is) in the Address bar and press ENTER. First, you are asked to log in. There is no default user name, so leave the field blank and enter the password. Press ENTER or click OK. You should see a screen similar to that shown in Figure 5-11.

In the Wireless section of the Setup tab, you will find most of the wireless access point settings with which you need to be concerned. The first setting enables or disables the access point; bear in mind that it is enabled by default with no security at all. The next option, Allow "Broadcast" SSID to Associate? (the question may be different on other devices but will refer to allowing SSID broadcast), controls whether the SSID of this wireless network is presented for everyone to see. Setting this to No doesn't guarantee security, but it will make your network a much more difficult target because other wireless users won't be able to tell that it is a wireless network. However, you will have to remember the SSID name to connect to it from clients manually.

Next is the Channel setting, which keeps you from conflicting with other access points or 2.4GHz devices.

The final settings are the WEP or Security settings. Depending on your model and how recent the firmware is, the device may refer to Security settings rather than WEP settings; if it refers to Security, the device supports WPA in addition to WEP. By default, WEP and WPA are disabled. See the "Configuring Security" section later in this chapter for more information.

If you make any changes in these settings, click the Apply button to save them in the router.

Configuring Advanced Wireless Settings Most users will never use a number of advanced settings for the wireless access point, but you should still know about

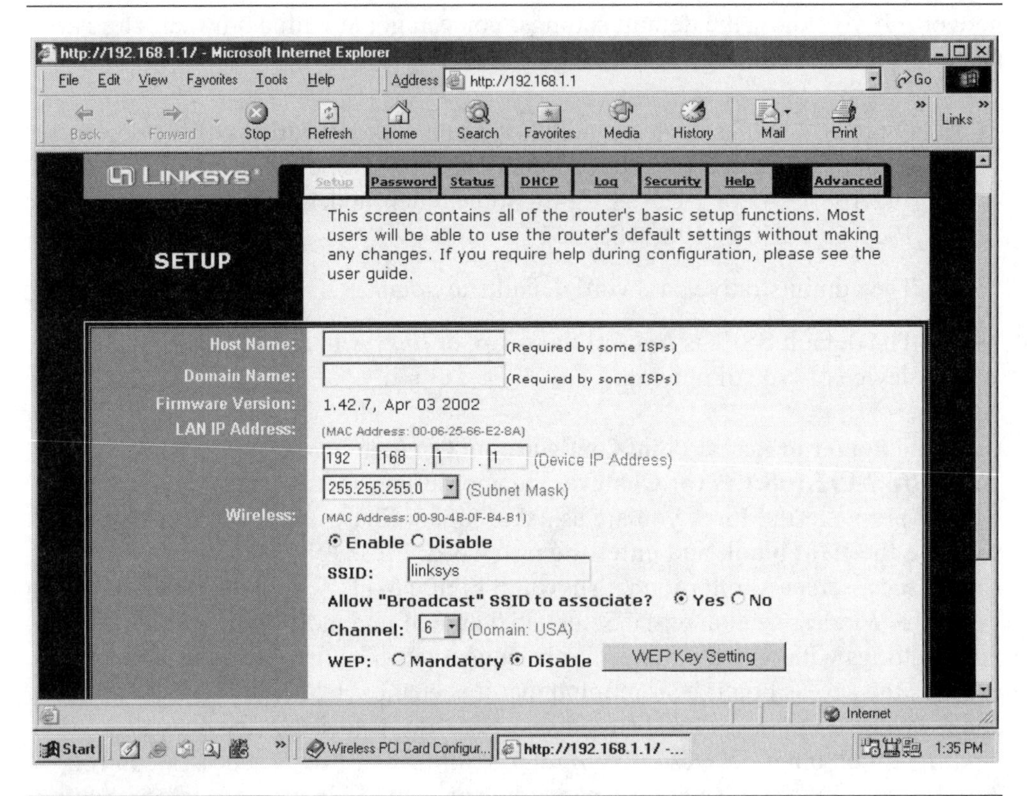

FIGURE 5-11 You program the wireless and other parameters of the router or access point through a Web browser.

them. In general, you should not change these settings unless directed to do so by Linksys Technical Support. The only exception to this is the Station MAC Filter, which is discussed in the next section.

Configuring Security

If you follow the computer trade press, you've seen many a story about deficiencies in wireless network security. Sadly, it turns out that WEP, the standard encryption system for the first versions of Wi-Fi products, is not as impenetrable as its designers originally thought. A talented and determined hacker with access to your physical proximity, and with some software tools that are available to anyone who knows where to look, can gain access to your wireless network.

How concerned are you about this? It's something to think about. I run a wireless network in my home. I eventually implemented all of the security features described in this section. I haven't always had them running, and they're not an absolute defense against attack. But I'm not going to deny myself the benefits of a wireless network just because it's possible for someone to hack into it. In the same way, I'm willing to live in my house even though it's possible for someone to break in and steal my belongings, even though I have good locks and a burglar alarm (and I do, so don't you go getting any ideas!).

Even if WEP is flawed, it's not the only security feature available to you. This section describes other measures you can take to make it very difficult for an attacker even to notice that you have a wireless network, let alone connect to it without permission.

So the good news is that while security in 802.11 has been less than pristine, it's still possible to protect yourself. Think of wireless security features like The Club for your car: a good car thief can still steal your car, but he's more likely to look for an easier target. So follow the advice in this section and you'll be doing what you can to make your wireless network safe from prying eyes. And there's even better news: the newest Wi-Fi products have support for a new security standard called WPA—Wi-Fi Protected Access.

Authentication

When configuring a wireless PC or other device for security, you'll see many references to authentication features. These features are designed to restrict access to the network based on their rights as defined by network administrators on servers, usually on what is called a RADIUS (Remote Authentication Dial-In User Service) server. Such features are irrelevant to small and home networks and you can safely leave any authentication-related options unselected.

Good Practices

Without ever getting into WEP or WPA encryption, you can follow a number of good practices that shut off the easier avenues of hacker attacks:

- Adapters, access points, and other hardware all come with default passwords and other settings. You should quickly change these values. Leaving manufacturer default passwords and settings unchanged basically opens up the door to strangers. The most important values to change are the SSID (from the default *linksys*) and the access point or router password (from the default *admin*). As with any important password, don't set it with something easily guessed about you, such as your birthday or pet's name. The SSID and password are always accessible from the configuration program that you access by browsing the device's IP address.

- If the access point supports it, as some Linksys models do, disable broadcast SSID. If you do this, the client and access point must be specifically set for an SSID and they will not pick up one off the Wi-Fi airwaves. You know the SSID that you have set, so it's only a minor problem for you, but if you disable broadcast SSID, hackers may not even see that there's a network.

NOTE *If you disable broadcast SSID, client systems won't see the wireless network and therefore you will not be able to select it. You will have to type in the name of the SSID yourself.*

- Place your access point as close as possible to the physical center of the home or office. This is good practice anyway to give you the best coverage inside your location, but it has the side benefit of minimizing coverage outside your location.
- In case you're curious enough and have a wireless-equipped notebook, take it outside and walk around. If your signal radiates several houses away, remember that your neighbors have access to it, as could someone in a car. If you live in an apartment building, you have even less wireless privacy. If your access point or adapter enables you to decrease transmission power through a software setting, as some Linksys models do, you might want to play with the setting to see how little power you can use and still achieve the coverage you need.

TIP *Many computer stores sell a very simple gadget that locates wireless signals. This palm-sized device has a button and a few LEDs. Press the button, and if there's a wireless signal around an LED lights up. Other LEDs indicate the strength of the signal. You can pick such a device up for around $20. These locators are great for walking around your property and making sure that you can get access where you need it—and it's a lot easier to manage than carrying around your notebook computer.*

- Many access points support MAC filtering. This feature lets you block out access to the wireless access point except to those adapters specified by their MAC addresses. All wireless adapters, indeed all network adapters of any kind, have a unique address in them called the MAC address, so telling your access point to support only your adapters is the best way you have to keep outsiders out. (See the "MAC Filtering" section later in this chapter for further instructions.)

- Check your log files. If your router or access point can create log files, glance at them every now and then to see whether any systems are accessing the network that shouldn't be there.

WEP

WEP is a system for encrypting the data on the wire. Its objective is to prevent unauthorized users within range of the network from "sniffing" the data on the network and seeing its contents. If you take some of the other precautions just mentioned, you can make it more difficult for someone to see the encrypted data.

Unfortunately, WEP is not as strong as its designers had hoped, and WEP's encryption weaknesses aren't its only problem—WEP is not easy to use. Implementations differ from product to product, even within the Linksys product line, and that makes things even more difficult because when you're using WEP, you need to use the same keys on all your systems and access points.

The common method across all products for entering a WEP password is to type in a string of hexadecimal values. See the sidebar "What Is Hexadecimal?" for an explanation of "hex."

Understanding Key Lengths

You may be confused at times by references to encryption being 40 bit, 64 bit, 104 bit, 128 bit, or even more. Without getting too deeply into the intricacies of cryptography, about which much larger books than this have been written, WEP uses what is called a 24-bit initialization vector in combination with a 40-bit or 104-bit key that you provide. So, 40 + 24 = 64, and 104 + 24 = 128, which is where all these numbers come from.

Some Linksys access points, such as the WAP54A Instant Wireless Access Point (an 802.11a product), implement a proprietary 152-bit WEP, in which the user-supplied key is a full 128 bits.

NOTE *WEP works fine on ad hoc (peer-to-peer) wireless LANs.*

Using WEP

When using WEP on any system, you need to use a set of up to four keys that the user supplies. The keys are used to encrypt data, and all systems and access points that communicate with each other must be set with the same keys and WEP settings. As a rule, you should use the largest key your system supports. However, since every system and access point needs to use the same keys and settings, you can use only the strongest keys supported by the weakest system on your network.

Keys are usually displayed as a series of hexadecimal values (see the sidebar "What Is Hexadecimal?"), and many WEP implementations actually make you type in literal hexadecimal sequences.

In some systems, including many Linksys systems, you can enter an English *passphrase*, which is essentially a password of up to a specified length. Usually,

What Is Hexadecimal?

You've seen several references in this book to *hexadecimal values*, which use numerical digits (0–9) and characters between *A* and *F*. The more computer stuff you read, the more references to this you'll see.

Hexadecimal originated as a convenient way to view data stored in computers. Computer data is organized into bytes, which are 8 bits long, and each bit can be in one of two states: on (1) or off (0). This type of number, in which each digit can be only a 1 or a 0, is referred to as *binary*. Because 2 to the 8th power is 256, an 8-bit byte can hold a number between 0 and 255.

If you're looking at a lot of binary data, it would quickly become tiresome and error-prone to look at the actual 1s and 0s. But looking at the regular decimal number equivalents—numbers between 0 and 255—is unappealing because these numbers don't obviously convey which bits are set and which aren't. That's where hexadecimal comes in.

One byte in hexadecimal is expressed as two digits that represent the first and second 4-bit binary halves of the byte. Each 4-bit half (sometimes called a *nibble*) can hold a value between 0 and 15. To keep each 4-bit half in a single digit, the letters *A* through *F* are used to represent the values *10* through *15*. So, hexadecimal is a base-16 system, where decimal is a base-10 system and binary is a base-2 system. The base number represents the number of values that can exist in a single digit: 0–F for hexadecimal, 0–9 for decimal, and 0–1 for binary.

To figure out the value of a hex number in decimal, take the decimal value of the first hexadecimal digit and multiply by 16; then add the value of the second nibble. Here's an example. To convert the number 7C in hexadecimal to its decimal equivalent, you would use $(7 \times 16) + 12$, or 124. (By the way, that same number in binary format would be 1111100.)

you click a button labeled "Generate" or something to that effect; the system then uses the passphrase to generate keys. Sometimes passphrase key generators will generate all four keys. Not all vendors' key generators are compatible, so don't assume that a passphrase used on one system will generate the same keys on another. (Windows XP needs to have the key entered manually in hexadecimal. Use the passphrase generator on the access point, and then copy whichever key you use into a Notepad document so you can enter the key into an XP station.)

Even though you can enter up to four keys, only one key is used at a time. The interface you use for the wireless connection (whether Windows XP or the WLAN Monitor) allows you to choose the key you want to use. In the case of a notebook computer, it's not difficult to see how being able to choose from preset keys could be useful, since you could use multiple keys for different wireless networks to which you connect and then switch among them when you move. It's less clear why storing multiple keys is useful for an access point, but they implement it as well.

Implementing WEP on Linksys Products

Even from one Linksys product to another you can see very different user interfaces for setting WEP, and it can be confusing. The exact layout of the WEP settings may differ somewhat in your model, but the essentials are the same from model to model.

Open a browser, go to *http://192.168.1.1/* (or whatever IP address you have set for your access point or router), and log in. The Setup screen will feature a button to change the WEP settings; in recent versions, it is labeled Edit WEP Settings, and it is called WEP Key Setting in others. You may have an option to enable WEP—select it—or to change the WEP enable setting to mandatory—select Yes. You should see the WEP Key Setting window; Figure 5-12 shows an example of how this window might look.

NOTE *If your router is WPA-enabled, you should see a button labeled Edit Security Settings in the Key Setting window. In such cases, you would not normally want to use WEP for security, but see the section "WPA" later in this chapter for instructions on how to do so.*

In some versions, you may have to select which key of the four to set. In others, all four may be set automatically. Make sure to set the first key, because that will be the default key used by client systems.

Select a key size, preferably the largest one available. In the Passphrase field, type in any phrase up to 31 characters. Sometimes you must click a Generate button to create the hexadecimal key in the Key field, but sometimes it is calculated

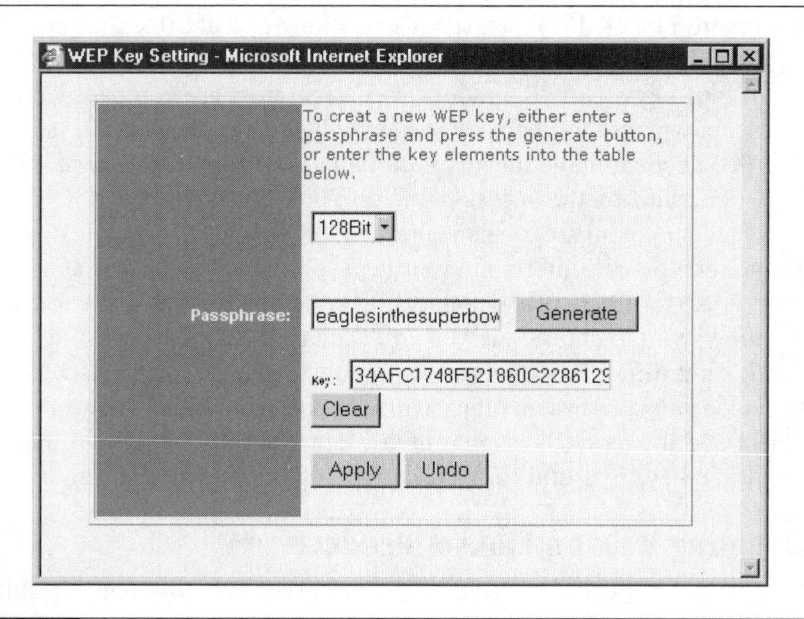

FIGURE 5-12 Most WEP-based products support a plain English passphrase to generate the hexadecimal key, but no standard on passphrases exists.

automatically. Remember that not all passphrase generators are compatible, so you should copy all of the keys, making sure to keep each one separated into a Word or Notepad document. This is very helpful for setting up client systems using Windows XP, which does not support the passphrase. Click Apply to save the changes to the router.

NOTE *Some older Linksys routers and access points do not have a generator routine. In these products, you must make up the hexadecimal string on your own. Check to see whether a firmware update is available that adds a generator routine.*

The wireless LAN will now be unavailable until client systems have the same WEP key set.

Managing WEP with WLAN Monitor The WLAN Monitor program, discussed in greater detail previously in the section "Using the Linksys WLAN Monitor Utility," comes with all Linksys products of recent vintage. WEP is managed in this program as part of the Profile Wizard.

To launch the program from the system tray, double-click the icon of a computer with an antenna. Click the Profiles tab. The first time you enter this window after each reboot, you will need to select a profile from the list of profile names and SSIDs. Select one and click the Edit button.

At this point, you are in the Profile Wizard. If you have run this wizard before, you will see your old settings as the wizard progresses through the screens, and you should be able to click Next until you reach the Security Settings window (see Figure 5-13), which you want to change.

First, select a WEP Level (64, 128, or 152 bits) to match all the other equipment on the network. In general, the larger the key size the better, but 152 bits is probably unsupported on non-Linksys hardware, so if you need to interoperate with other vendors' hardware choose 128 bit.

You can enter a passphrase that you will remember, and from this passphrase, the program will calculate a WEP key. However, the formula for computing a WEP key from the passphrase is proprietary to Linksys. If you are working with other Linksys devices, you can use the same passphrase and the WEP key will be the same, but if the WEP key on the Linksys device must match one on an existing non-Linksys device, you will have to enter the WEP key manually in hex in the WEP Key field. Alternatively, it may be easier to use the passphrase on the Linksys devices and enter the WEP key in hex only on the non-Linksys devices.

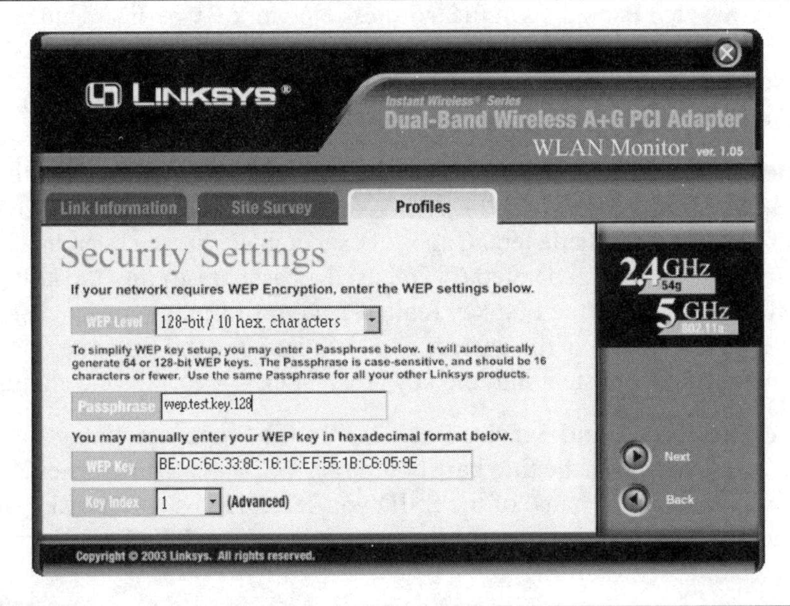

FIGURE 5-13 The WLAN Monitor utility automatically generates the WEP key from the passphrase.

Click the Next button until you reach the Confirm New Settings window, and then click Save to save the changes to the card.

Integrating WEP Support with Windows XP Windows XP integrates wireless network support, including WEP support. To access the appropriate screen, follow these steps:

1. Choose Start | Control Panel.
2. Select Network Connections.
3. Right-click the icon corresponding to your wireless network connection and select Status.
4. Click the Wireless Network tab.
5. In the lower list of preferred networks, select the appropriate network and click the Properties button.

Windows XP's behavior for the rest of this process differs quite a bit depending on the Service Pack you have installed.

- **Pre-Service Pack 1** On the Wireless Network Properties window, make sure the Data Encryption (WEP Enabled) box is checked and that the Network Authentication (Shared Mode) and The Key Is Provided for Me Automatically boxes are unchecked.

  Select a key length, preferably the longer one (104 bits, which is the same as what Linksys calls 128 bit). You can then select either ASCII characters or hexadecimal characters. Choose hexadecimal characters and paste the first key that you generated (if you used a passphrase) into the key area. Most of the time, the first key (called 1 on most Linksys products but in XP called Key 0) is the correct one. So just copy the first one on the document and paste it into the key area. Click OK to save the changes.

- **Service Pack 1 and Service Pack 2** On the Properties dialog for the wireless network (the title bar should say "*SSID name* Properties," where *SSID name* is the name of the SSID you selected in step 5), make sure the Network Authentication selector is set for Open and the Data Encryption selector is set for WEP.

Paste the value you generated (if you used a passphrase) into the Network Key field as well as the Confirm Network Key field. It's possible the access point or router generated different keys in the Key 1 through Key 4 fields, so make sure the key you just pasted corresponds to the Key Index Value below. Make sure that The Key Is Provided for Me Automatically box is unchecked. Click OK to save the changes.

TIP *With Windows XP it may be necessary to reboot the system after entering the WEP keys to access the network. Windows doesn't give you any indication that this may be necessary.*

When you subsequently connect to a different network, you may see the list of available networks, accessible through numerous Windows XP menus. Here, too, you must enter the WEP network key as a hexadecimal string.

WPA

Wi-Fi Protected Access (WPA) is part of a wireless security standard (named 802.11i) newer than the standard that includes WEP. The need for improved security was pressing enough that the industry has largely moved to adopt WPA, even though product roll-out is still in the early stages. The full 802.11i, now renamed WPA2, was finalized in the first quarter of 2004 and products should be available by the time you read this, but the release of the initial version of WPA has taken pressure off of the standards people, so you should expect WPA to be current and state of the art for some time.

NOTE *You can learn more about the WPA and WPA2 standards at the Wi-Fi Alliance site, http://www.weca.net/.*

Several new Linksys wireless products have implemented WPA, though for some you need to download and install a firmware update for the product to add WPA support. Even if a new product has WPA, earlier versions may not have it, so make sure to check the downloads page for that product on the Linksys support pages.

A WPA-enabled router or access point will have a button labeled Edit Security Settings on the main configuration page where an older one would have a WEP Settings button. Click the button to open a window like the one in Figure 5-14.

The Security Mode list lets you choose among a few security options.

WPA Pre-Shared Key

This Security Mode option is what you would normally want, but only if the devices connecting to the network—the network cards in the PCs—also support WPA. If

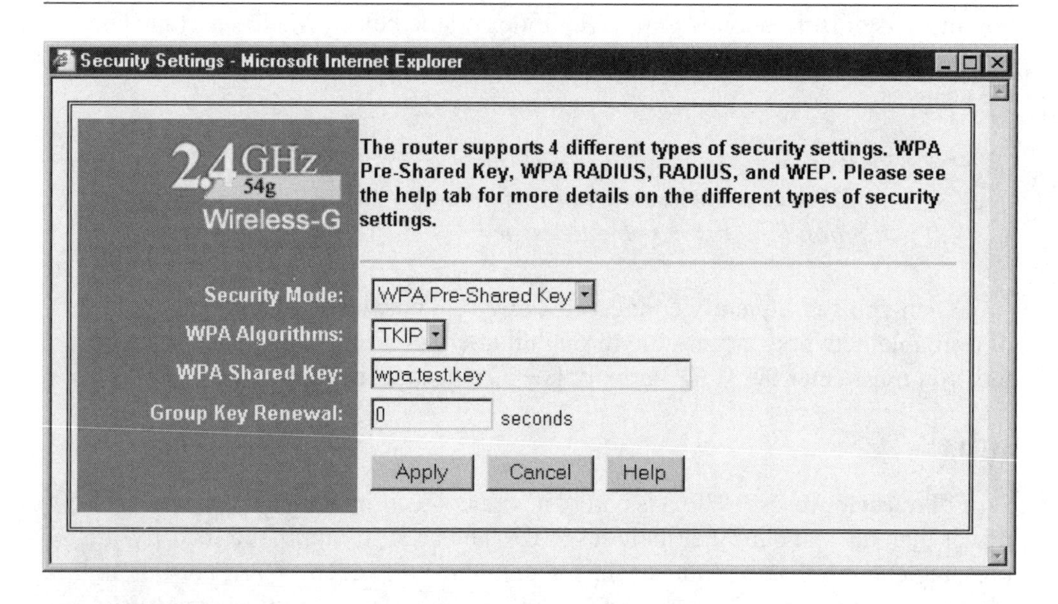

FIGURE 5-14 None of this hexadecimal nonsense exists with WPA, and the encryption is far more secure than WEP as well.

you make this selection, you will have to choose between two WPA algorithms that specify how the encryption key is determined.

TKIP (Temporal Key Integrity Protocol—pronounced "tee-kip") is the next generation of WEP and addresses the known flaws in the old version. Advanced Encryption Standard (AES) is the U.S. government's next-generation cryptography algorithm. It's important that you make sure you have the selection consistent across all your devices. TKIP has added features to defeat hackers, such as a Message Integrity Code that prevents tampering with data. TKIP clients change their keys frequently to defeat hackers who would attempt brute-force attacks. Finally, AES is not required for WPA implementation, so you may not be able to communicate with other WPA products if you rely on it.

After these selections, you should enter a WPA Shared Key of between 8 and 63 characters. You can leave the Group Key Renewal Interval setting at 0.

WPA RADIUS and RADIUS

These options are designed for corporate networks that have RADIUS-based authentication systems. RADIUS is a standard for authentication servers, such as dial-up servers, and access points and routers can be set to connect to them for the server to authenticate the user. RADIUS is rarely if ever found in small networks, but an experienced RADIUS administrator should have little trouble getting it to work. All you need to do on this screen is to enter the IP address of the RADIUS server, the port used (the default is set to the RADIUS standard of 1812), and the RADIUS shared key, also known as a shared secret.

The difference between RADIUS and WPA RADIUS is that the former uses WEP for wireless encryption and the latter uses WPA. The encryption settings are identical to those on the WPA and WEP screens.

WEP

This option allows you to use WEP instead of WPA. Unless you must support WEP clients, this setting is not advised. See the previous section "Implementing WEP on Linksys Products" for details.

WPA Client Configuration

Currently, Linksys supports WPA only on Windows XP clients and through the Windows XP native wireless configuration features described previously. Before too long, probably by the time you read this, Linksys will build WPA support into the WLAN Monitor program. Almost certainly you will access it in the Profile editor section of the WLAN Monitor, where you currently set the WEP configuration.

WPA support in Windows XP without SP2 is currently available through a special download from Microsoft. Go to the Microsoft Downloads page at *http://www.microsoft.com/downloads/* and enter **WPA** in the keyword search box. If you have SP2 installed, WPA support is already available on your computer.

After installing the Windows XP WPA update and rebooting, the normal Windows XP wireless configuration menus and windows include options for WPA. Here's how to access these:

1. Choose Start | Control Panel.
2. Select Network Connections.
3. Right-click the icon corresponding to your wireless network connection and select Status.
4. Click the Wireless Network tab.
5. In the lower list of preferred networks, select the appropriate one and click the Properties button.

On the Properties dialog for the wireless network (the title bar should say "*SSID name* Properties," where *SSID name* is the name of the SSID you selected in step 5), make sure Network Authentication is set for WPA-PSK and Data Encryption is set for TKIP (or AES if that's what you chose on the access point).

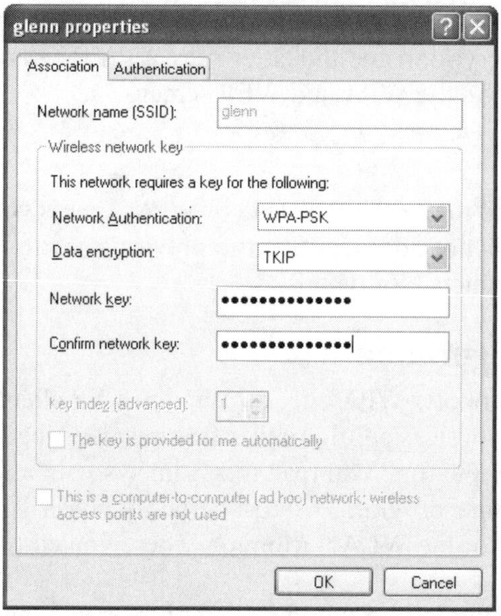

WPA-PSK stands for WPA Pre-Shared Key, the term used on Linksys access points for such a key. You also have Network Authentication options for WPA, in which case the key has been provided to you by a network administrator who built it into the adapter itself or on a Smart Card or some other device you were given for this purpose. Open and Shared allow you to use WEP.

In the Network Key fields, type in the key you used on other devices, such as the access point. You may enter the WPA shared key as regular human-readable text. Compared to WEP, WPA is remarkably easy to use. No more hex. No more silly key index stuff. Click OK to save the changes.

MAC Filtering

If you have a wired network, attackers would need to gain physical access to your building to put their computer on it. But with a wireless network it's possible for attackers to access your network from a car on the street, if they can get past the other security obstacles.

That's why wireless access points and routers have an additional feature called *MAC address filtering*. All network cards, including wireless cards, have a unique

MAC (Media Access Control) address. You can tell your access point or router to deny access to the network to NICs with specified MAC addresses or, more usefully, you can tell it to allow only NICs with specified MAC addresses access to the wireless network.

If you have a relatively small network and are not frequently allowing new users with their own cards onto it, it is important that you use MAC address filtering, as it will make it considerably more difficult for an outsider, even a sophisticated one, to hitchhike a ride on your wireless network.

Different access points and routers may implement this feature in different ways, depending on which versions of firmware are running. These features will all be available on the Advanced section of the access point or router configuration screens. In some cases, the Advanced section will include a Filters tab.

If you see a Filters tab, your device is probably a recent release and from the Filters tab, you should be able to access a screen something like the one shown in Figure 5-15. Select Enable to expose the fields that you need to configure to implement filtering. Check Permit PCs Listed Below to Access the Wireless Network. The

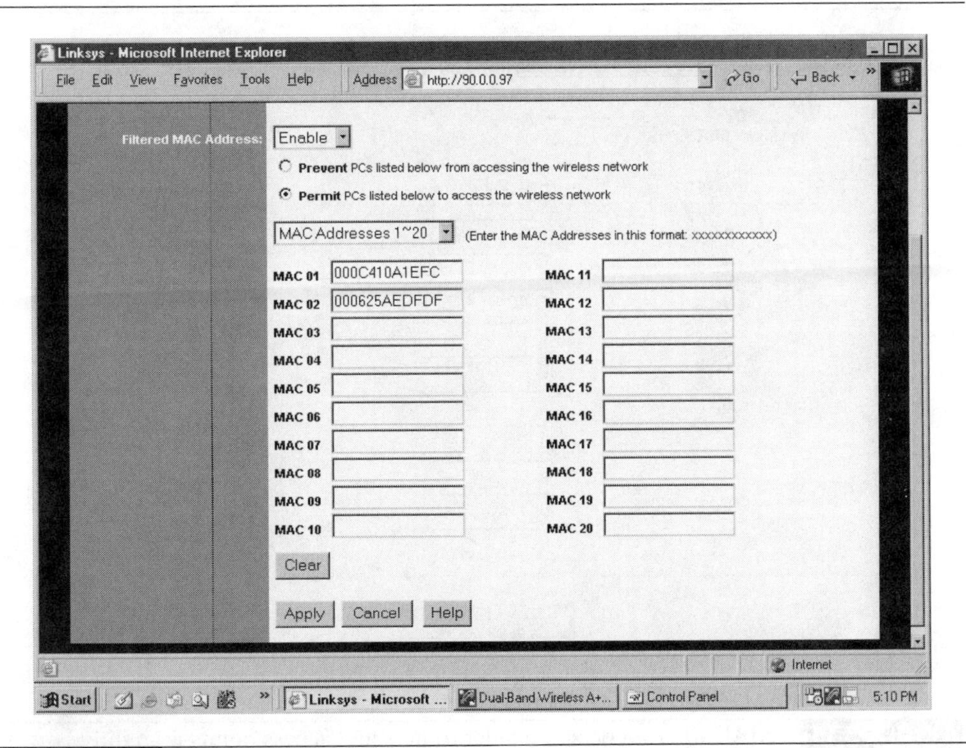

FIGURE 5-15 MAC filtering lets you specify only the network adapters that are allowed access to your wireless network.

MAC addresses consist of 12 hexadecimal characters. In many cases, the MAC address is printed on a label on the card itself. If the card is in a running Windows computer, you can get the MAC address by opening up a command prompt (also known as a DOS prompt) and typing **IPCONFIG /ALL**. (Note the space between the word *IPCONFIG* and the slash.) The resulting screen will list the MAC address as the Physical Address. Note that when you type this address into the MAC filtering page, you should not include the hyphens.

Older access points and routers may present a different tab (such as a Wireless tab) that includes two buttons: Active MAC Table and Edit MAC Filter Setting. Click the Active MAC Table button and a window will open showing the MAC addresses of every card connected to the wireless network. If you connect all the cards you want to allow, this window is a great shortcut for collecting the addresses to enter into the MAC filtering page.

After you have collected the MAC addresses, either through the Active MAC Table window or by running IPCONFIG on the clients, click the Edit MAC Filter Setting button to open the Wireless Group MAC Table window shown in Figure 5-16.

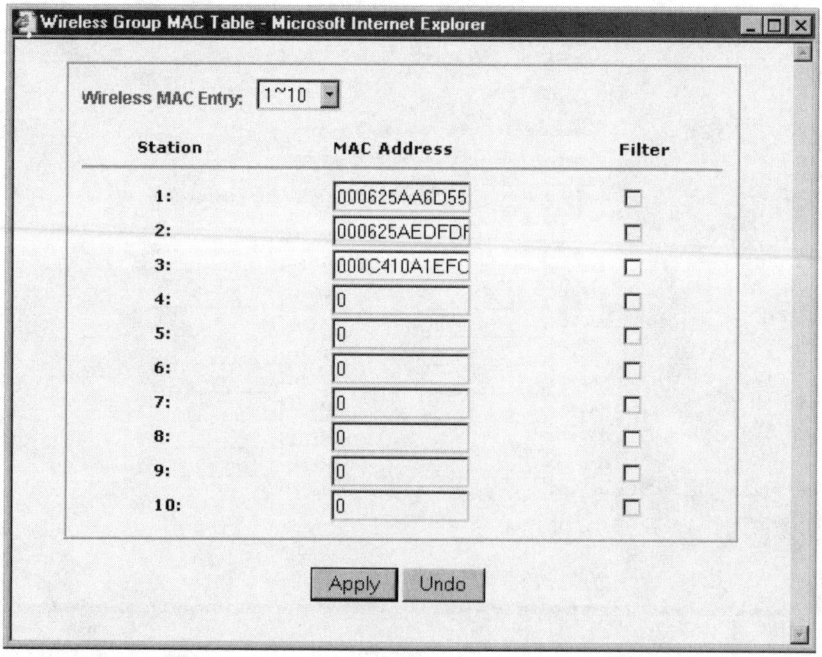

Wireless Group MAC Table - Microsoft Internet Explorer

Wireless MAC Entry: 1~10

Station	MAC Address	Filter
1:	000625AA6D55	
2:	000625AEDFDF	
3:	000C410A1EFC	
4:	0	
5:	0	
6:	0	
7:	0	
8:	0	
9:	0	
10:	0	

Apply Undo

FIGURE 5-16 MAC filtering on some older routers and access points is slightly different, but it works much the same way.

Enter the MAC addresses you want to allow and leave the Filter boxes unchecked. Click Apply.

It's still theoretically possible for attackers to slip past MAC address filtering, but it's difficult, and it's even more difficult for them to do it without attracting attention.

Improving the Wireless Signal

Wi-Fi uses radio signals, and you might think they're broadcast everywhere, but it's more complicated than that. Sometimes you just don't have enough signal where you need it and you have less than you think you should have.

Wi-Fi networking can work through most walls and other building structures, but the range is much better in open spaces. Linksys rates the range of its wireless adapters outdoors at up to 1500 feet (457 meters) and indoors at up to 300 feet (91 meters), but these ratings are under ideal circumstances, without interference. The indoor range is the most sensitive and depends on structural elements in the building. Radio engineers are hesitant to say what is the actual range of a wireless product because it depends on so many unpredictable factors. For example, metal in the walls as a base for plaster can interfere.

The best thing you can do with one access point or router to maximize the signal throughout the building is to place that device in the physical center of the building. This has the added security advantage of minimizing the signal outside the building. If you can't place the device in the middle, you may need to use more than one access point at different locations to get complete coverage, but this may be difficult and/or expensive.

If you have a wired network, you can utilize it to spread signals through the building by attaching more than one access point to it. If you join all of them to the same SSID (see "Wireless Broadband Routers and Access Points" earlier in this chapter), your clients can roam from one to the other as the signal from one moves to the other. Not many users will be in a position to do this, though, as it does require network wiring in the building, and most users deploy a wireless network in part to avoid laying cable.

Another option (albeit a complicated one) is to use home phoneline or powerline networking to bridge to wireless access points. The theory behind this option is that although you may not have Ethernet wiring in your building, you do have phone wire and power. Suppose you have a wireless router that has at least one Ethernet port in it. You could connect one of them to an Ethernet to a powerline or Ethernet to a phoneline bridge of the type sold by Linksys. Elsewhere in the building, you could connect another Ethernet to a phoneline or powerline bridge to an access point. The two physical wireless networks would be connected over the phone or powerlines. This is complicated and expensive, but it would work.

TIP *If you need just a little extra boost in your wireless range, Linksys offers a high-gain antenna set (HGA7T) that you can use to replace the antennas on your current router or access point. If you need to get wireless access to a point beyond the range of your existing 802.11g access point and don't want to install and configure an additional access point, you can also try the Wireless-G Range Expander, which essentially bounces access from your existing router or access point to new areas.*

Public Hot Spots

If you've got a portable computer with a wireless network card, you can experience the not-so-cheap thrill of connecting to the Internet at a public hot spot. Most of these hot spots are at travel-oriented establishments such as airport clubs and hotels, but many are at general public locations such as McDonald's and Starbucks. To find such hot spots, check the following sites:

- A general list searchable geographically: *http://www.hotspotlist.com/*
- Hotels, restaurants, offices, and so on: *http://www.boingo.com/*
- McDonald's: *http://www.mcdwireless.com/*
- Starbucks, Borders, some airports, and other locations: *http://www.t-mobile.com/hotspot/*

Usually, instructions will be available at the location, but it's better to be prepared by checking them on the Web beforehand and printing them out. Sometimes all you need is an 802.11b card and a Web browser, but some providers (Boingo, for example) have their own proprietary client software that you must install to access their network. This is another reason to investigate before going to the location. Finally, you can determine pricing in advance.

So have fun and remember this: your notebook computer is not a cup holder.

Chapter 6

Using Telephone Lines

Wiring your home or office for Ethernet can be a pain, but you probably already have telephone lines that you can use for computer networking. Under normal circumstances, you can use your telephones for voice communications while simultaneously using the same phonelines for your computer network.

Like the other types of networking described in this book, phoneline networking is based on an industry standard. This one is maintained by an organization called the Home Phoneline Networking Alliance (*http://www.homepna.org/*), which gave the name HomePNA to the standard. An early version of the HomePNA standard operated at a stingy 1 Mbps, but current products can work at 10 Mbps. (Equipment written to this specification switches down to 1 Mbps if any of the older equipment is on the network.) The 1 Mbps equipment supports up to 25 computers with a distance of up to 500 feet (152 meters) of cabling. The 10 Mbps equipment supports up to 30 computers with a distance of up to 1000 feet (305 meters) of cabling.

NOTE *The HomePNA has approved a third version of the specification, which supports network speeds up to 128 Mbps and allows both version 3 and 10 Mbps version 2 products to operate on the same lines at their native speeds. At the time of this writing, no products based on this specification are available. Some time later, possibly by the time you read this, HomePNA version 3 products may be available. Look for them on vendors' Web sites.*

HomePNA networking, like DSL, works on your phonelines while letting you use the lines for voice or fax communications. However, HomePNA and DSL aren't the same thing. In fact, while you can probably use both on the same phonelines at the same time, the DSL connection and the HomePNA connection can't communicate with each other. You'll need a DSL modem and optionally other hardware, such as the Linksys HPRO200 HomeLink PhoneLine 10M Cable/DSL Router, to make the network connection between the two.

NOTE *Some houses have wiring problems that can prevent HomePNA networking from functioning properly. If your wiring is nonstandard in any way, you should at least confirm that you can return products you purchased for phoneline networking before implementing them. Also, Synchronous DSL (SDSL) cannot coexist on the same phoneline with either HomePNA or voice. Only Asymmetric DSL (ADSL) can work this way.*

Installing Phoneline Hardware

As with any other networking scheme, phoneline networking requires a network adapter for each system on the network. Unlike some other networking schemes, phoneline networking doesn't necessarily call for a hub or hardware, although either can help at times.

After installing the adapter, you must configure Windows networking. See Chapter 8 for a full treatment of this topic.

USB Phoneline Adapter

You really have only one connection hardware choice for desktop PCs: a USB adapter. USB hardware is found in all systems sold in the last few years. You can install it simply by plugging in a cable between the device and the system (see Chapter 2 for general instructions on installing USB hardware). Check to make sure you have an available USB plug on the system for the network adapter. If you don't, you can buy a USB hub to expand the system.

The USB200HA HomeLink Phoneline 10M USB Network Adapter is remarkably easy to set up. You plug the phoneline into one of the two phone plugs, then connect the USB cable from the device to the system, and you are finished. You don't even need a power outlet, as this and many other USB devices draw their power directly from the system through the USB cable.

Four display lights appear on the USB adapter. The Power light indicates that the unit is drawing power from the system and is turned on. The Link light indicates that the adapter is connected to a phoneline network. The Tx light indicates that the device is transmitting data over a phoneline network, and the Rx light indicates that it is receiving data from the network. In the network adapter's normal course of operation, the Power and Link lights should be on constantly, but the Tx and Rx lights should flash a lot.

If you have Windows XP or later, when you plug the adapter into the system, Windows will recognize it and install the device drivers for it automatically.

If you have Windows 98, you must use a wizard to install the drivers:

1. When the Add New Hardware Wizard appears, if you have not already put the Phoneline 10M Network Card Driver floppy disk into your floppy drive, do so. Click Next.

2. On the next screen, the default selection is Search For the Best Driver For Your Device (Recommended). Leave the default selection and click Next.

3. On the next screen, select Floppy Disk Drives (or whatever source is appropriate) from the list of drives (Figure 6-1) and click Next again.
4. The next screen says that Windows is ready to install the Linksys USB 10M Phoneline Adapter and specifies the location. Click Next. Windows copies the driver from the floppy (or other source) to the computer. At this point, you may need to insert your Windows 98 CD-ROM, so have it ready. If you don't have a Windows 98 CD-ROM, you can usually specify c:\windows\options\cabs for any Windows files needed.
5. On the last screen, Windows tells you that it has finished installing the drivers for the card. Click Finish to exit the wizard. You may be prompted at this point to reboot the computer.

PC Card Phoneline Adapters for Notebooks

Most notebook computer users can also use USB devices, but almost all of them can use PC Cards (sometimes known as PCMCIA cards). See the preceding section, "USB Phoneline Adapter," for a discussion of USB devices. Most notebook computer users should use a PC Card such as the PCM200HA HomeLink Phoneline 10M Integrated PC Card.

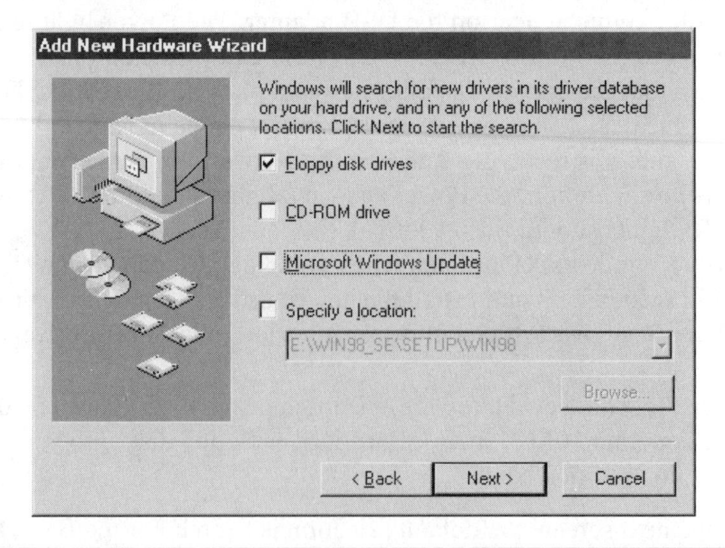

FIGURE 6-1 Make sure you have the driver disk in the appropriate drive and make the appropriate selection for the Add New Hardware Wizard.

NOTE *The PC Card requires a 32-bit CardBus slot, which some older notebooks lack. See Chapter 2 for more information on PCMCIA hardware.*

To install the PC Card, insert it into one of the notebook's PC Card slots so that the three lights on the card are pointed up. Push the card until you can feel it seat inside. The two rows of pins at the inside of the PC Card slot need to slide into the two rows of holes in the card.

With a PC Card, as with USB, you don't have to turn off the system before adding or removing hardware. If you just plug it in, Windows will recognize it and begin installing the software, or the hardware will work without software installation.

Three display lights appear on the PC Card. The Link light indicates that the card is connected to a phoneline network. The Tx light indicates that the device is transmitting data over a phoneline network, and the Rx light indicates that it is receiving data from the network. In the PC Card's normal course of operation, the Link light should be on constantly, but the Tx and Rx lights should flash a lot.

Insert a phoneline from the wall or from another phoneline system into one of the two RJ11 outlets on the PC Card. The two plugs are identical, even though one is labeled "Homelink" and the other "Phone."

Software Installation

Windows XP identifies the PCM200HA PC Card correctly, but note that the opening screen of the Found New Hardware Wizard identifies the card as a Broadcom iLine10 Cardbus Network Adapter (see Figure 6-2). This is simply a reference to the company that makes the chips in the card.

To install the software:

1. Insert the CD-ROM that came with the card into the notebook's CD-ROM drive. Leave the default set to Install the Software Automatically (Recommended) and click Next to continue.

2. You may see a warning that the hardware has not passed Windows Logo testing to ensure compatibility with Windows XP and that dreadful things may happen if you continue the installation. Fear not; it's safe to click Continue Anyway to install the device driver software, enabling the card.

3. The wizard installs the device driver files from the CD-ROM to the appropriate Windows directory. The installation should not require a Windows XP restart.

FIGURE 6-2 The PC Card is automatically recognized, but it's identified by its chipset, not as a Linksys adapter.

If you have Windows 98, the Add New Hardware Wizard appears when you insert the card:

1. If you have not already done so, insert the Phoneline 10M Network Card Driver CD into your CD drive. Click Next.
2. On the next screen, the default selection will be Search For the Best Driver For Your Device (Recommended). Leave the default selection and click Next.
3. Select the CD-ROM from the list of drives and click Next again.
4. The next screen says that Windows is ready to install the Linksys Phoneline 10M Network Card and specifies the location. Click Next. Windows copies the driver from the CD to the computer. At this point, you may need to insert your Windows 98 CD-ROM, so have it ready. If you don't have a Windows 98 CD-ROM, you can usually specify c:\windows\options\cabs for any Windows files needed.
5. On the last screen, Windows tells you that it has finished installing the drivers for the card. Click Finish to exit the wizard. At this point, you may be prompted to reboot the computer.

At the end of the process, your card should be active. If you connect the phone cables to the rest of the network, you should be able to communicate with other systems on the network as well as the Internet, if your network is connected to it. See Chapter 8 for more details on how to configure Windows networking.

Connecting to the Internet or Other Networks

As with other network types, you connect your phoneline network with the Internet in two ways. The cheaper (if not easier) way is to use Windows Internet Connection Sharing (ICS) or a similar third-party program to connect the Internet connection with the phoneline network. Chapter 8 explains in detail how to do this. The second way is to use a router, such as the Linksys HPRO200 HomeLink Phoneline 10M Cable/DSL Router, which makes the Internet connection easy to set up.

The Linksys Phoneline Router

The Linksys Phoneline Router (shown in Figure 6-3) provides dynamic Internet addresses for PCs on the network, which helps make setting up client PCs easy. The router can also connect an Ethernet PC or other Ethernet device or even an Ethernet hub to your phoneline network.

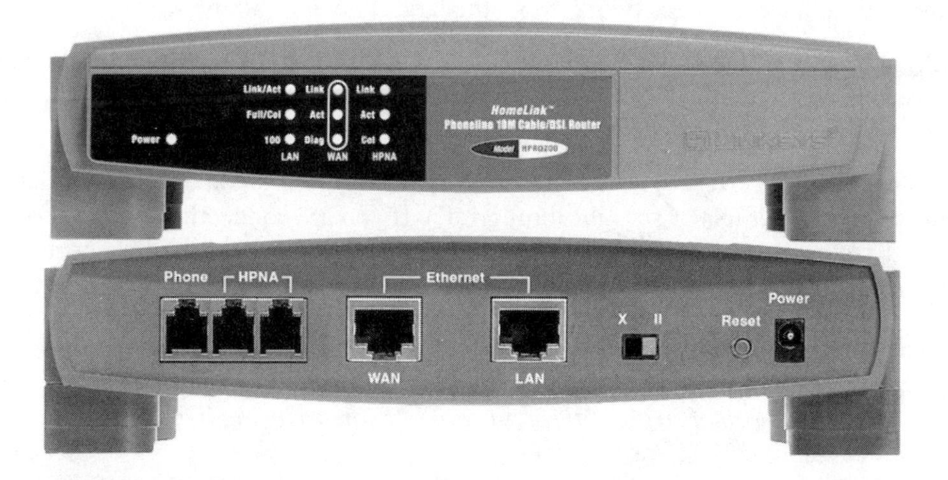

FIGURE 6-3 The Linksys HPRO200 HomeLink Phoneline 10M Cable/DSL Router connects to a HomePNA, phonelines, a broadband connection, and a local Ethernet LAN.

Unlike with ICS, no single PC is responsible for keeping the Internet connection going, so you can shut off any PCs on the network if you want and it won't affect the Internet connections of other computers. The Linksys Phoneline Router is set up for broadband routing, though, such as that attained with a cable modem or DSL service. If your Internet connection is through a dial-up modem, you will need to use ICS to share the connection with the rest of your phoneline network.

Router Ports

All the connections start (or end, depending on your point of view) at the back of your router. I'll go over each connection on the router, moving from left to right, according to the unit shown in Figure 6-3.

Phone This port is meant for a telephone, fax, or some other conventional telephony device. The manual says that it has special filter hardware for telephones and that you should not use your phones in any other port.

HPNA These two ports are for HomePNA network devices.

WAN Use the WAN port to connect the router to your DSL/cable modem. WAN (Wide Area Network) is a term that's usually applied to a network that's spread across multiple locations. (See the sidebar "LAN, WAN, and MAN" if you're interested in learning more about the various types of networks that are used to connect computers.) While the router doesn't really create a WAN, it does provide a separation point (and a barricade) between two networks: your LAN and the Internet (the Internet is a network, too—the largest network in the world).

LAN Use this port to connect the router to a wired Ethernet PC or hub. If you plan to use this port, read the following section on the nearby crossover switch, which controls the wiring of this connection.

Crossover Switch (X/II) This two-position switch sets the mode of the LAN port either to crossover (X) or straight-through (II). If you are connecting the LAN port directly to a computer, to another stand-alone device, or to the Uplink port in a hub, select the crossover (X) mode. For anything else, select straight-through (II).

NOTE *Remember that special crossover cables can do the same thing as the X mode in this switch. The preceding instructions presume that you are using a normal straight-through cable. If you are using a crossover cable, reverse the instructions.*

If you're confused about what selection to use or what kind of cable you have, there's no need to worry. Just plug it in and try both positions of the switch until it works.

Reset Button Like the Reset button on your computer, the Reset button on the router clears data and restarts the device. To use it, press and hold the button for 2 to 3 seconds and then release it. Use this button only in case of an emergency, if for some reason the links to the router are jammed and communications are frozen. Try following the tips in the troubleshooting section of your router's user guide before you press Reset.

It's possible, but unlikely, that the router could lock up like your computer sometimes locks up, to the degree that even the Reset button won't work. In these cases, remove the power cable from the router for 3 to 5 seconds and then reinsert it. There's a good chance that this procedure will retain network connections through the router, but if you leave the unit powered down much longer you may lose the connections.

Power This connector accepts the power adapter, the other end of which is plugged into a wall outlet (or, preferably, a surge protector).

LAN, WAN, and MAN

The methods for interconnecting computers vary depending on geographical circumstances. Each of the three basic types of networks—LAN, WAN, and MAN—has a variety of setup methods, but I'll stick to the basics here.

A LAN (Local Area Network) is a group of computers connected by a common communications line. That line is usually a cable, but it can also be a non-cable connection, such as telephone lines (within a house), powerlines, or wireless technology. Most small business networks and all home networks are LANs.

A WAN (Wide Area Network) is a group of computers, widely dispersed geographically, that use public communication lines as the connection methods. The public communication methods are telephone lines, high-speed connection lines, or the Internet. WANs are typically made up of multiple LANs communicating with one another over a distance.

A MAN (Metropolitan Area Network) is a group of computers that are geographically dispersed but in the same general area. The computers can be connected through public telephone lines or through the use of fiber-optic cable that's capable of withstanding the elements. For example, the computers in a group of adjacent buildings might be connected in this manner. Many college campus networks are connected as MANs, providing network connections in classrooms, dormitories, and other buildings.

The Front Panel LEDs

You'll notice 10 lights on the front panel of the Linksys Phoneline Router (see Figure 6-3). At the far left, on its own, is the Power light, which is on when the router is powered up. To the right are three columns, each with three indicators, labeled LAN, WAN, and HPNA. To power up the router, simply plug it in.

The LAN indicators show the status of the connection to the LAN port:

- Link/Act, the top indicator, is on continuously when a successful connection exists to a device on the LAN port. The LED flashes when the data is being sent or received through the port.
- If the Full/Col LED is on continuously, the LAN connection is full-duplex, which means that it is running at full speed both sending and receiving data. When it flashes, collisions on the connection are occurring, which means that the traffic load is heavy.
- The LED labeled 100 turns orange when the router is connected to the LAN at 100 Mbps.

The WAN indicators show the status of the connection to the WAN port:

- The top indicator, Link, is lit continuously when a successful connection to a device, such as a cable or DSL modem, exists on the WAN port.
- The Act LED flashes when data is sent or received on the WAN port.
- The Diag LED turns on during the router's self-diagnostic stage while starting up. It turns off if the test is successful. If it is on for a long period of time, the unit has a problem and you need help.

The HPNA indicators show the status of connections through the HPNA ports:

- The top indicator, Link, is on continuously when a successful connection to a HomePNA PhoneLine adapter is made on one of the HPNA ports or the Phone port.
- The Act LED flashes when data is sent or received on the HPNA or Phone ports.
- The Col LED flashes when collisions on the connection occur, which means that the traffic load is heavy. Heavy flashing may indicate a problem.

Making the Connections

Start by physically connecting your router to your DSL/cable modem and to the computers on your network. Depending on your current network topology (if a network is in place), making the physical connections can be merely a matter of moving some cable; however, you may need to install the cable from scratch, or you may have to do a little of both.

NOTE *Linksys advises that you power off all devices on the network while you make your connections.*

Attaching an Existing Hub/Switch to the Router If you have already set up a wired Ethernet network before deciding to add a HomePNA router, you don't have to abandon the hub or switch you're using (see Figure 6-4).

At first, this might seem a strange thing to do: if you have a wired Ethernet network, why would you need a HomePNA network? But there are good reasons for doing this. For instance, suppose that you have a wired Ethernet network in your office, with wires simply lying on the floor between systems and your Ethernet

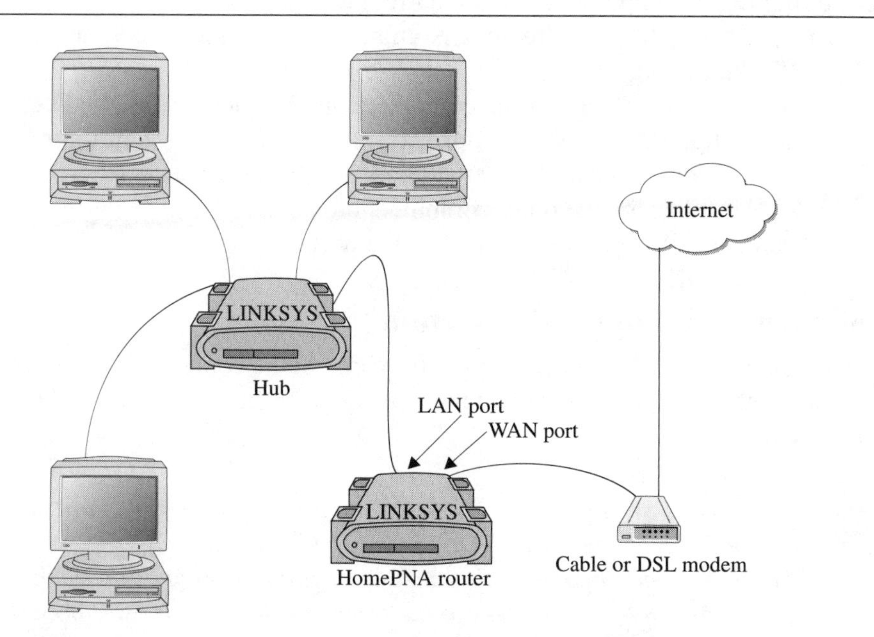

FIGURE 6-4 You can connect an existing hub or switch to the router.

hub. If you wanted to include computers elsewhere in the house on that network, you would have to run wires through the walls or perhaps down the stairs. Instead, you can use the router to connect your office network to a HomePNA network, and then you can network any PC within reach of a phone plug.

To make this connection, connect a regular port on the hub to the LAN port on the router. Make sure to switch the Crossover Switch to the X position. If you have an Uplink port on your hub, you can connect from it to the LAN port on the router, but make sure that you switch the Crossover Switch to the II position.

If you had been connecting a DSL or cable modem through the hub, it should be connected through the WAN port on the router, which might open up a port on your hub.

CAUTION *If you have an existing network, and you're using any form of ICS, you must disable it. The router takes care of sharing the connection.*

Configuring the Computers

You need to configure your computers to access the Internet through the router. (See Chapter 8 to learn how to access the TCP/IP settings for your NICs.) You must configure the computers to obtain an IP address automatically (the router takes care of issuing the IP addresses). Nothing else is enabled—no gateway, no DNS, no WINS, nothing.

If you have connected one of the computers on your network to the DSL/cable modem and configured its NIC for your ISP settings, you must reconfigure that NIC as a client to obtain an address and other TCP/IP information automatically (matching the settings for the other computers on the network). The original settings from the ISP are used to configure the router.

Configuring the Router Connection

You configure your router by accessing it from one of the connected computers. No special software has to be installed on that computer; the router is accessed through the browser.

NOTE *When you open the browser to begin configuring the router, you may receive an error message. That's because the browser can't get to the home page you configured (because until you finish configuring the router, you don't have access to the Internet). If your browser home page is set for About:Blank, however, you won't see an error message.*

Follow these steps to begin configuring your router:

1. In the browser Address Bar, enter **http://192.168.1.1/** and press ENTER to open the Enter Network Password dialog (it may take a few seconds for the dialog to appear).

NOTE *This dialog may look slightly different if you're not configuring this router on a Windows XP computer.*

TIP *Add the URL for the router to your Favorites list to make it easy to open the window later, in case you want to add or modify features.*

2. Leave the User Name field blank, and in the Password field type **admin** (in lowercase characters). Then click OK.

The Linksys Setup window appears with the Setup tab selected, as shown in Figure 6-5. The Setup window has multiple tabs for setting up all the features offered by your Linksys HomePNA router. I'll discuss the other tabs in the sections that follow.

In the Setup tab, you specify the basic options for your Internet connection. Before you set configuration options on the other tabs in the Setup window, you must configure the Setup tab, restart your DSL/cable modem, and restart the computers on the network to provide Internet access for your network. The Setup tab's options are as follows:

- **Host Name and Domain Name** These fields can usually remain blank, but if your Internet service provider (ISP) requires this information, fill in the data as instructed.

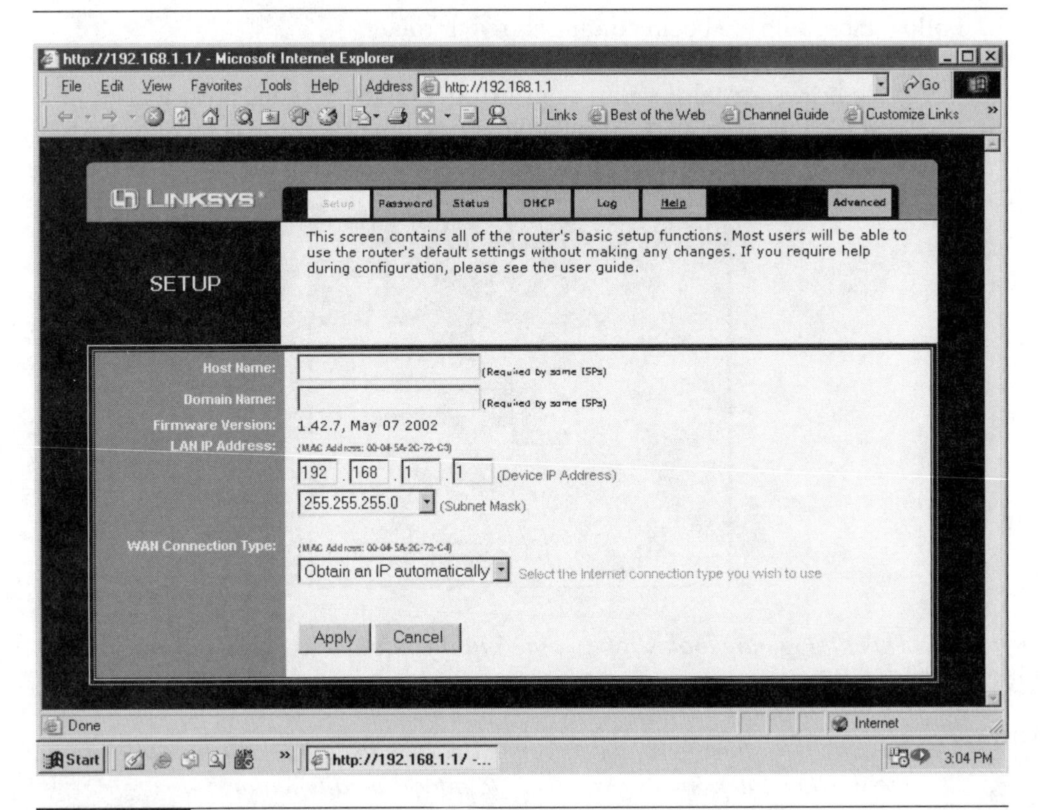

FIGURE 6-5 Configure your Internet connection through the Linksys router's Setup tab.

- **Firmware Version** This is the version number for the router's firmware, as well as the release date for the version. Firmware is programming code that is inserted into the read-only memory of a device. This technology provides a way to enhance the capabilities of hardware devices. When new firmware is available, you can download it from the Linksys Web site, along with instructions on how to insert the new code into the device's memory; however, Linksys does not recommend upgrading your firmware unless you're having trouble with the router.
- **Device IP Address and Subnet Mask** The default values for the router's IP address and subnet mask are preset and should not be altered.
- **WAN Connection Type** Click the arrow to the right of the text box and select a connection type. The WAN connection specifications must match

the instructions from your ISP. The Linksys HomePNA router supports five connection types, which are discussed next.

Obtain an IP Automatically This is the default selection, because it's the most common. Your ISP instructs you to use this setting when it provides DHCP (Dynamic Host Configuration Protocol) services. If this is the correct setting for your ISP, you have nothing more to do in the Setup tab.

Click Apply, and then click Continue to save your settings. Close the browser. Power your DSL/cable modem off and then turn it on again. Restart all the computers on the network so they can establish the router's settings. You can return to this Setup utility at any time to configure any other features you want to use.

Static IP Choose this option if the instructions from your ISP require a static IP address. The Setup window changes to display the fields you need for configuration (see Figure 6-6). Use the following guidelines to supply data in the fields:

- **Specify WAN IP Address** Enter the IP address for the router as seen from the WAN (Internet).
- **Subnet Mask** Enter the subnet mask as seen by the Internet and the ISP.
- **Default Gateway Address** Enter the IP address for the gateway.
- **DNS (Required)** Enter the IP address of the DNS server that your ISP wants you to use. Your ISP provides at least one DNS IP address. Many ISPs provide a secondary DNS IP address. The Setup window also has a field for a third DNS IP address if your ISP provided one.

Click Apply and then click Continue to save your settings. Close the browser. Power your DSL/cable modem off and on again. Restart all the computers on the network so they can establish the router's settings. You can return to this Setup utility at any time to configure any other features you want to use.

PPPoE If your DSL provider uses Point-to-Point Protocol over Ethernet (PPPoE), select this option to enable the protocol (see Figure 6-7). Then configure your connection, using the following guidelines:

- **User Name and Password** Enter the data provided by your DSL ISP.
- **Connect on Demand: Max Idle Time** You can configure the router to disconnect from your ISP after a specified amount of inactivity. Then,

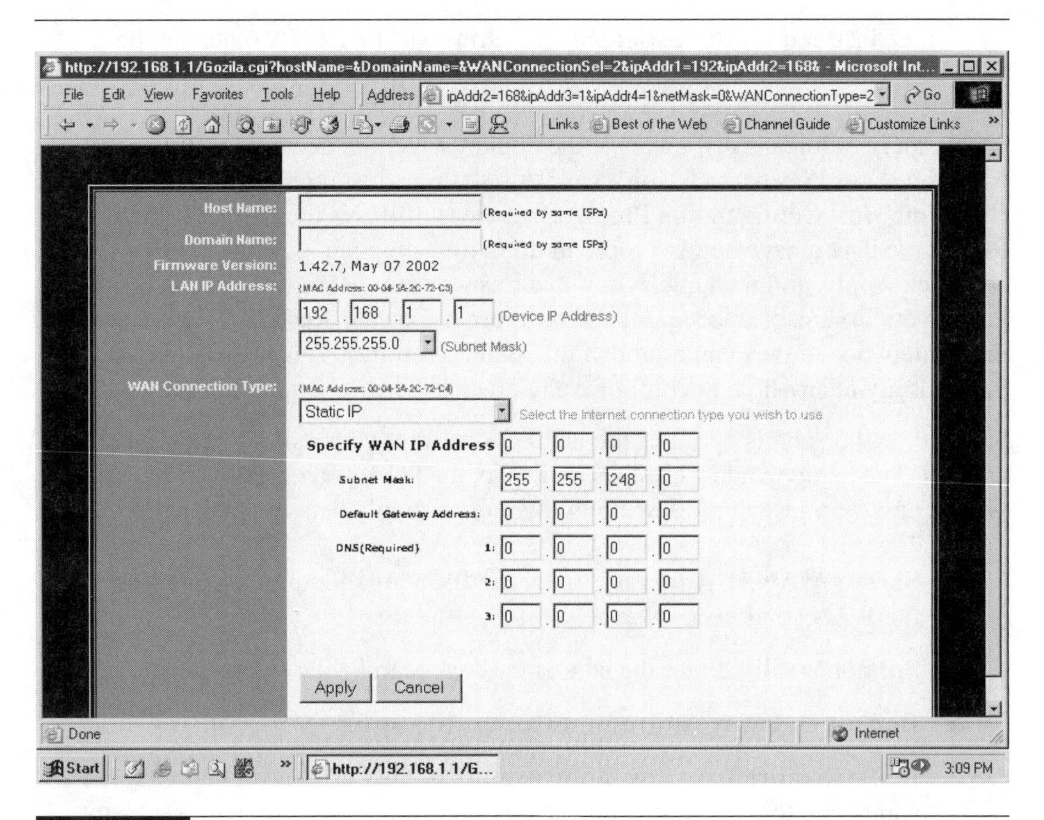

FIGURE 6-6 Use the information from your ISP to configure a static IP address.

whenever you're disconnected as a result of inactivity, the connection is reestablished as soon as a user attempts to access the Internet (by opening a browser or an e-mail application). Enter the number of minutes of inactivity that must elapse to cause the router to disconnect from your DSL ISP.

- **Keep Alive: Redial Period** Select this option to have the router periodically check the state of your Internet connection and reconnect to your ISP if the connection has been broken. Enter an amount of time that must elapse to cause the router to reconnect.

Click Apply and then click Continue to save your settings. Close the browser. Power your DSL modem off and on again. Restart all the computers on the network so they can establish the router's settings. You can return to this Setup utility at any time to configure any other features you want to use.

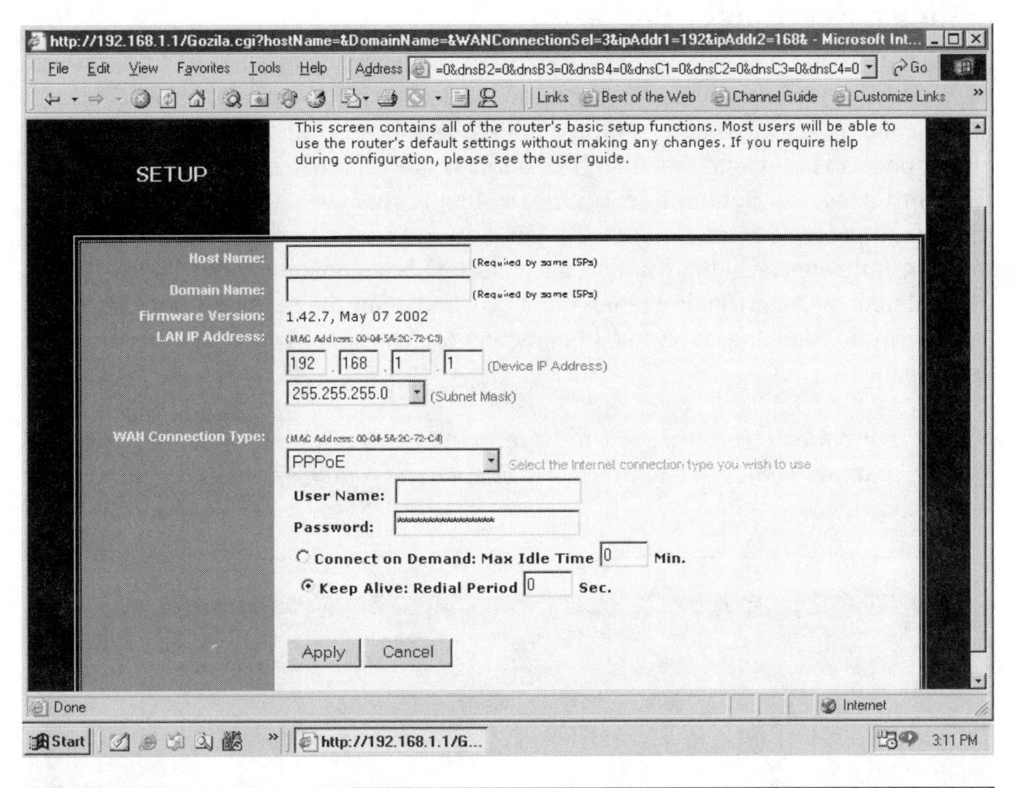

FIGURE 6-7 Enter your connection settings for PPPoE.

RAS and PPTP These services are less common and are used only outside the United States, as follows:

- RAS is used only in Singapore. Contact Singtel for information on the appropriate settings.
- PPTP (Point-to-Point Tunneling Protocol) is used mostly in Europe. Contact your ISP for information on settings. (PPTP is also used in Israel and Australia.)

Click Apply and then click Continue to save your settings. Close the browser. Power your DSL/cable modem off and on again. Restart all the computers on the network so they can establish the router's settings. You can return to this Setup utility at any time to configure any other features you want to use.

Setting a New Router Password

The default router password is the same for all Linksys routers, so unless you change the password, it's easy for any user on the local network to connect to the router and change the configuration settings. All the user needs to do is read the manual or this book to know that the default IP address is 192.168.1.1 and the default password is *admin*. Bottom line: one of the first things you should do is to change the default password (see Figure 6-8). On the Password tab, delete the asterisks that currently appear in the Router Password text box and enter a new password. Then, delete the asterisks in the next text box and enter the new password again to confirm it. You can use up to 63 characters for your password, but you can't use a space.

CAUTION *For added password security, don't enable the option to save the password and automatically log in when you open the router's configuration feature.*

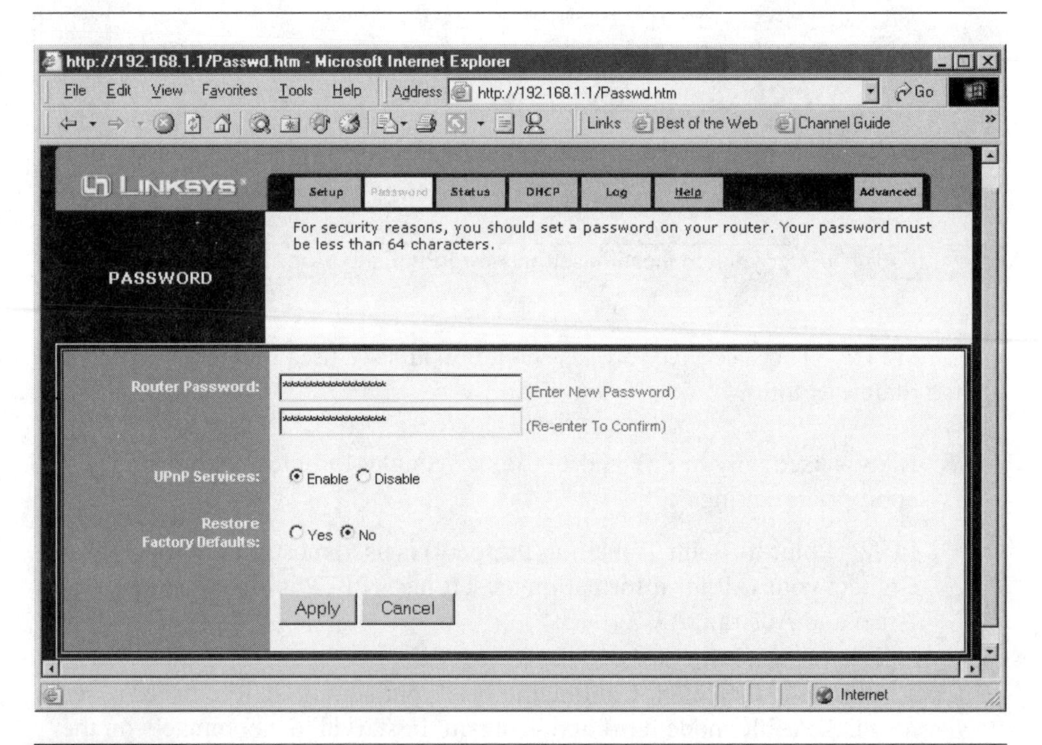

FIGURE 6-8 It's important that you change the default password on the unit so that others can't easily change the configuration.

Selecting UPnP Services

This is a Windows XP–only feature, and unless all the computers on your network are running Windows XP, you should select Disable. Even if all the computers on your network are running Windows XP, you may want to disable this option. The feature enables the Windows XP Universal Plug and Play service to reconfigure the router automatically if somebody on the network tries to use certain interactive Internet applications. A great many security problems have been reported as the result of using UPnP, and although Microsoft provides fixes and patches rather quickly, if you don't keep up with the patches and install them, you could compromise the security of your network. (Windows Me also has UPnP compatibilities.)

Restoring the Router to Factory Default

This is a selection that you must consider as a last ditch troubleshooting effort. If you select Yes and then click Apply, all of your router's settings are cleared and you have to start all over again. Rarely is such a drastic move necessary, and you shouldn't even think about using this option unless you've exhausted all troubleshooting suggestions from Linksys technical support and they've told you that this is the only solution. You can also press and hold the router's Reset button for 30 seconds to restore the factory defaults if you're unable to access the router through the Web-based interface.

Checking the Current Status of the Router

The Status tab (Figure 6-9) displays the current status of the router and its configuration. Most of the entries are self-explanatory, but the Login status may not be—it refers to whether or not Login is enabled for PPPoE, RAS, or PPTP connection types. If you're not using one of those connection methods, the Login status is disabled.

You cannot make changes to the values displayed on this page; it only reports your setup configuration. When you make changes to the Setup tab, the Status tab reflects those changes.

At the bottom of the Status page are three buttons related to DHCP management. The first two come into play if your router is a DHCP client on your ISP's network—in other words, if your router obtains an IP address automatically from the ISP's network. Clicking DHCP Release releases that address back to the ISP network. Click it and you will see all the WAN settings on the Status page revert to zeros. If you click DHCP Renew, the router will request a new address from the network.

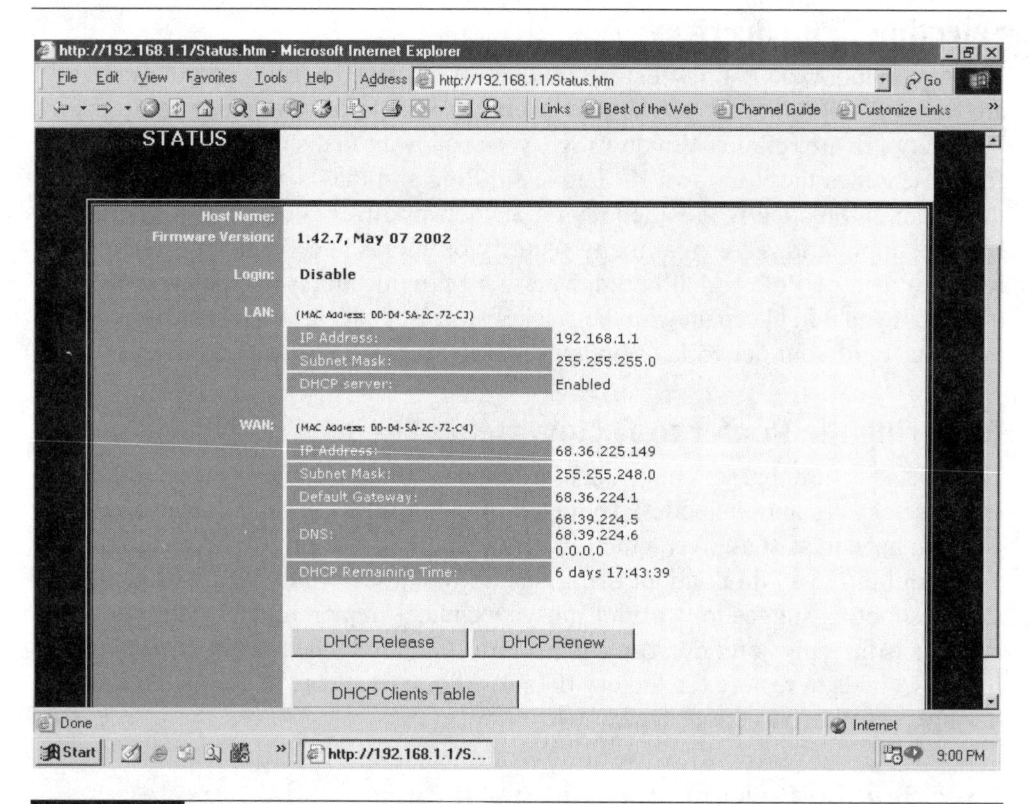

FIGURE 6-9 The Status tab displays network information and includes some buttons for managing DHCP functions.

The third button, DHCP Clients Table, opens a window that lists the hostname, IP address, and MAC address of devices with DHCP leases, and is identical to the button of the same name on the DHCP page.

Managing DHCP

When computers receive their IP addresses automatically instead of using an assigned static IP address, a DHCP server assigns the IP addresses. You can create a DHCP server on any network, using any computer—in fact, if you run ICS instead of using a router, the computer that is sharing the Internet connection becomes the DHCP server. Corporate network administrators set up DHCP servers to provide IP addresses for all the computers on the network.

It's best to let your router act as the DHCP server. Even if you had been running ICS, you had to disable it when you installed your router, so it would be unusual for a small network to use anything but the router for DHCP services. If you are running more than one router on your network, though (for example, if you have a standard Ethernet router and a PhoneLine router), you should make sure that only one device is acting as a DHCP server on your network.

DHCP servers don't assign IP addresses permanently; the servers lease the addresses to computers when the computers start up and request an IP address. When the lease expires, a new lease is assigned. (Computers don't have to reboot to request a new lease; it's an automatic process.) The default length of the lease appears on the DHCP tab (see Figure 6-10) along with other DHCP settings (some of which you set when you configure the Setup tab). There's no particular reason to change any of these settings.

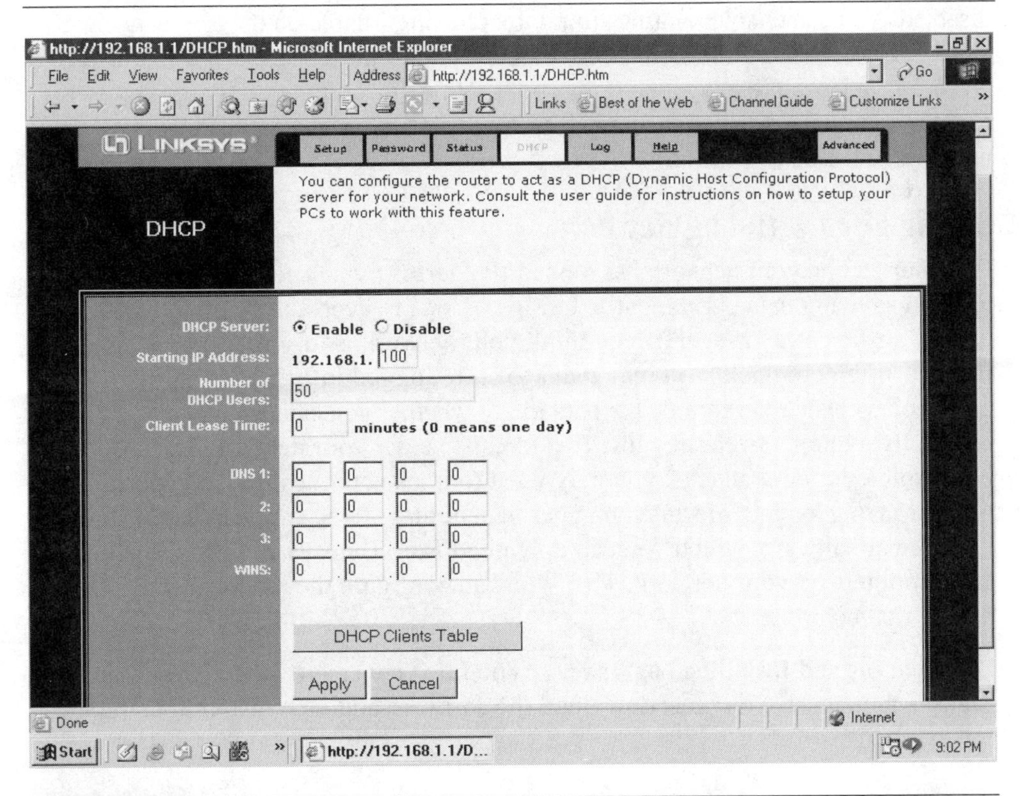

FIGURE 6-10 Configuration settings for your router-based DHCP server are displayed on the DHCP tab.

To see the current DHCP client data, click the DHCP Clients Table button. A window opens listing the hostname, IP address, and MAC address of devices with DHCP leases.

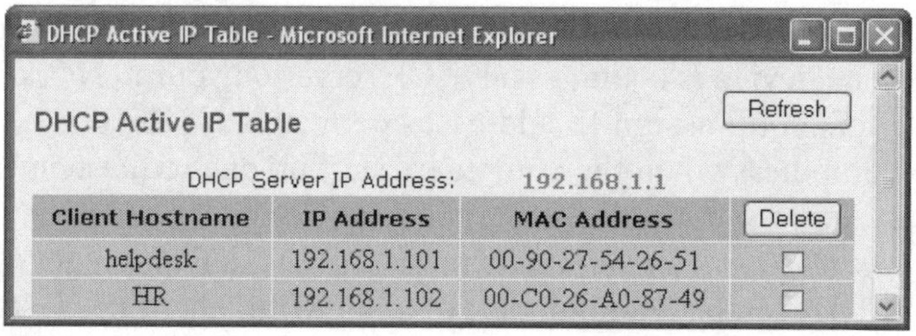

DHCP Active IP Table - Microsoft Internet Explorer

DHCP Active IP Table

Refresh

DHCP Server IP Address: 192.168.1.1

Client Hostname	IP Address	MAC Address	Delete
helpdesk	192.168.1.101	00-90-27-54-26-51	☐
HR	192.168.1.102	00-C0-26-A0-87-49	☐

Logging Events and Warnings

Use the Log tab to enable logging and to view logs. By default, logging is disabled. You can enable logging simply by clicking Enable on the Log page. You can view the information being collected by opening the logs. The Incoming Access Log button displays incoming Internet traffic, and the Outgoing Access Log button displays the URLs and IP addresses of Internet sites that users on the network accessed.

Saving Logs with LogViewer

If a computer on your network has a fixed IP address (which admittedly is unlikely), you can save log data permanently. Using the logs to keep an eye on the system is usually sufficient. However, if you think your network is in some serious danger from an Internet attack, you may want to store logged information in files. This gives you a chance to examine the data to see whether you can discern any patterns, especially attempts from the same IP address to enter your network. Even if you're not suspicious about attacks, you may want to track activities for some period of time by saving logged information in permanent files. To accomplish this, you need LogViewer software, which you can download from Linksys and install on one of the computers on your network. Then you can configure the router to send the log data to that computer.

Downloading and Installing LogViewer The LogViewer software is available from Linksys at no cost. You must download the software and then install it, using the following steps:

1. Open the browser on the computer that will install the viewer software and hold the log files, and enter **ftp://ftp.linksys.com/pub/befsr41/logviewer.exe** in the Address bar.

2. In the File Download dialog, choose Save This Program to Disk and click OK.

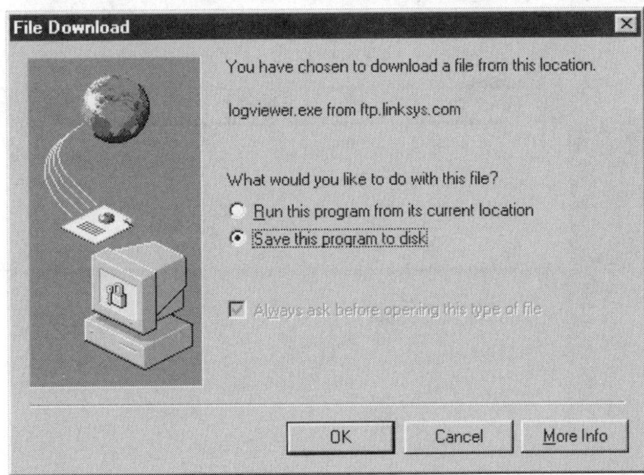

3. Select a folder to hold the downloaded file and click Save to save the file.
4. Close the browser and open My Computer or Windows Explorer to navigate to the folder where you saved the file (LogViewer.exe).
5. Double-click the file's listing to launch the LogViewer installation process. This is a wizard, so you click Next to move through each window.
6. Select a folder for the software or accept the default location (C:\Program Files\Linksys\LogViewer) and click Next.
7. The installation wizard displays the Programs menu item it will add to your system. Click Next.
8. Click Finish to complete the installation.

Configuring the Router to Save the Logs

On the Log tab of the router's Setup utility, as depicted in Figure 6-11, use the Send Log To field to specify the IP address of the computer that has the LogViewer software. Remove the default number (255) that appears for the last section of the IP address, and replace it with the last section of the IP address for the computer that's running LogViewer. Use the Active IP table, accessible via the DHCP Clients Table button on the DHCP tab (see the section "Managing DHCP" for an explanation) to determine the correct number if you have not assigned that computer a static IP. Click Apply and then click Continue to save your new settings.

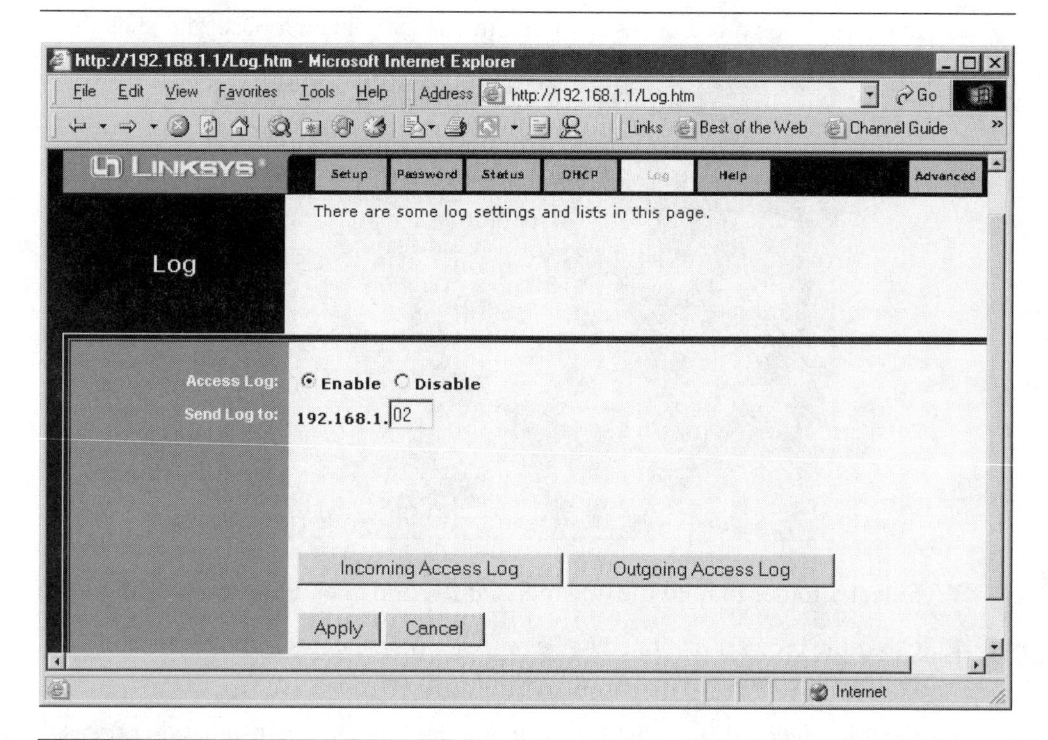

FIGURE 6-11 The router can send logs directly to one of the client systems specified by the IP address.

Viewing the Permanent Logs You can view the logs by opening LogViewer from the Programs menu. The logs continue to grow—unlike operating system logs, they don't have a finite size and use a first-in, first-out algorithm to get rid of older entries. Therefore, you must periodically clear them out or risk running out of disk space.

Getting Help

Use the Help tab to travel to specific support pages on the Linksys Web site (see Figure 6-12). In addition to finding answers to your questions, you can download a copy of the user guide, and you can even check to see whether a new firmware upgrade is available for your router.

Advanced Setup Configuration Options

Clicking the Advanced tab opens a whole new set of tabs you can use to tweak your router's settings. (To return to the original window, and the original tabs, click the Setup tab.) Most of the options available in these tabs are unnecessary for home

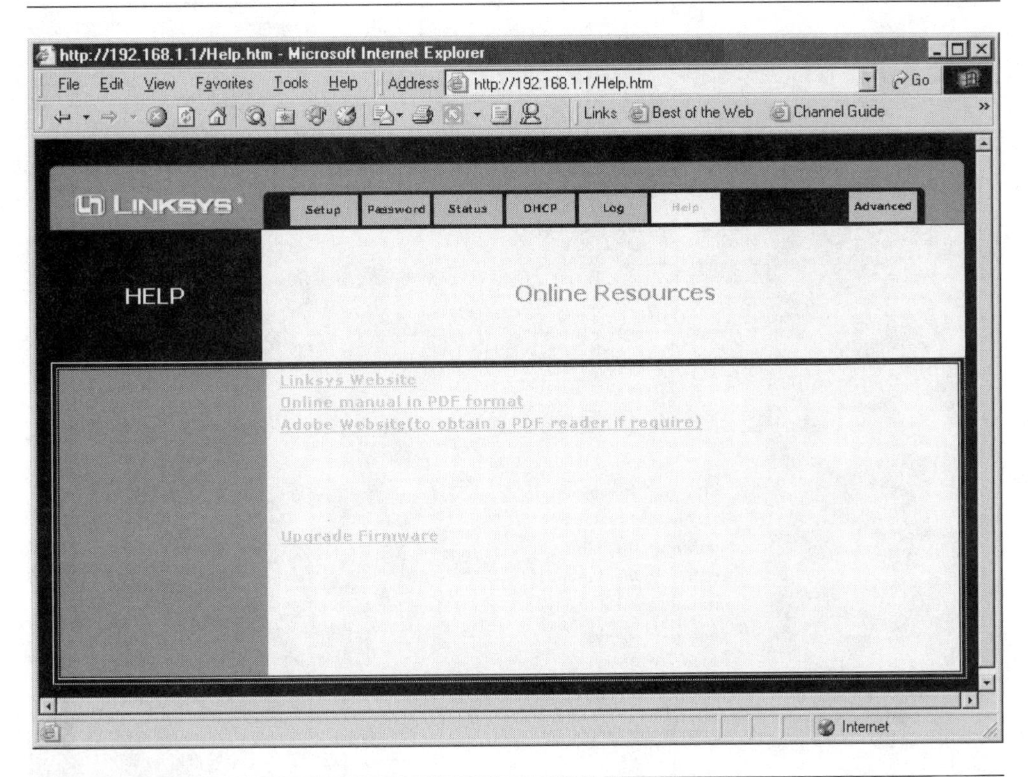

FIGURE 6-12 Click the appropriate link to get to the Linksys support pages.

and small business networks, but I'm going to offer brief descriptions of them because that gives you a better understanding about the way Internet communications work. (I believe that the more information you have about the way things work, the better off you are.) In addition, you may find a few options that are appealing to you as a way to enhance the security of your network or as a way to control network users.

Filtering Internet Traffic The Filters tab (see Figure 6-13) offers options you can use to enhance the security of traffic moving through your router. The Packet Filter option lets you deny access to certain types of traffic for specific computers. For example, you could establish a blockade against using certain protocols, such as FTP (File Transfer Protocol), so that a particular computer on your network can't download files from Internet servers. You can also establish blockades against certain Internet services in the other direction—forbidding computers on the Internet from sending particular types of data to a computer on the network.

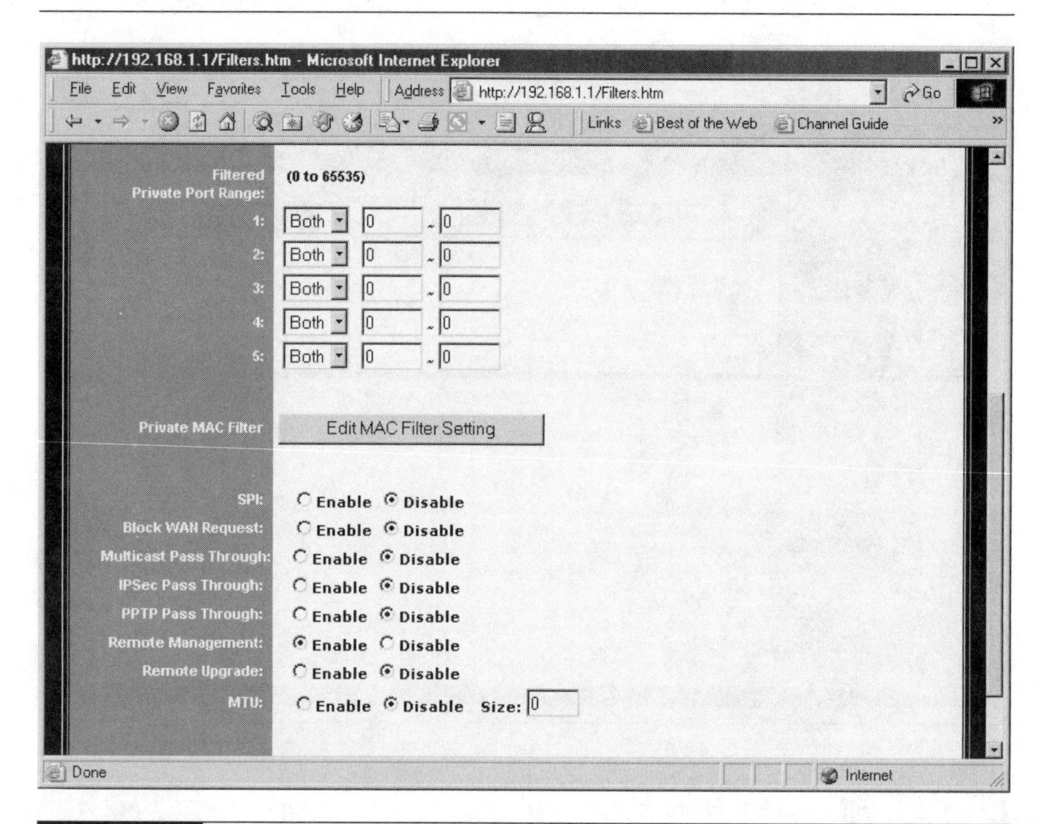

FIGURE 6-13 Tweak the router's settings with advanced options.

Even though I've only briefly described the way packet filtering can work, you can probably come up with several ways in which it would be helpful to use this technology to secure your network and control your network users. However, implementation requires a clear understanding of data types and the ramifications of restricting them—for home and small business networks, this is a job for a consultant (or detailed research) rather than a simple do-it-yourself task.

Forwarding Data Packets The Forwarding tab provides options that let you forward Internet traffic so that data intended for certain ports is intercepted and then forwarded to certain computers. These settings are useful if one of the computers on your network is actually running a service on the Internet (such as a Web server), which is highly unlikely (and often against your ISPs terms of service) for any small network—if you have a Web page, it's probably located on a server at a Web hosting company. To use forwarding, you will need to assign the computer that you wish to use an address that is outside of the DHCP scope (normally, this is 100–149); this means you can use the addresses 2–99 and 150–254.

Port forwarding can be used on only one PC at a time. In other words, you can forward a particular port only to one PC. If you need to forward a port to multiple ports, try port triggering.

Port Triggering Although port triggering is similar to port forwarding in opening ports, it works slightly differently. You can think of port triggering as a way to forward a port to a PC on your LAN, but only when the forwarding needs to happen. Here's an example of the difference between port forwarding and port triggering. With port forwarding, say you have incoming packets on port 12345 forwarded to IP address 192.168.1.20. All incoming packets to that port are forwarded to that address—all the time. With port triggering, the router waits until an outgoing request goes out on port 12345 and then "triggers" the router to open the incoming port range. (The triggered and incoming port ranges can be different or the same; if you're unsure which should be which, simply make them the same. You may also change the destination IP address.)

UPnP Forwarding This feature enables you to check which ports have been activated via UPnP. You can also manually forward ports here; however, it is not recommended.

Dynamic Routing The Dynamic Routing tab provides a way to make routing more efficient and has no effect on a router that's servicing a self-contained LAN. In large enterprises, where routers move data packets to remote servers in other physical locations, dynamic routing is a nifty technology, because you can instruct the router to find the quickest or cheapest way to move data.

Static Routing The Static Routing tab lets you set options that force routers to access other routers on your network in a specific way. Small networks don't use multiple routers, so you have no reason to use these options.

DMZ Host You can use the options on the DMZ Host tab to establish one of the computers on your network as a DMZ host.

A DMZ (Demilitarized Zone) is exposed to the Internet without any of the filtering and other protections the router may provide. For small networks, the DMZ can be useful for letting users perform actions that the router might normally prevent, such as playing certain interactive Internet games or participating in Internet conferences.

The DMZ is also a useful feature for a machine that is running multiple services such as HTTP and FTP. When using the DMZ, you do not have to forward multiple ports to that machine; simply put the machine into the DMZ.

NOTE

The DMZ does not disable the firewall completely. A computer in DMZ will still be under NAT (Network Address Translation). If you try to use a service that does not support NAT, it will not work through the DMZ.

MAC Address Clone The MAC Addr. Clone tab lets you change the MAC address of the router. A MAC address is a hardware-level ID number that uniquely identifies a hardware device. Some ISPs require you to register the MAC address of the device that's connected to the ISP. Before you installed your router, if you had a NIC in a computer to connect that computer to your DSL/cable modem—and therefore, to your ISP—the NIC's MAC address was registered with the ISP. After you installed your router, that router became the only connection your ISP sees, and its MAC address is not the one you originally registered with your ISP. Rather than go through a new MAC registration process with your ISP (not fun, unless you enjoy being transferred from technician to technician and spending a lot of time on hold), you can clone the original NIC's MAC address to your router. Your ISP will never know you changed the connection device.

TIP

If you ever do have to re-register your MAC address with your ISP, just tell the first technician you talk to that you got a new network adapter and need to register the MAC. The technician should transfer you to someone who can handle the request. If you are vague about what you want or tell them that you are having trouble with something, you'll end up spending more time on the phone as the primary technician walks you through a pre-written troubleshooting list.

To accomplish this, select the User Defined option and then enter the MAC address of the NIC that was originally connected to the DSL/cable modem. The tab displays the MAC address of the computer you're working on, so it's easiest to perform this task by accessing the router's Setup program (one of the CDs you received with the router) from the computer that was originally connected to the DSL/cable modem. Otherwise, check the Active IP Table, accessible using the DHCP Client Table button on the DHCP tab, to ascertain the MAC address of the computer that was originally connected to the ISP.

Connecting to Jacks

Almost any HomePNA adapter will have two RJ-11 phone plugs. On some adapters they will be labeled, as on a conventional modem, for "Line" and "Phone"; however, these plugs are interchangeable.

You have many options for wiring a home phoneline network, but basically a path through the phone wire must be present from every system on the network to every other system on the network. This path can be in the phone wires through the walls (see Figure 6-14) or it can just be a long wire that extends from one system to another (this is called *daisy-chaining*; see Figure 6-15). Once you accomplish this, you can use any free plugs to connect telephones, faxes, answering machines, or any other telephony device. You may also find it convenient to buy some phoneline splitter devices so you can run multiple phone wires.

Although it doesn't matter what rooms or floors the different phone outlets are in, they must be on the same phoneline. This means that they have a common junction at some point—at least at the point where the line enters the house.

NOTE *These phonelines must be conventional analog phonelines, not ISDN phonelines or digital PBX phonelines.*

Potential Interference Problems

Some very old telephone equipment creates noise in frequency ranges reserved for HomePNA equipment, preventing a reliable network connection. Some older home phone wiring cannot meet the signal requirements of HomePNA. If, after you install your HomePNA network equipment, you have connection problems with either the network equipment or your telephone equipment, you could be experiencing this problem.

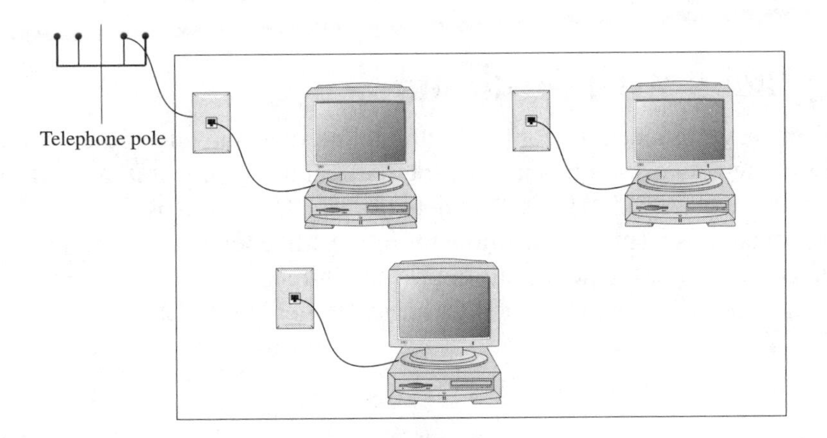

FIGURE 6-14 HomePNA adapters can use phone plugs in the same building if they are all on the same phoneline.

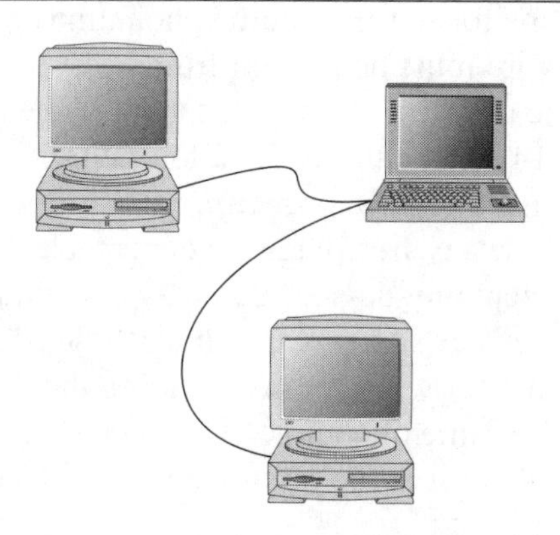

FIGURE 6-15 You can also daisy-chain HomePNA systems directly together. If all computers are in the same room, you don't even need to connect to a phoneline.

If you are having problems with your telephone equipment, an easy test is to unplug all the HomePNA equipment from the phone system and try the phones again. If the problem goes away, it was probably caused by the networking equipment.

If you are having problems with the HomePNA networking equipment, you should try unplugging telephone equipment from the lines, especially older telephone equipment, if you have any. Removing the phonelines from your walls is a bit much to ask.

See Chapter 12 for more on such troubleshooting techniques.

Sharing Jacks with Modems

Most users have a modem to connect with the Internet, and one of the main goals of most home networks is to share an Internet connection. But it's not all that uncommon for a user of a HomePNA network also to need to use a modem.

The situation is a simple one: modems are just like telephones and faxes, and you can connect your phonelines through your HomePNA adapters to modems, or from the phone jack on your modem into a HomePNA adapter.

Chapter 7

Plugging In to Electric Wires

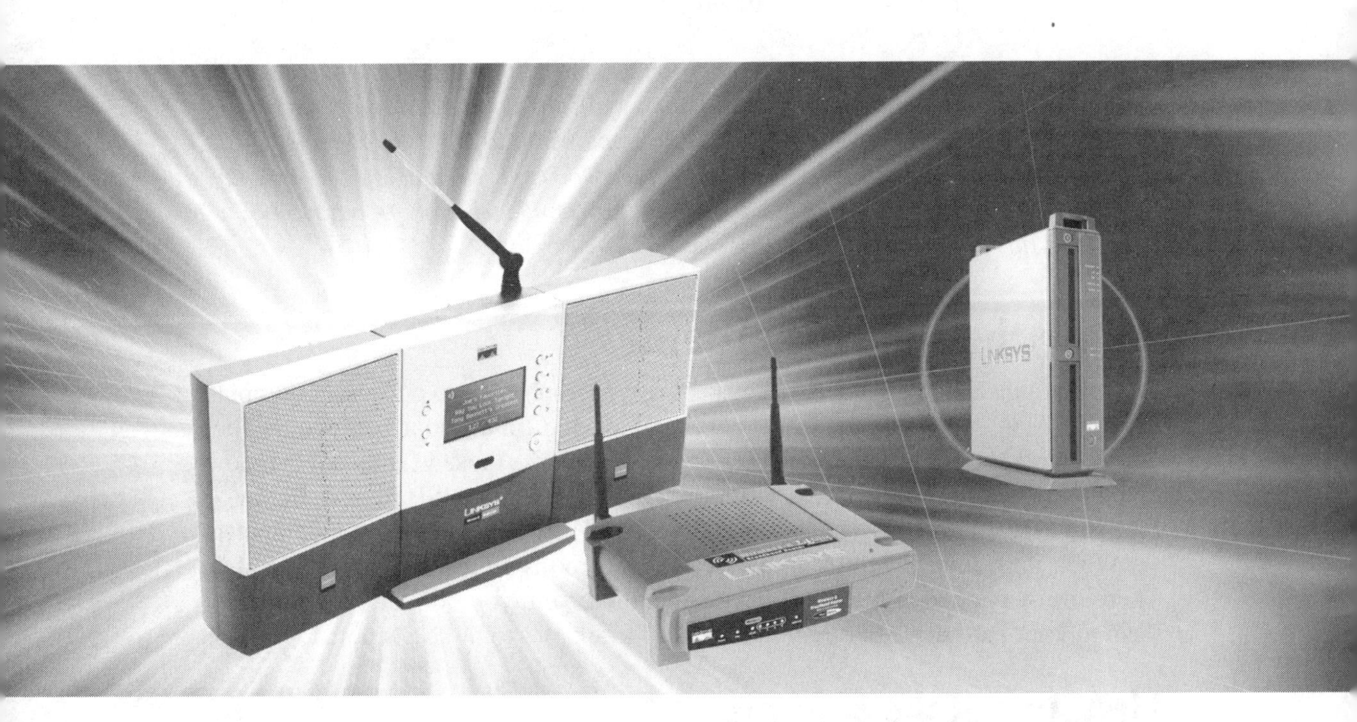

If you're loath to run cable through your home or office, an easy alternative is to connect your network by means of your existing powerlines. It's a safe bet that every room in your house or office has at least one electrical outlet, and it's a sure bet that any room you already chose to hold a computer has an electrical outlet. That convenience is certainly one of the attractions for choosing this network topology. The Linksys PowerLine Series provides networking that is incredibly easy to install. Two PowerLine products are available:

- **Instant PowerLine USB Adapter** can be installed on any computer that contains a USB port (including a laptop computer).
- **Instant PowerLine EtherFast 10/100 Bridge** can be used to connect your PowerLine network to an Ethernet device, such as a DSL/cable modem or router, to share the broadband access across the network. The bridge can also connect to a computer with an existing Ethernet network controller port. Most new computers have Ethernet ports built in, so this is a convenient way of not having to install additional drivers.

NOTE *Both of the Linksys PowerLine products are built to a PowerLine networking specification managed by an industry alliance named HomePlug, and you'll see subtle references to that name when using the products (for example, HomePlug is the default password set when using the built-in encryption with the Linksys products). You can learn more about HomePlug at http://www.homeplug.org.*

Installing the Network Adapter

The nifty thing about USB connections is that you don't have to open your computer to install them—and, in fact, you don't even have to turn off your computer. (They will not work, however, with Windows 95 or NT because those versions of Windows don't support USB.) As soon as you connect a device to a USB port, Windows Plug and Play wakes up and announces, "I've found new hardware on your computer."

When Plug and Play finds hardware, it wants to install the drivers immediately. Therefore, you need to have the drivers available, and you do that by installing them to your hard drive before you connect the adapter to the USB port.

First, Install the Software

You must install the software for your USB adapter before connecting the hardware to your computer. The software is on the CD that is in your USB adapter package.

The software has two components: drivers and a security program. (The security program is covered in the section "Securing Your PowerLine Network" later in this chapter.)

Insert the CD into your CD-ROM drive, and the installation program should launch automatically. If you've disabled the AutoRun feature that manages automatic startup of CD programs, you can start the installation program manually with either of the following actions:

- Choose Start | Run and enter **d:\setup.exe** in the text box (substitute the drive letter for your CD-ROM if it isn't *d:*).
- Open Windows Explorer or My Computer and display the contents of your CD-ROM drive; then double-click setup.exe.

The installation program is a wizard, which means you must click Next to move through the wizard's windows. The opening window displays a welcoming message, so click Next to get started with the installation program.

In the next window, enter your name and optionally enter your company name. If you're installing the USB adapter in Windows 2000 or Windows XP, you must also specify whether you want to make the adapter's drivers available to anyone who uses this computer or only to you whenever you log on to the computer. It would be rather unusual to limit the use of a network device to a single individual, so you should select the default option, which is to let anyone who logs on to the computer have access to the network.

The next wizard window displays the configuration settings you entered (your name and company name), as well as the location of the drivers on your hard drive (see Figure 7-1). You can click the Back button to change the user information, but you cannot change the destination folder for the software.

Click Install to begin the installation process. If you're running Windows 2000 or Windows XP, the system may display a warning message telling you that the driver does not have a proper digital signature. All this really means is that the driver has not been tested by Microsoft for compatibility. You do not need to worry about this, since your driver is coming from a reliable source (Linksys). Take the following action to indicate that you want to continue with installation:

- In Windows 2000, click Yes.
- In Windows XP, click Continue Anyway.

The wizard displays a progress bar as the software is installed to your hard drive (see Figure 7-2).

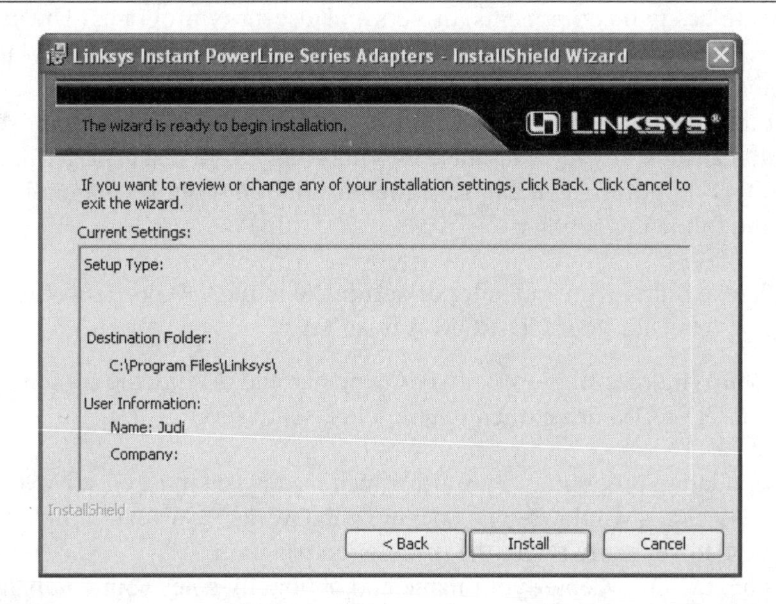

FIGURE 7-1 Your settings are displayed for your approval before the software is installed.

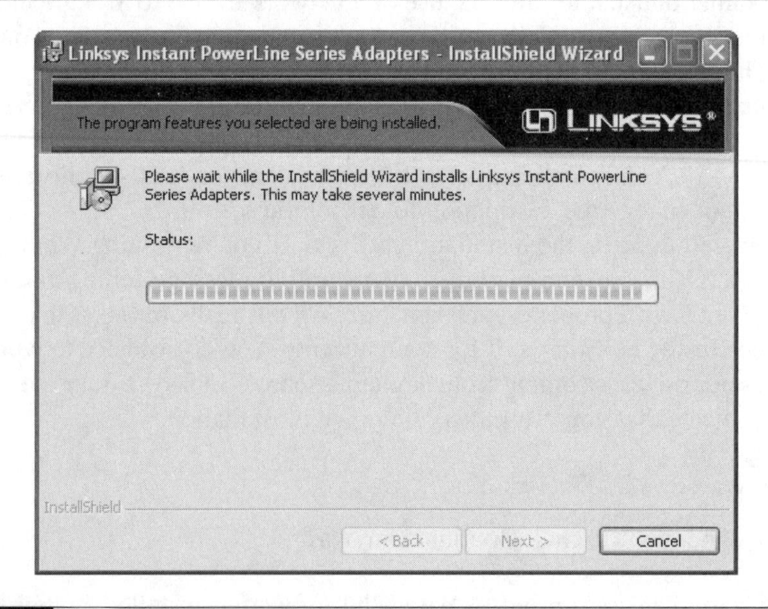

FIGURE 7-2 It takes only a minute or so to install the files on your hard drive.

After the files are copied, the wizard displays a message telling you that installation is complete. Click Finish. When the wizard displays a message telling you that you must restart the computer, click Yes.

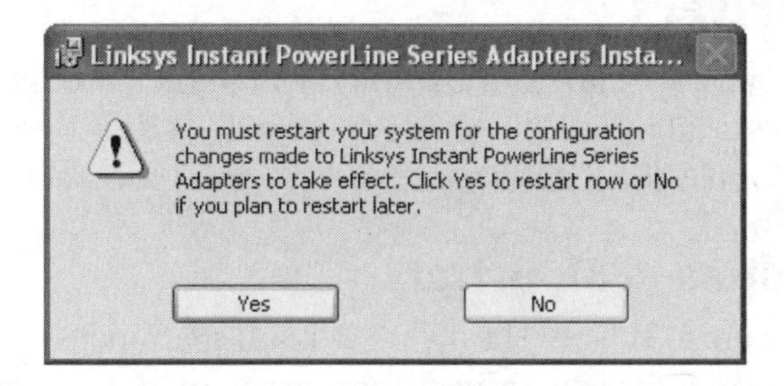

While Windows shuts down and restarts, you can prepare the hardware for the next step—the physical installation of your adapter.

Connect the USB Adapter

Your Linksys USB adapter has three components:

- The adapter itself
- A power cord
- A USB cable

The adapter has a connector at each end—one for the power cord and the other for the USB cable. Start by connecting the power cord and the USB cable to the adapter.

NOTE *USB cable has different connectors at each end. The Type A connector is a male rectangle, and it goes into the USB port on your computer (which is a female rectangle). The Type B connector is a small square, and it connects to the USB device—in this case, your Linksys network adapter.*

Connect the USB cable to the USB port at the back of your computer. Then plug the power cord into a wall outlet. (The USB adapter contains its own surge-protection technology, so you don't have to worry about plugging it into a surge protector.)

As soon as the cord is inserted into the outlet, Windows displays a message that the system has discovered new hardware. Now you're ready to install the

Windows drivers that you copied to your hard drive when you installed the software from your Linksys CD.

Install the Drivers

A wizard automatically appears to walk you through the process of installing the drivers for your USB adapter. The procedure varies slightly among Windows versions, and I'll discuss the details for each version in this section.

Installing Windows 98SE Drivers

Windows 98SE has an Add New Hardware Wizard that opens with a message saying that it will search for new drivers for your adapter. Click Next, and then follow these steps to install the drivers:

1. The wizard asks how you want to search for the drivers. Select the option Search For the Best Driver For Your Device (Recommended) and click Next.
2. Select the option Specify a Location. Then enter **c:\program files\linksys\usb drivers** in the location text box, or click the Browse button and navigate through the folders to reach that location (if you prefer clicking to typing). Then click Next.
3. The wizard displays a message telling you it has found the drivers and is ready to install them. Click Next.
4. The wizard asks you to insert your Windows 98 CD in the CD-ROM drive. After you insert the CD, click OK. (If you do not have the Windows 98 disk, then try c:\windows\options\cabs.)
5. When the wizard announces it has completed its task, click Finish.
6. Windows displays a message telling you that you have to restart your computer to complete the installation. Click Yes.

When Windows restarts, you can configure the adapter's network settings (IP address and other settings), which is covered in Chapter 8. After your adapter is set up, you must set up the security features (see "Securing Your PowerLine Network" later in this chapter).

Installing Windows Me Drivers

As soon as you plug in your new adapter, Windows detects its presence. The New Hardware Found dialog appears, asking for the location of the driver files. Enter **c:\program files\linksys\usb drivers** in the text box, or click Browse and then select that subfolder. Click OK, and when the drivers are installed, restart your computer.

When Windows restarts, you can configure the adapter's network settings (IP address and other settings), which is covered in Chapter 8. After your adapter is set up, you must set up the security features (see "Securing Your PowerLine Network" later in this chapter).

Installing Windows 2000 Drivers

Windows 2000 automatically senses the presence of the adapter and also automatically finds the drivers. The operating system displays a message telling you that the driver lacks a proper digital signature. This isn't a problem, so click Yes to install the drivers, and then restart the computer.

When Windows restarts, you can configure the adapter's settings (IP address and other settings), which is covered in Chapter 8. After your adapter is set up, you must set up the security features (see "Securing Your PowerLine Network" later in this chapter).

Installing Windows XP Drivers

Windows XP automatically senses the presence of the adapter and launches the Found New Hardware Wizard. The opening wizard window says you need the Linksys Installation CD, but you really don't (because you've already installed the drivers to your hard drive, right?). Click Next to begin using the wizard, following these steps:

1. Select the option Search For the Best Driver in These Locations, and also select the check box labeled Include This Location in the Search. Then enter **c:\program files\linksys\usb drivers**. Alternatively, you can click

the Browse button and locate that folder (if you prefer clicking to typing). Click Next.

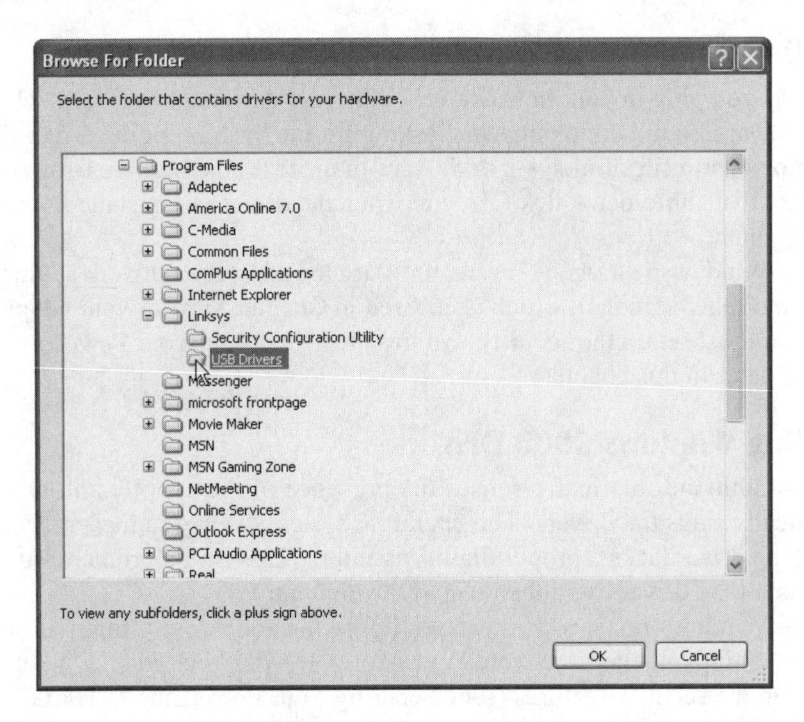

2. Windows displays a message telling you the driver isn't certified for the Windows Logo (don't worry—the driver is fine). Click Continue Anyway.
3. When the wizard announces the drivers have been installed, click Finish.
4. Restart the computer.

When Windows restarts, you can configure the adapter's network settings (IP address and other settings), which is covered in Chapter 8. After your adapter is set up, you actually have a working network—congratulations. However, before you pat yourself on the back, you must set up the security features (see the section "Securing Your PowerLine Network").

The PowerLine Adapter in Action

If you can see the USB adapter (sometimes the adapter is hidden from view behind your computer), you'll be able to tell what's going on by checking the lights:

- The Power light glows green when the adapter is powered on. If the light isn't lit, check the electrical outlet by plugging in a working device such as a lamp or clock. If the outlet is fine, and you think the problem may be with the adapter, contact Linksys support.
- The Link light glows green when the adapter is ready to interact with other computers. This green light should appear when the adapter is powered on, even if no other computers are attached to your network. If the light isn't lit, check the outlet, and if the outlet is fine, contact Linksys support.
- The Activity light glows green when the computer is exchanging data with other devices on the network.
- The Collision light flashes orange if a collision occurs on the network during an attempt to exchange data. A *collision* occurs when two computers try to send data to the same target at exactly the same time. You don't have to do anything, as both computers will try again, and the amount of time they wait is determined at random so it's unlikely they'll collide again. The flashing orange light is merely an indication that data collided and the system is taking care of the problem.

Securing Your PowerLine Network

When you use powerlines as your connection medium, you're sort of on a large peer-to-peer network that's centered at the transformer that supplies electricity to your home or office. Of course, that transformer also supplies electricity to other homes and offices. If anyone else in the area is using powerlines for networking, it's possible that one network could access data that's being transmitted across a different network. To prevent this, Linksys encrypts the data that's being transmitted on your network.

The range on PowerLine networks is short enough that people tapping into your PowerLine networks are not likely an issue if your network is a house or small office building. If you live in an apartment building and other tenants in the building also use PowerLine networks, it is possible that they would be able to intrude on your network. The encryption that Linksys uses does a good job of protecting your data as it is transmitted. Using a good firewall (read more about them in Chapters 8 and 9) and using good security techniques when sharing your files on the network (more about that in Chapter 10) also help keep your PowerLine network secure.

Understanding Encryption

Linksys uses Data Encryption Standard (DES) to encrypt your PowerLine network data. DES is a popular encryption scheme that uses secret keys that both the sending and receiving computers must know to decrypt data. A new key is created for each 64 bits of data, and DES technology chooses each key at random, from a pool of 72,000,000,000,000,000 (72 quadrillion) possible keys. This makes it statistically impossible for another set of computers to have the same keys at the same moment that those 64 bits of data are traveling through your network.

Running the Security Configuration Utility

The CD you used to install the Linksys PowerLine hardware drivers also installed a Security Configuration Utility. In fact, the installation process puts an icon for the security software on your desktop in addition to the listing on the Programs menu. You can configure the security features for each adapter on your network as soon as the following conditions are met:

- All the adapters are physically installed and plugged in.
- Drivers have been installed on each computer in the network.
- The adapters have been configured for IP addresses (see Chapter 8).

In fact, once these tasks are accomplished, you have a working network—it's just not secure, and you shouldn't begin sharing resources and transmitting data among your computers until you've guaranteed the security of those transmissions.

To add encryption to your network communications, follow these steps:

1. Double-click the Security Configuration Utility icon on your desktop (or choose the utility from the Programs menu). The Security Configuration Utility Wizard opens with a welcoming message. Click Next to get started.
2. In the Network Password field, enter the password you want to use for every computer on your network (see Figure 7-3). Your password must be between 4 and 24 characters (using any keyboard character except the space), and it's case sensitive.
3. Click Next to see the MAC address of the adapter that is now password-protected. When you move to the next computer and run the Security Configuration Utility, that computer's adapter is added to the list. The

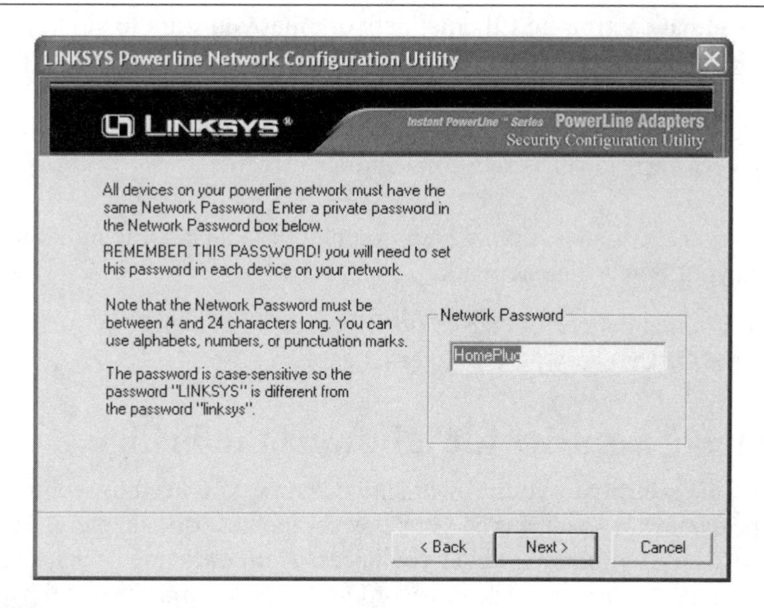

FIGURE 7-3 Linksys provides a default password, but you should replace it with a new password on all the computers on your network.

last computer you configure shows all the computers on your network that are protected with this password. (There's nothing you need to do with this data, it's just for your information.)

4. Click Next to see a congratulatory message on having successfully protected this adapter.
5. Click Finish.
6. Repeat these steps on every computer in your network, using the same password.

You now have a secure network. Congratulations!

Installing a Bridge to Connect to an Ethernet Device

If you want to connect your PowerLine network to an Ethernet device, you need to use a PowerLine bridge to cross the topology gap. The Ethernet device could be a hub or switch that controls an Ethernet network that you want to tap into, a router, a DSL/cable modem, or even an Ethernet print server. The bridge is particularly useful if you already have an Ethernet-based network and you are adding a computer to the network using PowerLine technology instead of running Ethernet cable to it.

The PowerLine bridge has two connectors:

- A PowerLine connection, which you plug into an electric outlet to have it join your PowerLine network.
- An Ethernet connector (RJ-45 port), which you connect to the Ethernet device via Category 5/5e/6 Ethernet cable.

Configuring Security for a PowerLine Bridge

To maintain the security of your PowerLine network, you need to secure the bridge in much the same way you secured your PowerLine network adapters. The bridge has a security utility program, which you access from the same Linksys CD you used to configure your adapter. The password for the bridge must match the password for each adapter on your network.

There's a small catch involved, however, because you can configure the bridge only if you've connected it to your PC via the bridge's Ethernet connector. To do that, you must have an Ethernet NIC in the computer. (Don't worry; this isn't as difficult or confusing as it may seem, and I explain everything in the next section, "Connecting the Bridge to Your Computer.")

You can opt to skip the configuration of the bridge. Skipping the configuration tasks affects only security; it doesn't interfere with the bridge's ability to communicate between your PowerLine network and your Ethernet devices. However, you'll have to alter the security settings for your network adapters so they match the bridge. Without configuration, the bridge maintains the default password (*HomePlug*), so you'll have to change the password of all your network adapters back to *HomePlug*. This may present a security risk if the following circumstances exist:

- Another network is using electric lines is in your area and is connected to the same transformer.
- That network is using the same password you're using. Under the laws of coincidence, this would occur only if the people who installed that network also use the default password—it's a real stretch to believe that another home or business would have created the same password you did.

Connecting the Bridge to Your Computer

If you want to communicate with the bridge to modify its settings, you must be able to access it, which requires an Ethernet connection between the bridge and the computer from which you're working.

Of course, because you opted for an electric line topology for your network, you didn't have any reason to purchase an Ethernet network adapter and install it in your computer. However, I've found that a majority of PowerLine networks have an Ethernet NIC in one of the computers, almost always as the result of one of the following:

- One computer (usually the newest computer on the network) came with an Ethernet NIC built in.
- After ordering DSL or cable Internet service, a technician installed an Ethernet NIC, or the ISP sent an Ethernet NIC along with installation instructions.

In fact, since it's most common to buy a bridge for the express purpose of hooking the PowerLine network to a DSL/cable modem or a router that connects to a DSL/cable modem, it's not unusual to find an Ethernet NIC you can use to configure the bridge.

If you don't have an Ethernet NIC, you can buy one—they're not expensive. To save yourself some work, make sure you get a USB Ethernet NIC; if you use an internal NIC, you have to open the computer and install it. In fact, you might be able to borrow a USB Ethernet NIC from someone; you need it only during the configuration process, and after that you can remove it and return it. Of course, if you want to reconfigure the bridge, you'll have to borrow it again.

Plug the bridge into an electrical outlet, and run Ethernet cable between the bridge's RJ-45 port and the Ethernet NIC on your computer. Then run the configuration program from the Linksys CD. The wizard (which assumes you've made the proper connections) walks you through the process of configuring the bridge with the password you're using for your network adapters. See, it's easy!

Connecting the Bridge to an Ethernet Device

After you've configured the bridge for password-protection, you no longer need to have the bridge connected to your computer. You've freed up the bridge's RJ-45 connector so it can be used to connect with the Ethernet device you want to add to your PowerLine network. Now it's time to make the connection. Just run Ethernet cable between the RJ-45 port on the bridge and the appropriate connection on the Ethernet device you're connecting to your network (see Figure 7-4).

The connection requires no work beyond plugging everything in—this is one of those gadgets that take care of themselves on automatic pilot. In computer jargon, we call this a "transparent" or "seamless" installation, which means that the user doesn't have to do anything to make it all work. As long as the password for the bridge is the same as the password for each network adapter, the bridge and the computers will find each other and communicate with the Ethernet device that's attached to the bridge's Ethernet port. Now your PowerLine network can share a DSL/cable Internet connection, access an Ethernet print server, or communicate with computers that are connected via Ethernet.

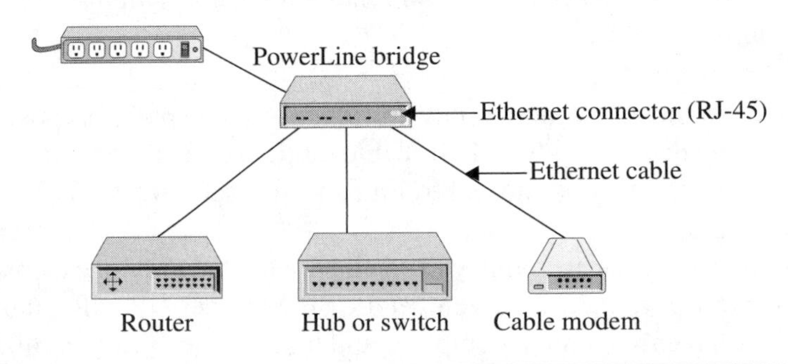

FIGURE 7-4 Connect your PowerLine network to an Ethernet device with the PowerLine bridge.

Chapter 8

Connecting Your Network to the Internet

After you've physically installed your networking equipment and the appropriate drivers on each computer, you still have several tasks in front of you, including making sure that all computers can communicate with one another and connecting your network to the Internet.

You can connect computers on a small network to the Internet in two ways:

- *Configure one computer with an Internet connection (telephone/DSL/cable modem) to share that connection with the other computers on the network.* To do this, you must make sure the Internet connection works on the primary computer and then use a built-in Windows feature named Internet Connection Sharing (ICS) to make the connection available to other computers. If you have a telephone modem Internet connection, using ICS will be your only choice.
- *Set up a hardware router that connects directly to your DSL or cable modem and then configure all the computers on the network to connect to that router.* While this method requires that you purchase an additional piece of equipment (a cable/DSL router), it offers a faster, more secure, and much more reliable connection than ICS. Personally, I recommend this option for all small networks.

NOTE *Actually, a third way exists, too. You could install a separate Internet connection on each computer. Of course, this method can get pretty expensive and complicated and really cancels out one of the big reasons you probably installed a network to begin with—to share a single Internet connection among all the computers.*

This chapter covers both using ICS to connect to the Internet and using a Linksys router. Since the ways that you configure the computers on the network differ depending on which Internet connection method you choose, I also talk about configuring client computers in each of these sections. Before getting started with that, however, you need to understand some important concepts that will help you when it comes time to set up the network.

Overview of Important Networking Concepts

I know you are eager to get your network configured and that sections on concepts can make people's eyes glaze over. However, you need to understand some important ideas before you dive in. I'll try to keep it short.

Protocols

A *protocol* is the language that computers use to send data, so it is important that each computer speak the same language. The most common protocol used is Transmission Control Protocol/Internet Protocol (TCP/IP), which is the protocol of the Internet and a native protocol in Windows operating systems. If you are configuring a home or small business network, you are going to be using TCP/IP. Although other protocols are available, none is as robust and flexible as TCP/IP, nor do the others support as many programs. TCP/IP is supported by every version of Windows. In fact, later versions, such as Windows 2000 and Windows XP, support *only* TCP/IP for most networking functions.

IP Addressing

On a TCP/IP network, every computer on the network must have a unique address, called an IP address, that distinguishes it from other computers on the same network. If you've worked with Windows, networks, or the Internet at all, you've probably seen an IP address, which looks something like the following:

192.168.001.104

The IP address is four numbers separated by periods (.). Each number can range from 0 to 255. The IP address is broken into two parts: one part (called a network ID) that identifies the network and one part (called a host ID) that identifies the computer on the network.

On a small network, every computer will share the same network ID, but each computer will have a different host ID. Another number, called a *subnet mask*, determines which portion of the IP address is the network ID and which portion is the host ID.

Here's how it works. Assume that a computer has the IP address 192.168.001.104 and the subnet mask 255.255.255.0. Line up these two numbers vertically, so that they look like this:

192.168.001.104
255.255.255.0

Each part of the IP address that matches the position of a *255* in the subnet mask is part of the network ID. Each part of the IP address that matches the position of a *0* in the subnet mask is part of the host ID. So in the example above, the network ID is *192.168.001* and the host ID is *104*.

On a small network, you will almost always see the subnet mask 255.255.255.0 being used, which means that the first three number groups in the IP address identify the network and the last number group identifies the computer. For example, on a small network, you might have four computers with the following IP addresses:

192.168.1.101
192.168.1.102
192.168.1.103
192.168.1.104

These addresses represent four computers (101, 102, 103, and 104) that are all on the same network (192.168.1).

Other variations on the subnet mask occur (such as 255.0.0.0 and 255.255.0.0) that you may encounter from the rare ISP. On large networks, you may even see custom subnet masks (such as 255.255.240.0), but that's a subject for another book.

Private Versus Public IP Addresses

The Internet is one, big TCP/IP network, so every device connected directly to the Internet must have its own IP address. This is called a *public address* because it is an address on the public Internet. If you have a single device attached to the Internet, that computer probably gets its public IP address automatically from your ISP.

If you have a small network, you will probably not have a public IP address for each computer on your network. Although many ISPs are happy to sell you a package that does provide public IP addresses for each computer, you really don't need it. The packages are considerably more expensive than having a single public IP address.

Instead, your small network will be a private network in which each computer has a private IP address that is part of a range of reserved addresses not found on computers connected directly to the Internet. A single computer or router on the network acts as a gateway between your network and the outside world. This device will be connected to the Internet and will have both a public IP address on the Internet and a private IP address on your network. You can think of this device (computer or router) as something like a switchboard operator at a business. The business may have one telephone number, but each employee in the business has a separate extension. The switchboard operator accepts the calls and switches callers to the appropriate extensions. In much the same way, all the network traffic between computers on your network and the Internet get routed through the gateway device (which is why it's usually called a router).

Dynamic Host Configuration Protocol (DHCP)

A computer on a network can get an IP address in two ways: you can assign one manually or you can let the computer obtain one automatically. Assigning IP addresses manually on a small network is not too big a chore once you understand how they work, but it does require some extra planning and effort, and there's really not much reason to bother with it except under special circumstances.

To obtain an IP address automatically, a network must have a special server known as a *DHCP server*. Your ISP has a DHCP server, so if you have a single computer that connects directly to the Internet, that computer can get its IP address from the ISP automatically (computers on the Internet need an IP address because the Internet is one big TCP/IP network).

On your private network, one device can act as a DHCP server and give out IP addresses to other computers on the network (a process known as *leasing*). If you are using ICS to share one computer's Internet connection with the rest of the network, the computer with the Internet connection acts as a DHCP server and provides IP addresses to the other computers on the network. If you are using a Linksys router to share an Internet connection, the router will act as a DHCP server. (In fact, the Linksys router will act as a DHCP server, leasing private IP addresses to other computers on the private network, and as a DHCP client, obtaining its own public IP from your ISP's DHCP server. You'll learn more about configuring this later in the chapter.)

NOTE

Many Linksys devices, including print and file servers, can also act as DHCP servers. It is important that you have only one DHCP server on your network, however. Fortunately, aside from routers, most Linksys products ship with this feature disabled.

If you're running Windows XP or Windows Me, you can configure the settings for a computer's network connection with the help of a wizard. The wizard can also configure ICS at the same time it sets up the adapter. See the section "Configuring the ICS Host Using the Windows Network XP/Me Wizard" for details.

In this chapter, I assume you want to share your Internet connection among all the computers on your network, so I don't cover the configuration of adapters in a network that doesn't have shared Internet access.

Using Internet Connection Sharing

If you're sharing your Internet connection with ICS, one computer has an Internet connection (telephone, DSL, or cable modem) and all the other computers access that connection through that computer. The computer that holds the modem is the *ICS host*, and all the other computers are the *ICS clients*.

Before you get started, you should make sure that your Internet connection is working on the ICS host computer. Then you should configure the network settings on the ICS host computer. The settings for the ICS host affect the settings for the client. If your ICS host computer is running Windows XP or Windows Me, a wizard is available for this task.

If the modem is a DSL or cable modem, the ICS host computer will contain two network adapters: one for the network and the other for the Internet connection. Each adapter must be configured for its role. If the Internet connection device is a telephone modem, the host computer doesn't contain a second network adapter. Instead of a second adapter, Windows installs a virtual connection called a *dial-up connection*. The modem is connected to the computer in one of the following ways:

- An internal modem has an RJ-11 port at the back of the computer. Use telephone cable to connect the port to the phone jack.
- An external modem is connected to the computer's serial port. Use telephone cable to connect the Line port at the back of the modem to the phone jack. Don't forget to plug the modem's power supply into an electrical outlet (or, even better, a surge protector).

Configuring the ICS Host Using the Windows Networking Wizards

If your ICS host computer is running Windows XP, you can use a wizard named the Network Setup Wizard to configure your network settings and your shared Internet connection. The wizard also creates a program for configuring the client computers and offers to copy the program to a floppy disk that you can run on the client computers. If you don't have a blank floppy disk, you can run the same program on the client computers from the Windows XP CD.

If your host computer is running Windows Me, you can use a wizard named the Home Networking Wizard to configure ICS, but I have experienced problems with this wizard. Go to *http://www.microsoft.com* and follow the links to the Windows Me section of the Knowledge Base. Enter **Network Wizard** in the search box to find all the articles on bugs, problems, and workarounds. Print the articles and use the information to solve any problems that occur.

In this section, I assume that you're using the Windows XP Network Setup Wizard. But if you're using the Windows Me Home Networking Wizard, the wizard windows are similar.

If the latest version of Windows on your network is Windows 98SE, and you're using a Windows 98SE computer as the ICS host, you don't have a wizard. See the section "Configuring the ICS Host in Windows 98SE" later in this chapter.

Configuring the ICS Host

In this section, I go over the steps for setting up your network by using the wizard on the Windows XP computer that has the Internet connection. I assume the settings for the telephone/DSL/cable modem have already been established, following the instructions from your ISP. Now, follow these steps to have the wizard set up your network and share the Internet connection (click Next to move through the wizard windows):

1. Choose Start | All Programs | Accessories | Communications | Network Setup Wizard to launch the wizard, which opens with a welcome message. Click Next.
2. The next wizard window presents a checklist for the tasks you should have completed before running this wizard (installing hardware and setting up the modem). Click Next.
3. Select the option that establishes this computer as the Internet connection host (see Figure 8-1).

NOTE *If your network card is disconnected, disabled, or not yet configured with drivers, you will see a warning here that lets you choose the NIC you want to use and allow the wizard to proceed by ignoring the fact that the connection's not working.*

4. Select the device that connects this computer to the Internet. The device is either a NIC attached to a DSL/cable modem, a wireless connection, or a dial-up connection for a telephone modem.
5. The next window begins the configuration for your LAN. Name the computer, and optionally enter a description (see Figure 8-2). The computer name must be unique on the network. Click Next.

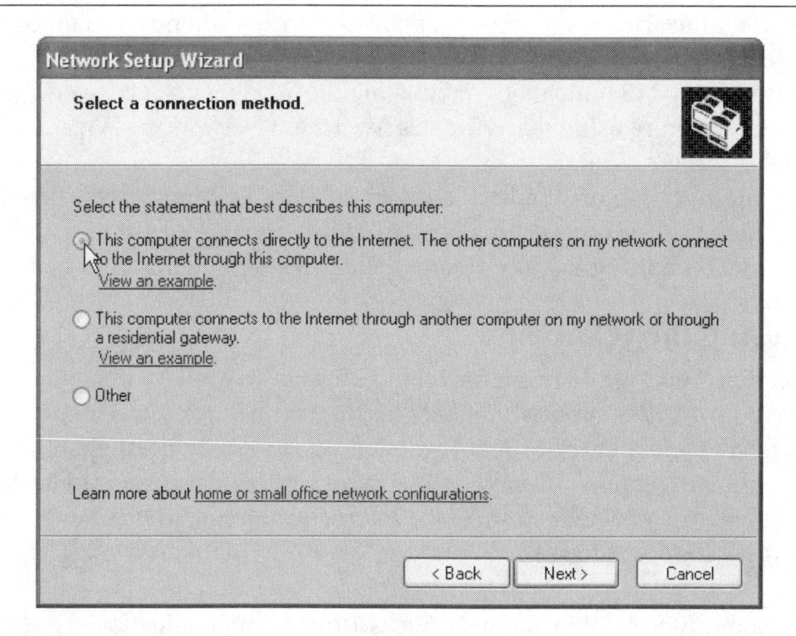

FIGURE 8-1 Tell the wizard that this computer is the ICS host.

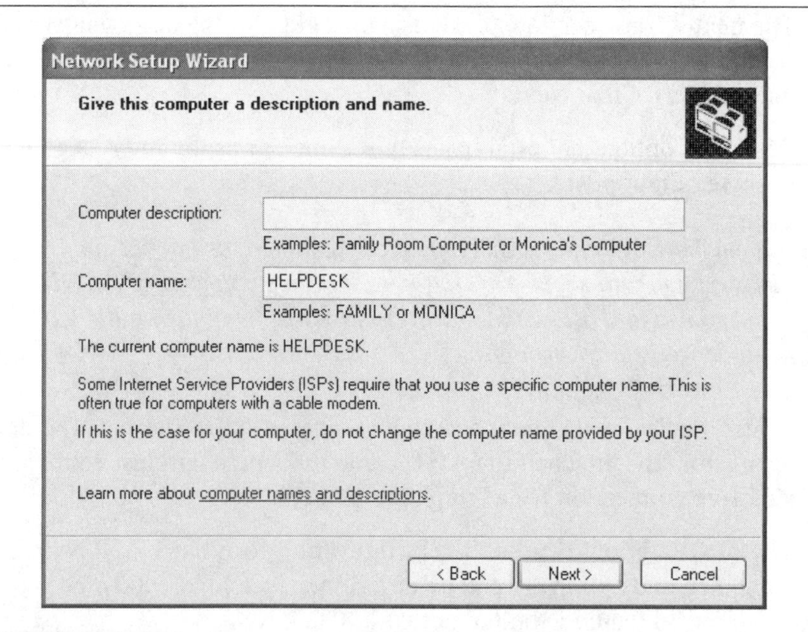

FIGURE 8-2 Each computer on the network must have a unique name.

6. Name the workgroup, which is the name you're giving your network. All the computers on the network must use the same workgroup name. You can use the name Windows suggests (MSHOME) or change the name to one you prefer. Click Next.

NOTE *If you are running Windows XP with Service Pack 2 installed, an additional page at this point will ask whether you want to turn on or off File and Printer Sharing. Turning this option on tells Windows Firewall that you want to allow other people on your network to access shared printers and files on your computer. Turning it off prevents any access to shared resources. Whichever option you choose, you can change it later. See Chapter 9 for more information about Windows XP Service Pack 2 and Windows Firewall. See Chapters 10 and 11 for more information about sharing files and printers on the network.*

7. The wizard displays a summary of all your selections. Click Back if you want to return to one of the previous windows and change an option. Otherwise, click Next to install the network and Internet connection settings. Follow the wizard prompts to complete the setup process.

The wizard sets up the files and settings, which takes a few moments, and then asks how you want to set up the other (client) computers (see Figure 8-3).

The easiest way to set up the client computers is to select the option Create a Network Setup Disk. The wizard installs a wizard setup program for client computers on a floppy disk. You can use the floppy disk on any version of Windows except Windows 2000.

Understanding TCP/IP Settings on the Host Computer

When you run the Network Setup Wizard on the host computer, you establish that computer as the DHCP server for your internal network. Since the ICS host has two network connections (one that is connected to the Internet and one that is connected to the private network), the ICS host also has two IP addresses—a public address for the Internet connection and a private address for the local network connection.

For the private address, Windows assigns the host computer the private IP address 192.168.0.1 (this is an assigned address that does not change). The ICS host then acts as a DHCP server, providing the client computers with their own private IP addresses automatically. You can see this private address by right-clicking the icon for the Local Area Network connection (the connection on the private

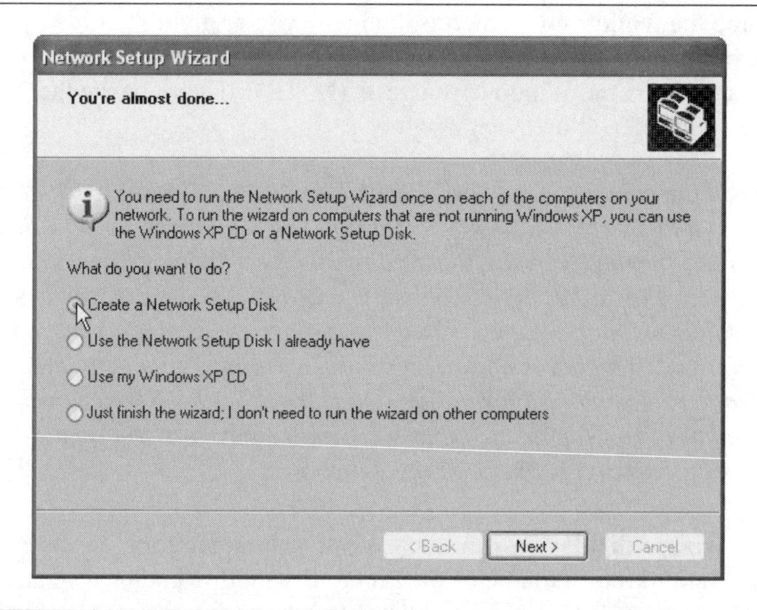

FIGURE 8-3 Select an option for setting up the ICS client computers.

network) and choosing Properties. Select the listing for Internet Protocol (TCP/IP) and click the Properties button to see the dialog shown in Figure 8-4. As you can see, the ICS host has the static IP address 192.168.0.1, which is assigned when you run the Network Setup Wizard.

The public address is assigned by your ISP and was configured when you set up the ICS host with Internet access. The Internet connection, which is either another network adapter (for a DSL or cable modem) or a software dial-up connection (for a telephone modem), usually does not have a fixed IP address. The ISP assigns the public address for this connection, while you're connected, so the correct TCP/IP setting is Obtain an IP Address Automatically. Click OK to return to the Internet Connection's Properties dialog box and then click OK again to close that dialog box and return to the Network Connections window.

To check the settings of your Internet connection, in the Internet Connections window, right-click the icon for the Internet connection and choose Properties. Then open the Properties dialog for TCP/IP as follows:

- For an adapter (DSL/cable modem connection), select the listing for Internet Protocol (TCP/IP) and click the Properties button.

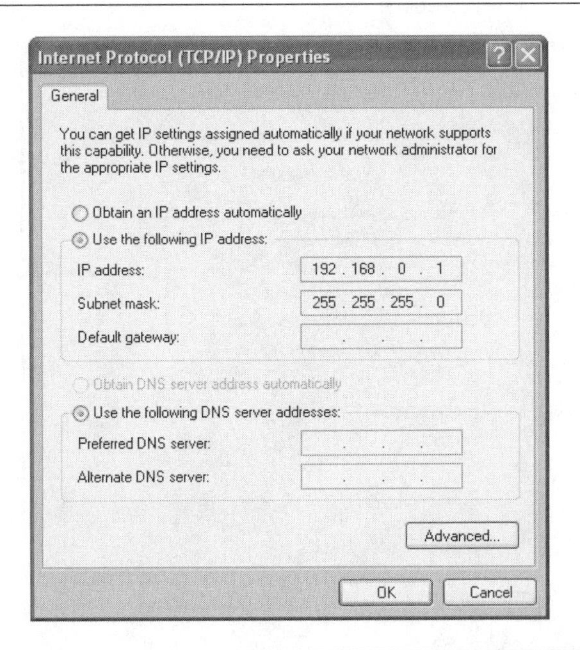

FIGURE 8-4 The wizard assigns a private IP address to the LAN connection on the ICS host.

- For a dial-up connection, take either of the following steps:
  - In Windows XP, go to the Networking tab, select the Internet Protocol (TCP/IP) listing, and click Properties.
  - In Windows 98SE/Me, go to the Server Type tab and click the TCP/IP Settings button.

Unless your ISP provided a public IP address for each computer on your network, only the host computer gets its public IP address from an ISP, so the settings for the Internet connection device are configured to obtain an IP address automatically (see Figure 8-5). If your ISP did provide public addresses, see the section "Configuring the Computers for Static IP Addresses" later in this chapter.

Configuring the ICS Host in Windows 98SE

If your network is made up of computers running Windows 98SE, you have to set up a host computer for the shared Internet connection, and you have to configure the other network settings. Windows 98SE does not have a wizard to help you set

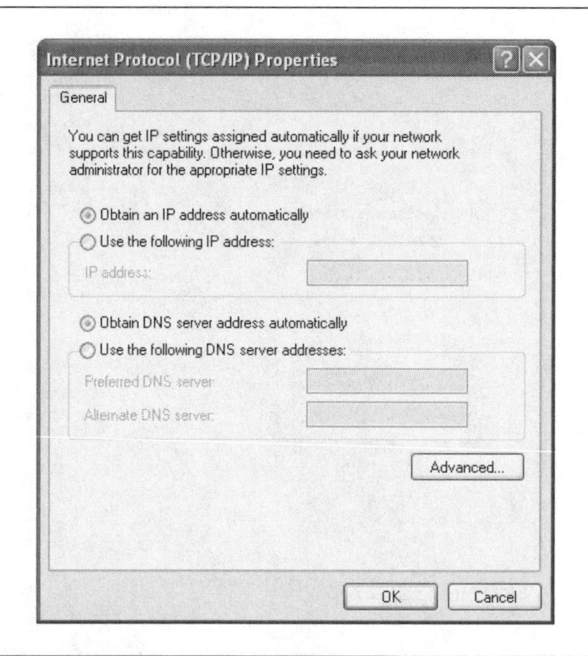

FIGURE 8-5 For an Internet connection, the ISP usually provides the IP address automatically.

up the network, but it does have a wizard to help you set up ICS. In this section, I cover the following topics:

- How to run the ICS Wizard on the host computer
- How to set up the client computers to share the Internet connection on the host
- How to set up the other network components on all the computers (host and clients)

Even if you have a Windows XP computer on your network, you need to configure a Windows 98SE computer as the Internet connection host if your telephone/DSL/cable modem is connected to a Windows 98SE computer and you don't want to move it to the Windows XP computer.

CAUTION *You must configure the host computer first, regardless of whether the client computers are running Windows 98SE or Windows XP.*

Installing Windows 98SE ICS

Windows 98SE ICS isn't installed by default when you install the operating system, so you must add it by following these steps:

1. Put the Windows 98SE CD in the CD drive, and if it automatically starts the Setup program, click Cancel. You aren't installing Windows 98SE; you just need to install some files from the CD.

TIP *You can stop the AutoRun feature by holding down the* SHIFT *key for a moment after you insert the CD.*

2. Choose Start | Settings | Control Panel to open Control Panel.
3. Double-click Add/Remove Programs.
4. Select the Windows Setup tab.
5. Scroll through the list and select Internet Tools—don't put a check mark in the check box; just select (highlight) the listing.

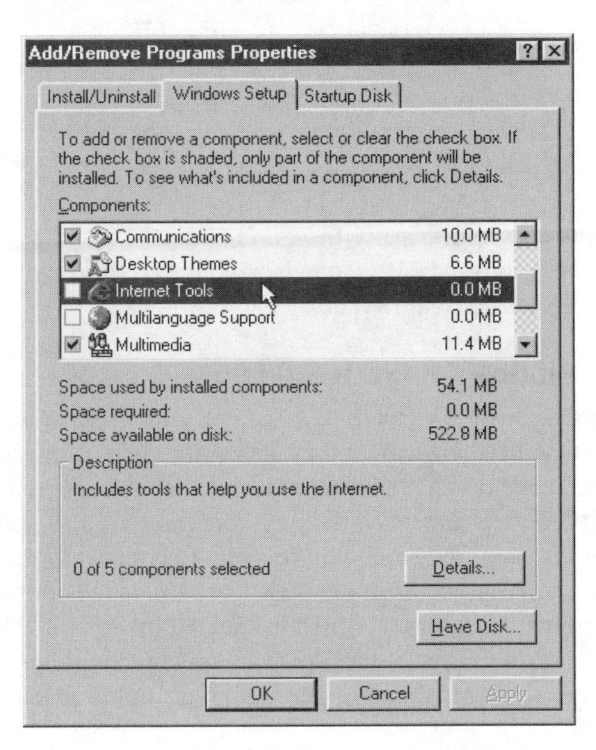

6. Click the Details button.
7. Place a check mark in the check box next to Internet Connection Sharing.

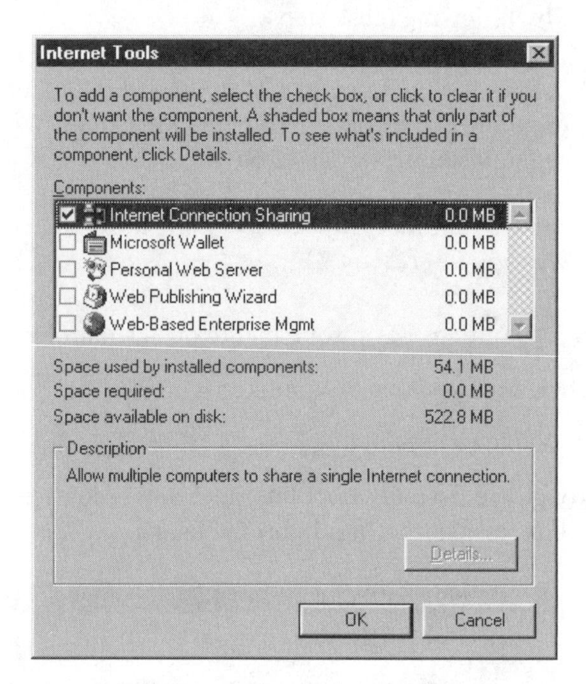

8. Click OK twice.

Windows transfers the necessary files, and when the installation process is complete, the system automatically launches the ICS wizard (which is actually called the Internet Sharing Setup Wizard).

Running the Windows 98SE ICS Wizard

The ICS wizard opens with a welcoming message; click Next to begin setting up the host computer. In the first wizard window, select the type of Internet connection device (telephone modem or DSL/cable modem) that's connected to the computer.

In the next window, the wizard displays the modem(s) installed on the computer. Select the specific device you're using to connect to the Internet.

If you're using a dial-up connection, the wizard offers the option Automatically Dial When Accessing the Internet, which is enabled by default. This means that when anyone opens browser or e-mail software on any computer on the network, the dial-up connection automatically opens and dials out to reach your ISP. If you disable this option, when anyone on the network wants to connect to the Internet, somebody has to be at this computer to launch the dial-up connection manually.

The wizard offers to create a client setup program on a floppy disk, so you can set up the Internet connection on the client computers. Put a blank floppy disk in the floppy drive and follow the prompts to create the client program. You could also set up the client computers manually—see the section "Configuring TCP/IP Settings Manually" later in this chapter.

Click Finish in the last wizard window. The wizard displays a message telling you the settings won't take effect until you restart your computer. Click Yes to restart.

Checking IP Addresses on the Windows 98SE Host

After your computer restarts, open the Network applet in Control Panel to see the changes ICS made to your setup. You'll see additional entries in the list of components, and they're all related to your ICS settings. For example, Figure 8-6 shows the new entries for a Windows 98SE host computer that connects to the

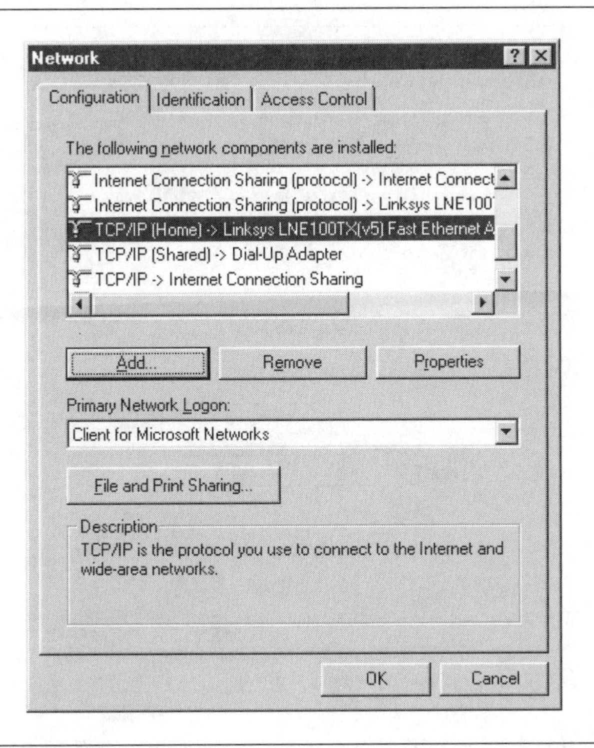

FIGURE 8-6 In Windows 98SE, ICS adds network components to your system.

Internet with a telephone modem. If your computer has a second adapter connected to a DSL/cable modem, you'll see entries for that adapter as well.

TIP

When you're viewing network properties in Windows 98SE, and you don't make any changes, always click Cancel instead of OK to close the windows. Windows 98SE isn't as sophisticated an operating system as Windows XP, and it always tries to install files from your Windows 98SE CD when you click OK (even if you haven't made any configuration changes).

Check the IP address for the network by selecting the TCP/IP component for the network adapter and then clicking Properties. As you can see in Figure 8-7, the host computer has a static IP address. For your LAN, the host computer becomes the DHCP server, and the client computers will get their network IP addresses from the host.

If you check the TCP/IP Properties for the Internet/dial-up adapter, you'll see that no IP address is assigned. Instead, you get your Internet IP address from your ISP.

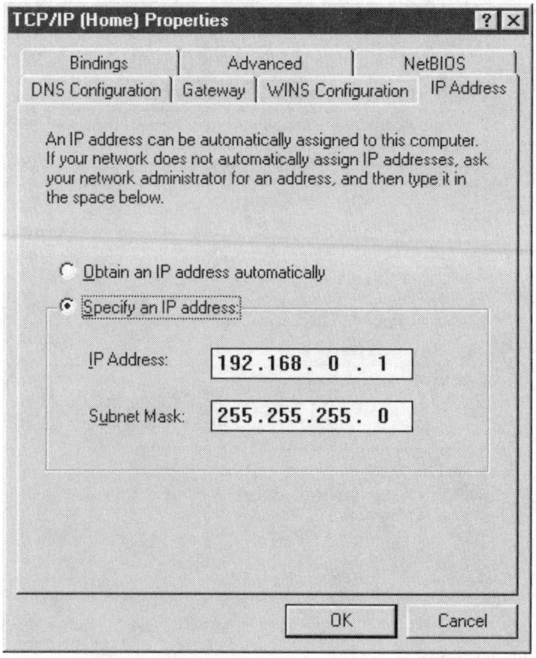

FIGURE 8-7 In Windows 98SE, the host computer also gets a static IP address.

Configuring ICS Client Computers

After you've set up the host computer to share its Internet device, you need to set up all the other computers (the clients). Make sure the original Windows CD for each computer is handy, because you may be asked to insert it so the system can copy files for setting up network services.

Using the Windows XP/Me Wizard on Client Computers

If you used the Windows XP/Me wizard to set up an ICS host, you can use the wizard for all client computers except those running Windows 2000. Launch the wizard in one of the following ways, and then follow the prompts to install the network files and configure the system:

- If you created a floppy disk for this purpose, insert the disk in the floppy drive, open Windows Explorer or My Computer to access drive A, and then double-click the file (netsetup.exe).
- If you're using the Windows XP CD, insert it in the CD drive. When the opening window appears, choose Perform Additional Tasks, and then choose Set Up Home or Small Office Networking.

NOTE *If you use the Windows XP CD and the opening window doesn't appear automatically, you must start the wizard manually. From My Computer, double-click the icon for the CD drive, and then double-click Setup.exe.*

Using the Windows 98SE ICS Wizard on Client Computers

The way you configure clients to communicate with a Windows 98SE host varies, depending on the version of Windows on each client.

For Windows 9*X*/Me computers, you can use the floppy disk you created with the ICS wizard. Put the floppy disk in the floppy drive and open Windows Explorer. Select the floppy drive and double-click Icsclset.exe. Then follow the prompts to set up the client computer.

For Windows XP client computers, you can use the Windows XP Network Setup Wizard and choose the option This Computer Connects to the Internet Through Another Computer on the Network. Then follow the prompts to finish setting up the Internet connection.

For Windows 2000, you must configure the IP address manually. (In fact, you can configure any client computers manually.)

Configuring TCP/IP Settings Manually

ICS client computers have just one adapter to configure—only the host has a second adapter for the Internet connection. Client computers need only Local Area Network settings, because to get to the Internet they have to connect only to the host. Use the following steps to configure the network adapter settings:

1. Open the Properties dialog for the network adapter (the steps vary, depending on the version of Windows).
2. Select the TCP/IP listing from the list of components and click Properties. (If TCP/IP isn't on the list of installed network components, see the next section, "Installing TCP/IP on Windows 98SE.")
3. If the option Obtain an IP Address Automatically is already selected, you don't have to do anything. If that option is not selected, select it now and click OK.

Windows copies the files it needs from the Windows CD; then you must restart the computer.

TIP *If you want to configure ICS clients to use a static IP address (instead of obtaining one from the ICS host), you can do so. Configure the client with an IP address that has a network ID of 192.168.0 and a host ID of anything between 1 and 254 that isn't already used on another computer (remember the network ID is the same on all computers, but the host ID must be unique). So, a valid IP address might be 192.168.0.23. Configure the client computer to use a subnet mask of 255.255.255.0 (to identify the network ID portion of the IP address correctly). Finally, configure the client to use a gateway address that matches the IP address of the ICS host (which is always 192.168.0.1). This tells the client to send data destined for the Internet to the ICS host first.*

Installing TCP/IP on Windows 98SE

Unlike Windows 2000/XP, Windows 98SE doesn't automatically install TCP/IP when you install a network adapter. If TCP/IP isn't on the list of installed network components, follow these steps to install it (you'll need to have your Windows 98SE CD at hand):

1. On the Configuration tab of the Network Properties dialog, click Add to open the Select Network Component Type dialog.

2. Select Protocol and click Add.
3. In the Manufacturers (left) pane, select Microsoft; then select TCP/IP from the Network Protocols (right) pane.
4. Click OK and follow the prompts to close the dialogs and transfer the files from the Windows CD.

Configuring Other Windows 98SE Network Components

Windows 98SE doesn't offer a network setup wizard—only an ICS wizard that establishes TCP/IP settings for your shared Internet connection. As a result, you must configure network components manually. Put your Windows 98SE CD in the CD drive. (If it automatically starts the Setup program, close that window, because you're not setting up the operating system—you only need to fetch some files from the CD.) Then begin installing and configuring network components as described in the following sections.

Enable File and Print Sharing

To participate in a network, a computer must be configured to share its resources. (To learn how to select the specific resources you want to share, see Chapter 11.) Click the File and Print Sharing button to display the File and Print Sharing dialog, and enable the file sharing feature. If the computer has a printer attached, also enable the printer sharing feature.

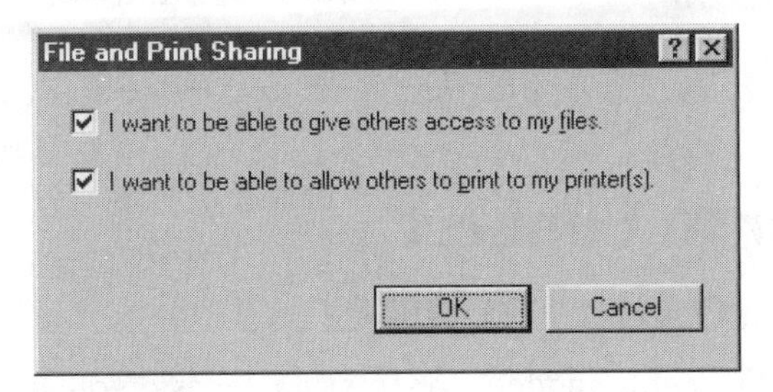

Click OK to return to the Network Properties dialog.

Enable Network Logon

In the Primary Network Logon drop-down list in the Network Properties dialog, select Client for Microsoft Networks as the logon option for this computer. (The other choice on the list, Windows Logon, refers to logging on to this computer when you start Windows, instead of logging on to the network.) The choice is available only if Client for Microsoft Networks is listed as an installed component. If you don't see Client for Microsoft Networks in the list of installed network components, you'll have to add it, as follows:

1. Click Add to open the Select Network Component Type dialog.
2. Select Client and click Add.
3. In the Manufacturers pane, select Microsoft; then select Client for Microsoft Networks from the Network Clients pane.
4. Click OK and then follow the prompts to return to the Network Properties dialog.
5. Click OK to let Windows copy the appropriate files from the Windows 98SE CD.
6. Restart the computer.

Identify the Computer on the Network

Click the Identification tab to make sure the computer's name and the name of your network workgroup are accurately entered. You can also optionally enter a description of the computer, which users on other computers will see when they open Network Neighborhood or My Network Places.

The Access Control tab on the Network Properties dialog enables password protection for shared folders and other resources. See Chapter 11 to learn about creating and password-protecting shared resources.

Using a Router to Connect Your Network to the Internet

If you're using a DSL/cable modem for Internet access, you should think about installing a router instead of running ICS. A router ties your Internet connection to your local network. Routers also provide a number of functions that benefit small networks and make network administration easy. For example, when you have a router, all the computers on the network can access the Internet all the time (with ICS, if the host computer is not running, none of the other computers can access the Internet). In addition, some of the Linksys routers include security features such as a firewall (see Chapter 9). All Linksys routers can act as DHCP servers, providing IP addresses to the computers on your network. In addition, you can buy a Linksys router with a built-in hub or switch. This means that with one device, you can connect all of your computers together on your LAN and connect your LAN to the Internet.

Connecting the Router to Your Network

Connecting a router to your network is quite easy, and very logical, although the steps vary, depending on the topology you've used to connect your network. The important logic is that the router sits between two networks: your LAN and the Internet (see Figure 8-8). All the computers on your network use the router to get to your ISP and then on to the rest of the Internet. The ISP and all the Internet users only "see" the public IP address of the router and not the private IP addresses of the computers on your network (we refer to these computers as being *behind* the router).

In the following sections, I go over the connection processes for routers. I assume the modem is already connected to the appropriate connection—the coaxial cable (for cable modems) or the phoneline that has your DSL connection.

Connecting Ethernet Routers

An Ethernet router has a number of ports, which you use to make all the connections you need. Use the WAN port to connect the router to the LAN port on your DSL/cable modem, using Ethernet cable. The modem's port may not be labeled "LAN" (it may say "Computer"), but you're looking for the port that connects the router to a computer. If the modem had previously been connected to a computer (before you installed a network), the connection to the router replaces the original connection to the computer. As far as the modem is concerned, the router is going to act like the computer with the Internet connection.

NOTE

WAN means Wide Area Network, which is a term that's usually applied to a network that's spread across multiple locations. While the router doesn't really create a WAN all by itself, it does provide a connection point between multiple networks—your network and the Internet.

Depending on the model you purchased, your router either has a single LAN port (for connecting to a separate hub or switch) or multiple numbered ports (if the router has a built-in hub or switch). These are the ports you use to connect your network to the router.

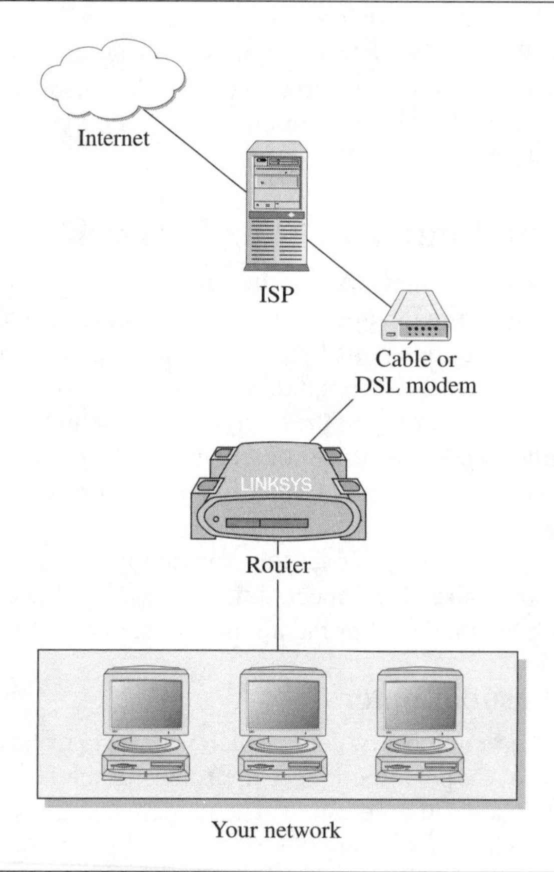

FIGURE 8-8 The router sits between your network and the Internet.

If the router has a single LAN port, connect that port to a port on your hub or switch, using Ethernet cable. Notice that the router has a Crossover Switch, which controls the wiring of the LAN port. The Crossover Switch sets the mode of the LAN port either to crossover (marked *X*) or straight-through (marked *II*). The choices relate to the way the cable pins meet at the connector. Regular Ethernet cable—the cable you use to connect computers to hubs—is straight-through cable.

If you are connecting the LAN port to the Uplink port in a hub or switch, select the crossover mode. If you're connecting the LAN port to a regular port in a hub or switch, select straight-through. You can buy special crossover cables that do the same thing as the X mode in this switch, but the switch makes it easier to create a proper connection using normal straight-through cable.

If the router has multiple numbered ports, you can use the router as a concentrator (which saves you the expense of buying a separate concentrator). Connect each computer to one of the numbered ports, using Ethernet cable. If you already have your computers connected to a hub or switch, use Ethernet cable to connect the hub/switch to one of the numbered ports.

Connecting a Router to a Wireless Network

If you have a wireless network, you can use either a wireless router or an Ethernet router to share your Internet connection. Connect the modem to the WAN or Internet port (the label differs depending on the router model) using Ethernet cable. If the modem had already been connected to one of the computers on the network, just move the connection from the computer to the router.

TIP *Linksys also provides devices such as the Wireless-G Broadband Router with SpeedBooster (model WRT54GS), which provide a cable/DSL router, wireless access point, and multi-port Ethernet switch all in one device. This is a great choice if you are starting your network from scratch and think you may eventually use both wired and wireless connections.*

Your wireless-equipped computers connect to a wireless router (providing the computers' network adapters are configured correctly, as covered later in the section "Configuring the Router").

If you have any Ethernet connections on your network (perhaps some computers are attached to a concentrator, while other computers use wireless and are connected with an access point), you can use an Ethernet router on your wireless network.

NOTE *Linksys wireless routers have built-in access points and Ethernet ports, so you can use the router as a hub to connect computers with Ethernet NICs, wired print servers, or other wired devices.*

Connecting a Router to a PhoneLine Network

Linksys makes a PhoneLine router for your PhoneLine network, or, if you have a PhoneLine bridge, you can use a standard Ethernet router (see Chapter 6 to learn about PhoneLine bridges).

To connect the PhoneLine router to your network, use Ethernet cable to connect the modem to the WAN port. Then connect one of the PNA ports on the router to a phone jack. If no phone jack is available (perhaps a computer is using the only phone jack), you can daisy-chain the router to a computer by using both

PNA ports (covered in Chapter 6). The PhoneLine router also has a telephone jack you can use to connect a phone instrument, so you can chat on the telephone while you're working on the computer.

Connecting a Router to a PowerLine Network

If you have a PowerLine network, you'll need an Ethernet router and a bridge to connect the two topologies. Connect the router to the modem and to the bridge, and then connect the bridge to a power outlet. See Chapter 7 to learn about PowerLine bridges.

Configuring the Router

I'm not going to discuss individual router models when walking you through the configuration steps, because you can refer to the user guide that came with your router for configuring specific features. For example, a router that provides firewall or Virtual Private Network (VPN) services has configuration tasks that other routers don't require.

Before you configure your router, disable any Internet-sharing features you might have set up (such as ICS or proxy server features). Linksys also recommends that you turn off all network devices when you add a new device to the network.

Regardless of the topology or the model, all routers require similar configuration efforts. Because a router sits between two networks, you must configure settings for each side of the router—the side that connects to your LAN and the side that connects to the Internet. Because the router acts as a DHCP server, make sure all the computers on your network have their TCP/IP settings configured to obtain an IP address automatically (unless you're using static IP addresses, in which case, see the section "Configuring the Computers for Static IP Addresses" later in this chapter).

Your router came with a CD that includes a setup program, but you can use your browser instead of the setup software to configure the device. I cover the browser-based configuration here, and if you use the software instead, you may find some minor differences. I don't cover all the screens available for configuration—just the basics. For the screens I omit, check the user guide that came with your router.

You can configure the router from any computer on the network that's connected to the router. Open your browser and enter the router's default IP address into the Address Bar: **http://192.168.1.1**. If your browser is configured to travel to a specific Web site when it opens (the site configured as your home page), you may receive an error message, because you're probably not able to connect to the Internet until you finish configuring the browser.

When you access a router, the device requires that you enter a username and password. Linksys uses the word *admin* for these values, but some differences in implementation exist among devices. For some devices, you will leave the User Name field blank and enter **admin** for the Password. For other devices, you will enter **admin** for both the User Name and Password fields. Consult the manual for your device to find out for sure (or just give both techniques a try).

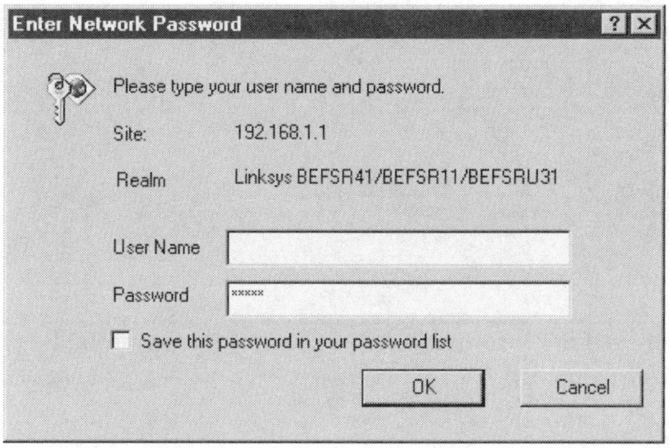

Enter Network Password
Please type your user name and password.
Site: 192.168.1.1
Realm Linksys BEFSR41/BEFSR11/BEFSRU31
User Name
Password *****
Save this password in your password list
OK Cancel

The router's configuration screen appears, and I go over the basic configuration options for routers in the following sections. Remember that your router model may have more tabs than I cover here, and some tabs may have different options available.

Setup Tab Configuration

The Setup tab, seen in Figure 8-9, contains fields for the information required to connect your network to your ISP through the router.

The Host Name and Domain Name fields can remain blank unless your ISP instructs you to enter information. I know of no DSL providers who require these fields (which doesn't mean that none of them do), but some cable providers require this information.

The LAN IP Address section of the tab has the following two fields:

- Device IP Address
- Subnet Mask

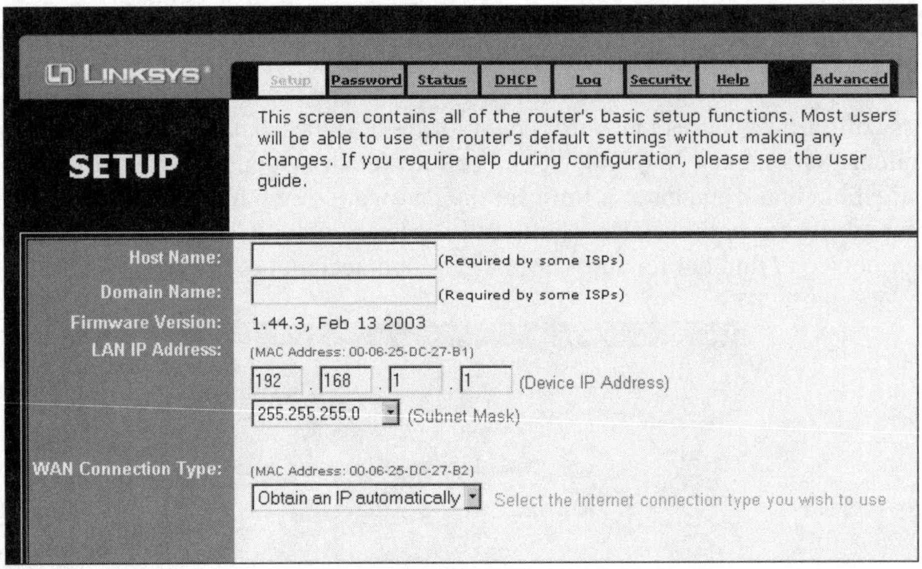

FIGURE 8-9 Most of the information you need to configure the Setup tab is available from your ISP.

The Device IP Address is the public IP address for the router. Unless you're using static IP addresses from your ISP, don't change the router's IP address. The subnet mask is 255.255.255.0 by default, and unless your ISP has told you to use a different subnet mask, don't change that value. (Usually, the only reason to change the subnet mask is to configure your network with static IP addresses.)

Select the WAN Connection Type from the drop-down list (matching the instructions from your ISP).

Obtain an IP Automatically This is the default selection, because it's the most common setting. Your ISP instructs you to use this setting when DHCP services are provided by the ISP. If this is the correct setting for your ISP, you have nothing more to do in the Setup tab except click Apply. Then click Continue to save your settings. Close the browser. Power your DSL/cable modem off and on again. Restart all the computers on the network so they can establish the router's settings. You can return to this Setup utility at any time to configure any other features you want to use.

Static IP Choose this option if the instructions from your ISP require a static IP address. The Setup screen changes to display the fields you need for configuration.

For instructions, read the section “Configuring the Router for a Static IP Address” later in this chapter.

PPPoE If your DSL provider uses Point-to-Point Protocol over Ethernet, select this option. The screen changes to display the fields required to enable and configure PPPoE (see Figure 8-10). Then configure your connection, using the following guidelines:

- **User Name and Password** Enter the data provided by your DSL ISP.
- **Connect on Demand: Max Idle Time** You can configure the router to disconnect from your DSL ISP after a specified amount of inactivity. Then, whenever you’re disconnected as a result of inactivity, the connection is reestablished as soon as a user attempts to access the Internet (by opening a browser or an e-mail application). Enter the number of minutes of inactivity that must elapse to cause the router to disconnect from your DSL ISP.
- **Keep Alive: Redial Period** Select this option to have the router periodically check the state of your Internet connection and reconnect to your ISP if the connection has been broken. Enter an amount of time that must elapse to cause the router to reconnect.

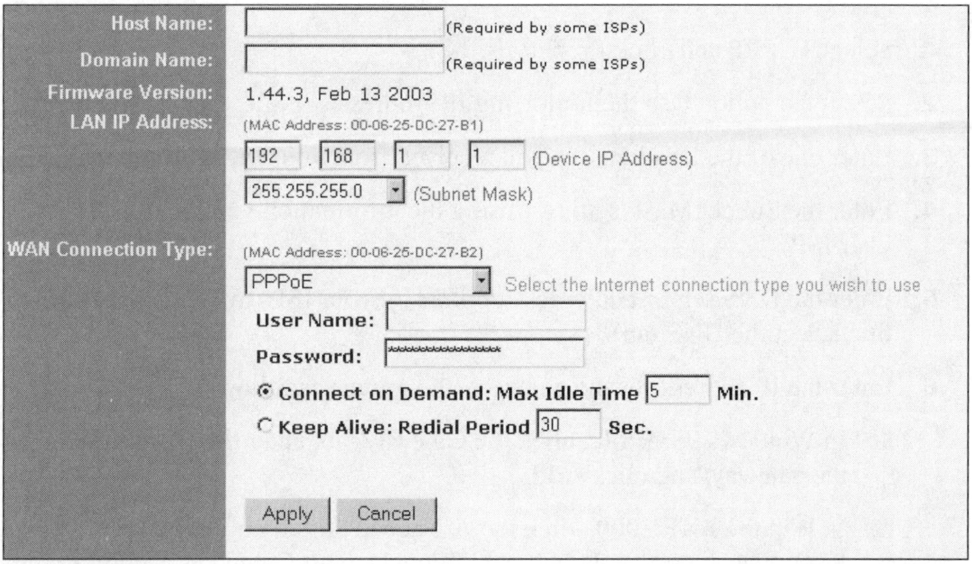

FIGURE 8-10 Enter your connection settings for PPPoE.

Click Apply, and then click Continue to save your settings. Close the browser. Power your DSL modem off and on again. Restart all the computers on the network so they can establish their settings from the router. You can return to this Setup utility at any time to configure any other features you want to use.

Other Protocols Depending on the router model, you may also see one or more of the following protocols in the drop-down list: RAS, PPTP, or HBS. These are country or continent specific. Your ISP can provide you with the settings you need.

Using Static IP Addresses

If your ISP service includes a range of static IP addresses, you must enter those addresses manually. Static IP addresses work for a DSL/cable connection only where you're sharing your Internet connection by attaching all the computers to a router. In the following sections, I go over the procedures for operating networked computers with assigned static IP addresses.

Configuring the Computers for Static IP Addresses

To assign static IP addresses to the computers on your network, open the Properties dialog for the LAN connection using the appropriate steps for the version of Windows running on the computer. Then take the following steps to configure your network adapter for a static IP address:

1. Select TCP/IP and click Properties.
2. Select the option Use the Following IP Address.
3. Enter one of the IP addresses you received from your ISP.
4. Enter the Subnet Mask settings, using the information you received from your ISP.
5. Enter the DNS server addresses supplied by your ISP (in Windows 98SE, first select the DNS tab).
6. Enter the IP address for the gateway (the router) as follows:
   - In Windows 98SE/Me, click the Gateway tab, enter the IP address of the gateway, and click Add.
   - In Windows XP/2000, click the Advanced button on the TCP/IP Properties dialog, and click Add in the Default Gateways section of the Advanced TCP/IP Settings dialog. Enter the IP address of the gateway.

7. Click OK.
8. If Windows prompts you to restart the computer, do so.

Repeat this process on each computer, making sure you don't use any IP address twice (each IP address must be unique on the network).

Configuring the Router for a Static IP Address

Choose Static IP Address if the instructions from your ISP require a static IP address for your router. The Setup window changes to display the fields you need for configuration (see Figure 8-11). Use the following guidelines to supply data in the fields:

- **Specify WAN IP Address** Enter the IP address for the router as seen by the Internet and the ISP.
- **Subnet Mask** Enter the subnet mask as seen by the Internet and the ISP.
- **Default Gateway Address** Enter the IP address your ISP gave you for the gateway.

Static IP Addresses and the Windows XP Network Wizard

When you set up your Windows XP computer for static IP addresses, you'll probably see the Network Setup Wizard, even though you want to do a manual configuration. The wizard just pops up—it's impossible to suppress it. On the third wizard window (the window that asks for your connection type), select Other and click Next. In the next window, select the first option (which describes a scenario in which all computers connect to the Internet through a concentrator) and click Next.

In the next window, select the network adapter as your Internet connection. Because your adapter is configured to connect to a DSL router or a concentrator, and it has a static IP address, your adapter is also an Internet connection device. Click Next. The wizard warns you that you should enable Windows Firewall on your computer. Continue to respond to the wizard's prompts, clicking Next to move through the wizard windows. When you exit the wizard, open the Properties dialog box for the LAN connection and manually configure the IP addresses the way you want.

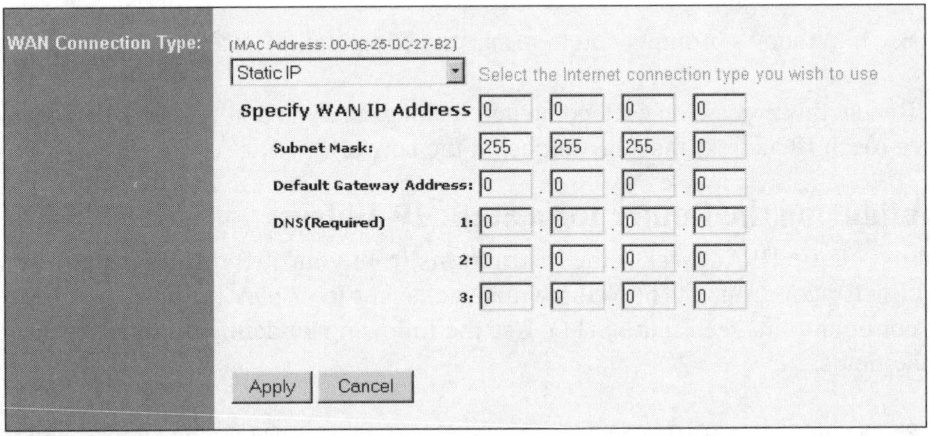

WAN Connection Type: (MAC Address: 00-06-25-DC-27-B2)
Static IP — Select the Internet connection type you wish to use
Specify WAN IP Address 0 . 0 . 0 . 0
Subnet Mask: 255 . 255 . 255 . 0
Default Gateway Address: 0 . 0 . 0 . 0
DNS(Required) 1: 0 . 0 . 0 . 0
2: 0 . 0 . 0 . 0
3: 0 . 0 . 0 . 0
Apply Cancel

FIGURE 8-11 Use the information from your ISP to configure a static IP address.

- **DNS (Required)** Enter the IP address of the DNS server your ISP wants you to use. Your ISP provides at least one DNS IP address, although many ISPs provide a secondary DNS IP address. The Setup window also has a field for a third DNS IP address if your ISP provided one (which would be unusual).

Click Apply, and then click Continue to save your settings. Close the browser. Power your DSL/cable modem off and on again. Restart all the computers on the network so they can access the router and its settings. You can return to this Setup utility at any time to configure any other features you want to use.

Managing the Router's Password

The Password tab provides the opportunity to change the router's password. The default router password is the same for all Linksys routers, so any user on the local network could connect to the router and change the configuration settings. All a user would have to do is read the manual or this book to know that the default IP address is 192.168.1.1 and the default password is *admin*. As a result, you should change the default password by using the fields available in the Password tab (see Figure 8-12).

Delete the asterisks that currently appear in the Router Password text box, and enter a new password. Then delete the asterisks in the next text box and enter the

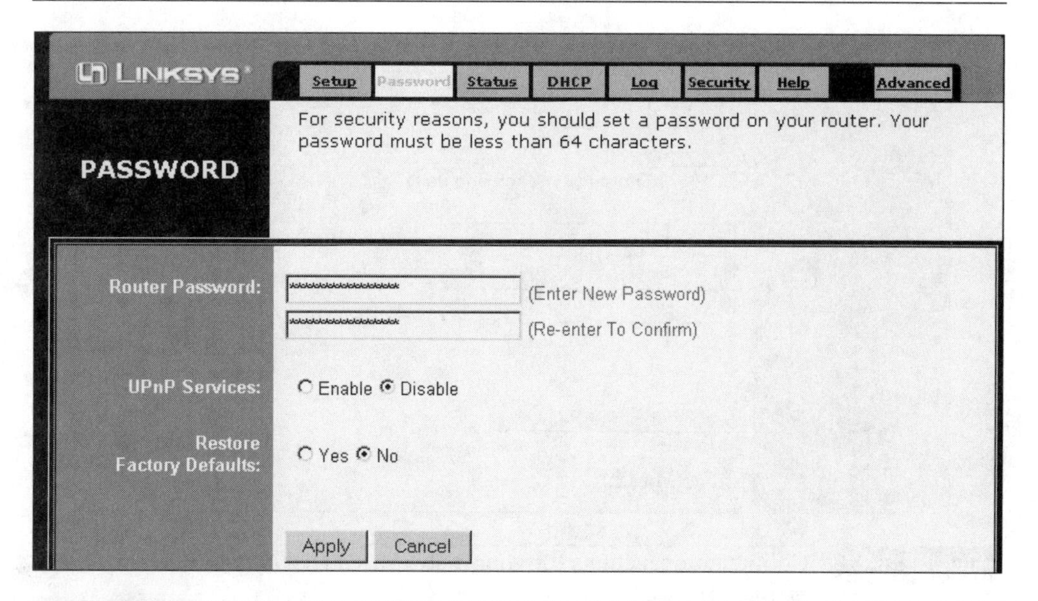

FIGURE 8-12 Change the default password so other users can't change the configuration.

new password again to confirm it. You can use up to 63 characters for your password, but you can't use a space.

NOTE *The option to enable Universal Plug and Play (UPnP) is related only to Windows XP. If you enable the option, Windows XP can automatically configure the router for certain Internet applications, such as gaming and videoconferencing. It's quite possible that Windows XP can manage these applications without your enabling this option, so test first.*

Managing DHCP

When you install a Linksys router, the router can act as the DHCP server for your network. DHCP servers don't assign IP addresses permanently; they're leased to computers when the computers start up and request an IP address. When the lease expires, a new lease is assigned (computers don't have to reboot to request a new lease; it's an automatic process). The settings for providing DHCP services are displayed on the DHCP tab (see Figure 8-13).

DHCP Server: Enable Disable
Starting IP Address: 192.168.1. 100
Number of DHCP Users: 50
Client Lease Time: 0 minutes (0 means one day)

DNS 1: 0 . 0 . 0 . 0
2: 0 . 0 . 0 . 0
3: 0 . 0 . 0 . 0
WINS: 0 . 0 . 0 . 0

DHCP Clients Table

Apply Cancel

FIGURE 8-13 Configuration settings for your router-based DHCP server are displayed on the DHCP tab.

The Starting IP Address and Number of DHCP Users fields tell you the range of addresses that will be assigned by the server. For example, if the starting address is 192.168.1.100 and the number of users is 50 (which really means up to 50), DHCP addresses will be in the range 192.168.1.100 through 192.168.1.149. To see the current DHCP client data, click the DHCP Clients Table button.

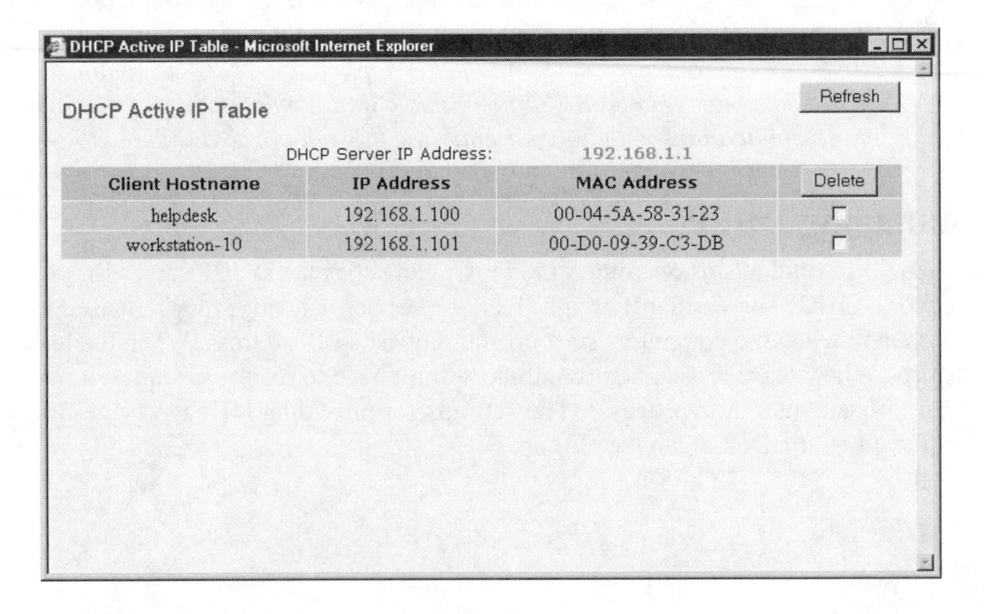
DHCP Active IP Table - Microsoft Internet Explorer

DHCP Active IP Table

Refresh

DHCP Server IP Address: 192.168.1.1

Client Hostname	IP Address	MAC Address	Delete
helpdesk	192.168.1.100	00-04-5A-58-31-23	
workstation-10	192.168.1.101	00-D0-09-39-C3-DB	

Routers and AOL

If you're an America Online (AOL) subscriber, setting up a router isn't quite as straightforward as it is for people who don't use AOL. A router is an IP device and until recently, the AOL network would not use an IP device because it didn't fit the way AOL wanted to build its client software. (Non-AOL users don't have to use special client software from their ISP. They are free to use standard e-mail software and Web browsers.) However, because of the demand by AOL users for IP addresses (mostly Xbox and Playstation 2 devices), AOL changed its network infrastructure to permit IP devices.

When you set up your router, you need to enter **america online** as the User Name and skip the Password (the opposite of the instructions for non-AOL users). The Password field continues to display asterisks (as though a password were entered), but you can ignore them. Click Apply to save the settings.

For more information about configuring your router, contact AOL support or head to *http://www.linksys.com* and go to the Support section. Select the Knowledge Base and search on the term *AOL*.

Part III

Working with Your Network

Now that you have learned how to choose hardware for your network, install different types of networks, and get your network connected to the Internet, it's time to put your network to work. The following chapters show you how to secure your network and computers, share files and printers, and bring media stored on computers into exciting new places like your home entertainment center. You will also learn some troubleshooting tips and tricks that help you make sure your network works properly.

Chapter 9

Security

Security is a much bigger issue that it used to be. Since more computers are now connected permanently to the Internet through broadband connections, more opportunities exist for malicious user activity. While the risk of evil-doers that want to break into your home or small business network and steal *your* files is relatively small, other bad things *can* happen. Those same evil-doers could use the computers on an unprotected network as a launching point for automated attacks against bigger targets. In addition, e-mail can deliver viruses and other nasties right to your desktop.

Fortunately, you can take some easy steps to protect yourself. In this chapter, I cover what I like to call the "big three" security measures:

- *Use firewalls*. Firewalls work by blocking unwanted traffic from entering or exiting your network. You should use a good hardware firewall (such as those from Linksys) to protect your entire network. You should also use a good software firewall on each computer on the network.
- *Update your software*. Security holes in software are discovered regularly. This is not always because of shoddy design; it's because a continual tug-of-war exists between software companies that try to design secure software and bad guys who try to break into it. Keeping your software (especially your operating system) up to date with the latest patches is essential.
- *Use anti-virus software and keep it updated*. Viruses (and other malicious programs) tend to come through e-mail and downloading software from the Internet—two sources that you specifically allow into your computer. Using good anti-virus software and keeping it continually updated with the latest virus signatures can save you a world of trouble.

In addition, I talk about a few other security measures you can take. One relatively new annoyance called *pop-up messages* (which haven't yet proven to be virulent—but it's probably only a matter of time) are actually pretty easy to take care of. *Spyware* is software that installs itself on your computer and can do things like report your activities to someone on the Internet or even allow that person access to your computer. Spyware is a bigger problem than pop-up messages, but I cover good ways to protect yourself from it. I also give you an overview of a feature called *Virtual Private Networking (VPN)*, which provides security for online participants in a network.

Using Firewalls

Firewalls are like the guards at castle gates. Their job is to keep out the traffic you don't want on your network but allow in the traffic you do want. In this section, I give you an overview of how firewalls work. I then cover how to protect your network with a hardware firewall and how to protect each computer with a software firewall.

Understanding Firewalls

A hardware firewall provides a blockade between your computers and the Internet, preventing the unauthorized exchange of data. To understand how a firewall works, and to be able to configure a firewall for maximum protection, you have to understand the components of Internet communication: IP addresses, data packets, and ports.

IP Addresses

When a computer is connected to the Internet, it has a public IP address, which is also called an Internet IP address. The same computer may have a private IP address that's used to facilitate TCP/IP communication within the network, but that private IP address doesn't work on the Internet. Several ranges of numbers have been assigned for private IP addresses, and they're not recognized as true Internet IP addresses:

- 10.0.0.0 to 10.255.255.255
- 169.254.0.0 to 169.254.255.255
- 172.16.0.0 to 172.31.255.255
- 192.168.0.0 to 192.168.255.255

If your computer is on a private network, it probably falls into one of these private ranges. However, when your computer connects to the Internet, it must use a public IP address, and frequently this address is assigned to the device directly connected to your DSL/cable modem (for always-on connections) or by your ISP at the time of connection. Today, some DSL services are not always-on connections, so you may have to reconnect to your DSL provider when you want to use the Internet; you'll receive an IP address each time you connect. All telephone modem connections are assigned an IP address each time they dial out and connect to the ISP. (Chapter 8 covers the configuration of computers on your network, including the options for assigning IP addresses.)

NOTE *Some small networks have public IP addresses assigned to each computer, because the ISP provides those addresses (for a fee). Business DSL and cable modem services sell public IP addresses as part of the package, and if you use public IP addresses for each computer, you can enter those addresses in the TCP/IP options when you're configuring your connection, because they're valid on the Internet.*

When you're on the Internet with your public IP address, that address is a doorway between you and every other computer on the Internet. Network traffic flows through that doorway in both directions. It's possible that a malicious hacker can access your computer through that IP address doorway, unless you've prevented that with a firewall.

Internet intruders work by selecting an Internet IP address and then trying to connect to that IP address. They usually don't pick an IP address themselves; they're not specifically looking for your computer (even if you have the secret Swiss bank account numbers of famous people in a document on your hard drive). They use software that selects an IP address at random and then tries to access the computer that's using that address on the Internet. If the attempt fails, either because the IP address is not currently on the Internet or because a firewall blocked the attempt, the software selects another IP address and tries again.

If your IP address comes up and you're not protected by a firewall, the attempt to access your computer succeeds, and the intruders have access to your computer and its contents. You won't know that anything is going on, even if you're working at the computer, because all of this occurs in the background without interfering with anything you're doing.

Here are some of the common nefarious acts that are known to be performed by intruders:

- Sending viruses to your computer.
- Renaming or removing important system files.
- Copying your documents back to their own systems to gain personal and sensitive information.
- Sending an enormous number of files just for the fun of filling up your drive.

- Bombarding your computer with data in a way that overwhelms the computer, which is called a *Denial of Service* (DoS) attack. A variety of methods are available for DoS attacks, and they can do harm well beyond merely freezing up the computer.
- Using your computer to run software that performs DoS attacks on other computers (this turns your computer into a *zombie*). Often, thousands of zombies bombard a particular Internet address with DoS attacks in a massive attack known as a *distributed DoS* (DDoS) attack.

NOTE *Don't think that using passwords on folders or setting up restricted access via the NTFS security features protects you. Intruders who gain access to your computer have tools to assist them in getting past those security blocks, which are really designed for security within the network.*

Data Packets

The Internet uses the communications protocol TCP/IP, which operates with two layers:

- TCP (Transmission Control Protocol, the higher layer)
- IP (Internet Protocol, the lower layer)

The TCP layer breaks data transmissions into small packets of information, called data *packets*. The TCP layer on the sending computer disassembles the original data into these packets and sends them across the Internet. The travel route across the Internet may not be the same for each packet, and some packets may hop across one set of servers, while other packets may use a different set of servers. In the end, when all the packets arrive at their destination, the TCP layer at the receiving computer reassembles the packets to put the data into the right order.

The IP layer keeps track of the IP addresses involved in the data transmission, to ensure that each packet gets to the correct recipient computer. Even if packets are routed through different Internet servers, all the packets land at the correct recipient because the IP layer knows the recipient's IP address. If a packet is damaged or lost during its travels, the IP layer knows the sender's IP address and can request a resend of that packet.

A true firewall checks every data packet that passes through. It checks the data in the IP layer to determine whether or not an IP address is approved or unapproved. An unapproved IP address is one that you haven't specifically configured as an

IP address from which you're willing to receive data. (The IP addresses of other computers on your network, or the range of IP addresses included in your DHCP configuration, are configured as those from which your computer *will* accept data.)

Data Ports

Some programs need to communicate with programs on other computers on the network or on computers on the Internet. For example, when you try to access a file that is shared on another computer on your network, your operating system must communicate with the operating system on the other computer. When your e-mail program needs to check for new messages, it communicates with a mail server, which is usually a program that is running on a computer on your ISP's network. To keep track of what data goes to what program, your computer assigns each of these programs a data port. This port is just a number that identifies the program. The information about the port is included in every packet of data that crosses the network so that the computer on the other end knows what to do with it.

All communication processes use ports, and most types of communication are programmed to use specific ports. These data ports are numbered from 0 to 65536, and the port numbers between 0 and 1024 are reserved for specific data communication services. (For example, HTTP, the protocol you use when you're viewing a Web page, uses port number 80.) Ports work by listening for data and will usually automatically accept data if it's the right type of data for that port. A port that is listening is open, waiting to accept data, and because it's open, it's vulnerable.

Internet hackers also need to use ports if they want to communicate between their computers and your computer. Lots of software is available to aid these folks in testing whether a port on a remote computer is listening. Frequently, the software tests only certain ports, by pretending to send data of the type that's supported by that port. This technique is called *port scanning*, and it's a popular method of testing whether a computer is vulnerable to attack. It enables Internet hooligans to scan the ports on computers, see which services are currently listening for connections, and determine the ports on which they are listening. Then, the hacker software uses that information to create a data stream that masquerades the appropriate type of data for the listening port.

Even the most basic router on a network acts as a sort of firewall by blocking incoming traffic from the Internet on ports you don't use. If you run programs that users need to access from the Internet, you can unblock the appropriate port on your router. A good example of this would be if you ran Web server software on your computer that hosted a Web site that people on the Internet could access. To gain that access, your router would have to allow traffic to come in on the appropriate port, and then direct that data to the computer that is running the Web server software. The router does all of this using a protocol known as *Network Address Translation* (NAT). As you learned earlier, a router shows only one public IP address to the Internet, protecting the private IP addresses of computers on your network. The router translates the network addresses as they pass through so that each computer on the network can communicate with computers on the Internet as though they were directly connected—hence the name Network Address Translation. On a NAT router (as they are called), all incoming ports are blocked by default. You have to configure the router specifically to let in incoming traffic on certain ports. However, all outgoing ports are unblocked. The assumption is that you are the one initiating outgoing traffic, so why block it? Many people refer to NAT routers incorrectly as firewalls, and while they do offer pretty decent protection for your network, NAT routers are not really *true* firewalls.

A true firewall does more than just block or unblock ports and act as a traffic director; it also checks the virtual ports to see whether data passing through each port is of the correct data type. This process is called *stateful packet inspection* (SPI). SPI checks the actual content of the data passing through ports (rather than just allowing it through), which enables the firewall to catch data packets that identify themselves as being appropriate for the port; but when the data is examined closely, the firewall discovers that the data type has been faked. At that point, the firewall blocks communication. This procedure is performed in addition to the IP address check, making the firewall more effective. The Linksys firewall router performs stateful inspections.

Protecting Your Network with a Linksys Firewall Router

The advantage of using a hardware firewall is that it's always protecting all the devices on your network; it doesn't produce loading errors when a computer is low on RAM or resources; and users can't accidentally uninstall a hardware firewall, remove it from the Startup folder, or "exit" a hardware firewall.

In this section, I go over the setup and basic configuration tasks for configuring Linksys firewall routers. The user guide that comes with your product has the detailed instructions for all the tasks. Because so many permutations and combinations are available for the options you might choose, it's too space-consuming to have an exhaustive discussion here.

Router Ports

All the connections start (or end, depending on your point of view) at the back of your router. I go over each connection on the router, moving from left to right.

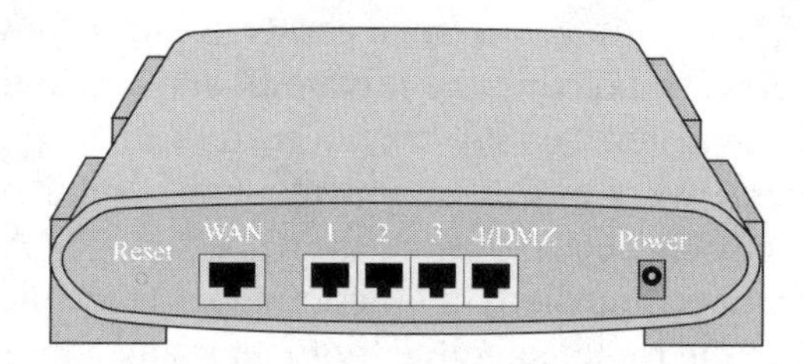

Reset Button Like the Reset button on your computer, the Reset button on the router clears data and restarts the device. To use it, hold the button for 2 or 3 seconds and then release it. Use this button only in case of an emergency, if for some reason the links to the router are jammed and communications are frozen. Try following the tips in the troubleshooting section of your router's user guide before you press Reset.

WAN Port Use the WAN port to connect the router to your DSL/cable modem. WAN (Wide Area Network) is a term that's usually applied to a network that's spread across multiple locations and connected via telephone lines. (See the sidebar "LAN, WAN, and MAN" in Chapter 6, if you're interested in learning more about the various types of networks that are used to connect computers.) While the router doesn't really create a WAN, it does provide a separation point (and a barricade) between two networks: your LAN and the Internet (the Internet is a network too—the largest network in the world).

Ports 1, 2, and 3 Use these ports to connect your network devices to the router. Usually, the network devices are computers, so if your network is made up of three (or fewer) computers, the router becomes your hub. However, you can also use these ports to connect hubs or switches to which you've already connected multiple PCs, or any other type of node (for example, a stand-alone print server).

Port 4/DMZ This port is capable of playing either of two roles:

- Providing the same connection as the ports numbered 1 through 3
- Providing a DMZ

A DMZ (Demilitarized Zone) is "firewall-neutral" (just as an army general would describe a wartime DMZ as "neutral"). If you set up a DMZ (covered later in this chapter in the sections on advanced configuration of the router), the computer you connect to this port becomes the DMZ node.

NOTE *All four of the numbered ports will automatically detect whether you're connected to another hub or switch and will use the proper setting, so you won't need a crossover cable.*

Power This connector accepts the power adapter, the other end of which is plugged into a wall outlet (or, preferably, a surge protector). The router lacks an On/Off switch, so the power connector is the only way to turn the router on and off.

Making the Connections

You need to start by physically connecting your router to your DSL/cable modem and to the computers on your network. Depending on your current network topology (if a network is already in place), making the physical connections can be merely a matter of moving some cable, installing the cabling from scratch, or a little of both.

NOTE *Linksys advises that all nodes on the network be powered off while you make connections.*

Using the Router as Your Hub If you have a network consisting of four or fewer computers, you can build your network around the router (see Figure 9-1), which has a built-in hub or switch.

- Run cable from the NIC in each computer to one of the numbered ports on the router.
- Connect the Ethernet cable from your DSL/cable modem to the WAN port on the router. (Be sure to use the same cable that came with the modem. If you're unsure which cable to use, just pull the computer cable to which the modem was connected and connect it to the WAN port of the router.) The other end of your DSL/cable modem, of course, remains attached to the outside world—to your DSL phone wire or to your cable company's cable.

If a DSL/cable modem was already installed on a stand-alone computer and connected to a NIC in that computer, move the cable connector from the NIC to the router. The NIC in the computer becomes the network NIC and will have to be reconfigured for the network settings. (See Chapter 8 for information about configuring NICs.)

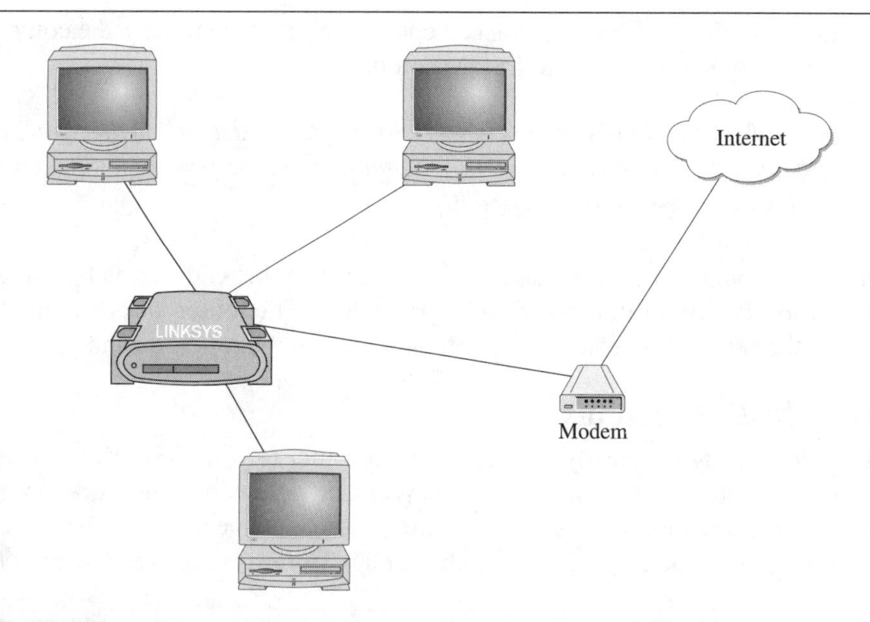

FIGURE 9-1 The firewall router has a built-in hub or switch, connecting all computers on the network.

Attaching an Existing Hub/Switch to the Router If you already set up your network before deciding to add a firewall router, you don't have to abandon the hub or switch you're using. You can connect the hub or switch to the router (see Figure 9-2).

- Connect a regular port on the hub to one of the numbered ports on the router. If all the ports on the hub are used, move one of the computer connections from the hub to a numbered port on the router to free up the hub port for the connection to the router.
- Connect the Ethernet cable from your DSL/cable modem to the WAN port on the router.

NOTE *If you have an existing network and you're using any kind of software Internet Connection Sharing (Windows ICS), you must disable it. The router takes care of sharing the connection.*

If your network consists of four or fewer computers, you may want to consider using the router and selling the hub to a friend or neighbor who has voiced an

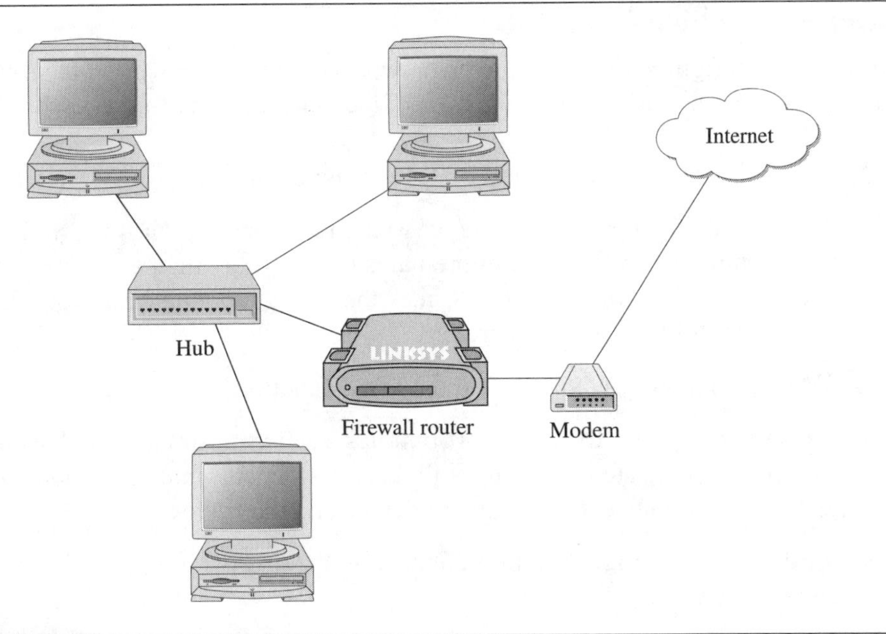

FIGURE 9-2 You can connect an existing hub or switch to the firewall router.

interest in creating a home network (or sell it on an online auction). The advantage of keeping the hub (outside of the obvious advantage of saving yourself the work of moving cable) is that it makes it easier to "grow" your network. When you want to add computers to your network, you can use the router for the new machines instead of buying a larger hub or buying another hub and linking it to the existing hub.

Configuring the Computers

You need to configure your computers to access the Internet through the router. (See Chapter 8 to learn how to configure the TCP/IP settings for your NICs.) You must configure the computers to obtain an IP address automatically (the router takes care of issuing the IP addresses and other TCP/IP settings, such as DNS server addresses).

If one of the computers on your network had been connected to the DSL/cable modem and its NIC is configured for the ISP settings, that NIC must be reconfigured as a network client (matching the settings for the other computers on the network). The settings you received from your ISP, originally used for this NIC, are used to configure the router.

Power Up the Firewall Router

After you've configured the NICs on the network computers, power up the router by plugging it in. The LED lights in the front of the router should respond as follows:

- **Power** is green as soon as the router is plugged in.
- **Diag** is red after power-up while the router runs a self-diagnostic procedure, and then it turns off. If the light remains red for more than a minute or so, the router may have a problem. Check the user guide that came with the router, or call Linksys for service.
- **DMZ** is green if you've enabled the DMZ function.
- **Link/Act** is green for each port that has a network device (such as a computer) connected. If the light flickers, it indicates that communication is in progress between the network device and the router.
- **Full/Col** is green for each port connection that is operating in full-duplex mode.
- **100** is yellow if the port connection is operating at 100 Mbps (otherwise, the connection is operating at 10 Mbps, and no light appears).

Configuring the Router Connection

You configure your router by accessing it from one of the connected computers. No special software has to be installed on that computer, as the router is accessed through the browser.

NOTE *When you open the browser to begin configuring the router, you may receive an error message. That's because the browser can't get to the home page you configured (until you finish configuring the router, you don't have access to the Internet). If your browser home page is set to load a blank page (using the special address about:blank), you won't see an error message because your browser isn't trying to access an Internet server.*

Follow these steps to begin configuring your router:

1. In the browser Address Bar, enter **http://192.168.1.1/** and press ENTER to open the Connect To dialog (it may take a few seconds for the dialog to appear).

NOTE *This dialog looks slightly different if you're not working on a Windows XP computer.*

TIP *Add the URL for the router on your Favorites list to make it easy to open the window later, in case you want to change the configuration.*

2. Leave the User Name field blank, and then go to the Password field and enter **admin** (in lowercase). Then click OK.
3. The Linksys Setup window appears with the Setup tab selected, as seen in Figure 9-3.

NOTE *The Setup window has multiple tabs for setting up all the features offered by your Linksys firewall router. I discuss the other tabs later in this chapter.*

The Setup tab is where you specify the basic options for your Internet connection. You must configure this tab and restart your DSL/cable modem, and you may need to restart the computers on the network to provide Internet access for your network and before you set configuration options on the other tabs in the Setup window.

- **Host Name and Domain Name** These fields can usually remain blank, but if your ISP requires this information, fill in the data as instructed.
- **Firmware Version** This is the version number for the router's firmware, as well as the release date for the version. Firmware is programming code that is inserted into the read-only memory of a device. This technology provides a way to enhance the capabilities of hardware devices. When new firmware is available, you can download it from the Linksys Web site, along with instructions on how to insert the new code into the device's memory.

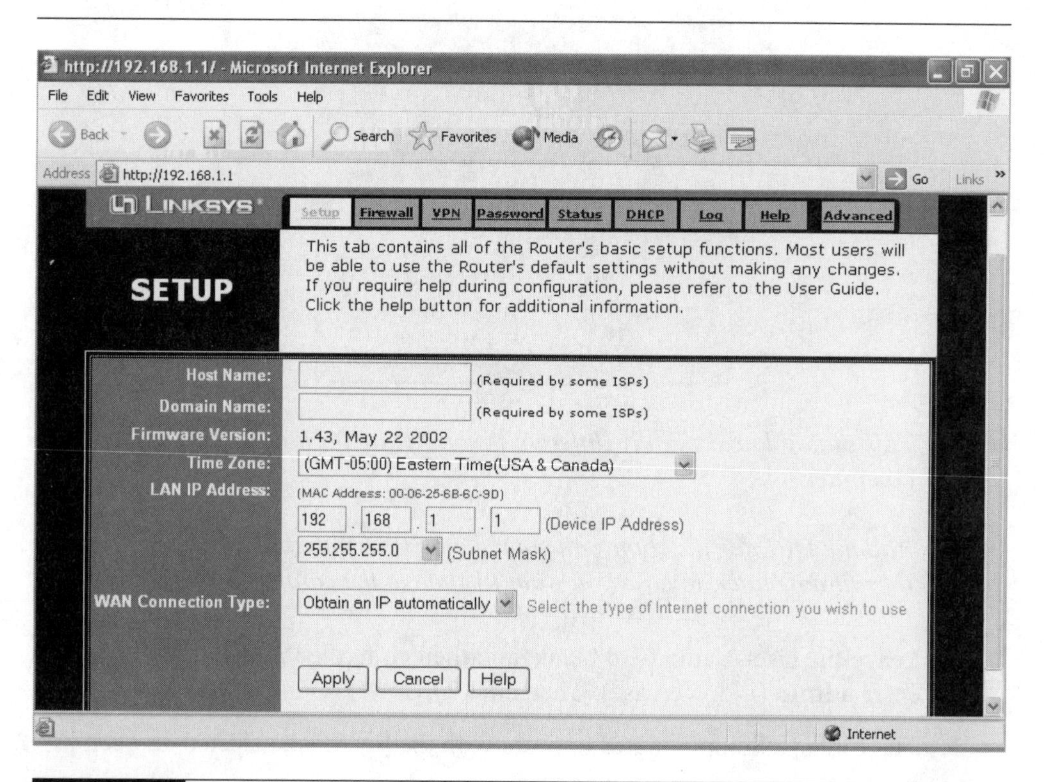

FIGURE 9-3 Configure your Internet connection through the firewall router's Setup tab.

NOTE *Linksys does not recommend upgrading the firmware unless you're having problems with the router.*

- **Time Zone** Use the drop-down menu to select your local time zone.
- **Device IP Address and Subnet Mask** The default values for the router's IP address and subnet mask are preset and should not need to be altered unless you have a special configuration that is needed (such as VPN).
- **WAN Connection Type** Click the arrow to the right of the text box and select a connection type.

The WAN connection specifications must match the instructions from your ISP. The Linksys firewall router supports six connection types, which are discussed next.

Obtain an IP Automatically This is the default selection, because it's the most common. Your ISP instructs you to use this setting when DHCP services are provided by the ISP. If this is the correct setting for your ISP, you have nothing more to do in the Setup tab.

Click Apply and then click Continue to save your settings. Close the browser. Power your DSL/cable modem off and on again. Restart all the computers on the network so they can establish the router's settings. You can return to this Setup utility at any time to configure any other features you want to use.

Static IP Choose this option if the instructions from your ISP require a static IP address. The Setup window changes to display the fields you need for configuration (see Figure 9-4). Use the following guidelines to supply data in the fields.

- **Specify WAN IP Address** Enter the IP address for the router as seen from the WAN (Internet).
- **Subnet Masks** Enter the subnet mask as seen by the Internet and the ISP.
- **Default Gateway Address** Enter the IP address for the gateway.
- **DNS (Required)** Enter the IP address of the DNS server your ISP wants you to use. Your ISP provides at least one DNS IP address. Many ISPs provide a secondary DNS IP address. The Setup window also has a field for a third DNS IP address if your ISP provided one (which is unusual).

Click Apply and then click Continue to save your settings. Close the browser. Power your DSL/cable modem off and on again. Restart all the computers on the network so they can use the router's settings. You can return to this Setup utility at any time to configure any other features you want to use.

PPPoE If your DSL provider uses Point-to-Point Protocol over Ethernet, select this option to enable the protocol (see Figure 9-5). Then configure your connection using the following guidelines:

- **User Name and Password** Enter the data provided by your DSL ISP.
- **Connect on Demand: Max Idle Time** You can configure the router to disconnect from your ISP after a specified amount of inactivity. Then, whenever you're disconnected as a result of inactivity, the connection is reestablished as soon as a user attempts to access the Internet (by opening

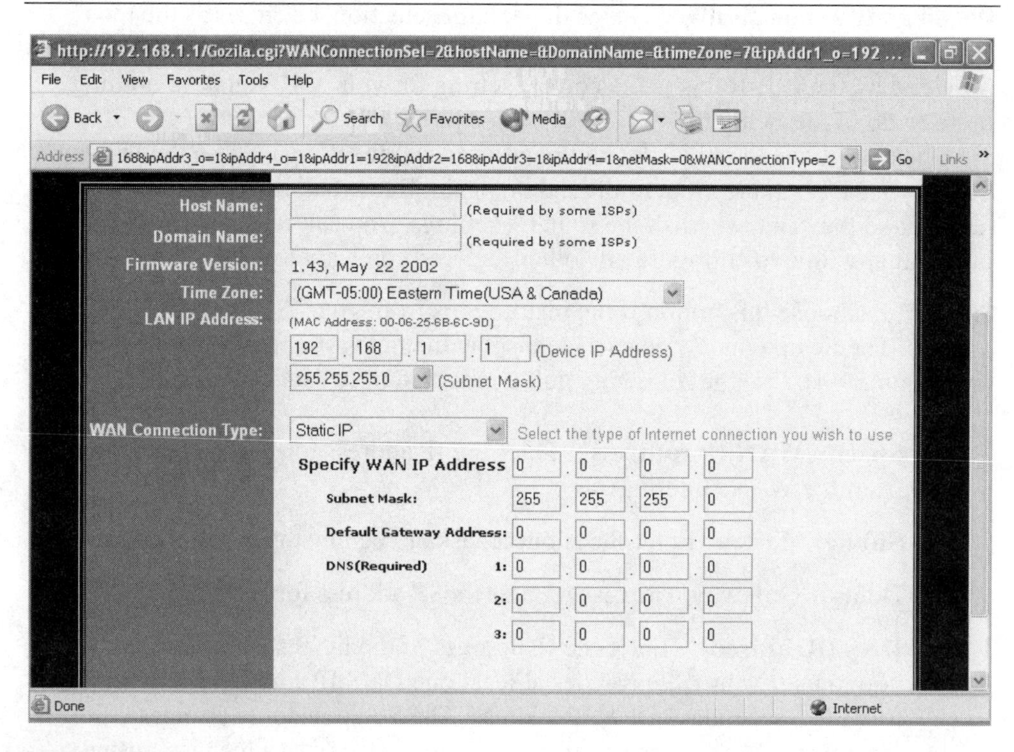

FIGURE 9-4 Use the information provided by your ISP if you have to configure a static IP address.

a browser or an e-mail application). Enter the number of minutes of inactivity that must elapse to cause the router to disconnect from your DSL ISP.

- **Keep Alive: Redial Period** Select this option to have the router periodically check the state of your Internet connection and reconnect to your ISP if the connection has been broken. Enter an amount of time that must elapse to cause the router to reconnect.

Click Apply and then click Continue to save your settings. Close the browser. Power your DSL/cable modem off and on again. Restart all the computers on the network so they can establish the router's settings. You can return to this Setup utility at any time to configure any other features you want to use.

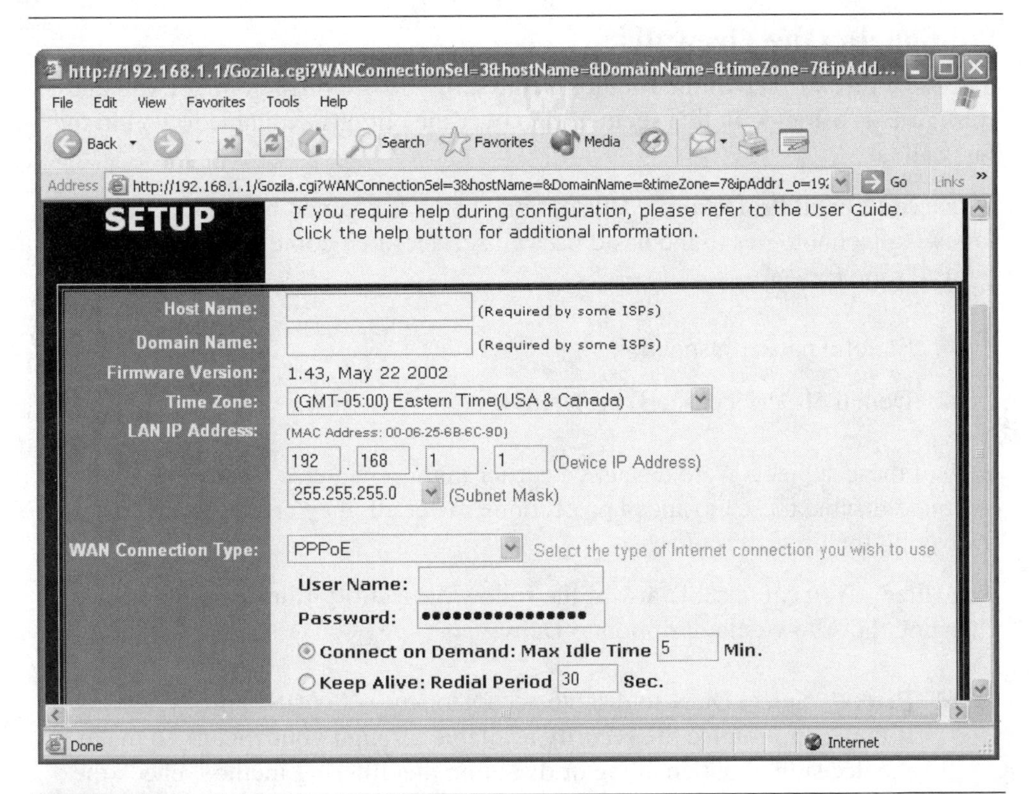

FIGURE 9-5 Enter your connection settings for PPPoE.

RAS, PPTP, and HBS These services are less common and are used only outside the United States, as follows:

- RAS is used only in Singapore. Contact Singtel for information on the appropriate settings.
- PPTP is used only in Europe. Contact your ISP for information on settings.
- HBS is used only in Australia. Contact your ISP for information on settings.

Click Apply and then click Continue to save your settings. Close the browser. Power your DSL/cable modem off and on again. Restart all the computers on the network so they can establish the router's settings. You can return to this Setup utility at any time to configure any other features you want to use.

Configuring the Firewall

Select the Firewall tab of the router's Setup utility to establish your firewall and configure its settings. In this section, I go over the options available to you in the Firewall tab.

Advanced Firewall Protection This option, which is enabled by default, adds the following technologies to the basic firewall services that come with your Linksys firewall router:

- Stateful packet inspection
- Denial of Service (DoS) protection

Both of these subjects were discussed earlier in this chapter. I can't think of any reason to disable these advanced protections. After all, they are the main reason for buying the firewall router.

Web Filter You can disable any of the following security filtering methods by changing the Allow default option to Deny:

- **Proxy** Select Deny to disable access to any WAN (ISP) proxy servers if they compromise the security available through your router. To make the decision about enabling or disabling this filtering method, check the documentation on your ISP's Web site or discuss this issue with support personnel.
- **Java** Many Web sites, especially sites with a lot of interactive content, use Java programming. If you deny Java, the router strips Java files from Web pages and you may not be able to use the functions on those sites.
- **ActiveX** ActiveX controls are used on many Web site programs, and if you disable this technology, the router strips ActiveX files from Web pages and you won't be able to use those features.
- **Cookie** If you deny cookies, the router permits Web sites to write cookies to computers but denies access when the site attempts to retrieve the cookie. This means you won't be able to save passwords or save any customized settings on Web sites.

Blocked URL Contents You can deny access to specific Web sites, to Web pages with certain text in the site's content, and to file types. You have 10 fields in which to enter the specific blockades you want to impose. In each of the fields, you can enter any of the following:

- A URL (the address of a specific Web page)
- Text you want the firewall to discriminate against by stripping files that contain that text from Web pages
- A file extension (such as *.bmp) to block files of that type

Time Filter You can use the Time Filter feature to block access to your network, from your network to the Internet, or in both directions, for specific periods of time. The default setting is Disable, which means every computer on your network has access to the Internet all the time. Click the arrow to the right of the Time Filter text box to select one of the following options:

- **Block Incoming Traffic** Prevents data packets from entering the computers on your network
- **Block Outgoing Traffic** Prevents access to the Internet
- **Block Bidirectional Traffic** Stops all data from moving between your network and the Internet in either direction

Once you enable any of these options, the window on the Firewall tab displays the fields necessary to configure the time periods (see Figure 9-6). Even though the option uses the word *block*, you enter the time periods for which you'll *allow* Internet traffic—all other times are blocked.

NOTE *The Time Filter feature uses a 24-hour clock (military time).*

It's not common to use the blocking feature, but there are some circumstances under which you might want to consider it. If yours is a business network, you might want to prevent employees from staying after work (or returning to the office at night) to download nonbusiness files (music or video). If yours is a home network, you can use these features to prevent your children from trolling the Internet at night. Of course, you must keep the password for accessing the router's configuration dialogs a secret, or users could easily reset the options at will. Particularly industrious users could also figure out how to reset the router to use

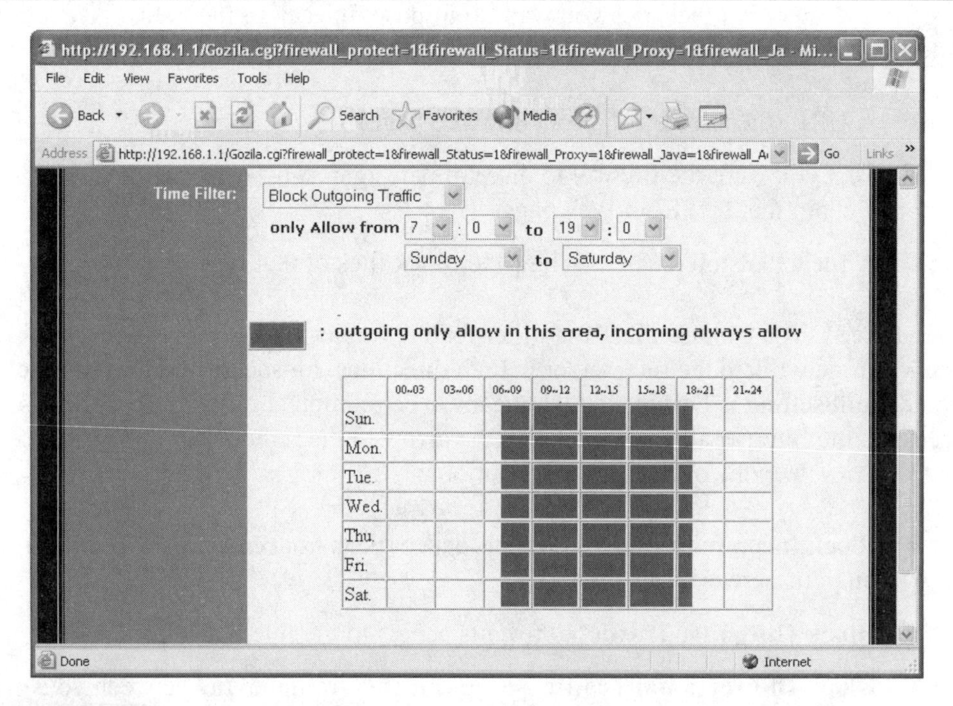

FIGURE 9-6 Users on this network can't generate outgoing data packets during overnight hours, so no late night Internet access.

the default password, so you should check the configuration once in a while to make sure it's the way you set it.

Firewall Report and View Logs Click these buttons to view the logs your router keeps. The same logs are available on the Log tab, and you must enable logging in the Log tab before you can view logs. See the user guide for instructions.

When you finish configuring the Firewall tab, click Apply, and then click Continue. Move to another tab to continue configuring your router, or close the browser.

VPN Tab

This tab is used for configuring Virtual Private Networks, a complicated technology adopted mostly by corporations with branch offices or headquarters in various geographical locations. If you're interested in setting up a VPN, you probably should think about bringing in a consultant, because most home and small business networks don't have an IT professional with sufficient knowledge on staff (or hanging around).

The Linksys Firewall router provides VPN services with a software solution. For a router that provides a hardware solution, you can purchase the Linksys VPN router model BEFVP41. For an overview of VPNs, see the section "Using VPNs" later in this chapter.

Managing Configuration Security

Use the Passwords tab to set security for the router configuration functions (see Figure 9-7). Anyone can access the router configuration windows from any computer on the network by entering its address (*http://192.168.1.1/*). You need to make sure that network users can't make wholesale changes that could mess up your ability to connect to the Internet. Just as important, you need to make sure nobody can undo the firewall protections you've configured.

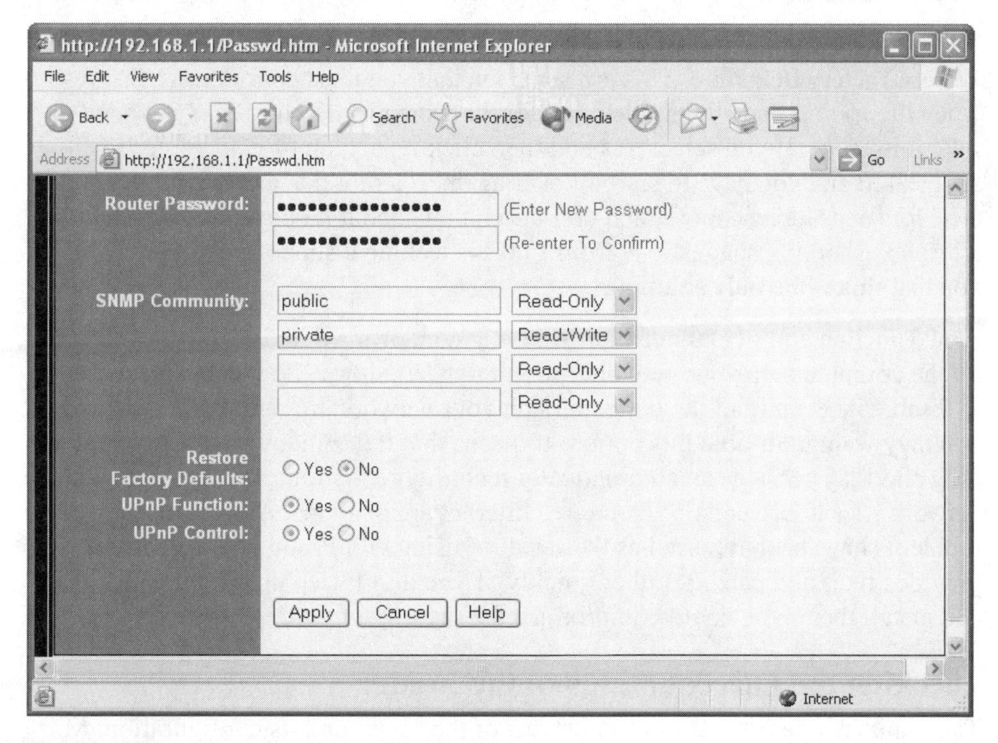

FIGURE 9-7 Protect the settings you spent so much time on from inadvertent (or purposeful) modifications.

Router Password You should create a new password to replace the default password (*admin*), to prevent the immediate world from accessing the router's configuration. Delete the asterisks that currently appear in the Router Password text box and enter a new password. Then do the same thing in the next text box to confirm the new password. You can use up to 63 characters for your password, but you can't use a space.

For added password security, don't enable the option to save the password and automatically log in when you open the router's configuration feature.

SNMP Community Simple Network Management Protocol (SNMP) is used to manage computers, routers, and lots of other devices. Network administrators use a management information base (MIB) to track the objects they're controlling. If you see options in this section of the Password page, that means the Linksys router supports the MIBs. This is well beyond the scope of any management tasks needed for a small network, so you can just skip the SNMP options and leave the default settings intact.

Restore Factory Defaults This is a selection that you must consider as a last resort; when life as you know it has changed for the worse, and you're ready to send up a flare for rescue. If you select Yes and then click Apply, all of your router's settings are cleared and you have to start all over again. It's rare that an occasion would arise for such a drastic move, and don't even think about it unless you've exhausted all troubleshooting suggestions from Linksys technical support and they've told you that this is the only solution.

UPnP Function and UPnP Control This is a Windows XP–only feature, and unless *all* the computers on your network are running Windows XP, you must select No to disable it. Even if all the computers on your network are running Windows XP, you may want to disable this option. It means that the Windows XP Universal Plug and Play service can automatically reconfigure the router if somebody on the network tries to use certain interactive Internet applications. A great many security problems have been reported as the result of using UPnP, and although Microsoft provides fixes and patches rather quickly, if you don't keep up with the patches and install them, you could compromise the security of your network.

Checking the Current Status of the Router

The Status tab displays the current status of the router and its configuration. Most of the entries are self-explanatory, but the Login status may not be—it refers to whether or not Login is enabled for PPPoE, RAS, PPTP, or HBS connection types.

If you're not using one of those connection methods, the Login status is marked Disabled.

You cannot make changes on this page; it's a report of your setup configuration. When you make changes to the Setup tab, those changes are reflected in this Status tab.

Managing DHCP

When computers receive their IP addresses automatically, instead of using an assigned static IP address, the IP address assignments are handled by a Dynamic Host Configuration Protocol (DHCP) server. You can create a DHCP server on any network, using any computer—in fact, if you run Internet Connection Sharing (ICS) instead of using a router, the computer that has the modem becomes the DHCP server. Corporate network administrators set up DHCP servers to provide IP addresses for all the computers on the network.

It's best to let your router act as the DHCP server. Even if you had been running ICS, you had to disable it when you installed your router, so it would be unusual for a small network to use anything but the router for DHCP services.

DHCP servers don't assign IP addresses permanently; instead, they're leased to computers when the computers start up and request an IP address. When the lease expires, a new lease is assigned. (Computers don't have to reboot to request a new lease, because it's an automatic process.) The default length of the lease appears on the DHCP tab (see Figure 9-8) along with other DHCP settings (some of which you set when you configured the Setup tab). There's no particular reason to change any of these settings.

To see the current DHCP client data, click the DHCP Clients Table button.

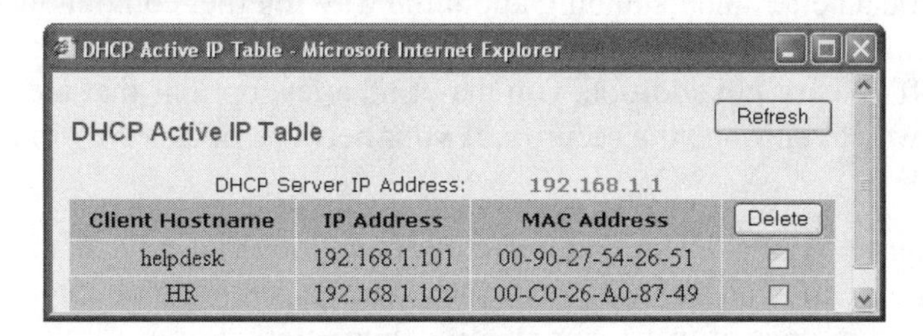

Advanced Setup Configuration Options

Clicking the Advanced tab opens a whole new set of tabs you can use to tweak your router's settings. (To return to the original window, and the original tabs, click the Setup tab.) Most of the options available in these tabs are unnecessary for home and small business networks, but I offer brief descriptions of them because

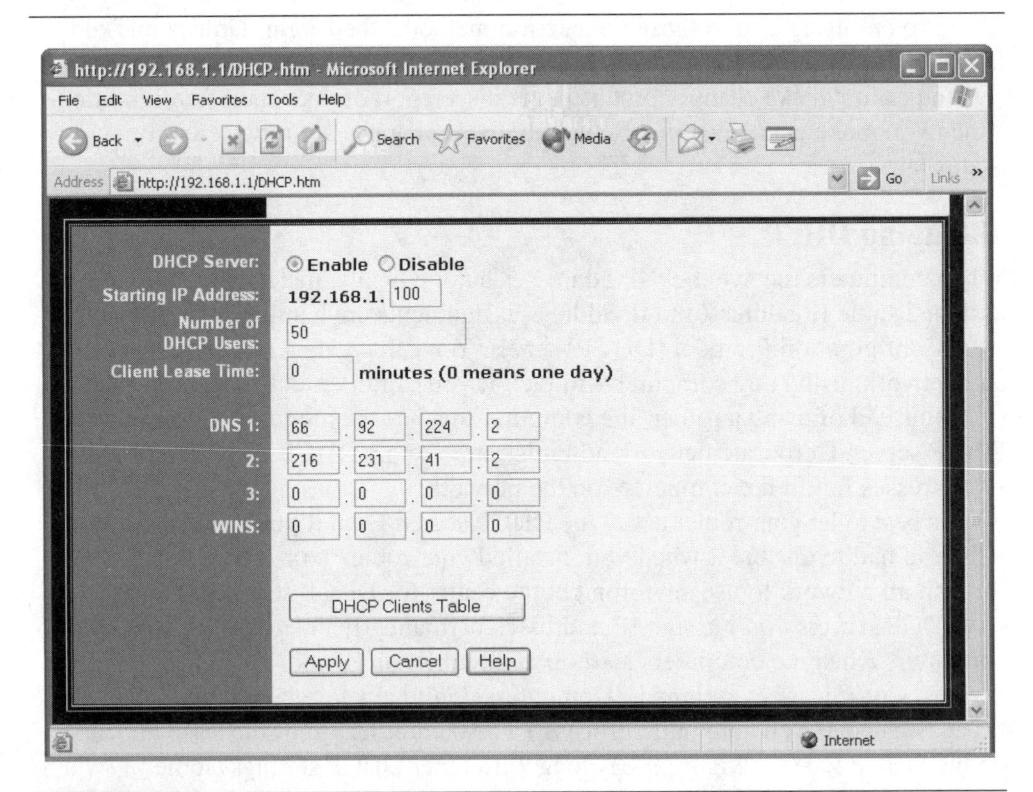

FIGURE 9-8 Configuration settings for your firewall router-based DHCP server are on the DHCP tab.

that gives you a better understanding about the way Internet communications work. (I believe that the more information you have about the way things work, the better off you are.) In addition, you may find a few options that are appealing to you as a way to enhance the security of your network or as a way to control network users.

Filtering Internet Traffic The Filters tab offers options you can use to enhance the security of traffic moving through your router. The Packet Filter option lets you deny access to certain types of traffic for specific computers. For example, you could establish a blockade against using certain protocols, such as FTP (File Transfer Protocol), so that a particular computer on your network can't download files from Internet servers. You can also establish blockades against certain Internet services in the other direction—forbidding computers on the Internet from sending particular types of data to a computer on your network.

Even though I've only briefly described the way packet filtering can work, you can probably think of several ways in which it would be helpful to use this technology to secure your network and control your network users. It's actually quite an attractive idea. However, implementation requires a clear understanding of data types and the ramifications of restricting them—for home and small business networks, you should do your research or hire a consultant rather than do it yourself.

Forwarding Data Packets The Forwarding tab provides options that let you forward Internet traffic so that data intended for certain ports is intercepted and then forwarded to certain computers. These settings are useful if one of the computers on your network is actually running on the Internet. Since most ISPs prohibit running services like Web or FTP servers on small networks, you may not have to worry about it at all. However, at times you may want to allow traffic into your network and forward it to the appropriate computer. A good example of this is when you play multiplayer games that require an Internet connection. If you (or your child) and your friends want to play a game together, usually one person in the group must run the game as the host and then allow other players to connect. The host will need to allow access on the appropriate ports to reach the host computer so that other players can locate and communicate with it (you'll have to check the documentation for the game or other program to see what ports it uses).

To use forwarding, the computer to which you want to forward traffic will need a static IP address, rather than an automatic address assigned by the router using DHCP. You will need to assign the computer that you wish to use an address that is outside of the DHCP scope (normally 100–149), so this means you can use the addresses 2–99 and 150–254.

The router can forward a particular port only to one PC at a time. If you wish to forward ports to multiple ports, try port triggering—one of the two other options available on this tab:

- **Port Triggering** This is similar to port forwarding in the aspect of opening ports; however, port triggering works slightly differently. With port forwarding, all incoming packets on port 12345 are forwarded to IP address 192.168.1.20. With port triggering, the router waits until an outgoing request goes out on port 12345 and the router is "triggered" to open the incoming port range. (The triggered and incoming port ranges can be different or the same. If you're unsure which is which, simply make them the same.)

- **UPnP Forwarding** This feature enables you to check which ports have been activated via UPnP. You can also manually forward ports here; however, it is not recommended.

Dynamic Routing The Dynamic Routing tab provides a way to make routing more efficient, and it has no effect on a router that's servicing a self-contained LAN. In large enterprises, where routers move data packets to remote servers in other physical locations, dynamic routing is a nifty technology, because you can instruct the router to find the quickest or cheapest way to move data.

Static Routing The Static Routing tab lets you set options that force routers to access other routers on your network in a specific way. Small networks don't need multiple routers, so you have no reason to use these options.

DMZ Host You can use the options on the DMZ Host tab to establish one of the computers on your network as a DMZ host. As explained earlier in this chapter, that computer must be connected to port 4 of your router.

A DMZ host ignores the firewall (or it may be more accurate to say that the firewall ignores the DMZ host). DMZ hosts can send data packets back and forth between the two networks (your LAN and the Internet) without obeying any rules. The other nodes (your network computers) continue to be protected by the firewall, and they use the DMZ node as the "sacrificial lamb" that sends and receives data from the outside network. In large corporate networks, a DMZ is normally used to gain access to the company servers that are exposed to the Internet, while keeping the internal network secure from users who are visiting the company Web site. (That's why, when you visit a Web site such as *http://www.linksys.com*, you can't issue commands that would let you access data on the Linksys internal servers or the employees' computers, even if you know the commands that would permit such access.) DMZ is also a useful feature for a machine that is running multiple services such as HTTP and FTP. You do not have to forward multiple ports to that machine; simply put it into the DMZ.

NOTE *The DMZ will override port forwarding, so do not run both services at once.*

For small networks, the DMZ can be useful for letting users perform actions that the firewall would usually prevent, such as playing certain interactive Internet games or participating in Internet conferences without having to unblock ports. However, establishing a network node that is unprotected by the firewall for any length of time invites trouble. Be sure to take the computer out of the DMZ when it doesn't need to be there. If you think you need to set up a computer to reside permanently in the DMZ, you should call a consultant to help you set this up.

NOTE *The DMZ does not bypass the firewall completely. The computer that is in the DMZ will still be under NAT (Network Address Translation). If you try to use a service that does not support NAT, it will not work through the DMZ.*

MAC Address Clone The MAC Addr. Clone tab lets you change the MAC address of the router. A MAC (Media Access Control) address is a hardware-level ID number that uniquely identifies a hardware device. Some ISPs require you to register the MAC address of the device that's connected to the ISP. Before you installed your router, if you had a NIC in a computer to connect that computer to your DSL/cable modem—and therefore, to your ISP—the NIC's MAC address was registered with the ISP. After you installed your router, that router became the only connection your ISP sees, and its MAC address is not the one you originally registered with your ISP. Rather than go through a new MAC registration process with your ISP (not fun, unless you enjoy being transferred from technician to technician and spending a lot of time on hold), you can clone the original NIC's MAC address to your router. Your ISP will never know you changed the connection device.

To accomplish this, select the User Defined option and then enter the MAC address of the NIC that was originally connected to the DSL/cable modem. The tab displays the MAC address of the computer you're working on, so it's easiest to perform this task by accessing the router's Setup program from the computer that was originally connected to the DSL/cable modem. Otherwise, check the DHCP Client Table on the DHCP tab to ascertain the MAC address of the computer that was originally connected to the ISP.

Protecting Your Computer with a Software Firewall

In addition to using a hardware firewall to protect your network, you should also use a software firewall on each computer connected to the network to provide an extra layer of protection. Think of it as living in a gated community—just because everyone must pass through a gate to get into the neighborhood doesn't mean you shouldn't lock your doors. Good software firewalls also do something that many hardware firewalls don't do: they prevent access *to* the Internet by programs that you haven't specifically given permission to have that access. This helps prevent programs such as viruses and spyware (which you'll learn more about later in the chapter) from being able to contact the outside world.

If you are using Windows XP, you already have access to a very good, free software firewall. All you have to do is let Windows install an update named Windows XP Service Pack 2 (SP2). In fact, if you have a computer with Windows XP that is connected to the Internet and you routinely apply the latest updates, you probably already have SP2 installed. If you don't update your computer routinely, check out the section, "Enabling Automatic Updates in Windows XP," to find out more.

If you are not using Windows XP, you can still get a good software firewall from companies such as ZoneLabs (*http://www.zonelabs.com*), Agnitum (*http://www.agnitum.com*), or McAfee (*http://www.mcafee.com*). In this section, I cover using Windows Firewall, the firewall that comes with Windows XP SP2. If you're using Windows 98, Me, or 2000, consider buying a firewall product from another vendor.

Internet Connection Firewall Versus Windows Firewall

When Windows XP first shipped, it included a built-in firewall named Internet Connection Firewall. This software was actually not a great firewall and was not very configurable. With the release of Windows XP SP2, the built-in firewall was renamed Windows Firewall and completely redesigned.

In addition to being far easier to use, thanks to a streamlined interface, Windows Firewall boasts a number of enhancements:

- It is turned on by default. The old version, Internet Connection Firewall, was disabled by default when you installed Windows. When you install Windows XP SP2, Windows Firewall is turned on by default, so chances are it's already working for you.
- On computers with multiple network connections (such as portable computers that you move between the office, the airport, and home), you can configure the firewall settings on each connection independently.
- Windows Firewall begins protecting your network early during Windows startup, so that you are safe long before you even see the Windows desktop.

How to Tell Whether You Have SP2

If you are running Windows XP and your computer is configured to download critical updates automatically, or if you bought your computer recently, you should already have SP2 installed. To find out, use these steps:

1. On the Start menu, right-click the My Computer icon and click Properties.
2. In the System Properties dialog box that opens, on the General tab, look at the System section (where it says Microsoft Windows XP). At the bottom of that section, under the version number, you'll see the words *Service Pack 2* if SP2 is installed.
3. Click OK to close the System Properties dialog box.

TIP *If you don't have Windows XP SP2 installed, check out the section "Enabling Automatic Updates in Windows XP," for information on how to get it.*

How to Enable or Disable Windows Firewall

To make changes to Windows Firewall, you must be logged on with a user account of the Administrator type. As I mentioned earlier, you can enable or disable Windows Firewall for each network connection on a computer, or you can enable or disable it for all connections at once. If you have only one connection, you should use these steps to configure it globally.

To enable or disable Windows Firewall for all network connection, use these steps:

1. Choose Start | Control Panel.
2. In the Control Panel window, select Network And Internet Connections.
3. In the Network And Internet Connections window, select Windows Firewall.
4. On the General tab of the Windows Firewall dialog box, shown in Figure 9-9, select the On (Recommended) option to enable the firewall for all connections. Select Off (Not Recommended) to disable the firewall for all connections.
5. Click OK.

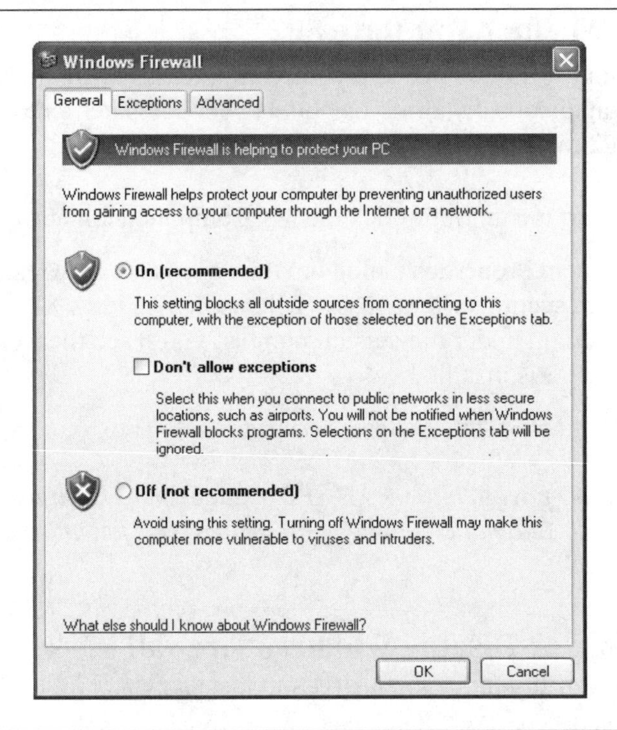

FIGURE 9-9 Turning Windows Firewall on or off for all connections

If you have multiple network connections on your computer and you want to enable or disable Windows Firewall for a specific network connection, use these steps:

1. Choose Start | Control Panel.
2. In the Control Panel window, select Network And Internet Connections.
3. In the Network And Internet Connections window, select Network Connections.
4. In the Network Connections window, right-click the connection for which you want to enable or disable Windows Firewall, and then choose Properties.
5. In the Properties dialog box of the network connection, select the Advanced tab.
6. On the Advanced tab, click Settings.
7. In the Windows Firewall dialog box, switch to the Advanced tab, shown in Figure 9-10.

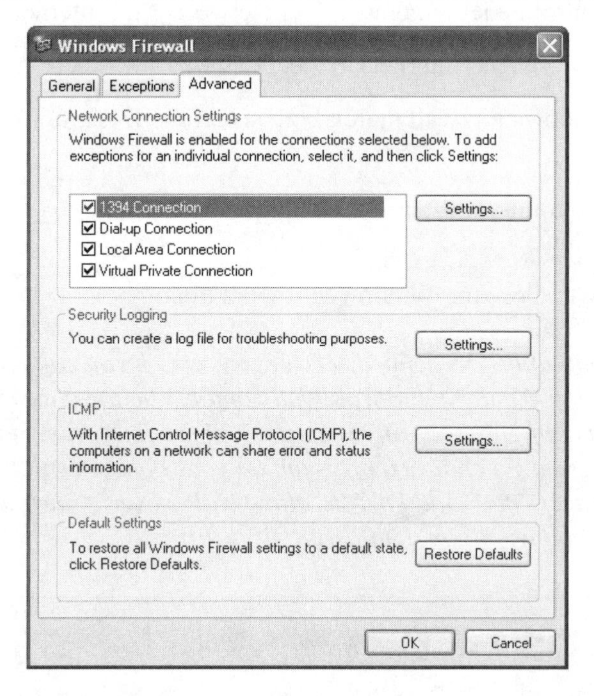

FIGURE 9-10 Turning Windows Firewall on or off for one connection.

8. To enable Windows Firewall for a connection, select the check box for that connection. To disable Windows Firewall for a connection, clear the check box for that connection.
9. Click OK to close the Windows Firewall dialog box.
10. Click OK to close the Properties dialog box for the network connection.

How to Create an Exception for a Service or Application

By default, Windows Firewall blocks all unsolicited traffic. You can create exceptions so that particular types of traffic are allowed through the firewall (such as FTP traffic, for example).

To create a global exception that applies to all network connections for which Windows Firewall is enabled, use these steps:

1. Choose Start | Control Panel.

2. In the Control Panel window, select Network And Internet Connections.
3. In the Network And Internet Connections window, select Windows Firewall.
4. In the Windows Firewall dialog box, select the Exceptions tab, shown in Figure 9-11.
5. On the Programs And Services list, select the check box for the service you want to allow.
6. Click OK to close the Windows Firewall dialog box.

TIP *In addition to the predefined services for which you can create an exception in Windows Firewall, you can also define a custom service and then configure it as an exception. On the Exceptions tab, just click Add Program (to choose a program on your computer that should be allowed access) or Add Port (to allow traffic over a particular port—much as you would on a hardware firewall).*

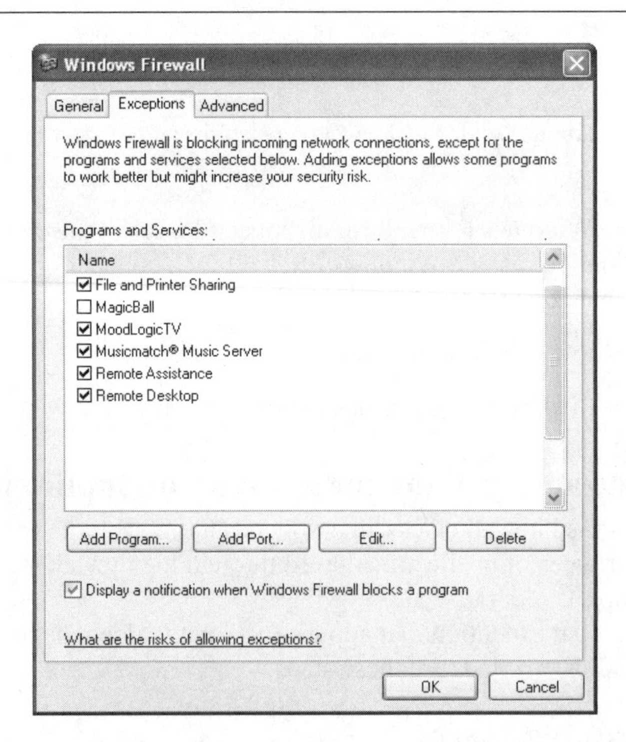

FIGURE 9-11 Creating a global exception for all connections in Windows Firewall

To create an exception for a particular network connection for which Windows Firewall is enabled, use these steps:

1. Choose Start | Control Panel.
2. In the Control Panel window, select Network And Internet Connections.
3. In the Network And Internet Connections window, select Windows Firewall.
4. In the Windows Firewall dialog box, select the Advanced tab.
5. In the Network Connection Settings section, select the connection for which you want to configure an exception and click Settings.
6. On the Services tab of the Advanced Settings dialog box, shown in Figure 9-12, select the check box for the service you want to allow.
7. Click OK to close the Advanced Settings dialog box. Click OK again to close the Windows Firewall dialog box.

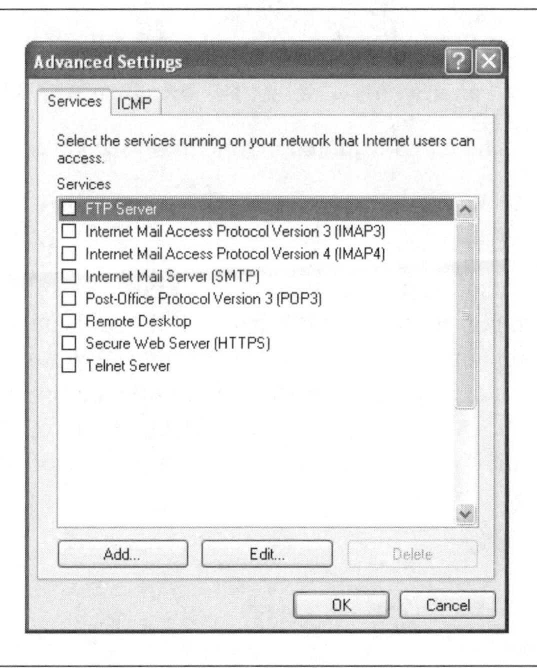

FIGURE 9-12 Creating an exception for a particular network connection in Windows Firewall

Enabling Automatic Updates in Windows XP

Software updates help keep computers protected from new vulnerabilities that are discovered (and new threats that are created) after the operating system ships. Updates include security patches and other critical fixes and are vital to keeping computers secure and functioning properly.

Most versions of Windows (including Windows Me, Windows 2000, and Windows XP) feature an automatic updating service named Automatic Updates that can download and apply updates automatically in the background. Automatic Updates connects periodically to Windows Update on the Internet. When Automatic Updates discovers new updates that apply to the computer, it can be configured to install all updates automatically (the preferred method if you have a broadband connection) or to notify the computer's user that an update is available.

Enabling Automatic Updates works pretty much the same way in all versions of Windows that support it, so I cover the feature in Windows XP only. You'll have no trouble figuring it out for other versions.

To enable Automatic Updates in Windows XP, use the following steps:

1. Choose Start | Control Panel.
2. In the Control Panel window, select Performance And Maintenance.
3. In the Performance and Maintenance window, select System.
4. On the Automatic Updates tab, select the Automatic (Recommended) option, as shown in Figure 9-13.
5. Select how often and at what time of day updates should be downloaded and installed. For users with high-bandwidth, dedicated connections (such as a cable modem), you should configure Windows to check for updates daily at a time when the user is not using the computer (the default setting of 3:00 A.M. works pretty well). Users with lower-bandwidth connections may want to check less frequently or even use one of the manual options.
6. Click OK.

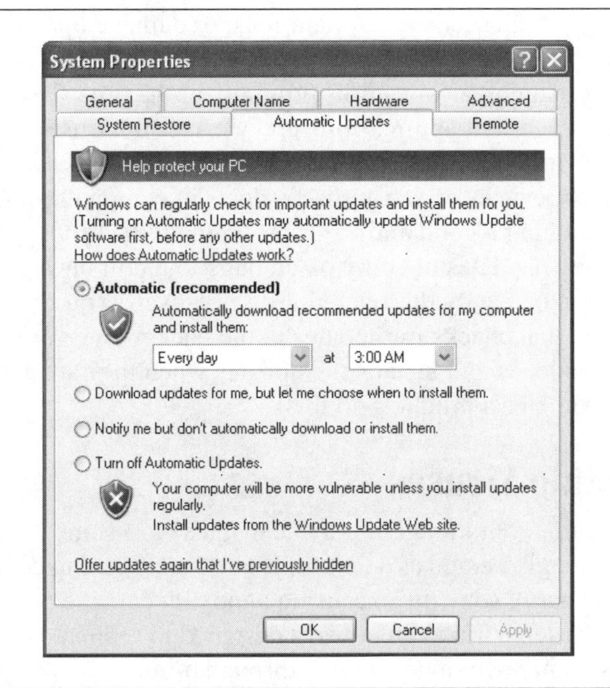

FIGURE 9-13 Use Automatic Updates to download and install updates in the background so you don't have to worry about it.

TIP *If you don't like the idea of Windows updating itself without you, or if you just like the hands-on approach, you can visit the Windows Update site to search for and install updates for your computer. In addition to providing a more hands-on experience, Windows Update also provides access to updates beyond just critical fixed and security patches. You can often find feature updates, new versions of Windows programs (such as Media Player), and even the occasional hardware driver update.*

Anti-Virus Software

Computer viruses are an enormous problem, and the spread of a variety of forms of this rogue programming code has grown to epidemic proportions. Viruses erase data, change program files, change system files, or damage operating system files so the computer can't boot.

You should be running an anti-virus program all the time. Two of the most popular and well-regarded applications are McAfee's VirusScan (*http://www.mcafee.com*) and Symantec's Norton AntiVirus (*http://www.symantec.com*). You can also check reviews of anti-virus products in computer publications. As important as running a good anti-virus program all the time is keeping it continually updated. Updates not only patch bugs found in the software, but they contain information on newly discovered viruses as well. You should choose an anti-virus program that checks for updates in the background for you and then automatically downloads and installs the updates when they are available (both Symantec's and McAfee's products do this).

Understanding Viruses

A *virus* is a program, even though it may be disguised as something else (including something as seemingly benign as a text file). The programming code of a virus is designed to cause harm, sometimes causing annoying damage and sometimes inflicting utter disaster. Viruses are always designed to replicate themselves to other computers, either over a network or through e-mail.

The fact that part of the definition of a virus is that it's a program confuses some people, because they know they can get a virus through a document prepared in Microsoft Word or Microsoft Excel (there has certainly been plenty of press coverage of that fact). However, the virus you may get from an e-mail attachment of a Word or Excel document is indeed from a program, because the virus travels in a macro that's linked to (and essentially, part of) the document. Microsoft uses Visual Basic Script (VBS) programming code for macros, and VBS produces executable code just like any other programming language. Therefore, Word and Excel macros qualify as programs.

TIP

If you don't use VBS and don't need to run .vbs files, change the file association for .vbs files to Notepad. Then, if you accidentally open a file containing a virus in the VBS code, the file opens as a text file in Notepad. Check your Windows help files to learn how to change file associations.

Types of Viruses

Viruses arrive in many forms and categories, and within each category are many subcategories. Covering all of these variants and explaining what they do would take forever (and fill a thick book). Therefore, I present a brief, albeit somewhat simplified, overview of some of the basic types of viruses.

File Infector Viruses

File infector viruses are the oldest type of virus, and they've been around as long as the PC has existed (although in those early days viruses were transmitted by infected floppy disks, as nobody was surfing the Internet back then).

A file infector virus attaches itself to an existing program file, perhaps a file you open frequently. When you launch the program, you launch the virus, which then does its damage and plants itself somewhere on your drive so it can spread itself to other computers. These viruses can use any executable file type, although they most commonly use .com and .exe files. However, other executable file types, including .sys and .mnu files, can also be targets of their parasitic behavior.

NOTE *Some file infector viruses arrive as fully contained programs (frequently as scripts) instead of attaching themselves to other programs.*

When I tell people who have been victimized that the virus was linked to an executable file, they're usually surprised (or tell me I'm wrong). They point out that they examined the filenames of e-mail attachments, looking for a file extension that indicates an executable file. They saw an attachment with the file extension .txt and assumed the attachment was safe.

Sigh! Unfortunately, they didn't see the actual, full, filename. In designing Windows, Microsoft decided that the default behavior of Windows is to hide the display of file extensions that are associated with programs—probably the idea being to hide the intricacies of Windows from novices. This means a file that displays its name as readme.txt could actually be named readme.txt.exe. You should change that behavior immediately, which you can do by taking the following steps:

1. Open any system folder such as Windows Explorer, My Computer, or Control Panel.
2. Choose Tools | Folder Options (or View | Folder Options in Windows 98).
3. Click the View tab, and locate the item Hide Extensions for Known File Types. Click the check box to remove the check mark.
4. Click OK.

Macro Viruses

Macro viruses are programmed to do the same type of damage as file infector viruses, but they use a different method of transportation. Instead of being attached to a program file, they're linked to a macro in a Word or Excel document. They launch when the document file to which they're attached is opened, carry out their nefarious tasks, and replicate themselves into other documents.

Boot Sector Viruses

A boot sector virus places its code in the Master Boot Record of a hard drive (or the boot sector of a floppy disk). As the computer boots, during the time the computer reads and executes the programs in the boot sector (before the operating system starts), the virus launches itself into memory. Once it's in memory, the virus can control computer operations and replicate itself to other drives on the computer or to other computers on the network. Some boot sector viruses are programmed to destroy the computer's ability to boot, while others let the computer boot normally and then perform their ugly tasks.

Worms

A worm is a self-contained program that doesn't need to attach itself to another program to do damage. A worm counts on users opening the rogue file manually, at which point it performs whatever damage it's programmed to do and replicates itself. Worms commonly replicate themselves by mailing themselves to all the recipients in an Outlook or Outlook Express address book and by installing themselves on hard drives, including those across a network.

Because they don't have to attach themselves to other programs, worms propagate themselves faster and easier than the proverbial rabbit. They just lay down anywhere they feel like it and clone themselves all over your drives. Sometimes their propagation scheme is designed in a way that gives each clone a different assignment, so when all of them go into action, they can do incredible damage.

Trojan Horses

A Trojan horse performs the same type of evil tasks as a virus does, but it's technically not a virus because it doesn't replicate itself. Since replication is part of the strict definition of a virus, the term *Trojan horse* was adopted to create a distinction between this type of rogue code and true viruses. If you've been victimized by a Trojan horse, however, you don't care much about those technicalities.

One serious challenge in dealing with Trojan horses is that even if your anti-virus software can remove the file, the attendant damage to your system may not be easy to remove. You should always contact your anti-virus software vendor to get instructions. You may have to undo changes to the registry or replace system files to rid your system of the damage. Fortunately, companies such as Symantec (the makers of Norton AntiVirus and other products) and McAfee (the makers of McAfee VirusScan and other products) provide detailed information about getting rid of Trojan horses and often provide tools to help you do the job. You can obtain software that's dedicated to managing Trojan horses; two companies that offer these products are PestPatrol (*http://www.safersite.com*) and Tauscan (*http://www.agnitum.com*).

Understanding Anti-Virus Software

Anti-virus software is complicated and powerful, because it operates in multiple ways, using multiple components. The software contains two main components: the engine and the virus definition data files (often called virus signature files).

The engine, which is responsible for running all the processes, has two different programs:

- A background scanner that automatically checks for viruses any time a file is saved to your hard disk, whether that file comes through e-mail, a Web site, from another computer on the network, or from a removable disk (floppy or CD-ROM, for example)
- A regular scanning component, which performs a scan of the files on your computer to check for viruses—usually scheduled to do a full scan of your computer periodically

The virus definition data files contain information about known viruses, which makes it possible for the software to spot them.

The software works by intercepting operations such as reading files or opening e-mail messages to check a file for viruses before permitting the operation to continue. Checking the file involves several steps:

- Comparing the data with the information in the virus data information files, looking for a string of characters or bytes that's found in a particular virus (called a virus *signature*)

- Checking for a change in a file's attributes since the last time the file was checked—for example, looking for a change in the size of an executable file
- Using heuristic scanning to check for suspicious data (see the sidebar "Heuristic Scanning")

When the software detects a virus in a file, it displays a message asking you what you want to do. The choices vary depending on the software, but usually you have the following options:

- *Clean the file.* This choice is available when a virus has infected an existing file. The software tries to clean the virus out of the file to return the file to its original condition. If cleaning fails (it frequently does), the software usually suggests that you delete the file, using the Delete option in the anti-virus software window.
- *Delete the file.* The file is permanently deleted, and it is not sent to the Recycle Bin.
- *Isolate the file.* The file is placed in a special folder that's created and managed by the anti-virus software (to prevent the virus from launching). Later, you can delete the files in that folder or send them to the anti-virus software company (if you're participating in a program to alert the company of any found viruses).

The software names the viruses it finds, and it's a good idea to go to the software company's Web site to learn more about that virus. You'll find instructions for taking additional steps to rid your system of the effects of the virus.

Heuristic Scanning

Heuristic scanning is a behavior-based method for analyzing an executable file and determining whether it may be a threat. Anti-virus software uses heuristic scanning to try to catch viruses that are new and for which virus definition files are not yet available. The anti-virus software is looking for viruslike behavior. Using heuristic scanning does slow down the scanning process a bit and sometimes causes false alarms, but these are minor inconveniences compared to what a virus can do to your system.

Other Security Measures

In addition to the big three security measures I've already described, you should be aware of some other issues. In this section, I cover three additional security measures you can take:

- Ending pop-up messages that appear on your desktop
- Getting rid of spyware installed on your computer
- Using VPN to connect networks securely over the Internet

Ending Pop-Up Message Intrusions

A relatively new annoyance has appeared on Windows 2000/XP/2003 desktops in the form of pop-up messages from advertisers. I'm not talking about pop-up ads you see when you're on the Internet with your browser—I'm talking about messages that appear directly on your desktop. They can appear when you're not connected to any Web site, and even your browser isn't open.

These are "desktop spam" items—spam from direct advertisers that appears on your monitor, looking like a message from another computer—no graphics, no links, just text. Most of the ads I've seen are from institutes of higher education that offer degrees, and the message hints that you can get a degree without buying books, attending classes, or, apparently, even straining your brain with any need to study.

What's interesting from a technical point of view is the way these messages get to your desktop over the Internet. Essentially, the spammers are using a "back-door" technique to overcome any security efforts you think you've made to protect your computer from Internet interlopers.

Without getting into deep technical waters, I'll just explain that the advertisers are using the `net send` command (covered in Appendix B), which uses the Windows messenger service. That's why the ads look like the standard, regular, intercomputer messages you'd see if you used `net send`. The messenger service is a Windows service that transmits `net send` messages that are created manually by users and messages that are sent automatically through the alerter service (usually from servers to workstations, such as automatic messages that alert administrators to a problem on a server). The Windows messenger service is also used by the operating system and software programs to send messages to users (such as the message that tells you a print job is complete and the message sent by an anti-virus program to tell you a virus has been found and deleted). The

Windows messenger service is not related to your browser, your e-mail software, or Windows Messenger (the Instant Messaging program).

You may believe that the ads are neither a major problem nor a security threat, they're just annoying. However, the technical reality is that the back-door method the advertisers use can also be used to disrupt network communications. Most of the software the advertisers purchase takes advantage of port availability and uses UDP 135. The good news is that if you are running a good software firewall on your computer (such as Windows Firewall in Windows XP with SP2), you will already be protected from pop-up message intrusions.

If your firewall isn't configurable, you can stop the messenger service from loading automatically when you start Windows, using the following steps:

1. In Windows 2000, choose Start | Settings | Control Panel; in Windows XP, choose Start | Control Panel, and then click Performance and Maintenance.
2. Double-click the Administrative Tools icon.
3. Double-click the Services applet.
4. Double-click the messenger service to open its Properties dialog.
5. Click the Stop button, and wait for Windows to stop the service.
6. Change the Startup type as follows:
   - Select Disable if you don't need to use the `net send` command.
   - Select Manual if you occasionally use the `net send` command. When you want to send a message, repeat these steps to open the Properties dialog for Services and click the Start button. After you've sent the message, click the Stop button.
7. Click OK.

Getting Rid of Spyware

Spyware (sometimes called adware) are programs that secretly run on your computer, gather information about your activities, and send that information to companies or bad guys on the Internet. Sounds scary, doesn't it? The reason that spyware was initially developed was to let companies that provide you services (such as free, downloadable music, games, or other programs) also provide you with advertisements to offset the costs of giving you free stuff. While this intention seems harmless enough, spyware causes all kinds of problems.

For one thing, even the most well-intentioned spyware consumes your system resources and can cause problems with your operating system or other programs. In addition, companies that use spyware often do not tell you that you are going to allow programs to install themselves except somewhere in the very fine print of their terms of agreement (and I'm sure we all read those things thoroughly). To make the situation even worse, in addition to just sending you advertisements, companies also use spyware to track your activities—information like what Web sites you visit—and send that information back to the company. And if that isn't enough, spyware is typically poorly written software that causes crashes, poor performance, and generally strange behavior on your computer. Spyware is also used by unscrupulous people as a mechanism for hacking into your computer or delivering you viruses.

Fortunately, you can take some really good steps to make sure you are not a victim of spyware:

- *Watch what you download.* The best way to take care of spyware is not to let it get to your computer in the first place. While it's hard to resist trying out free offers, be very careful from whom you accept these freebies. Download programs only from reputable sources. File-sharing programs, such as those that let people trade music and other copyrighted material freely over the Internet, are notorious for installing spyware on your computer.
- *Don't say yes.* If you are browsing the Web and a site asks you do download and install content (usually by popping up a browser window where you can click Yes or No), say No unless you are absolutely sure you need the content. Some sites do use special browser extensions to display media content, so you may need to say Yes sometimes. Just be careful and be sure to read those agreements—even the long ones.
- *Use a good spyware scanner.* Many companies, such as Symantec and McAfee, sell spyware scanners that scan your computer, identify spyware, and remove it. But two spyware products are available that really stand out—and they're free as well: AdAware Personal (*http://www.lavasoftusa.com*) and SpyBot Search & Destroy (*http://www.safer-networking.net*). Follow the onsite instructions for downloading, installing, and using these programs. Also, be sure to update the programs regularly (much the same way you update anti-virus programs), because new spyware is discovered all the time.

TIP

I use both AdAware Personal and Spybot Search & Destroy on my computers because each finds spyware the other misses. I run both programs once every couple of weeks.

If you want to download SpyBot Search & Destroy, be sure to visit http://www.safer-networking.net instead of http://www.safer-networking.com. The latter address is for a company that sells a product named SpyKiller—a fine spyware scanner, but it's not free.

Using VPNs

A VPN is a secure connection between two or more LANs to form a larger network. The word *secure* means that the VPN employs technology to guarantee that only authorized users can use the VPN and to ensure that data cannot be intercepted while it travels between locations.

In this section, I present an overview of VPNs so you understand what they are and why they exist. Because it would be highly unusual for a home or small business network to need a VPN, it's beyond the scope of this book to provide detailed instructions for setting up and managing VPNs. The software and security issues are extremely complicated, and without an experienced IT professional on hand, you need to hire a consultant if you find you need a VPN.

When you create a LAN, it's a private world consisting of computers that are connected by the topology you selected (Ethernet, wireless, PhoneLine, or PowerLine). This is true for home networks, small business networks, and large corporate networks. Any user who wants to access resources on the network must be working at a computer that's connected to the LAN.

Suppose your business has another office with its own LAN on the other end of town, or in another town. Or suppose you have users who want to work from home but connect to the company network. How do you create a network environment between the two locations? Obviously, you can't just extend the topology—you can't run Ethernet cable from one location to the other, nor can you plug into the phone or powerlines, and you certainly can't put a wireless antenna in a position that would extend the network. You have two choices for creating this extended private network:

- Install a direct connection to create a WAN, which is a private network.
- Use the Internet, which is public, along with security features, to create a VPN.

Direct Connections for WANs

A direct connection is a physical device that connects multiple LANs, and you must look to the telephone company for the physical device. You can use regular telephone lines to have a modem dial in to one LAN from another LAN, or you can use a dedicated high-speed telephone line (such as a T1 line) to establish an always-on connection. You don't need an ISP to make the connection—essentially you make a telephone call from one phone number to another, and the paradigm is called *remote access*.

NOTE *When you dial in to your ISP for your regular Internet browsing sessions, you're using remote access to connect from your computer (the remote access client) to the ISP's computer (the remote access server).*

To enable this method for a WAN, you must install a remote access server that manages the phone connection, the user logons, and the security issues. Windows provides software and tools for creating, configuring, and managing remote access services.

However, modems are too slow to produce any level of efficiency, and high-speed lines are very expensive. In addition, you have to set up a security system that prevents outside users from using phonelines to invade your network. Because you're probably using peer-to-peer networks (this book makes that assumption, because it's written for small business and home networks, which are almost always peer-to-peer), you lack the authentication features available in client/server networks. Some ISPs provide T1 WAN services (most ISPs connect to the Internet via T1 lines), but the cost, on top of the cost of the line, can be prohibitive.

Rather than use physical devices to connect computers that are at different locations, why not use communication lines that are already in place? Why not use the existing public infrastructure that the Internet provides to create your own private network? The Internet is not only the largest network in the world, it's a network that's accessible by any computer in the world.

Because it doesn't use direct wiring the way a LAN does, this method results in a "virtual" private network. In essence, a VPN is a secure, private networking connection that works on top of (or, as we say in the IT business, tunnels through) the Internet. In addition, if you have a broadband Internet connection, the computers in your VPN can communicate at an efficient speed. What makes the network "private" is the fact that only authorized users can access network resources. To make that a reality, you have to apply security features that are designed to ensure that only authorized users can connect to the VPN. In addition, you have to make sure the data that moves between network nodes is secure, which involves encrypting the data. After all, the data is moving along the Internet's public lines, and unless the data is secure, any reasonably efficient hacker can intercept it. A VPN must provide the same security that a self-contained LAN provides. The technical term for a secure communication channel is *tunnel*, and a tunnel is created by applying a variety of security functions, usually referred to as *IPSec* (which stands for IP security).

Using a VPN Router

The security services are the most complicated issues in a VPN, and you can maintain security with a router that's specifically designed to provide secure communication between LANs on a VPN. Linksys has VPN routers that apply the controls and technologies you need to ensure safe exchanges of data. If you choose a VPN router, you can use either of the following connection methods:

- Connect a VPN router on one LAN to a VPN router on another LAN.
- Connect a VPN router on one LAN to a computer running client VPN software that supports IPSec on another LAN.

The Linksys VPN routers have the following features:

- LAN ports, so you can use the router as your hub if your network has no more than four computers. Otherwise, use one of the ports to connect your hub or switch to the router.
- A WAN port to connect to your DSL/cable modem.
- DHCP services to assign IP addresses to all the computers on the LAN.
- Configuration options you access using the browser of any computer on the LAN.
- Security configuration options to create a secure tunnel (including configurable encryption and authentication functions).
- Backup and restore functions for your configuration data.
- A DMZ zone to enable Internet access to a computer on the LAN.

For full, detailed instructions on configuring the VPN, see the user guide that comes with your router.

Accessing a Network with a VPN Network Adapter

If your home or small business network has a VPN router, and you want to access network resources from an external location, the Linksys VPN network adapter provides the client side of VPN communications in a hardware device. Using this adapter saves you the trouble of installing and configuring complicated VPN client software. The adapter connects to your computer via a USB connector, and it can be used to access the Internet over a DSL or cable modem. Once you're connected to the Internet, you can establish a VPN tunnel to your network. You have the same access to network resources, and the same security, that you would have if you were on-site, using a computer that's physically connected to the LAN.

Chapter 10

Sharing Files and Folders

In a network environment, you can share certain components on one computer with the other computers on the network. These components are called *shared resources*, and they include drives, folders, and printers. When you create a shared resource, the commonly used jargon for that resource is a *share*. Other standard terminology you'll encounter for shared resources includes the following:

- **Sharename** The name of a share (all shares are named)
- **Local computer** The computer at which you're currently working
- **Local user** The user who is working at a specific computer
- **Remote computer** Another computer on the network
- **Remote user** The user who is accessing a share from a remote computer

NOTE *Appendix A is a glossary of networking terms, and you should check it whenever you come across a phrase you don't understand.*

Linksys also offers dedicated storage devices that attach directly to a network. These devices are often called *network attached storage* (NAS) devices. Using a NAS device to store shared files that network users need frees individual computers from having to share files and offers other advantages as well.

Sharing Files

To share files across the network, you share their containers, which are drives and folders. Windows does not provide a way to share individual files; you must share the drive or folder that contains the file. Sharing does more than provide access to files for other users on the network; it's also handy when you want to work on your own files, but the computer you usually use isn't available at the moment, or if you want to access the files on your main computer from another computer, such as a notebook. In most home networks, there are more users in the household than computers, so it's common to share computers. If Dad usually sits at the computer in the den and saves his documents on that computer, when his daughter is using the den computer Dad can go to any computer in the house and access the documents stored on the den computer. In fact, he can work on those documents as if he were sitting in front of the den computer.

File Sharing Is Hierarchical

When you share a drive or folder, every part of the container is shared. This means that if you share a drive, you share every folder, subfolder, and file on that drive. If you share a folder, you share every subfolder and file contained in that folder.

To keep your system safe, it's best not to share a drive. In addition, you should limit your shares to the folders that contain document files rather than software and system files, because sharing software and system files can be very dangerous—for example, remote users could inadvertently change or remove those files. Share your document folder, or share only specific subfolders within your document folder.

TIP *Many people create a special folder named something like Shared Files and make that the only shared folder on their computer. To share files or other folders, they just place the objects in the Shared Files folder. This makes it easy to keep track of what they have and haven't shared.*

The exception to this safety rule is a removable-media drive such as a CD-ROM or a Zip drive. When you share such an external drive, you cannot share a folder on that drive, because the folder structure changes depending on the media that's inserted in the drive. Instead, you share only the drive, making its current contents available to remote users.

Sharing a CD-ROM drive (or other removable-media drive) is also a good way to make the drive available to computers that may not have that type of drive. For example, some lightweight notebook computers do not come with a built-in CD-ROM drive. Instead of having to purchase and then connect an external drive to the notebook, you can pop a CD into a shared drive on another computer and access it from the notebook.

Shares and the Network Browse Window

Once you understand that sharing is hierarchical, your logical brain tells you that the best way to share a large number of files is to share the highest container in the hierarchy. For example, if your My Documents folder contains many subfolders (each dedicated to a particular type of document), you should share My Documents. Then, when anyone on the network (including yourself if you're working on a different computer) needs to access any file in any subfolder, it takes only a couple of double-clicks to open the hierarchical set of folders to get to the target subfolder and then to the file.

However, regardless of the logic and its apparent efficiency, it's actually more effective (and safer) to share subfolders. You can skip any subfolders that hold files you deem "private" and don't want to share with other users on the network. In fact, for your "private" subfolder, you can create a hidden share that only you can access when you're working on a different computer (see the section "Using Hidden Shares" later in this chapter).

In addition, shares automatically appear in the network browser window (Network Neighborhood in Windows 98SE, and My Network Places in Windows XP/Me/2000), so any user can quickly get to any shared folder from a remote computer, regardless of that folder's hierarchical standing.

Additionally, a share can be mapped to a drive letter, which means a remote user can access the files in a share without opening the network browser window. See the section "Mapping Shares to Drive Letters" later in this chapter.

Sharing Folders and Drives in Windows XP

When you run the Windows XP Network Setup Wizard, file sharing is enabled as part of the process. Windows XP uses a feature called Simple File Sharing, in

Working Without Simple File Sharing

Because Simple File Sharing is all that's available with Windows XP Home Edition (and that's the edition most home and some small business networks use), this chapter covers sharing files using Simple File Sharing. If you are running Windows XP Professional on a network, you can disable Simple File Sharing and use a more sophisticated configuration in which you create user accounts on each computer and assign detailed permissions to those user accounts for each folder you share. This lets you control which users can access a shared folder and, to some extent, the precise control the users have over the shared folder (for example, whether they can just open documents to read them or can actually change or delete those documents).

If you are running a small business network, you should consider the added security offered by disabling Simple File Sharing. However, given that using standard file sharing requires more configuration and some expert knowledge, you may be better off even on small business networks to continue using Simple File Sharing and teach employees about its risks. You can learn more about Simple File Sharing and standard file sharing by reading the Microsoft support article "How to configure file sharing in Windows XP," available at *http://support.microsoft.com/default.aspx?scid=kb;en-us;304040*.

which a share is either available or it's not. You cannot limit access to certain users by forcing the use of passwords, as you can with Windows 98SE shares. If you're using Windows XP Home Edition, you cannot turn off Simple File Sharing. If you're using Windows XP Professional with NTFS, you can turn off Simple File Sharing and use NTFS security to restrict the activity of remote users (for example, permitting remote users to read files but not change or delete them).

NOTE *The Windows XP Network Setup Wizard even creates a special folder named Shared Documents, which is automatically shared using the sharename SharedDocs. Although this share is designed to make its contents available to all the users who log on to the computer, you can also make it a network share that's available to remote users.*

Sharing Folders in Windows XP

Most of the time, you'll want to share your My Documents folder or one or more of the subfolders you created to hold documents of specific types (for example, budgets, letters, contracts, and so on). To share a folder in Windows XP, follow these steps:

1. In My Computer or Windows Explorer, right-click the folder and choose Sharing and Security from the shortcut menu to open the folder's Properties dialog. Click the Sharing tab to bring it into the foreground (see Figure 10-1).
2. In the Network Sharing and Security section, select Share This Folder on the Network.
3. Enter a sharename for this folder, which is the name remote users see when they view the folder in Network Neighborhood or My Network Places. By default, Windows uses the folder name, but you can change it.

NOTE *Changing a sharename doesn't change the folder name.*

4. If you don't want remote users to be able to create, change, or delete files in this folder, clear the check box labeled Allow Network Users to Change My Files.

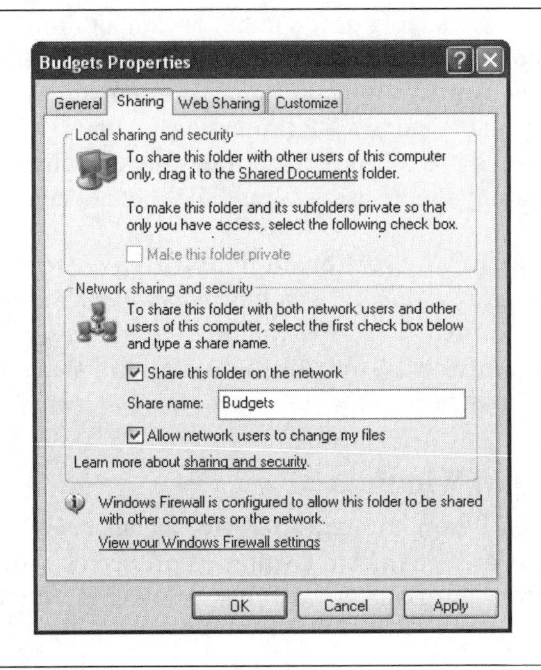

FIGURE 10-1 Enable sharing and name the share.

CAUTION *If you prevent remote users from creating or changing files in a shared folder, that restriction also affects you when you're working with the files from a remote computer.*

5. Click OK to create the share.

NOTE *Sharenames that are longer than 12 characters can't be seen in Network Neighborhood on Windows 98/Me computers.*

To stop sharing a folder, deselect the sharing option. After you create a share, the folder icon you see in My Computer or Windows Explorer changes to include another graphical element—a hand cradling the folder icon. This gives you a quick way to determine which folders are shared.

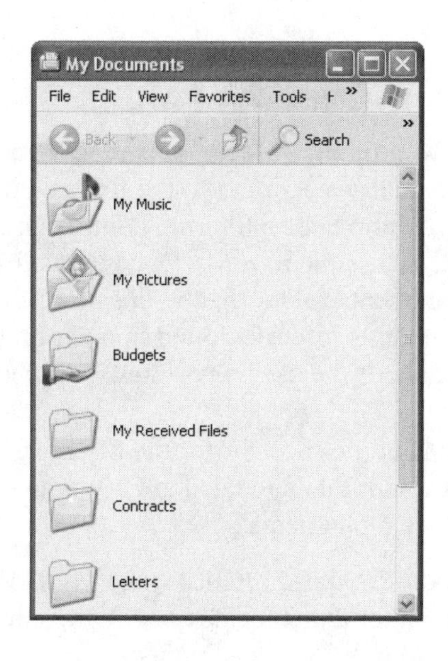

Sharing Drives in Windows XP

When you attempt to share a drive in Windows XP, the system issues an admonition, citing the dangers of exposing all the folders and files contained on the drive to remote users.

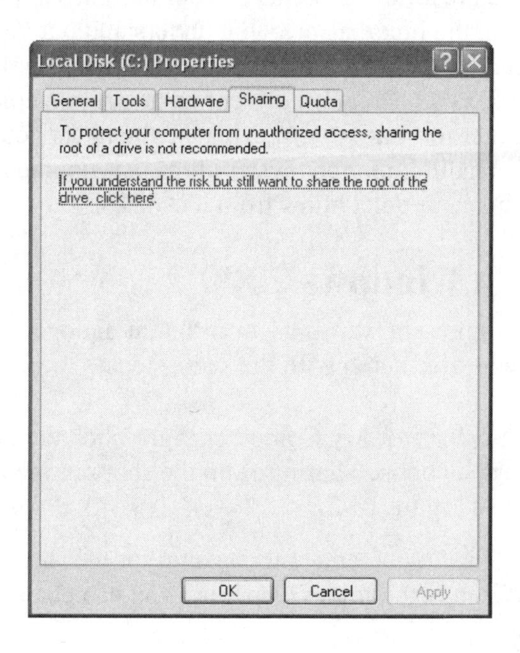

Sharing the My Documents Folder

The icon for the My Documents folder you see in Windows Explorer isn't really the folder—it's actually a shortcut to the folder. When you right-click the My Documents icon, you don't see a Sharing command; the Sharing command appears only when you access the *real* My Documents folder. The shortcut is pointing to the My Documents folder that belongs to the currently logged-on user. The *real* My Documents folder is found in one of the following locations (substitute the logon name of the user for <*UserName*>):

- In Windows 98/Me, the shortcut for the My Documents folder is pointing to a folder that's located at C:\Windows\Profiles\<*UserName*>\My Documents.
- In Windows 2000/XP, the shortcut for the My Documents folder is pointing to a folder that's located at C:\Documents and Settings\<*UserName*>\My Documents.

The warning is valid, and you should consider it carefully. However, if you have some reason to share all the contents of your hard drive, you can display the Sharing tab by clicking the link that says you understand but you want to share the drive anyway. Incidentally, the same warning appears for any drive, even removable drives such as a CD or Zip drive. Sharing removable drives doesn't present the same danger to your system, because the disks you insert in those drives don't usually contain important system files that remote users could change or remove. In fact, you can't delete files from CD disks.

Sharing Files in Windows 2000

Windows 2000 doesn't present warnings, or different dialogs, for folders and drives—both containers are shared with the same steps:

1. In Windows Explorer or My Computer, right-click the drive or folder you want to share and choose Sharing from the shortcut menu to open the Sharing tab (see Figure 10-2).
2. Select Share This Folder, and enter a name for the share (the system automatically enters the folder name, but you can change it).

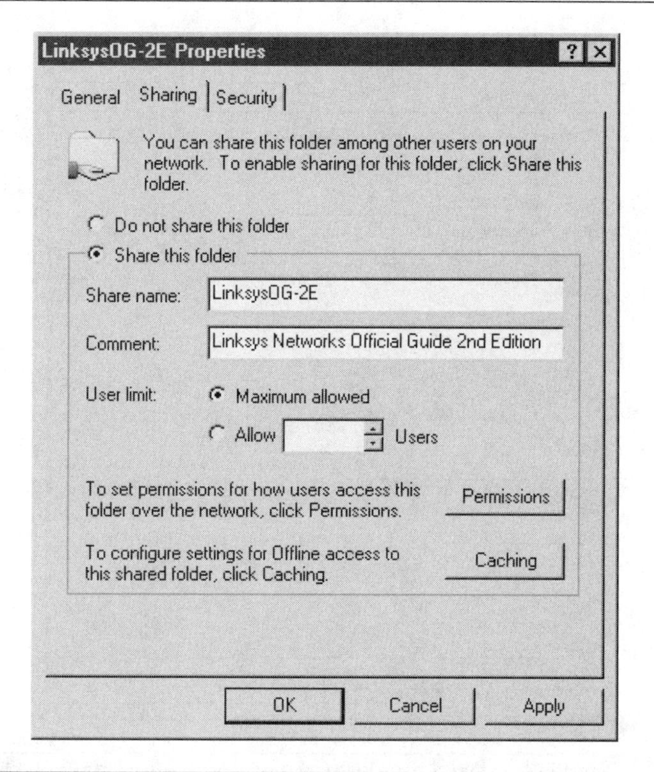

FIGURE 10-2 If you're not using NTFS, the Permissions button and the Security tab are missing from your dialog.

3. Optionally enter a description of the share (which is displayed in Network Neighborhood and My Network Places if the view is set for Details).
4. If you're running NTFS, set Permissions.
5. Click OK.

Sharing Files in Windows 98SE/Me

In Windows 98SE and Me, you can share a drive or a folder using identical steps, because those operating systems don't issue a warning about the dangers of sharing a drive. Follow these steps to create a share:

1. In Windows Explorer or My Computer, right-click the drive or folder you want to share and choose Sharing from the shortcut menu, which will open the Sharing tab of the Properties dialog (see Figure 10-3).

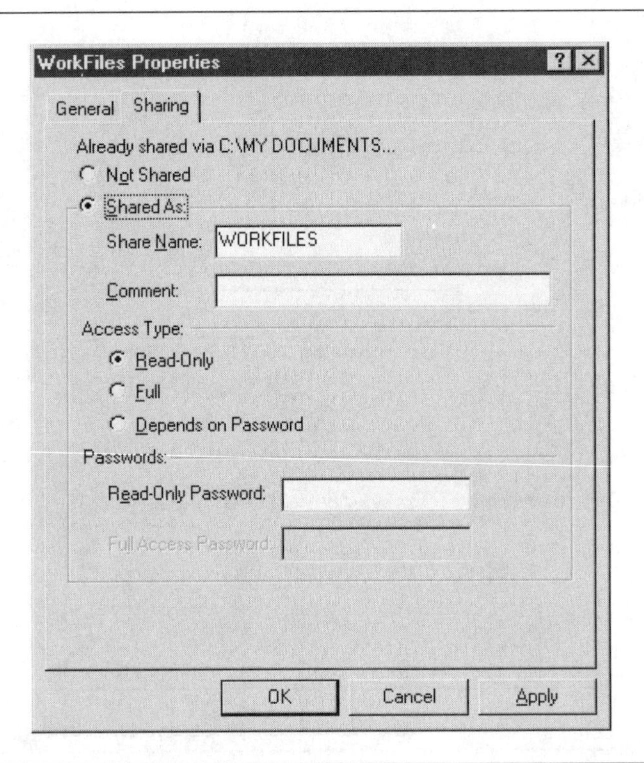

FIGURE 10-3 Windows 98/Me provides password-protection for each shared folder.

2. Select Shared As and enter a name for the share (the system automatically enters the folder name, but you can change it).
3. Select the type of access you're permitting for remote users, as follows:
   - **Read-Only** Lets users open and copy files but not change or delete files. You can create a password to let people into the folder for read-only access, or skip the password requirement to let all users access the share with read-only permissions.
   - **Full** Lets users do whatever they wish in the folder. You can create a password to let people into the folder for full access, or skip the password requirement to let all users access the share with full permissions.
   - **Depends on Password** Allows different access levels, depending on the password the user enters.
4. Click OK to create the share.

Notice that Windows tells you when the share you're creating is a subfolder of a folder that's already shared (see the text at the top of the Sharing tab in Figure 10-3). You can create the new share anyway, to make it appear in the network browse window. That way, a remote user (including yourself, if you're working on a different computer) can open the folder quickly or can map a drive to the share.

Using Windows 98SE/Me Passwords for Shares

The password feature for shares is very handy. You can share the folder and then give the password only to certain people. In fact, you can keep the password to yourself, and you'll be the only person who can get into the folder—which is helpful when you're working at a different computer.

When a remote user (who could be you) attempts to open the folder, a dialog appears for entering the password:

If the user doesn't enter the correct password, she can't open the share. However, if the share is a subfolder of a shared folder (that isn't password-protected), a remote user can open the parent folder and then enter the password-protected folder without encountering a password dialog. This is another example of why it's important to share only specific subfolders.

NOTE *In Windows XP with Simple File Sharing enabled, you can't password-protect or control the specific level of access. You must be using Windows XP Professional with Simple File Sharing disabled to control specific users and access levels.*

Using Hidden Shares

A hidden share doesn't show up in the network browse window, so remote users won't know the share exists just by browsing the network. However, anyone who knows the share exists (which would usually be only the person who created the hidden share) can access it if he knows the share's exact name. Hidden shares are handy for keeping private documents away from remote users, while maintaining the option to access the private files when you're working at a different computer.

NOTE *Only the share is hidden, not the folder itself—which means its hidden attribute works only on remote users. The folder is a normal accessible folder to anyone working on the computer.*

A hidden share isn't hidden if any of the containers above it are shared. If you create a hidden share for a subfolder in My Documents, don't share My Documents or the drive on which My Documents exists. If you do share the parent container, remote users see the folder you thought you'd hidden. If you want to share My Documents, and you also want to create a hidden share, create a separate folder outside of the My Documents folder and use it to save your personal stuff. Don't share the drive.

Creating a Hidden Share

To hide a share, all you have to do is make the last character in the sharename a dollar sign (*$*).

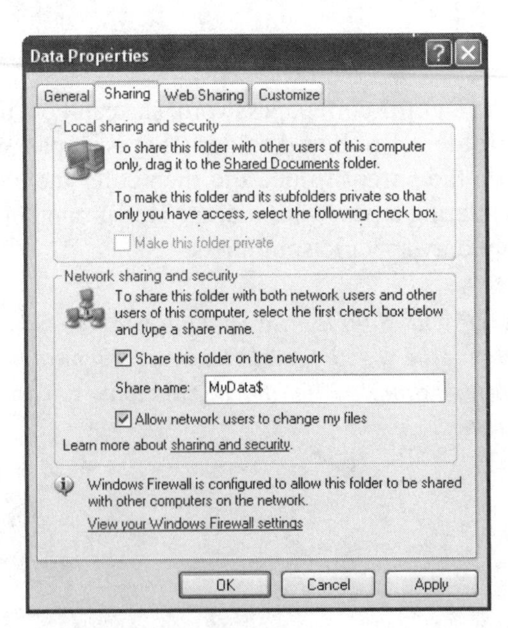

Because you're probably the only person who ever accesses this share from a remote computer, be sure of the following:

- If you're running Windows XP, make sure the hidden share has the option Allow Network Users to Change My Files enabled.
- If you're running Windows 98SE/Me, be sure to provide Full Access (you don't need a password for a hidden share—that would be overkill).

Accessing a Hidden Share from a Remote Computer

To access a hidden share from a remote computer, choose Start | Run and enter the path to the share, using this format: **\\ComputerName\ShareName**. Then click OK. For example, enter **\\bigdesk\mynovel$** to get to the hidden share named mynovel$ on the computer named bigdesk (you can use uppercase or lowercase characters, and don't forget that dollar sign!). A window opens, displaying the contents of the share, and you can go to work.

This format (a double backslash before a computer name and a single backslash before a sharename) is called the Universal Naming Convention (UNC), and it's designed to let network users access resources on the network without opening the network browse window.

Mapping Shares to Drive Letters

Mapping is the technical term for assigning a drive letter to a share on a remote computer. The mapped drive letter acts just like another drive on your local computer. This is a useful trick for shares you access constantly, because all the drives on your computer appear in My Computer and Windows Explorer, which means you don't have to open a network browse window to get to a particular share.

You can also use the mapped drive letter in your software programs when you want to open or save a file that's in a remote share. Using a drive letter is much easier than browsing the network to get to a specific remote folder to open or save a document.

TIP *Some older programs simply won't recognize network shares or do not provide access to a network browse window. For these applications, mapping a network share to a drive letter lets the program access the share, because the program thinks it's just another drive.*

You can map a drive letter only to a share, not to a subfolder of a share. For example, assume that drive C on a remote computer is shared and that there is a folder on drive C named My Novel. You cannot map a network drive to the My Novel folder, even though drive C is shared. You would have to explicitly share the My Novel folder in order to map a network drive to it.

NOTE *The fact that you can map a drive only to a resource that's been explicitly shared is a Windows rule. If you've worked in a corporate setting and your company used Novell NetWare, you know it's possible to map a drive to any subfolder. This feature is called Map Root, and it's not available in Windows.*

Creating a Mapped Drive

To map a drive letter to a share, open the network browse window (My Network Places in Windows XP/Me/2000, or Network Neighborhood in Windows 98SE). Double-click the icon for the computer that has the share you want to map, which displays all the computer's shares. Select the icon for the share you need, and then select Map Network Drive from the Tools menu. The Map Network Drive dialog opens so you can assign a drive letter to the share and also decide whether you want to make the mapping permanent. (If the Map Network Drive command does not work, read the section "Network Browse Window Shortcuts Are Confusing.")

Click OK or Finish (depending on the version of Windows you're using) to map the drive. A window opens to show you the contents of the mapped share. You can work on files or close the window if you're merely creating the mapped drive and you aren't ready to work with the files.

Selecting a Drive Letter In all versions of Windows except Windows XP, the system automatically selects the next available drive letter on your computer. The next available drive letter changes depending on whether you have multiple drives on the computer or you've previously mapped a drive letter to a share.

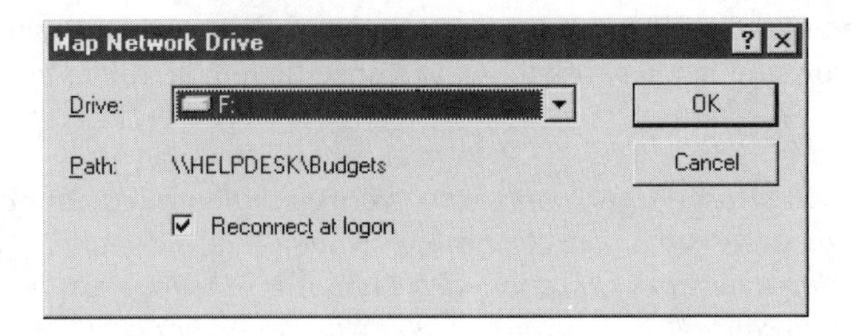

In Windows XP, mapped drives start with *Z* and then work backward through the alphabet. For example, if this is the second mapped drive you're creating, its default drive letter is *Y*.

Regardless of the version of Windows you're using, you don't have to accept the default drive letter. You can click the arrow to the right of the Drive field and select another drive letter from the drop-down list.

Permanent Mapping Versus Temporary Mapping You can decide whether you want this mapped drive to be persistent, which means when you shut down Windows, the next time you start up the share is remapped and once again becomes a drive letter on your computer. By default, Windows assumes you want to map this drive permanently, and the Reconnect at Logon option is selected. If you want to map the drive only temporarily, click the check box to clear the check mark.

Automatic reconnections of mapped shares can be tricky, however. If you select the option to reconnect your mapped drive at logon, the order in which you start your computers becomes important. The computer that holds the shared resource should boot before the computer that has the mapped drive. That way, when the computer with the mapped drive searches for the resource to complete the mapping process, the resource is available. This, of course, presents a seemingly insurmountable problem if you have two computers on the network and each of them is mapping drives to shares on the other.

Don't worry, though, because this is all workable. When a computer that has drives mapped to remote shares boots and cannot find the computer that holds the drives, an error message appears at the end of the startup process. The error message tells you that the permanent connection is not available, and it will ask whether you want to reconnect the next time you start the computer. Click Yes.

After both (or all) computers have booted, open My Computer or Windows Explorer. You can see the mapped drive, but there's a red *X* mark under the icon, which indicates the connection is "broken." Click the icon to access the mapped share—because the remote computer is now available, the red *X* goes away and you can access the files you need.

Windows 98SE actually has a better idea: an option that stalls the attempt to connect to a mapped drive until you actually access it. You can configure this option with the following steps:

1. Put the Windows 98SE CD in the CD drive (exit the setup program if it starts automatically).
2. Choose Start | Settings | Control Panel.
3. Open the Network applet in Control Panel.
4. Select Client for Microsoft Networks and click Properties.
5. Select Quick Logon.
6. Click OK twice to close the Network Properties dialog and to transfer files from the Windows 98SE CD to your hard drive.

Network Browse Window Shortcuts Are Confusing

If the Map Network Drive command is not available on the shortcut menu when you right-click a shared resource, the resource is not explicitly shared and you cannot map it. However, that statement isn't as straightforward as it seems. Windows XP automatically browses the network on a frequent basis and puts a shortcut for each share it finds in the My Network Places window. Shortcuts are not really icons for shares, so you won't see the command for mapping a drive on the menu that appears when you right-click the icon. The shortcuts are handy when you want to access a share, but the only way to map a share is to get to the icon for the share instead of the icon for its shortcut. To do this, you must click the Entire Network icon or the Workgroup icon to access these shares, and open the appropriate computer window to see its shares. (Incidentally, some users find all those shortcuts overwhelming and confusing, and if that statement applies to you, just delete them!)

TIP

In Windows XP, in the My Network Places window, you can create new network places (which are essentially shortcuts to a shared folder on another computer or to an Internet resource) by clicking Add a Network Place in the Network Tasks list on the left-hand side of the window. (If you don't see the Network Tasks list, try making your window bigger. If you still don't see it, select Tools | Options and make sure the Show Common Tasks in Folders option is selected.) The shortcut becomes available in the main My Network Places window from then on. Also, if you are browsing the network, you can also create a shortcut to a network share the same way you create a shortcut to any folder or program on your local computer. For example, you could drag a network share to your desktop to create a handy shortcut to that shared folder—no more opening the My Network Places window at all!

Using Linksys Network Attached Storage Devices to Share Files

Network attached storage devices offer a way to add shared storage space directly to a network instead of sharing folders on a specific computer. Using a NAS device offers several advantages:

- NAS devices usually respond faster than shared folders on computers because they are dedicated to sharing files—it's all they do. Computers are often engaged in other activities that can slow down the responsiveness of delivering files to remote users.
- NAS devices are more consistently available than shared folders on computers because you can leave them on all the time. Computers get restarted or turned off (or just crash), which can make shared files suddenly unavailable—not good if you are in the middle of working with a file.
- NAS devices can be simpler to configure because you don't need to worry as much about what version of Windows you are running or what type of file sharing is used.
- NAS devices are controlled through a Web browser interface, so you can reconfigure file sharing from any computer on the network that has a Web browser (which will likely be all computers).

Linksys offers two types of NAS devices:

- A network attached storage device, which is basically a dedicated computer with a hard drive built-in.
- The Network Storage Link for USB 2.0 Disk Drives, which is a network attached storage device that doesn't have a built-in hard drive but features two USB 2.0 ports to which you can attach your own high-speed external disk drives.

Sharing Files with the Linksys NAS Device

Linksys offers two models of NAS devices: EtherFast Network Attached Storage (EFG120), which includes a 120GB hard drive and a bay for an additional drive, and EtherFast Network Attached Storage (250GB with PrintServer) (EFG250), which includes a 250GB hard drive, a bay for an additional drive, and a built-in print server.

Both devices offer built-in utilities for running self-tests, scanning, and defragmenting the hard drives. If you install a second disk drive, you can also use a built-in tool to back up the primary hard drive to the second drive. You can even purchase quick-connect drive trays that are easy to slide in and out of the device so that you can create rotating backup systems.

NOTE *This chapter focuses on the EFG250, though the EFG120 works pretty much the same way.*

The EtherFast Network Attached Storage (250GB with PrintServer)

The front of the EFG250, shown in Figure 10-4, features the following:

- The Power button turns the device on and off. Pressing this button while the device is turned on initiates an internal shutdown sequence that safely turns off the device, so you should not worry about simply turning off the device (though you should *never* simply unplug it when it's on). You can also safely turn off the device using a command in the device's Web-based utility (more about that in the section "Setting up the EFG250").
- The two drive bays each accept a hard drive that is installed in a quick-connect hard drive tray. The device has two drive trays—one that includes

the 250GB drive that comes with the unit and one empty tray that you can use to install an additional drive. The bottom bay (as the unit stands vertically) is for the first drive and the top bay is for the second drive.

- The Ready/Status LED is solid green when the device is turned on and working properly. The light blinks green during startup and shutdown. If the light turns orange, an error has occurred.
- The LAN LED is solid green when the device is connected to the network. The LED blinks green when data is transmitted to or from the device.
- The Disk LED flashes green when the device is reading or writing data from either disk.
- The Disk Full LED is off during normal operation. When a disk drive reaches 98 percent of its capacity, the light blinks green. When the disk drive is full, the light is solid green.
- The Backup LED blinks when the device's built-in backup utility is operating.
- The Disk 2 LED blinks when the unit is writing or reading data from the drive in the second drive bay.
- The Disk 1 LED blinks when the unit is writing or reading data from the drive in the first drive bay.

The back of the EFG250, also shown in Figure 10-4, features the following:

- The LAN port is used to connect the device to your network.
- The Printer Port lets you add a standard printer that uses a parallel printer cable to the unit.
- The Reset button returns the unit to its factory default settings if you press and hold the button for 3 seconds. Using the Reset button does not erase any data stored on the drives, nor does it alter the sharing profiles of folders on the drive. The Rest button resets the unit's IP address and administrative passwords. You can use this button if you forget the device's IP address or password.
- The Power port is used to plug in the power adapter for the unit.

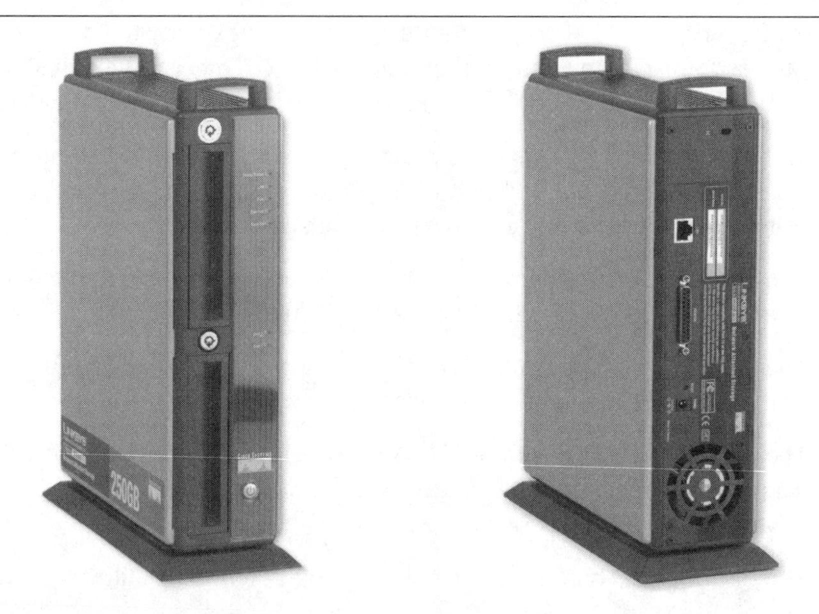

FIGURE 10-4 The front and back of the EtherFast Network Attached Storage (250GB with PrintServer).

Installing the EFG250

The EFG250 is simple to install. Just follow these steps:

1. Connect the device directly into your existing network using an Ethernet cable (as you would a computer). Connect the other end of the cable to a hub, switch, or computer with network adapter installed.
2. Connect a printer to the printer port if you want to.
3. Connect the power supply to the unit, and then plug the other end into a power outlet (or surge protector unit).
4. Press the Power button on the front of the EFG250. The unit beeps once to indicate that it has been turned on, runs a self-test, and then starts up. During startup, most of the LEDs will flash or light up. After a few minutes, only the Ready/Status and the LAN LEDs should remain lit and the other LEDs should not be lit. At this point, the unit has started up.

NOTE *If you hear multiple beeps during the startup process (usually a sequence of two, three, or five beeps that repeat every so often), or if you see the Error LED flashing, a hardware problem has occurred. Consult the documentation that came with the device to interpret the error and find the solution.*

Setting up the EFG250

After connecting and turning on the EFG250, you will need to run the EFG's Setup Wizard to configure the unit so that it is accessible on the network. The Setup Wizard works the same whether you are using Windows 98, Me, NT 4.0, 2000, or XP. To run the Setup Wizard, use these steps:

1. On any computer that is connected to the network, insert the Setup Wizard CD that came with the EFG250. When you insert the CD, the Setup Wizard should start automatically. If it does not (for example, if you have Windows AutoRun feature disabled), you can start the wizard by choosing Start | Run and typing **d:\SetupUtility.exe**, where *d* is the drive letter for your CD-ROM drive. On the first page of the Setup Wizard, click Setup.

2. The Setup Wizard automatically searches the network for the EFG250 (and will also detect the unit if it's attached directly to your computer).

NOTE *If the Setup Wizard fails to locate the EFG250, be sure that you have given the unit enough time to start up. Click Search Again to have the Setup Wizard try again to find the device. If it still cannot locate the device, you should make sure that it is correctly attached to your network.*

3. After the Setup Wizard locates the EFG250, it lets you know of its success. In the Selected Drive list, click the unit to view its configuration.

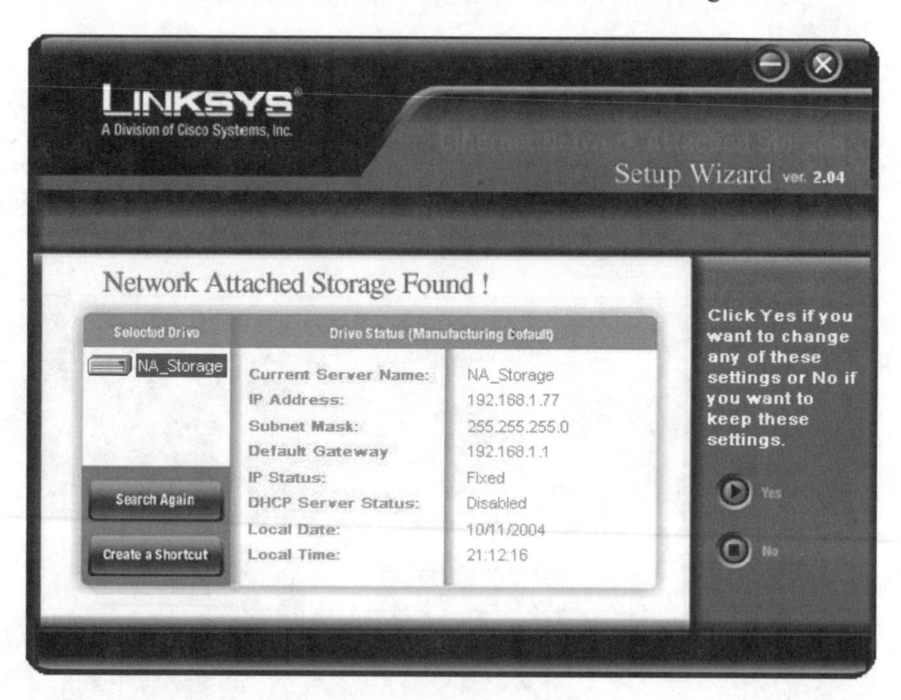

4. If the configuration looks correct, click No (indicating that you don't want to change any settings). The Setup Wizard closes and you are ready to share folders on the device. If you want to change the configuration, click Yes to go on with the Setup Wizard.

5. The first setting you can change is how the device obtains its IP address. Choose Fixed IP Address if you want to create a static IP address for the device. Choose Dynamic IP Address if you want the device to act as a DHCP client and obtain its IP address from a DHCP server (such as a router on your network). Most likely, you will want to choose Dynamic IP Address—the default setting. Click Next after making the appropriate settings.

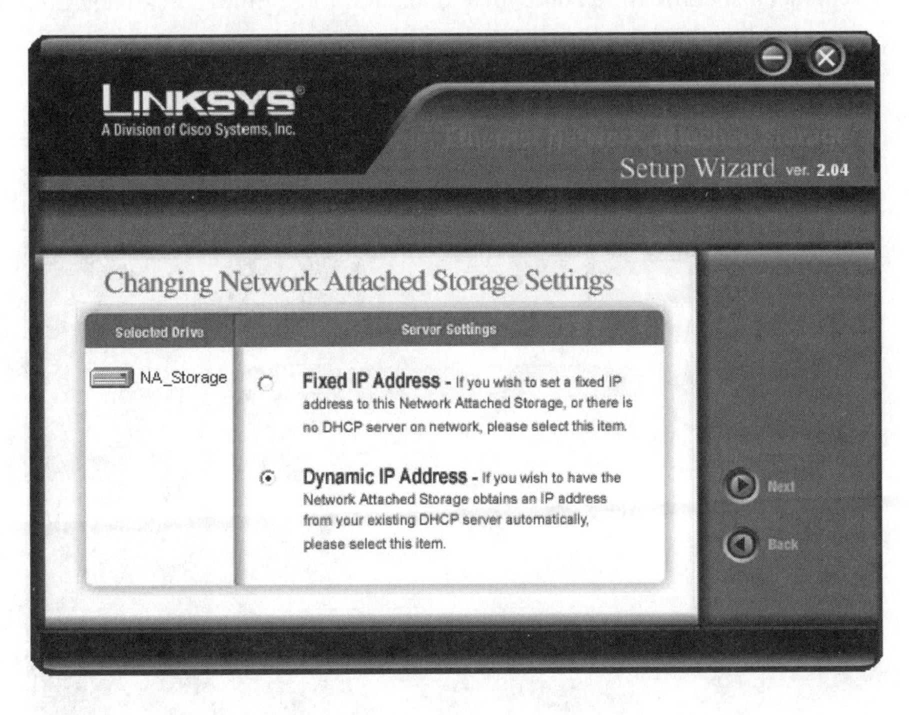

NOTE *If you configure the device to use a fixed IP address, you will see two additional pages in the Setup Wizard. The first page lets you change the IP address (the default address used is 192.168.1.77—an address that should work perfectly well on most Linksys-based networks) and other IP addressing information. The second page lets you configure the EFG250 to act as a DHCP server, which it can do only if it has a fixed IP address. For more information on using DHCP and on configuring IP addresses, see Chapter 8.*

6. The next option you can change is the time and date for the EFG250. You can set a specific time zone, local date, and local time. Click Next after making the appropriate settings.

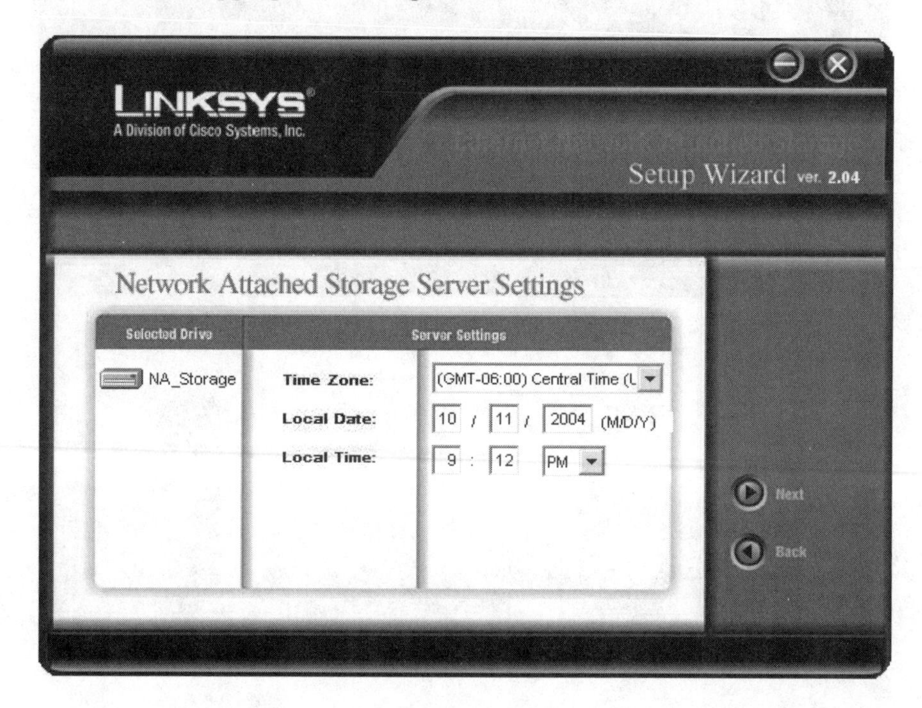

7. The next page shows you a summary of the EFG250's settings. If you're happy with the way you've set it up, click Save. Otherwise, you can click Back to work your way back through the wizard and make changes.

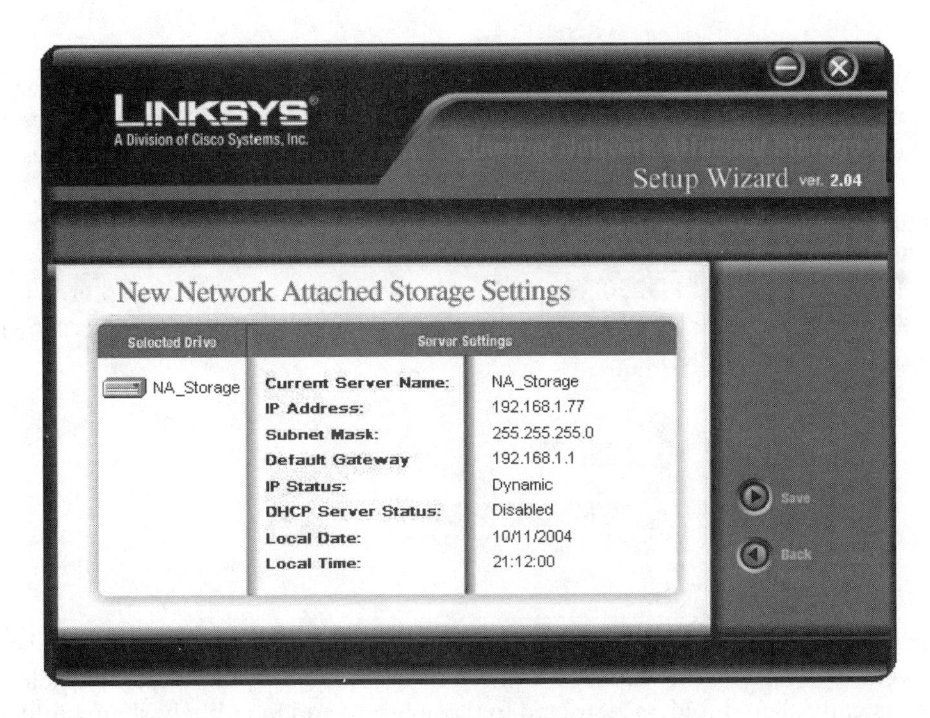

TIP *Write down the configuration information for the unit—especially the IP address, as you will use it to connect to the device and share folders. In Windows, you can also press* ALT-PRINT SCREEN *(or* PRTSCN*) to save an image of the page to the clipboard. Open any image-editing program (such as MS Paint) or word processor (such as Word), and then press* CTRL-V *to paste the image. Print the image for easy reference.*

8. After saving the configuration changes, the Setup Wizard displays a message that warns you that changes will be made to the unit. Click OK to save the changes or Cancel to return to the wizard.
9. After the changes are successfully saved, the Setup Wizard displays a Congratulations page. Click Exit to close the wizard.

At this point, your EFG250 is connected, configured, and ready to go. As you'll see in the next section, accessing the unit and sharing folders is as easy as using a Web browser.

Connecting to the EFG250

After connecting the EFG250 to your network and running the Setup Wizard, you can access the EFG250 from any computer that has a Web browser. This makes the EFG250 easy to manage from anywhere on your network. The Web-based administration tool uses the familiar tabbed interface common to other Linksys network devices.

To connect to the EFG250, open a Web browser such as Internet Explorer. In the Address bar of the Web browser, type the IP address of the EFG250, as shown here, and then press ENTER.

Using the Home Tab

The Home tab, shown in Figure 10-5, is intended as an easy way for users on the network to connect to the EFG250 and view files in their private folders (which are basically shared folders restricted to those users) and in publicly shared folders (which are accessible to everyone on the network). The main Home tab also shows the basic status of the unit, including the server name, the version of firmware installed, the unit's IP address, and the status of each disk on the system.

Private User Files The User Log in (Private Data) link offers access to a user's private folder. When you click this link, your Web browser prompts you for a username and password. Entering this information identifies the user to the system and then displays that user's private folders, as shown in Figure 10-6. (You'll see how to set up users and passwords a bit later in the section "Using the Administration Tab.")

A user's private folders offer a way to store private documents that the user can access from anywhere on the network. On some networks, you might also want to encourage users only to store documents on the EFG250 and then back up the device using the built-in backup utility. This offers the advantage of having a single backup system in place that backs up all user files.

Public Files The Disk 1/Disk 2 (Public Data) links offer access to shared folders on the EFG250 that are accessible to everyone.

Accessing Shares Directly from Windows While you can use the Web interface built in to the EFG250 to access and browse shared folders, users will typically

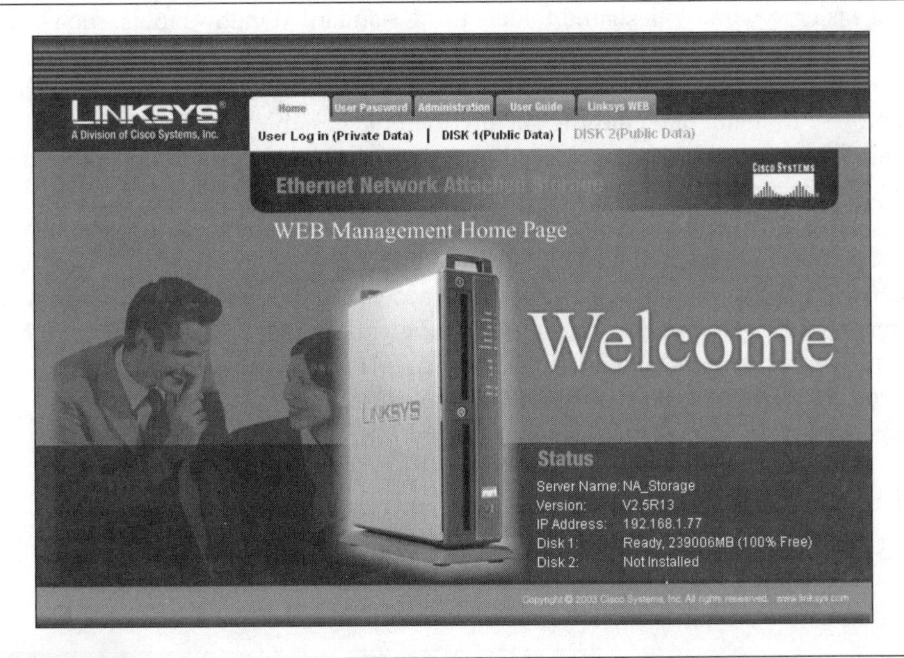

FIGURE 10-5 The main home page offers easy access to users' folders.

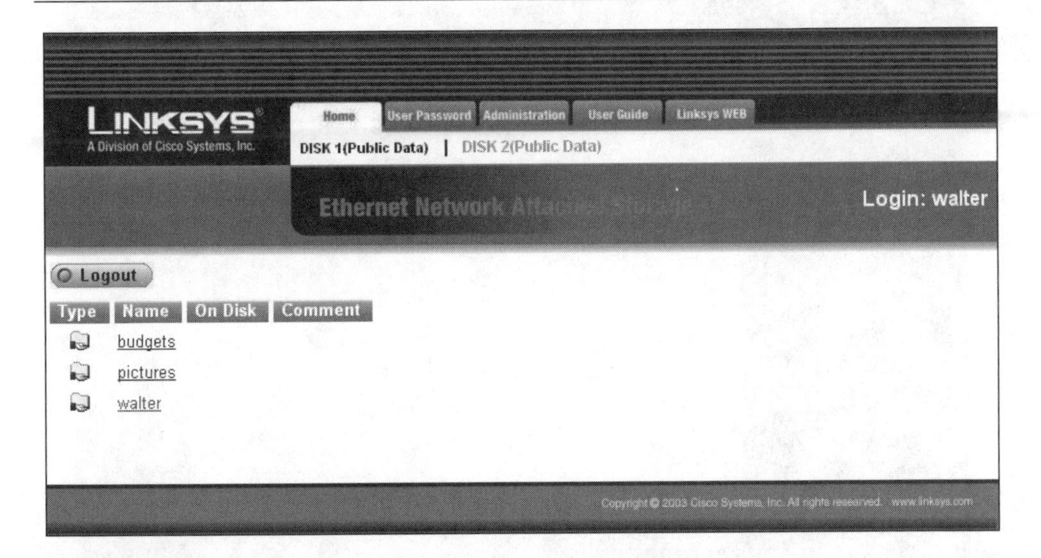

FIGURE 10-6 Private folders are accessible only after entering a username and password.

find it easier to work with shared folders using standard Windows tools, such as My Network Places. The EFG250 shows up in My Network Places (Windows 2000/XP) or Network Neighborhood (Windows 98/Me) just like any other computer. You can browse to it and open the files in any folder accessible to you. While you can see all folders on the device (including other users' private folders), you are prompted for a password if you attempt to open a folder that is password-protected.

If, however, you are logged on with a username that is identical to your username (same password, too) on the EFG250, you will be able to access your own private folders (or any that you have permission to access) without having to type in your username and password. For example, assume your Windows username is Bob and you are logged on to Windows. If the username Bob and the same password are used on the EFG250, you will be able to access the folders on the EFG250 without being prompted for a username and password.

Using the User Password Tab

The User Password tab, shown in Figure 10-7, allows a user to change his or her password. Simply type in the username and enter the current password. Type

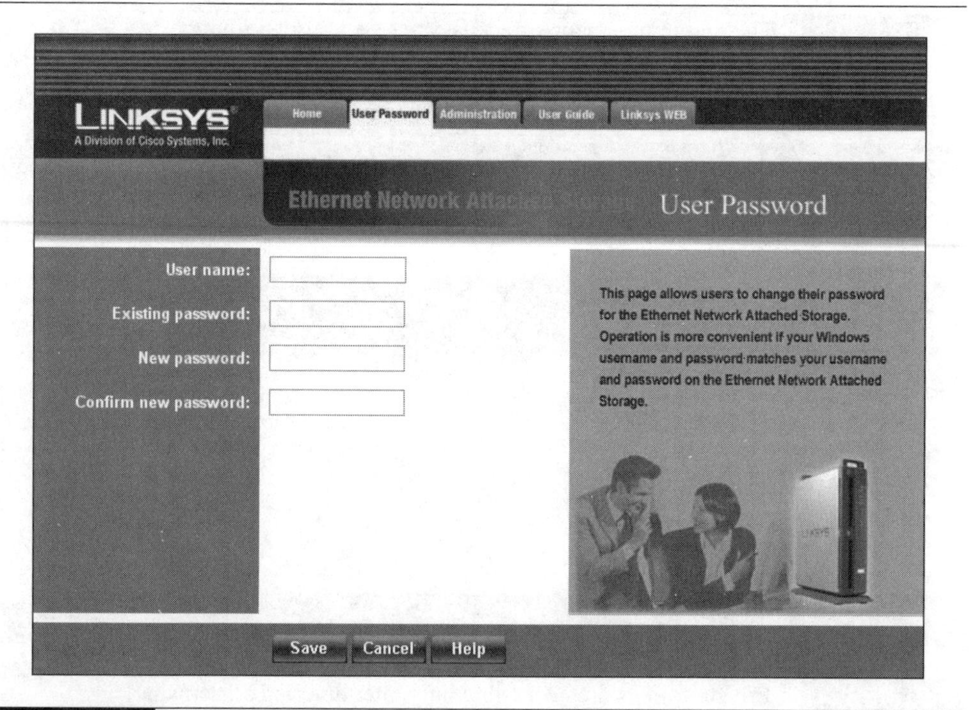

FIGURE 10-7 Users can change their own passwords.

and confirm the new password, and then click Save. The new password takes effect immediately.

Using the Administration Tab

As you might expect, the Administration tab is a little more complicated than the tabs you've seen so far. In fact, the tab is divided into two major groups of pages: Setup and Advanced. You use the Setup pages to manage basic system and network functions and to create new users. You use the Advanced pages to create groups and new shares, and to access disk functions such as backing up, scanning, and defragmenting.

When you click the Administration tab, you are prompted for a username and password. If you've never logged in before, the default administrator username *and* password for the device is *admin*. After logging in, you can access the pages (which are covered in the following sections). To the far right of the list of pages (LAN, System, and so on), you'll see a link named Advanced. Click it to access the Advanced pages. (While you're viewing the Advanced pages, the link name changes to Setup. Click it to return to the Setup pages.)

Setup—LAN Page The LAN page, shown in Figure 10-8, lets you configure how the EFG250 communicates with your network. You can configure the following settings:

- **IP Address section** Specify whether the EFG250 obtains an IP address automatically from a DHCP server or has a fixed IP address. If you use a fixed IP address, you must also specify a network mask and default gateway that is appropriate for your network. See Chapter 8 for more on configuring these network settings.
- **DHCP Server section** Enable the EFG250 as a DHCP server. You should enable this option only if a DHCP server is not currently on the network.
- **DNS Server section** Specify a DNS server that the device should contact to resolve DNS names. You do not have to configure these settings if the EFG is configured to obtain an IP address automatically—the DNS server information is also obtained automatically. If you are using a fixed IP address, you should specify whatever DNS servers the other devices on your network are configured to use (the DNS server addresses specified by your ISP). This is particularly important if you are using the E-Mail Alerts feature of the EFG250 (see the section, "Setup—Status Page" for more on this).

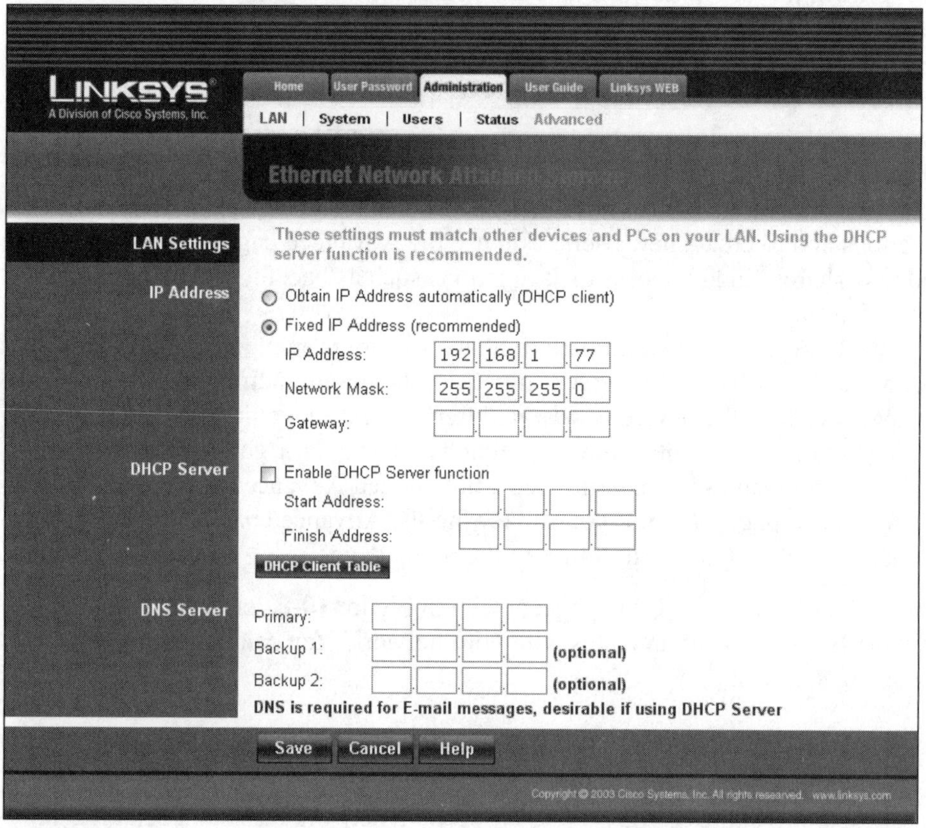

FIGURE 10-8 Configure LAN settings for your EFG250.

Setup—System Page The System page, shown in Figure 10-9, allows you to configure a number of settings that govern how your EFG250 is identified on the network and how it allows access. In particular, you can configure the following settings:

- **Identification section** Specify a server name (the name that appears in My Network Places or Network Neighborhood in Windows), the Windows workgroup of which the EFG250 is a part (you will usually configure only one workgroup on a small network), and the sharename of the printer connected to the EFG250.

- **Location section** Change the language, time zone, date, and time for the unit.
- **WINS section** Enable the EFG250 as a Windows Internet Naming Service (WINS) client. WINS is used in place of DNS on some older Windows networks. On a small network, you should never have to worry about this setting.
- **Options section** Configure the following options:
  - **Enable Guest Logins** Allows users who do not have a username to access public shares on the EFG250. Use the Convert Failed Logins to "Guest" Logins option to force users that enter an invalid username or password to log in as guests.
  - **Enable FTP Server** Lets the EFG250 be accessed by File Transfer Protocol (FTP) clients. FTP is widely used for transferring files on the Internet. Typically, on a small network, you won't need to worry about this option. Some users, though, may be more comfortable using FTP than browsing for shared folders. Also, the EFG250 can allow FTP access from the Internet (though you must configure your router to forward FTP traffic to the EFG250's IP address).
  - **Enable Https** Allows the EFG250 to handle secure Web traffic.
  - **Enable UPnP Support** A Windows XP–only feature; unless all the computers on your network are running Windows XP, you should not select this check box. Even if all the computers on your network are running Windows XP, you may want to disable this option. The feature enables the Windows XP Universal Plug and Play feature to reconfigure the router automatically if somebody on the network tries to use certain interactive Internet applications.
  - **Enable Printer Icon** Causes an icon for the printer to appear when users browse to the EFG250 using My Network Places or Network Neighborhood. If no printer is connected to the EFG250 (or if you do not want users to be able to connect to the printer directly), disable this option.

Setup—Users Page The Users page, shown in Figure 10-10, lets you view, add, and delete users. The Existing Users area shows a list of all users configured on

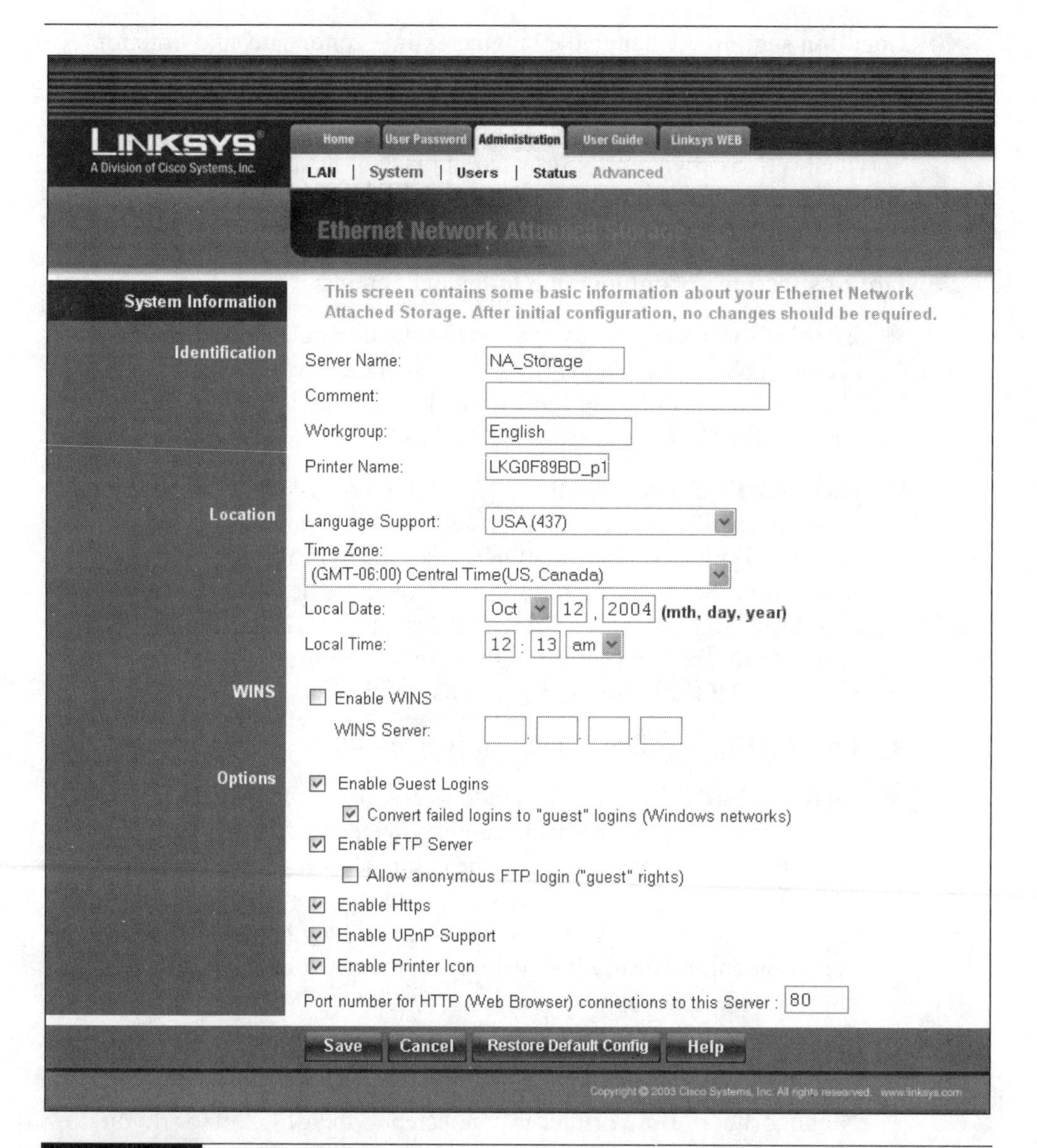

FIGURE 10-9 Configure the name and location of the printer, as well as several other connection options.

the EFG250. Select a user and click Groups to manage the groups to which the user is a member (you'll learn more about groups in the "Advanced—Groups Page" section). Select a user and click Delete to remove the user.

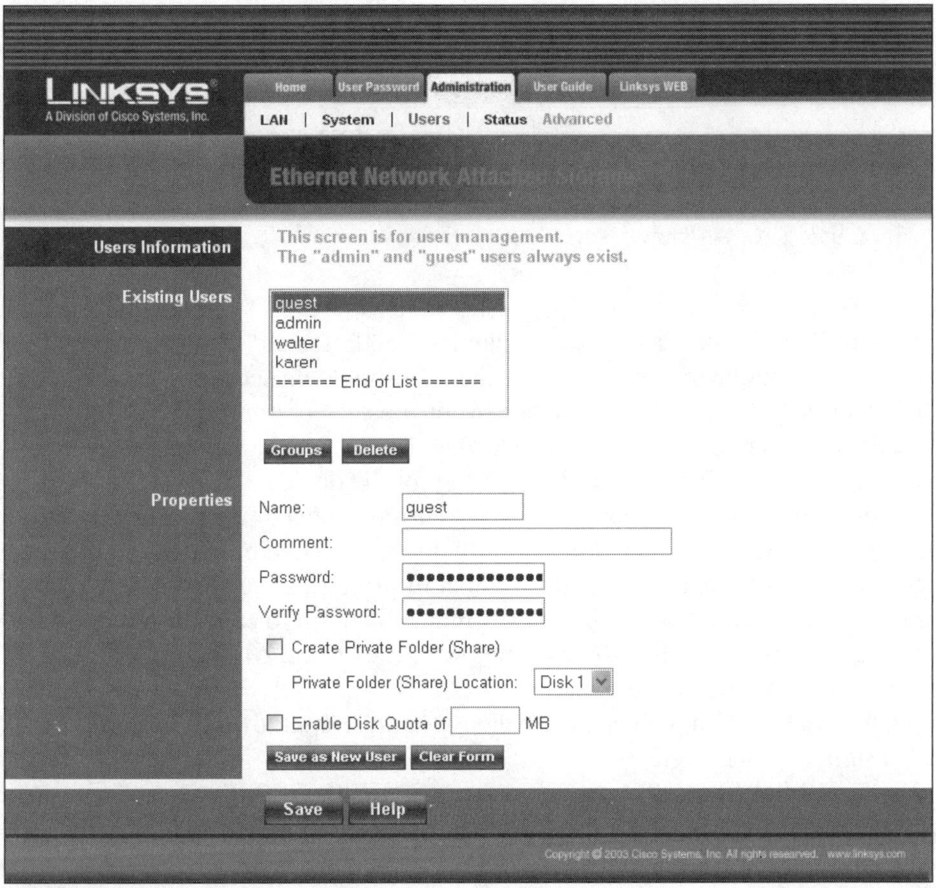

FIGURE 10-10 Configure users on the EFG250.

To create a new user, follow these steps:

1. In the Properties section, type the username in the Name field.
2. If you want, you can also type a comment to help identify the user. (I find that the best use for this field is to enter the user's full name. That way, you can enter a shortened version of the name as the actual username to make it easier for the user to type.)
3. Enter the same password in both the Password and Verify Password fields.

4. If you want to create a private folder for the user (a folder with the same name as the username), select the Create Private Folder (Share) option. If you have two disks in the EG250, you can specify the disk on which the private folder should be created.
5. If you want to limit the amount of disk space the user is allowed to use, select the Enable Disk Quota Of option and enter the limit in MB.
6. Click Save As New User.

Setup—Status Page The Status page, shown in Figure 10-11, shows information about the EFG250, such as the server name, IP address, and the device's current status. Click Shutdown Now to initiate the safe shutdown sequence for the device. Click Restart Now to restart the device (often a useful first troubleshooting step if the device is having problems). Click View Log to see administrative events (shutdowns, restarts, and disk utility results) for the device.

In the Printer section, you can view the current status of the printer attached to the EFG250—whether it is ready, currently printing, is out of paper, or an error has occurred. You can also view the number of print jobs (documents) currently waiting to be printed. Use the Delete Current Job button to cancel printing of the document that is first in line to be printed. Use the Delete All Jobs to cancel printing of all waiting documents.

In the Disk section, you can view the type and amount of free space for each disk installed in the EFG250.

In the E-Mail Alerts section, you can configure the EFG250 to send an e-mail message to one or two addresses if a problem occurs with the EFG250. This is a handy option, as it "checks in" on the unit for you and sends alerts so you don't have to. To use e-mail alerts, your EFG must have the IP address of at least one DNS server configured. See the section "Setup—LAN Page" for more details.

Advanced—Groups Page The Groups page, shown in Figure 10-12, is the first of the Advanced pages (which you access by clicking the Advanced link on the Administrative tab). On the EFG250, access to folders is controlled using groups. When you create a shared folder, you grant permission for one or more groups to access that folder, and then you place user accounts into the appropriate groups. While it seems like an extra step to take when assigning permissions, using groups actually accomplishes two things: it forces you to think carefully about how you assign permissions (preventing them from getting too complicated), and it allows you to grant or remove access quickly to multiple users down the road.

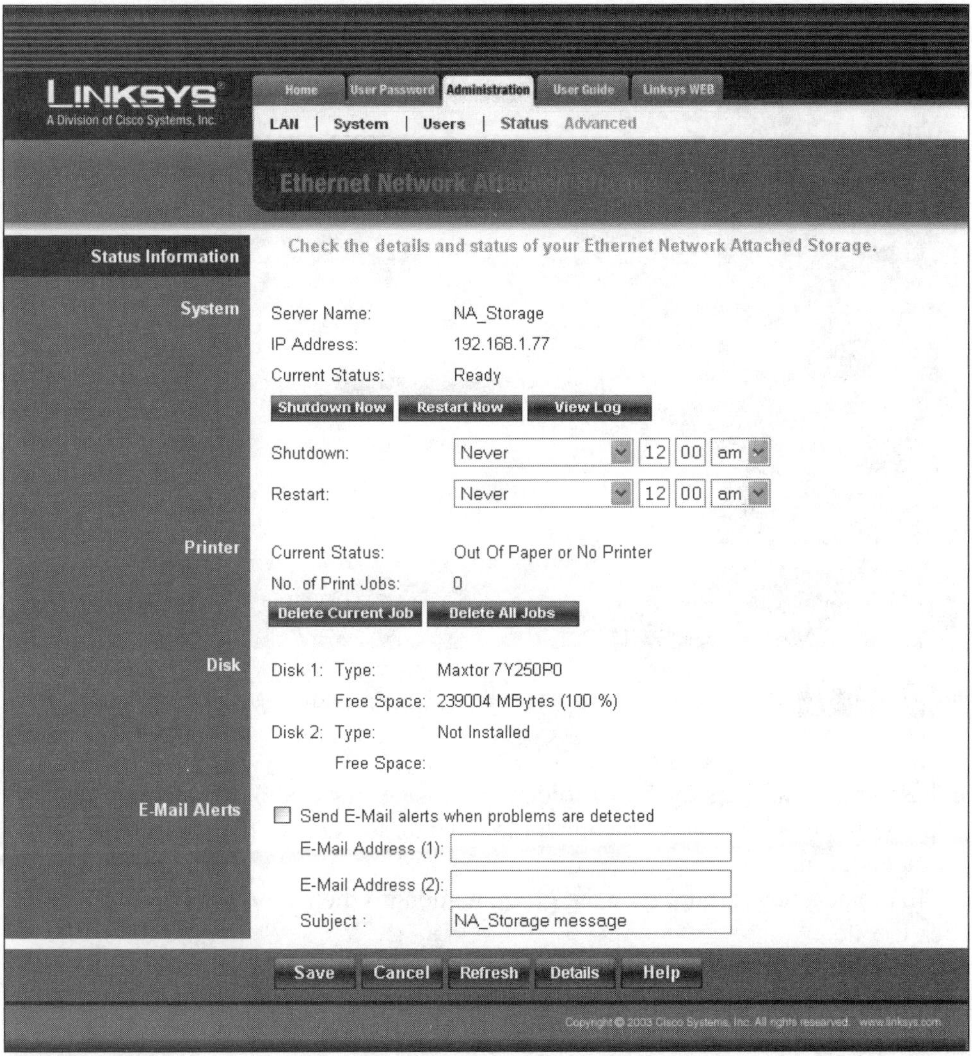

FIGURE 10-11 Use the Status page to monitor the EFG250.

For example, assume you are running a small business network in a company with two managers and ten employees. You could create a group named Managers and a group named Staff. You would then place users into the appropriate groups

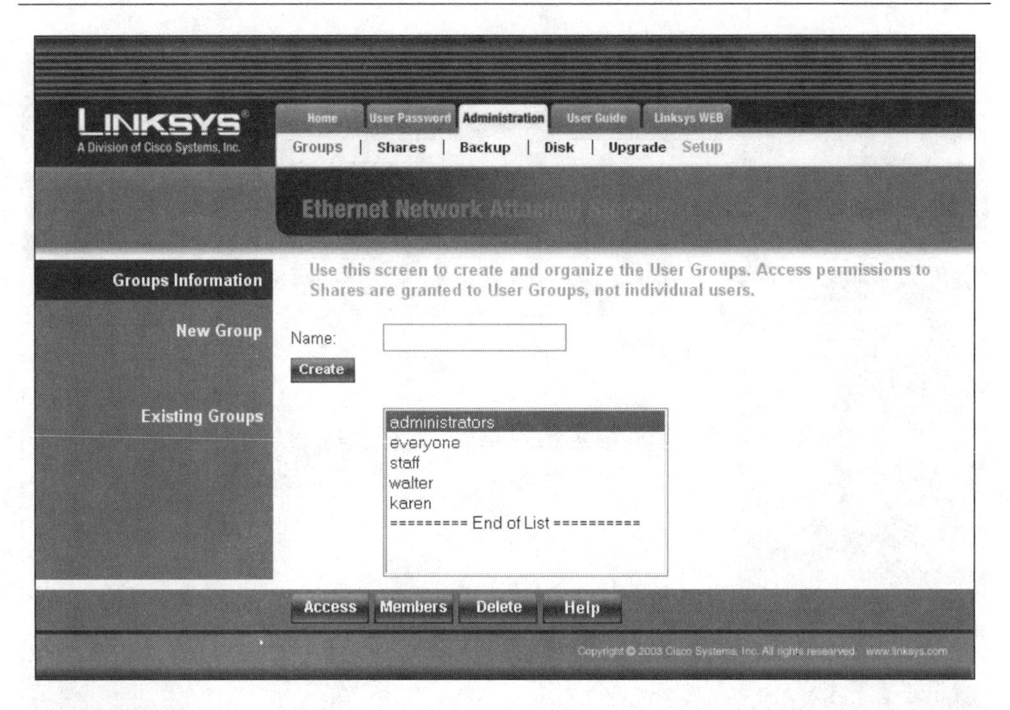

FIGURE 10-12 The EFG250 controls access to shared folders using groups.

and assign permissions to shared folders to those groups. Should an employee be promoted to a manager, all you would have to do is move that user to the Managers group.

To create a new group, type the group name into the Name field and then click Create.

To administer an existing group, select the group in the Existing Groups list and then do one of the following:

- Click Access to choose which shared folders the group can access. A group can have three levels of access to a shared folder: No Access, Read access (which allows users to open files, but not modify or delete them), and Read/Write access (which allows users full control of files).
- Click Members to choose which users are members of the group.
- Click Delete to remove the group.

Advanced—Shares Page The Shares page, shown in Figure 10-13, is where you will create and manage the shared folders that users access. The Existing Shares list shows all folders currently shared on the EFG250. Select a folder and perform one of the following actions:

- Click Access to choose which groups have access to the folder and which of the three levels of access they have.

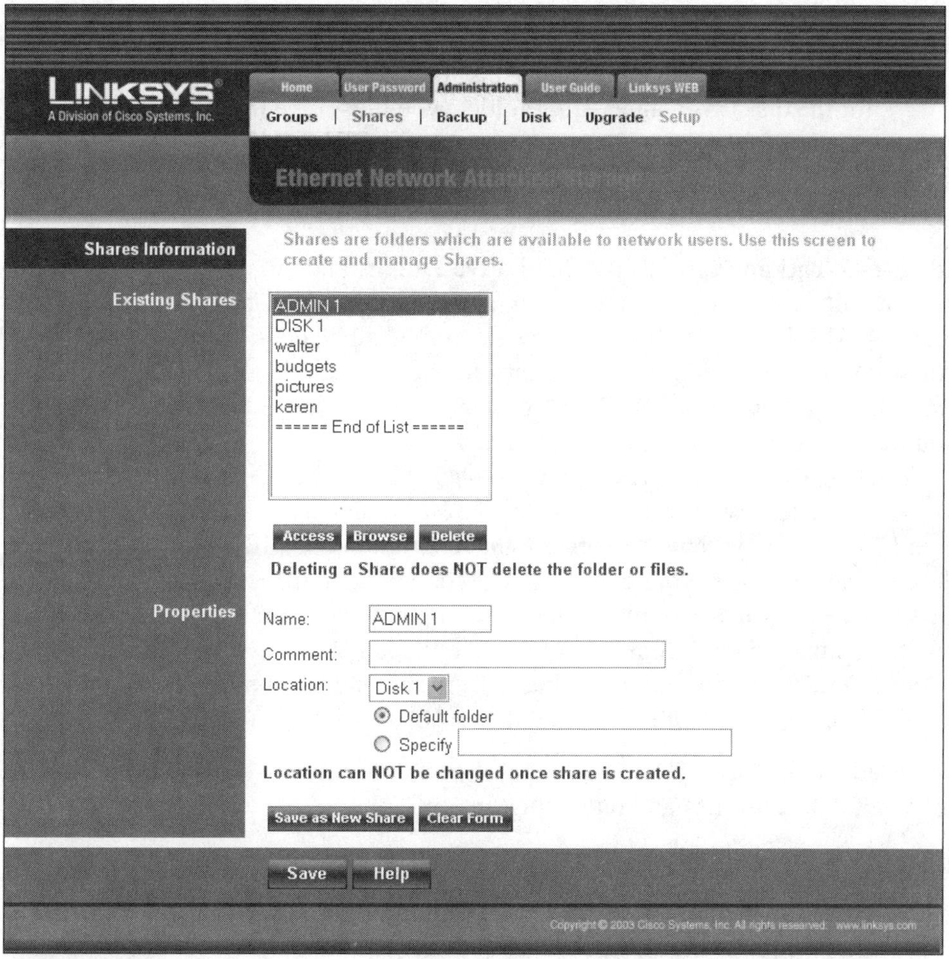

FIGURE 10-13 Create and manage shared folders using the Shares page.

- Click Browse to open the folder in Windows Explorer.
- Click Delete to remove the group.

To create a new group, use the following steps:

1. In the Properties section, type the group name in the Name field.
2. If you want, type in a comment that helps further identify the group.
3. If you have two disks in the EFG250, you can select on which disk you want to create the folder.
4. Choose whether to create the share in the default folder (the main folder for the disk) or in an existing folder (you must type in the name of the existing folder).
5. Click Save As New Share.

Advanced—Backup Page If two hard drives are installed in the EFG250, you can use the built-in backup tool to back up all the data on Disk1 to Disk 2, as shown in Figure 10-14. If you want to back up data immediately, click Start Backup Now. If you want to schedule automatic backups to happen periodically, select the Enable Data Backup From Disk 1 to Disk 2 option and then choose the interval at which you want to back up data.

You can also use the Backup page to back up the EFG250's configuration data to your computer—a good precaution to take on the off chance something happens to your EFG250 and you need to restore that configuration. Click Download to save the configuration file to your computer. The configuration file is named configfile.bin. Be sure to save it in a safe place on your computer and name the folder that you put it in so that you will remember what the file is for (for example, I named my folder EFG250 Configuration Backup). To restore a configuration from a file back to the EFG250, click Upload and tell the EFG250 where configfile.bin is located.

Advanced—Disk Page The Disk page, shown in Figure 10-15, provide access to four useful disk utilities and one important option:

- **Format Disk section** Format a newly installed disk. Formatting a disk erases all data on the disk, so you should use this with caution. The disk included with the EFG250 is already formatted, so you will not need to format it (except in the rare circumstance in which you want to erase all

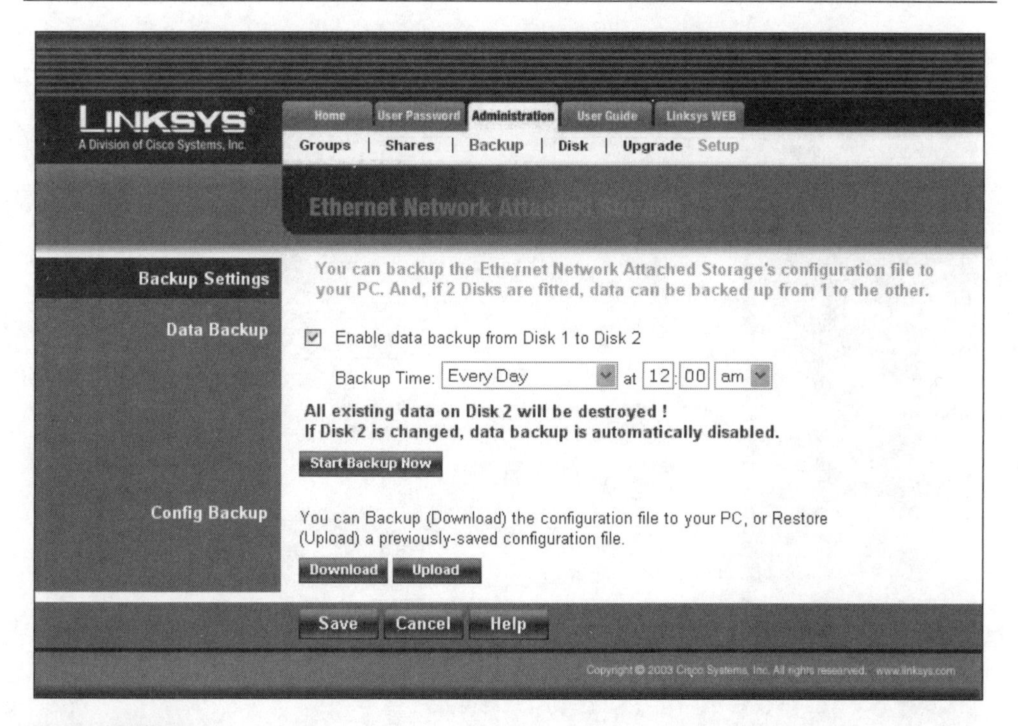

FIGURE 10-14 Use the Backup page to back up data from Disk 1 to Disk 2 and to back up the EFG250's configuration data to your computer.

the data on the disk and start from scratch). When you install a new disk in the EFG250, you will need to format the disk.

- **Self-Test (S.M.A.R.T) section** Test the status of a disk. S.M.A.R.T stands for Self-Monitoring, Analysis, and Reporting Technology, and it is a standard developed by several disk manufactures that allows software to test several disk attributes and determine how likely the disk is to fail. Click Test Now to test all installed disks.
- **Scandisk section** Check the directory structure, available space, and condition of files on the disk.
- **Defrag section** Defragment the disks. Disk fragmentation occurs naturally over time as files are deleted and added to a disk. When a file is deleted, the space on the disk that the file inhabited is marked as available to be overwritten. When a new file is written, part of the file may be written to

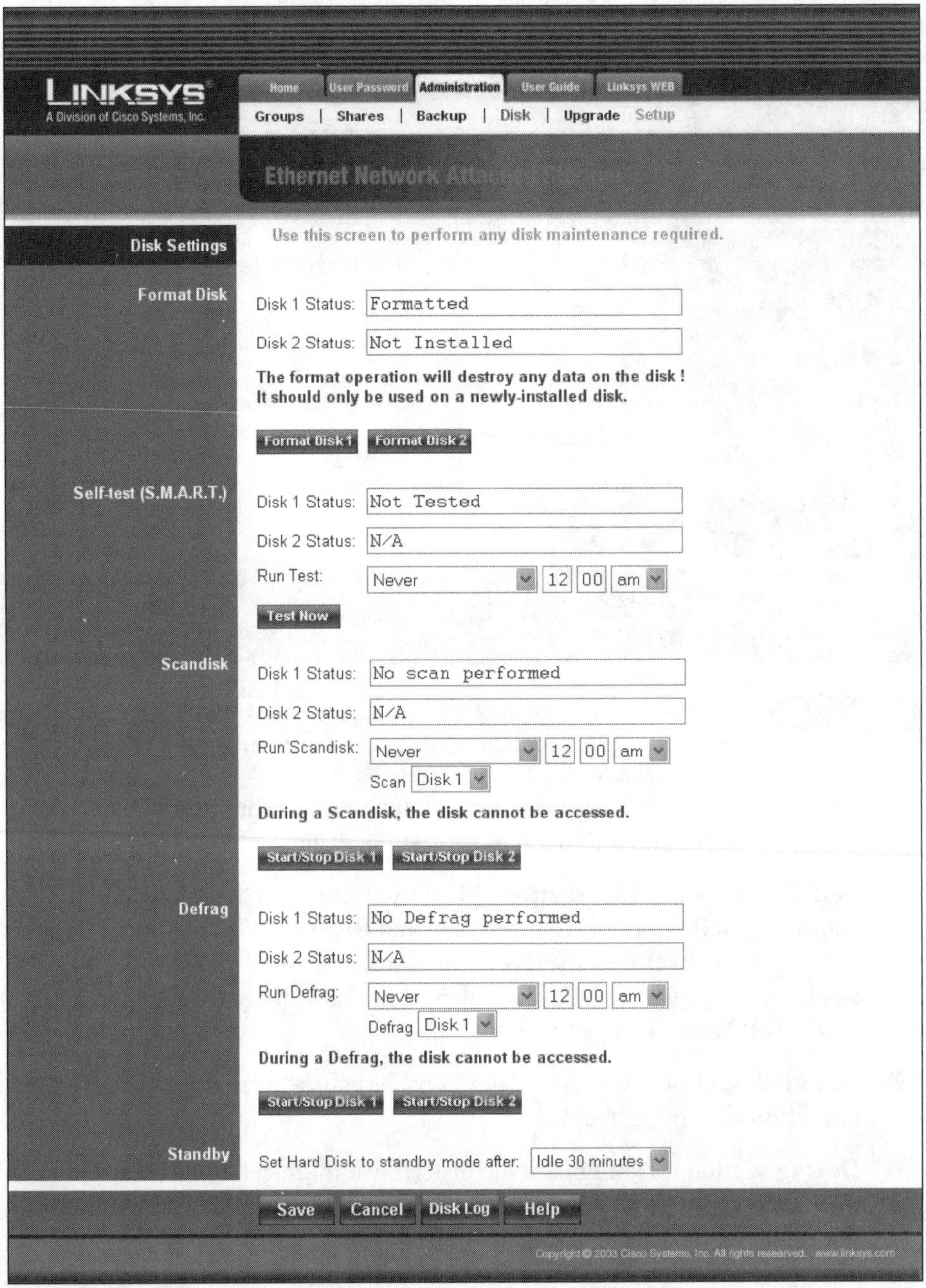

LINKSYS
A Division of Cisco Systems, Inc.

Home | User Password | Administration | User Guide | Linksys WEB

Groups | Shares | Backup | Disk | Upgrade Setup

Ethernet Network Attached Storage

Disk Settings

Use this screen to perform any disk maintenance required.

Format Disk

Disk 1 Status: Formatted

Disk 2 Status: Not Installed

The format operation will destroy any data on the disk !
It should only be used on a newly-installed disk.

Format Disk 1 | Format Disk 2

Self-test (S.M.A.R.T.)

Disk 1 Status: Not Tested

Disk 2 Status: N/A

Run Test: Never 12 00 am

Test Now

Scandisk

Disk 1 Status: No scan performed

Disk 2 Status: N/A

Run Scandisk: Never 12 00 am

Scan Disk 1

During a Scandisk, the disk cannot be accessed.

Start/Stop Disk 1 | Start/Stop Disk 2

Defrag

Disk 1 Status: No Defrag performed

Disk 2 Status: N/A

Run Defrag: Never 12 00 am

Defrag Disk 1

During a Defrag, the disk cannot be accessed.

Start/Stop Disk 1 | Start/Stop Disk 2

Standby

Set Hard Disk to standby mode after: Idle 30 minutes

Save | Cancel | Disk Log | Help

Copyright © 2003 Cisco Systems, Inc. All rights reserved. www.linksys.com

FIGURE 10-15 Use the Disk page to access the EFG250's built-in disk utilities.

one section of the disk, part to another, and so on. While such *fragmentation* is a normal occurrence and does not pose a real threat to your data, it can slow down access to the drive. Click Start/Stop Disk 1 or Start/Stop Disk 2 to start or stop the defragmentation process on a drive. You can also schedule periodic defragmentation to happen automatically.

- **Standby section** Control whether the EFG250 moves the drives into standby mode after a period of not being accessed. Standby helps conserve power, and some people say it prolongs the life of a disk. The default setting is to enter standby mode after 30 minutes of no activity. Use the drop-down list to change the amount of idle time required to send a disk to standby or to disable the feature.

Advanced—Upgrade Page The Upgrade page, shown in Figure 10-16, allows you to upgrade the firmware (built-in software instructions) for the EFG250 using an upgrade file you download from Linksys. Click the Check for Update button and your system will automatically check with Linksys for updates on the Linksys support site. Download any files as indicated. After you have downloaded a file, click Browse to specify the location of the file on your computer. Click Start Upgrade to upgrade the firmware.

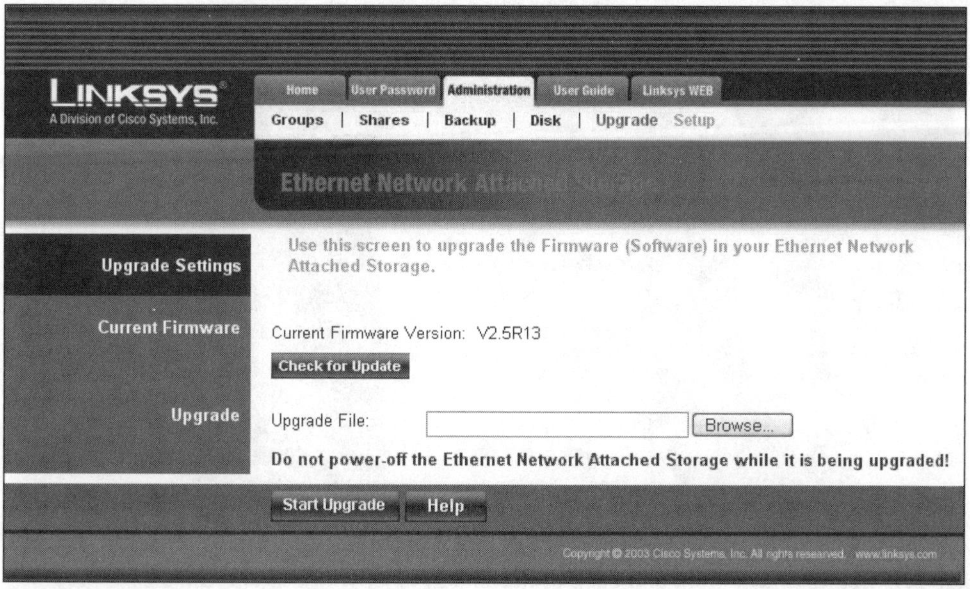

FIGURE 10-16 Use the Upgrade page to update the EFG250's firmware.

Sharing Files with the Linksys Network Storage Link

The Linksys Network Storage Link for USB 2.0 Disk Drives (NSLU2) works in much the same way as the EtherFast Network Attached Storage (250GB with PrintServer) that I covered in the last section, with one very important difference: Instead of containing built-in hard drive bays, the NSLU2 has USB ports on the back of the unit to which you can hook up your own external drives. One of the ports can be used for any USB hard drive, and the other can be used for a USB hard drive or a USB flash drive (such as a Linksys Instant USB Disk). Figure 10-17 shows the front and back of the unit.

The front of the NSLU2 features the following:

- The Power button turns the device on and off. Pressing this button while the device is turned on initiates an internal shutdown sequence that turns off the device safely, so you should not worry about turning off the device (though you should never simply unplug it while it's on). You can also

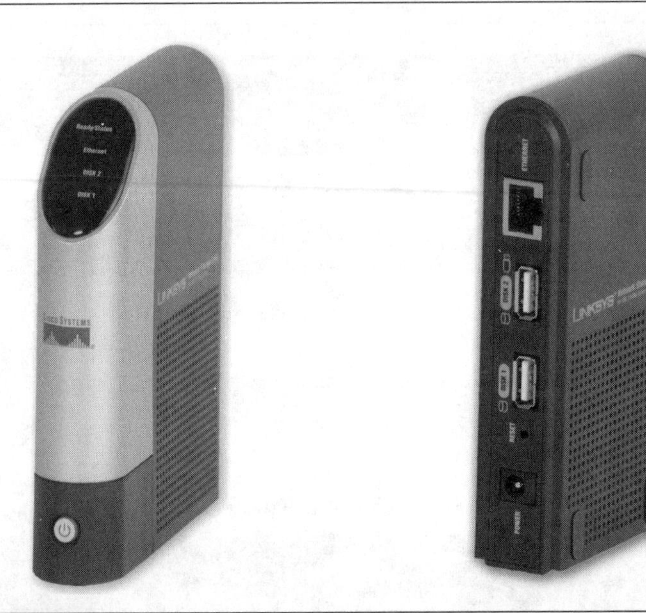

FIGURE 10-17 The front and back of the Linksys Network Storage Link for USB 2.0 Disk Drives.

turn off the device safely using a command in the device's Web-based utility (more about that in the section "Setting Up the NSLU2").

- The Ready/Status LED is solid green when the device is turned on and working properly. The light blinks green during startup and shutdown. If the light turns orange, an error has occurred.
- The Ethernet LED is solid green when the device is connected to the network. The LED blinks green when data is transmitted to or from the device.
- The Disk 1 LED blinks when the unit is writing or reading data from the drive in the first drive bay.
- The Disk 2 LED blinks when the unit is writing or reading data from the drive in the second drive bay.

The back of the NSLU2 has the following features:

- The Ethernet port is used to connect the device to your network.
- The Disk 1 port is used to connect a USB hard drive. The Disk 1 port does not recognize flash drives.
- The Disk 2 port is used to connect a USB flash drive or a USB hard drive.
- The Reset button on the NSLU2 has two functions: If you press and hold the button for 3 seconds, the unit resets to the default fixed IP address (192.168.1.77). The unit beeps once when this has occurred. If you hold the button down for 10 seconds, the unit resets the administrator's password to its default setting (*admin*). The unit beeps again when this has happened. Note that to reset the password, you must also reset the IP address.
- The Power port is used to plug in the power adapter for the unit.

Installing the Linksys Network Storage Link for USB 2.0 Disk Drives

The NSLU2 is easy to install. Just follow these steps:

1. Connect the device directly into your existing network using an Ethernet cable (the same as you would a computer). Connect the other end of the cable to a hub, switch, or computer with a network adapter installed.

2. Connect the USB storage devices to the ports on the back of the NSLU2. If you are using a flash drive, you must insert it in the Disk 2 port.

3. Connect the power supply to the NSLU2, and then plug the other end into a power outlet (or surge protector).

4. Press the Power button on the front of the NSLU2. The unit runs a self-test and then starts up. During startup, most of the LEDs will flash or light up. The Ready/Status light will flash orange, then flash green, and then finally settle down to a solid green. After a couple of minutes, only the Ready/Status and the LAN LEDs should remain lit (green) and the rest of the LEDs should be unlit. At this point, the unit will beep once to indicate that it has started up and is ready to go.

NOTE *If you hear multiple beeps during the startup process (usually a sequence of two, three, or five beeps that repeat every so often) or if you see the Ready/ Status LED flashing orange after startup, a hardware problem has occurred. Consult the documentation that came with the device to interpret the error and find the solution.*

Setting Up the NSLU2

After connecting and turning on the NSLU2, you will need to run the Setup Wizard to configure the unit so that it is accessible on your network. The Setup Wizard works the same whether you are using Windows 98, Me, NT 4.0, 2000, or XP and is nearly identical to the Setup Wizard described in the previous section on the EFG250. To run the Setup Wizard for the NSLU2, use these steps:

1. On any computer that is connected to the network, insert the Setup Wizard CD that came with the NSLU2. The Setup Wizard should start automatically. If it does not (for example, if you have Windows AutoRun feature disabled), you can start the wizard by choosing Start | Run and typing **d:\SetupUtility.exe**, where *d* is the drive letter for your CD-ROM drive. On the first page of the Setup Wizard, click Setup.

2. The Setup Wizard automatically searches the network for the NSLU2 (and will also detect the unit if it's attached directly to your computer).

NOTE *If the Setup Wizard fails to locate the NSLU2, be sure that you have given the unit enough time to start up. Click Search Again to have the Setup Wizard try again to find the device. If it still cannot locate the device, check to make sure that the device is correctly attached to your network.*

3. After the Setup Wizard locates the NSLU2, it lets you know of its success. In the Selection list, click the name of the unit to view its configuration status.

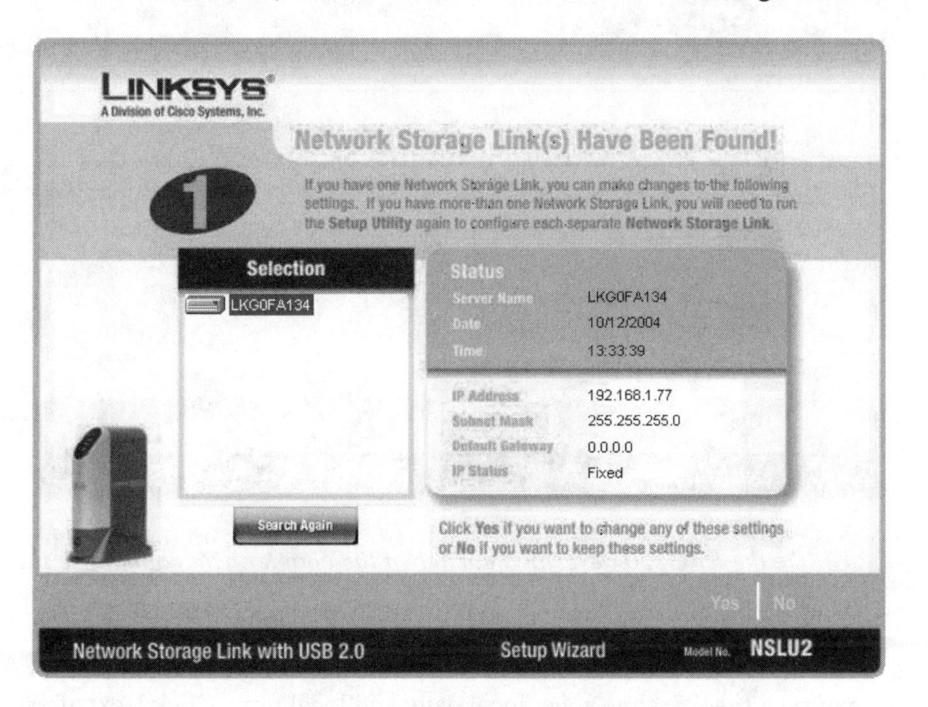

4. If the configuration looks correct, click No (indicating that you don't want to change any settings). The Setup Wizard closes, and you are ready to share folders on the device. If you want to change the configuration, click Yes to go on with the Setup Wizard.

5. The first setting you can change is how the device obtains its IP address. Choose Set IP Configuration Manually if you want to create a static IP address for the device. Choose Automatically Obtain an IP Address (DHCP) if you want the device to act as a DHCP client and obtain its IP address from a DHCP server (such as a router on your network). Most

likely, you will want to choose Fixed IP Address—the default setting. Click Next after making the appropriate settings.

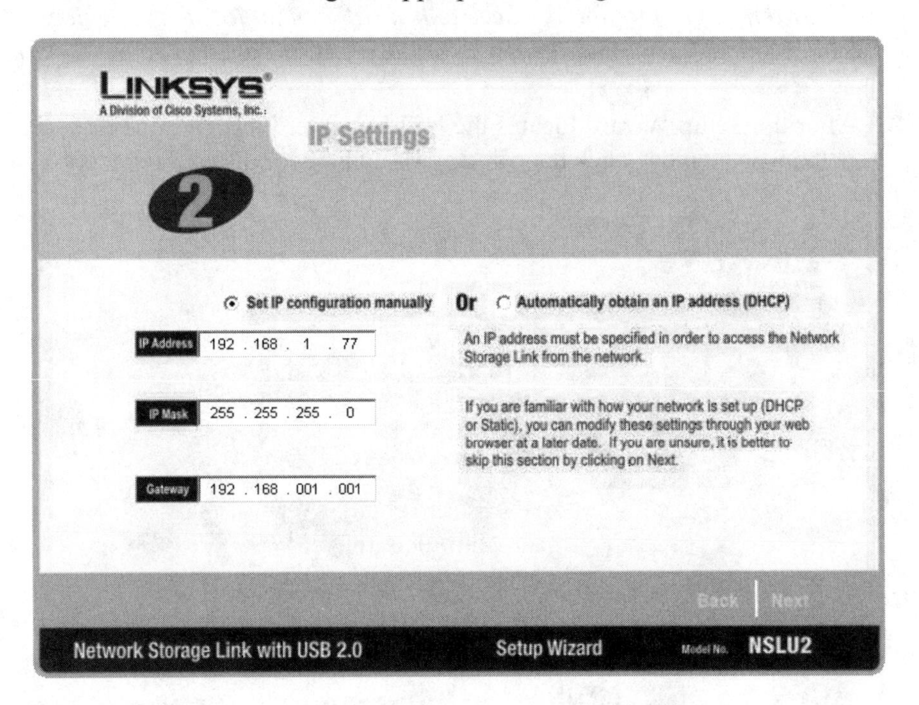

NOTE *Unlike the EFG250 described earlier in the chapter, you cannot use the NSLU2 as a DHCP server.*

6. The next option you can change is the time and date for the NSLU2. You can set a specific time zone, local date, and local time. Click Next after making the appropriate changes.
7. The next page shows you a summary of the NSLU2's settings. If you're happy with the way you've set it up, click Save. Otherwise, you can click Back to work your way back through the wizard and make changes.
8. After saving the configuration changes, the Setup Wizard displays a message that warns you that changes will be made to the unit. Click OK to save the changes or Cancel to return to the wizard.
9. After the changes are successfully saved, the Setup Wizard displays a Congratulations page. Click Exit to close the wizard.

At this point, your NSLU2 is connected, configured, and ready to go.

Managing the NSLU2

After connecting the NSLU2 to your network and running the Setup Wizard, you can access the NSLU2 from any computer that has a Web browser. This makes the NSLU2 easy to manage from anywhere on your network. The Web-based administration tool uses the familiar tabbed interface common to other Linksys network devices. Just point your browser to the IP address you configured during the Setup Wizard to access the NSLU2 administration utility.

Actually, the NSLU2 uses a set of management tools that are almost identical to those of the EFG250, described in detail earlier in the chapter. So instead of repeating everything here, I offer you a summary of what you can do with the NSLU2 and refer you back to the section "Sharing Files with the Linksys NAS Device" for the details.

- **Home tab** Provides an easy way for users to log in and view their private shares and access public data on any installed disks.
- **User Password tab** Allows a user to change his or her password without having to ask someone with an administrative password to do it.
- **Administration tab** Requires an administrator's password to access The default password is *admin*). It features a host of management tools, including these:
  - **LAN page** Lets you change the IP address of the unit and configure the addresses of one or more DNS servers (not necessary if you obtain an IP address automatically).
  - **System page** Lets you change the server name and the workgroup to which the unit belongs. You can also change time and date information, enable a WINS server, permit guest logins, and enable UPnP support.
  - **Users page** Lets you view, create, and delete users. You can also view the groups to which a user belongs.
  - **Status page** Provides the current status of the unit. It also lets you shut down, restart, and even schedule automatic shutdowns and restarts. You can view a log of any administrative functions that have occurred and configure the unit to send an e-mail message to one or two addresses when a problem occurs.
  - **Groups page** Allows you to view, create, and delete groups. You can also control to which folders each group has access (and what level of

access—none, read only, or read/write) and control the users that are members of each group.

- **Shares page** Shows existing shares on the unit's hard drives and allows you to browse, delete, or create new shares. You can also control the groups that have access to each share (and the level of access).
- **Backup page** Lets you back up the configuration of the NSLU2 to your computer, as well as backup information on Disk 1 to Disk 2 if you have two disks installed. You can even schedule automatic data backups.
- **Disk page** Provides access to the two disk tools available on the NSLU2: formatting disks (necessary when you install a new disk) and scandisk (which scans the directory structure and file conditions on the disk).
- **Upgrade page** Lets you update the firmware on the NSLU2 with an update file you have downloaded from the Linksys support site.

Chapter 11

Sharing Printers

The ability to share printers in a network is almost as big a motivation for installing a network as the desire to share an Internet connection. Without a network, households and small businesses with multiple computers have two choices for printing:

- Buy a new printer every time you buy a new computer.
- Make users copy documents to a floppy disk, walk to the computer that has the printer, insert the floppy disk, open the appropriate software, load the document in the software, and print the document—whew!

Of course, when you have a network, you *can* buy a printer for each computer—perhaps a high-speed laser printer for one computer and a color inkjet printer for another computer—and then everyone can use either printer, depending on the type of document they're printing.

You have two choices for setting up printer sharing in your network:

- Use a hardware device called a *print server*.
- Use the Windows software features to share a printer that's attached to a computer.

Using Linksys Print Servers to Share Printers

You gain several benefits when you use a hardware-based print server to share printers on a network instead of the standard printer sharing features offered by Windows:

- **Speed** The Linksys print servers soup up the speed at which data is delivered to the printer, and the device is dedicated to printing instead of having to perform all the other activities your computer does.
- **Location** You can put your printers in a place that's convenient for all users on the network, instead of attaching individual printers to individual computers (this is especially important if the computers aren't near each other).
- **Availability** The print server is available all the time, while printers attached to computers aren't available when the computer isn't running.

Linksys offers several types of print servers. I happen to use the 3-Port Print Server (EPSX3) because it fits my network setup best, so I use that model as the basis of this discussion. However, setting up any Linksys print server is very much the same, regardless of the model. Installing a Linksys print server requires several easy steps:

1. Physically connect the print server to your printer(s) and your network.
2. Install the drivers for the print server.
3. Configure the print server.
4. Install the drivers for the printers that are attached to the print server on each computer that will use the printers.

Physically Installing the Print Server

You must make all the physical connections for your print server before you can start setting up the print server and the printers.

Attach your printer to the printer port at the back of the print server. Depending on the print server model, the port is either a parallel port or a USB port. If your printer is currently attached to a computer, remove the connector from the back of the computer and connect it to the print server (turn off the computer first if the printer is connected to a parallel port). If you're attaching multiple printers to a print server that has multiple printer ports, repeat this step for each printer.

- If you're using a wired print server, use the RJ-45 port (the LAN port) on the back of the print server to attach the print server to your network hub or switch (or router, if you're using a router as a concentrator). Use a standard Ethernet patch cable to make the connection.
- If you're using a wireless print server, you have to connect the print server to an Ethernet device to install the drivers and configure the print server. Afterward, it communicates with your network with RF technology, using its antenna. You can use a router or an access point as the Ethernet device.

Connect the power supply to the print server, and plug it into an outlet. The print server lacks an on/off switch—you power it up by plugging it in. As soon as you power up the print server, the LED lights on the front of the device should glow to indicate the presence of power, printer connections, and computer connections.

Installing the Print Server Driver

All the computers on the network use the print server to access printers, so you must install the print server's driver on all of those computers. You can take the Linksys CD that came with your print server to each computer, or use the CD on a computer that shares the CD-ROM drive and access that drive across the network to install the driver on all the other computers.

Linksys is constantly upgrading and tweaking its installation programs, so the CD that came with your print server may take any of the following actions after you insert it in the CD-ROM drive:

- No action, which means that no program automatically opens and you access the drive to run the software you need.
- Run the BiAdmin program, which is software that lets you change configuration options for the print server.
- Run the driver installation program, which automatically installs the drivers for the print server and sets basic configuration options.

Even though it's possible to run the BiAdmin configuration program before you install the drivers, it's best to close that program if it runs automatically. Install the drivers and the basic configuration options first, and then, if necessary, you can use either the BiAdmin software or the Web-based software to make changes to the configuration of the print server. The drivers must be installed on every computer that accesses the print server, but the BiAdmin or Web-based configuration software has to be installed only on one computer.

Launch the print server setup wizard, which is the driver installation program, by using either of the following methods:

- Choose Start | Run, enter **d:\driver\win9xnt\setup.exe**, and click OK (substitute the drive letter for your CD drive if it isn't *d*).
- Open Windows Explorer or My Computer and navigate to the driver\win9xnt folder on the CD; then double-click setup.exe.

When the wizard opens, click Next to have the setup program copy the files from the CD to the computer's hard drive. By default, the wizard creates subfolders under the Program Files folder to hold the software, but you can change the location to a different folder if you prefer to install software and drivers to discrete folders.

The wizard also displays the menu item it will create on your Programs menu. When the wizard displays the Setup Complete window, the option Configure Print Driver Now is preselected.

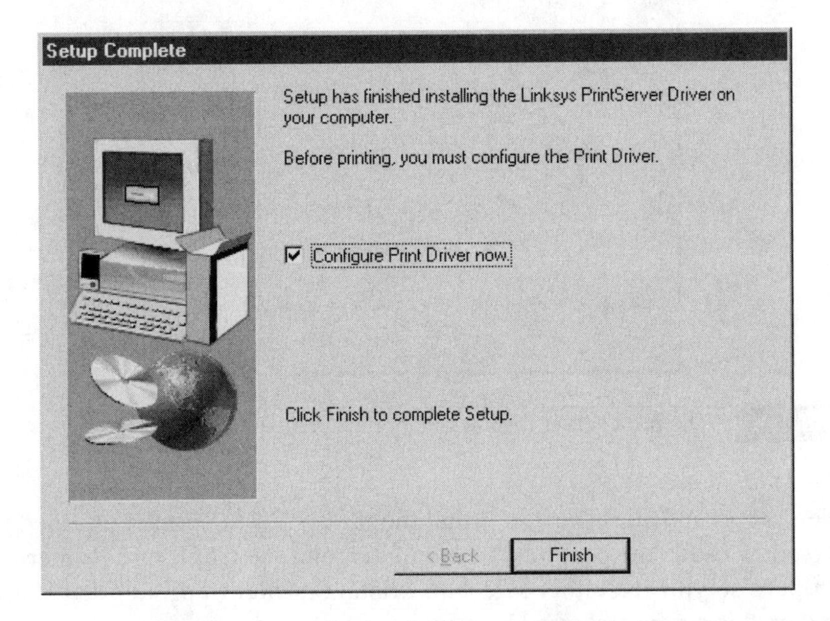

This configuration program is where you configure the printer port(s) on the print server, so you can install the drivers for the printers that are connected to the print server. Note that this is not the same as making configuration changes to the print server (which is covered in the subsequent sections on BiAdmin and the Web-based configuration utility); this configuration is for the printers attached to the print server.

If your network is using DHCP to assign IP addresses, your print server has received an IP address and you can move immediately to the configuration of the printers. If your network is using assigned IP addresses, you must give the print server an IP address before you can do anything else. See the section "Understanding the Print Server Configuration Tools" later in this chapter.

Installing Printer Drivers

To install print drivers, double-click the Print Driver Setup icon (or start the Print Driver Setup program from your Programs menu if you stopped to assign an IP address to the print server). This is the phase in which you install the drivers for the printers you've attached to the print server. The wizard displays its printer port(s) and the printer(s) attached to the port(s), as seen in Figure 11-1.

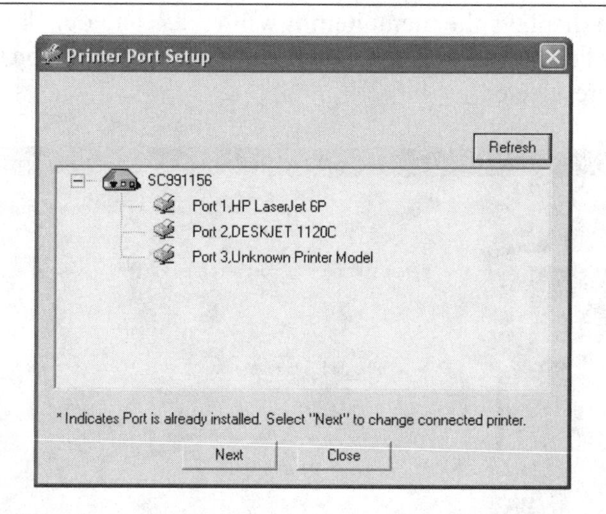

FIGURE 11-1 The print server displays its ports and attached printers.

Select a port and click Next to install the drivers for the printer attached to the port. Windows adds the port to your computer, and the Configure Printer Port dialog opens so you can either select an existing printer (a printer that's already installed on this computer) or add a printer.

NOTE *The port that's added to your computer's configuration is the port on the print server, and the port is named for the print server, which is named SCXXXXXX (substitute numbers for each X). The print server's name is on a label on the bottom of the device.*

If the printer you're configuring had previously been installed on this computer, you'll see an existing driver. Select its listing and click Connect. Windows links the printer that's attached to the print server to its already-installed driver and returns you to the Printer Port Setup dialog. Click the Refresh button to update the display—the port listing displays an asterisk to indicate that both the port and the printer are installed.

If the printer you're configuring isn't on this computer (no listing appears in the Configure Printer Port dialog box), click Add New Printer. The Windows Add Printer Wizard opens, and you need to work through the wizard screens to add the printer, using the same steps you'd use if you were adding a printer that's attached to this computer. Windows includes drivers for a lot of printers, but if you have drivers from the printer's manufacturer, choose the Have Disk option and follow the wizard's prompts to install the printer. When you're returned to the Printer Port Setup dialog, click the Refresh button to update the list of printer ports—the port listing includes an asterisk to indicate that both the port and the printer are installed on this computer.

If you open the Printers and Faxes folder in Control Panel, you'll see the printer (or multiple printers) you installed. This means the name of the printer also shows up when you open the Print dialog in the software program you're using, so you're all set for printing, no matter which computer on the network you're using.

Restart the computer so Windows can add the new port to your computer's hardware configuration settings.

Understanding the Print Server Configuration Tools

You can configure many of the features on your print server with either of the configuration tools that are available:

- The Web-based configuration utility, which uses your browser and requires no software installation.
- The BiAdmin software program, which is on the CD that came with your print server.

NOTE *The name Web-based is a misnomer, because when you're working on your network you're not accessing the print server over the World Wide Web—the utility should probably be named Browser-based instead.*

Both tools offer functions for configuring and managing your print server (covered in the section "Using the Print Server Management Tools" later in this chapter).

The Web-based configuration utility is easier to use, because you don't have to install any software—you can use any computer on the network to access the print server in a browser. However, because you access the print server by entering its IP address in the browser address bar, there's a catch:

- To use the Web-based utility, you must know the print server's IP address.
- To ascertain the print server's IP DHCP-supplied address, you must run the BiAdmin software.

- To give the print server an assigned IP address (if your network doesn't use DHCP), you must run the BiAdmin software to find the print server by using its name (the name is on the label on the bottom of the print server).

In the following sections, I cover installation of the BiAdmin software as well as the tools you can access in that software or in your browser.

Installing the BiAdmin Utility

You don't have to install the BiAdmin software on every computer, because the software is used only if you have to configure or manage the print server. In addition, most of the commonly used management utilities are available in the Web-based utility. Since the BiAdmin software is used so rarely, if at all, you can install it on only one computer. To install the software, put the Linksys CD in the CD drive and take one of the following actions:

- Choose Start | Run and enter **d:\utility\biadmin\setup.exe** (substitute the appropriate drive letter if your CD-ROM drive isn't *d*).
- Open the CD drive in Windows Explorer or My Computer, navigate to the \utility\biadmin subfolder, and double-click setup.exe.

When you launch BiAdmin, the program opens a window that asks you to confirm the protocol you're using for network communication (TCP/IP is selected by default). Click OK to start the program, which first scans your network to find the Linksys print server you've installed.

Assigning a Static IP Address to the Print Server

If you're using static IP addresses on your network, the BiAdmin program won't find the print server when it scans your network. You must take the following steps to attach your print server to your network by assigning it a static IP address:

1. Find the print server's name on the bottom of the device, and make a note of it. The name is in the format SC*XXXXXX*.
2. In the BiAdmin software window, choose InitDevice | Set IP Address to open the Set IP Address dialog.
3. In the Default Name field, enter the name you copied from the label at the bottom of the print server.

4. Enter the IP address you're assigning to the print server.
5. Enter the gateway IP address you use on your network (if you have a gateway).
6. Enter the subnet mask you use on your network.
7. Click Set.

The software searches the network, finds the print server, and displays it in the BiAdmin window.

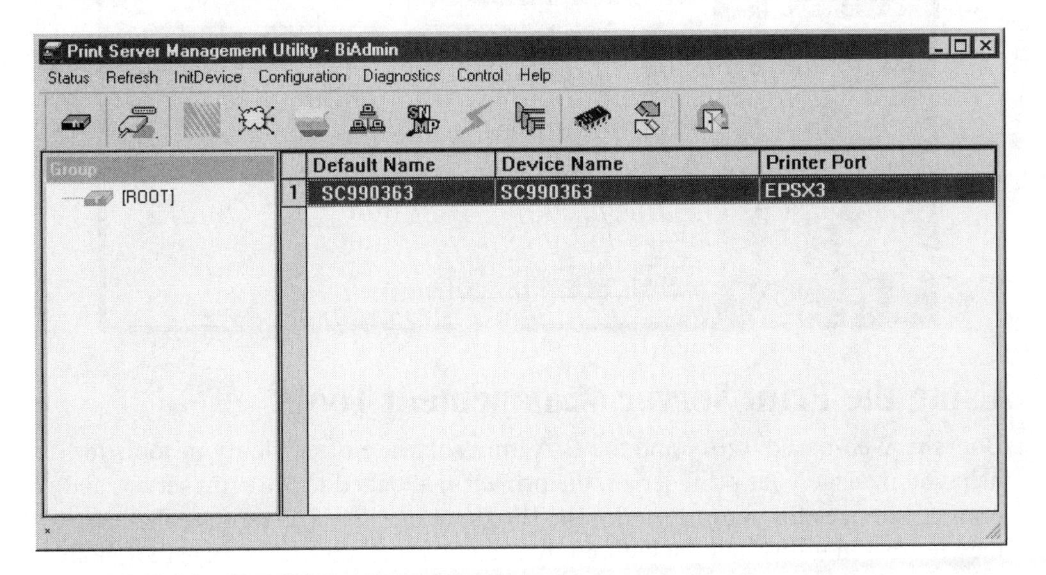

If you're using DHCP to assign IP addresses to network nodes, it's a good idea to assign a static IP address to your print server instead of letting it receive a leased address from your DHCP server. That way, you don't have to use the BiAdmin program to discover the print server's current IP address if you want to use the Web-based utility to view or manage the device. Assign an IP address that's unlikely to be leased to a computer on your network by choosing a number high in the address range. For instance, you can use an address that the DHCP server won't assign to a computer, such as 192.168.1.99 (DHCP assigns numbers starting at *100*). Write the address you assign on a label or a piece of paper and affix it to the print server so you don't have to rely on your memory.

Opening the Web-Based Configuration Utility

To use the Web-based configuration tool, open a browser and enter the print server's IP address in the Address Bar. Your browser window displays a dialog with tabs that contain the configuration and management options for the print server.

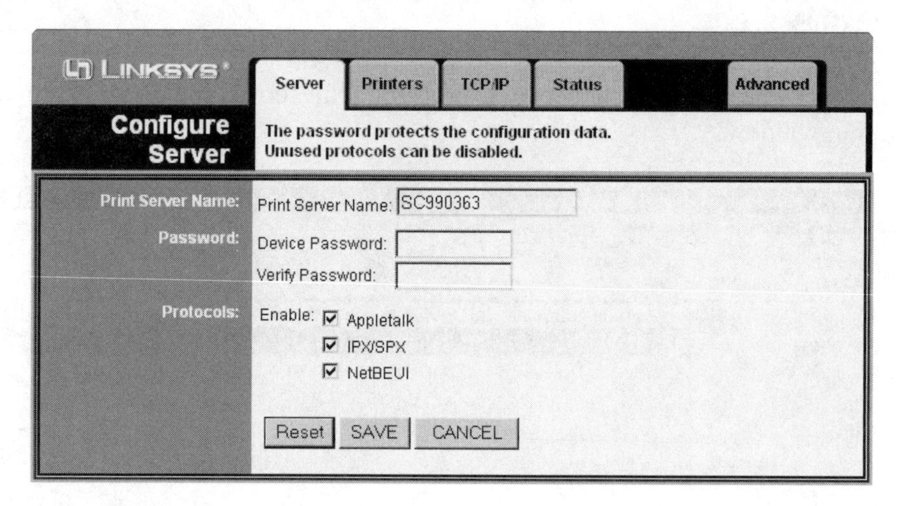

Using the Print Server Management Tools

Both the Web-based utility and the BiAdmin software offer plenty of tools to help you manage your print server, the printer(s) attached to the print server, and printing services for your network. The BiAdmin program has more tools than the Web-based utility, but the commonly used (and most useful) tools are in both programs. I go over a few of the useful utilities here.

Changing the Print Server Name

If you wish, you can change the name of the print server, although there's probably no need to do this unless you have two print servers and need to distinguish between them. It's difficult to remember which is which if they both have similar names in the default format SC*XXXXXX*—it's easier to remember Hallway and Bob (for the print server that's near Bob's computer).

In the Web-based utility, the name appears on the Server tab. In the BiAdmin software window, choose Configuration | System to open the System Configuration dialog. Select the current name and replace it with a new name.

Password-Protecting the Print Server

You can assign a password to the print server so that only users who know the password can view or manage the device. In the Web-based utility, the password fields are on the Server tab. In the BiAdmin software, choose InitDevice | Set Password. Enter a password, and then reenter it to set the password.

Unless you have a user on your network who habitually messes around with equipment (and wreaks havoc), you shouldn't bother with a password. If you do assign a password, write it down and hide the paper. If you forget it, you can't get into the print server's administration tools unless you reset the print server to return its settings to their defaults. In that case, you'd have to start your print server configuration again, performing every configuration task.

Enabling and Disabling Protocols

By default, the print server supports multiple protocols, even though your network almost certainly requires only TCP/IP support from the device. You can disable the protocols you don't need, although leaving them enabled is harmless. In the Web-based utility, deselect unneeded protocols on the General tab. In BiAdmin, choose Configuration | System.

Checking the Status of the Print Server

You can view the status of the print server and save the current settings to a file, which is useful if you have to reconfigure the device in the future.

In the Web-based utility, move to the Status tab to see the current configuration. To save the configuration settings to a file, choose File | Save As from the browser menu bar. By default, the system uses the filename Server Status. It's best to select Text as the file type.

In BiAdmin, choose Status | Backup/Restore Device Information (or click the leftmost icon on the toolbar). Click Save to File to save a text file with the configuration settings.

Checking the Status of the Printers

You can see whether a printer is accepting data through the print server by sending a test page. If you send a test page from the printer's Properties dialog on your computer and the test page fails to print, you don't know whether the problem is with the printer, between the computer and the print server, or between the print server and the printer. If you send a test page from the print server to the printer and it fails, you know the problem is with the connection between the print server and the printer, or with the printer itself. If you send a test page from the print server to the printer and it succeeds, you know the problem is between the computer and the print server.

In the Web-based utility, move to the Printers tab. If the status for the printer is set to Offline, the problem is clearly between the print server and the printer, or with the printer itself. If the status is set to Online, click Print Test Page. If the test fails, you need to check hardware and connections.

In BiAdmin, choose Status | Port Status. Select the appropriate parallel port to see the current status. If the printer is marked Offline, a problem exists between the print server and the printer, or with the printer itself. Check hardware and connections. If the status is set to Online, print a test page by choosing Diagnostics | Print Test Page. Select the appropriate parallel port for the printer you're testing. If the test fails, you need to check hardware and connections.

Troubleshooting Printer Problems

If a printer that's supposed to be online is marked Offline in the status screen, or if a printer text page fails to print, you have to correct the problem.

Check the printer. Make sure all the lights that indicate its status are on or off as appropriate. Check the paper tray to make sure it's not empty. Check for a paper jam. Make sure the parallel or USB connector is properly attached.

Check the network connections for the computer and the print server. Make sure the computer and the print server are properly connected to the network:

- For an Ethernet network, make sure everything is connected properly between the concentrator, the computers, and the print server.
- For a wireless network/print server, make sure nothing is blocking the signal. Try moving the print server.
- For a PowerLine or PhoneLine network, check the connection between the print server and the bridge.

Using Windows Printer Sharing

If you don't have a print server hardware device, you can use the built-in Windows printer sharing features to give everyone on the network a way to use any printer attached to a computer on the network. This makes any computer that is attached to a printer a print server for that printer—so, for example, if you have three computers with printers, you have three print servers on your network.

In this section, I go over the steps involved for sharing a printer and for installing and using a printer that's attached to another computer. I assume you've already taken the steps to install printers and their drivers on your computers. I use a lot of the standard terminology that's applied to discussions of shared printers, so here are some guidelines to make this section easy to understand:

- The printer that's attached to the computer you're working on is a *local printer*.
- A printer that's attached to another computer on the network is a *network printer* (sometimes called a *remote printer*).

Sharing a Printer in Windows XP

To share a printer that's connected to a computer running Windows XP, follow these steps:

1. Choose Start | Control Panel to open the Control Panel window.
2. Select Printers and Other Hardware, and then select View Installed Printers or Fax Printers.
3. In the Printers and Faxes window, right-click the icon of the printer you want to share, and choose Sharing to open the Sharing tab of the printer's Properties dialog.
4. Select Share This Printer, and name the share. Windows usually suggests a name based on the printer's model, but you can change the sharename to suit yourself.

NOTE *If you create a printer sharename that has more than 12 characters, Windows 98SE users won't see the printer share when they open Network Neighborhood. As a result, be sure to count the characters as you create a sharename for the printer.*

5. Click OK.

6. The icon for the printer now sports a hand cradling the printer graphic, indicating that this is a shared printer.

TIP *When you install a printer on a Windows XP computer that's attached to a network, during the installation process you're asked whether you want to share the printer with other users. In this section, I assume you either installed your printer before you installed your network or you didn't share the printer if you installed it after you created your network (and you're ready to share it now).*

NOTE *You can provide printer drivers for this printer for remote users who are running earlier versions of Windows. See the sidebar "Installing Additional Drivers" for more information.*

Sharing a Printer in Windows 2000

To share a printer that's connected to a computer running Windows 2000, follow these steps:

1. Choose Start | Settings | Printers to open the Printers folder.
2. Right-click the icon for the printer, and choose Sharing from the shortcut menu.
3. Select Shared As and either accept the default sharename or change it.
4. Click OK.

If you create a printer sharename that has more than 12 characters, Windows 98SE users won't see the printer share when they open Network Neighborhood. You can provide printer drivers for this printer for remote users who are running other versions of Windows. See the sidebar "Installing Additional Drivers" for more information.

Sharing a Printer in Windows 98SE/Me

To share a printer that's attached to a Windows 98SE/Me computer, follow these steps:

1. Choose Start | Settings | Printers to open the Printers folder.

Installing Additional Drivers

Windows XP and Windows 2000 have a button labeled Additional Drivers on the Sharing tab. If you click the button, you see a list of Windows versions for which you can preinstall drivers for this printer. This means that users working on a computer running Windows 98SE, for example, can install the printer drivers using files on the Windows XP/2000 computer, instead of accessing driver files from the Windows 98SE CD or a printer manufacturer's driver disk.

However, to provide the drivers, you must preinstall them on the Windows XP/2000 computer. To accomplish this, you must insert the Windows 98SE CD or a printer manufacturer's driver disk. Personally, on small networks, I think it's easier just to let each user install his or her own drivers. However, on larger networks, on networks where you don't expect users to have disks available, or on networks with users who you don't want to provide disks, installing additional drivers can be a nice thing to do.

2. Right-click the icon for the printer, and choose Sharing from the shortcut menu.
3. Select Shared As and either accept the default sharename or change it.
4. Click OK.

NOTE *You can password-protect the printer in the same way you can password-protect folder shares. However, it's unusual to have a reason to do that.*

Installing a Remote Printer

To use a printer that's on a remote computer, you must install it on your local computer (which means installing the printer drivers on the local computer). To locate and install a remote printer, follow these steps:

1. Open Network Neighborhood or My Network Places.
2. Double-click the computer that has the printer you want to install to display all the shares for that computer (including printer shares).

3. Right-click the icon for the printer you want to install, and then choose the appropriate command:

    - In Windows XP/2000, choose Connect from the shortcut menu.
    - In Windows 98SE, choose Install from the shortcut menu.

4. The Add Printer Wizard opens to begin installing the printer. Follow the wizard's prompts to install the printer. You may be asked to insert the Windows CD. If you're using drivers from the printer's manufacturer, click Have Disk or enter the path to the drivers when the wizard asks for it.

Windows XP Remote Printer Installation

The manner in which Windows XP handles any hardware installation could be described as "semi-magical." If the operating system recognizes a Plug and Play device and has built-in drivers for the device, it automatically installs it. You don't see a dialog box, you don't have to walk through a wizard—you don't have to do anything.

Windows XP manages remote printers in the same way. If you share a printer on another computer and Windows XP has the drivers for the printer already installed on the local hard drive, you don't have to install that remote printer. Wait a few minutes and then open the Printers and Faxes window from Control Panel. Voilà! You'll see the remote printer listed as an installed printer. You see, Windows XP browses the network every few minutes, behind the scenes, looking for anything new. When it finds a new shared printer for which it has installed drivers, it automatically adds the printer. If it doesn't have an installed driver, it ignores the printer until you manually install it. This phenomenon is common when the same or similar printers (printers that use the same driver) are installed on both the Windows XP and other computers (which is the case on many small networks).

Chapter 12

Tips, Tricks, and Troubleshooting

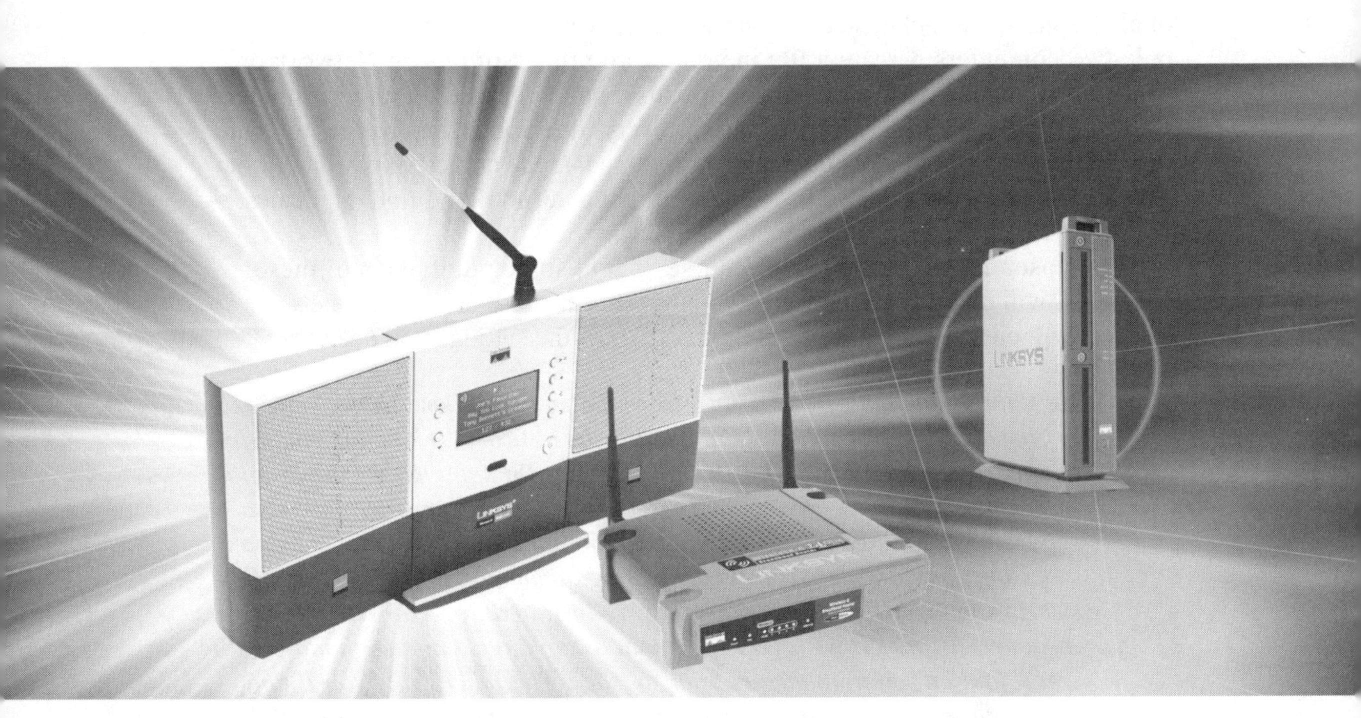

After you've created a network, you automatically earn the title "network administrator." The administrator is the person in charge of the network, and in most home and small business networks, that title belongs to the person who took time to read books, read the documentation that came with the equipment, install the hardware and software, and configure the network.

Networking is complicated. Hundreds of thick, complicated books have been written about networking, which is not to say that you need to know all that stuff when you're running a small network. But things can go wrong. In this chapter, you learn about the things you should do to make sure your network runs smoothly all the time. In the process, you'll pick up some of the tricks used by network administrators of large corporate networks.

Document Everything

You need to keep a record of everything you do. You won't remember the details of all the steps you took to set up your network, even if your network consists of only two computers. Create a file in your word processor (call it Network or something similar), back it up to a floppy disk, put a copy on another computer on the network, and print a copy for filing. Every time you make changes to your network, document those changes in your file, update the copies, and print out the new file. Make the first line of the file the current date, so if you find duplicates, you know which is the latest copy.

The reason for doing this is, of course, that at some point, each of these computers will die or some important component (the hard drive or the network adapter) will die. When you replace it, you'll know the settings you need.

TIP *Get a three-ring binder and a hole punch. Label the binder "Home Network" or something else that helps you identify the network. Whenever you print out documentation or receive documents from ISPs, punch the paper and insert it in the binder. If you have several computers, consider making a separate section in the binder for each computer. In a computer's section, place information such as troubleshooting documentation, printouts of the system summary (hardware and software installed), and other information. As your network grows (and it will) and as computers change hands, you'll find information much easier to track. The other thing you'll find after you create your own network is that your friends and family will want your help with their own networks. Keep a binder for each.*

Track Your ISP Settings

Your Internet service provider (ISP) provided instructions about setting up your Internet connection. Those instructions include the way the computers on your network get their IP addresses, whether or not you have to specify a DNS server, and other important information. Copy the important settings into the file you're creating so you have complete documentation of your network's setup.

Track Hardware Settings

Some devices require specific settings, such as interrupt request (IRQ) levels and I/O addresses. (It doesn't matter whether you understand what they are; it just matters that you can find them if you need technical support or you have to replace a device.) Windows has a feature called Device Manager that tracks this information, and you should copy this information. (If your computer or drive dies, you won't be able to get to Device Manager.) To open Device Manager, right-click My Computer—located on the desktop or on the Start menu—and choose Properties from the shortcut menu. Click the Hardware tab, and then click the Device Manager button. (Windows 98 and Windows Me both include a Device Manager tab, so you save yourself a mouse click.)

When Device Manager opens, it displays each type of hardware component in your computer. When you expand a component type by clicking the plus sign (+) next to its listing, you see the specific device of the type that's installed in your computer. Figure 12-1 shows the Network Adapter expanded in Device Manager to display the specific adapter in this computer.

Right-click the device (not the device type) and choose Properties from the shortcut menu. In the Properties dialog for the device, shown in Figure 12-2, the General tab, the Advanced tab, the Resources tab, and the Driver tab all provide information about the device and its settings.

You could write down the settings and then type them in your network documentation file. Or you could take a shortcut, as follows:

1. Click the title bar on the device's Properties dialog to make sure that the window is active.
2. Hold down the ALT key while you press the PRINT SCREEN key. This copies a picture of the window into the clipboard's memory. (The ALT key tells the clipboard to capture only the active window; otherwise, everything you see on your monitor is copied, which is more than you need.)

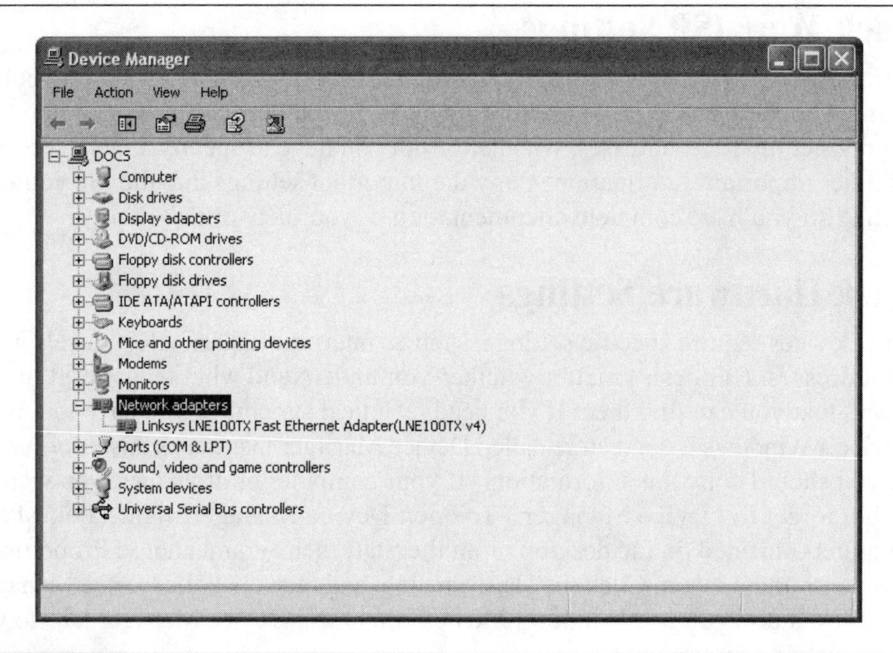

FIGURE 12-1 Expand a device type to see the specific device that's installed on your computer.

3. Choose Start | Programs | Accessories | Paint to open the Paint program.
4. Choose Edit | Paste from the Paint menu bar. The image is pasted from the clipboard into the Paint window.
5. Choose File | Save and save the file (use a filename that reminds you of the contents, such as KitNICDrivers for the Drivers tab of the NIC in the computer named Kitchen).
6. Repeat these steps for each set of information you want to keep about devices.

If you save the file on the local computer, copy it to the computer on which you're saving your network documentation file. Or, better still, when you save the file, navigate across the network to that computer right in the software window. (See Chapter 10 to learn how to access folders on other computers.)

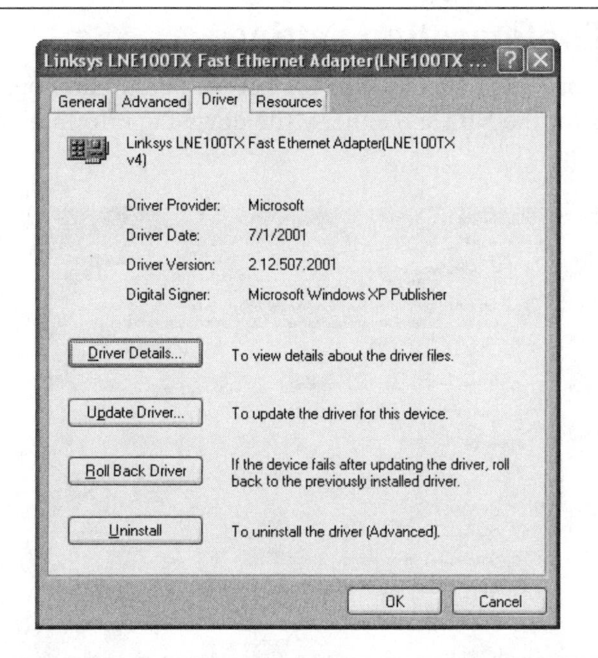

FIGURE 12-2 Use the Properties dialog for the network adapter to find information about the device, software drivers, and also to configure device-specific settings.

TIP *Programs are available that automatically gather your computer's settings and save them in a simple file format (such as text files you can view in Notepad or HTML files you can view with a Web browser). Two good, free programs are AIDA32 (http://www.webattack.com/get/aida32.shtml) and WinAudit (http://www.pxserver.com/WinAudit.htm).*

You can save each of these image files separately—put each of them, along with your documentation file, in its own folder. Or you can import each image file into your documentation file. (In Microsoft Word, choose Insert | Picture | From File, and then choose the file you saved.) Your network documentation file will grow large, because everything is in one place.

Track NIC Configuration Settings

To capture the information about the NIC's network configuration, open the Properties dialog for the NIC and either write down the information or capture an image.

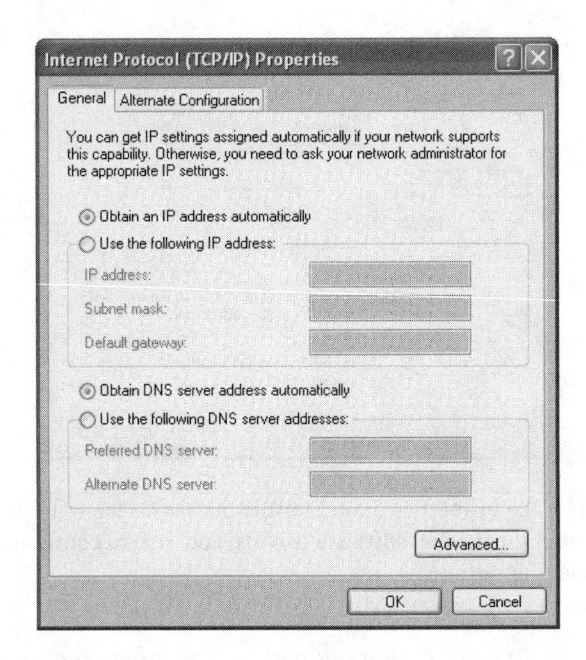

If all your NICs get IP addresses from a DHCP server (either the host computer for a shared Internet connection on your network or a hardware device such as a router), you really don't have to track each computer. However, if you're using static IP addresses, or if you're buying multiple public IP addresses from your ISP, you must keep track of each computer's configuration. Even if you are using DHCP, you might want to list all of your computer's IP addresses, because many of the troubleshooting tools you will use on a TCP/IP network rely on knowing the IP address of devices on the network.

The easy way to accomplish this is to create a table in your word processor, with an entry for each IP address you plan to use (including extra addresses for network growth), an example of which is shown in Table 12-1.

Track Cable Connections

If you're using Ethernet cable, it's a good idea to label the connectors so you know which cable is attached to which computer. This makes troubleshooting easier if a

Computer Name	IP Address
AcctsPy	192.168.1.101
AcctsRec	192.168.1.102
FrontDesk	192.168.1.103
Docs	192.168.1.104
HelpDesk	192.168.1.150
Apps	192.168.1.151
Server-2	192.168.1.152
DNS Server (ISP)	216.231.41.2 216.231.41.3
Router (ISP Public IP Address)	216.231.41.5
Router (Private network IP Address)	192.168.1.1

TABLE 12-1 Charting IP Addresses Eliminates Problems with Duplicate Numbers and Helps with Troubleshooting

computer has a problem when it attempts to join the network (the cable connection is always the first suspect). Tape a paper label to each end of the cable, near the RJ-45 connector (don't put tape on any part of the connector), or use a permanent marker to write the computer name on the cable.

In fact, it's a good idea to label all connections for a computer. The back of every one of my computers is filled with notes that I wrote with a thick marker (which makes it so much easier to find everything if I have to open the computer—reattaching all those connections is much quicker). I have a big *M* and *K* next to each of the PS/2 ports that connect my mouse and keyboard. I wrote *CAM* next to the serial port to which I attach my camera, and *MOD* next to the serial port to which I attach my modem. (I keep a modem for faxing and for a backup Internet connection in case my broadband connection goes down.) I have an arrow pointing to the jack that accepts the speakers on my sound card (I got tired of plugging the speakers into the microphone jack and then having to go back to move the plug).

Expanding Your Network

Most networks grow, and even if you may be sure at the moment that your household won't need more than two computers, you'll probably change your mind later. You'll decide that another computer might be really useful in the kitchen, or the kid's room, or even the garage. Or you might decide to hook up a few network media gadgets to your home entertainment system. If you're putting your network in a small business environment, growth is expected (and hoped for). As businesses grow, new employees arrive, and each new employee needs a computer. So regardless of the current size of your network, your life will be easier if you plan for growth.

Expanding Ethernet Networks

If you have a cabled network and your concentrator runs out of ports, you can connect another hub or switch to the concentrator, which is called *uplinking*. Linksys hubs are built to let you perform this task easily, but you do have to pay attention to the documentation for your specific hub model.

Uplinking is a great way to connect more than one computer in a room without having to run a cable for each computer. Just run one cable from the main concentrator to the room. Connect a hub or switch to that cable, and then hook up as many computers as the hub or switch allows.

Adding Concentrators

The number of ports on your concentrator (hub or switch) depends on the Linksys model you purchased. Linksys concentrators come in 5-, 8-, 16-, and 24-port configurations, and most people buy a concentrator that has more ports than the number of computers they're planning to install on the network (because networks almost always grow). In fact, the Linksys Network in a Box kit contains two NICs and a 5-port concentrator, because even small home networks eventually gain at least one additional computer beyond the two computers that motivated the move to a network. The Linksys 5-port concentrator includes a port that's clearly marked as an Uplink port, which means the port isn't used to connect a computer; it's used to connect another concentrator.

The other, larger Linksys concentrators have one port (the highest number) that can be used for either a computer connection or for a connection to another concentrator. To uplink the concentrator, connect the cable from the Uplink port to any port on the next concentrator. Figure 12-3 shows a multiple-concentrator solution for managing an expanding network.

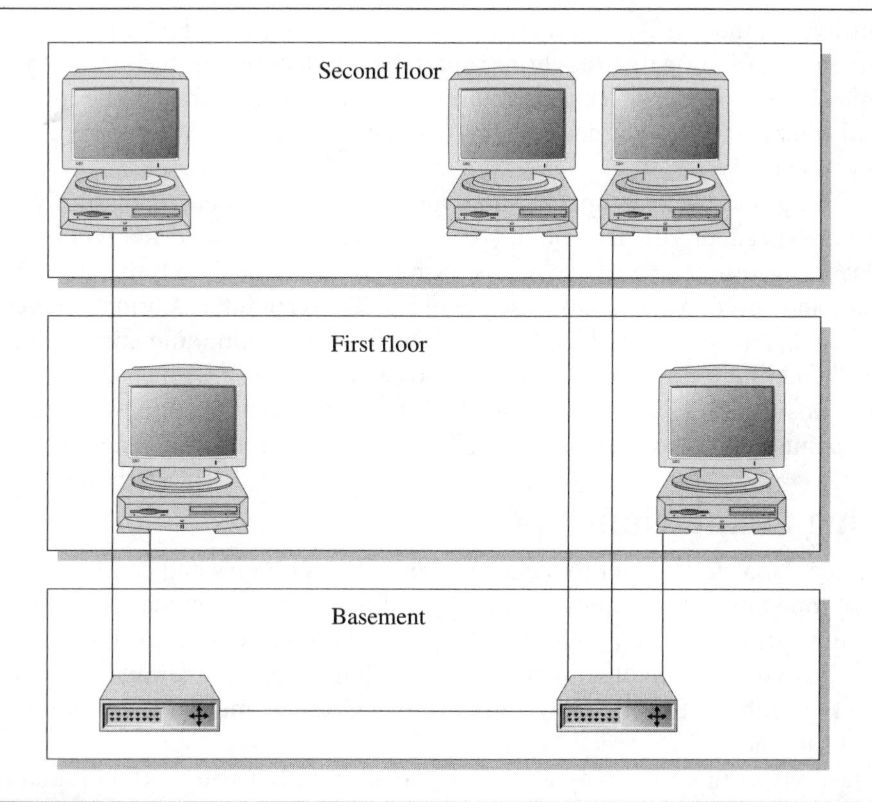

FIGURE 12-3 Cable the computer to multiple concentrators, and then connect the concentrators.

Using Multiple Concentrators for Difficult Cabling Environments

Figure 12-3 is also a good illustration of using multiple concentrators to solve difficult cabling problems, even if you don't have more computers than ports. If the physical layout of your home or office is such that there's no easy-to-reach midpoint at which to locate a single concentrator logically, you can split your network between two sets of cable runs. One set of cables can connect to one concentrator, and the other set can connect to another concentrator. Then you connect the concentrators to create one network.

Expanding Wireless LANS

Wireless communication has some distance limits, so the computers on your wireless network may have to be located in a manner that enhances communication. This is not always the most efficient way to position computers, especially in a business environment. Additionally, the farther apart the wireless nodes, the slower the communication. The distance limitations vary, depending on the number of walls (and whether metal pipes or ducts are in those walls) and other possible impediments to wireless communication.

If you need to place computers more than 300 feet (91 meters) apart, if you want more speed, or you need both, you can install a wireless *access point* or a wireless *range extender*. Access points push the communication limits for both distance and speed. You can also use a wireless access point as a bridge to merge a wireless LAN with a wired LAN (see the next section on mixing connection types). In addition, Linksys has a signal booster you can use with an access point that extends the range of wireless signals. Chapter 5 has instructions for installing access points, signal boosters, and range extenders in wireless LANs.

Mixing Connection Types

Sometimes, growth is easier to manage by mixing topologies and combining your original topology with new connection types. For example, you may start with two computers connected by wireless adapters, phonelines, or powerlines. Then you add two more computers that are physically near each other and easy to connect via Ethernet cable. Now you have two LAN segments: one Ethernet, one not Ethernet.

Or, it works the other way around—you start with a couple of computers connected through an Ethernet hub, and the new computers are far removed, or on a different floor, and there's no easy method of joining each of them to a cabled network. You decide to use wireless, PhoneLine, or PowerLine connections.

Perhaps you need only one non-Ethernet LAN segment, and you have no need to connect computers via Ethernet. However, you've installed a DSL/cable modem, which requires an Ethernet connection, and you need to be able to connect your non-Ethernet computers to the modem so everybody can get to the Internet.

You can merge these diverse setups into a single network, thanks to a clever device called a bridge. A *bridge* (including an access point) is a connection point where two topologies meet. (Actually, bridges can perform a number of useful functions, but for this discussion, I cover only their ability to link Ethernet LAN segments with other LAN segments that are using a different topology.)

Linksys provides a bridge for each combination of Ethernet and non-Ethernet connection types:

- Wireless/Ethernet

- PhoneLine/Ethernet
- PowerLine/Ethernet

Installing a bridge is easy (and logical), because the device has multiple connector types (that match the technologies it's bridging). Plug an Ethernet cable into the Ethernet port, and then attach the other technology through the appropriate port. Some bridges may require a setup program; if so, the package includes a CD.

Troubleshooting and Tweaking Network Communication

On a day-to-day basis, networks run smoothly and efficiently without any help from human beings. In fact, some networks run for long periods of time without encountering a single problem. However, sometimes communications break down, and one computer can't access the rest of the network.

NOTE *A computer must have at least one shared resource (usually a folder) to be seen on the network. Until a share is created, the computer cannot be accessed by other computers on the network. See Chapter 10 to learn how to create a network share on a computer.*

When you need to troubleshoot a network problem, you need to follow a pecking order for your investigative efforts. Luckily, the things you look for first are also the easiest tasks to accomplish: start with the connectors, then move to the cable, then to the adapters, and finally to the software settings.

Checking Network Connections

The first thing to check is the connection. Is everything attached as it should be? Are all the components working properly? Following are some guidelines to consider as you check your network for problems.

Troubleshooting Ethernet Connections

For an Ethernet network, make sure the RJ-45 connector is plugged into both the NIC and the concentrator properly—fully inserted. Windows XP displays a pop-up message to announce the fact that a connection seems to be unplugged. (Of course, to see these indicators, you must enable the option to display the network connection icon on the taskbar, which is not the default setting. Open the Properties dialog of your network connection and choose the option to put an icon on the taskbar.)

If you extended the length of any cable segment by using a coupler to combine two cable lengths, check the connectors in the coupler. Disconnect the RJ-45 connectors and use canned air to clean the port. Then order a patch cable of the appropriate length so you can get rid of the coupler.

Check to make sure the cable isn't passing close to anything that could cause interference, such as fluorescent lights, uninterruptible power supplies, or other sources of strong electromagnetic signals.

Make sure the adapter is connected to the computer properly. If you're using an internal NIC, open the computer and make sure the card is seated firmly in the bus. If you're using a USB connector, make sure the connector is inserted firmly.

NOTE *You cannot assume that the USB port on the back of your computer is working. I've run into a number of computers in which the USB port is not activated by default and must be turned on by entering the BIOS Setup program that's available while the computer is booting. Check the documentation for your computer to see whether this could be your problem.*

Check the cable for any of the following problems:

- Be sure the cable isn't coiled tightly (some people do this when the cable is longer than is necessary). Coiled cable can create electromagnetic fields that may disrupt data communication. If you must coil, try to keep the cable fairly slack, about 5 to 6 inches in diameter.
- Be sure your computer is within the listed maximum range of the concentrator.
- For short cable runs, test the cable by replacing it with cable that is currently connected to a computer that is working properly.

Troubleshooting Phoneline Connectors

For a PhoneLine network, check the RJ-11 connectors at both ends of the telephone cable to make sure they're fully engaged. If your home has more than one telephone line, make sure all the RJ-11 connectors are plugged into wall jacks for the same telephone line. You cannot "cross" telephone lines for PhoneLine networking, in the same way you cannot pick up a telephone that's attached to one line and join a conversation taking place on the other line. Swap your cable for a new cable that you know is working.

NOTE *Even though your PhoneLine network adapter has two RJ-11 ports, one marked for the network and the other marked for a phone or fax, it really doesn't matter which port you use—they're identical.*

Troubleshooting Powerline Connectors

For a PowerLine network, make sure the adapter is securely attached to the USB port. (See the earlier note on making sure the USB port is activated on the computer.) Make sure the plug from the adapter is fully inserted in the electrical outlet.

If the outlet is switched (controlled by an on/off switch on the wall), be sure the wall switch is in the on position.

NOTE *It's not really a good idea to plug anything related to computers or networks into a switched outlet.*

If the adapter is plugged into a surge protector strip (or any other type of strip), be sure the strip's on/off switch is set to on. To test whether the strip is damaged, remove the adapter from the strip and plug it into a wall outlet. (The PowerLine network adapter has its own surge protector built in, so you don't need to plug it into a surge protector; in fact, some strips may have circuitry that interferes with your PowerLine adapter, so it's best to use a wall outlet.)

Be sure you've run the security configuration utility on every computer on the network, using the same network password. You cannot enable security on some computers and omit security on other computers.

Troubleshooting Wireless Connections

For a wireless network, although no connectors are used, you should check the antenna (which is the equivalent of a connector). Make sure the antenna doesn't have something on it. (I've seen books, purses, and backpacks on antennas.) Make sure the computer, and therefore the antenna, isn't under a metal desk or in a location that puts metal between it and the rest of the network. For example, if a metal file cabinet sits next to the computer, it's probably interfering with your ability to transmit or receive data.

Don't forget to check the antenna on your access point, if you're using one.

Make sure you're not having a problem with distances, because you really have no way of knowing the maximum range of your wireless network until you test it. Too many factors can interfere with the range, such as leaded glass, metal, reinforced concrete floors, and walls with metal pipes or ducts. Bring two computers (or a computer and an access point) into the same room and see if they can communicate. Then move them farther apart and test again, repeating this until you determine whether distance is the problem.

Be sure other RadioFrequency (RF) devices aren't interfering with the signal. Cordless telephones are frequently a problem; check the frequency range to make sure you're not overlapping.

See Chapter 5 for more details on wireless networks.

Checking Network Configuration Settings

If the configuration and condition of the physical components of your network seem to be okay, you must investigate the software side: drivers and settings.

Device Manager

Start with Device Manager, which can reveal problems with drivers, hardware resource conflicts, and settings. To open Device Manager, take the appropriate steps, as follows:

- In Windows XP and Windows 2000, right-click My Computer and choose Properties from the shortcut menu. Click the Hardware tab, and then click the Device Manager button.
- In Windows 98 and Windows Me, right-click My Computer and choose Properties from the shortcut menu. Click the Device Manager tab.

Device Manager displays all hardware devices by category. To see a specific device, you must click the plus sign (+) next to its category to expand the display to include the specific device(s) of that category that are installed on your computer. However, if a device has a problem, Device Manager displays changes in the following ways:

- The device category is automatically expanded to show the troublesome device.
- The device's listing shows a yellow icon with an exclamation point.

For example, in Figure 12-4, my Windows 98SE Device Manager opened with the SCSI controller category expanded and displayed a SCSI device with an exclamation point.

To investigate further, right-click the device listing (not the category) and choose Properties. The tabs and information that appear on the Properties dialog depend on the type of device and the operating system. All device Properties dialogs open to the General tab, which isn't always terribly specific about the problem affecting a device that isn't working (see Figure 12-5). However, sometimes Device Manager knows exactly what's wrong. (For example, if you never installed the driver for the device, the General tab will display "No Driver Installed.")

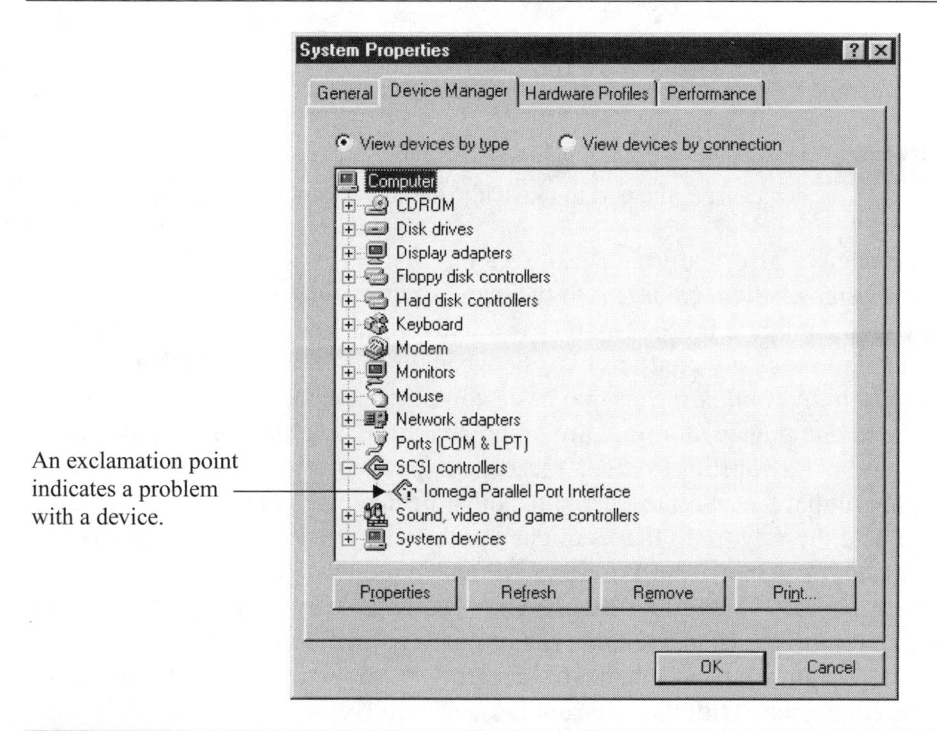

FIGURE 12-4 Device Manager marks devices for attention when it knows that Windows is unable to communicate with the device.

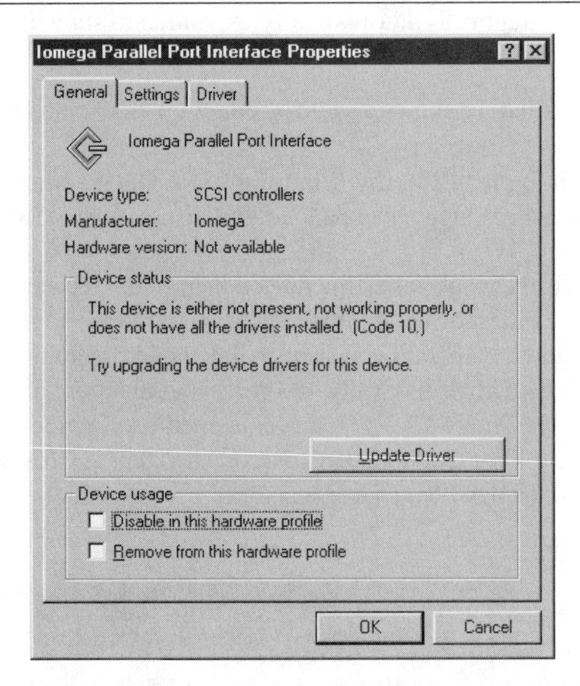

FIGURE 12-5 Device Manager isn't specific about this problem; I'd disconnect the device from the port to move it to another computer for testing.

Some devices also feature a Resources tab that lets you control whether Windows assigns system resources to the device automatically and sometimes allows you to configure those resources manually. If the device has a Resources tab, check it to see if any conflicts exist between this device and any other device in your system. A *conflict* means that basic computer resources that are supposed to belong to one device at a time are being shared by two devices, which just doesn't work. If a conflict exists, a message appears on the Resources tab to inform you of that fact. You must find the other device that's grabbing the same resource, and the way to do that is to change the way Device Manager displays devices, which you can do in Windows XP and Windows 2000 only. In Device Manager in Windows XP/2000, choose View | Resources by Connection to display the system resources. Then, expand each resource listing to determine whether two devices are assigned the same resource. Figure 12-6 shows a display of resources, sorted by connection, with the Interrupt Request (IRQ) resource expanded. If you see two devices on the same IRQ, it's not a conflict as long as the devices are on a PCI bus, because PCI manages resource allocation. However, if two devices are on the same IRQ on an ISA bus, you have a problem: one of those devices isn't working.

You have to change the IRQ assignment for one of the devices, and to accomplish this, you must check the documentation that came with the device or call the manufacturer for technical support.

Network Adapter Configuration

All the configuration settings for your network adapters must follow the same pattern. The protocol you're using for network communication (usually TCP/IP) must be installed for every adapter. File and printer sharing must be enabled. If a configuration problem occurs, it's most likely to be in the TCP/IP settings. Read Chapter 8 to learn about the permutations and combinations of IP addresses and make sure the settings on each computer are correct.

Turn Off Internet Connection Firewall in Windows XP Without Service Pack 2

During the network setup on Windows XP, the system usually enables the Internet Connection Firewall (ICF) automatically, especially if you tell the setup wizard you're using an always-on Internet connection. ICF is a primitive firewall that

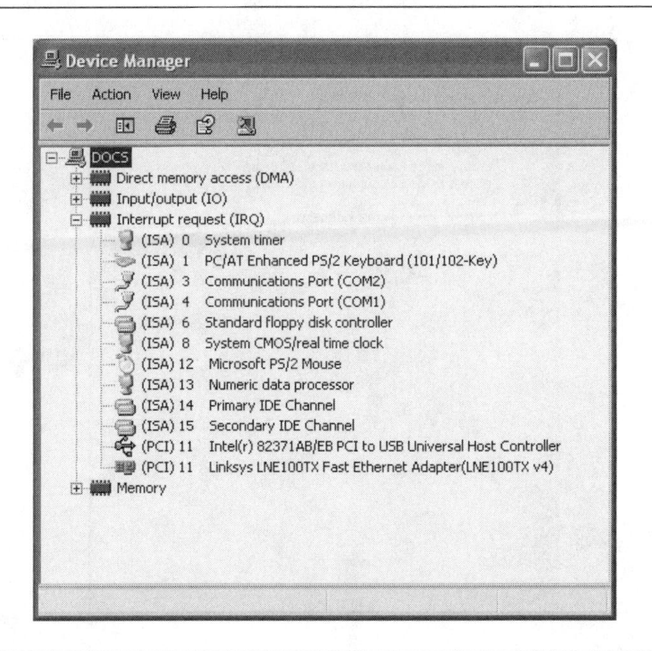

FIGURE 12-6 It looks as though two devices are sharing IRQ11, but it's okay because the devices are on a PCI bus that can manage the resource.

doesn't let you configure it to allow incoming network traffic. This means no computer on your network can access a Windows XP computer that's running ICF.

Disable ICF and replace it with either of the following firewall utilities:

- A hardware firewall, which you can use with DSL/cable modem devices (see Chapter 9 to learn about firewall routers)
- A third-party software firewall such as ZoneAlarm or BlackIce

To disable ICF, follow these steps:

1. Choose Start | Control Panel | Network and Internet Connections.
2. Click Network Connections.
3. Right-click the listing for your Local Area Connection and choose Properties from the shortcut menu.
4. Select the Advanced tab.
5. Deselect the option to use ICF, and then click OK.

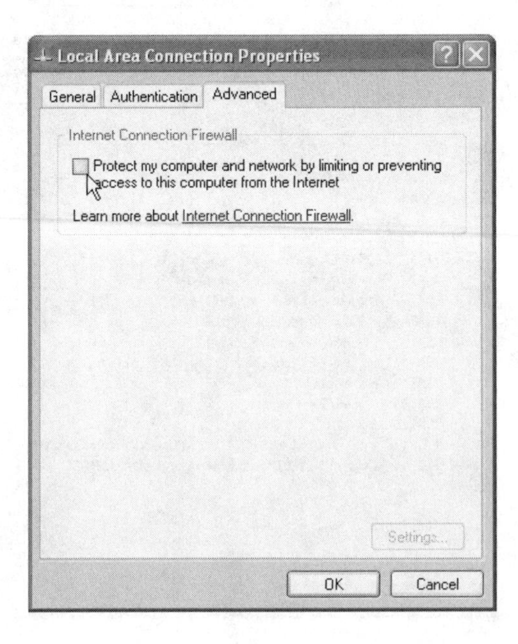

Check Windows Firewall Settings in Windows XP with Service Pack 2

With the upgrade to Windows XP Service Pack 2 (SP2) comes a new version of the built-in firewall named Windows Firewall. If you update your computer regularly (or if you've purchased your computer recently), the chances are that SP2 is already installed on your computer. If not (or if you're not sure), see Chapter 9 for more information on making sure you are updated. Windows Firewall is much more robust than its predecessor, and you should leave it running even if you also have a hardware firewall in place (though you will want to disable it if you are running another software firewall on the same computer). For Windows Firewall to allow other computers to access shared files and printers, you must enable File and Printer Sharing.

To enable File and Printer Sharing when Windows Firewall is turned on, follow these steps:

1. Choose Start | Control Panel | Network and Internet Connections.
2. Click Network Connections.
3. Right-click the listing for your Local Area Connection and choose Properties from the shortcut menu.
4. Select the Advanced tab.
5. In the Windows Firewall section, click Settings.
6. In the Windows Firewall dialog box, on the Exceptions tab, select File and Printer Sharing, and then click OK.
7. Click OK again to close the network connection Properties dialog box.

NOTE *Read Chapter 9 for more information on Windows Firewall and Windows XP SP2.*

Troubleshooting and Tweaking Internet Connections

Troubleshooting Internet connection problems can be complicated and time-consuming. The problems are varied—one computer can't reach the Internet, none of the computers can reach the Internet, or all but one computer fails to connect with the Internet. Patience pays off when you attempt to solve these problems, and you may have to consider many possibilities before discovering the actual source of the difficulty.

No Internet Connection

This particular problem has a large number of potential explanations, so you probably have to check a large number of things on your system. Sometimes, the reason for a faulty or missing Internet connection is beyond your control, such as problems with your ISP. Some problems, on the other hand, turn out to be stupid things you would never anticipate, such as the dog knocking the router's power outlet out of the wall.

Just because you can't get to your home page, don't jump to the conclusion that your Internet connection is down; it may be that the Web site is down. Try another site. If you can't get to anything from your browser, try to reach a site without the browser, using the `ping` command. To do this, open a command window and do the following:

- In Windows 98, choose Start | Programs | MS-DOS Prompt.
- In Windows Me, choose Start | Programs | Accessories | MS-DOS Prompt.
- In Windows 2000, choose Start | Programs | Accessories | Command Prompt.
- In Windows XP, choose Start | All Programs | Accessories | Command Prompt.

In the command window, enter **ping *sitename***, substituting the name of an Internet domain for *sitename*. For example, you could enter **ping linksys.com** or you could ping your ISP. If the site replies to your ping, your Internet connection is working and your browser has a problem. Check the settings.

```
Command Prompt

C:\>ping linksys.com

Pinging linksys.com [66.161.11.20] with 32 bytes of data:

Reply from 66.161.11.20: bytes=32 time=100ms TTL=105
Reply from 66.161.11.20: bytes=32 time=90ms TTL=105
Reply from 66.161.11.20: bytes=32 time=90ms TTL=105
Reply from 66.161.11.20: bytes=32 time=91ms TTL=105

Ping statistics for 66.161.11.20:
    Packets: Sent = 4, Received = 4, Lost = 0 (0% loss),
Approximate round trip times in milli-seconds:
    Minimum = 90ms, Maximum =  100ms, Average =  92ms

C:\>_
```

If the `ping` command fails with an error message (usually "host not found"), it means either you don't have an Internet connection or you are connected to the Internet but you're not getting DNS services from your ISP. DNS services translate domain names to domain addresses, which are needed because when you travel to a domain, you're really traveling to a specific IP address on the Internet. You can try pinging the IP address of a Web site directly, with the command `ping xxx.xxx.xxx.xxx` (substituting the IP address for all the `x`s). Of course, unless you have the IP address of a Web site memorized (rather unlikely), you'll need to find out what it is. Call a friend and ask her to ping the site you're using for your test, and tell you the IP address that the `ping` command returns. If the `ping` command fails, you have no Internet connection.

TIP

While you have a working Internet connection, ping a Web site on the Internet that you know is reliable (such as http://www.linksys.com). The `ping` *command returns the IP address. Write down the IP address in your documentation so that you can use it to test connections later.*

Try connecting to the Internet from another computer on your local network. If only one computer has trouble connecting to the Internet, the problem is not network-wide and therefore is probably not caused by your Internet connection hardware.

NOTE

See Appendix B to learn more about using the `ping` *command.*

Check the Equipment Connections

Make sure that all the equipment involved in the Internet connection—from the computer to the modem to any routers you have installed, and any hubs or switches in the middle—are plugged into power outlets and turned on.

Similarly, check to see that all cable is connected properly. Whether at a router, hub, or NIC, there's almost certainly a light that shines green when a connection is made. If you don't see lights where you expect them, manually check the plug. If the plug is tight, move a working cable (a green light glows at its connection point) to the problem connector. If the connection now works, the problem is the cable.

TIP

Make sure you know what all the LED lights represent on your network equipment. Make a list in a word processor document, which makes it easy to find the information when you need it (instead of trying to find the manual for each piece of equipment). If you're really industrious, print out the lists on a small piece of paper, laminate the paper, and slide it under the device where you can always find it.

Check the Internet Connection Device

Is your DSL/cable/telephone modem actually connected? Check the lights on this device carefully, as one or more lights indicate a connection to the Internet. On a DSL/cable modem, a light named Internet, Cable, or something similar usually glows a solid green when a good connection exists. If you see the light flashing slowly, a connection problem is likely.

If no connection exists, try resetting the device. If it is a DSL device or cable modem, it should try to reconnect itself to the Internet. If you still have no connection, the problem is at the ISP end. You may want to wait a while to give the ISP a chance to clear it up, or call the ISP on the phone (if your phones are working).

If your broadband connection appears to be functional, but your computer connections still don't work, and this device is connected through a hub or router, you should try reconnecting the modem directly to a single PC. You may have to reconfigure that PC temporarily for the ISP settings—for example, if you have a static IP address from your ISP and have been using a router to provide NAT and DHCP, you will have to reconfigure the PC to use the static address.

Check TCP/IP Settings

If TCP/IP were not installed on the computer, you would never have been able to get on the Internet. Nevertheless, it's possible that something happened that affected the TCP/IP configuration.

In Windows 98/Me, choose Start | Settings | Control Panel, and then double-click the Network applet to open it. The list of protocols and devices should contain both your network adapter and TCP/IP bindings to them. Scroll through the list to confirm this. Select TCP/IP and click Properties to see the TCP/IP properties. Confirm that the settings are correct.

In Windows 2000, choose Start | Settings | Network and Dialup Connections. Right-click the icon for Local Area Connection and check the settings.

In Windows XP, choose Start | Control Panel. Click the link for Network and Internet Connections, and then click the link for Network Connections. Right-click the icon for Local Area Connection and select Status. If an obvious error message such as "Network cable unplugged" appears, plug in the cable. If the connection is disabled, right-click its listing and select Enable. If you still don't have a functioning connection at this point, right-click the connection again and select Repair. If this fails, make sure the TCP/IP properties are set properly.

Check Network Communications

If you can communicate between two computers on the local network but cannot connect to the Internet, you've probably proved that the problem exists in the Internet connection hardware or in the Internet connection itself.

The easiest way to check whether you can communicate between two computers is to open Network Neighborhood or My Network Places and try to access a shared resource on a remote computer. Or, you can use the `ping` command, with the syntax `ping` *`computername`* (substitute a real computer name for *`computername`*—for example, `ping den`). If you get an error message, you may have a network communication problem. To make sure, you should also try pinging a remote computer by its IP address. To determine the IP address, go to the remote computer you're trying to ping and open a command window. On Windows 98/Me computers, type **winipcfg** and press ENTER. The computer opens a dialog box that shows the IP addressing information. On Windows 2000/XP computers, type **ipconfig** and press ENTER. The system displays the current IP address (along with other information about the network adapter) right in the command window. Write down the IP address so you can use it with the ping tool.

From another computer on the network, open a command window and type **ping *x.x.x.x*,** where ***x.x.x.x*** is the IP address of the computer on which you ran ipconfig. If the `ping` command returns a series of error messages, such as "Request timed out," the computer on which ping is running cannot see the other computer. This could mean anything from a disconnected cable to a software crash. But you know that the problem is probably not with your Internet connection equipment.

Check the Gateway

TCP/IP networking requires a computer or other device to function as a gateway, which is the device that sits between your network and the Internet. If you are using a router, it's probably acting as the gateway. Otherwise, the gateway is probably your ISP.

To determine your gateway, open a command window and type **ipconfig**. The system displays the IP address of the gateway (in addition to other information about the network adapter). Type **ping** ***x.x.x.x*** (where ***x.x.x.x*** is the IP address of the gateway system specified by ipconfig). If you get a series of error messages, such as "Request timed out," that means that your computer cannot communicate with the gateway.

If your gateway is a router, read the troubleshooting section of the user guide that came with your router (the user guide may be on the CD instead of a printed booklet). You might have to reset the router by pressing the Reset button and holding it for several seconds. The router will restart and attempt to reconnect to the local network and Internet. If it still fails, you need to contact Linksys technical support. If your gateway is at your ISP's site, contact your ISP.

Invalid DHCP Lease

You may see a message about an invalid DHCP lease in Internet Explorer when you're trying to connect to a Web page. It's likely that your Internet access device tries to retrieve an Internet address automatically from the ISP, and sometimes the

What APIPA Addresses Mean

Sometimes a network PC or some other network device, such as a print server, won't connect to the network. If you run the ipconfig tool, you learn that the device has an IP address of 169.254.*x.x* (where each *x* value is between 0 and 255—the specific number is unimportant). Addresses in this range are called APIPA (Automatic Private IP Addressing) addresses, and their presence indicates that the device is set to obtain an IP address automatically from a DHCP server, but that no DHCP server could be found. When this happens on a computer running Windows XP, APIPA kicks in and Windows assigns itself an IP address in this range.

When you see an address in this range, it means that the computer could not communicate with a DHCP server to obtain an address, either because the network connection to the DHCP server is not working or because there is a problem with the DHCP server. You should check your DHCP server first to make sure it's functioning, and then work through basic network troubleshooting steps for the computer.

ISP's DHCP server is slow to respond to your system's request for an IP address. Before the ISP can supply an address, Windows times out (gets tired of waiting) and assigns the network adapter an APIPA number (see the sidebar "What APIPA Addresses Mean").

To fix the problem in Windows 2000/XP, follow these steps:

1. Choose Start | Run, type **cmd**, and then press ENTER.
2. Type **ipconfig** and press ENTER. The system displays the IP address assigned to each network adapter on this computer. The network adapter connected to the Internet should have an address of 169.254.*x.x*, where each *x* is a number between 0 and 255. This indicates that Windows could not obtain an IP address automatically and so assigned itself one.
3. Type **ipconfig /release** to set the address to 0.0.0.0.
4. Type **ipconfig /renew** to request a new address for the adapter.

To fix the problem in Windows 98/Me, follow these steps:

1. Choose Start | Run, type **winipcfg**, and then press ENTER.
2. The dialog box that opens displays the IP address assigned to each network adapter on this computer. The network adapter connected to the Internet should have no IP address at all, indicating that it likely could not reach a DHCP server.
3. Click Release to make sure any lease is released.
4. Click Renew to request a new address for the adapter.

Tricks and Tips for Network Printing

When you go through the installation process for a printer (installing the drivers), an icon for that printer is placed in the computer's Printers folder (called Printers and Faxes in Windows XP). That icon represents a *virtual printer*, which means it's a collection of settings and configuration options that are used by the operating system when it sends a print job to the physical printer. You actually send a print job to the virtual printer, and the operating system passes the job to the physical printer.

When you select the Print command in your software applications, you can set print options that are supported by the printer and the operating system. These options could include selections such as the tray from which to fetch the paper (if the printer has multiple trays), choosing between color or monochrome (if the printer is a color printer), and even whether to print the job to a file instead of to paper.

Once you understand the fact that you're printing to a virtual printer, and the operating system is the only user that can communicate with the physical printer, you can take advantage of this scenario.

Creating Preconfigured Printers

Because you print to a virtual printer, not the physical printer, you can create multiple virtual printers for the same physical printer. This makes it easier to use specific features in the printer.

If you have a printer with multiple trays (perhaps you have checks or letterhead in one tray and plain paper in the other tray), you must select the appropriate tray every time you use the Print command. By creating a separate virtual printer for each tray, you can make sure you don't accidentally use the wrong tray. (Isn't it annoying to print a letter on a check form, or the other way around?)

If you have a color printer, you can print in monochrome automatically, selecting the virtual printer configured for color only when color is necessary. This means you won't have to replace the color cartridge as frequently, which results in substantial cost savings.

To create a separate virtual printer for each feature, you must install the same printer multiple times, using the same Add Printer Wizard you used to install the original printer. Go through all the steps, selecting the same printer and the same port (usually LPT1). Windows doesn't complain if you add multiple printers to the same port. The wizard asks whether you want to use the same driver you already installed (when you installed the first instance of the printer), and of course you do, and that means you won't have to install files from the Windows CD. The wizard adds the printer to your system with a parenthetical number after the printer model name, such as HPLaserJet(Copy *X*) where *X* is a sequential number.

Install as many copies of the printer as there are features you want to isolate. For example, if you want to set up a printer for Tray 1 and another printer for Tray 2, install two copies of the printer. If the printer also has a manual feed tray, and you use it frequently (perhaps to print envelopes), create a third instance of the printer.

TIP

Don't bother sending a test document to the printer. If Windows asks if you want to share the printer, choose No (only Windows 2000 and Windows XP automatically ask). It's easier to configure the printers first and share them later.

Right-click one copy of the printer and choose Properties from the shortcut menu. Find the Properties page that holds the configuration settings for the printer, which differs depending on the printer—there may be a Settings tab or a Setup button. Configure the printer to reflect a single set of default options.

Rename the printer icon to reflect its settings. For example, suppose the printer has two trays: tray #1 holds checks, and tray #2 holds blank paper. For the printer that has only tray #2 available (because you configured tray #1 as Not Available), a good name is Paper. Then configure a copy of the printer to make tray #2 unavailable, and name it Checks. Share each printer, using a sharename that also reflects the settings (in fact, it's easiest to use the new printer icon name as the sharename).

The configuration options you select vary according to the printer's resources and features. For example, you may want to preconfigure a printer for each of the following features:

- Plain paper for printing in Portrait mode
- Plain paper for printing in Landscape mode
- Letterhead
- Plain paper for printing in Landscape mode, 1200dpi printing
- Plain paper for printing in Landscape mode, 600dpi printing
- Envelope (even if it requires manually feeding the envelope)

For color printers, you may want to create numerous multiple printers, each with preconfigured settings for any of the choices the printer offers. For example, you can create virtual printers for different resolutions in addition to making the printer color-only or monochrome-only.

Remember that in addition to renaming the printer to reflect its settings, you can use the Comment field on the General tab of the printer's Properties dialog to add information about the printer's settings. The text you add to the Comment field is visible to users on the network when they view the printer's listing in Network Neighborhood or My Network Places.

Limiting the Time a Printer Is Available

If a printer is attached to a computer running Windows 2000 or Windows XP, you gain additional advantages in your ability to control network printing. These advantages are especially important in business networks. One important feature is the ability to control the times during which a printer is available. I've had innumerable small business clients talk to me about controlling color printers. The owners couldn't figure out why they were spending a small fortune replacing color cartridges, because color printing was limited to certain types of documents that were printed infrequently. In every case, they discovered that employees were staying after hours or returning to the office in the evenings or on weekends to use the color printer for personal documents. In many cases, the print jobs were generated by parents who were printing documents for their children—school work, party invitations, and even comic books that children were writing. More than one business owner told me that these employees had color printers at home but used the office printer to avoid the need to replace expensive color cartridges on their own printers.

You can control the hours that a printer is available in the Advanced tab of the printer's Properties dialog (the Advanced tab is available only in Windows 2000/XP).

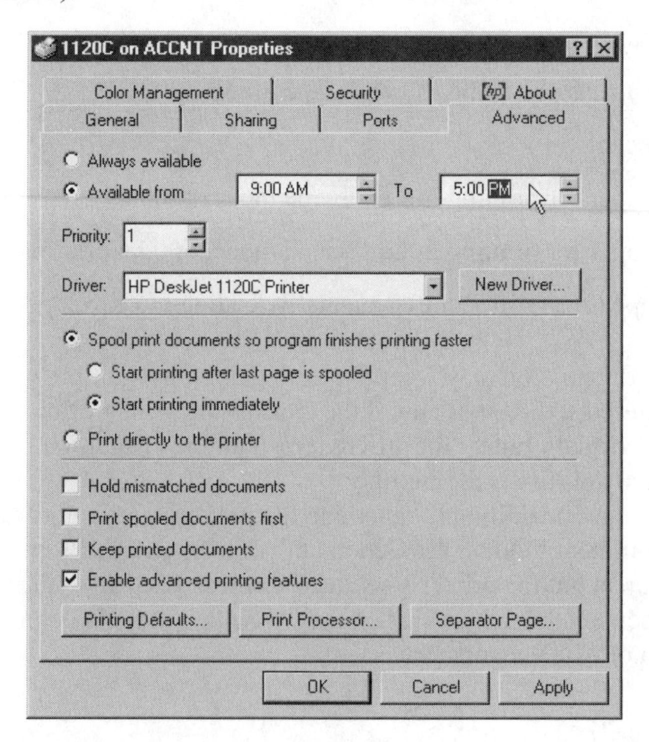

You might think you could solve printer access problem by shutting down the computer that holds the printer, but that won't work because all someone has to do to make the printer available is turn on the computer. Windows does *not* require a completed logon to make a shared printer available—anyone can print as soon as Windows is running, even before the logon dialog is displayed on the screen.

To prevent aggressive (and knowledgeable) users from changing the availability settings on the Advanced tab, be sure you're running NTFS on all your Windows 2000/XP computers and restrict access to the Properties dialog. A remote user who is working at a computer that's running Windows 2000/XP can open the Properties dialog, access the Advanced tab, and make changes—unless the security features stop him.

Creating a Printer for Text Files

Sometimes it's useful to print a document to a file instead of to a printer. For instance, you may have created a document at work (such as a report from a database or an accounting software application) that you want to take home and load into your word processor. If you use the Print command from the software window, and select the option to print to a file instead of to the printer, the resulting printer file can be sent only to the same printer model, which may not be the printer you have at home. That's because the printer driver controls the print file, which is filled with special codes that can be interpreted correctly by that printer only.

You can create a print file that works with every printer in the world. The file has no special codes, so anybody can print it to any printer. You can also load the file into any word processor, or into Notepad or WordPad, and print it. Additionally, if you create a printer that's preconfigured to print to a file, you don't have to remember to choose the Print to File option on the Print dialog box.

To create a printer that automatically creates plain text files, start the Add Printer Wizard. Select Local Printer and deselect the option to have Plug and Play look for the printer (it wouldn't find it, since the printer doesn't physically exist). Select the manufacturer named Generic, and select the model Generic/Text only. Choose FILE as the port for this printer. Don't share this printer; instead, install it as a local printer (on LPT1) on every computer on the network.

Moving Laptops Between Home and Office Networks

Many corporate network administrators provide laptop computers for employees who travel, to make sure those employees can easily fetch their e-mail, access corporate databases, save documents to corporate servers, and otherwise stay in touch with the home office. Today, this is such a common corporate paradigm that an entire army of mobile users travels the world, hooking into networks from remote locations.

Mobile users bring their laptops home, of course, and if there's a home network available, joining that network provides printers, Internet access, and any other features that have been installed on the network.

Moving your laptop between two networks isn't terribly difficult, because it's not technically complicated. You just have to spend time changing network configuration options to match the configuration settings of the network you're about to join. Before I go through all the physical and software stuff you need to know about, I offer one piece of advice to all of you running Windows 98 on your laptops: if at all possible, upgrade your laptop to Windows XP. If your laptop won't support Windows XP, see if you can upgrade to Windows 2000 Professional. Your life as a laptop user who wants to switch between networks is much more difficult with Windows 98.

Topology Differences

Your company network is almost certainly cabled with Ethernet, but many corporate IT administrators are installing access points throughout the Ethernet enterprise to make it easier for mobile workers to join the network when they're in the office. Before the development of reliable wireless network communication, administrators had to provide docking stations or spare RJ-45 connectors at an empty desk. Today, as a mobile user equipped with a wireless network adapter, you can plunk down anywhere you can find space and hook into the corporate network. This means that if your laptop is company-supplied, you have either an Ethernet or wireless network adapter.

NOTE *If your employer is a small business, you may have a network adapter for any type of topology, because PhoneLine and PowerLine networks are occasionally found in small businesses. However, for the purpose of this discussion, I assume standard corporate topology choices—Ethernet or wireless.*

If your home network uses the same topology as your corporate network, you don't have to worry about the physical side of networking. You do, however, have to be concerned about network configuration settings, which are covered later in this section.

If your corporate network uses a different topology than your home network, buy another network adapter that's designed for the topology of your home network. Linksys offers both USB and PC Card network adapters for all topology choices. Most laptops have two PC Card slots, so you can have both adapters available at all times. In fact, if your laptop runs Windows 2000 or Windows XP, each adapter will have its own icon and its own settings (Windows 98 and Windows Me don't recognize more than one adapter).

Differences in Settings

Three sets of configuration settings must match the network you're logging on to, and therefore you probably have to change them to log on to a specific network:

- The name of the computer
- The name of the domain or workgroup you want to join
- The TCP/IP settings

You can change the network settings that are configured for your network adapter in several ways:

- Manually change the settings.
- Use a third-party software program that switches between settings.
- Use a command-line tool to automate a change in settings (only in Windows 2000/XP).

I discuss all these approaches in the following sections.

Changing Settings Manually

Manual changes aren't complicated, because you're essentially repeating the steps you learned in Chapter 8, where you set up your network configuration settings. Make your changes just before you shut down your computer, when you know the next time you boot your computer it will be joining the "other" network. So you don't have to flip back to Chapter 8, I present an overview of the dialogs you must open to make the changes.

Changing the Computer Name and Domain/Workgroup

You can make this step a bit easier by using the same computer name on both networks—just use the computer name for your corporate network when you set up your computer for your home network. Your corporate network is probably a client/server network, and you and your computer must both log on to a domain (*companyname.com*), while your home network is a peer-to-peer network (a workgroup). In the following sections, I give you information about the dialogs you have to open and configure to make the changes. When you make these changes, Windows displays a message telling you that the changes take effect after you restart the computer. Windows also offers a dialog in which you can click a button to restart the computer. *Don't restart the computer.* Instead, say No to the offer to restart the computer, and then shut down the computer instead of restarting it. Restarting the computer with the new settings won't work, because those settings are designed for the "other" network, the one you're planning to join the next time you start your computer.

Windows 98/Me Computer Name and Domain/Workgroup Options In Windows 98/Me, open the Network applet in Control Panel and move to the Identification tab. Enter the computer name and the domain/workgroup name you use for the network you'll be logging on to the next time you boot.

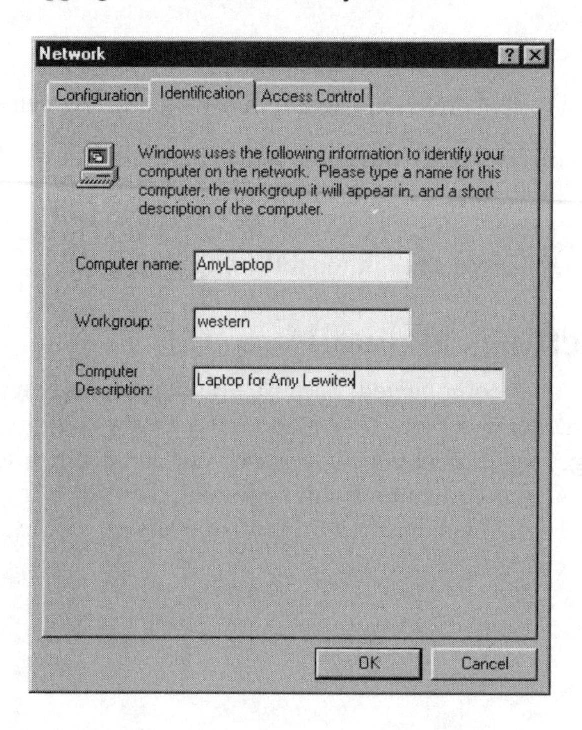

Windows 2000 Computer Name and Domain/Workgroup Options In Windows 2000, right-click My Computer and choose Properties. In the System Properties dialog, move to the Network Identification tab. Click the Properties button to open the Identification Changes dialog. Make the changes you need for the network you'll be logging on to the next time you boot.

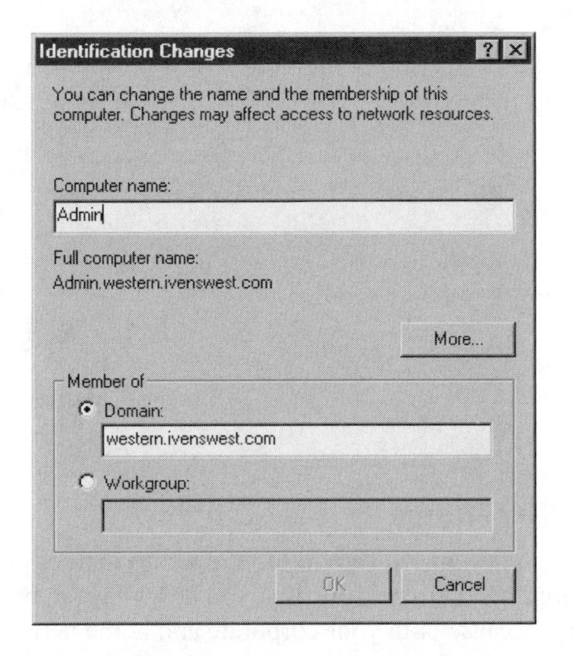

Windows XP Computer Name and Domain/Workgroup Options In Windows XP, right-click My Computer and choose Properties. In the System Properties dialog, move to the Computer Name tab. Click the Change button to open the Computer

Name Changes dialog. Make the changes you need for the network you'll be logging on to the next time you boot.

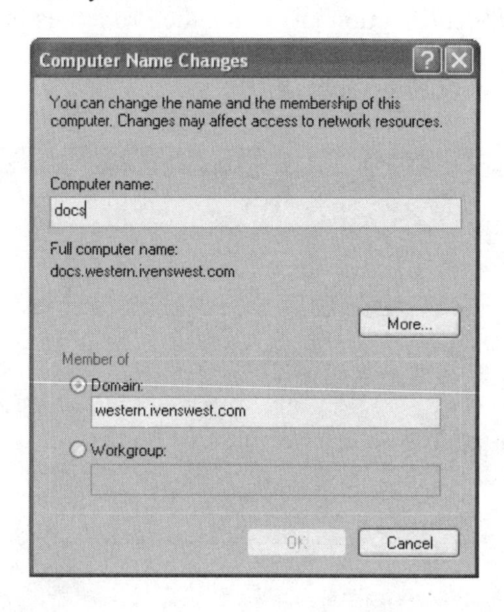

Changing TCP/IP Settings

The TCP/IP settings for your NIC are in the Properties dialog for your Local Area Network connection. It's quite possible that you don't have to make changes to the IP Address setting, because both your corporate and home network may require the option Obtain an IP Address Automatically. This is the most common IP address setting in both client/server and peer-to-peer networks. On a client/server network, which is probably the way your corporate network is set up, one or more computers running Windows Server have been configured to act as DHCP servers. On a peer-to-peer network, which is the way most home and small business networks are set up, DHCP services are provided by the ICS host computer (if you're running ICS), a router (if you've installed one), or your ISP (if you're making a direct connection from your computer to the ISP).

If you don't obtain your IP address automatically on one or both of the networks you connect to, you must fill in the static IP address assigned to your computer for the network that requires static IP addresses. You may be able to automate this process if all of the following conditions exist:

- Your computer is running Windows XP.

- One network has a DHCP server that provides an IP address automatically.
- The other network requires a static IP address.

See the next section, "Automatic Alternative Settings in Windows XP," to learn more.

Automatic Alternative Settings in Windows XP

Windows XP has a nifty feature called alternative settings for network adapters. If the network you're logging on to doesn't accept the regular settings for your NIC, instead of failing to join the network and issuing an error message, Windows XP says, "Okay, network, you didn't like those settings, so try these settings," and presents another set of configuration options (which you've created) to the network. The only rule is that the basic settings must include the option to obtain an IP address automatically, and the alternative settings must have assigned (static) IP addresses. Most of the time, that rule works for both your home and corporate network. When you attempt to log on to your network, the primary setting, Obtain an IP Address Automatically, is offered to the network. If no DHCP server exists, Windows XP automatically switches to the alternative configuration setting, which is a static IP address.

Understanding APIPA

You can configure the alternative settings to obtain an Automatic Private IP Address instead of a static address if a DHCP server can't be found (which is what makes the alternative configuration kick in). APIPA is the automatic assignment of an IP address within the range 169.254.0.1 through 169.254.255.254, along with a subnet mask of 255.255.0.0. Networked computers can communicate with each other with APIPA, but since APIPA does not assign a gateway, a DNS server, or Windows Internet Name Services (WINS), it's not possible to reach the Internet through a shared Internet connection.

The computer uses Address Resolution Protocol (ARP) to check the other computers on the network to make sure that another computer on the network isn't already using the address the computer wants to use. After the computer has assigned itself an IP address, it can communicate over TCP/IP with other computers on the network that are either configured for APIPA or are manually set to the correct address range and a subnet mask value of 255.255.0.0.

Configuring the Alternative Configuration Dialog

To configure the alternative TCP/IP settings, follow these steps:

1. Open the Properties dialog for the LAN connection.
2. On the General tab, select the listing for Internet Protocol (TCP/IP) and click the Properties button.
3. In the TCP/IP Properties dialog, move to the Alternate Configuration tab (which doesn't exist unless the TCP/IP settings are configured to obtain an IP address automatically).

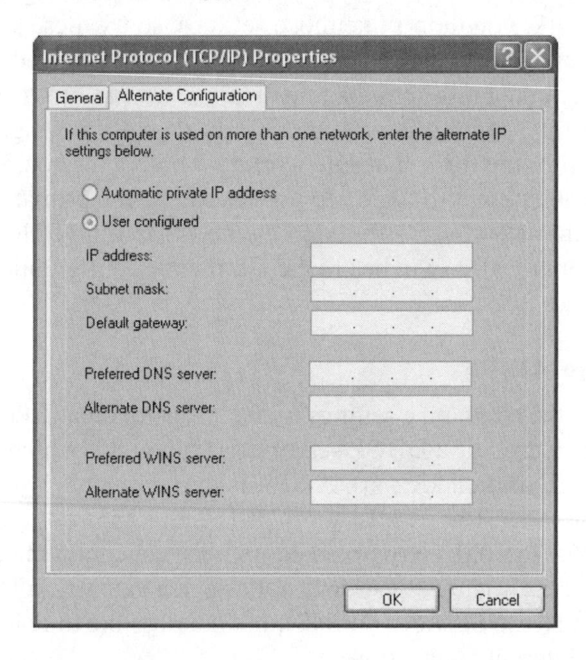

4. Select Automatic Private IP Address if your network is using this setting.
5. Select User Configured if your network is using assigned IP addresses. Don't forget to fill in the IP addresses for DNS services and WINS (if WINS is required by your network or your ISP).

Using Software to Change Network Settings

A number of software programs are available to let you automate the process of changing settings to match multiple networks. Two of these applications,

NetSwitcher and Mobile Net Switch, seem to get the best reviews, so I discuss both in this section.

NetSwitcher saves your network settings and then loads the settings you need as you boot into a network. When you install NetSwitcher, the program immediately asks whether you want to save the current configuration so you can load it later. After you save these settings, NetSwitcher lets you define a different set of network configuration options (the settings for the "other" network). Each set of configuration options is called a *location*. When you boot the computer, you select the location you need for the network you're joining. You can learn more about NetSwitcher at *http://www.netswitcher.com.*

Mobile Net Switch works similarly to NetSwitcher, but it supports only Windows 2000/XP/2003. However, if your laptop is running Windows 98, the program works as long as you install the Windows Management Instrumentation (WMI) component. This Windows component isn't installed by default, but you can add it to your system from the Windows Setup tab of the Add/Remove Programs applet in Control Panel. Select Internet tools, click Details, and then select Web-Based Enterprise Mgmt. After the component is installed, reboot and then install Mobile Net Switch. You can learn more about Mobile Net Switch at *http://www.mobilenetswitch.com.*

Using the Netsh Tool

If your laptop is running Windows 2000 or Windows XP, and you're comfortable using command-line tools, you can use the built-in program Netsh.exe to save and load network settings. Using Netsh.exe is a two-step process:

1. Save the network settings to a file.
2. Load the file to insert the contents into your network settings.

You have to perform these steps twice, once for each set of network configuration options (so I guess it's really a four-step process).

Storing Network Settings with Netsh.exe

Start by storing a copy of the current settings with the following syntax:

```
netsh -c interface dump > c:\foldername\filename.txt
```

The target location can be any folder (*foldername*) and any filename (*filename*), but it's best to use a filename that reflects the settings, such as work.txt (unless the current settings are for your home network, in which case you'd name the file home.txt).

When you're ready to shut down the computer, and you're going to log on to the other network the next time you start, manually change the settings to reflect the other network's configuration requirements. Then repeat the `netsch` command, saving the settings to another filename (home.txt or work.txt, depending on which settings you're saving).

You now have both sets of settings saved in files.

Loading Network Settings with Netsh.exe

Before you shut down your laptop, use the `netsh` command to load the settings you'll need the next time you start the computer. To accomplish this, use the following syntax:

```
netsh -f c:\foldername\filename.txt
```

Chapter 13

Linksys Media Devices

So far in this book, you've learned how to set up and use a basic small network. Now it's time to have some fun. In recent years, networking in the home has become about more than just sharing files, printers, and Internet access. More and more, networking is moving into new and exciting areas. In this chapter, I talk about using two Linksys media devices to bring your music and pictures away from the computer—to other rooms and even to your home entertainment center.

In particular, I cover the following products here:

- Linksys Wireless-B Media Link (WMLS11B), which is a stand-alone, portable "boom-box" that accesses music files stored on your computer and which you can also connect to your home stereo.
- Linksys Wireless-B Media Adapter (WMA11B), which is a device that connects to your television or home entertainment center and lets you view pictures and listen to music files stored on your computer. You control the Media Adapter using graphical menus on your television with a simple remote control.

NOTE *The actual name of the WMLS11B is the Wireless-B Media Link. However, on the product packaging, the name Wireless-B Music System appears. Most likely, the name Music System refers to the device and the software that supports it. Throughout this chapter, I refer to the device as the Media Link—the actual name of the device and the name you'll see on the device, user manuals, and the Linksys support site.*

The Linksys Wireless-B Media Link

Imagine being able to access all of your music at the touch of a button anywhere within your wireless network's range. Imagine not having to listen to digital music on your computer speakers and not having to fire up your computer when you want to listen to music. The Linksys Wireless-B Media Link lets you do just that. All you have to do is install software on your computer that makes music files available, connect the Media Link to your network, and you're ready to listen. And if that's not enough for you, you can also use the Media Link to listen to hundreds of Internet radio stations.

The front of the Media Link device, shown in Figure 13-1, features the following:

- The LCD screen provides access to the menus that let you select and play music. When music is playing, the screen shows you the name of the song and album (or Internet radio station) currently playing.

FIGURE 13-1 The front of the Media Link provides easy-to-use controls for navigating and playing your music.

- The Up and Down buttons to the left of the LCD screen allow you to scroll through the various menus you will see when using the device. When music is playing, these buttons control volume.
- The Play/Pause button plays an album or a music track (depending on the menu you're looking at). When music is playing, the button pauses and resumes the music.
- The Stop button ends the music currently playing and returns you to the menu you were previously viewing.
- The Left and Right buttons allow you to move through menus on the LCD screen. You'll use the Right button to select a highlighted item on a menu (which you can think of as moving forward). The Left button returns you to a previous menu (sort of like moving back in a Web browser).
- The Power button turns the device on and off.

The back of the Media Link device, shown in Figure 13-2, features the following:

- The Power port is for plugging in the power adapter provided with the Media Link.

- The Speaker DC port lets you connect the power cord for the speakers provided with the Media Link. The other end of the power cord plugs directly into the right speaker.
- The Crossover (X/II) switch is used when you are connecting the Media Link to a network or to a PC using an Ethernet cable instead of connecting wirelessly. If you're connecting to a network via a switch or hub, the switch should be in the Parallel (II) position. If you're connecting directly to a PC (as you might do when you first set up the Media Link), the switch should be in the Crossover (X) position.
- The Ethernet port lets you attach the Media Link to your network using an Ethernet cable. This is useful if you do not have a wireless network, or if you are connecting the device in a location where you already have Ethernet cabling and you don't expect to move the device (such as when you connect it to your home stereo).
- The Digital Output port lets you attach the Media Link to a home stereo that accepts optical input, which provides crystal clear digital sound. The Media Link does not come with an optical cable, so you'll need to buy one separately if you want to use this port.
- The 2 CH Output port lets you attach the Media Link to the external speakers that come with the device (both cables plug into ports on the right speaker). You can also use this port to connect the Media Link to a home stereo that does not have a digital input. The Media Link comes with a short two-channel cable that just reaches the external speakers. You'll probably have to buy a longer cable if you want to connect to your stereo.
- The Reset button lets you reset the Media Link to its factory default settings. Just press the button and hold it for about 5 seconds.

Setting Up the Media Link

You can set up your Media Link in several ways. The recommended (and arguably easiest) way is to connect the Media Link directly to your PC or to your network using an Ethernet cable, and then run the setup program that comes on the CD-ROM provided with the device. You can also set up the device to use the wireless network or a wired network by using the LCD screen on the device and skip using the setup program on your computer. The advantage of this method is that you don't have to connect the device first using an Ethernet cable.

FIGURE 13-2 The back of the Media Link lets you connect the power, speakers, and possibly a home stereo to the device.

Setting Up the Media Link with the Setup Program

I find it easier to set up the Media Link using the LCD screen instead of using the Setup program (and the procedure for this is covered in the next section). The advantage of using the setup program, however, is that it provides clearer instructions. The disadvantage is that you must first connect the Media Link to your wired network and run the setup program, and then disconnect it from the wired network and move it wherever you want it to go.

To set up the Media Link using the setup program, follow these steps:

1. Connect the external speakers to the device.
2. Plug in the power adapter and connect it to the Power port on the back of the device.
3. Plug one end of an Ethernet cable into the Ethernet port on the back of the Media Link and plug the other end into your concentrator or directly into your PC.
4. If you are connecting to a concentrator, make sure the Crossover switch on the back of the device is set to Parallel (II). If you are connecting to a PC, make sure the switch is set to Crossover (X).
5. Turn on the Media Link.

6. Insert the Setup CD into the CD-ROM drive on a computer that is connected to the network (or on the computer connected to the Media Link if you're using a direct PC connection). When you insert the CD, the Setup Wizard should start automatically. If it does not (for example, if you have disabled Windows AutoRun feature), you can start the wizard by choosing Start | Run and typing **d:\Setup.exe**, where *d* is the drive letter for your CD-ROM drive. On the first screen that appears, click Setup.

NOTE *You can run the setup program from any computer on the network, since all you're doing right now is configuring the device to operate with the network. When it comes time to install the Media Server software, you'll want to install it on the computer that contains your music files. You can also install the Media Server software on multiple computers and then access the music on any of them.*

7. Read the licensing agreement and then click Next.

8. You'll see a screen informing you that the Media Link must be connected to a wired network to use the setup program. Click Next to continue.

9. The setup program searches for the Media Link and then displays the results. Make sure the Media Link is selected (it will be selected by default if only one device is on your network), and then click Next.

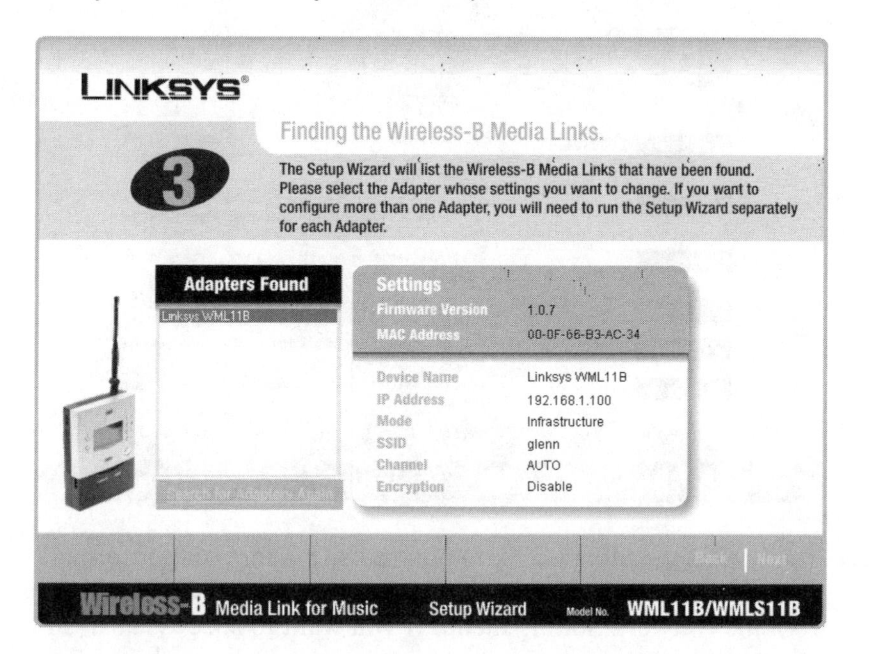

TIP

If you see an error stating that the setup program cannot locate the Media Link, make sure that the Crossover switch on the back of the unit is in the correct position. Also make sure that you have a DHCP server on your network that can assign an IP address to the Media Link. See Chapter 8 for more information on this.

10. On the next screen, choose whether you want to connect the Media Link via a wireless or wired network, and then click Next.

11. On the Basic Settings screen, you can control the basic network settings for the Media Link. By default, the network name of the adapter is Linksys

WML11B (after the model name for the device), but you can type in any name that helps you identify the device.

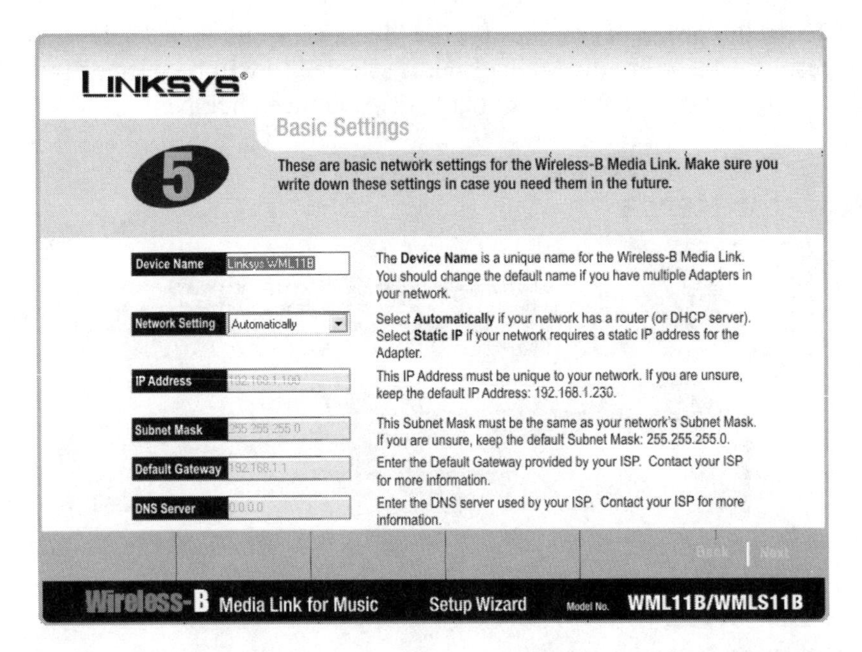

12. If you want the Media Link to obtain its IP addressing information automatically using a DHCP server on your network, choose Automatically from the Network Setting menu. If you want to specify an IP address, subnet mask, default gateway, and DNS server address, choose Static IP from the Network Setting menu and then enter the appropriate information. (See Chapter 8 for information on configuring DHCP and IP addressing information.) Click Next to proceed.

13. If you chose to connect the device to a wireless network, you'll see a screen that lets you configure wireless settings (if you are connecting to a wired network, skip to step 17). If you are using a wireless router or access point, choose Infrastructure from the Mode menu. If you are connecting to wireless-equipped PCs without using a router or access point, choose Ad Hoc from this menu.

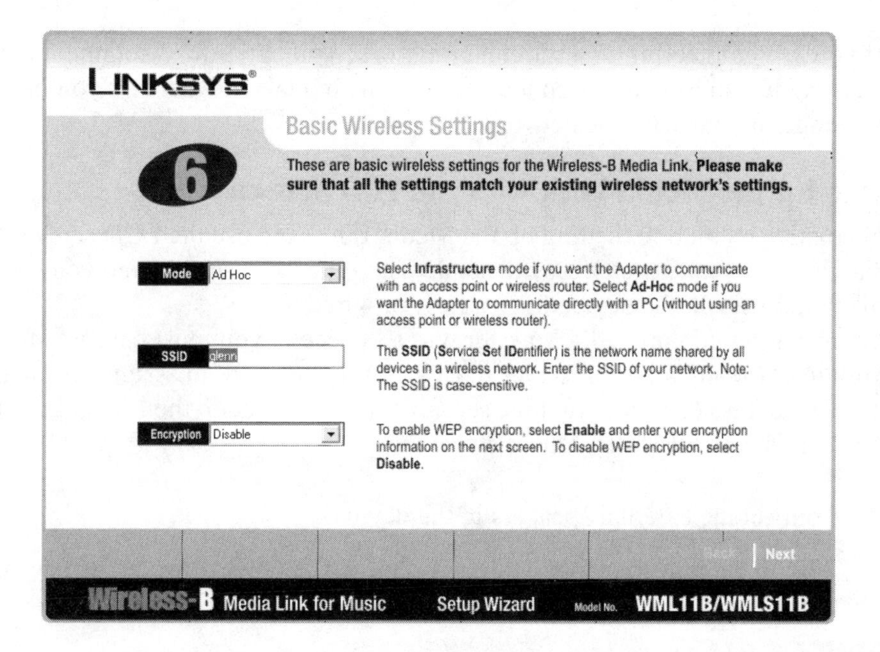

14. Type in the Service Set Identifier (SSID) name for your network. If you're unsure of this name, you can usually determine it by logging on to your router or access point.
15. If your network uses WEP encryption, select Enable from the Encryption menu. Otherwise, leave this setting at Disable. If you enable Encryption, you will see an additional screen where you can enter details about the level of encryption and your network's passphrase.

NOTE *You can learn more about what these wireless settings mean in Chapter 5.*

16. Click Next to continue.
17. The setup program displays the settings you have chosen. If you want to change any settings, click Back to work your way back through the setup program's screens. Otherwise, click Save to save the new settings to the Media Link.
18. The Media Link stores the settings and then restarts itself. When it restarts, it will contact the router or switch, obtain an IP address, and then be ready to go. In the setup program, click Finish.

If you are connecting to a wireless network, you can now disconnect the Ethernet cable you used to set up the Media Link and take it wherever you like within range of your wireless network.

Setting Up the Media Link with the LCD Screen

An alternative method for setting up the Media Link is to use the LCD screen. The Media Link is actually pretty easy to set up using the LCD screen, and you can use this method to set up the device for wireless or wired access.

When setting up the Media Link for wireless access, you must have a wireless network in place and a DHCP server must be on the network to assign the Media Link an IP address (for more on this, see Chapter 5). To set up the Media Link to use a wireless network, follow these steps:

1. Connect the external speakers to the device.
2. Plug in the power adapter and connect it to the Power port on the back of the device.
3. Turn on the Media Link.
4. On the main Menu screen, use the Down button on the front of the device to scroll to the Network Setup option, and then press the Right button.
5. On the Network Setup screen, use the Down button to scroll to the Wireless option, and then press the Right button.
6. On the Wireless screen, select the Site Survey option and then press the Right button.
7. The Media Link shows you the wireless networks that it has found.

NOTE *The Site Survey option works only if your wireless router or access point is configured to broadcast its SSID name. If it is not configured this way (the option is sometimes turned off for security purposes), on the Wireless screen, select the SSID option and then enter the SSID for your network. Use the Up and Down buttons to select characters and the Right button to move to the next character in the name.*

8. Select the network to which you want to connect and then press the Right button.

9. The Media Link stores the settings and then restarts itself. When it restarts, it will contact the wireless router or access point, obtain an IP address, and then be ready to go.

TIP *On the Main menu of the Media Link, scroll to the Network Status option and press the Right button to determine the wireless settings. Use this feature to determine whether the Media Link has successfully connected to the network.*

To set up the Media Link to use a wired network, follow these steps:

1. Connect the external speakers to the device (unless you are planning to connect the device to your home stereo).
2. Plug in the power adapter and connect it to the Power port on the back of the device.
3. Plug one end of an Ethernet cable into the Ethernet port on the back of the Media Link and plug the other end into your concentrator or directly into your PC.
4. If you are connecting to a concentrator, make sure the Crossover switch on the back of the device is set to Parallel (II). If you are connecting to a PC, make sure the switch is set to Crossover (X).
5. Turn on the Media Link.
6. On the main Menu screen, use the Down button to scroll to the Network Setup option, and then press the Right button.
7. On the Network Setup screen, use the Down button to scroll to the Change to wired option, and then press the Right button.
8. A message appears on the screen asking you to connect the Ethernet cable and confirm that you want to change to a wired setup. Press the Right button to confirm.
9. The Media Link stores the settings and then restarts itself. When it restarts, it will contact the router or switch, obtain an IP address, and then be ready to go.

After setting up the Media Link (whichever method you use), the device is connected to the network and ready to play music. If your network is connected to the Internet, you can use the LCD screen to browse through Internet radio stations and listen to them; using Internet radio does not require that any special software be installed on your computer.

To listen to music that is stored on your PC, you must install the Media Server software that comes on the CD provided with the Media Link. This installation is the focus of the next section.

Installing the Media Server Software

After setting up the Media Link, your next step is to install the Media Server software on the computer that holds your music collection. This software (which is actually named MUSICMATCH Jukebox and does a whole lot more than just act as a media server) scans your computer for music files and then makes them available over the network to the Media Link.

To install the Media Server software, follow these steps:

1. Insert the Setup CD into the CD-ROM drive on the computer that stores your music files. When you insert the CD, the Setup Wizard should start automatically. If it does not (for example, if you have disabled Windows AutoRun feature), you can start the wizard by choosing Start | Run and typing **d:\Setup.exe**, where *d* is the drive letter for your CD-ROM drive. On the first screen that appears, click Install Media Server to launch the MUSICMATCH Jukebox setup program.
2. On the welcome screen for the setup program, click Next.
3. Read the licensing agreement and then click Yes to accept it.
4. On the Installation Options page, leave the Express option selected and then click Next.

NOTE *You can choose the Advanced option if you want to specify where the program is installed on your computer. When using the advanced installation, the screens you see will differ slightly.*

5. The setup program installs the software. When it is done, you are prompted to restart your computer. Select Yes, I Want to Restart My Computer Now and then click Finish.

After installing the MUSICMATCH Jukebox software and restarting your computer, the next step is configuring it to serve your music files to the Media Link. The software runs in the background and starts automatically whenever you start Windows. You can tell it's running by the MUSICMATCH Jukebox icon that appears in the system tray (near your clock). Double-click this icon to start the software.

NOTE *The first time you start the MUSICMATCH Jukebox software, you are prompted to register. Follow the steps in the registration wizard to enter your registration information.*

You can do a lot with the MUSICMATCH Jukebox software. You can use it to copy music to and from CDs, find music on the Internet, listen to and organize your music, and much more. Here, I cover how to have the software search your computer for existing music files, add them to the MUSICMATCH Jukebox library, and make them available to the Media Link device. You can learn more about the MUSICMATCH Jukebox software's other features by consulting its Help menu.

To add your music files to the MUSICMATCH Jukebox library, follow these steps:

1. Start the MUSICMATCH Jukebox software by double-clicking the icon in the system tray or by choosing Start | All Programs | MUSICMATCH | MUSICMATCH Jukebox. The main MUSICMATCH Jukebox window, shown in Figure 13-3, provides quick access to all the software's many features.
2. Click the Add to Library button to open the Add Tracks to Music Library dialog box.

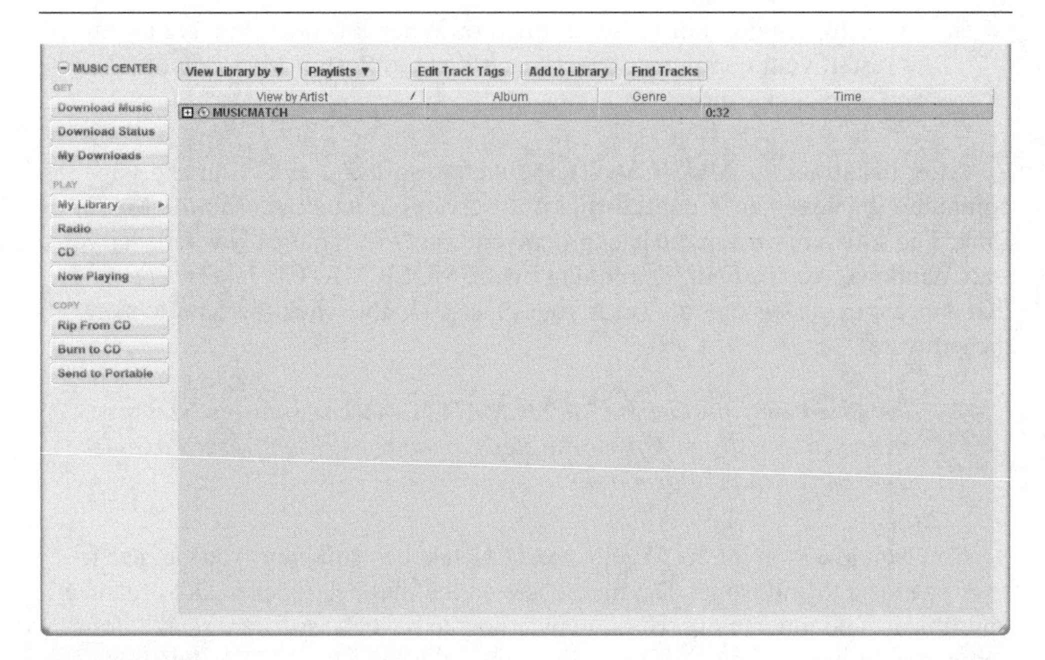

FIGURE 13-3 The main MUSICMATCH Jukebox window lets you manage and listen to your music.

3. Locate and select the music files that you want to add, and then click Add.

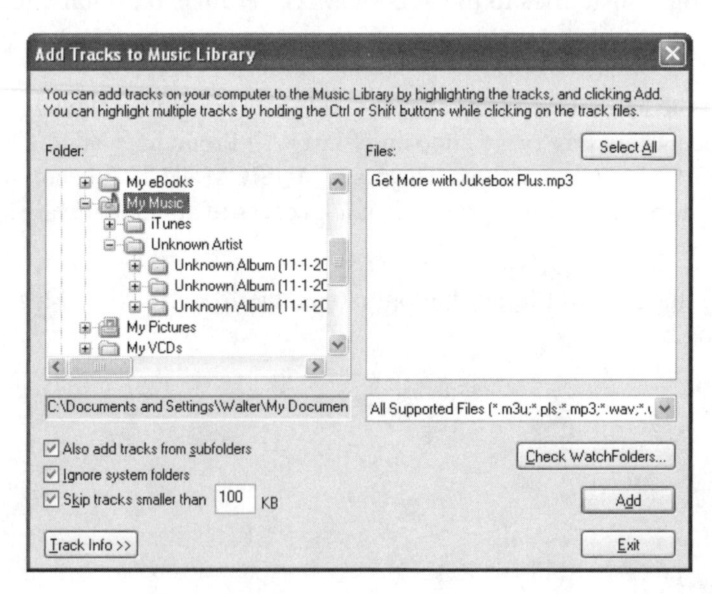

TIP *In the Add Tracks to Music Library dialog box, you can add all your music in one step by selecting the main folder where you store your music (usually the My Music folder) and making sure the Also Add Tracks From Subfolders option is selected.*

4. After you have added all the tracks you want, click Exit to return to the main window.

At this point, all tracks you have added to your library are made available automatically to the Media Link device and you're ready to listen to music.

Using the Media Link

You'll use the Media Link's LCD screen to listen to music. All of the functions on the Media Link are organized in menus that you can access using the Up, Down, Left, and Right buttons on the front of the device. Following is a list of those menus and the functions they provide:

- **Browse** The Browse menu categorizes your music files so that you can easily locate the tracks you're looking for. You can browse by album, artist, genre, and custom playlists you create using the MUSICMATCH Jukebox software. When you select a track, album, or playlist you want to listen to, just press the Play button to start listening.
- **Internet Radio** The Internet Radio menu lets you browse all the Internet radio stations available on your Media Link (and there are a lot). You can browse by genre or country (or look through a single list of all stations, but that can get a little tedious). When you select a station, press Play to listen. The Media Link accesses the station and begins streaming the music into a memory buffer, so a slight delay may occur before you hear anything. The buffer helps avoid gaps in listening due to Internet traffic.
- **Media Server** If you have more than one computer on your network acting as a media server (you installed the MUSICMATCH software on more than one computer), you can use this menu to select the server from which to access files. After selecting a server, you see the Browse menu for that server.
- **Network Setup and Network Status** These menus let you configure the Media Link to access your network and view the network connection settings. See the earlier section, "Setting Up the Media Link with the LCD Screen," for more on using these menus.

- **Update Radio List** By default, the Media Link periodically updates the Internet radio stations in its list automatically. This menu lets you enable or disable the automatic updating (though I'm hard pressed for a reason to disable it). If you disable automatic updating, this menu also provides the option for updating the list manually.
- **EQ** This menu lets you select from a preconfigured list of equalizer settings that affect the tone of the music to which you are listening. You can select settings such as Classical, Acoustic, Jazz, Rock, Pop, and Flat (the default, unequalized setting). Experiment with these settings to find the best tone for your music.
- **Playlists** This menu provides quick access to custom playlists you create using the MUSICMATCH Jukebox software.
- **Favorites** In addition to creating custom playlists, you can also use the MUSICMATCH Jukebox software to designate favorite music tracks. This menu provides access to your favorites.

The Linksys Wireless-B Media Adapter

While the Media Link lets you play music "boom-box" style or through your home stereo, the Media Adapter is designed to connect to your television or home entertainment center. The Media Adapter lets you listen to your music through your stereo or television speakers and view pictures stored on your computer on your television screen. In fact, you can even watch slideshows of your digital pictures while listening to your favorite music—much better than hauling out that old slide projector. You control the Media Adapter using simple, graphical menus on your television screen via a remote control that comes with the device.

The front of the Media Adapter, shown in Figure 13-4, features the following:

- The Ready LED flashes when the Media Adapter is starting up to indicate that it is connecting to the host computer. The LED is solid when the device has established a connection.
- The Wireless LED lights a solid green when the Media Adapter has a connection to a wireless network. The LED flashes when data is being transmitted between the device and the host computer.
- The Ethernet LED lights solid green when the Media Adapter has a connection to a wired network. The LED flashes when data is being transmitted between the device and the host computer.

FIGURE 13-4 The front of the Media Adapter has a Power button and status LEDs.

- The Power button lets you turn the Media Adapter on and off.

The back of the Media Adapter, shown in Figure 13-5, features the following:

- The Power port is used for plugging in the power adapter provided with the Music Adapter.
- The LAN port is used for connecting an Ethernet cable. You connect one end of the cable to the Media Adapter and one end to a PC or a concentrator.
- The Uplink button is used only when the Media Adapter is connected to a wired network. If you are connecting directly to a PC, you should depress the Uplink button. If you are connecting to a concentrator, you should not depress the Uplink button.
- The Video port is used to connect the video for the Media Adapter to a television (or to a receiver with video-switching capability) using a standard RCA cable such as the one included with the device. The included cable is a combination cable with jacks for video (yellow), right audio channel (red), and left audio channel (white).

FIGURE 13-5 The back of the Media Adapter lets you connect the power, your home entertainment center, and an optional Ethernet cable.

- The Left and Right ports are used to connect the audio for the Media Adapter to your television or stereo.
- The S-Video port may be used instead of the standard Video port if your television supports an S-Video connection.
- The Reset button lets you reset the Media Adapter to its factory default settings. Just press the button and hold it for about 10 seconds.

Connecting and setting up the Media Adapter works much like connecting and setting up the Media Link. First, you set up the Media Adapter to connect to your network. Next, you install software on the host computer that allows the Media Adapter to access music and pictures on the host computer.

Setting Up the Media Adapter

As with the Media Link, you can set up your Media Adapter for use in a variety of ways. The recommended way is to connect the Media Adapter directly to your PC or to your network using an Ethernet cable and then run the setup program on the CD provided with the device. You can also set up the device to use the wireless network or a wired network by using the onscreen menus on your television and skip using the setup program on your computer. The advantage of this method is that you don't have to connect the device using an Ethernet cable first.

Setting Up the Media Adapter with the Setup Program

To set up the Media Link with the setup program, follow these steps:

1. Connect the Media Adapter to your television or home entertainment center. The details of this step vary depending on your setup, but it goes basically like this: Connect a video cable from either the Video or S-Video port (not both) on the back of the Media Adapter to a video port on your television (or a video port on a video-capable receiver if you are using one). Connect the right and left audio cables from the Right and Left ports on the back of the Media Adapter to audio ports on your television or home stereo.

TIP

If you don't have an Ethernet cable long enough to reach from your computer to your home entertainment center, don't worry. You really don't need to connect the Media Adapter to the television and stereo before running the setup program. Instead, hook up the device to your wired network or computer, run the setup program, and then connect the device to the home entertainment center.

2. Plug in the power adapter and connect it to the Power port on the back of the device.
3. Plug one end of an Ethernet cable into the Ethernet port on the back of the Media Adapter and plug the other end into your concentrator or directly into your PC.
4. If you are connecting to a concentrator, make sure the Uplink button on the back of the device is not pushed in. If you are connecting to a PC, make sure the button is pushed in.
5. Turn on the Media Adapter.
6. Insert the Setup CD into the CD-ROM drive on any computer that is connected to the network (or on the computer connected to the Media Link if you're using a direct PC connection). When you insert the CD, the Setup Wizard should start automatically. If it does not (for example, if you have disabled Windows AutoRun feature), you can start the wizard by choosing

Start | Run and typing **d:\Setup.exe**, where *d* is the drive letter for your CD-ROM drive. On the first screen that appears, click Setup.

7. The setup program asks whether you want to install the Adapter Utility (the software that makes the music and pictures available to the Media Adapter). If you are setting up the Media Adapter from the computer that contains your music and picture files, you can go ahead and click Install to install the utility (this is covered in the section "Setting Up the Media Adapter Utility") and come back to the rest of this procedure later. If you want to install the utility on a different computer, click Skip and go on with the remainder of this procedure.

8. You'll see a screen informing you that the Media Adapter must be connected to a wired network to use the setup program. Click Next to continue.

9. The setup program searches for the Media Adapter and then displays the results. Make sure the Media Adapter is selected (it will be selected by default if only one adapter is on your network) and then click Next.

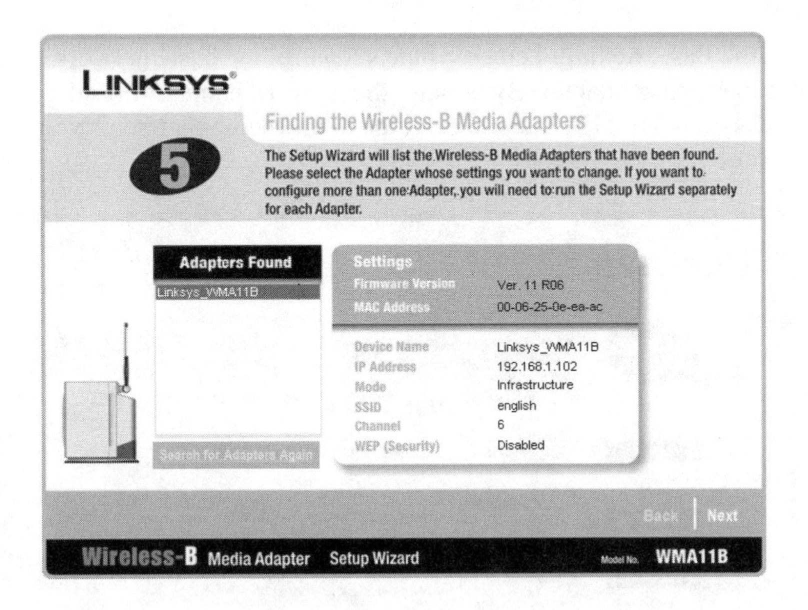

TIP *If you see an error stating that the setup program cannot locate the Media Adapter, make sure that the Uplink button on the back of the unit is in the correct position. Also make sure that you have a DHCP server on your network that can assign an IP address to the Media Adapter.*

10. On the next screen, choose whether you want to connect the Media Adapter via a wireless or wired network, and then click Next.

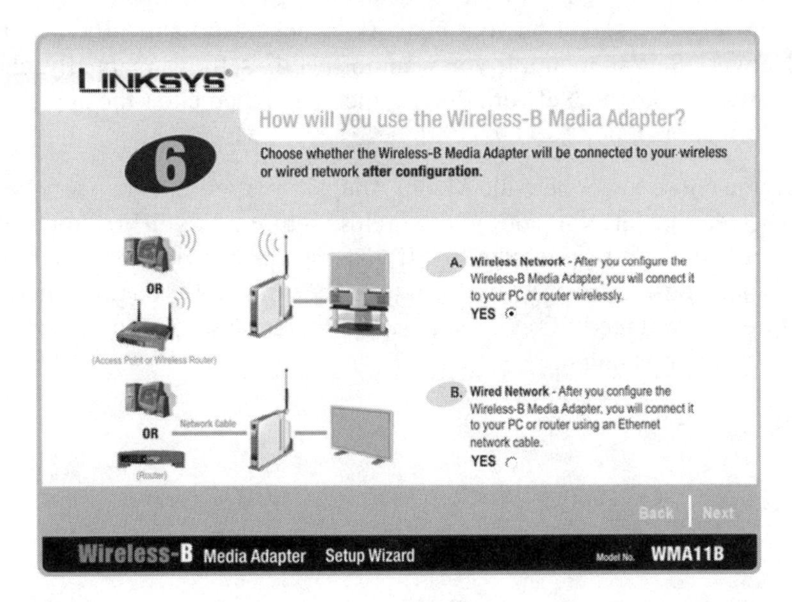

11. On the Basic Settings screen, you can control the basic network settings for the Media Adapter. By default, the network name of the adapter is Linksys_WMA11B, but you can type in any name that helps you identify the device.

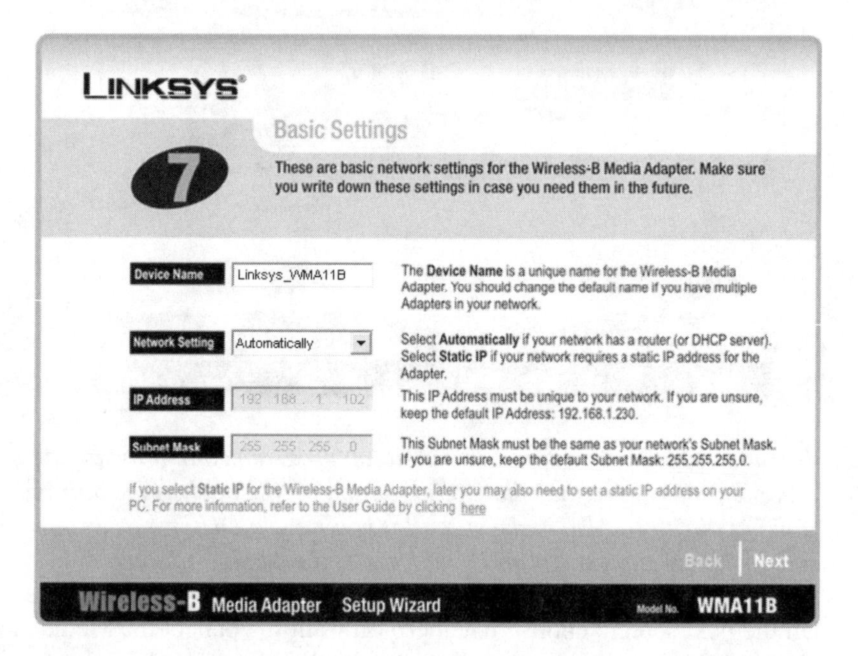

12. If you want the Media Adapter to obtain its TCP/IP information automatically from a DHCP server on your network, choose Automatically from the Network Setting menu. If you want to specify settings manually, choose Static IP from the Network Setting menu and then enter the appropriate information. Click Next to continue.

13. If you chose to connect the Media Adapter to a wireless network, you'll see a screen that lets you configure wireless settings (if you are connecting to a wired network, skip to step 17). If you are using a wireless router or access point, choose Infrastructure from the Mode menu. If you are connecting to wireless-equipped PCs without using a router or access point, choose Ad Hoc from this menu.

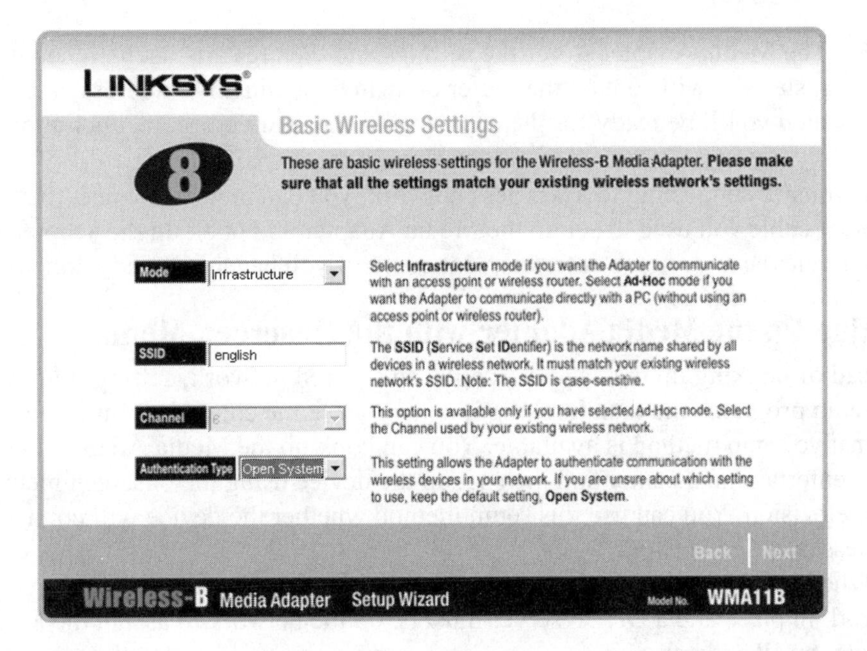

14. Type in the SSID name for your network. If you're unsure of this name, you can usually determine it by logging on to your router or access point.
15. If your wireless network requires authentication between devices, select Shared Key from the Authentication Type menu. Otherwise, leave this setting at Open System. After configuring your wireless network settings, click Next to continue.
16. You'll see a screen that lets you configure wireless network security. If your network uses WEP encryption, select the level of encryption (64-bit or 128-bit) from the WEP menu. Otherwise, leave this setting at Disabled. If you enable WEP, you will also need to enter your network's passphrase or a WEP key.
17. The setup program displays the settings you have chosen. If you want to change any settings, click Back to work your way back through the setup program's screens. Otherwise, click Save to save the new settings to the Media Adapter.

18. The Media Adapter stores the settings and then restarts itself. When it restarts, it will contact the router or switch, obtain an IP address, and then you'll be ready for the next step. In the setup program, click Finish.

If you are connecting to a wireless network, you can now disconnect the Ethernet cable you used to set up the Media Adapter and hook up the adapter to your television or home entertainment center if you haven't already done so.

Setting Up the Media Adapter with the Onscreen Menu

Instead of hooking up the Media Adapter to a wired network, setting it up with the setup program, and then hooking it up to your home entertainment center, an alternative setup method is available. You can hook up the Media Adapter to your home entertainment center and then set up the device using the onscreen menus on your television. You can use this setup method whether the device will connect via wireless or wired network.

When setting up the Media Adapter for wireless access, you must have a wireless network in place and a DHCP server must be on the network to assign the Media Adapter an IP address.

To set up the Media Adapter for a wireless network using the onscreen menus, follow these steps:

1. Connect the Media Adapter to your home entertainment center.
2. Plug in the power adapter and connect it to the Power port on the back of the device.
3. Switch your television or video-capable receiver to the proper channel (this depends on how you have set up your system).
4. Turn on the Media Adapter.
5. On your television screen, you'll see a black screen with the words "Waiting for Host" in big white letters. Near the bottom of the screen, in smaller lettering, you'll see the text "Press Setup to enter the TV Setup Screen." On the remote control that came with the device (don't forget to install the batteries), press the Setup button.

6. The television screen will change to a screen named "Media Adapter Setup" and will show some familiar configuration options, such as IP address and wireless network settings. Using the directional controls on the remote, configure the network settings to match your network setup.

7. When you have configured the network settings, press the Setup button on the remote control again. The Media Adapter will reset itself and begin searching for a host.

After setting up the Media Adapter, you must configure the host computer with the Adapter Utility software. This installation is covered in the next section.

Setting Up the Media Adapter Utility

After setting up the Media Adapter, your next step is to install the Media Adapter utility software on the computer that holds your music and digital picture collection. This software acts as a server that provides access to your collection to the Media Adapter across the network.

To install the Adapter Utility software, follow these steps:

1. Insert the Setup CD into the CD-ROM drive on the computer that stores your music files. When you insert the CD, the Setup Wizard should start automatically. If it does not (for example, if you have disabled the Windows AutoRun feature), you can start the wizard by choosing Start | Run and typing **d:\Setup.exe**, where *d* is the drive letter for your CD-ROM drive.

2. On the welcome screen for the setup program, click Install Utility on PC.

3. On the welcome screen for the Utility Wizard, click Next to continue.

4. Read the licensing agreement and then click Next to accept it.

5. On the Select Music and Picture Folders screen, commonly used folders (My Music and My Pictures) are already selected for you. Use the Add

button to browse for any other folders you want to add to your collection. Click Next when you are done adding files.

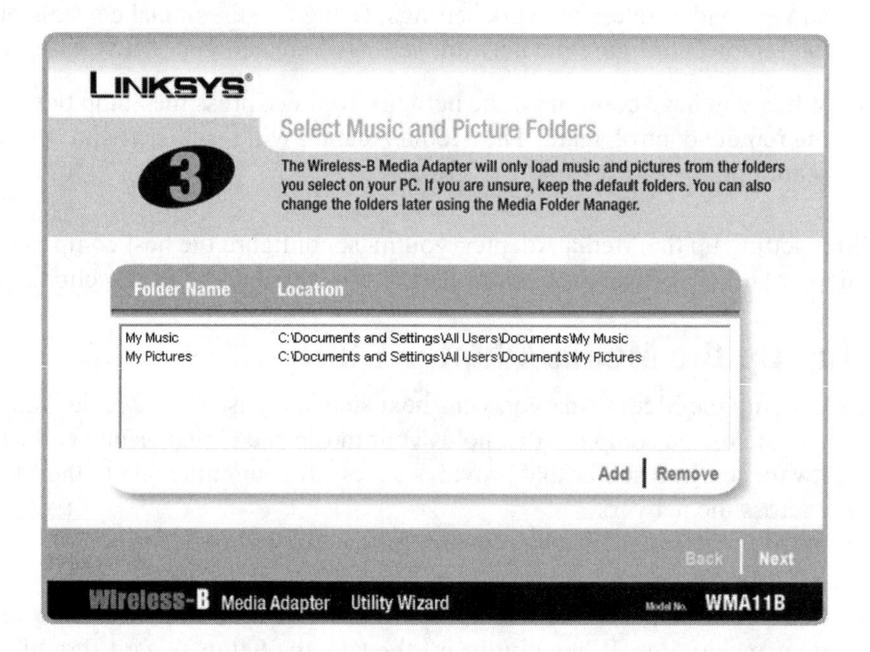

6. The Utility Wizard installs the Adapter Utility on your computer. When it is finished, click Exit to close the Utility Wizard. Click Exit again to close the setup program.

After installing the Adapter Utility software, the host computer automatically makes the files you selected available to the Media Adapter, so you're ready to enjoy your digital media. You can tell the program is running by the Linksys Wireless-B Media Adapter icon that is added to your system tray. If you want to add files to your collection after installation, click the Linksys Wireless-B Media Adapter icon in your system tray, then click Media Folder Manager on the shortcut menu, and then use the window that appears to select the files you want to add.

Using the Media Adapter

After setting up the Media Adapter and installing the Adapter Utility software, you're ready to use your new toy. The interface on your television is simple and effective. When you switch to the channel on your television that corresponds to the video port you chose and turn on the Media Adapter, you'll see a main navigation screen. Use the directional controls on the remote control to select options. The three options available are as follows:

- **Music** Selecting Music takes you to a submenu that lets you browse music by artist, genre, folders on your computer, or custom playlist. Select a music track or group of tracks and press the Play button to listen.

TIP *The Media Adapter does not let you sort by album, so browsing through long lists of tracks can be daunting. I recently digitized my entire music collection and ended up with more than 500 albums—quite a chore to sort through. In the My Music folder on my computer, I created folders for each letter of the alphabet and used them to alphabetize my album folders. That way, I can use the Folders option when browsing for music and view an alphabetized collection.*

- **Pictures** The Pictures menu works much like the Music menu, letting you browse through the folders of pictures on the host computer. Highlight a picture using the directional controls on the remote and then press the Select button to view the picture full screen. Select a folder and press the Play button to view a slideshow.

TIP *The Media Adapter lets you play music while looking at pictures. Use the Music menu to start listening to music and then use the Picture menu to start up a slideshow.*

- **Help** The Help menu provides brief reminders of how to play music and look at pictures. Selecting Help takes you to sort of a slideshow of several screens that each provide advice. Use the Left and Right directional buttons on the remote to move between the screens. Use the Menu button to return to the main menu.

Part IV

Appendixes

All computer books have at least one appendix, and we're no different. This part has a glossary of networking terms and instructions on using software utilities for tweaking and troubleshooting your network.

Appendix A

Glossary of Network Terminology

10Base2 Commonly known as *coaxial cable* or *Thinnet cable,* this network cable looks like a thin version of the cable that your cable television company uses. 10Base2 used to be the standard cable for Ethernet, but most companies have abandoned their 10Base2 systems in favor of 10BaseT. (See also *10BaseT.*)

10BaseT Also called *twisted-pair cable,* 10BaseT is the current standard in Ethernet cable. 10BaseT looks like telephone cable, but it is manufactured differently, and it's designed to transmit data rather than voice. The cable's wires are twisted along the length of cable; hence the name *twisted-pair* cable. Two types of 10BaseT are available: unshielded twisted pair (UTP) and shielded twisted pair (STP). In STP, the cable wires are encased in metal foil, which lessens the possibility of interference from other electrical devices, radar, or radio waves. Using 10BaseT requires the purchase of a hub. Each network computer's NIC is connected to a length of 10BaseT cable, which is then connected to the hub. The hub disseminates data to the computers' NICs.

100BaseTX A networking standard that supports data transfer rates up to 100 Mbps, 10 times faster than the original Ethernet standard. Often referred to as *Fast Ethernet.* The official standard is IEEE 802.3u.

1000BaseT A networking standard that provides 1000 Mbps (gigabit) Ethernet service.

Active Application The software application in which you are currently working. Its window is in the foreground of your screen. Other applications that may be open are in the background of your screen and are called *inactive* applications.

Adapter A card installed in a PC or a device connected to a PC through an external port that provides connectivity to a network.

ADSL Asymmetric Digital Subscriber Line. This technology uses standard telephone lines to produce high-speed connections to the Internet. ADSL supports data rates of 1.5 to 9 Mbps when receiving data (*downstream rate*) and from 16 to 640 Kbps when sending data (*upstream rate*).You need a special ADSL modem, telephone lines that support the technology, and an Internet host server that maintains ADSL modems that can connect to your modem. (See also *SDSL.*)

ASCII American Standard Code for Information Interchange. This standard assigns a number to each key on your keyboard. Internally, your computer uses the number to read and write keyboard characters.

ASCII Text File A file that contains nothing but ASCII characters without special formatting.

Bandwidth The transmission capacity of a device, including how much data the device can transmit in a fixed amount of time. Bandwidth is usually expressed in bits per second (bps).

Banner The NetWare term for a separator page, which is a form that accompanies each print job. (See also *Separator Page.*)

Barrel Connector A tube-shaped device that enables you to join two lengths of 10Base2 cable in a network. (See also *10Base2.*)

Baud Rate The speed at which information is transferred. Also referred to as bits per second (bps).

BIOS Basic Input/Output System. The part of a PC that controls and manages the hardware in the computer.

Bit The smallest unit of digital information. A bit is either on or off (to the computer, on is 1 and off is 0).

Bit Error Rate (BER) In a digital transmission, the percentage of bits with errors, divided by the total number of bits that have been transmitted, received, or processed over a given time period. The rate is typically expressed as 10 to the negative power. BER is the digital equivalent to signal-to-noise ratio in an analog system.

Bit Error Rate Test (BERT) A procedure or device that measures the bit error rate of a transmission. (See also *Bit Error Rate.*)

Bitmap A graphic image stored as a pattern of dots (called *pixels*).

Bits Per Second (bps) Measurement of the speed at which data is transferred.

BNC Connector A round device shaped like a fat ring, a BNC connector looks like a smaller version of the connector at each end of your cable television cable. Installed at each end of a length of coaxial cable (also called *10Base2* or *Thinnet*), the BNC features a center pin (connected to the center conductor inside the cable) and a metal tube (connected to the outer cable shielding). A rotating ring on the metal tube turns to lock the male connector ends to any female connectors. (See also *10Base2.*)

Boot The process of starting the computer and loading the operating system. Some people think the term originates from the adage "pulling oneself up by one's bootstraps."

Bottleneck A delay in the transmission of data through the circuits of a computer's microprocessor or over a TCP/IP network. The delay typically occurs when a system's bandwidth cannot support the amount of information being relayed at the speed it is being processed.

Bridge A device that connects different networks.

Broadband A data transmission technology in which multiple signals share the bandwidth of a device.

Brownout A drop in electrical voltage that can destroy a variety of computer components (hard drive, chips, and so on). You can prevent brownout damage by purchasing a voltage regulator. (See also *Voltage Regulator.*)

Buffer Underrun A problem that occurs when burning data to a CD. It indicates that the computer is not supplying data quickly enough to the CD writer. Recording to a CD-R (for compact disc, recordable) is a real-time process that must run nonstop without any interruption, and the CD-R drive stores incoming data in a buffer so that slowdowns in the data flow will not interrupt the writing process. A buffer underrun error occurs when the flow of data is interrupted long enough for the recorder's buffer to empty.

Bus A slot on your computer's motherboard into which you insert cards, such as network interface cards. (Technically, the name of the slot is *expansion slot*, and the bus is the data path along which information flows to the card. However, the common computer jargon is *bus.*)

Byte The amount of memory needed to specify a single ASCII character (8 bits). Kilobytes (1000 bytes) and megabytes (1,000,000 bytes) are usually used to describe the amount of memory a computer uses.

Cable Modem A modem that connects to your cable television company's cable lines (but doesn't interfere with TV transmissions). Cable modems are significantly faster than standard telephone modems but aren't yet available everywhere. Their speeds are measured in millions of bytes per second rather than in thousands of bytes per second like standard modem speeds. (See also *Modem.*)

Cache Random-access memory (RAM) that is set aside and used as a buffer between the CPU and either a hard disk or slower RAM. The items stored in a cache can be accessed quickly, speeding up the flow of data.

Cascading Menu A menu that is opened from another menu item. Also called a hierarchical menu or submenu. In Windows, a menu item displays a right arrow if it opens a cascading menu.

Cat 5 (Category 5) An American National Standards Institute/Electronic Industries Association (ANSI/EIA) standard for twisted-pair cable that is the standard for Ethernet networks. See also *Cat 5e (Category 5e)* and *Cat 6 (Category 6)*.

Cat 5e (Category 5e) An updated standard for twisted-pair cable that provides specifications for 100 Mbps network speeds. See also *Cat 5 (Category 5)* and *Cat 6 (Category 6)*.

Cat 6 (Category 6) The newest standard for twisted-pair cable that provides tighter restrictions that Cat 5 or 5e cabling. See also *Cat 5 (Category 5)* and *Cat 5e (Category 5e)*.

CD-ROM Compact Disc–Read-Only Memory. Discs that contain programs or data. CD-ROMs can hold more than 600MB of data. You can only read data on a CD-ROM; you cannot write (save) data.

Centronics Interface The connector on a parallel (printer) cable that attaches to the printer.

Check Box A small square box in a dialog that can be selected or cleared to turn an option on or off, respectively. When the check box is selected, an *X* or a check mark appears in the box.

Client A computer that uses hardware and services on another computer (called the *host* or *server*). Also called a *workstation.*

Client/Server Network A network scheme in which a main computer (called the *host* or *server*) supplies authentication services and sometimes supplies files and peripherals shared by all the other computers (called *clients* or *workstations*). Each user who works at a client computer can use the files and peripherals that are on his individual computer (called the *local computer*) or on the server.

Clipboard An area of memory devoted to holding data you cut or copy, usually used to transfer data between applications or between parts of a data file. Typically, you transfer data to the clipboard by using an application's Copy or Cut command, and you insert data from the clipboard by using the application's Paste command.

Cluster A unit of data storage on a hard disk or floppy disk.

Coaxial Cable Cable used in 10Base2 networks. (See also *10Base2.*)

COM Port Also called a *serial port.* A connector where you can plug in a serial device cable, usually attached to a modem. Most PCs have two COM ports, COM1 and COM2.

Computer Name A unique name assigned to a computer on a network to differentiate that computer from other computers on the network.

Concentrator See *Hub.*

CPU (Central Processing Unit) The computing component of a computer. Also called the *processor.*

Credentials Permissions and rights given to users when they log on to Windows that control the access users have to various resources.

CSMA/CD Carrier Sense Multiple Access/Collision Detection. The LAN access method that Ethernet uses. When a device wants access to the network, it checks to determine whether the network is quiet (senses the carrier). If the network is not quiet, the device waits a random amount of time before retrying. If the network is quiet and two devices access the cable at exactly the same time, their signals collide, and both devices retreat to wait another random amount of time before trying again.

Daisy Chain A configuration in which devices are connected in a series, one after another. Transmissions go to the first device, then the second device, and so on.

Data Packet A frame in a packet-switched message. Most data communication processes divide messages into packets. For instance, Ethernet packets can be from 64 to 1518 bytes long.

Database A collection of data that is organized in a way that makes the data easy to access.

Default Button In some dialogs, a command button that is selected automatically if you press ENTER. In most dialogs, the default button has a bold border to make it discernible.

Default Gateway The routing device that is used to forward all traffic that is not addressed to a device within the local LAN.

Defrag To take fragments of files and put them together so that every file on a hard drive has all of its contents in one place. Defragging makes opening files a much faster process because the operating system doesn't have to look all over your hard drive for all the pieces of a file that you want to open.

Device Driver A set of software files that allow your operating system to communicate with hardware such as network interface cards or peripherals such as printers. For example, a printer driver translates information from the computer into information the printer can understand and manage. (Also called *drivers.*)

DHCP Dynamic Host Configuration Protocol. A protocol that lets network administrators manage the assignment of IP addresses. Each computer using TCP/IP gets an IP address automatically.

Dial-Up Networking A feature in Windows that enables your modem to dial out and connect to a server, either on the Internet through an Internet service provider (ISP) or to a server in a company network.

Directory Part of the structure for organizing your files on a disk. A directory can contain files and other directories (called subdirectories). In Windows, directories are usually called *folders*.

DMZ Demilitarized Zone. Allows one IP address to be exposed to the Internet, creating a host for the other computers that access the Internet.

DNS Domain Name System. A function that controls how domain names are located and translated into IP addresses.

Document A data file that you create in a software program.

Document Window The window within a software program's window that holds the document. More than one document window can be open at a time.

Domain On a Windows network, a group of computers under the control of a central security database. On a TCP/IP network, a group of computers and devices that share a common naming scheme and are managed according to common procedures.

Download To receive a file transmitted over the network (including the Internet). The opposite of *upload*, which means to send a file out over the network.

Driver Software that provides the operating system with information about a device, enabling the operating system to control the device.

Dynamic IP Address An IP address that is assigned automatically, usually by a DHCP server.

Dynamic Routing Forwarding data via different routes, based on the current condition of network circuits.

Embedded Network Card A network interface card that is built in to a computer's systemboard, or motherboard.

Ethernet The most widely used of the several technologies available for cabling Local Area Networks. (See also *LAN*.)

Expansion Slot A slot on your computer's systemboard, or motherboard, into which you insert cards, such as network interface cards. Also called a *bus*.

Extension The period (.) and characters at the end of a filename that usually identify the kind of information a file contains. For example, text files usually have the extension *.txt*, and Microsoft Word files usually have the extension *.doc*.

Failover A backup operation that automatically switches to a standby database, server, or network if the primary system fails or is shut down.

Fast Ethernet Ethernet that communicates at 100 Mbps.

Fault Tolerance The ability of a system to react automatically to an unexpected software or hardware failure. Many levels of fault tolerance exist, from being able to continue operations in the event of a power failure (using backup battery systems) to mirroring all operations (by performing every operation on one or more duplicate systems).

Firewall Software or hardware that protects a computer on the Internet from unauthorized, outside intrusion. Companies that have one or more servers exposed to the Internet use firewalls to allow only authorized employees access to the servers.

Firmware Programming code that is written into read-only memory, so it is retained even when the device is not on.

FTP File Transfer Protocol. A protocol used to transfer files over TCP/IP.

Full Duplex The ability of a device to transmit data in both directions simultaneously.

Gateway A device that interconnects networks.

Gigabit When used to describe data storage, a gigabit equals 1024 megabits. When used to describe data transfer rates, it equals 10^9 (1,000,000,000) bits.

Gigabits per Second (Gbps) A measurement of data transfer speed. A gigabit equals 1,000,000,000 bits.

Gigabyte (GB) When used to describe data storage, a gigabyte equals 1000MB.

GPF General Protection Fault. In Windows, this means the memory protection feature detected an illegal instruction from a program, causing the program to crash.

Graphical User Interface (GUI) A way of interacting with a computer using graphics instead of text. GUIs use icons, pictures, and menus to display information and accept input through a mouse and a keyboard.

Half Duplex Data transmissions that can travel in only one direction at a time.

Home Phoneline Networking Alliance (HPNA) An association working to ensure adoption of a single, unified home telephone line networking standard and to bring home telephone line networking technology to the market.

Host The main computer on a client/server network that supplies the files and peripherals shared by all the other computers. Also called a *server*.

HTML HyperText Markup Language. The language used to create Web pages, it defines the location and characteristics of each element on the Web page.

HTTP HyperText Transfer Protocol. The protocol used for transferring files to and from World Wide Web (WWW) sites.

Hub The home base of a 10BaseT network to which all lengths of cable from the network computers are attached. (One end of each cable length attaches to the hub; the other end of each length attaches to a computer's network interface card.) Also called a *concentrator*.

IDE Integrated Drive Electronics. A type of hard drive controller.

IEEE Institute of Electrical and Electronics Engineers. An organization that oversees standards.

Internet Connection Firewall The built-in software firewall included with Windows XP Professional prior to the Service Pack 2 update.

Interrupt A signal that a device sends to the computer when the device is ready to accept or send information. (See also *IRQ*.)

I/O Input/Output. The process of transferring data to or from a computer. Some I/O devices handle only input (keyboards and mice), some handle only output (printers), and some handle both (disks).

IP Internet Protocol. The method by which data is sent from one computer to another computer on the Internet, or on a network using TCP/IP.

IP Address A number that identifies a computer's location on the Internet or on a network using TCP/IP.

IPSec Internet Protocol Security. A series of protocols used to implement security during the exchange of data over a network.

IRQ Interrupt Request. An assigned location in memory used by a computer device to send information about its operation. Because the location is unique, the computer knows which device is interrupting the ongoing process to send a message.

ISA Bus ISA (Industry Standard Architecture) is a standard bus that has been used for a number of years. It's a 16-bit card, which means that it sends 16 bits of data at a time between the systemboard (or motherboard) and the card (and any device attached to the card). (See also *Bus* and *PCI Bus*.)

ISDN Modem A modem that offers faster transmission speeds than a standard modem. (ISDN stands for Integrated Services Digital Network, in case you were wondering.) ISDN modem is generally more expensive than a standard modem and requires a special ISDN phoneline (which is more expensive than a standard phoneline).

ISP Internet service provider. A company that provides Internet access to individuals and businesses.

Java A programming language produced by Sun Microsystems. Java is used to provide services over the Web. A Web site can provide a Java application (called an *applet*), which you download and run on your own computer.

JPEG A format for graphic image files. JPEG images are usually smaller than other types of image files, due to compression features. However, the compression features are sometimes rather primitive, so it may be difficult to reproduce the image properly.

Jumper A small piece of plastic in a network interface card that "jumps" across pins. Whether or not pins are "jumpered" determines settings components in a computer.

Kbps Kilobits per second. A measure of data transfer speed. One Kbps is 1000 bits per second.

Keyboard Buffer An area in memory that keeps track of the keys you typed, even if the computer did not immediately respond when you typed them. If you hear a beep when you press a key, you've exceeded the size of the buffer.

Kilobyte 1024 bytes. Usually abbreviated K, as in 1024K. Used to describe the size of memory and hard drive storage.

LAN Local Area Network. Two or more computers connected to one another so that they can share information and peripherals.

Latency The delay between the time a communication or process request is made and when it begins.

LCD Liquid Crystal Display. Technology used for laptop and desktop computer displays as well as many other electronic devices.

LMHOSTS File In Windows, a plain text file that tells your computer where to find another computer on a network. The file resides in the Windows directory, and it lists the IP addresses and computer names of computers on the network.

Local Computer The computer you sit in front of when you access a remote computer. (See also *Remote Computer.*)

Local Printer A printer attached to the computer you're using.

LPT1 The name used to refer to the first parallel port on a computer. The second parallel port, if there is one, is named LPT2.

LVDS Low Voltage Differential Signaling. A low-noise, low-power, low-amplitude method for high-speed data transmission over copper wire. LVDS differs from normal input/output. Normal digital I/O uses 5 volts as a high (binary 1) and no volts as a low (binary 0). The differential adds –5 volts as a third option, which provides another level for encoding, therefore providing a higher maximum data transfer rate, using fewer wires.

MAC Address Media Access Control address. A unique number assigned by the manufacturer to an Ethernet networking device (such as a network adapter), which lets the network identify the device at the hardware level.

Mapping To assign a drive letter to a shared resource on another computer to access that shared resource more easily. You can map another computer's drive, folder, or subfolder. The drive letter that you use becomes part of the local computer's set of drive letters. The drives you create are called *network drives*.

Mbps Megabits per second. A data transmission measurement of 1 million bits per second.

Megabit When used to describe data storage, 1024 kilobits. When used to describe data transfer rates, 1 million bits.

Megabyte 1024 kilobytes (approximately 1 million bytes). Usually abbreviated MB.

Megahertz The speed at which a computer runs, set by the processor. Usually abbreviated MHz.

MIDI Musical Instrument Digital Interface. The protocol for communication between electronic musical instruments and computers.

MIME Multipurpose Internet Mail Extension. The standard for transferring binary information (files other than plain text files) via e-mail.

Modem A communications device that enables a computer to transmit information over a telephone line (telephone and DSL modems) or coaxial cable (cable modem).

Modular Duplex Jack A device that plugs into a telephone wall jack to convert that single telephone jack into two jacks so that you can plug in two phones; a phone and a modem; or, in the case of a telephone line network, a telephone and a telephone line network cable. Also called a *splitter*.

Monochrome Printer A printer that prints in black and shades of gray (rather than a color printer, which prints in colors). Some people call this a black-and-white printer, despite the fact that no white ink is involved.

Motherboard For a PC, a plane surface that holds all the basic circuitry, and the CPU. Also called a *systemboard*.

Multimedia PC A PC that contains a CD-ROM drive, sound card, and speakers.

Multiprocessor A computer system that uses more than one CPU running simultaneously for faster performance.

NAT Network Address Translation. The translation of an IP address used within a network to a different IP address that is known within another network.

NDIS Network Driver Interface Specification. A Windows device driver feature that enables a single NIC to support multiple network protocols (for example, both TCP/IP and NetBEUI).

NetBEUI NetBIOS Extended User Interface. The transport layer for NetBIOS communication.

NetBIOS Network Basic Input/Output System. A software program that permits applications to communicate with other computers that are on the same cabled network.

Network Two or more computers that are connected so they can exchange data.

Network Drive A drive that is located on another computer on the network.

Network Interface Card (NIC) The primary hardware device for a network, a NIC attaches a computer to the network cable. Technically, *NIC* refers only to internal cards, because network controllers are available for USB and other ports. However, the term is often used generically to describe any network controller.

Network Printer A printer attached to a remote computer on the network. (A printer attached to a local computer on the network is called a *local* printer.)

Network Resource A device located in a computer other than the local computer.

Node A connection point for distributing computer transmissions. The term is usually applied to computers on a network.

Object Linking and Embedding (OLE) A software system that allows programs to transfer and share information. When a change is made to a shared object in the first program, any document in any program that contains that object is automatically updated.

Packet A chunk of information sent over a network (including the Internet).

Parallel Port A connection on a PC, usually named LPT1 or LPT2, where you plug in a cable for a parallel device (usually a printer).

Pathname In DOS, a statement that indicates a filename on a local computer. When you use a pathname, you tell your computer that the target folder is on the local computer. Anyone working at another computer on the network must use a UNC statement to access that folder. (See also *UNC.*)

PC Card A device for a laptop computer that is designed to use PCMCIA slots on the computer.

PCI Bus Peripheral Component Interconnect bus. The PCI bus is built for speed and is found in most new computers. It comes in two configurations: 32-bit and 64-bit (32-bit means that the bus sends 32 bits of data at a time between the systemboard and the card; 64-bit means that the bus sends 64 bits of data at a time). Its technology is far more advanced—and complicated—than that of the ISA bus. (See also *Bus* and *ISA Bus.*)

PCMCIA A device for a laptop computer, such as a NIC or a modem, that works like an expansion slot (bus) in a desktop computer. A PCMCIA card is about the size of a credit card. Also called a *PC Card.*

Peer-to-Peer Network A network in which all the computers are connected without any network-wide authentication procedures (which is the case in a client/server network).

Peripheral Any device connected to a computer: a monitor, keyboard, removable drive, CD-ROM drive, scanner, speakers, and so on.

Permission Level A setting that controls users' access to shared resources on a network. The person who creates a shared resource decides which type of permission level to grant, such as Read-Only, Full, or Depends on Password.

Persistent Connections Mapped drives linked to a user (a logon name) rather than a computer. If multiple users share a computer, the mapped drives that appear are those created by the user who is currently logged on. (See also *Mapping.*)

Plug and Play A software feature that reviews all the hardware in your computer during startup. When a new Plug and Play hardware component is detected, the software installation procedure begins automatically.

POP Post Office Protocol. A protocol for downloading e-mail from an e-mail server.

Port A connector located on the back of your computer into which you can plug a peripheral device, such as a keyboard, mouse, printer, and so on. Computers also have virtual ports. (See also *Virtual Port.*)

POST Power-On Self-Test. The internal circuitry, memory, and installed hardware that a computer performs on itself when you turn it on.

PPP Point to Point Protocol. A protocol for communication between two computers using a serial interface (usually a telephone line). Usually used to describe the way an ISP provides a connection so the provider's server can respond to your output, pass it on to the Internet, and bring Internet responses back to you.

PPPoE Point to Point Protocol over Ethernet. A method of encapsulating PPP in a way that provides authentication processes in addition to transporting data. Used by some cable/DSL ISPs.

PPTP Point to Point Tunneling Protocol. A protocol that allows PPP to be tunneled through an IP network. Usually used for secure access from one location to another over a Virtual Private Network (VPN).

Print Queue The lineup of documents waiting to be printed.

Print Server On a network, a computer to which a shared printer is attached.

Print Spooler The place on your hard drive where printer jobs are lined up, waiting to be sent to the printer. (See also *Print Queue.*)

Profile The computer environment that belongs to a particular user.

Protocol Standardized rules for transmitting information among computers.

Proxy Server A server that acts in place of a client computer. For example, a proxy server performs all the functions of a Web browser for all the individual computers accessing the Internet.

RAM Random-Access Memory. The memory used by the operating system and software to perform tasks. The term *random-access* refers to the ability of the processor to access any part of the memory.

Registry A database that keeps track of the configuration options for software, hardware, and other important elements of your Windows operating system.

Remote Computer On a network, a computer other than the one you're working on.

Remote User A user who's accessing one computer but sitting in front of another computer.

Resolution The number of dots (pixels) that make up an image on a screen or printed document. The higher the resolution, the finer and smoother the images appear.

RG-58 cable The specific type of coaxial (10Base2) cable used in networks. (See also *10Base2.*)

RIP Routing Information Protocol. A routing protocol (part of TCP/IP) that determines the route to a destination based on the smallest number of hops.

RJ-11 Registered Jack-11. The connector at each end of a length of telephone cable for telephones and telephone line networking schemes.

RJ-45 Registered Jack-45. The connector at the end of Ethernet twisted-pair cable.

Root Directory A section of your hard drive that is not part of a directory (folder). It holds files needed for booting.

Router A device that connects subnetworks together.

SDSL Symmetric Digital Subscriber Line. A technology that allows a high-speed connection to the Internet over standard telephone lines. SDSL supports data rates up to 3 Mbps. It differs from ADSL in the fact that it supports the same data rates for both upstream and downstream traffic. (See also *ADSL.*)

Separator Page A form that accompanies each print job and prints before the first page of the job. The form displays the name of the user and prints ahead of the first page of each document so that multiple users of a printer can easily identify their documents. Also called a *banner* (in NetWare).

Server A computer on a network that functions as a supplier of services to users. Also called a *host*.

Shared Resources Files, folders, printers, and other peripherals attached to one computer on a network that have been configured for access by remote users on other computers on the network. (See also *Remote User.*)

Slot See *Expansion Slot.*

SMTP Simple Mail Transfer Protocol. The protocol used to transfer e-mail between computers on the Internet. It is a server-to-server protocol, so other protocols (such as POP) are needed to transfer e-mail to a user's computer.

Sneakernet The inconvenience you have when you don't have a network. With sneakernet, information is exchanged between computers by copying files to a disk from one computer, walking to another computer (not necessarily wearing sneakers), and then loading the files from the disk into the second computer.

SOHO Small Office/Home Office. A description of computer (usually network) environments.

Splitter See *Modular Duplex Jack.*

Static IP Address A permanent IP address assigned to a node in a TCP/IP network.

Static Routing A permanent routing system for forwarding data in a network, which cannot adjust to changing conditions. (See also *Dynamic Routing.*)

STP Cable Shielded Twisted-Pair cable. A type of 10BaseT cable in which metal encases the cable's wires, lessening the possibility of interference from other electrical devices, radar, radio waves, and so on.

Subnet Mask A method of splitting IP networks into a series of subgroups (subnets). Usually LANs are computers that have the same subnet mask.

Switch A device that connects network devices, allowing a large number of network devices to share a limited number of ports.

System Files The files that Windows installs to make the operating system run.

T-Connector A T-shaped connector used to connect 10Base2 to a NIC on a network without interrupting the cable run. (See also *10Base2* and *Network Interface Card.*)

TCP/IP Transmission Control Protocol/Internet Protocol. A set of standardized rules for transmitting information. TCP/IP enables Macintosh, IBM-compatible, UNIX, and other dissimilar computers to jump on the Internet and communicate with one another, as long as each computer uses TCP/IP.

Terminator A device with BNC connectors that lets you "cap off" the empty cross-bars of T-connectors at the beginning and end of a 10Base2 cable run. (See also *10Base2, BNC Connector,* and *T-Connector.*)

TFTP Trivial File Transfer Protocol. A version of FTP that has no security (password) capabilities.

Thinnet See *10Base2.*

Topology The physical or logical layout of a network.

Twisted-Pair Cable See *10BaseT.*

UNC Universal Naming Convention. A formatted style used to identify a particular shared resource on a particular remote computer. The format is *Computername**sharename*.

Uninterruptible Power Supply (UPS) A mega-battery that plugs into the wall outlet. You plug your computer and monitor into the UPS outlets. If power fails, your computer draws power from the battery to give you enough time to shut down your computer properly.

Upload To send data over a network (including the Internet). Opposite of *download* (receive data).

URL Uniform Resource Locator. Used on the World Wide Web (WWW) to identify the address of a resource on the Internet. For example, *www.microsoft.com.*

User Account A collection of settings and preferences that are applied to a user when the user logs on to a computer.

UTP Cable Unshielded Twisted Pair cable. 10BaseT cable that does not have a metal shield. (See also *STP Cable.*)

Virtual Drive A drive that doesn't really exist; you add a new drive letter, but you don't add any new physical drives to a computer. (See also *Mapping.*)

Virtual Port A nonphysical port through which a computer accepts data from remote computers (including over the Internet). For example, HTTP (the protocol you use when interacting with a Web page) uses port 80. Ports work by "listening" for data and will usually automatically accept data if it's the right type of data for that port.

Voltage Regulator A device connected on one side to an outlet and on the other side to a computer. The device measures voltage coming from the outlet and then adjusts the voltage to make sure the voltage delivered to the computer is within a safe range.

VPN Virtual Private Network. A technique for creating private communication channels (called *tunnels*) between LANs.

Wake-on-LAN A technology (built into network adapters) that allows a computer to be powered on remotely over a network.

WAN Wide Area Network. A network connected by public networks (usually telephone lines), covering remote geographical areas, consisting of two or more LANs.

Windows Firewall The built-in software firewall provided with Windows XP Service Pack 2.

Wizard An interactive program that walks you through a software installation process.

Workgroup The group to which the computers on a peer-to-peer network belong.

Workstation See *Client.*

Y-Connector An adapter shaped like the letter *Y* that connects two devices to one input device. For example, you can use a Y-connector to connect both a modem and a telephone line NIC to a length of cable that's inserted in a wall jack for a telephone line network. The two ends at the top of the *Y* connect to the back of the computer (one end connects to the modem; the other connects to the NIC). The single end at the bottom of the *Y* connects the cable between the computer and the wall jack. (See also *Network Interface Card.*)

Appendix B

Advanced Network Tools

If all goes well (and it usually does), after you connect all the hardware and finish all the software configuration chores, the computers on your network will recognize each other and find the Internet, and you can start using your network. Every once in a while, however, you may encounter a small problem with the way your network is functioning, and you may have to dig around the operating system to find and solve the problem. Luckily, lots of tools exist to help you dig. In addition to diagnosing and solving problems, you can use network tools to learn about the way networks work.

Windows Graphical Network Tools

Windows works in a GUI (pronounced *gooey*, and which stands for graphical user interface), so it's not surprising that many of its built-in tools are GUI tools. However, few of Microsoft's network tools are GUI tools. Most of the network tools and utilities are text-based programs that you run from the command line, and they're discussed later in this chapter in the section "Command-Line Tools." However, the few GUI network tools that come with Windows or are available from Microsoft's Web sites are important and useful.

Winipcfg

Winipcfg is available in Windows 95/98/98SE/Me and presents a graphical view of a computer's TCP/IP configuration. It provides a way to renew the computer's DHCP lease of the IP address. To run winipcfg, choose Start | Run, type **winipcfg**, and click OK. The program opens with a display of the basic TCP/IP information for the network adapter(s) installed in the computer.

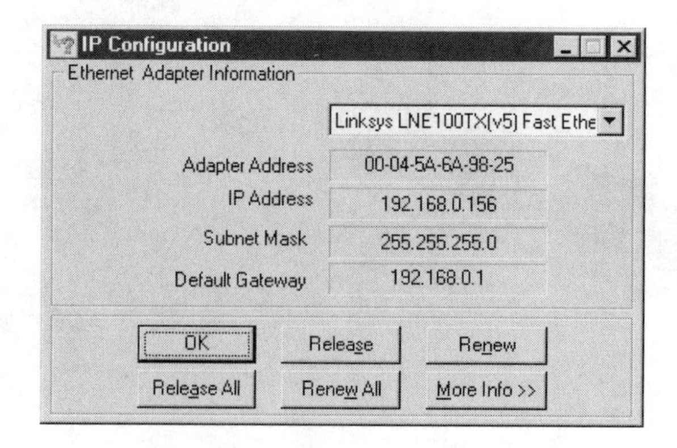

If you have multiple network adapters (perhaps one adapter for a DSL/cable modem and another for the LAN), select an adapter from the list in the drop-down box at the top of the window to see its configuration settings.

The Release, Renew, Release All, and Renew All buttons are available only for adapters that have DHCP addresses (IP addresses assigned by a DHCP server). If you run the program on the computer that's acting as the DHCP server (your ICS host), the buttons are grayed out.

Here's an overview of the options on the dialog:

- Click Release to remove the DHCP lease for the selected adapter, which removes the adapter's IP address.
- Click Renew to retrieve a new address for the selected adapter from the DHCP server.
- Click Release All to remove the DHCP leases from all the adapters in the computer.
- Click Renew All to retrieve new addresses for all the adapters in the computer.
- Click More Info to expand the window so it reveals more information about the computer's TCP/IP configuration (see Figure B-1).

While it's unusual to need to release and renew IP addresses, under some circumstances you may have to perform this task.

If a computer fails to find the DHCP server during startup, Windows assigns an Automatic Private IP Address (APIPA) to the LAN adapter. APIPA addresses are assigned in the range 169.254.*x.x,* and they permit computers to communicate over a LAN but won't work for Internet Connection Sharing. If the failure to find the DHCP server resulted from the order in which computers started up (you should always start the DHCP server first), after the DHCP server is up and running, the client computers usually find the DHCP server and get a leased IP address. You can force the computer to obtain an IP address from the DHCP server by using the Release and Renew buttons in the winipcfg window.

If you move a computer from one LAN to another (a scenario that usually involves a laptop), you can use the Release and Renew buttons to assign the computer an IP address that is guaranteed to be unique on the network.

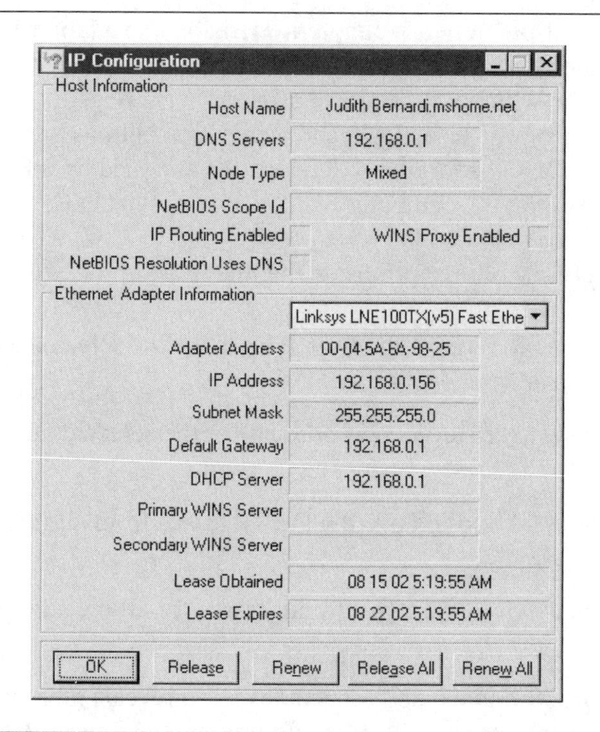

FIGURE B-1 The detailed view of winipcfg provides plenty of information about the TCP/IP settings for this computer.

Wntipcfg

Wntipcfg is the Windows NT/2000/XP version of winipcfg. Unfortunately, it isn't built in to the operating system, but you can download it from *http://www.microsoft.com/windows2000/techinfo/reskit/tools/existing/wntipcfg-o.asp*. If you've purchased the Windows 2000 Resource Kit, it contains a copy of wntipcfg.exe, so you don't have to download it.

Click the link labeled Wntipcfg_setup.exe and save the file on your hard drive. To install the program, double-click the downloaded file and follow the prompts to complete installation.

To run wntipcfg, open Windows Explorer or My Computer and navigate to the folder in which you installed the program (the default installation folder is C:\Program Files\Resource Kit). Double-click the program's listing to open a window that offers the same information and tools as winipcfg.

NOTE *For Windows NT/2000/XP, a command-line tool, ipconfig, is available. This tool is a more powerful version of wntipcfg. Ipconfig is discussed later in this chapter in the section "Command-Line Tools."*

Network Connection Properties

You can use the Properties dialog of the network adapter to check settings and repair errors. A great deal of information about configuring adapter settings is found throughout this book in the chapters specific to the network topology you're using (Ethernet, wireless, and so on). However, you can also do some troubleshooting from the Properties dialog. The following sections cover some of the settings you should check if you're having problems with network communications.

Workgroup Name

Be sure every computer on the network is logging on to the same workgroup. By default, Microsoft names the workgroup MSHOME or WORKGROUP (depending on the version of Windows running on the computer), but if you chose a different name, you may have forgotten to make the change on one computer.

In Windows 98SE, follow these steps to determine the name of the workgroup:

1. Choose Start | Settings | Control Panel to open the Control Panel window.
2. Double-click the Network applet to open the Properties dialog for your network adapter(s).
3. Click the Identification tab to see the workgroup name.

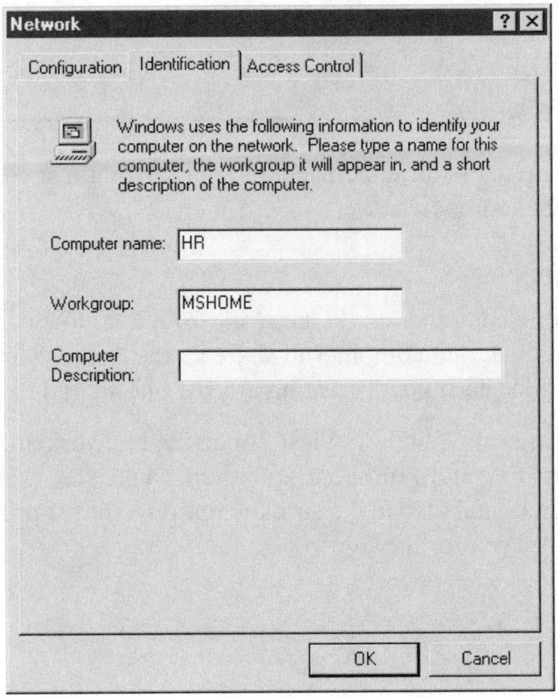

In Windows XP, follow these steps to see the name of the workgroup:

1. Choose Start | Control Panel.
2. Click Network and Internet Connections.
3. In the left pane (the Network Tasks list), click My Network Places.
4. In the left pane, click View Workgroup Computers and look for the workgroup name at the bottom of the left pane.

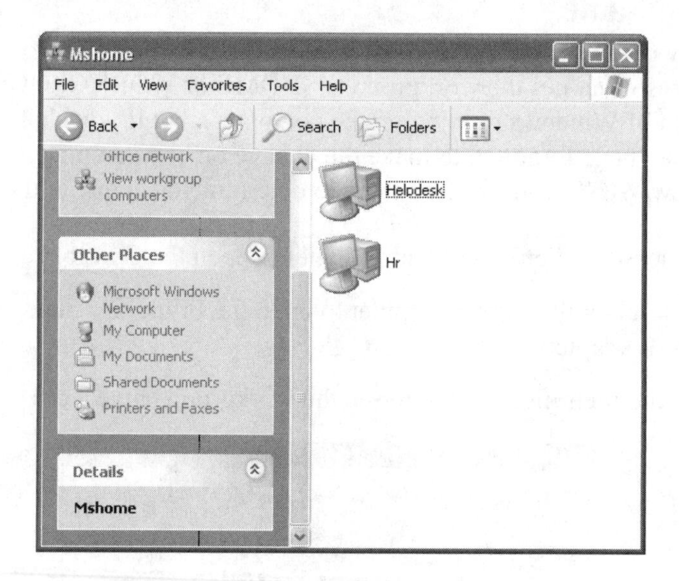

If the workgroup name differs on any computer, you must correct the errant entry and reboot that computer.

Shared Resources

You can't access one computer on the network from a remote computer unless you've configured the target computer to share its resources. This is a two-step process: enabling file sharing and creating at least one shared resource.

Enabling File Sharing In Windows 98SE, open the Network applet in Control Panel, and click the File and Print Sharing button. Make sure that the option to share files is selected (and also make sure the option to share printers is selected if the computer has a printer).

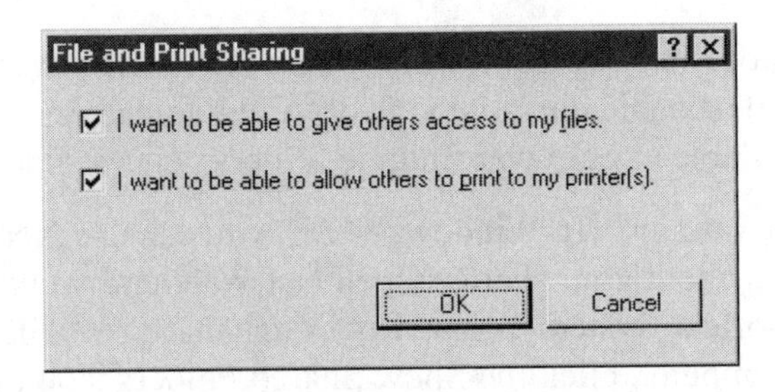

In Windows XP, right-click the icon for the LAN connection, choose Properties, and on the General tab, make sure the option File and Printer Sharing for Microsoft Networks has a check mark in the check box.

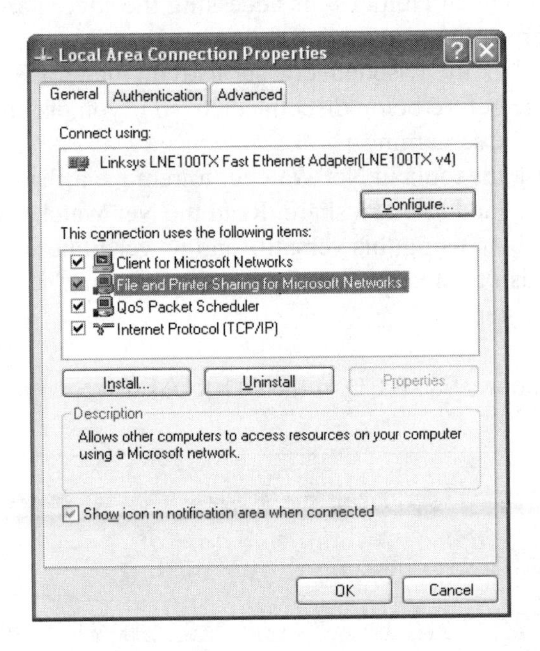

NOTE *If you are using Windows XP with Service Pack 2 installed, you must also make sure that Windows Firewall is configured to allow file and print sharing. See Chapter 9 for more on this.*

Checking Shared Resources

Make sure at least one folder (or drive) is shared on each computer. The quickest way to check is to open Windows Explorer or My Computer and look for drive and folder icons that include a picture of a hand. However, if your shared folders are subfolders, or subfolders of subfolders, it's more difficult to check for shared folders (you have to navigate down into the drive and folder structure). Fortunately, some tools are available to help you find the folders you've shared.

Windows 98SE Net Watcher In Windows 98SE, you can use Net Watcher to display information about your shares. Open Net Watcher by choosing Start | Programs | Accessories | System Tools | Net Watcher. To see a list of the shared resources on the computer, click the Show Shared Folders icon on the toolbar (see Figure B-2).

When you select a share, the right pane displays the name of any remote computer that's connected to that share. In Figure B-2, you can see that a user from the computer named Helpdesk is accessing the share named Linksys. To ascertain the name of the user, click the Show User icon on the toolbar. To disconnect a user, click the Disconnect User icon on the toolbar. (The user gets no warning message before being disconnected, so if you use this tool be prepared to hear some screaming.)

You can also use the tools in Net Watcher to remove a share (the icon is named Stop Sharing) and to add a share. Read the Net Watcher Help files for more information about using this versatile and powerful networking tool.

If Net Watcher isn't listed on your System Tools menu, you need to install it using the following steps:

1. Put the Windows 98SE CD in the CD-ROM drive.

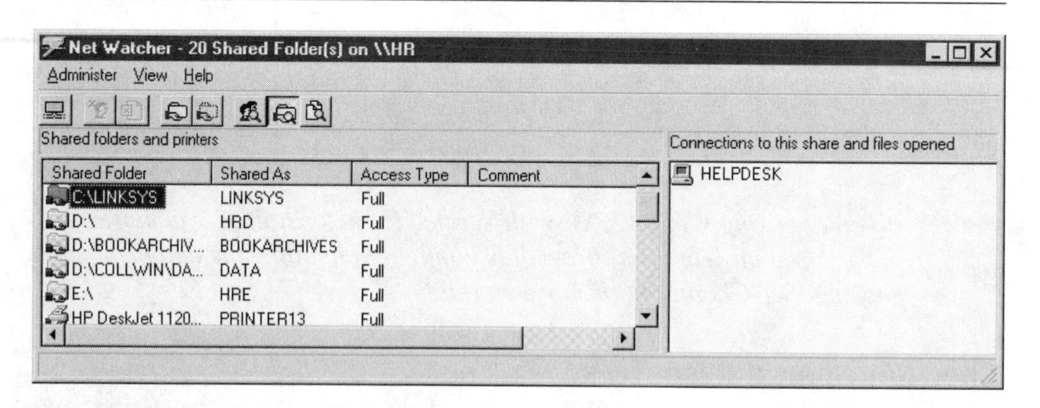

FIGURE B-2 Net Watcher displays information about all of the shared resources on the computer.

2. Choose Start | Settings | Control Panel to open the Control Panel window.
3. Open the Add/Remove Programs applet.
4. Click the Windows Setup tab.
5. Select the System Tools listing and click Details.
6. Click the check box next to the Net Watcher listing to place a check mark in the check box.
7. Click OK twice and follow the prompts to install Net Watcher.

Windows XP Shared Folders In Windows XP, you can use the Computer Management tool to view information about the shares on the computer. To open Computer Management, choose Start, right-click the My Computer listing, and choose Manage from the shortcut menu. In the Computer Management window that opens, expand the System Tools folder in the console pane (the left pane) by clicking the plus sign, and then expand the Shared Folders folder as well. This reveals listings for the three categories of information you can view: Shares, Sessions, and Open Files.

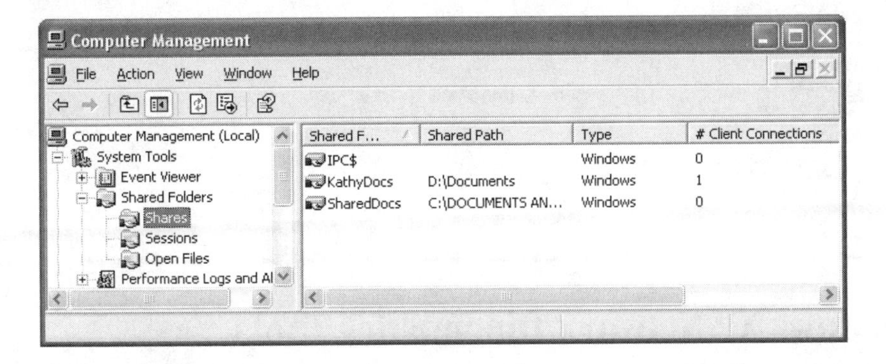

Click the Shares listing in the console pane to view a list of all the shares on the computer. Notice that you can also see whether any users are connected to any shares.

Click the Sessions listing in the console pane to see which users are connected to this computer's shares. The Action menu offers a command to disconnect all the sessions if you have some reason to do so.

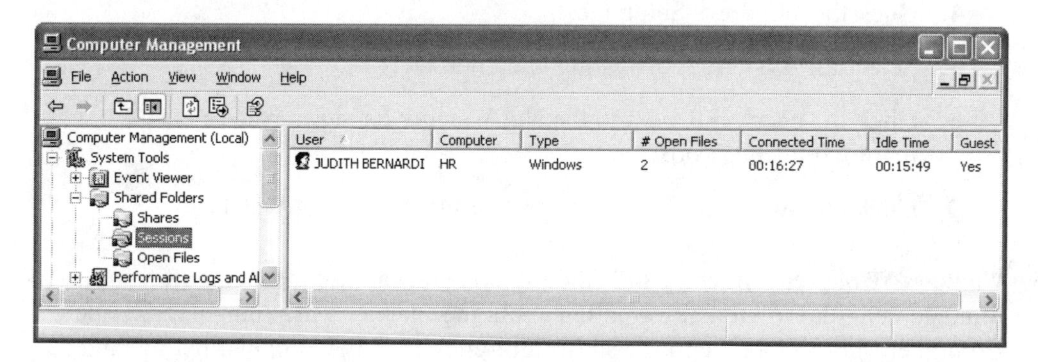

Click the Open Files listing to see the files being used by remote users. The Action menu offers a command to disconnect (close) all open files.

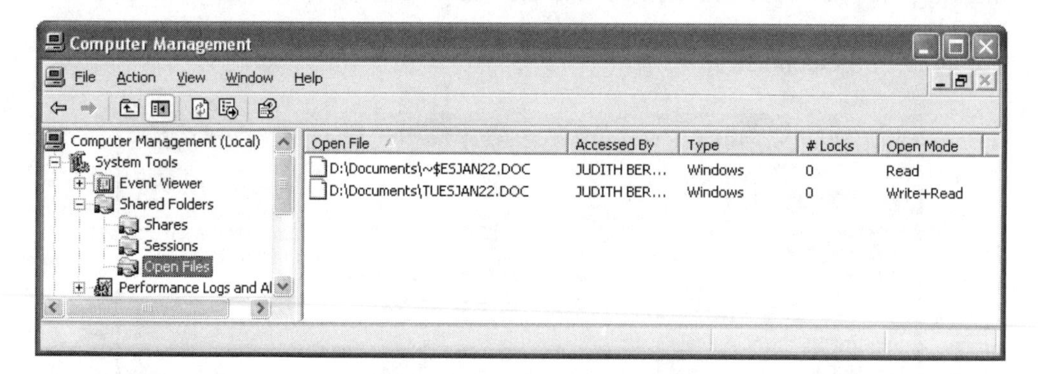

Windows XP Network Diagnostics Tools

If you're running Windows XP, you have some additional graphical tools built in to the operating system for diagnosing and solving network connectivity problems. You can access these tools with the following steps:

1. Choose Start | Help and Support to open the Help and Support Center.
2. Under Pick a Task, click the link labeled Use Tools to View Your Computer Information and Diagnose Problems.
3. In the Tools list (the left pane), click Network Diagnostics.

You can click Scan Your System to have Windows XP look at all the settings involved in your network and Internet connections. Or you can customize the scanning process by clicking Set Scanning Options. This tool is most useful if you're working with Microsoft support personnel, because it checks settings in the registry (the database that controls Windows). However, the tool performs a couple of tests on network hardware and indicates the results with a Passed/ Failed indicator.

After scanning your system, the Network Diagnostics tool displays a report on the screen, as seen in Figure B-3. The report displays the categories the tool uses to analyze your network settings.

You can expand any category by clicking the plus sign so you can see the details for that category. Most of the details won't make sense to you, unless you

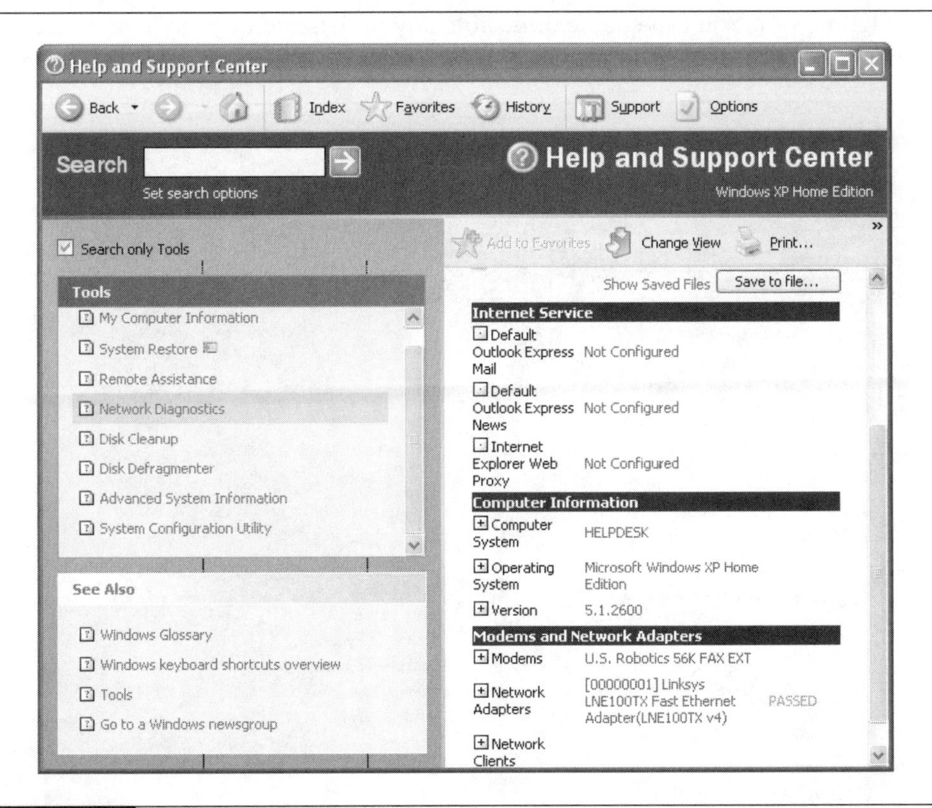

FIGURE B-3 The Windows XP Network Diagnostics tool reports its findings sorted by category.

have a good understanding of the registry. To maintain a permanent copy of the report, click Save to File. The system saves the file in two places on your hard drive.

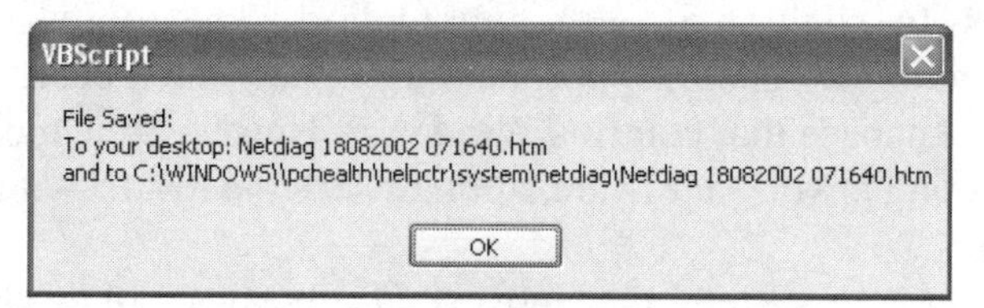

The filename is Netdiag *XY,* where *X* is the date (in the format *DDMMYYYY*) and *Y* is the time (in the format *HHMMSS*). You can retrieve the file later by clicking Show Saved Files.

If you find the test results overwhelming, you can focus on specific network settings by selecting the option Set Scanning Options. A window opens to display the actions the tool performs and the categories for which the tool checks settings (see Figure B-4). You can enable or disable any of these settings by inserting or removing a check mark. To make your selections permanent, click Save Options.

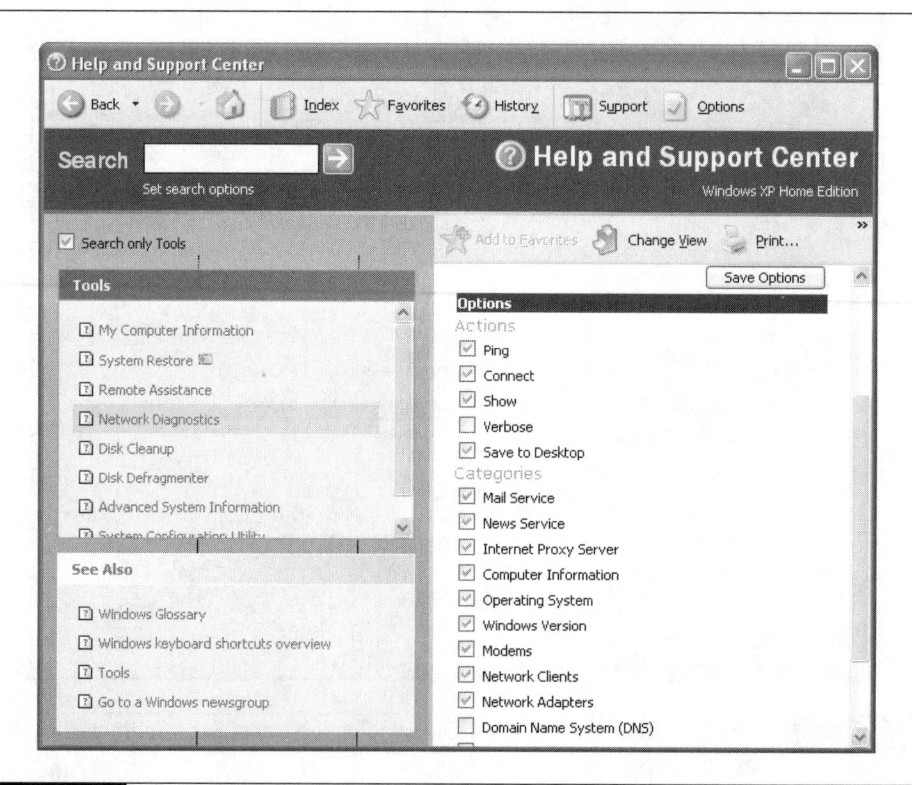

FIGURE B-4 Select the actions and categories you want Network Diagnostics to cover when it scans your system.

Command-Line Tools

Even though the interface that Windows sports has introduced new and fancier graphics, command-line tools continue to be part of the operating system. There's a good reason for this: text-based tools are very powerful. Working in text mode is often faster than working in a GUI tool, and some text-based commands aren't even available in a graphical format.

Some of us are very comfortable working at the command line (called *text mode*), because we started working with computers before graphical interfaces such as Windows existed. At that time, text mode was the only mode available. However, people who were introduced to computers after graphical interfaces became the norm often have a tough time with command-line tools.

Among us older—uh, make that more experienced—folks you'll find a lot of command-line junkies; we move to text mode whenever possible because it's faster than the graphical interface. For those of you who avoid text mode, I urge you to try it because you'll like the speed (especially if you're a good touch typist).

Command-line tools operate in a command prompt window, which you reach in either of the following ways:

- In Windows XP, choose Start | All Programs | Accessories | Command Prompt.
- In Windows 98SE, choose Start | Programs | MS-DOS Prompt.

NOTE *Type **exit** to close a command window.*

Most of the command-line tools return information, which is displayed on your screen. If you want to save the information to a file that you can open and examine at any time, you can invoke a feature called *redirection*. Saving output data permanently can be useful for working with support personnel. To redirect the data provided by a command-line tool, use the following syntax: *command* > `filename.txt` (substitute the real command name and a real filename for these placeholder names).

Ipconfig

Ipconfig is a command-line tool that's available in Windows 98/Me/NT/2000/XP. It's a particularly useful tool on systems running DHCP, because it allows you to see which TCP/IP values have been configured by DHCP. (If you have an assigned

IP address, you can see it by viewing the Properties dialog for the LAN connection if you don't want to use ipconfig.)

To see the current IP address, open a command prompt, type **ipconfig**, and press ENTER. The system returns information about the current IP address.

```
Command Prompt
C:\>ipconfig

Windows IP Configuration

Ethernet adapter Local Area Connection:

        Connection-specific DNS Suffix  . :
        IP Address. . . . . . . . . . . . : 192.168.0.1
        Subnet Mask . . . . . . . . . . . : 255.255.255.0
        Default Gateway . . . . . . . . . :

PPP adapter Mindspring:

        Connection-specific DNS Suffix  . :
        IP Address. . . . . . . . . . . . : 63.14.144.236
        Subnet Mask . . . . . . . . . . . : 255.255.255.255
        Default Gateway . . . . . . . . . : 63.14.144.236

C:\>_
```

To gain more information and perform additional tasks, you can use parameters with ipconfig, as follows:

ipconfig [**/all** | **/renew** [*adapter*] | **/release** [*adapter*]] (for WinNT/2000/XP)
ipconfig [**/all** | **/renew_all** | **/release_all**] (for Win98/Me)

where

- **all** displays all information about all connections. As you can see in Figure B-5, both the LAN connection and the dial-up Internet connection settings are shown. Note that the computer in Figure B-5 is the ICS host and therefore doesn't need DHCP services to gain an IP address for the LAN connection.
- **/renew** [*adapter*] - **/renew_all** renews the DHCP configuration parameters (IP address lease). This option is available only if the computer is running the DHCP Client service. If you have multiple adapters and want to renew the lease for only one adapter, type the adapter name that appears when you use ipconfig without parameters.
- **/release** [*adapter*] - **/release_all** releases the current DHCP lease. This option is available only if the computer is running the DHCP Client service. The option disables TCP/IP on the local system or on a specific adapter.

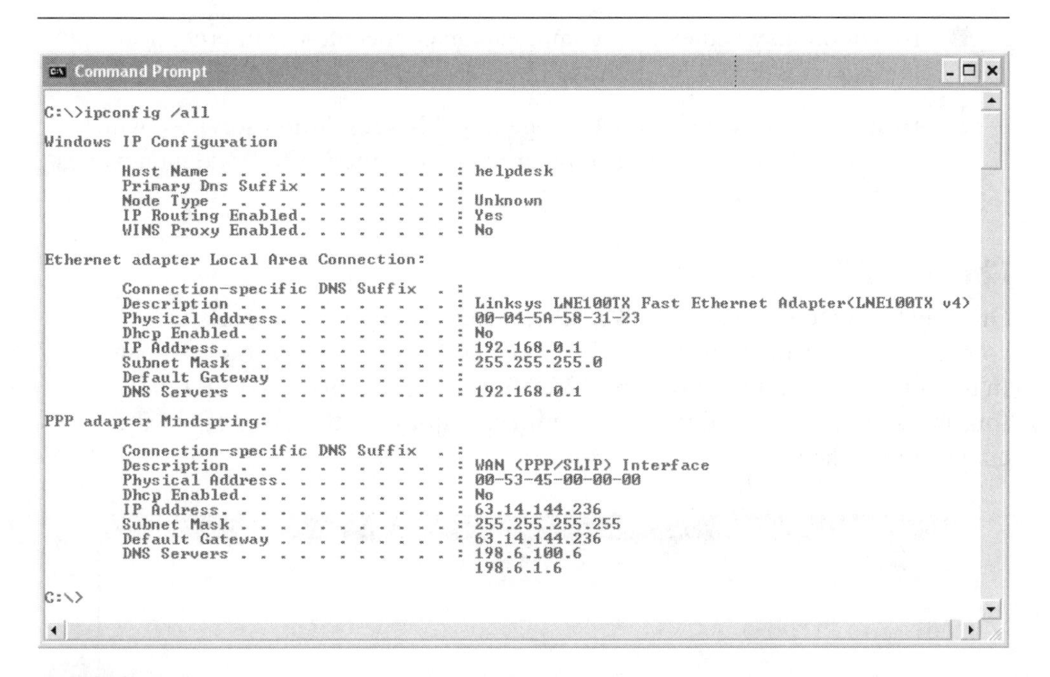

FIGURE B-5 Everything you need to know about a computer's TCP/IP configuration is available when you use the /all parameter with ipconfig.

Ping

Ping is a command-line tool that lets you verify the connection to a remote computer. It's available in all versions of Windows and requires the TCP/IP protocol. Ping works by sending an Internet Control Message Protocol (ICMP) Echo Request message to a remote computer. ICMP is a message control and error-reporting protocol that uses IP datagrams, where the messages are processed by the IP software and are not seen by the user. The messages all request a reply, and the user can see whether a reply is received and the length of time it takes to receive that reply. You can use ping for a variety of tasks, depending on the function you need to check:

- To make sure that the TCP/IP protocol is installed and running on your computer
- To determine whether your computer is correctly connected to the network and receiving an IP address from a DHCP server

- To determine whether your computer can connect to the Internet host computer on the LAN or on the Internet
- To see whether your computer is getting DNS resolution services, which translates IP addresses to computer names (on the LAN) or domain names (on the Internet)

Check TCP/IP

One quick way to see whether TCP/IP services are running properly on your computer is to perform a test, called a *loopback test*, with the `ping` command. In the command window, type ping 127.0.0.1 and press enter. TCP/IP sends four message packets and waits for replies, displaying the progress in the command window.

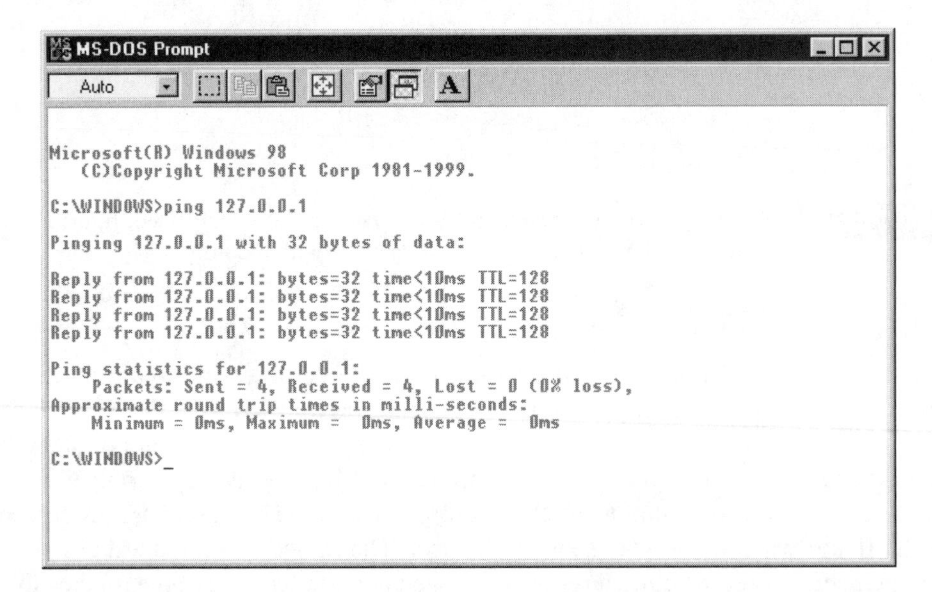

If the loopback test fails, it means the IP stack on the local computer isn't working properly. This could mean the TCP drivers are corrupted or the network adapter has failed. Remove and reinstall the TCP/IP protocol, and if the loopback test still fails, replace the adapter.

Check Network Services

You can use ping to make sure your computer is getting IP address and gateway services from a host computer on your network. First, use winipcfg or ipconfig to determine the IP address of the computer. Then, enter **ping *x.x.x.x*** (replace *x.x.x.x* with the IP address) and press ENTER. If the network routing system is correct, this command merely forwards the packet to the loopback address of 127.0.0.1. The resulting display should look similar to the results from pinging the loopback address. If the loopback test succeeds, but pinging the local IP address fails, you probably have a problem with the driver for your network adapter or with the routing taking place on the ICS host computer.

Check Connection to the Gateway

To make sure your computer can reach the Internet gateway on your LAN, ping the IP address of the gateway. Usually, the gateway is the computer or the Linksys router acting as the Internet connection host on your LAN, but if you have static IP addresses, the gateway may be at your ISP. In a command window, enter **ping *x.x.x.x*** (substitute the IP address of the gateway for *x.x.x.x*) and press ENTER. The system returns the information about the replies.

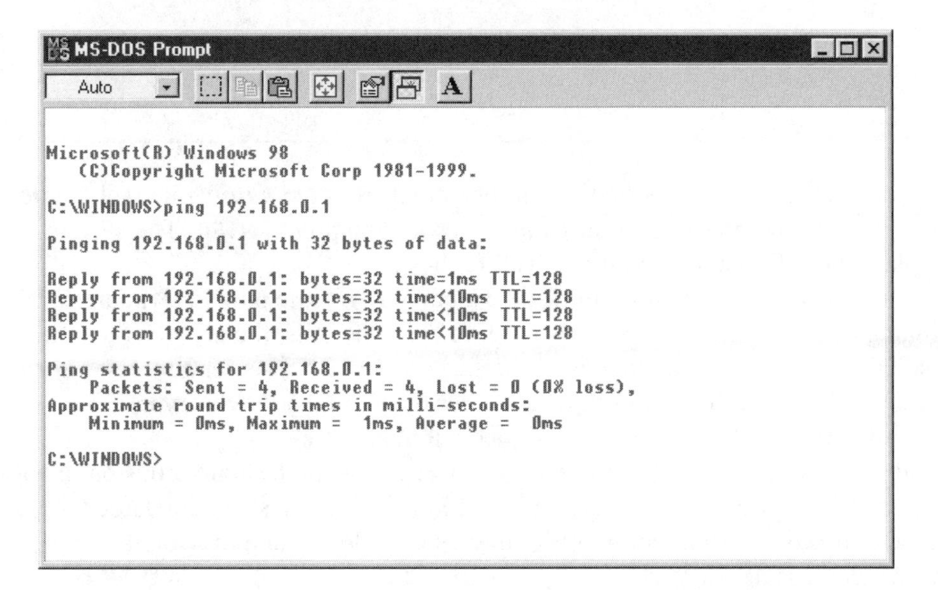

If ping fails, it's likely you have a problem with the gateway device (the computer NIC or the router) or the cabling.

Check DNS

To make sure the DNS functions are operating properly, you should check both the local network and the Internet. To check the local network, enter **ping *ComputerName*** (substitute the name of a computer on your network for *ComputerName*) and press ENTER. The system displays the information about received replies, along with the IP address to which the name resolved.

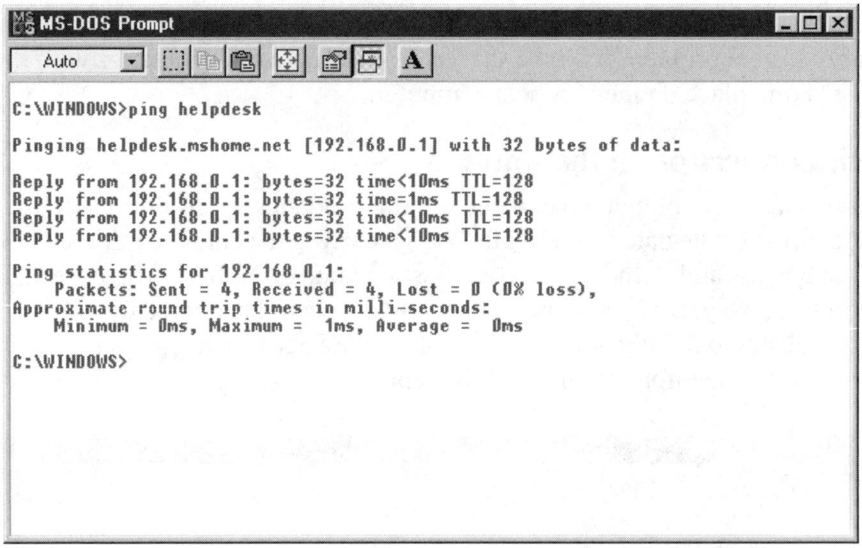

```
MS-DOS Prompt
Auto

C:\WINDOWS>ping helpdesk

Pinging helpdesk.mshome.net [192.168.0.1] with 32 bytes of data:

Reply from 192.168.0.1: bytes=32 time<10ms TTL=128
Reply from 192.168.0.1: bytes=32 time=1ms TTL=128
Reply from 192.168.0.1: bytes=32 time<10ms TTL=128
Reply from 192.168.0.1: bytes=32 time<10ms TTL=128

Ping statistics for 192.168.0.1:
    Packets: Sent = 4, Received = 4, Lost = 0 (0% loss),
Approximate round trip times in milli-seconds:
    Minimum = 0ms, Maximum =  1ms, Average =  0ms

C:\WINDOWS>
```

To check DNS services on the Internet, enter **ping *DomainName*** (substitute the URL for any Internet site for *DomainName*) and press ENTER. The system displays the information about received replies.

Ping uses name resolution to resolve a computer name into an IP address. If pinging by IP address succeeds but pinging by name fails, the problem is name resolution, not network connectivity. Make sure that DNS server addresses are configured properly for the computer (either by naming a DNS server or by indicating that DNS services are assigned automatically).

Ping is a powerful and useful command-line tool and has numerous parameters you can use to perform a variety of tasks. Many of those tasks are outside the scope of this discussion, but if you're interested in learning more about ping, see the Windows Help files.

Tracert

When you connect to an Internet server, your computer doesn't establish a direct connection to that computer—instead, you move through a number of Internet servers to get there. You start at your ISP, then move through the Internet backbone, and then move through other servers. Each move is called a *hop*. Tracert (which stands for *trace route*) traces and reports the hops. If you use the `ping` command to verify connectivity to a computer on the Internet, and ping doesn't return all four packets properly (you see a result that says timeout), you can use the `tracert` command to try to identify the location of the problem.

To use tracert, open a command window and enter **tracert *DomainName*** (substitute the URL for a Web site for *DomainName*).

```
Command Prompt

C:\>tracert ivens.com

Tracing route to ivens.com [64.226.173.212]
over a maximum of 30 hops:

  1    <1 ms    <1 ms    <1 ms  ds1092-230-065.phl1.dsl.speakeasy.net [66.92.230.65]
  2    16 ms    15 ms    16 ms  gw-081-239.dsl.speakeasy.net [66.92.239.1]
  3    10 ms     9 ms    10 ms  border1.fe5-14.speakeasy-27.ext1.phi.pnap.net [216.52.67.91]
  4    11 ms    11 ms    11 ms  core1.fe0-1-bbnet2.phi.pnap.net [216.52.64.65]
  5    11 ms    12 ms    12 ms  sl-gw26-pen-5-1-0.sprintlink.net [144.232.190.201]
  6    11 ms    12 ms    12 ms  sl-bb25-pen-0-7.sprintlink.net [144.232.5.185]
  7    11 ms    12 ms    12 ms  sl-bb21-pen-8-0.sprintlink.net [144.232.5.237]
  8    13 ms    13 ms    13 ms  sl-bb23-rly-0-0.sprintlink.net [144.232.20.32]
  9    15 ms    14 ms    13 ms  sl-bb21-rly-9-0.sprintlink.net [144.232.14.133]
 10    28 ms    26 ms    26 ms  sl-bb20-atl-10-1.sprintlink.net [144.232.9.198]
 11    27 ms    26 ms    26 ms  sl-gw21-atl-9-0.sprintlink.net [144.232.12.110]
 12    29 ms    30 ms    29 ms  sl-il-3-0.sprintlink.net [160.81.204.10]
 13    30 ms    30 ms    30 ms  64.224.0.99
 14    31 ms    30 ms    30 ms  ivens.com [64.226.173.212]

Trace complete.
```

If any hop produces a timeout or takes an excessive length of time (50 milliseconds or more) to return a packet to tracert, you've probably discovered the source of your Internet connectivity problem. If the errant server is at your ISP, you can call the support number to see what's going on. Frequently, when an ISP is performing maintenance tasks on servers, connectivity is slow or temporarily unavailable. If the errant server is out on the Internet, you can't do anything except wait for the problem to be resolved. At least you know the problem is on the Internet, and not in your configuration settings.

NOTE *If you see asterisks instead of an IP address at any hop, it means that server is configured for extra security, to avoid displaying its IP address to the world. Doing a tracert to microsoft.com produces such a result.*

Pathping

Pathping, which is available only in Windows XP and Windows 2000, is a useful utility that combines the power of ping with the power of tracert. You can use pathping to show each hop across the Internet as you travel to a target site and see statistics about the way the data packets were handled by each server. The statistics are computed by continuous pinging of servers, which is time-consuming (so you don't want to try this with the slow speed of a telephone modem).

To accomplish its mission, pathping sends data packets to each server (actually, to the routers on each server) and then computes results based on the packets returned from each hop. The returned data shows the degree of packet loss at any given hop, so you can determine which server might be causing connectivity problems.

Nbtstat

Nbtstat is a powerful diagnostic tool that displays information about current TCP/IP connections that are using NBT (NetBIOS over TCP/IP). You're most likely to use this tool at the direction of a technical support person, but if you're having connectivity issues, this program is a good way to determine whether the problem stems from duplication of a computer name or IP address.

Windows computers communicate with each other using the Server Message Block (SMB) network command protocol. (SMB is now called Common Internet File System, or CIFS, for no apparent reason, because I think the word "Internet" is confusing—SMB is used on LANs. Maybe Microsoft just likes having the word "Internet" in all the cute names it gives its technology features.)

SMB hosts use the computer name (called the *friendly* name) to identify computers, and the friendly name used to be called the NetBIOS name. SMB doesn't use the NetBIOS interface, but the phrase *NetBIOS name* dates back to earlier days in networking, when NetBIOS was the communication protocol—today we use TCP/IP. TCP/IP doesn't know (or care about) friendly names, so Windows uses an application called NetBIOS-Over-TCPIP Helper (NBT) to translate friendly names to IP addresses.

NBT registers the friendly name of each computer on the network, as each computer boots into Windows. It uses a Windows Internet Naming Service (WINS) database to store the information. If you're using WINS for name-to-IP address resolution (and you're probably not—instead, you're probably using DHCP), you can access the information that NBT has stored with the nbtstat command-line tool. If you're not using WINS, NBT gathers the information it needs by periodically browsing the network.

Ntbstat has many parameters, and you can see all of them, along with explanations, by entering **nbtstat** at the command line. It's important to note the following two syntax rules for ntbstat:

- You enter parameters with a minus sign instead of a forward slash.

- Capitalization counts—entering the parameter `-R` is not the same as entering the parameter `-r`.

For this discussion, I'll go over some of the commonly used parameters when investigating network connectivity problems.

- **nbtstat -a *RemoteComputerName*** lists the remote computer's name table, indicating whether or not the computer name is registered on the network. For instance, to see information about a computer named helpdesk, entering **nbtstat -a helpdesk** produces a display that shows the computer named helpdesk is registered (several times, due to periodic browsing) as a unique name. The display also indicates the name of the workgroup (MSHOME), and the MAC address of the adapter on the computer named helpdesk. Unique names are imperative, because any computer name that isn't unique to the network has serious connectivity problems.

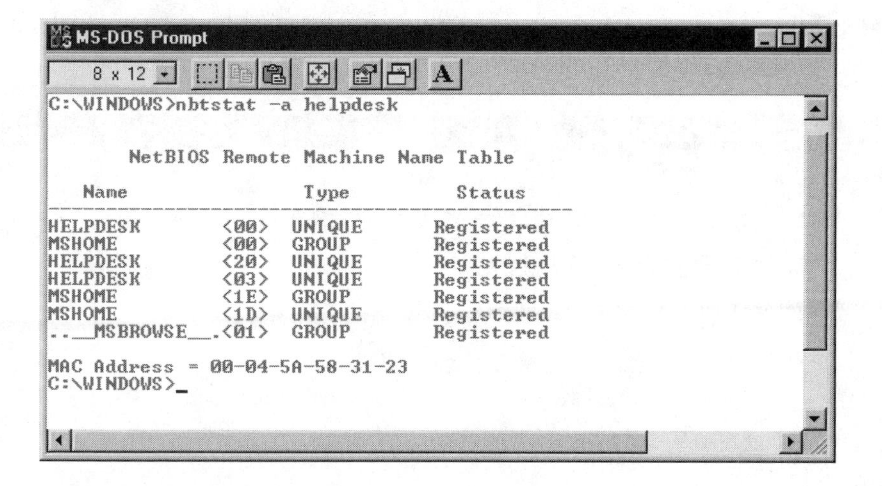

- **nbtstat -A *RemoteIPaddress*** is the same as using `-a` except instead of using the computer's friendly name, you enter its IP address.

- **nbtstat -n** displays the NetBIOS name for the local computer, also indicating whether the name is unique to the network. A status of Registered indicates that the name is registered by broadcast or WINS.

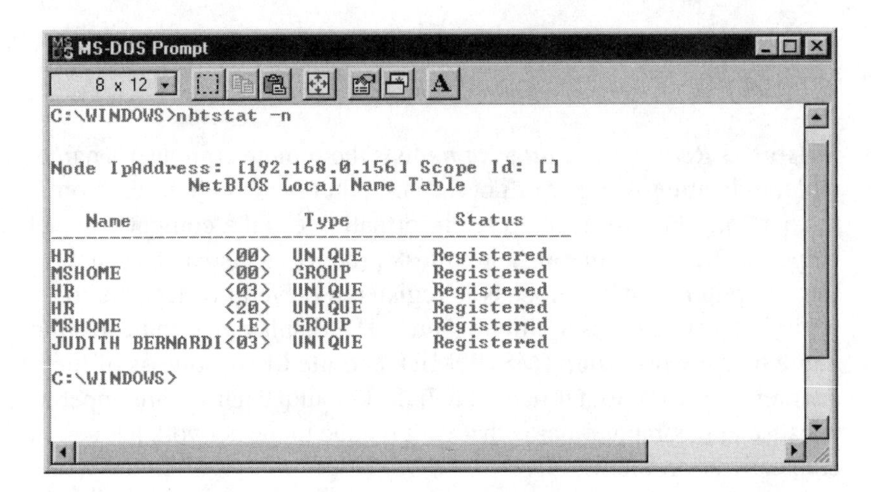

- **nbtstat -r** lists the names of remote computers that have been resolved and registered via broadcast or via WINS.

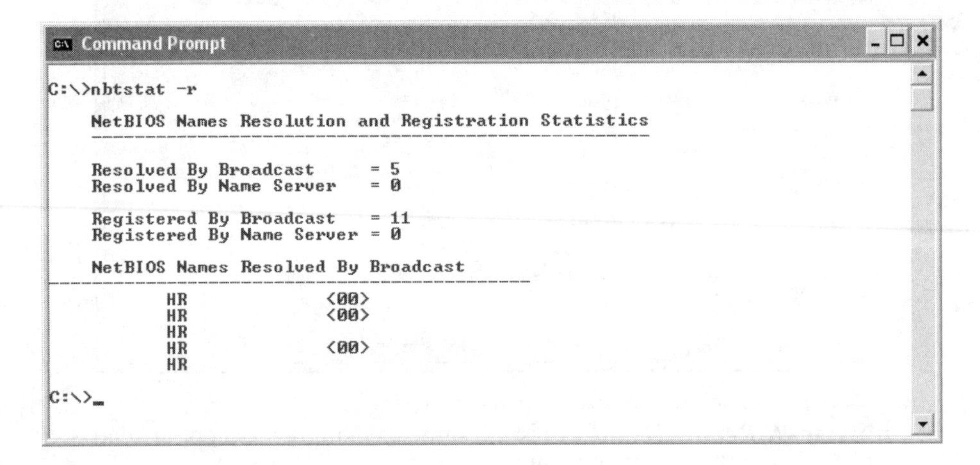

Net Commands

Windows has a slew of commands you can use to view network settings, perform network tasks, and troubleshoot network problems. All the commands start with the word *net* and have a second word that calls the specific net command. In this section, I'll discuss several of the useful net commands that run in a peer-to-peer (workgroup) environment.

Net Config

In Windows 98SE, entering **net config** at the command line returns information about the current computer and network software.

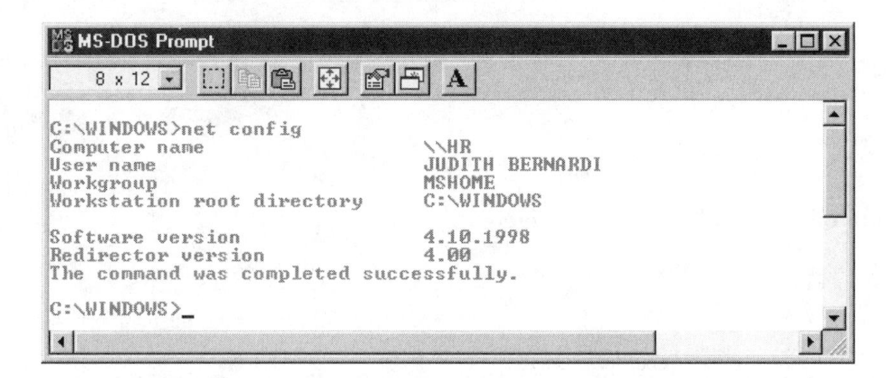

In Windows XP, entering **net config** at the command line returns information about the network services that are running on the computer: Server and Workstation. You can obtain additional information about the services (see Figure B-6) by entering **net config server** and **net config workstation**.

Net File

Available only on Windows XP/2000, this command displays the filenames of files currently accessed by remote users and also allows you to close files that are in use by remote users.

To see the names of files in use, enter **net file** at the command prompt and press ENTER. The system returns the following information:

- An ID number for the file
- The complete path to the file
- The name of the remote user who is using the file
- The number of locks on the file (if the file has locks, it cannot be accessed by anyone else, including you)

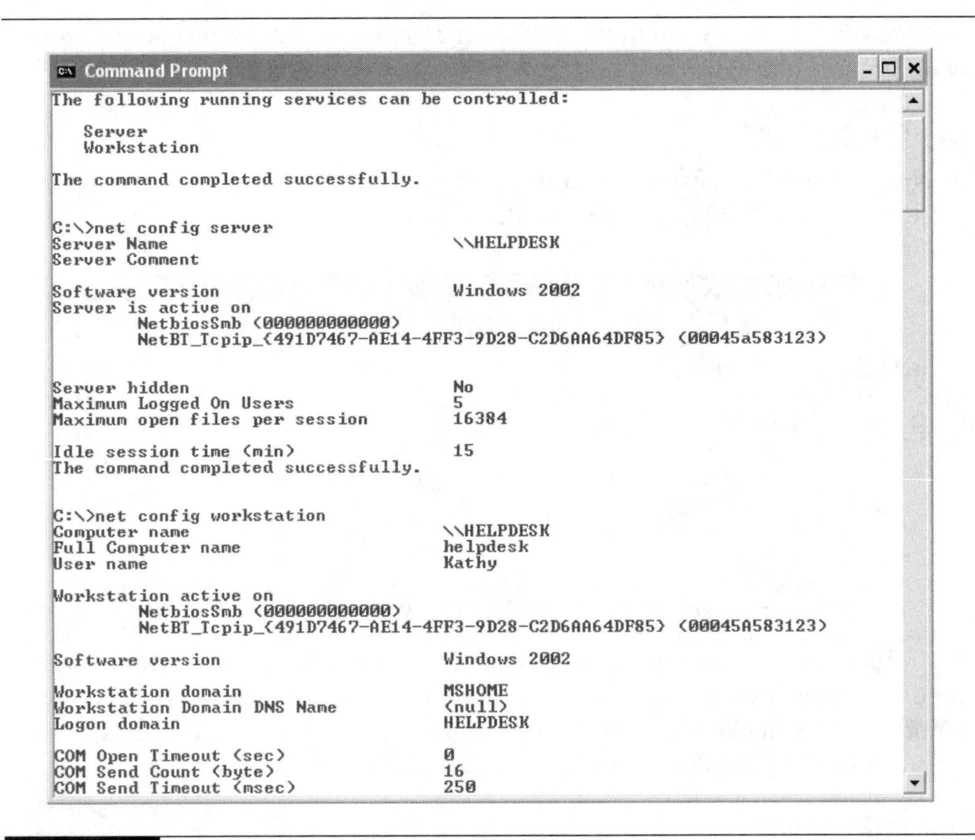

FIGURE B-6 You can view detailed information about the Server and Workstation services on a Windows XP computer.

To close a file that's in use (and release the lock if it's locked), enter **net file *ID#* /close** (substitute the ID number you saw when you entered the command net file for *ID#*).

Net Send

Available only in Windows XP/2000/NT, this command lets you send messages to other computers on the network. The messages are displayed on the screen. To send a message to another computer in your workgroup, enter **net send *ComputerName MessageText*** (substitute the name of a computer for *ComputerName* and the text of your message for *MessageText*) at the command prompt and press ENTER.

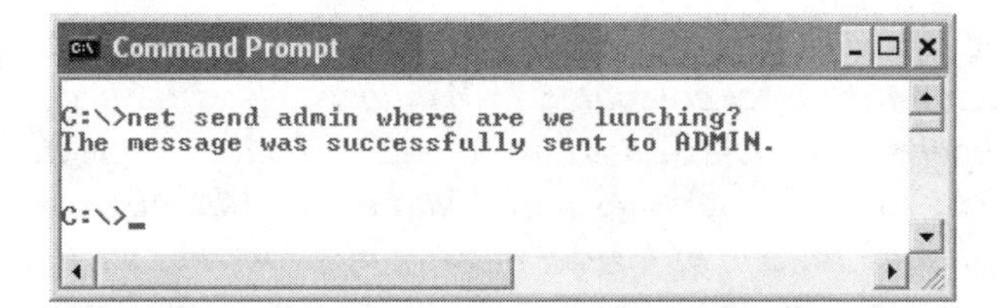

At the target computer, a pop-up window displays the message:

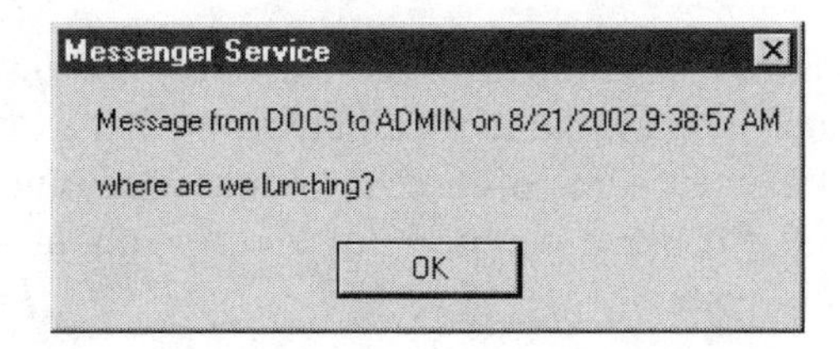

The `net send` command supports additional useful syntax values, as follows:

- **net send * *MessageText*** sends the message to all the computers in the workgroup.
- **net send *UserName MessageText*** sends the message to the user who is logged on as *UserName* (useful if you don't know which computer that user is working on). If the user isn't logged on, no message is sent.
- **net send /users *MessageText*** sends the message to all logged-on users.

You need to be aware of the following rules for using net send:

- If a *UserName* or *ComputerName* contains a space, enclose the name in quotation marks.
- The message text cannot exceed 128 characters, including spaces.
- The messenger service must be running on all the computers involved in the transaction.

By default, the messenger service starts automatically when Windows starts, but some users disable the messenger service because of a new annoying Internet intrusion called Pop Up Messages (not to be confused with pop-up advertisements that appear when you're using your browser). See Chapter 9 to learn about this new annoying intrusion.

NOTE *Sending console messages requires that a service named Messenger be running on the target computer. In Windows XP with Service Pack 2, the Messenger service is disabled by default. You can enable the Messenger service by using the Services tool found in the Administrative Tools folder, though the use of instant messaging programs such as Windows Messenger may be much more useful to you on a small network.*

Net Share

Available only in Windows XP/2000, you can use net share to manage the shared resources on a computer. The available parameters and syntax rules for net share are quite robust, and I discuss some of the commonly used (and useful) methods for using this command. (You can get more information about net share in the Windows XP/2000 help system.)

- Entering **net share** (with no parameters) lists all the shared drives and folders on the computer.
- Entering **net share *ShareName*** displays information about that share, including the name of any user who is currently accessing the share.

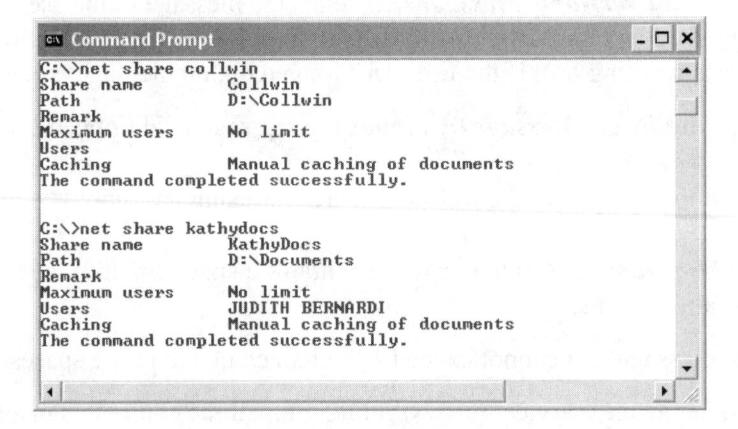

- Entering **net share *ShareName* /users:*number*** sets the maximum number of users (the number you enter for *number*) who can simultaneously access the share.
- Entering **net share *ShareName* /unlimited** specifies that an unlimited number of users can simultaneously access the share.

- Entering **net share *ShareName* /delete** stops sharing the resource named in *ShareName* (the folder isn't deleted, it's just no longer shared).

Net Time

Use the `net time` command to synchronize your computer's clock with the clock of another computer on the network that you know has the correct time. For computers logging on to a Windows 2000 domain, time synchronization is automatic, and Windows 2000 domain controllers are set to synchronize the time with an external reliable clock, over the Internet. When you're working in a peer-to-peer network (a workgroup), you can use a Windows XP computer as the computer that synchronizes its clock over the Internet, and then use the `net time` command to synchronize all the other computers on the network to that computer. See the section "Synchronizing Time over the Internet" later in this appendix to learn how to use a Windows XP computer as a network timekeeper.

To synchronize a computer's clock with the clock of another (reliable) computer on the network, enter **net time *ComputerName* /set /yes** (substitute the name of the reliable computer for *ComputerName*) at a command prompt and press ENTER. The system performs the following tasks automatically:

- Displays the current time of the computer to which you synchronized your computer
- Resets the time (and the date, if the current date is incorrect) of your computer

Net Use

The `net use` command lets you control connections to shared resources on remote computers. The most common use of this command is to map a remote shared folder to a drive letter. *Mapping* is the technical term for assigning a drive letter to a share on a remote computer. The mapped drive letter becomes another drive on your local computer. This is a useful trick for shares you access constantly, because all the drives on your computer appear in My Computer and Windows Explorer, which means you don't have to open a network browse window to get to this share. Using a drive letter is much easier than browsing the network to get to a specific remote folder to open or save a document.

NOTE *You can also map drives from the network browser (My Network Places or Network Neighborhood), which is discussed in Chapter 12.*

To map a remote share to a local drive letter, enter the following command at the command prompt and then press ENTER:

```
net use x: \\ComputerName\ShareName
```

where

- ***x:*** is the drive letter you want to use for this share.
- ***ComputerName*** is the name of the computer that has the share.
- ***ShareName*** is the name of the share.

If you're unsure about which drive letter is available, enter an asterisk (*) instead of a drive letter, followed by a colon. Windows will assign the share the next available drive letter on your computer, using the following rules:

- Windows XP starts at z: and works backward.
- All other versions of Windows start at the first unused drive letter on the computer and work forward.

To see the mapped drives on your computer, enter **net use** at the command prompt and press ENTER. The system returns information about mapped drives, the status, the local drive letter that's been assigned to a share, and the name of the share on the remote machine:

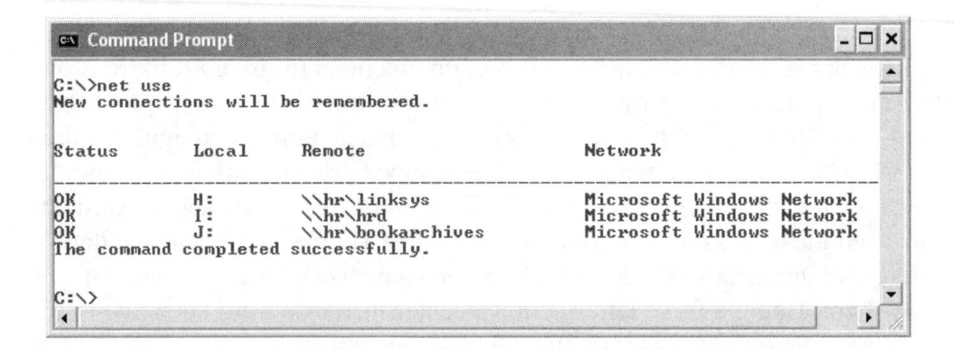

```
C:\>net use
New connections will be remembered.

Status       Local     Remote                    Network

-------------------------------------------------------------------------------
OK           H:        \\hr\linksys              Microsoft Windows Network
OK           I:        \\hr\hrd                  Microsoft Windows Network
OK           J:        \\hr\bookarchives         Microsoft Windows Network
The command completed successfully.

C:\>
```

- To disconnect a mapped drive, enter **net use *x*: /delete** (substitute the drive letter you want to disconnect for *x*) and press ENTER.
- To disconnect all mapped drives, enter **net use * /delete** and press ENTER.

The real beauty of the `net use` command is the ability to use it in batch files to automate transfer of files between computers. I use the command in a batch file that backs up files from one computer on my network to another. Following is a copy of one of my batch files for backing up important files. You can see I create a mapped drive (the share is drive C of the computer named admin), and then I use `xcopy` (and its powerful parameters) to back up my files to a parent folder named adminbu (which stands for admin backup) that I created on the local computer. (Note that some of these lines of code have been broken into two or more lines to fit on this page.)

```
REM SET UP A MAPPED DRIVE FOR THE SOURCE SHARE
net use i: \\admin\admin-c
REM BEGIN COPYING
xcopy i:\figures\*.* c:\adminbu\figures /s/e/h/i/r/c/v/y
xcopy i:\"documents and settings"\administrator.WESTERN\
"mydocuments"\*.* c:\adminbu\"my documents" /s/e/h/i/r/c/v/y
xcopy i:\cuteftppro\*.* c:\adminbu\cuteftpro /s/e/h/i/r/c/v/y
xcopy i:\eudora\*.* c:\adminbu\eudora /s/e/h/i/r/c/v/y
xcopy i:\quickbooks\*.qbw c:\adminbu\quickbooks /s/e/h/i/r/c/v/y
REM REMOVE THE MAPPED DRIVE (TO AVOID AN ERROR
THE NEXT TIME THE BATCHFILE RUNS)
net use i: /delete
```

Net View

Net view displays information about the computers on your network that share resources. Entering **net view** at the command prompt returns a list of all the computers on the network that have at least one share defined (including the local computer).

To see a list of all the shares available on a specific computer, enter **net view *ComputerName***. If you've mapped a drive to any of the shares, the drive letter is displayed.

Synchronizing Time over the Internet

A Windows XP computer that's operating in a workgroup can synchronize its clock with an Internet time server that's accurate to the millisecond. After the Windows XP computer has synchronized its clock, you can use the `net time` command on the other computers in the workgroup to sync their clocks to the accurate Windows XP clock.

Making sure that the computer clocks (including the date) are accurate isn't just an exercise for the terminally fussy—it's important for time-stamped data. For example, if users on your network are accessing a network-wide database (including accounting software), the time stamp for each addition or modification of a record is important. Additionally, your e-mail software inbox is probably sorted by date/time, and the date/time stamp on your outgoing messages may be important to recipients.

Understanding Time Synchronization

To use the time sync feature, you designate one Windows XP computer on your network as the time source. That computer's clock is synchronized with an Internet time server once a week. This is, obviously, much easier to accomplish if you have an always-on Internet connection through a DSL/modem cable. If, however, you're using a telephone modem or a DSL connection that isn't always on, you can elect to sync the computer's clock manually.

The time sync works automatically—the Windows XP computer reads the time from the Internet time clock and resets its own clock (unless the clocks already match, of course). However, before attempting the synchronization, the Windows XP computer must have the correct date (some Internet clocks won't provide information

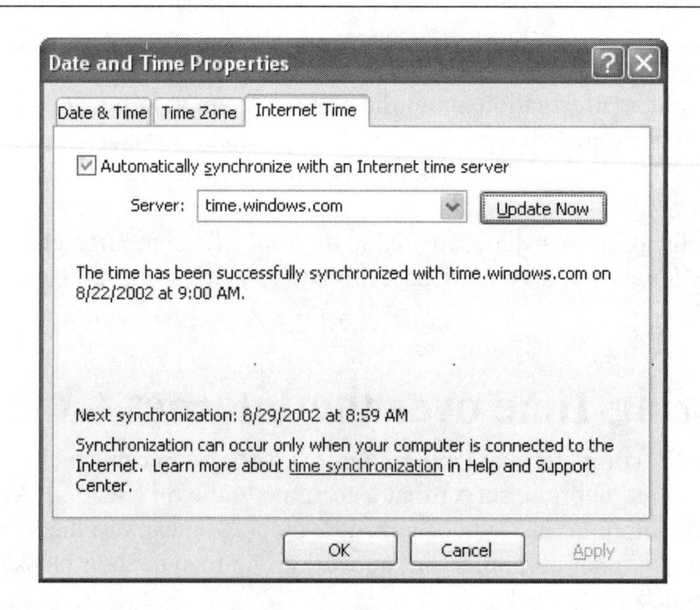

FIGURE B-7 Be sure synchronization is enabled, and choose an Internet time server.

to a computer that has the wrong date). You can check the computer's date setting by hovering your mouse over the time display at the right edge of your taskbar. If the date is wrong, double-click the time display to open the Date and Time Properties dialog and specify the correct date. Click OK to close the dialog and reset the computer's date.

To establish the settings for synchronizing time on your Windows XP computer, double-click the time display at the right edge of the taskbar to open the Date and Time Properties dialog. Click the Internet Time tab, shown in Figure B-7.

Changing the Time Server

You can change the Internet time server if you wish (the default time server is run by Microsoft). If you click the arrow to the right of the Server field, you'll see an entry for a time server run by the United States government *(time.nist.gov),* which you can select.

You can also enter the name of a time server you prefer if you want to use one that is not in the drop-down list (useful if you live outside the United States).

NOTE *Only time servers that use the Simple Network Time Protocol (SNTP) will work. You can't use an Internet address that uses the HyperText Transfer Protocol (HTTP).*

Time servers, which are available around the world, are maintained in a hierarchy. Primary (stratum 1) servers are the most accurate, but secondary (stratum 2) servers are generally either synchronized perfectly with stratum 1 servers or are only slightly off the clock ticks of the stratum 1 servers. The difference, a matter of a few nanoseconds, certainly won't create a problem for you. Big deal!

- For a list of stratum 1 servers, visit *http://www.eecis.udel.edu/~mills/ntp/clock1a.html.*
- For a list of stratum 2 servers, visit *http://www.eecis.udel.edu/~mills/ntp/clock2a.html.*

NOTE *Because stratum 1 time servers are very busy and can time out, you should select stratum 2 servers as your external NTP servers.*

Each list contains the NTP time servers available for public access, including any restrictions on their use. The lists are sorted by country code.

Synchronizing the Time Manually

If you don't have an always-on Internet connection, or if your Windows XP computer was not running during the last scheduled sync, you'll see a failure message when you open the Internet Time tab of the Date and Time Properties dialog. You can, however, update the Windows XP clock manually. Start your Internet connection and then click Update Now.

You may want to use the manual update method even if you have an always-on Internet connection. For instance, if your Windows XP clock doesn't maintain its accuracy over the course of a week, you can sync time daily or semiweekly.

Updating Clocks on the Network Computers

Once you have a reliable clock on the network, you should update the time on all the other computers on your network by using the `net time` command and pointing the computers to the reliable Windows XP computer. See the discussion on the `net time` command earlier in this appendix.

Index

See Appendix A, "Glossary of Network Terminology," for a comprehensive list of terms.

B

C

D

E

F

G

H

I

J

K

L

M

N

P

R

S

T

U

V

W

X

Z

INTERNATIONAL CONTACT INFORMATION

AUSTRALIA
McGraw-Hill Book Company
Australia Pty. Ltd.
TEL +61-2-9900-1800
FAX +61-2-9878-8881
http://www.mcgraw-hill.com.au
books-it_sydney@mcgraw-hill.com

CANADA
McGraw-Hill Ryerson Ltd.
TEL +905-430-5000
FAX +905-430-5020
http://www.mcgraw-hill.ca

GREECE, MIDDLE EAST, & AFRICA (Excluding South Africa)
McGraw-Hill Hellas
TEL +30-210-6560-990
TEL +30-210-6560-993
TEL +30-210-6560-994
FAX +30-210-6545-525

MEXICO (Also serving Latin America)
McGraw-Hill Interamericana Editores
S.A. de C.V.
TEL +525-1500-5108
FAX +525-117-1589
http://www.mcgraw-hill.com.mx
carlos_ruiz@mcgraw-hill.com

SINGAPORE (Serving Asia)
McGraw-Hill Book Company
TEL +65-6863-1580
FAX +65-6862-3354
http://www.mcgraw-hill.com.sg
mghasia@mcgraw-hill.com

SOUTH AFRICA
McGraw-Hill South Africa
TEL +27-11-622-7512
FAX +27-11-622-9045
robyn_swanepoel@mcgraw-hill.com

SPAIN
McGraw-Hill/
Interamericana de España, S.A.U.
TEL +34-91-180-3000
FAX +34-91-372-8513
http://www.mcgraw-hill.es
professional@mcgraw-hill.es

UNITED KINGDOM, NORTHERN, EASTERN, & CENTRAL EUROPE
McGraw-Hill Education Europe
TEL +44-1-628-502500
FAX +44-1-628-770224
http://www.mcgraw-hill.co.uk
emea_queries@mcgraw-hill.com

ALL OTHER INQUIRIES Contact:
McGraw-Hill/Osborne
TEL +1-510-420-7700
FAX +1-510-420-7703
http://www.osborne.com
omg_international@mcgraw-hill.com